How to...

P9-BHV-166

Linux Network Servers

seven

Craig Hunt

San Francisco   Paris   Düsseldorf   Soest   London

Associate Publisher: Guy Hart-Davis
Contracts and Licensing Manager: Kristine O'Callaghan
Acquisitions & Developmental Editor: Neil Edde
Editor: Emily Wolman
Technical Editor: Will Deutsch
Technical Galley Reviewer: Don Hergert
Book Designer: Bill Gibson
Graphic Illustrator: Tony Jonick
Electronic Publishing Specialist: Nila Nichols
Project Team Leader: Jennifer Durning
Proofreaders: Richard Ganis, Emily Hsuan, Catherine Morris, and Shannon Murphy
Indexer: John S. Lewis
Cover Designer: Ingalls + Associates
Cover Illustrator/Photographer: Ingalls + Associates

Library of Congress Card Number: 99-63817
ISBN: 0-7821-2506-9

Manufactured in the United States of America

10 9 8 7 6 5 4 3 2 1

To Norman Hunt and Frank McCafferty, who showed me what it means to be a man.

Acknowledgments

The millennium bug bit my family, and 1999 became a year of many changes. My eldest daughter got married. My son graduated from college and is busily pursuing a career. My youngest daughter graduated from high school and moved to New England for college. I changed jobs. And I found a new publisher.

This is my fourth book (fifth if you count second editions), but it is my first book for Sybex. I admit to having felt very nervous about starting a book with a new team. Writing a book is both a very personal and a very public thing. For an author, the book is your "baby." You want everyone to like it, and the editor's job is to help you make sure everyone does. It's not easy to hear from your editor that your baby isn't perfect—an excellent rapport is needed between the author and the editors. So I worried! But my fears were groundless. The Sybex team is a tight-knit group of consummate professionals.

A special thanks goes to acquisitions and developmental editor Neil Edde. Without Neil and Maureen Adams, also from Sybex, this book never would have been written. They first approached me at Networld+Interop, where I teach a tutorial about Linux network servers, with the idea of writing this book. Neil also took the time to introduce me to the Sybex team and to show me the Sybex way of doing things. Without him, I would have been lost.

The hand of Emily Wolman, my editor, can be seen throughout the book. Emily deserves special praise for keeping me on track through the final phases of the book. If you haven't experienced it, it is hard to understand the amount of mayhem that ensues in the final weeks of finishing a book. Emily kept her humor and my focus during those final critical weeks.

Will Deutsch (University of California at Davis) was the book's technical editor. He provided key technical insights that make this a much better book. His knowledge of the latest Linux kernel was very helpful and enhanced the technical accuracy of the text.

The Sybex team produces a superior publication. Thanks to production players Jennifer Durning, Richard Ganis, Emily Hsuan, Catherine Morris, Shannon Murphy, Nila Nichols, Tony Jonick, and Ted Laux.

Finally, thanks to my family, Kathy, Sara, David, and Rebecca, for being so understanding.

Contents at a Glance

Table of Contents

Introduction

It's not just for enthusiasts anymore! Linux is gaining widespread acceptance as one of the world's leading operating systems. International Data Corporation (IDC) reports that as of October 1998, a minimum of 7.5 million copies of Linux were in use. Further, IDC expects the sales of Linux by Red Hat and Caldera, leading suppliers of Linux, to grow by 43 percent in 1999. At ISPCON Fall 98, Intel announced that it has purchased a minority position in Red Hat. Compaq and IBM are set to ship PCs with Linux pre-installed.

The growth of Linux has not gone unnoticed. With companies like Intel, Netscape, and Novell investing in Linux and companies like Oracle, Sybase, and IBM endorsing it, it can't be long before your company begins to investigate Linux. When it does, you need to understand how to use Linux to build a network server that is reliable and robust enough for business applications. This book will give you that understanding. As part of Sybex's *24seven* series, this book focuses on providing computer professionals with the information they need to "do the job right"—and fast.

The Linux Operating System

This book focuses on running Linux on PC hardware. Linux runs on other hardware plat-forms, but the real market for Linux is as a PC operating system, and most of you will never run Linux on anything but PC hardware. The real power of Linux is the amazing ability of this low-cost software to turn low-cost hardware into a real network server.

Linux is an efficient, modern operating system. But it is more than that. It is both the product of one man and the product of global cooperation. Linus Torvalds wrote Linux as a student project, incorporating many of the latest ideas in operating system design. However, the development of Linux did not stop there. The creation of Linux became a global, grassroots effort. Volunteers from every part of the technical community work on porting existing applications, creating new ones, and fixing bugs. These enthusiasts work not for money, but for the love of what they are doing. They have created what I believe is the most complete network server for the PC platform, and they have created a system of exceptional quality.

The Linux distribution supports all of the following network server features:

- All TCP/IP protocols
- NetBIOS SMB (Server Message Block) protocols
- NetWare clients
- Remote login access including dial-up access with PPP and SLIP
- FTP server including anonymous FTP

- Network News server
- Full TCP/IP mail server (`sendmail`)
- Post Office Protocol (POP) and Internet Message Access Protocol (IMAP) for mailbox services
- Web server
- JAVA software development kit (SDK)
- Application server
- A complete software development environment—C, C++, Perl, and many more programming languages

None of these features are extra-cost options. All are included as part of the basic Linux distribution.

Many business managers ask their technical people if Linux is "serious enough for business." Funny—this is the same question that was asked ten years ago about the Internet. Many traditional telephone companies lost a major opportunity by declaring that the Internet was not suitable for business. Don't ignore Linux. It may be an opportunity to make your computer operation more efficient and your company more profitable.

The Benefits of Linux

There are many reasons for the amazing popularity of Linux. First, of course, is its low cost. Even the CD-ROM versions are almost free. However, organizations with serious business requirements know that initial software cost is an insignificant portion of the total cost of operating a 24seven computer service. The cost of hardware, desktop licenses, optional software, maintenance, and support staff all contribute to the total cost of operation.

In all of these areas, Linux is extremely cost effective. The PC hardware that Linux runs on is very inexpensive, and clients don't have to be licensed to use a Linux server. So many features are bundled in Linux that the need for optional software is minimized. Maintenance and support costs are also reasonable, as explained in the following paragraphs.

Another reason that Linux is popular is that it is a Unix-like operating system. Programmers, support staff, and users who are familiar with Unix need very little training to work with Linux. In fact, a book like this one is all that a Unix system administrator needs to master installation and configuration of a Linux network server.

Unix has a twenty-year history. Linux benefits from that already substantial base of skilled support personnel. As this book demonstrates, the complexity of installing and configuring a Linux server is very comparable to installing and configuring a Windows NT server. Therefore, even system administration professionals who do not have a Unix background should have no more difficulty learning Linux than they would learning Windows NT Server.

The high quality of Linux support is also a reason for the popularity of the system and is an important factor in its growing acceptance as a business operating system. There is, of course, the worldwide network of Linux enthusiasts who quickly discover and fix bugs. For this reason, kernel updates and patches are constantly posted that can be downloaded at no cost and used to improve your system. Additionally, the companies that produce Linux distributions for the business market also sell support services. Finally, it is possible to contract with a third party for Linux support.

Third-party Linux support is arguably better than third-party support for commercial operating systems. Most businesses prefer to depend on commercial operating systems because they think they will get better support for those systems. I call this the "myth of commerciality" for the following reasons. Commercial PC software is so inexpensive that it is financially impossible for the manufacturer of the software to provide free support. Most businesses, however, do not purchase the optional support directly from the manufacturer, because they do not think it is worth the price when they find themselves competing with millions of other customers for the attention of one large software manufacturer. Instead, they use in-house support staff or turn to third parties for support. However, the third parties that support commercial software are hampered by the fact that they do not have access to the operating system's source code. They can master the techniques of using the system, but without the source code, they can never know exactly how the system is implemented or directly repair problems in the system.

Thus, Linux in-house support and third-party support is better because the support personnel have access to all of the operating system source code. Nothing is hidden. Linux support personnel can solve their own problems; they do not have to rely on the kindness of strangers.

The importance of the availability of source code can hardly be exaggerated. Your mission-critical applications are dependent on the operating system, and your ability to influence its development is very limited. When I began my computer career, the U.S. government required that manufacturers provide the source code for operating systems that would host critical business and military applications. They knew that source code was the last resort for resolving disputes over what could be fixed or improved. With access to the source code, you can always hire someone to make the fixes that are critical to your business. Without it, your critical business applications are hostage to the whims of a company that may not even know your business exists.

In short, Linux is low cost, high quality, and well supported. It is an excellent choice for your Internet and departmental servers.

Who Should Buy This Book

You should! This book is for anyone who wants to learn how to build a departmental server or a network server using Linux. The book doesn't assume that you know much about Linux, but it does assume that you have a good understanding of computers and IP networks, as well as a basic understanding of Linux commands.

> **TIP**   If you're a system administrator but you don't know the basics of Unix or Linux, start with *Mastering Linux,* by Arman Danesh (Sybex, 1999). It is an excellent introduction to Linux and will give you all the background you need.

This book does not provide yet another review of the basics. Instead, it provides insight into how to get things done and how to avoid pitfalls along the way. This book helps you understand the role Linux can play in a business network and shows you how to run a 24seven network server operation with Linux.

If you're a Unix professional, you'll benefit from this book's design and planning information by avoiding problems when selecting hardware and installing the system. Additionally, you'll be pleased by the number of servers included in the Linux distribution that are costly options on other systems. If you're a Microsoft professional, you'll be surprised at the ease with which Linux performs remote access services, TCP/IP e-mail services, and Web services.

How This Book Is Organized

This book is divided into five parts: *Planning and Installation*, *Internet Server Operations*, *Departmental Server Operations*, *Security and Troubleshooting*, and *Appendices*. The five parts are composed of fifteen chapters and three appendices.

The coverage of some network services spans multiple chapters. In particular, e-mail server coverage spans Chapters 7 and 13 and Appendix C, and the topic of Domain Name Service is discussed in Chapter 6 and Appendix B. However, most topics are covered in a single chapter.

Though individual chapters can be read alone—for example, you could jump directly to Chapter 8 to read about the Web server configuration files—this book was designed as a unit. Most chapters reference material covered in other chapters. When such a reference is made, it contains a pointer to the chapter that covers the referenced material. If you have a specific task to study, such as setting up a Samba server, feel free to jump directly to that topic. But if like many system administrators you need to support the entire range of Linux network services, you will benefit from reading the entire text.

Part 1—Planning and Installation

To lay the foundation for a reliable network server, the first part of the book contains three chapters that provide essential information for properly planning a Linux installation, detailed instruction for installing Linux, and an explanation of what happens when you boot your new Linux server.

Chapter 1: Getting Started   This chapter explains the abundance of Linux distributions and how to obtain them. It gives guidance for selecting hardware that will help you avoid installation and reliability problems. Further, it provides suggestions for planning your Linux installation.

Chapter 2: Basic Installation   A detailed example of installing the **Red Hat 6 Linux** distribution is provided in this chapter along with tips on troubleshooting the installation. Disk partitioning with Disk Druid and fdisk are explained, as are the structure and purpose of fstab.

Chapter 3: The Boot Process   This chapter details the boot process, including Linux runlevels. This chapter describes the Linux Loader, the role of the kernel in initializing devices, and the role of init in starting all of the system services. It covers the lilo.conf and inittab configuration files and emphasizes the key startup files that a network server administrator needs to understand.

Part 2—Internet Server Operations

Part 2 covers operation of traditional Internet services. It provides the information you need to configure the network interface and the essential Internet services that run over that interface. The chapters in this part of the book give detailed instructions for configuring login services, Domain Name Service (DNS), sendmail, Apache Web service, and IP routing.

Chapter 4: The Network Interface   An interface to the physical network is required for every network server. This chapter covers the installation and configuration of an Ethernet interface, which is the most commonly used network interface. Linux systems can also provide network service through the serial interface, which is described along with the getty and login processes that support serial communications. Linux can run TCP/IP over a serial line using PPP software. Both client and server PPP configurations are covered.

Chapter 5: Login Services   Linux provides complete application server features. Users can access applications running on the server remotely through rlogin and telnet. This chapter covers the configuration of these as well as the configuration of an FTP server.

Chapter 6: Linux Name Services   Domain Name Service (DNS) is essential for the operation of your network. Linux provides the Berkeley Internet Name Domain (BIND) software that is the most widely used, most thoroughly tested, and most reliable DNS server software available. This chapter provides detailed information on configuring the new BIND version 8 DNS software. It also covers the host table and how DNS and the host table are used together.

Chapter 7: Configuring a Mail Server   The most powerful and complex system for handling Internet mail service is sendmail. Linux bundles sendmail as part of the system. This chapter shows you how to simplify sendmail configuration by concentrating on what is important; it also discusses how to create your own custom configuration.

Chapter 8: The Apache Web Server   The Apache Web server, which is the most widely used Web server in the world today, is included as part of the Linux distribution. This chapter explains the installation and configuration of a secure, reliable Web service.

Chapter 9: Network Gateway Services   All internets require routers. Linux provides a full range of both static and dynamic routing. It includes the commonly used routing daemon (routed) and the full-featured gateway daemon (gated). Some networks use address translation, which is available for Linux as *address masquerading*. This chapter explains the administration of all of these services.

Part 3—Departmental Server Operations
Part 3 describes the operation of services that are essential for a departmental server that supports desktop clients. Its four chapters provide information about:

- Creating configuration servers—both DHCP and BootP
- Configuring the servers that provide file sharing—both NFS and Samba
- Configuring print servers—both LPD and Samba
- Configuring mailbox servers—both POP and IMAP

Chapter 10: Desktop Configuration Servers   Configuring a TCP/IP client can be complex. A configuration server relieves your users of this task. Linux provides configuration servers for both Windows and Unix desktops through the Dynamic Host Configuration Protocol (DHCP) server and the Bootstrap Protocol (BootP) server. This chapter covers the administration of both.

Chapter 11: File Sharing   The most important feature of a departmental network is that it allows desktop computers to transparently share files. Linux provides this capability through the Samba server that provides native file sharing for Windows systems, and the

NFS server that provides file sharing for Unix clients. This chapter provides detailed information about both of these services, and about the native Linux file system.

Chapter 12: Printer Services   Linux provides printer services to desktop clients through Samba and the Line Printer daemon (LPD). This chapter explains how printers are shared through these services, as well as how to install and configure local printers.

Chapter 13: More Mail Services   Most desktop systems cannot directly receive Internet mail; they rely on a mailbox server to collect and hold the mail for them until they are ready to read it. Linux includes two techniques for providing this service. Post Office Protocol (POP) is the most widely used mailbox server, and Internet Message Access Protocol (IMAP) has advanced features that are making it increasingly popular. This chapter covers the installation, configuration, and administration of both services.

Part 4—Security and Troubleshooting

Part 4 focuses on tasks that, while not specifically linked to network services, are essential to maintaining a secure and reliable server. This part contains two chapters. The first explains the security threats that face your server and what you can do to minimize those threats. The second tells you what to do when things go wrong with the server and the network to which it is connected.

Chapter 14: Security   A sad fact of life on the Internet is that there are people out there who will do you harm if they have the chance. To run a reliable server, you must run a secure server. This chapter tells you how to keep up-to-date on security issues, how to take advantage of the exceptionally good security features included in Linux, how to monitor your system for security problems, and how to add extra security features if you need them.

Chapter 15: Troubleshooting   Things can—and will—go wrong with your Linux system. When they do, you need to locate and fix the problem. This chapter helps you test and debug the network, and analyze and resolve problems. It discusses when you need to upgrade your Linux kernel and how to do it. It also describes the tools used to analyze network problems.

Part 5—Appendices

Part 5 concludes the book with a series of appendices.

Appendix A: X Windows Configuration   This appendix provides information about installing the XFree86 X Windows system on your computer. The XF86Setup, xf86config, and Xconfigurator installation tools are all covered, as well as the structure of the XF86Config configuration file.

Appendix B: BIND Reference   This appendix provides a summary of the BIND 8 configuration commands for the `named.conf` file. It also provides a summary of the BIND 4 configuration commands for the `named.boot` file. Administrators of Linux systems who are still running BIND 4 will need to use this reference.

Appendix C: The `m4` Macros for `sendmail`   This appendix provides a summary of the `m4` macros that are available to build a custom `sendmail` configuration.

Help Us Help You

This book contains many Web page references. The Web is an important source of Linux information. Unfortunately, Web page addresses change so frequently that those listed in a book rapidly become outdated. Only one tool can keep up with the Web, and that is the Web itself. The `www.24sevenbooks.com/linux.html` Web site will be used to keep the Web page references up-to-date and to provide other corrections and updates for this book.

To help us keep this text as accurate as possible, please contact us whenever you find a stale link or other error in this book. You may either go to the `www.24sevenbooks.com` Web site and follow the Support link, or you may send an e-mail to `support@sybex.com`.

Part 1

Planning and Installation

Topics Covered:

- Selecting a Linux distribution

- Choosing the correct server hardware

- Planning a Linux installation

- Basic Linux installation

- Using `fips` to coexist with Windows

- Partitioning disks with Disk Druid and `fdisk`

- Understanding mount points and the `fstab` file

- Understanding the Linux boot process

- Knowing when to use LOADLIN

- Configuring the Linux loader LILO

- Providing input to the kernel during initialization

- The roles of run levels, the `init` process, `inittab`, and the startup scripts

- Managing loadable modules and why they are needed

1

Getting Started

Linux is about choices–more choices than most other operating systems. Many Unix systems limit your choice of hardware vendors because the system only runs on one type of hardware. Microsoft Windows limits your choice of operating systems vendors because Windows is only available from Microsoft. With Linux, you can choose from many different distributions, all of which run on a wide array of hardware.

And choices mean decisions. This chapter will help you make the decisions necessary to select the software and hardware upon which to build a Linux server.

First, you'll learn how to determine which version of Linux best suits your individual needs. There are several excellent Linux distributions. Though all are based on the Linux kernel, each has its own unique features. No matter what your needs, you're sure to find a Linux distribution that is right for you.

In addition to Linux software, this chapter looks at what hardware is right for your server. Linux runs on a wide variety of PC hardware, so you might think that any system will do, but mistakenly picking incompatible or under-powered hardware can be a big headache. Read on to make sure you know how to determine what you need to get your job done, as well as what to avoid.

It's also important to plan for the installation by getting all of the information you'll need before you start. Linux allows you to direct the installation and configuration process, and the installation program asks you to make many decisions. Most of these decisions are easy, but it is always best to be prepared ahead of time.

> **NOTE** Different readers should use this chapter in different ways. If you're just starting out with Linux, you need to learn as much as you can about selecting the hardware and software for your server; the entire chapter will be helpful for you. If you already have the PC hardware and the Linux software for your system, you can skip most of this chapter for now and come back to it when you plan to upgrade your system. However, most system administrators, even those who have already installed Linux, can benefit from the "Understanding Your Hardware" and "PC Hardware Basics" sections of this chapter.

Linux Distributions

Linux is an efficient, full-featured Unix-like operating system. But even for Unix professionals, the Linux world can be confusing. Computer professionals learning Unix often voice the concern that "there are too many versions of Unix." By this they mean that Solaris, Irix, AIX, and BSD are all different. Each has a different installation process. Each has a different location for key files. And each has its own set of administrative tools. For system professionals coming from the conformity of a shop that uses just one vendor's operating system, this variety can be daunting.

Like Unix, there are many different versions of Linux. Yet at the core, there is only one Linux–all versions of Linux run the same operating system kernel. The differences that you see among the various Linux distributions are superficial but extremely important, because the differences often occur in those areas in which the administrator is most deeply involved: installation, location of key configuration files, administrative tools, and the user interface.

Which Features Are Right for You?

Given that at heart all Linux systems use the same kernel, how do you decide which distribution is right for you? Good question! In the traditional Unix world, the hardware drives the choice. If you have a Sun system, you use Solaris; if you have an IBM system, you use AIX. But all versions of Linux run on the same PC hardware. For Linux, the choice is driven by the features you want.

There are several features used to differentiate distributions. Low cost is one. The Debian distribution is the winner here, because Debian is completely free. Students love this feature. But for most businesses running a 24seven service, the difference between a free distribution and a $50 distribution is not significant.

For a serious business operation, the quality of support is a more significant feature. The type of support programs offered, the probability that the Linux vendor will stay in business and be able to meet their support obligations, and the presence of training and certification programs for support personnel all need to be evaluated. Red Hat and Caldera are winners in this category, because they both offer support plans and formal training.

Ease of maintenance and administration are important features for reducing the total cost of ownership. Red Hat pioneered simplifying the software update process, Yggdrasil was an early developer of graphical system administration tools, and Debian's .deb software update system is highly rated.

Even the look and feel of the desktop and the availability of user applications can be decisive features. What is appealing in a desktop environment is highly personal. I like Caldera because they were the first to bundle both the KDE and Looking Glass Desktop environments along with all of the other more common choices.

> **NOTE** See the "Personal Choices" sidebar later in this chapter for my personal experience with some Linux distributions.

If you're fairly new to Linux, and you probably are, the distribution names in the preceding paragraphs don't mean much to you. You can find out more about these popular versions of Linux from the Web sites listed below:

OpenLinux (`www.caldera.com`) OpenLinux is the distribution produced by Caldera. Caldera, which has close ties to Novell, introduced NetWare client support into Linux and was the first distributor to ship Linux with Netscape Navigator. OpenLinux also includes the StarOffice Suite and the Metro X Windows server. Many Microsoft Windows users like the Caldera 2.2 Linux Wizard (`lizard`) installation tool.

Red Hat (`www.redhat.com`) The leading seller of Linux in the United States, Red Hat developed the Red Hat Package Manager (RPM) that simplifies the installation of optional Linux software and, more important, the task of keeping the server software updated. Red Hat is still well known for a simple, automated installation. Check out their Web site for information and software downloads. Red Hat 6 includes both the GNOME Enlightenment and the KDE desktop window managers.

Slackware (`www.CD-ROM.com`) Slackware is one of the first Linux distributions to gain wide acceptance in the United States. It ships as a four-CD-ROM set with many optional software packages. The Walnut Creek Web site provides product information and software downloads.

Plug-and-Play Linux (www.yggdrasil.com) Plug and Play introduced a "control panel" for system administration that has since been adopted by other popular distributions. This version of Linux provides a completely buildable source tree for system software developers.

S.u.S.E. (www.suse.com) This is the best-selling Linux in Europe. Both English and German versions are available.

Debian (www.debian.org) Debian is a completely free version of Linux. The folks at Debian do not even produce a CD-ROM version, for which they would have to charge. They do, however, list many companies from which you can buy a CD-ROM version of their system. Debian also provides an advanced software package manager.

NOTE The distributions listed above are only the tip of the iceberg. There are many other Linux distributions; to learn more go to www.linux.org and click the Distributions button.

Which Distribution Is Right for You?

So how do you figure out which distribution has the features that are right for you? First, I suggest visiting the Web site of each distribution that interests you, some of which are listed in the previous section. Read what they have to say about their products, and evaluate the style and presentation of their Web sites. Remember, you're going to be using Linux for a serious business system. Does the Linux vendor appear to be addressing a business audience? Do they appear to have a quality, professionally-run Web site? If they are not willing to invest in sales (i.e., the Web site), will they be willing to invest in support?

Also, evaluate the support offered for each version of Linux. Is professional support available from the vendor? Do they appear to be substantial enough to really provide support if you purchase their product?

Next, look for references for each distribution. Check with some computer professionals who use Linux. If you have local third-party support, find out the distribution they prefer to work with. Third-party support is generally better if you let the support personnel select the distribution they know best.

TIP Go to your local Linux users group for plenty of opinions about various distributions and to find out about local third-party support. Follow the Users Group path from www.linux.org to locate the user group nearest you.

Further, use a distribution that comes with high-quality installation documentation. I usually buy the Red Hat or Caldera boxed set that includes the CD-ROM, boot diskette, and printed installation guide. I recommend you do the same. Installation procedures can change dramatically from one release to another, and the most current documentation is your best protection against being caught off guard by these changes.

NOTE See Chapter 2, *Basic Installation*, for a detailed example of installing a Linux system.

If you have time, and I know that is a big if for a network administrator, pick a few distributions and work with them. Installing several different distributions can give you lots of insight into the workings of Linux and increased confidence in dealing with Linux problems. This side-by-side comparison will help you select the Linux you like best. Linux distributions are so inexpensive that money is not the problem with this approach. The problem is, of course, time.

Personal Choices

I have personal experience with three distributions: Slackware, Red Hat, and Caldera. Unfortunately I'm not much help in choosing between them, because I like them all.

Slackware

I have a soft spot in my heart for Slackware, because it was the first Linux I used in a serious way. Because I was a Solaris user, I liked the fact that Slackware included the Sun textedit program in the default desktop. I also like that it has the least-automated install process of the three distributions I have used. I often find that it is harder to undo the mistakes of an automated process than it is to exercise manual control over the process in the first place.

Caldera

I like Caldera because of its desktop interface and selection of tools. Desktop interface preferences are a personal thing, but I think Caldera has a good one. It also has a good set of administrative tools. I appreciate the fact that Caldera promotes Linux as a supportable, commercial operating system for business use, which is something in which I firmly believe. The reason I bought my first copy of Caldera was that it comes with Netscape Navigator. All major distributions now come with Netscape Navigator, but Caldera was a pioneer in bundling premier commercial applications in a Linux distribution.

Personal Choices *(continued)*

Red Hat

As for Red Hat, I like its excellent administrative tools, such as the Red Hat Package Manager. Red Hat tools are so good that they are widely used in other Linux distributions. Red Hat is also quick to adopt good administrative tools, like `linuxconf`, when they become available. For me, simplifying system administration is always important. Most of the examples in this book are based on Red Hat, though there are examples from other vendors.

And the Winner Is . . .

Red Hat and Caldera. Both are substantial companies, and both offer support. Red Hat offers direct support, and they have a network of "Support Partners," which are third-party support companies selected by Red Hat. Caldera offers direct telephone support that can be purchased on a per incident basis or as a yearly contract. Both of these companies want to promote Linux for business use, and they offer training and certification for support personnel. Red Hat and Caldera are good choices when you're building a network server.

Slackware, though I dearly love it, does not have the level of professional support and training necessary for business customers.

Selecting the Hardware

In addition to deciding upon a Linux distribution, you need to select the hardware on which the operating system will run. Linux runs on almost any PC hardware, from an obsolete 486 to the latest processor. Nevertheless, take care when selecting hardware to avoid unnecessary problems. The cost of even the most powerful PC is modest compared to the labor costs that can be spent on tracking down a problem.

Linux-PC Compatibility

The performance and CPU compatibility of Linux is impressive. I recently ran a classroom demonstration system on a 33MHz 486. When asked, no one in the class guessed that we were using a system of such low power. In another class, I used an old 100MHz AMD/NexGen Nx586. After demonstrating that Windows NT refused to install on this "unrecognized" CPU, I installed Linux without a hitch. Linux compatibility demonstrates a design built upon the premise that you, not the operating system, know what is best. You select the hardware, and Linux will do its darndest to get it running. Once I demonstrated Linux compatibility by attempting to install Windows NT 4 (SP3) on a system with an existing FAT32 Windows 98 installation. Windows NT objected to the unknown file system and would not install. Linux installed without complaint and even dual-booted this "unknown" operating system, though at that time it could not share files with FAT32.

While these classroom demonstrations show the power of Linux, I don't recommend using an old clone chip for a critical server system. Some problems have been reported with early AMD 486DX chips, early AMD K6 chips, and older Cyrix chips. I have never encountered any CPU incompatibilities, but then again, I have never built an operational server with an old clone chip. To be safe, use a standard Pentium-class CPU. All current chips should work.

CPU Requirements

There are currently three families of Pentium-class processors used in new Linux systems. They are the AMD K6 processors, the Cyrix MII processors, and the Intel Pentium and Celeron processors. These processors provide a wide range of choices in price and performance.

While Linux will run on almost any CPU, the CPU you choose should be sized for the task at hand. Though most network services are not CPU intensive, a powerful CPU never hurts—but it may not have as much effect on performance as, say, more memory for certain services. If, however, you allow users to run jobs directly on the server, a powerful CPU is critical. As a general rule, you'll never be disappointed if you purchase the most powerful CPU your budget allows.

In today's PC market, it is unlikely that you will buy a new server system that has less than a 350MHz Pentium II processor. But you may not be buying new equipment for your Linux server; you may be installing Linux on existing equipment. If you are, size the load to fit the equipment. Split the users and the tasks among multiple low-end systems if that is all you have. Some vital services that can be provided by low-end systems are:

DNS server A dedicated DNS server needs very little CPU power or disk storage. A 133MHz Pentium with a 500MB disk drive is enough for a dedicated DNS server.

Mail server A dedicated mail server needs substantial disk storage but little CPU power. The number of e-mail users determines the size of the disk you need. Allow anywhere from 5MB of storage per user for light e-mail users to 25MB per user for heavy e-mail users. A 233MHz Pentium with 4GB of disk storage should be able to handle at least 100 e-mail users.

Print server A dedicated print server needs enough disk storage to hold the print queue, but it needs very little CPU power. A print server could be run on a 133MHz Pentium with a 1GB disk drive.

Subnet router A dedicated subnet router needs little CPU power and almost no disk storage. A 233MHz Pentium with a 500MB disk drive would work fine.

Linux allows you to put obsolete equipment to use in vital tasks. Splitting important tasks among several systems instead of concentrating everything in one large server avoids a single point of failure. It also puts essential services onto systems that do not allow user logins.

TIP Using dedicated servers improves reliability and security. I'll talk more about this in Part 4 of this book.

Memory Requirements

A Linux server must have a minimum of 16MB of RAM. I always use at least 64MB for a server, because when it comes to memory, more is usually better. However, increased memory enhances the performance of a system only if the computer can effectively handle the memory.

All Pentium-class systems benefit from memory up to 64MB. Memory above 64MB, however, is not effectively handled by some systems that have only a 512KB L2 cache. An L2 cache of that size can cache only 64MB of memory. For a larger server with more than 64MB of memory, you need a system that has a larger L2 cache or additional hardware for managing the larger memory.

The use planned for the server determines how much memory it really needs. A server that is dedicated to a single function, such as a dedicated DNS server, does not really require much memory. For this type of system, 16MB may be adequate. However, a system that runs many processes or serves a large number of users, such as a busy Web server, requires more memory. Use a minimum of 64MB for a departmental server. If you can afford it, adding memory to a server that needs it will decrease swapping and increase performance.

Disk Storage Requirements

The minimum disk space required for a Linux server installation is 250MB. This minimum space might be adequate for a dedicated router or DNS server, but the least amount of disk space I have ever used is 500MB. Frankly, it is unlikely that a modern PC will have such a small hard drive. It is more likely that a new IDE disk drive will contain more than 8GB of storage. Disks this large can be an installation problem for Linux.

Users consume lots of disk storage. Users generally split their files between their desktop system and the file server, and most want to keep a large amount of their data on their desktop computers. User storage on a server is used primarily for file sharing and backup. A departmental server can often start out with a single large disk and add additional disks later, as they are needed. Allocate a minimum of 200MB for file sharing to each user. An 8GB disk with 2GB allocated to the system can support up to 30 users.

SCSI Adapters

To maximize the disk storage on your server as well as to enhance its performance, install a Small Computer System Interface (SCSI) adapter. Each SCSI adapter allows you to add up to eight peripheral devices.

> **TIP** For the best performance, use an ultra-wide SCSI adapter and ultra-wide SCSI disk drives.

A SCSI adapter also allows you to connect a SCSI tape drive to your server. Every server needs a backup device, and a SCSI tape drive is a good choice for a Linux server, because Linux provides excellent support for SCSI tapes devices, and these drives provide good performance.

Even if you have a SCSI adapter, use the built-in IDE controllers for some of your storage requirements. Most new systems come with two IDE controllers, each of which can support up to two IDE devices. Current IDE disk drives provide good performance and high-density storage for very low cost.

> ***TIP*** A Linux system has no problem supporting a mixture of SCSI and IDE devices. Use the SCSI disk drives for high-performance storage and IDE drives for less demanding applications.

CD-ROM Requirements

A perfect use for the IDE interface is to connect a CD-ROM drive. Don't waste a high-performance SCSI interface on a CD drive. Use an IDE CD-ROM that complies with the ATAPI standard.

> ***TIP*** Never use an old CD-ROM that runs off of a sound card on your server. CD drives are very inexpensive and easy to install; the cost of the CD-ROM drive is much less expensive than the staff time that is wasted fooling with obsolete equipment.

Additional Hardware Considerations

Beyond the basics of a CPU, memory, disk drives, and CD-ROM, you need to select a video adapter card, monitor, Ethernet card, and three-button mouse for your server. A few rules of thumb will help you make hardware selections:

- Check Patrick Reijnen's "Linux Hardware Compatibility HOWTO" at `sunsite .unc.edu/mdw/HOWTO/Hardware-HOWTO.html`. (Version 98.2 of this document is printed as Appendix F in *Mastering Linux* by Arman Danesh [Sybex, 1999].) Also check the home page of the Linux distribution you plan to use. See if the vendor lists any hardware incompatibilities before you buy. When possible, stick to the hardware list provided by the vendor.

- Don't purchase the very latest model of any piece of hardware. Most adapter cards are delivered initially with Microsoft Windows drivers. It takes a while before drivers are available for other operating systems, including Linux. So don't try the newest Ethernet card; use last year's model. See the case study at the end of this chapter for an example of the problems I encountered when I first upgraded my network to Fast Ethernet.

- A network server does not need high performance graphics. You'll use the server console to run administrative applications, not video games. Don't invest in the latest high-performance 3D graphics or the largest high-resolution monitor. Purchase a well established video card and monitor that are documented to work with Linux. Use the money you save for more memory or a faster CPU.

- Don't buy things you don't need. For example, network servers don't require sound cards or speakers. Avoid buying equipment that complicates configuration and adds no value.

- Never buy any "Win" hardware. Some internal modems are called "Winmodems" because they are designed to work with Microsoft Windows. Some printers, called GDI printers, depend on the Windows Printing System. These devices are so dependent on the Windows operating system that they cannot work without it. I have personal experience with this problem. I had an NEC Ready 9725 with a pre-installed Aztech multi-function board. The Aztech board is both a sound card and a modem. A quick check of Windows 95 shows the modem configured as a "Winmodem." I was able to use the sound function of the Aztech card under Linux, but not the modem. The solution was to purchase a separate modem, so I bought an external Hayes modem that works fine.

> **TIP** Sometimes the best deals on PCs are on systems that come pre-configured with lots of features. If you find yourself with such a system, remove all of the unneeded equipment and use it to enhance your desktop system. A cool sound system is a nice addition to your desktop, but it is unnecessary on a server. Superfluous equipment is just a source of trouble on a server system.

Most organizations buy PCs with Microsoft Windows pre-installed. It is also possible to buy computers with Linux pre-installed. (A link to vendors that sell pre-installed Linux systems can be found by following the Hardware path from www.linux.org.) This is often very cost effective, because the cost of in-house staff time is frequently higher than the small premium involved in purchasing systems with pre-installed software. Despite the cost effectiveness of this approach, I don't recommend it for all installations. You should install Linux several times yourself, even if you use some systems with pre-installed software. The reason is simple: In order to properly maintain a network server, you need to feel confident about installing and re-installing Linux.

> **TIP** Get an obsolete or underutilized system—an old 486 with 16MB of memory will do—and use it as a training tool. Take the system apart. Remove unneeded hardware, such as the sound card. Add in the type of Ethernet card you'll use on your real server. Then install Linux repeatedly until you feel at ease about tearing apart hardware and installing Linux software.

Understanding Your Hardware

Thus far, I have been speaking as if you will be able to select the exact hardware for your server. That would be nice, but often it is not the case. Frequently, you are given an existing system and told to turn it into a Linux server. Regardless of how you come by your computer, you need to know exactly what hardware components it contains.

If you select your own hardware and assemble the system, you will know all you need to know about the hardware. Many times, however, someone else asks you to configure a system for them that you know very little about. Don't be afraid to pull off the system case and examine the cards and devices installed in the system. Check the cables on the back of the system to see how everything is connected. Look at the documentation that comes with the system and, if Windows is installed, use the information in the Microsoft Windows configuration.

> **TIP** To check the hardware configuration through Microsoft Windows, open the Control Panel and double-click System. Select the Device Manager tab, click the Print button, and select the All Devices And Systems Summary report to get a hard-copy report of all the devices that Windows has configured.

Disk Drives

Understanding the hard drives is essential, because one of the installation tasks is to partition the hard drives and assign the partitioned space. Know the make, model, and capacity of each drive, and know if it is a SCSI or IDE drive. If you have an IDE drive, know if it runs in Logical Block Addressing (LBA) mode, which many large IDE disk drives do. LBA mode maps the physical sectors on the disk drive to logical sectors that are compatible with MS-DOS. LBA mode is defined in the computer's ROM setup.

The documentation that comes with your disk drive should provide all of this information. Unfortunately, many systems come without a complete set of hardware documentation. Don't despair. Many PCs display the disk drive characteristics during the boot process. If yours doesn't, check the settings in the BIOS setup program. To do this, boot the PC. Interrupt the boot process and enter the BIOS setup program. Go to the part of the setup that defines the IDE disk drives. Note everything about the drives: type, cylinders, heads, sectors, and mode. Frequently the drive type is "auto," which means that the drive configuration is automatically detected by the BIOS. In this case, the details of the disk drive structure may not be displayed by the BIOS setup program. If all else fails, you can always remove the drive from the PC to see if the drive characteristics are printed on the case—they frequently are.

CD-ROM Drives and Other Peripheral Devices

The CD-ROM is used to install the operating system and future upgrades. You should know if it is an IDE drive or a SCSI drive. It doesn't hurt to know the make and model of the drive, as well as its performance characteristics. As noted above, if it is not an IDE or SCSI CD-ROM, replace it. Of course, if you're helping a friend install Linux on their system, you may not be able to replace the CD-ROM drive. In that case, it is critical that you know the make and model of the device and that you check the hardware compatibility list to find out if it is even worth the effort to try the installation.

If you have a SCSI adapter, know the exact make and model of the card. The same goes for your Ethernet card.

For the mouse, you need to know if it is a serial, PS/2, or bus mouse. If it is a serial mouse, find out which port it is connected to. You need to know the protocol used by the mouse—Microsoft, Logitech, PS/2, IntelliMouse, or MouseMan. The mouse protocol can often be determined from the make or model of the mouse, or by flipping it over and looking at the label on the bottom of the mouse. You even need to be aware of the number of buttons on the mouse. You can use a two-button mouse with Linux, but it's not worth the bother. Get a three-button mouse.

Configuring X Windows is the main reason for understanding the mouse. Even more important for X configuration is understanding the video adapter and the monitor. For the video adapter, know the make and model as well as the amount of video RAM it contains. You also need to know the performance characteristics of the monitor. This includes the horizontal and vertical sync ranges. Also knowing the highest resolution the monitor can support doesn't hurt.

NOTE X configuration is not covered in this part of the book; you can read about it in Appendix A.

PC Hardware Basics

Before leaving the topic of hardware, a short review of the fundamentals of PC hardware is in order. Most system administrators do not have a good grasp of the underlying hardware of the system. Many Unix administrators work with expensive systems that have separate hardware support contracts and thus are discouraged from touching the hardware. Many Windows NT administrators don't see the details of the hardware either, because Windows does a good job of hiding those details.

Linux, on the other hand, openly displays detailed hardware information that can be confusing if you don't understand the details. (You'll see several examples of this in Chapter 3, *The Boot Process*.) Additionally, most Linux administrators are expected to handle software and hardware problems. For these reasons, it is important for you to have some idea of how PC hardware works.

Figure 1.1 is a block diagram of a personal computer. The figure simplifies the PC down to four basic components: the CPU, the system memory, the I/O bus, and the peripheral devices.

Figure 1.1 PC block diagram

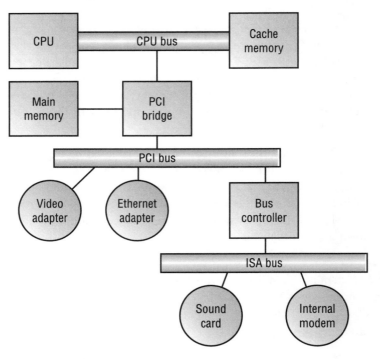

All system administrators know what processor is in the PC. They can tell you if it has a 450MHz Pentium III or a 350 MHz AMD K6, and they know how much memory the system has. However, the CPU and the memory are only part of the hardware story. Networks are really I/O devices. Therefore, the I/O bus architecture is a part of the system that the network administrator must also understand. And because it is the part of the PC that devices like the Ethernet adapter connect to, you should know how these peripheral devices interface to the bus.

At least seven different bus architectures have been used in the history of PCs. Currently, only two peripheral bus standards are commonly used: Industry Standard Architecture (ISA) and Peripheral Component Interconnect (PCI).

The ISA Bus

The ISA bus was introduced with the PC AT. This bus has been around for a long time, but its roots are even older. It is physically and electrically compatible with the 8-bit cards of the original PC, but it expanded the original PC bus from eight data lines to 16, and from six interrupt lines to 11. Adding data lines doubled the effective speed of the bus. Just as important, adding interrupts made it possible to expand the number of peripherals attached to the computer.

Additional interrupt lines are important because two ISA adapters cannot reliably share the same interrupt line. The reason for this goes back to the design of the original PC bus. Interrupts on the PC bus are edge-triggered, which means that the transition of the signal on the line causes the system to detect an interrupt. Specifically, IBM defined the interrupt as a transition from low to high. If more than one card attempts to use a single interrupt line, the interrupts can be lost.

This limitation of the PC bus caused IBM to increase the number of interrupt request lines when they designed the ISA bus. The original PC bus had only five bus slots. Since there were no multi-I/O cards when the bus was designed, six interrupts seemed sufficient. However, once multi-I/O cards came into existence, the number of interrupt request lines was clearly inadequate. The designers of the AT bus added another five lines, making a total of 11 lines. But even 11 IRQs can prove inadequate when a system is stuffed full of I/O cards.

Newer bus designs avoid this limitation by using level-sensitive interrupts. Level-sensitive interrupts are triggered by the level of the signal on an interrupt line. Therefore, it is electrically possible to have multiple adapters share a single interrupt.

The PCI Bus

The PCI bus uses the local bus for peripheral I/O. The local bus is the pathway that connects the CPU to the memory; it is a "fast and wide" bus that is at least 32 bits wide and clocked at the CPU's external clock rate. This means that the local bus can move at least 32 bits of data, a full four bytes, every clock cycle.

The PCI bus has several advantages:

> **Broad industry acceptance** Hundreds of companies make PCs with the PCI bus and PCI adapter boards.

Standard clock speed   The local bus runs at the external clock rate of the CPU. This might be 100MHz on one system and some other speed on another. The PCI interface is standardized on a fixed 33MHz clock rate, thus simplifying the manufacture of the adapter boards.

Standard connector   The PCI bus connector is the same on all systems.

Intelligent bus   The PCI bus protects the vital communications between the CPU and memory, and at the same time allows multiple devices, some of which may be bus masters, to use the local bus. The bus also supports automatic adapter board configuration through Plug and Play. The board, the bus, and the system cooperate to find and assign unused hardware configuration values.

Low cost   Compared to adapters for earlier types of intelligent peripheral buses, PCI boards are very inexpensive.

Systems based on the PCI bus maintain compatibility with the older adapter cards by including a second bus. The most common configuration is to have a PCI bus for high speed I/O and an ISA bus for compatibility with older cards and for lower speed I/O.

> **WARNING**   In addition to PCI and ISA connectors, many systems have an Advanced Graphics Port (AGP) adapter slot. AGP is only used for graphics cards, but on rare occasions, the AGP adapter can interfere with an Ethernet card if the Ethernet card is plugged into the PCI slot next to the AGP slot. To avoid problems, don't use that specific PCI slot if you don't have to.

PCI cards are better than ISA cards, not just because they are faster, but because they are easier to configure. ISA hardware must be configured via DIP switches, jumpers, and software. The default configuration values are often correct, and the best new ISA cards have intelligent software configuration programs that help you avoid setting the wrong configuration value. Nonetheless, correct hardware settings are required for the adapter to function correctly.

Adapter Card Configuration

ISA PC adapter cards require up to four distinct hardware configuration parameters: the Interrupt Request number (IRQ), the Direct Memory Access (DMA) Request number (DRQ), the I/O port address, and the adapter memory address. Each parameter has a range of possible values:

- The IRQ values available for adapter cards are 2–7 and 9–12. IRQs 0, 1, 8, 13, 14, and 15 are used by functions on the system board.

- The available DRQ values are 0–3 and 5–7. DRQ 4 is used by the system board.
- The I/O port addresses available for peripheral bus I/O are hex values in the range from 100 to 3FF. The I/O addresses from 000 to 0FF are reserved for the system board.
- The adapter memory address is the address in system memory where the ROM on the adapter card is mapped. The addresses available for adapter memory are from C0000 to DFFFF.

Planning and Installation

PART 1

> **WARNING**   Take care to ensure that each card has unique configuration values. Cards cannot share configuration values, or I/O conflicts can occur.

The Linux kernel displays the configuration of your ISA devices during startup. These messages are discussed in detail in Chapter 3; for now, let's look at what they show you about the adapter card configuration values:

```
eth0: SMC Ultra at 0x340, 00 00 C0 4F 3E DD, IRQ 10 memory 0xc8000-0xcbfff.
```

Without an understanding of the four basic adapter configuration values, this message would be meaningless. With such an understanding, this message provides useful information that is often difficult to dig out of other server operating systems. This message tells us that an SMC Ultra Ethernet adapter is installed in the system. The Ethernet address of the adapter is 00:00:C0:4F:3E:DD. The message tells us that the card is using I/O port address 340 and adapter memory address C8000 to CBFFF. The card is using IRQ 10. No DRQ is mentioned, because the SMC Ultra does not use DMA I/O.

IRQ Assignments   Of the four configuration values, IRQ assignment causes the most trouble. A quick look at the information in the previous list might make you think that the configuration resource in shortest supply is the DRQ. That's not the case. Seven DRQ numbers are enough, because few cards use Direct Memory Access to perform I/O. However, almost all ISA cards use interrupts and require an IRQ number. Some cards use more than one. For example, a multi-I/O card with two serial and two parallel ports might use four IRQ numbers. Additionally, several of the IRQ values are "pre-assigned" to commonly used I/O devices, which further limits your choices. Table 1.1 shows the traditional assignments of IRQs.

Table 1.1   Traditional IRQ Assignments

IRQ Number	Traditional Assignment
0	System timer
1	Keyboard
2	Cascade to second interrupt controller
3	Second serial port (COM2)
4	First serial port (COM1)
5	Second parallel printer port (LPT2)
6	Floppy disk controller
7	First parallel printer port (LPT1)
8	Real-time clock
9	Available for general use
10	Available for general use
11	Available for general use
12	Available for general use
13	Coprocessor
14	Hard disk controller
15	Available for general use

Avoid using an IRQ that is traditionally assigned to another I/O device when installing ISA network hardware. It's not always possible, but it's a good idea even if the device that uses the interrupt is not currently installed in the system. In the future, someone may install an ISA I/O card that contains the device, and it will probably default to its traditional IRQ assignment. If you've already installed an ISA network card using that IRQ, expect a call saying that "the network is broken," because IRQs cannot be shared reliably by ISA devices.

I/O Port Address Assignments   Some I/O port addresses are traditionally assigned to devices that are probably already installed in your system; Table 1.2 lists some of the common address assignments. These I/O port addresses should be avoided when configuring a network device to prevent possible conflicts.

Table 1.2   Traditional I/O Port Assignments

I/O Port	Assignment
1F0–1F8	Hard disk controller
200–207	Game port I/O
278–27F	Parallel printer port 2 (LPT2)
2F8–2FF	Serial port 2 (COM2)
378–37F	Parallel printer port 1 (LPT1)
3F0–3F7	Floppy disk controller
3F8–3FF	Serial port 1 (COM1)

Installation Planning

The next chapter walks you through a full installation of a Red Hat Linux system; it illustrates the basic steps of a Linux installation and points out the similarities in all operating system installations. But before you start, you need to collect all of the information you will need to provide the installation program to install and configure your system.

Hardware Information

You have begun to collect some of that information by learning about the server's hardware. Here is a list of the hardware information that is useful to have on hand during the installation:

Hard drive characteristics   These include the total storage of the drive; the drive geometry, which is the number of cylinders, heads, and sector; and the interface of the drive, either SCSI or IDE.

SCSI adapter information   This is the make and model of the adapter.

Ethernet adapter information   This is the make and model of the Ethernet adapter.

Video monitor characteristics These include the horizontal and vertical sync ranges of the monitor as well as its maximum resolution.

Video interface characteristics These include the make and model of the video card, the amount of video memory on the card, and whether the card has a clock chip (and if it does, the model of the clock chip).

CD-ROM characteristics These include the type of interface: SCSI, IDE, or "other." If an "other" interface is used, the make and model of the CD-ROM is also needed.

Network Information

In addition to information about the system's hardware, you need information about the network in order to configure a networked system. The required network configuration information is:

- An Internet address
- A network mask
- A host name
- A domain name
- The addresses of the domain name servers
- The default gateway address, unless a routing protocol will be used

Software Considerations

Finally, when you plan your server installation, you should consider what the server will be used for. Many servers are general purpose systems that provide a wide range of services. On those systems, you will install all of the system software. Other servers, however, have a dedicated purpose that only requires some of the system software. Don't install everything on these dedicated systems. Choose only the software that is needed.

Linux systems group related software packages together so that you can select the appropriate software for your system. Slackware defines 14 different groups that it calls *disk sets*; Red Hat 6 provides 34 different software groups that it calls *software components*.

Each Red Hat software component has a descriptive name that can help you determine whether or not it is useful for your server. Several of the components are clearly identifiable as network server packages. For example, News Server, NFS Server, Anonymous FTP Server, Web Server, and DNS Server are all software components. From the name alone, it is easy to tell what package would be required for a dedicated DNS server.

> ***TIP*** The installation program provides much more information than just the component name. How to obtain information, down to a description of an individual program, is covered in Chapter 2.

Several other Red Hat components provide the software packages needed for the client side of a network connection. Mail/WWW/News Tools, DOS/Windows Connectivity, Networked Workstation, Dialup Workstation, SMB (Samba) Connectivity, and IPX/NetWare (tm) Connectivity provide traditional Unix tools as well as tools to connect to NetBIOS and NetWare servers.

Finally, there are many components, such as the software development components, that are not directly related to a network server but may be needed on your system for development and maintenance. In the planning phase, it is useful to think of all of the groups of software that will be required for your server to fulfill its purpose.

Linux Services

If you know what you want your system to do, selecting the software required to get that job done is simple.

The network services started at boot time by Linux are closely related to the software that is installed. Red Hat allows you to choose these services. Again, you should not choose services you don't need, but you should run all of the services required for the server to meet its purpose. Table 1.3 lists each service offered by Red Hat and provides a short description of its purpose.

Table 1.3 Services Offered by Red Hat Linux

Service	Function
amd	The automount daemon mounts NFS file systems on demand.
apmd	The power management daemon monitors battery status.
arpwatch	This daemon keeps track of the Address Resolution Protocol (ARP) IP to Ethernet address mappings.
atd	The at daemon runs commands scheduled by the at command.
autofs	The auto file system mounts files when needed and unmounts them when they are not in use.

Table 1.3 Services Offered by Red Hat Linux *(continued)*

Service	Function
bootparamd	This is an obsolete daemon for booting diskless Sun workstations.
crond	The cron daemon runs user programs at periodic scheduled times.
dhcpd	The Dynamic Host Control Protocol (DHCP) server is used to configure network clients.
gated	The gateway routing daemon turns a Linux computer into an Internet Protocol router.
gpm	The general purpose mouse program provides mouse support for text-based applications.
httpd	The Apache software turns a Linux computer into a Web server.
inet	The Internet Server daemon (inetd) starts a large number of network services on demand.
innd	The Internet News daemon is a TCP/IP network news server.
keytable	This script loads the keyboard map.
linuxconf	This script starts linuxconf, the Red Hat system administration tool.
lpd	The Line Printer daemon provides printer services.
mars-nwe	The MARS NetWare system provides file and print services for NetWare networks.
mcserv	The Midnight Commander is a file manager that runs in a text window.
named	The Name Server daemon turns a Linux computer into a Domain Name Service (DNS) server.
netfs	This script mounts and unmounts all NFS mount points.

Table 1.3 Services Offered by Red Hat Linux *(continued)*

Service	Function
network	This script activates/deactivates all network interfaces configured to start at boot time.
nfs	This script turn a Linux computer into a Network File System (NFS) file server.
nscd	The Name Switch Cache daemon stores lookups for NIS clients.
pcmcia	This script installs PCMCIA support for laptops.
portmap	The portmapper daemon manages RPC connections for protocols such as NFS and NIS.
postgresql	This back-end daemon services SQL database requests.
random	This daemon provides higher quality random number generation.
routed	The routing daemon runs the Routing Information Protocol (RIP).
rstatd	The Remote Statistics daemon allows remote users to retrieve statistics from this system.
rusersd	This daemon allows remote users to locate users on any machine on the network.
rwalld	This daemon allows remote users to display messages on all of the active terminals on the system.
rwhod	This daemon allows remote users to list all of the users logged into a machine.
sendmail	This daemon turns the Linux system to an e-mail server.
smb	The Samba server turns the Linux system into a Server Message Block (SMB) server.
snmpd	The Simple Network Management Protocol (SNMP) daemon reports SNMP statistics to the SNMP monitor on your network.

Planning and
Installation

PART 1

Table 1.3   Services Offered by Red Hat Linux *(continued)*

Service	Function
sound	This script saves and restores sound card settings.
squid	This daemon is an Internet caching server.
syslog	This daemon provides a unified system log file.
xntpd	The Network Time Protocol (NTPv3) daemon provides NTP time synchronization.
ypbind	This daemon turns the Linux system into a Network Information Service (NIS) client.
yppasswdd	This daemon is the RPC server for setting NIS passwords.
ypserv	This daemon turns the Linux system into a Network Information Service (NIS) server.

This table shows the surprisingly large number of services that are available with Linux. All of them are useful, but not all of the time or on every system. What services you use depends on how you plan to use your system. Some services, like inetd and network, are required by every networked system. Others, like bootparamd, are rarely used. Few systems need to run a routing protocol like routed or gated. Server systems rarely have sound cards. Only the NIS server needs to run ypserv. Only a NetBIOS server needs to run smb. ruserd, rwhod, and rwalld are potential security problems that shouldn't be run on a server connected to the Internet.

This book covers many of the services in this table. As you go through the book, think about when and where you want to use these services. Don't expect to understand every service right away. If you're not sure about a service, you can start by enabling it and then change it later when you decide you don't need the service.

You can run linuxconf or tksysv at any time to change the services your system will offer. Both of these tools are user-friendly X Windows applications. tksysv, which runs on all Linux systems, is covered in Chapter 3; linuxconf, which is provided with Red Hat systems, is covered here.

Change to the root user account and enter **linuxconf** at the shell prompt. This opens the
linuxconf window. From the menu on the left side of the window, select Control ➤
Control Panel ➤ Activate Configuration to display the Service Control dialog box in the
right side of the linuxconf window (see Figure 1.2).

Figure 1.2   Selecting services with linuxconf

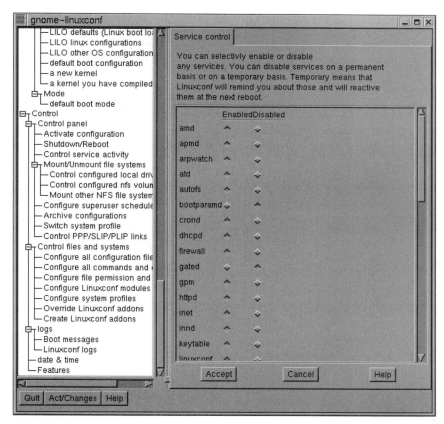

To enable or disable a service, click the appropriate button in the Service Control area of
the window.

> **NOTE** This process can be run at any time, allowing you to fine-tune the con-
> figuration after the system is running.

An Unnecessary Problem

An example of the problems that unneeded services can cause recently occurred at one of my customer's sites. A user installed Linux and enabled everything, including gated, which is intended for use on routers. It marks an interface as "down" when it doesn't receive routing information through the interface. So because the network interface appeared to be down, the user reported an intermittent hardware failure.

Final Words

As you saw in this chapter, there are several steps that must be taken before you can begin a Linux installation. Planning is often disregarded by technical people. I say, "One Linux vendor is as good as another," or "The newest and fastest hardware must be the best." Later I come to regret my rashness.

Planning doesn't have to be a chore. Shopping for the best distribution and the right combination of hardware can be fun! And I always enjoy exploring the hardware of a system. But regardless of whether or not you enjoy planning, it is essential.

Equipped with new software and hardware and armed with all of your planning information, you're ready to begin the installation. In Chapter 2, you'll put the plans into practice by installing Red Hat Linux 6.

Not-So-Fast Ethernet

A network support staff needs to keep ahead of its users. A few years ago, when Fast Ethernet switches became available, my staff and I purchased them for our own network. We purchased switches that could run at either 10Mbps or 100Mbps and that were auto-sensing. The auto-sensing capability meant that a switch would detect the speed of the traffic on an individual port and adjust its speed to the speed of the system connected to that port. This allowed us to continue supporting our 10Mbps Ethernet customers while experimenting with 100Mbps Fast Ethernet.

I couldn't stand to watch the Windows 95 systems get 100Mbps cards while the Linux systems had 10Mbps cards. I broke my own rule about using the newest hardware and searched for a Fast Ethernet card that would work on Linux. I found a driver for the DEC 21140 Fast Ethernet chipset in the Slackware system I was using at the time, and I found an SMC 10/100 Ethernet card that used the DEC chipset. I installed

the new adapter and configured the system to load the driver. The system reported the card and the correct configuration for the card during the boot. It also reported the correct IP configuration for the card. In fact, all of the diagnostic tools reported that the card was correctly configured.

There was only one problem—it didn't work! I was so convinced that I had it right that I tried swapping cables and changing ports on the Ethernet switch. I even tried a second SMC 10/100 card in case the first one was bad. None of this worked. The only thing that did work was admitting that I'd moved too fast in my hurry to get to Fast Ethernet. We had to re-install the old 10Mbps Ethernet cards and wait for the correct Fast Ethernet driver to be developed.

Chapter 4 returns to this little drama to see what the long-term solution was for our Fast Ethernet problem…

24*seven* CASE STUDY

2

Basic Installation

Now that you know how to select the Linux software distribution and the hardware to build your server, it's time to install that software onto that hardware. In some ways, this initial task is more challenging than that of configuring the various network services once the operating system is installed. This chapter examines the basic installation tasks and looks at the pitfalls that can make this the most frustrating part of building a Linux network server.

This chapter also illustrates one of the subtle reasons that Linux has a very low total cost of ownership. Some operating systems require you to master the installation of the operating system and then to master equally complicated installations to add remote access, routing support, or Web services. By the end of this chapter, everything will be installed— no additional complicated installations are required—and you'll be ready to configure any service.

Regardless of the distribution you are working with, when you install Linux from a CD-ROM, the installation process is basically the same. You begin by creating any necessary boot materials. For most systems, this means creating boot floppies and, for first-time installations, creating Linux boot floppies from DOS.

After creating the boot materials, you reboot the system so that it is running Linux and then run the Linux installation program. Many Linux distributions automatically start the install program; on others, you manually start the program. Either way, the system is running Linux when the Linux installation begins. You then partition the disk and load the Linux software into the new disk partition. When the loading is finished, you have a permanent Linux installation.

The following sections discuss each of these steps in detail. Red Hat Linux 6 is used as the primary example, but similar steps are taken for every Linux distribution. The details vary, but the overall pattern is the same.

Selecting an Installation Method

Linux can be installed from several different sources: FTP (File Transfer Protocol), NFS (Network File System), SMB (Server Message Block), HTTP (Hypertext Transfer Protocol), local hard drive, or CD-ROM. On your server system, you should install from a CD-ROM. It is the simplest and fastest installation method, and the CD-ROM provides a reliable backup media when you need to re-install.

You will *never* install from a local hard drive. This is an obsolete installation method that involves copying the operating system twice: first to a DOS partition on the local disk and then, as part of the actual installation, from there to the Linux partition. This installation method dates from the time when most systems had neither a CD-ROM nor a network interface.

All of the other installation methods depend on a network interface. FTP is primarily used to download files from the Internet, and the FTP method installs via the network from an FTP server. This method is used to directly load free Linux software across the Internet to a desktop system. You will not use this method on your server or network; downloading from the Internet is too slow and unreliable for a production environment. If you decide to use FTP installation at all, place the Linux files on an anonymous FTP server on your local area network and use the FTP installation mode to install client systems attached to that network.

The HTTP installation method is very similar to the FTP method and has similar constraints. The only real difference is the protocol used to move the files across the network: one uses FTP and the other uses HTTP.

If you use a network installation method, which you should only use for Linux desktop clients, it will probably be either NFS or SMB. SMB is the protocol used by NetBIOS servers for file sharing among Microsoft Windows systems. If the primary file server on your network is a Windows NT server, place the Linux distribution files on that server and use SMB to install Linux on your network clients.

Most likely, you will use NFS rather than SMB to share files between two Linux systems. NFS is the most popular file-sharing protocol for Unix systems. Place the Linux distribution files on a Linux server, and your desktop Linux clients can use NFS to install Linux.

> **NOTE** To find out more about using NFS or SMB, refer to Chapter 11, *File Sharing.*

Making the Boot Disk

Insert the Linux CD-ROM in the CD drive, insert the boot disk into the floppy drive, and turn on the computer. On most computers, that's all it takes to boot the Red Hat installation program. In fact, if you have a computer that can boot from a CD-ROM, you don't even need the floppy.

Unfortunately, it's not always that easy. First, the preceding paragraph assumes you purchased the Red Hat boxed set that includes both a CD-ROM and a boot disk. That's not always the case. Not every Linux distribution ships with a boot disk, and for that matter, not even every vendor sells the Red Hat boxed set that includes the floppy. Sometimes you have to make your own boot disk.

Making a boot floppy is easy, and the process is essentially the same for all Linux distributions: A boot image is copied from the CD-ROM to the floppy using either `rawrite` under DOS or `dd` under Unix. An example of each command illustrates how they are used.

In the Red Hat 6 distribution, the boot image is stored in the `images` directory, and the `rawrite` program is stored in the `dosutils` directory. The following sample code creates a Red Hat boot disk from files stored on a CD-ROM mounted on DOS drive D:

```
D:\>dosutils\rawrite
Enter disk image source file name: images\boot.img
Enter target diskette drive: a:
Insert a formatted disk into drive A: and press -ENTER- :
D:\>
```

Creating Additional Installation Disks

Boot disks are not the only disks that might be needed for an installation. While a server installation probably will not require additional installation disks, you may be called upon to install a system that does. A laptop that needs to install Linux through a PCM-CIA network adapter or through a CD-ROM drive attached to a PCMCIA SCSI controller is an excellent example of a system that may need an additional installation disk; for example, to install Red Hat 6 on such a laptop, you need a `pcmcia.img` disk. The following sample code creates that disk on a Linux system:

```
# mount /dev/cdrom /mnt/cdrom
mount: block device /dev/cdrom is write-protected, mounting read-only
# cd /mnt/cdrom/images
# dd if=pcmcia.img of=/dev/floppy
2880+0 records in
2880+0 records out
#
```

The first line of this listing attaches a physical device to a mount point with the `mount` command. The device, `/dev/cdrom`, is the CD-ROM drive. The mount point, `/mnt/cdrom`, is an empty directory on the Linux system. The directory structure of the CD-ROM is now available through the mount point, as illustrated by the change directory (`cd`) command that puts us in the `images` directory of the CD-ROM. The actual creation of the diskette is done by the `dd` command, which copies the input file `pcmcia.img` to the output file `/dev/floppy`. In this case, the output file is a physical device. On most Linux distributions, the device name `/dev/floppy` is equivalent to the device name `/dev/fd0`.

Linux Device Names

A few Linux device names are used in the example above, and more are used later in this book. If you're not familiar with Unix, Linux device names can be confusing. A quick look at the structure of device names will be useful for the uninitiated. The format of a device name is type, unit, and possibly partition. For example, `hda1` is an IDE drive (`hd`), the master unit on the first IDE controller (`a`), and the first partition (`1`) on that device. Another example is `sda2`. This is a SCSI drive (`sd`), the first disk drive on the SCSI chain (`a`), and the second partition (`2`). CD-ROM drives are not partitioned, so the partition number is not used, but because they attach to the same IDE controller, CD drives use the same device names as hard drives.

Table 2.1 lists the device names used by Linux, which are used repeatedly throughout this book.

Table 2.1   Device Names Used by Linux

Device	Linux Name	DOS Equivalent
IDE drives	hda to hdd	Available drive letters (e.g., C)
SCSI drives	sda to sdh	Available drive letters (e.g., C)

Table 2.1   Device Names Used by Linux *(continued)*

Device	Linux Name	DOS Equivalent
Modem	cua0 to cua3	COM1 to COM4
PS/2 mouse	/dev/psaux	No special name
Serial mouse	ttyS0 to ttyS3	COM1 to COM4
Parallel printer	lp0 or lp1	LPT1 or LPT2
Serial printer	ttyS0 to ttyS3	COM1 to COM4
SCSI tape	st0 to st1	No special name

These names lack consistency. The first IDE disk drive is "a" (hda) while the first SCSI tape drive is "0" (st0). The first serial port is called cua0 when a modem is attached to it and ttyS0 when a serial mouse or a serial printer is attached to it.

The reason for this seemingly inconsistent naming convention is that Linux device names are designed to be equivalent to the device names in Unix. Unix was developed over a long period of time by many different people, and the inconsistency is an artifact of that long and varied development. Linux addresses this complexity by providing logical device names for some of the most commonly used devices. Examples of this are the names /dev/floppy and /dev/cdrom used above. In addition to these, most versions of Linux also use /dev/modem for the modem, and /dev/mouse for the mouse.

> **NOTE**   All valid device names can be found in the device directory (/dev).
> Devices are frequently referred to buy their full path names (e.g., /dev/hda).

Slackware Boot Images

Both Red Hat and Caldera use a general purpose boot image and rely on the CD-ROM to provide all of the additional files needed to handle a variety of system hardware. Slackware, on the other hand, uses a different approach. The bootdsks.144 directory on the Slackware distribution contains many boot images that are all customized for certain hardware configurations.

Slackware counts on the system administrator to pick the boot image that is best for their situation. The net.i image provides the drivers needed for a network-based boot, the scsi.i image provides support for SCSI devices, and the bare.i image provides only the basic IDE device support found in all of the images.

The first step in installing Slackware is to pick the correct boot image and copy it to disk. (Even though I load Linux from an IDE CD-ROM, I prefer net.i, because it gives me immediate support for an Ethernet card.) Slackware also requires you to select and then copy a ramdisk image to a diskette from the rootdsks.144 directory. The ramdisk contains a root file system that includes the Slackware installation program. (I always use color.gz except for those times when I need pcmcia.gz for a laptop.)

Reading the paragraphs above, you might be concerned about the apparent confusion of directories and filenames found among the different distributions. Everyone seems to have decided to call the boot image something different and to store it in a different directory. Remember, installation and file placement are areas in which distributions differ. But also remember, you won't be working with three different distributions. You will pick one and stick with it until you have a good reason to change. So don't be overly concerned. For the purposes of this book, I point out these variations, but you should also notice the similarities. In all cases, the same commands (rawrite and dd) are used to do the same thing: copy images from CD-ROM to floppy disk. And in all cases, when you are done, you have a floppy that you'll need to boot the installation program.

Booting the Installation Program

When you boot the installation program, a screen full of information is displayed, and you are given a boot prompt. The information you receive varies from distribution to distribution. In our example, Red Hat uses it to tell you about help features for the installation program.

But the important thing on this screen is not the information, it's the boot prompt. Most distributions have it, and it serves the same purpose for them all: It gives the system administrator an opportunity to provide input to the boot process. For example, on a Red Hat system, you might enter:

```
boot: linux hda=1244,255,63
```

This tells the installation program the correct geometry for the hard disk.

Most systems don't need input at the boot prompt, so the first time you run the installation program on any system, just press the Enter key. Only if the installation fails should you try it again with input at the boot prompt. An example of this is if the installation program was not able to automatically detect all of the storage on the hard drive through normal probing. This can happen with very large disk drives on systems where the BIOS reports the wrong disk geometry to the operating system.

> **NOTE** See Chapter 3, *The Boot Process*, for more information about the commands that can be entered at the boot prompt.

Respond to the boot prompt to start the Linux kernel. Linux will detect some essential hardware during this phase. As it does, it displays information about that hardware on the screen. At this time, Linux also constructs a runtime environment for the installation program. Some systems, such as Slackware, prompt for a second disk to create this runtime environment. Other distributions, like Caldera and Red Hat, do not require a second disk. Take note of the hardware detected during the boot and the construction of the runtime environment.

When the system completes the initialization of the runtime environment, it displays a welcome message. Red Hat reminds you to register your purchase for free installation support and then asks you to select the language and keyboard you're using. If it detects a PCMCIA chipset, it asks you if you need PCMCIA support. At this point in the installation process, PCMCIA support is only required for laptops that have a CD-ROM attached through a PCMCIA interface card or for laptops that are installing over the network using a PCMCIA Ethernet card. If you answer that you do need PCMCIA support, you must provide a supplemental disk. Create it ahead of time with rawrite or dd by copying /images/pcmcia.img from the Red Hat CD-ROM.

The Red Hat installation next asks for the installation method. For a server, this is always Local CDROM. If you have an IDE CD-ROM drive, make sure the Red Hat CD-ROM is in the drive, because the installation program attempts to detect the correct drive by locating the CD-ROM. If the installation cannot detect the CD-ROM in an IDE drive, it will ask you what type of drive you have. The choices are SCSI and Other. Some servers use a SCSI CD-ROM drive. If you select SCSI, you will be asked to tell the installation program which SCSI device is the CD-ROM. The Other category is reserved for CD-ROM drives connected through sound cards or other proprietary interfaces. If you select Other, you will be given a list of supported CD-ROM drives. Select the make and model of your drive from that list.

NOTE If you have an IDE drive that was not detected, you must reboot the system and pass the name of the CD-ROM device to the installation program at the boot prompt. For example: `linux hdc=cdrom`.

After the CD-ROM is located, the Red Hat installation asks if this is a basic installation or an upgrade. The first time you install, it is a basic installation, so select that. Subsequently, however, use the Upgrade option to speed the installation and to save configuration files you have customized for your system. An upgrade installation runs faster, because only the kernel and packages that have been updated since your last installation are replaced. Configuration files are saved with the extension `.rpmsave` so that they can be reused. For example, `sendmail.cf` becomes `sendmail.cf.rpmsave`.

Next, Red Hat asks if you want a Workstation, Server, or Custom installation. As the system administrator, you should know as much as possible about how your server is installed and configured, so select Custom. Choosing Server will work, but you won't have as much control over the installation. The main difference between a server installation and a custom installation is the disk partitioning, which is discussed next.

Partitioning the Disk

Red Hat offers two different disk partitioning tools: Disk Druid and `fdisk`. Many Red Hat administrators use Disk Druid, but `fdisk` is used by the administrators of all Linux distributions. Though you'll only use one of these tools during the installation, this section will discuss both so that you're prepared to install any Linux distribution.

For most administrators, partitioning the hard drive is the installation task that creates the most tension. It doesn't need to be, particularly for a server installation. People worry about partitioning because they do not want to lose the data that is already on the disk.

The first time you install a server, there isn't anything on the disk that you want. Even if the PC came from the hardware supplier with Windows 98 pre-installed, it doesn't matter. You don't need it. Sometimes desktop client systems can *dual-boot*, which means that they have more than one operating system installed, and the user of the system boots the different systems for different applications. Servers do not dual-boot. A server needs to be available 24 hours a day, 7 days a week—it cannot be offline running Windows 98 when a client needs service. Therefore, extra operating systems installed by the hardware vendor are not needed. Because of this, you can start your server with clean disks, and you can partition your disks with less worry.

Working with a Windows Partition

When you install a server, you don't need to worry about retaining the data in a Windows partition. However, not every installation is a server installation. Frequently you *do* need to be concerned about the Windows partition.

To partition a disk that contains Windows, follow these steps:

1. Save the Registry.

2. Run a full system backup of Windows.

3. Open the Properties sheet for drive C, select the Tools tab, and click Defragment Now.

4. After the disk is defragmented, select the General tab and look at how much disk space is currently used. Add to this figure the amount of growth you want to allow for your Windows system. This gives you the minimum size for your Windows partition.

5. Copy the `fips` program from the Linux CD-ROM to the `c:\windows\temp` directory. (I always copy `fips` to the hard drive, because I find that many users do not have CD-ROM support when their systems are booted in DOS mode.)

6. Reboot the PC in DOS mode.

7. Run `fips`.

The `fips` program splits the hard disk into two partitions. The first, called the *old partition*, contains Windows and is just large enough to hold the data currently stored by Windows. Use the cursor keys to adjust the size of the old partition until it is at least the minimum size you calculated for the Windows partition. The remaining space, which `fips` calls the *new partition*, is the space that will be available for installing Linux.

`fips` is provided without warranty and is not supported by any of the Linux vendors, so, though I have used it many times with great success, I can't guarantee it will work for you.

> **Working with a Windows Partition** *(continued)*
>
> Another product that I have used that allows you to partition a disk without deleting an existing Windows partition is Partition Magic. It is a well-documented commercial product that I find easy to use. I'm sure there are other similar products, as well. Select the one you like best, but regardless of what you use, *always* back up your data before using any partition tool.

Partition Planning

Before you partition your disk drives, plan exactly how you want them partitioned. In order to do this properly, you need to understand what partitions are and why they are used. If you have a Unix background, this is probably something you understand well, but if you're coming from a Microsoft background, an explanation is probably needed.

Despite the fact that the DOS partitioning program and the Linux partitioning program share the same name (fdisk), the concept of partitioning for these two operating systems is subtly different. The DOS fdisk program divides a large disk drive into smaller logical drives. Using fdisk, for example, the C drive might become both C and D. Each of these logical drives has it own root file system and looks to the operating system and to the user as if they are physically separate devices. Conceptually, the DOS fdisk command is used to divide things.

On the other hand, the Linux fdisk command is part of a system that unifies things. Linux (and all other Unix-like operating systems) unifies all of the physical disk drives under a single root. Instead of seeing a separate device or partition as a logical drive (C or D), the user sees the partition as a directory in the file system, such as /home.

The directory to which a device or partition is "attached" is called a *mount point*. This term springs from the fact that Unix has been around for a long time. Back in the dark ages, a computer operator had to manually mount a "disk pack" on the spindle in the disk drive assembly. Disk packs are no longer used, but the flexibility of mounting and dismounting physical devices to directories within the file system lives on in the mount and umount commands.

The partition table you create is written directly to the disk drive. The mount points and the partitions that are mapped to them are written to the /etc/fstab file from where they are read during the boot process and mounted using a mount -a command. You saw an example of the mount command earlier in this chapter, and you'll see more examples of it before long.

The philosophy of the DOS and Linux file systems may be different, but the ultimate purpose of partitioning is the same. Partitions keep incompatible data separated, and they divide a large storage space into pieces that are more manageable and can be more effectively used. At a minimum, Linux requires two partitions: a swap partition and a root partition.

Most administrators use more than two partitions. Providing a partition to hold user files and another to hold the operating system software is an example of what administrators do to organize and manage their disk space. Table 2.2 lists the most common partitions and describes the purpose of each.

Table 2.2   Common Partitions

Partition Name	Description
swap	Required. It holds the swap space for the operating system.
root (/)	Required. The root is the foundation of the entire file system. On many systems it holds all of the files needed to boot the system.
/boot	Some distributions place the boot files in a separate directory so that a boot partition can be created separate from the root partition.
/usr	The usr partition contains most of the system software. With everything installed, it requires about 700MB.
/home	The home partition contains all of the user home directories and almost all of the user files.
/var	The var directory holds all of the printer spool files, the mail files, the news file, and the system log files.
/opt	The opt directory holds optional software. Some third-party software packages assume that the /opt directory is available and install themselves there by default.

Swap Partitions

The *swap partition* is needed to provide swap space for the operating system. Linux, like all Unix operating systems, uses virtual memory. In other words, it uses disk storage as an extension of the RAM memory. Inactive processes are swapped out of memory and held on disk whenever the RAM they occupy is needed by an active process.

The disk drive, and therefore swapping, is very slow. You want to design your server to avoid swapping to the greatest extent possible. If you need more memory, add more RAM—not more swap space. Swap space should only be needed for spikes of activity that temporarily create an unusually large number of processes.

The less real memory available to your machine, the more important swap space becomes. For systems with 32MB or less memory, you should plan for a swap partition of 32MB. If the memory is greater than 32MB, the swap space should be the same size as the memory up to 64MB, which is plenty of swap space for most servers.

NOTE   Regardless of the RAM size, the swap partition should *never* be larger than 127MB. That is the largest single swap partition Linux can use; besides, a larger swap space should not be needed.

Root Partitions

Planning the swap partition is easy: You must have one, and it will probably be 64MB. Planning the other partitions takes a little more thought. There are two basic schools of thought on partitioning: One school says to take all of the remaining disk space and create one large root partition, and the other says to create several carefully-sized partitions. Each school of thought has some merit.

The main advantage of creating a single large root partition is that it is easy. It also avoids the "root file system full" error that occurs when /tmp or /opt grow too large. If the entire disk is dedicated to the root directory, you won't have a full root file system until the entire disk really is full of data.

The problem with this approach is that it is *too* easy. It doesn't take the variability and load of a server into account. It works fine for a single-user client system with a single disk drive. But a server environment is more complex:

- A server usually has more than one disk drive. A single partition cannot span multiple disk drives.
- A server supports many users. The /home directory holds the files for these users and often grows very large.

Which Partitioning Scheme Is Right for You?

A single partition is simply not flexible nor reliable enough for a server. Placing all files in the root partition reduces the reliability of that critical partition by increasing the chance that the partition may become corrupted.

The root partition is critical, because it contains the files necessary to boot the system. Some Linux distributions consider this important enough to place the critical boot files in /boot so that a separate partition can be created just for them. In fact, if either the Workstation or Server installation classes are selected on a Red Hat system, a /boot partition is created. The Workstation installation class creates a swap partition, a /boot partition, and a root partition. This is a slight variation on the "single large root" partition scheme described above. The server installation class creates a swap partition, a /boot partition, a root partition, a /usr partition, a /home partition, and a /var partition. While different Linux vendors recommend different partitioning schemes, they all recommend more than one partition for a large server.

It is possible to create too many partitions. This creates a confusing structure and can waste space. The Red Hat server installation class provides a reasonable example of partitioning for a server. I use a similar structure for multiuser, multidisk servers:

- A swap partition of 64MB.

- A root (/) partition of 200MB.

- A /var partition of 300MB. Create a /var/tmp directory and symbolically link /tmp to it. The size of the /var partition can vary greatly depending on the number of users who leave their mail on the server and whether or not the server is a news server. Network news consumes a very large amount of space. If this is the enterprise news server, you need a larger /var partition. However, if the users don't store mail on the server and it isn't the news server, a /var partition is not needed at all. A 300MB /var partition is adequate for most servers.

- A /usr partition of 1.5GB. Create a /usr/local directory to contain local software. Create a /usr/opt directory and symbolically link /opt to it.

- A /home/user1 partition encompassing the remainder of the first disk drive, a /home/user2 partition encompassing the entire second disk drive, and so on. User storage is the major use for disk space. If you have multiple disk drives, it is probably to hold user data. User data is placed in the /home directory. Segmenting the directory in this way allows it to span multiple disks.

TIP To simplify the path names for the users and to simplify things when I want to move users between physical disks, I sometimes create a small /home partition on the first disk that only contains symbolic links to the users' real home directories that reside on other disks. (See the discussion about creating user accounts in Chapter 5, *Login Services.*)

Symbolic Links

This discussion of partitions may be confusing to readers who don't have a Unix background. I mentioned earlier that each partition is attached to the file system at a mount point. Thus, each partition appears as a directory within the file system and can be manipulated like any other directory. In Linux, directories can be "linked" together by creating a pointer from one directory to another. These pointers are called *symbolic links*. Use the ln command to create symbolic links. For example, this command creates a "directory" named /opt and links it to the real directory /usr/opt:

```
ln -s /usr/opt /opt
```

Once this symbolic link is created, any reference to the link /opt has a corresponding effect on the directory /usr/opt. An ls of /opt lists the directory contents of /usr/opt. A file stored in /opt is really stored in /usr/opt. Symbolic links increase the flexibility of the Linux file system.

No suggestions from anyone, no matter how experienced, can take the place of your own judgment. You know what you want to do with the server, you know how many people it will serve, and you know the tasks it will perform. Use this knowledge to plan your partitions.

Once you have developed a partition plan, you need to write the partition scheme onto the hard disk. You may use the Linux fdisk program to do this; on Red Hat systems, an alternative to fdisk is Disk Druid.

Partitioning with Disk Druid

If you select a custom installation, the Red Hat installation program asks you which Linux partitioning tool you would like to use. You can select the traditional fdisk program or Disk Druid, which uses a full-screen interface (see Figure 2.1). Use the tab key to move between fields on the screen, the spacebar to select items, and the cursor control keys to scroll through lists.

Figure 2.1   Disk Druid's main screen

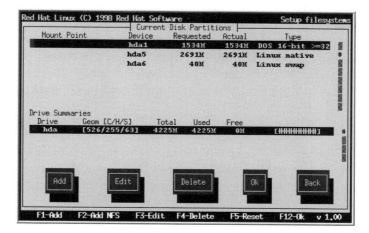

The top of the screen displays the current partition information for the disk. The first column of the display is the mount point. When you first install Red Hat, no mount points are listed.

The second column is the device name. These names follow the rules for device names described earlier, so the numbers at the end of each name are the partition numbers.

The next two columns define the space requested for a partition and the space that is actually allocated to the partition. The requested space is the minimum size for the partition you requested when it was created. The actual size may be larger than that if you clicked the Growable? checkbox when creating the partition. (More on this later.)

The last column displays the partition type. To install Linux, you need two types of partitions—one Linux swap partition and at least one Linux native partition.

In the middle of the screen, Disk Druid displays a summary of the disk drives installed in the system. Any of these can be partitioned. The disk drive summary lists the device name of each drive. Next, its geometry in the form of the number of cylinders (C), heads (H), and sectors (S) is listed. This is followed by the total storage in megabytes of the drive, the amount that is used, and the amount of storage that is still available.

At the bottom of the screen are the buttons that indicate the action you wish to take. You can add, edit, or delete a partition; for example, to delete a partition, you highlight the partition in the partition list at the top of the screen and then click Delete. When you're done, you can click OK to exit Disk Druid.

Deleting a Partition

Deleting a partition is frequently the first step in partitioning a disk; regardless of the type of system being installed, you usually start by removing unwanted partitions from the disk to make room for the new partitions. For example, new computers often come with Windows 98 installed in a partition that consumes the whole disk. As mentioned earlier, for a server installation, you start by deleting the Windows 98 partition, because servers do not normally dual boot.

If you are installing Linux on a client system that will be dual booting, you don't delete the Windows 98 partition, but you do start by deleting the other partition created by fips. (See the discussion of fips earlier in this chapter.)

Adding a Partition

To add a new partition to a disk, simply tab to the Add button in the Disk Druid main screen and press Enter. This displays the box shown in Figure 2.2. Here you enter the mount point for your new partition and the size of the partition in megabytes. If you check the Growable? checkbox, the size you enter for the partition will be its minimum size. If you do not check the Growable? checkbox, the size you enter for the partition will be its maximum size.

Figure 2.2   Adding a partition in Disk Druid

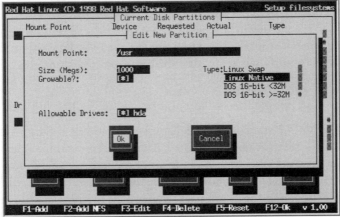

From the Allowable Drives list, select the disk drive for which you are creating this partition. Make sure that only one drive is selected. Otherwise Disk Druid can place the new partition on any one of the selected drives, which may not be where you intended.

Finally, from the Type list, select the partition type. The swap partition is of the type Linux Swap. All of the other partitions you create with Disk Druid will be Linux Native and will be used to hold the Linux operating system.

> **NOTE** You can create DOS partitions with Disk Druid, but you shouldn't need to, because even if Linux is going to share a disk with Microsoft Windows, Windows should already be on the disk when you install Linux. Linux is very tolerant of other operating systems, and many of the installation tools are built with the assumption that Windows will be there when Linux is installed. Windows, on the other hand, is not designed to fit itself into the space left by other operating systems. Things run most smoothly if you let Windows take what it wants first and then install Linux.

Using Disk Druid to delete old partitions, add new ones, and edit existing partitions, you can develop the partition table that you want. The partition table listed back in Figure 2.1 shows the partition plan of a desktop client. This same partition structure could be written to the disk using the traditional `fdisk` command.

Partitioning with `fdisk`

`fdisk` is a command-driven, text-based utility. At the `fdisk` prompt, enter any of the utility's single-character commands, which are listed in Table 2.3.

> **TIP** Use the m command to display a similar command list on your console.

Table 2.3   Single-Character `fdisk` Commands

Command	Function
a	Toggle the boot flag
b	Edit a BSD disk label

Table 2.3 Single-Character fdisk Commands *(continued)*

Command	Function
c	Toggle the DOS compatibility flag
d	Delete a partition
l	List the partition types
m	Display a list of fdisk commands
n	Add a new partition
p	Print the partition table
q	Quit without saving changes
t	Set the partition type
u	Select either sectors or cylinders as the units used to display partition size
v	Verify the new partition table
w	Write the partition table to the disk and exit
x	Enter experts mode

To partition a disk using fdisk, start by displaying the current partition table with the p command. Next, use the d command to delete any unneeded partitions. On a server, the 49unneeded partition is probably the partition created by fips. This client example shows these initial steps:

```
# fdisk
Using /dev/hda as default device!

Command (m for help): p

Disk /dev/hda: 32 heads, 63 sectors, 827 cylinders
Units = cylinders of 2016 * 512 bytes
```

```
Device     Boot Start   End Blocks Id System
/dev/hda1   *     1      76 76576+  6 DOS 16-bit >=32M
/dev/hda2         77     827 757008 6 DOS 16-bit >=32M


Command (m for help): d
Partition number (1-4): 2
```

After making sufficient space on the hard drive for the Linux installation, create the Linux partitions with the n command. This example creates two partitions for a client system:

```
Command (m for help): n
Command action
   e   extended
   p   primary partition (1-4)
p
Partition number (1-4): 2
First cylinder (77-827): 77
Last cylinder or +size or +sizeM or +sizeK ([77]-827): +32M


Command (m for help): n
Command action
   e   extended
   p   primary partition (1-4)
p
Partition number (1-4): 3
First cylinder (110-827): 110
Last cylinder or +size or +sizeM or +sizeK ([110]-827): 827
```

The first thing fdisk asks is whether you want to create a primary partition or an extended partition. Primary partitions are sometimes called *physical partitions*, because they exist as physical entities on the disk; extended partitions are sometimes called *logical partitions*, because they are logical entities that provide a way of referring to different parts of a physical partition. The example shows two primary partitions being created, partition number 2 and partition number 3. The first four partition numbers, partitions 1 to 4, are reserved for primary partitions. All other partition numbers are for extended partitions.

How Extended Partitions Really Work

When extended partitions are created, a physical partition is used to host the logical partitions. Refer back to the Disk Druid example shown in Figure 2.1. That figure shows three partitions: one physical partition and two logical partitions. In reality, the partition table contains four partitions: hda1, hda2, hda5, and hda6. The first partition, hda1, is a physical partition containing Microsoft Windows. The other partitions created by Disk Druid are logical partitions contained in physical partition 2, hda2. To see this, use fdisk to display a partition table created by Disk Druid:

```
# fdisk

Using /dev/hda as default device!


Command (m for help): p


Disk /dev/hda: 255 heads, 63 sectors, 526 cylinders

Units = cylinders of 16065 * 512 bytes


Device     Boot Start End    Blocks  Id System

/dev/hda1    *    1   191   1534176   c Win95 FAT32 (LBA)

/dev/hda2        192   526  2690887+  5 Extended

/dev/hda5        192   521  2650693+ 83 Linux native

/dev/hda6        522   526    40131  82 Linux swap


Command (m for help): q
```

How Extended Partitions Really Work *(continued)*

Notice in this example that the physical partition hda2 and the logical partition hda5 start at exactly the same physical location—cylinder 192. Further, notice that the physical partition ends at exactly the same cylinder—526—as the logical partition hda6. This view shows that extended partitions are really a way of subdividing primary partitions into additional parts.

I prefer to limit the partition table to the primary partitions when working with fdisk. Four partitions per disk are generally enough; too many partitions create an unnecessarily complex structure. Disk Druid, on the other hand, works with extended partitions, because Linux has more control over logical partitions, making it simpler to implement "growable" partitions. When fdisk prompts for the partition type you can choose either primary or extended. There is really very little operational difference between them.

After selecting the partition type, fdisk asks you to select the specific cylinder where the partition will start. Generally, you use the first free cylinder on the disk. The size of the partition is then indicated either by selecting an ending cylinder for the partition or an absolute size in megabytes. For example, +32M for 32 megabytes.

After creating the new partitions, use the p command to view them. You'll notice that all new partitions are created as Linux native partitions:

```
Command (m for help): p


Disk /dev/hda: 32 heads, 63 sectors, 827 cylinders
Units = cylinders of 2016 * 512 bytes


Device    Boot  Start End Blocks Id System
/dev/hda1 *        1  76 76576+  6 DOS 16-bit >=32M
/dev/hda2         77 109 33264  83 Linux native
/dev/hda3        110 827 723744 83 Linux native
```

Use the t command to set the correct partition types. The 32MB partition in the example is supposed to be a Linux swap partition. As shown in the following example, a Linux swap partition is a type 82 partition:

```
Command (m for help): t
Partition number (1-4): 2
Hex code (type L to list codes): l

  0 Empty            75 PC/IX
  1 DOS 12-bit FAT   80 Old MINIX
  2 XENIX root       81 Linux/MINIX
  3 XENIX usr        82 Linux swap
  4 DOS 16-bit <32M  83 Linux native
  5 Extended         93 Amoeba
  6 DOS 16-bit >=32  94 Amoeba BBT
  7 OS/2 HPFS        a5 BSD/386
  8 AIX              b7 BSDI fs
  9 AIX bootable     b8 BSDI swap
  a OS/2 Boot Manag  c7 Syrinx
 40 Venix 80286      db CP/M
 51 Novell?          e1 DOS access
 52 Microport        e3 DOS R/O
 63 GNU HURD         f2 DOS secondary
 64 Novell Netware   ff BBT
 65 Novell Netware
Hex code (type L to list codes): 82
Changed system type of partition 2 to 82 (Linux swap)
```

As the list of types shows, fdisk allows you to define a much wider range of partition types than Disk Druid does. However, you rarely need to use these. Most Linux installations only need Linux native and Linux swap partitions. Once, however, I was able to use this feature of fdisk to save a Windows NT user from a major headache. See the following sidebar for the full story.

Planning and
Installation

PART 1

---

fdisk to the Rescue

When Windows 98 was first introduced, a user attempted to install Windows NT 4 on a system that had a Windows 98 FAT 32 system on it. The user wanted to keep Windows 98, but he didn't back up the system, because he thought that two Microsoft products would be completely compatible. The Windows NT installation failed, but not until it had corrupted the Windows 98 partition in such a way that Windows 98 would no longer boot.

I used a set of Slackware installation boot disks to boot the system and run fdisk. I reset the first partition to type b (FAT 32) and made the partition bootable. After writing the corrected partition table to the disk, the system successfully booted Windows 98, and the user was able to back up his files.

Finish your new partition table by making the Linux native partition active. In this case, an active partition is a bootable partition. This is useful because it provides more flexibility when configuring the Linux loader (LILO), as you'll see in the "Installing the LILO Boot Loader" section later in this chapter. Only one partition should be bootable, so for this example, I made the DOS partition inactive (non-bootable):

```
Command (m for help): a
Partition number (1-4): 3
Command (m for help): a
Partition number (1-4): 1


Command (m for help): p


Disk /dev/hda: 32 heads, 63 sectors, 827 cylinders
Units = cylinders of 2016 * 512 bytes


Device    Boot Start End Blocks  Id System
/dev/hda1          1  76 76576+   6 DOS 16-bit >=32M
/dev/hda2         77 109  33264  82 Linux swap
/dev/hda3    *   110 827 723744  83 Linux native
```

```
Command (m for help): w
The partition table has been altered!

Calling ioctl() to re-read partition table.
Syncing disks.
Reboot your system to ensure the partition table is updated.

WARNING: If you have created or modified any DOS 6.x
partitions, please see the fdisk manual page for additional
information.
```

Notice that the a command is a toggle. When used on an inactive partition, it makes it active. When used on an active partition, it makes it inactive.

The completed partition table is written to the disk with the w command. fdisk then terminates with a series of status messages. The final warning message is always printed. It tells you to create DOS partitions with the DOS fdisk program and Linux partitions with the Linux fdisk program. For this reason, I recommend that if you are configuring a dual-boot client system, install Windows 98 first. Then use fips or Partition Magic to adjust the DOS partition before you install Linux.

As you can see, fdisk differs from Disk Druid in several ways. Disk Druid is used on Red Hat systems; fdisk runs on all versions of Linux. fdisk supports a wide range of partition types; fdisk doesn't support the concept of "growable" partitions. Additionally, when you create a partition, fdisk does not allow you to assign the mount point to the partition as Disk Druid does. You must define the mount points separately.

Defining Mount Points

After you write the partition table to the disk with the w command, the Red Hat installation program jumps to Disk Druid so that you can enter the mount points for the partitions. The process is simple:

1. Disk Druid displays the partition(s) you just created. Highlight the partition whose mount points you would like to enter.

2. Use the tab key to select the Edit button and press Enter. This displays a dialog box very similar to the box shown earlier in Figure 2.2.

3. Enter the mount points.

NOTE   Other versions of Linux do not use Disk Druid, but all give you a way to define mount points for the partitions.

Despite the fact that you can use Disk Druid to define mount points, they are not really stored as part of the partition table. Whether you enter the mount points in Disk Druid or later in the installation process, mount points are stored in the file system table, fstab, which is read during the boot.

The fstab File

The file system table, /etc/fstab, defines the devices, partitions, and remote file systems that make up a Linux computer's file system. The fstab file is a critical part of the system. It is used by swapon and mount during the system boot. It is read by several processes, but it is only written by the system administrator. The basic file is built from your input to the installation process. After that, it is maintained by you. You'll see more of this file in Chapter 11.

The installation program builds the basic fstab file for you. Assuming the partitions defined above in the Disk Druid example, the computer would have the following fstab:

```
/dev/hda5    /              ext2     defaults    1 1
/dev/hda6    swap           swap     defaults    0 0
/dev/fd0     /mnt/floppy    ext2     noauto      0 0
/dev/cdrom   /mnt/cdrom     iso9660  noauto,ro   0 0
none         /proc          proc     defaults    0 0
```

Each line in the table describes an individual piece of the file system. These pieces can be hard disk partitions, devices such as the floppy drive or the CD-ROM drive, or a file system from a remote NFS server. The first line in the sample file defines the root partition, the second line defines the swap partition, the third line is the floppy disk drive, and the fourth line is the CD-ROM drive. The last line defines /proc—the process information pseudo file system.

NOTE   The sample above does not have any NFS entries. (You'll see some examples of NFS entries in Chapter 11.) But the sample file, which was created by the Red Hat installation program, does have pretty much everything else that appears in an `fstab` file.

Every Linux system has a `/proc` directory. It is not a real file system, thus there is no device name in the first field of the `/proc` entry in the `fstab` file. Instead, it is an interface into the kernel data structures that provide information about running processes. A system administrator does not work directly with the `/proc` directory. Instead, you use administrative tools that extract the information from the `/proc` directory for you. All you really need to know is that every Linux `fstab` file must have a `/proc` entry, and you should *not* modify that entry.

The Entries in an `fstab` File

Each line in the `fstab` file is composed of six fields. The first field contains the file system name. It is either the keyword "none" for the `/proc` pseudo file system, the path name of a remote NFS file system, or the name of a local device. If it is a local device name, it must be the name of a "block special device." Linux systems have two types of devices: character devices, which provide data one character at a time, and block devices, which provide chunks of data. Use the `ls -l` command to find out which type a device is:

```
$ ls -l /dev/hda1
brw-r----- 1 root operator 3, 1 Jan 8 1998 /dev/hda1
$ ls -l /dev/ttyS0
crw-rw---- 1 root uucp    4, 64 Jan 8 1998 /dev/ttyS0
```

The first character in the output of the `ls` command shows the device type. If it is a c, the device is a character device. If it is a b, the device is a block device. All of the local devices in the `fstab` file are block devices.

The second field in each `fstab` entry is the mount point for the file system. Most of these are self-explanatory; they are the same mount points you entered when partitioning the disk. The clear exception is the swap space; it does not have a mount point. On Linux systems, the keyword `swap` appears in this field for the swap partition entry.

The third field defines the file system type. Table 2.4 lists the file system type keywords that are valid for this field and what they mean.

Table 2.4 Valid File System Type Keywords

Keyword	Meaning
minix	An obsolete local file system derived from the Minux operating system
ext	An obsolete local file system that has been replaced by the ext2 file system, and should no longer be used
ext2	The Linux native file system
xiafs	A little-used alternative to ext2
msdos	The MS-DOS file system
hpfs	The OS/2 HPFS (High Performance File System) file system
iso9660	The ISO standard for CD-ROM drives used by Linux
nfs	A remote NFS file system
swap	The swap partition
ignore	The entry is ignored; used to mark disk partitions as currently unused

The fourth field is a comma-separated list of options. The defaults option identifies file systems that:

- Can be mounted at boot time by the mount -a command
- Are mounted as read and write file systems
- Allow set uid and set gid processes
- Support both character and block devices

In other words, these are average Linux file systems.

The noauto option indicates file systems that are not automatically mounted at boot time. In the current example, these are the floppy and CD-ROM devices. The ro option on the CD-ROM indicates that it is a read-only device. There are many more options that can appear in the fstab file, all of which are discussed when I cover NFS and the mount command in Chapter 11.

The fifth field is used by the dump command to determine which file systems should be backed up. If this field contains a 0, dump will not back up the file system. If it contains a 1, dump will back up the file system every time dump is run. The dump command, of course, has its own syntax and commands. However, marking certain file systems in the fstab file with a 0 prevents dump from unnecessarily searching file systems, like /proc, that should never be backed up.

The sixth and last field in each entry is used by fsck to determine the order in which file systems should be checked. fsck is like the Windows ScanDisk program—it checks the file systems for damage and repairs any problems that it finds. File systems become corrupted, particularly when the system loses power or shuts down in an unexpected way. If the sixth field contains a 0, the file system is not checked. The file system is checked first if it contains a 1, second if it contains a 2, and so on. This permits you to define the order in which the systems are checked so that critical systems are checked before less critical ones.

> **NOTE**   The root partition should *always* be checked first.

fsck also allows you to specify that file systems should be checked in parallel to speed the process. For example, assume that you have two different partitions of similar size on two different disks. If you placed a 2 in the sixth field for both of these partitions, they would both be checked second.

> **TIP**   If you specify parallel checking, only do it for partitions that are on different physical disks, and only for those that are of similar size. Otherwise, you get no real performance gain.

Formatting Partitions

Once the disk is partitioned and the mount points are defined, the Red Hat installation process asks which partitions it should format. There are three things to remember when formatting partitions:

- Do not format partitions that contain any data you wish to keep.
- Never format a partition that contains another operating system if you intend to dual boot.
- Don't format partitions during an upgrade.

When initially formatting the Linux swap and Linux native partitions, check for bad blocks. Doing so takes longer, but it can save you a serious headache later on.

When you designate which partitions to format, the installation program does the work for you. The Linux native partitions are built with the `mke2fs` command. You can enter this command yourself if you ever need to manually build a partition. For example, if you add a new disk to an existing system, you can run `fdisk` to partition the disk and then run `mke2fs` to check and format the partitions. If you add a fourth disk to the IDE controller and want to format the third partition on that disk, you could use the command `mke2fs -c /dev/hdd3`.

The swap partition is built with the `mkswap` command and then is enabled with the `swapon` command. `swapon` is run every time the system is rebooted, so the command can be found in one of the boot scripts. You only need to run `mkswap` manually if the swap partition becomes corrupted. This is rare, but it does occur on systems that run more than one operating system. A boot message such as "Unable to find swap-space signature" indicates that the swap partition is corrupted. The following example shows a system administrator repairing a corrupted swap partition:

```
bash# mkswap -c /dev/hda4
Setting up swapspace, size = 65798144 bytes
bash# swapon /dev/hda4
```

In this example, `mkswap` rebuilds the swap space on partition `/dev/hda4`. The `-c` option causes `mkswap` to check for bad blocks. Based on the status message displayed by `mkswap`, the partition is 64MB. After the swap space is initialized, the administrator enables it with the `swapon` command. Now the corrupted swap space is repaired and ready for use.

NOTE Thankfully, the installation program hides all of these details from you when you first install a system. But it is nice to know about these commands if you ever need them.

Installing the Software

After you decide what partitions should be formatted, the installation program asks you to select the software to install. Red Hat, Caldera, and Slackware all provide similar choices. You can select related groups of software (Red Hat calls these components), individual packages, or everything.

Planning and Installation

PART 1

Installing everything is both simple and useful. It gives you a chance to play with all of the software when you are first learning about Linux. It is also useful when all functions from compute server to mail server are concentrated on one system.

WARNING   Installing everything is not the best approach for most operational servers. Avoid putting software on a system that doesn't need it. Unneeded software wastes disk storage and can open a hole for a security cracker to crawl through.

Selecting individual packages gives you the most control over the installation, but it also requires the most knowledge about each piece of software—and it is very time consuming. When you select individual package installation on Slackware, it provides a single-screen summary of each software package as it is ready to be installed. After reading the summary, you can choose to install the package or skip it.

Selecting components is a good compromise for most systems. It is faster than reviewing individual packages for installation, and it gives you more control over the configuration than installing everything.

Red Hat combines the speed of component installation with the ability to review individual packages. After you select the software components you want installed, highlight a component and press Enter to see a listing of the packages that make up that component. You can then press the spacebar to select or deselect any individual package.

If you want a description of a package, highlight it and press F1. Use these descriptions to help you select the minimum software needed to effectively run the server. Sometimes this is not obvious. For example, you might plan on creating a dedicated mail server. You know you need sendmail and the TCP/IP network software, but what about programming languages like C? You may want to download and compile the latest version of sendmail, which would require C. And you need m4 to create the sendmail configuration file. One possibility is to have a separate development machine compile sendmail and build the configuration files before placing them on the mail server. This is a more secure configuration than having a compiler sitting on the mail server, but many system administrators prefer to have the compiler on the machine where it is needed.

Red Hat has a nice feature that searches for software dependencies and warns you if you are trying to install a package that is dependent on another without installing the package it is dependent on. Once it alerts you to the problem, Red Hat will automatically install the required packages if you tell it to.

TIP   Loading the selected software packages is the most time consuming part of installing a Linux system. Go have a cup of coffee. When you come back, the system will be ready for configuration.

Configuring the Essentials

The Red Hat installation wraps up with the configuration of several devices and services. In these final steps, a mixed bag of devices and services are configured ranging from the mouse and the printer to the system clock and the root password. Not all of these are absolutely essential for booting an operational Linux system; I recommend skipping those that are not absolutely required and focusing on those that are essential for a running system. After the system successfully reboots as an operational Linux system, you can finish the configuration of the less essential services.

Each configuration step is described below in the order that they appear during the Red Hat installation.

The Mouse

The Red Hat installation program attempts to determine the type of mouse that is installed. It displays its best guess, allowing you to either approve its selection or to select another mouse from the list it displays. If you have a two-button mouse, make sure you check the Emulate 3 Button checkbox. If you have a serial mouse, identify the port it is attached to—ttyS0 to ttyS3 for COM1 to COM4.

NOTE   Linux works best with a three-button mouse.

The Ethernet Adapter

Configuring the network interface is the next step in the installation process. If this is a desktop client system that was installed via the network, you're given the option of keeping the temporary configuration created for the installation. For all other systems, you enter the configuration at this time. To configure a server, you need a host name, a domain name, an IP address, a network mask, a default gateway address, and up to three DNS server addresses.

First, the Red Hat installation asks you whether you will be using a static address, BOOTP (Bootstrap Protocol), or DHCP (Dynamic Host Configuration Protocol). Server systems always use static addresses. Once a static address is selected, you must enter all of the network configuration information manually.

NOTE   Red Hat makes best guesses about several network configuration values based on the IP address you enter. Check these values to make sure they are what you really want.

In contrast to servers, client systems can use BOOTP or DHCP. If either one of these options is selected, the network configuration is complete, because the BOOTP server or the DHCP server provides all of the configuration information. To use BOOTP or DHCP, you must, of course, install, maintain, and operate the appropriate server. (Chapter 10, *Desktop Configuration Servers*, describes how to set up a configuration server.)

After filling in the network configuration forms, set the system clock. To do this, simply pick your time zone from the list that is displayed.

System Services

The next step is to select the services that Red Hat should start each time the system boots. At this point, you should just accept the defaults. After the basic configuration is completed and the system successfully boots, log in as root and run ntsysv. Scroll through each service in the list. If there is a service you don't understand, highlight it and press F1 to see a short description of its function.

> **WARNING**   Select only those services that you actually need. Running an unneeded service wastes resources and can offer an entryway for Internet crackers.

> **NOTE**   To help you plan for this configuration step, all of the available services are listed in Table 1.3 in Chapter 1, *Getting Started*.

The Printer

Once you have chosen the system services to launch at boot, Red Hat asks if you would like to configure your printer. Again, I suggest you say No at this point and skip printer configuration until after you have the basic system running. Printer configuration can be complex, particularly if you're not familiar with the way Linux or Unix handles printers. I usually wait until after I have X running so that I can use the excellent X-based system administration tools to configure and manage the printer. See Chapter 12, *Printer Services*, for more information about Linux printer services and printer configuration.

The Root Password

After skipping the printer configuration, enter a root password for your first logon. Red Hat and Caldera put the selection of the root password in the installation program to ensure that you don't forget to select one. Any account without a password is an open invitation to a system cracker, which could lead to a security disaster. Be sure to pick a password, and make it a good one.

> **NOTE**   If you're not sure how to pick a good password, see the guidelines for doing so in Chapter 14, *Security*.

Selecting an Authentication Type

In addition to selecting a root password, Red Hat 6 gives you the opportunity to select optional password security. Traditionally, Linux stores passwords in the /etc/passwd file, and it encrypts the passwords stored there using standard Unix password encryption. There are two problems with this. First, Unix password encryption uses only the first eight characters of the password. Limiting passwords to eight characters limits a user's choice of passwords and makes them easier to guess. Second, the /etc/passwd file must be "readable" by every user and process on the system. Storing encrypted passwords in a file that everyone can read makes them vulnerable to attacks with password guessing programs.

The Authentication Configuration window in the Red Hat 6 installation gives you a way to address these security problems. Select the Use Shadow Passwords setting to store the encrypted passwords in the /etc/shadow file, which cannot be read by all users. Next, select the Enable MD5 Passwords checkbox to use the Message Digest 5 (MD5) algorithm to encrypt your passwords. MD5 encryption allows for passwords up to 256 characters in length, far larger than any user will ever need. Figure 2.3 shows the Authentication Configuration window with both security enhancements selected.

Figure 2.3   The Red Hat 6 Authentication Configuration setup

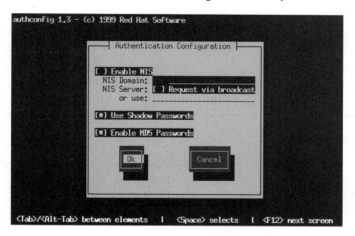

In addition to these two security enhancements, the Authentication Configuration window can be used to enable NIS passwords. Network Information Service (NIS) stores several administrative databases on a networked server. One of these databases is /etc/passwd. If your system gets its passwords from a NIS server, select Enable NIS and provide the name of your network's NIS domain. If you use NIS passwords, shadow passwords and MD5 passwords do not apply.

The Boot Floppy

The next installation step is to create a boot floppy for the new system. This is not the same as the installation boot floppy that was created earlier in this chapter. The floppy you create during this step contains the Linux kernel, and the basic configuration files need to boot a fully operational server with the configuration you have just created. It is absolutely essential.

WARNING   Don't skip this step! The boot disk is essential if you make a mistake in the Linux loader (LILO) configuration. This disk has saved me more times than I care to remember.

Installing the LILO Boot Loader

Once you have all of the essentials configured, the Red Hat installation asks you where you want to install the LILO boot loader: in the master boot record (MBR) or in the first sector of the boot partition. By default, Red Hat installs LILO in the MBR. Caldera, on the other hand, prefers to install LILO in the Linux root partition. Why the discrepancy between these two major vendors, and what difference does it make where LILO is installed?

There are advantages and disadvantages to both approaches. If LILO is installed in the MBR, anything in the existing MBR is destroyed. Most of the time, this is unimportant. LILO is designed to be compatible with the standard function and structure of the master boot record. See the "A Master Disaster" sidebar for information about what can go wrong when you write over the master boot record.

A Master Disaster

It is possible that your system is already using the MBR for some special purpose. I once lost the use of an entire hard drive by installing LILO on the master boot record. The system had an older Western Digital hard drive that was using the EZ Drive software. The computer itself was also an older system that was not able to address all of the hard drive's capacity without the help of the EZ Drive software. EZ Drive modified the MBR to load the software necessary to access the large disk. When LILO overwrote the MBR, the disk stopped working. The only way to recover was to reinstall EZ Drive. Luckily, the user still had the EZ Drive floppy and was able to find it.

If LILO is installed in the root partition's boot sector, the MBR is unaffected, but another problem may appear. The problem occurs when the boot partition is a logical partition, because a standard MBR only boots an active physical partition. The partitions created in the Disk Druid program are logical partitions; here is a sample fdisk listing of a partition table created by Disk Druid:

```
Device    Boot Start  End   Blocks  Id System
/dev/hda1 *      1    191  1534176   c Win95 FAT32 (LBA)
/dev/hda2      192    526 2690887+   5 Extended
/dev/hda5      192    521 2650693+  83 Linux native
/dev/hda6      522    526    40131  82 Linux swap
```

This partition table illustrates the problem that can be encountered. The active partition shown here is hda1, which contains MS-DOS. The Linux root partition, hda5, is not marked as active. This is despite the fact that the user completed the installation of LILO in the boot sector of the root partition and selected /dev/hda5 as the default partition for LILO to boot. Since a standard MBR only boots the active partition, it will boot Windows 95, not Linux.

However, the problem is not only that the MS-DOS partition is active and the Linux partition is not. You can test this by running fdisk and using the a command to change the active partition, assuming you have the all important boot floppy with which to reboot the system. First make the Windows 95 partition inactive. Then make the hda5 partition active. Try to boot from the hard drive, and the system tells you that there is no bootable disk installed. Reboot with the floppy. This time make hda5 inactive and make hda2, the physical partition that holds the logical partitions, active. Now the system will attempt to boot but it will hang.

Clearly, the issue is not only that the MS-DOS partition is active and the Linux partition is not. The underlying problem is that the standard MBR cannot boot an operating system that is located on a logical partition. To avoid this problem when working with Disk Druid logical partitions, install LILO in the master boot record.

To put LILO in the root partition, you must use fdisk to partition your disk, and you must put the Linux root partition in a physical partition. With Linux in a physical partition, you can install LILO in either the MBR or the boot sector of the root partition. I prefer using fdisk to create primary partitions and installing LILO in the boot sector of the root partition. In this manner, I avoid both of the problems described above—I can even install Red Hat on an old PC that depends on EZ Drive!

Planning and Installation

PART 1

After you select the location where LILO will be installed, the Red Hat installation program gives you a chance to enter any required boot input. Most systems do not require any input at this time, but if you had to use boot input in order to run the Linux installation program, you may need to use that same input *every* time Linux boots.

NOTE   See Chapter 3 for more information about boot input.

Finally, the installation program displays a list of all of the partitions that it thinks you might want to boot. It will list the Linux root or /boot partition as the default and assign it the boot label "linux." This means that LILO will boot this partition by default, or it will boot this partition if the keyword "linux" is typed at the boot prompt by the user.

If the disk has a DOS or Windows partition, the Red Hat installation program assigns it the boot label "dos." Change the boot labels with the Edit button or accept things the way Red Hat has them configured. Generally, there is no reason to change the labels.

X Windows

If you have installed X, Red Hat 6 starts Xconfigurator to configure it. Make sure you know the horizontal and vertical sync ranges of your monitor, the monitor's maximum resolution, the make and model of your video card, the amount of memory on the video card, and whether or not the video card has a clock chip (and if it does, the model of that chip). Armed with this information, you'll have no problems running Xconfigurator.

If you don't have all of the required information at your fingertips, you may want to skip X configuration for now, though this may be easier said than done. Many Linux systems make configuring X Windows an option that you can put off until later, but Red Hat 6 automatically starts the Xconfigurator. If you're not really ready to configure X, answer the questions to the best of your ability and then tell Xconfigurator *not* to automatically start X when you boot. Then you can boot the system and re-run Xconfigurator after you have all of the required information on hand.

WARNING   Do *not* run X Windows unless you know you have the correct setting for your monitor. The wrong settings can harm the monitor.

X configuration can be complex. If you have trouble configuring X, don't worry—you can boot the system with no problems, because this is the last item in the configuration, and X is not essential to get the system running. Also, it is easier to play with various X configuration options after the basic system is running because, while Xconfigurator is the only X configuration tool that can be used during the Red Hat installation, there are other configuration tools to choose from after the system boot.

> **NOTE** For complete information on configuring X Windows, see Appendix A, *X Windows Configuration*.

You're done! Red Hat warns you that it will reboot the system; when it does, the system should boot up under Linux. The next chapter covers the boot process in detail.

Final Words

Most of the installation steps in this chapter are integrated into a single installation program. Nonetheless, each step is distinct and requires your thought and input. Ninety percent of the time everything goes smoothly, but as the following case study shows, things can—and do—go wrong. To deal with the times when things don't go so smoothly, you need to fully understand the installation process.

A Real Installation, Warts and All!

I once had to install Linux on a "pre-packaged" PC. I installed Red Hat 5.2 on the user's brand new 450MHz Pentium II with 128MB of memory, a 10GB IDE hard drive, a 24X IDE CD-ROM, a 3COM 3c905 Ethernet card, and Windows 98 pre-installed. The user wanted to retain Windows 98 and dual-boot the system.

The first step was to boot Windows 98 and run ScanDisk and Disk Defragmenter. Next, I copied fips from the Red Hat CD to the C:\Windows\Temp directory. I restarted in MS-DOS mode and ran fips to divide the disk into an old partition of 3.7GB for Windows and a new partition of 6GB for Linux.

The system had a bootable CD-ROM, so I didn't make an installation boot floppy. Instead, I rebooted the system and the Red Hat installation program directly from the CD-ROM.

Everything ran fine until I started to partition the disk with Disk Druid. That's when I noticed that the system was reporting 8.4GB of space on a disk that contained 10GB! Despite the fact that the computer had a new IDE controller and a new ROM BIOS, it could not see more than 1024 cylinders. With the disk geometry that was defined for the disk, this gave me a maximum of 8.4GB. At this point, I had to abandon Disk Druid and use fdisk. (The Back button allowed me to move back through the installation until I was again prompted to select either Disk Druid or fdisk. This time I chose fdisk instead of Disk Druid.)

At the fdisk prompt, I typed **x** to enter expert mode. Once in expert mode, I was able to enter the real disk geometry as shown in the following example:

```
# fdisk
Using /dev/hda as default device!

Command (m for help): p

Disk /dev/hda: 255 heads, 63 sectors, 1024 cylinders
Units = cylinders of 16065 * 512 bytes

   Device Boot    Start     End    Blocks   Id  System
/dev/hda1    *        1      67   3538146    c  Win95 FAT32 (LBA)
/dev/hda2            68    1244   6454252    c  Win95 FAT32 (LBA)
Partition 3 has different physical/logical endings:
     phys=(1023, 254, 63) logical=(1243, 254, 63)

Command (m for help): x
```

```
Expert command (m for help): c
Number of cylinders (1-[1024]-65535): 1244
The number of cylinders for this disk is set to 1244.
This is larger than 1024, and may cause problems with:
1) software that runs at boot time (e.g., LILO)
2) booting and partitioning software from other OSs
   (e.g., DOS FDISK, OS/2 FDISK)

Expert command (m for help): r

Command (m for help): p

Disk /dev/hda: 255 heads, 63 sectors, 1244 cylinders
Units = cylinders of 16065 * 512 bytes

   Device Boot    Start      End   Blocks   Id  System
/dev/hda1    *        1       67  3538146    c  Win95 FAT32 (LBA)
/dev/hda2             68     1244  6454252    c  Win95 FAT32 (LBA)

Command (m for help): d
Partition number (1-4): 2

Command (m for help): n
Command action
   e   extended
   p   primary partition (1-4)
p
Partition number (1-4): 2
First cylinder (68-1244): 68
Last cylinder or +size or +sizeM or +sizeK ([68]-1244): +64M

Command (m for help): t
Partition number (1-4): 2
Hex code (type L to list codes): 82
Changed system type of partition 2 to 82 (Linux swap)

Command (m for help): n
Command action
```

24seven CASE STUDY

```
  e    extended
  p    primary partition (1-4)
p
Partition number (1-4): 3
First cylinder (77-1244): 77
Last cylinder or +size or +sizeM or +sizeK ([77]-1244): 1244

Command (m for help): W
```

The fdisk p command showed several interesting and important things. First, it told me that the current geometry for the disk was 255 heads, 63 sectors, and 1024 cylinders, which gives a maximum of 8.4GB of storage. Second, it told me that the physical addresses and the logical addresses didn't agree; specifically, the addresses disagreed on the last cylinder address: 1023 versus 1243. Counting from a first cylinder address of 0, the physical address was claiming that there were a total of 1024 cylinders, and the logical address was claiming a total of 1244 cylinders. I entered expert mode to fix this discrepancy.

The x command put me in expert mode. Once there, I set the number of cylinders with the c command, the number of heads with the h command, and the number of sectors with the s command. The physical and logical addresses agreed about the number of sectors and heads; they both had the maximum of 63 sectors and 255 heads. (Actually, you can specify 256 heads, but I have never seen it used.)

The difference was the number of cylinders. Therefore, I used the c command to define a physical limit of 1244 cylinders. fdisk warned me that a setting above 1024 can be incompatible with the boot loader and with other operating systems. However, I wasn't worried about this, because Microsoft Windows already had been installed within the first 1024 cylinders, and LILO would be installed within that limit. Furthermore, the user had no plans to ever install any other operating systems on this disk. So I entered the r command to exit expert mode and return to the regular fdisk menu.

When I entered p at the fdisk prompt, it displayed the true storage of the disk and did not complain about an address conflict. I then deleted the hda2 partition, which was the "new" partition created by fips, and created a 64MB swap partition and a 6GB root partition. I used this simple partition scheme because it was a desktop client system for a single user; a server would have had a more complex partition scheme.

I proceeded through the rest of the installation without incident and then rebooted. This installation wasn't smooth, but it did get done after one false start. However, we are not done yet—Chapter 3 will revisit this case study to see how I resolved some lingering problems from the disagreement between the physical and logical disk geometry.

3

The Boot Process

At the conclusion of the Linux installation in Chapter 2, *Basic Installation*, the PC rebooted under Linux. This chapter looks at what happens during a Linux boot. It examines the processes that take place and the configuration files that are read. Booting is a critical part of the operation of a server. If the server will not boot, it is unavailable to all of the users and computers that depend on it. For this reason, it is essential that you create a boot floppy during the initial installation as described in Chapter 2.

It is also important for the administrator of a network server to understand the boot process and the configuration files involved in that process. After all, you're the person who will maintain those configuration files and who will be responsible for recovering the system when it won't boot.

The term *boot* comes from *bootstrap loader*, which in turn comes from the old saying "pull yourself up by your bootstraps." The meaning of this expression is that you must accomplish everything on your own without any outside help. This is an apt term for a system that must start from nothing and finish running a full operating system. When the boot process starts, there is nothing in RAM memory—no program to load the system. The loader that begins the process resides in non-volatile memory. On PC systems, this means that the loader is part of the ROM BIOS.

Booting a Linux PC is a multi-step process. It involves basic PC processes as well as Linux processes. This complex process begins in the PC BIOS; it starts with the ROM BIOS program that loads the boot sector from the boot device. The boot sector either contains or loads the Linux loader (LILO), which then loads the Linux kernel. Finally, the kernel starts the init process, which loads all of the Linux services. The next few sections discuss this process in detail.

Loading the Boot Sector

The ROM BIOS is configured through the BIOS setup program. Setup programs vary among different versions of the BIOS, but all of them allow the administrator to define which devices are used to boot the system and the order in which those devices are checked. On most PC systems, the floppy drive (A) and the first hard drive (C) are the boot devices, and they are checked in that order. Of course, this is not always the case. Newer systems that permit booting from the CD-ROM usually list the CD-ROM as the first boot device followed by the first hard drive.

For an operational Linux server, set the ROM BIOS to check the floppy first and then the hard drive, even if you used a bootable CD-ROM for the initial installation. The reason for this is simple: The floppy is used to reboot an operational system when the hard drive is corrupted; the CD-ROM is only used to install or upgrade a system. During an installation, the system is offline, and you have plenty of time to fiddle with a BIOS setup program. But during an outage of an operational server, time is critical. You want to be able to reboot Linux and fix things as quickly as possible.

The first 512 bytes of a disk contain a boot sector. The ROM BIOS loads the boot sector from the boot device into memory and transfers control to it. The bootstrap program from the boot sector then loads the operating system.

Floppy disks have only one boot sector, but hard disks may have more than one, because each partition on a hard drive has its own boot sector. The first boot sector on the entire hard disk is called the *master boot record* (MBR). It is the only boot sector loaded from the hard drive by the ROM BIOS. The MBR contains a small loader program and a partition table. If the standard DOS MBR is used, it loads the boot sector from that active partition and then passes control to the boot sector. Thus both the MBR and the active partition's boot sector are involved in the boot process.

> **NOTE**   LILO can be used in place of the DOS MBR. If it is, booting is not limited to the active partition of the boot disk, because LILO has much more capability than the DOS MBR does. LILO is covered in the next section.

Figure 3.1 shows how the boot process flows from the BIOS to the MBR and then to the partition's boot sector. This figure assumes a DOS MBR and LILO in the boot sector of the active partition. Alternatively, LILO can be installed as the MBR to eliminate one step in the boot process.

NOTE   Chapter 2 discusses the pros and cons of placing LILO in the MBR.

Figure 3.1   The boot process flow

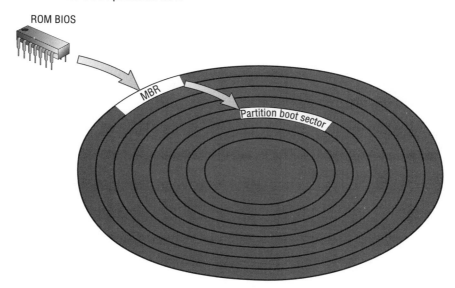

The BIOS may introduce some limitations into the Linux boot process. Linux can be installed anywhere on any of the disks available to the system, but if it is, it might not boot. The Linux loader depends on BIOS services. Some versions of BIOS only permit LILO to access the first two IDE hard drives, /dev/hda and /dev/hdb. Additionally, only the first 1024 cylinders of these disks can be used when booting the system. These limitations are at their worst on old systems. New systems have two IDE disk controllers providing access to four disk drives, and these controllers address up to 8GB of disk storage within the 1024 cylinder limit. An old system might only address 504MB in 1024 cylinders!

For a server installation, this is not a real problem. Since servers do not dual boot, everything can be removed from the disk, and the Linux boot files can be installed in the first partition without difficulty.

A desktop client is a different matter. Most desktops have Microsoft Windows installed in the first partition. If there is available space within the first 1024 cylinders on the first disk drive, use `fips` to create empty space and install the Linux root partition there. (This process is discussed in detail in Chapter 2.) Otherwise a client system that dual boots is forced to use one of the following options:

- Install LILO in the MBR of the first disk and install the Linux root partition in the first 1024 cylinders of the second disk.

- Use LOADLIN to boot Linux from Microsoft Windows instead of using LILO. (More on LOADLIN in the next section.)

- Make a complete backup of Microsoft Windows and repartition the disk in such a way that both Windows and Linux are in the first 1024 cylinders. This, of course, requires a complete re-installation of Windows.

- Create a Linux boot directory within the Windows directory structure that contains the Linux kernel and all of the files from the `/boot` directory. A current release of Linux is needed for this to work if Windows is using a FAT32 file system. You'll see an example of this approach later in the chapter.

- Upgrade the BIOS. This is not as difficult as it may sound. Most systems I have worked with allow the BIOS to be upgraded, and many motherboard manufacturers and many BIOS manufacturers have BIOS upgrades on their Web sites. However, don't undertake this lightly! A problem during the upgrade can leave the system unusable and send you scurrying to the computer store to buy a replacement BIOS chip.

TIP Don't be overly concerned about this potential problem. I have installed many Linux systems and have only had this problem once. In that case, it was an old system that could only directly address 504MB per disk drive. My solution was to give the user a 250MB drive from my junk drawer as a second disk. (I never throw anything away.) I installed LILO in the MBR of his first disk and Linux on the second disk. The user was happy, Linux was installed, and I had less junk in my drawer.

LOADLIN

LOADLIN is a program that loads Linux directly from DOS. Because it requires a system that boots DOS first, it is used on desktop clients more often than it is used on network servers. Use it to overcome the 1024 cylinder limitation described above, or to initialize hardware that can only be initialized in DOS. The latter problem occurs when the hardware has a special configuration or initialization program that must run under DOS and no equivalent program for Linux. To use LOADLIN:

1. Boot Linux using the boot floppy created during the installation. Make sure the DOS partition is mounted so that you can write to it from Linux.

2. Download LOADLIN from `metalab.unc.edu` (it's stored in the `/pub/Linux/system/boot/dualboot` directory under the name `lodlin16.tgz`). Use the `z` option on the `tar` command line to decompress and restore the file. Store the resulting executable in the DOS partition. Remember to place it in a DOS directory that is in the DOS execution path.

3. Copy the `kernel` to DOS.

4. Reboot the system to DOS. Enter the LOADLIN command in the form: `loadlin kernel root` `ro`, where `kernel` is the path name of the Linux kernel stored in the DOS partition, `root` is the Linux root partition, and `ro` is an argument that is required to tell LOADLIN to mount the Linux root directory as read-only. For example, assume you have copied the kernel to the DOS root directory on C, and assume that the Linux root partition is /dev/hda3. You would use the following LOADLIN command to boot the system: `loadlin c:\vmlinuz root=/dev/hda3 ro`.

> **NOTE** LOADLIN is not the only alternative to LILO. The system can be booted by SYSLINUX, which is another DOS program similar to LOADLIN, or by a commercial boot loader such as System Commander. If you have special boot requirements, there are a number of choices available.

Even though there are several options for loading Linux, on the vast majority of systems, the boot sector either contains LILO or loads an active partition that contains LILO. The remainder of this chapter treats LILO as *the* means for loading the Linux kernel.

Loading the Kernel with LILO

LILO, the Linux loader, is used on most Linux systems and is the loader you will most likely use. It is a versatile tool that can boot Linux from a floppy disk or from a hard disk. LILO can manage up to sixteen different boot images, and it can be installed on a floppy disk, in a hard disk partition, or as the master boot record. Yet with all of this power and flexibility comes complexity, which is illustrated by the large number of LILO configuration options.

Most installation programs lead you through a basic LILO configuration during the initial system installation, as we saw in the Red Hat example in Chapter 2. However, LILO configuration is not limited to initial installation; the LILO configuration file is accessible to the system administrator at any time.

LILO Configuration Options

Most of the time you don't need to think about the complexity of LILO; the installation program will lead you through a simple LILO installation. It is for those times when the default installation doesn't provide the service you want that you need to understand the intricacies of LILO.

LILO is configured by the /etc/lilo.conf file. Listed below is the lilo.conf file created by the Red Hat 6 installation program on one of my PCs. Other than the fact that I inserted three comments to make the file more readable, it is exactly as Red Hat 6 created it.

```
# gobal section
boot = /dev/hda3
map=/boot/map
install = /boot/boot.b
prompt
timeout = 50
# default boot image
image = /vmlinuz
    label = linux
    root = /dev/hda3
    read-only
# additional boot image
other = /dev/hda1
    label = dos
    table = /dev/hda
```

With this configuration, the user has five seconds to input either **dos** to boot Microsoft Windows or **linux** to boot Linux. If the user enters nothing, LILO boots Linux after the five seconds have expired. The following section examines each line in this file to see how LILO is configured.

A Sample `lilo.conf` File

A `lilo.conf` file starts with a global section that contains options that apply to the entire LILO process. Some of these entries relate to the installation of LILO by `/sbin/lilo` and are only indirectly related to the boot process.

> **NOTE**   The program `/sbin/lilo` is not the boot loader. The LILO boot loader is a simple loader stored in a boot sector. `lilo` is the program that installs and updates the LILO boot loader.

Comments in the `lilo.conf` file start with a sharp sign (#). The first active line of the global section in the sample file identifies the device that contains the boot sector. The option, `boot = /dev/hda3`, says that LILO is stored in the boot sector of the third partition of the first IDE disk drive. This tells us two things: where LILO is installed and where it isn't installed. LILO is not installed in the MBR of this system; it is installed in `hda3`, which must be the active partition.

The configuration option `map = /boot/map` defines the location of the map file, which contains the physical locations of the operating system kernels in a form that can be read by the LILO boot loader. `/boot/map` is the default value for the `map` option so it does not really need to be explicitly defined in the sample configuration file.

The `install = /boot/boot.b` line defines the file that `/sbin/lilo` installs in the boot sector. (`boot.b` is the LILO boot loader.) In this case, the line is not actually required, because `/boot/boot.b` is the default value for `install`.

The `prompt` option causes the boot prompt to be displayed. If the prompt option is not included in the `lilo.conf` file, the user must press a Shift, Ctrl or Alt key, or set the Caps Lock or Scroll Lock key to get the boot prompt.

The `timeout` entry defines how long the system should wait for user input before booting the default operating system. The time is defined in tenths of seconds. Therefore, `timeout = 50` tells the system to wait five seconds.

> **WARNING**   Don't use `prompt` without `timeout`. If the `timeout` option is not specified with the `prompt` option, the system will not automatically reboot. It will hang at the boot prompt waiting for user input and will never timeout. This could be a big problem for an unattended server.

If the timeout is reached, the default kernel is booted. The first kernel listed in the `lilo.conf` file is the default. In the sample configuration above, the `image` statement identifies the default kernel, which is `/boot/vmlinuz-2.2.5-15`. The `image` option allows you to put the Linux kernel anywhere and name it anything. For example, the same kernel on a Caldera 2.2 system is `/boot/vmlinuz-2.2.5-modular`.

> **NOTE**   The ability to change the name of the kernel comes in very handy when you want to do a kernel upgrade, which is discussed in Chapter 15, *Troubleshooting*.

There are several "per-image" options that can be used in the configuration file, some of which are specific to kernel images. The `label = linux` option defines the label that can be entered at the boot prompt to load the `vmlinuz-2.2.5-15` image. Every image defined in the sample file has an associated label entry; if users want to boot an image, they must enter its label.

The `root = /dev/hda3` option is also kernel-specific. It defines the location of the root file system for the kernel. The `lilo.conf` file should have a root option associated with the kernel image. If it is not defined here, the root file system must be defined separately with the `rdev` command. However, don't do that; define the root in the LILO configuration.

The next option, `read-only`, is also kernel-specific. It applies to the root file system described above. The `read-only` option tells LILO that the root file system should be mounted read-only. This protects the root file system during the boot and ensures that the file system check (`fschk`) runs reliably. Later in the startup process, the root will be re-mounted as read/write after `fschk` completes.

The last three lines in the sample file define the other operating system that LILO is able to boot. The other OS is located in partition 1 of the first IDE drive, `other = /dev/hda1`. As the `label = dos` entry indicates, it is Microsoft Windows. The `table` option points to the device that contains the partition table that should be passed to the other operating system. In this case, it is `hda`, which stands for the master boot record—the place where Microsoft Windows expects to find the partition table.

Only Linux and one other operating system appear in the sample file, which is the most common case. However, LILO can act as the boot manager for up to sixteen different operating systems. It is possible to see several `other` and `image` options in a `lilo.conf` file. Multiple image options are used when testing different Linux kernels. The most common reason for multiple `other` options is a training system where users boot different OSs to learn about them. In an average operational environment, only one operating system is installed on a server, and no more than two operating systems are installed on a client.

Additional `lilo.conf` Options

There are many more `lilo.conf` configuration options than those described above, but you won't need to use most of them. The sample configuration file from Caldera is almost identical to the one built by the Red Hat installation program, which is almost identical to the one built by the Slackware installation program. Basically, the small subset of options just described are the options used to build 99 percent of all LILO configuration files.

The one percent of systems that cannot be configured with the usual commands are often those systems with hardware difficulties. The `lilo.conf` file provides several options for dealing with hardware problems.

The `linear` option is sometimes necessary to handle large SCSI disks. The Red Hat installation program displays a Use Linear Mode checkbox in its Lilo Installation dialog box. The `linear` option forces the system to use linear sector addresses—sequential sector numbers—instead of traditional cylinder, head, and sector addresses.

NOTE   The Red Hat documentation of the Use Linear Mode checkbox is a little confusing. It implies that all disks that use LBA mode should use the checkbox. That's not true. Most IDE disks that use LBA do not require linear address mode.

It is possible to define the disk geometry directly in the LILO configuration file. For example:

```
disk = /dev/hda
  bios = 0x80
  sectors = 63
  heads = 32
  cylinders = 827
  partition = /dev/hda1
    start = 63
  partition = /dev/hda2
    start = 153216
  partition = /dev/hda3
    start = 219744
```

This example defines the geometry for the first disk drive, which normally has the BIOS address of hexadecimal 80. The sectors, heads, and cylinders of the disk are defined. In the example, the linear address for the start of each partition is also given. This is an extreme example of defining the disk drive for the system; I have never had to do this.

The `append` command is another LILO option related to defining hardware. (I have used this one.) The `append` option passes a configuration parameter to the kernel. The parameter is a kernel-specific option used to identify hardware that the system failed to automatically detect. For example:

```
append = "ether=10,0x210,eth0"
```

I have used this command to tell the kernel about the non-standard configuration of an Ethernet card. This particular option line says that the Ethernet device `eth0` uses IRQ 10 and I/O port address 210. (The format of the parameters that can be passed to the kernel are covered in "The Linux Boot Prompt," later in this chapter.)

> **NOTE**   Recent releases of Linux have gotten much better at detecting the configuration of Ethernet hardware, and software configurable cards are better at reporting their settings. Additionally, new PCI cards do not require all of these configuration values. Given these developments, I have not used this command lately. By and large, optional input is not needed to boot the system.

Setting Server Security

Two LILO configuration commands are useful for enhancing the security of your network server. If your server is in an unsecured area, it is possible for an intruder to reboot your system and gain unauthorized access. For example, an intruder could reboot your system into single-user mode and essentially have password-free root access to part of the system. (You'll read about single-user mode more later. For now, just take my word that this can be done.)

To prevent this, add the `password` and the `restricted` options to the `lilo.conf` file. The `password` option defines a password that must be entered to reboot the system. The password is stored in the configuration file in an unencrypted format, so make sure the `lilo.conf` file can be read only by the root user. The `restricted` option softens the security a little. It says that the password is required only when passing parameters to the system during a boot. For example, if you attempt to pass the parameter "single" to the system to get it to boot into single-user mode, you must provide the password.

The following example includes restricted password protection for booting the Linux kernel. The example is based on the `lilo.conf` file you saw earlier with a few lines removed that contain default values, for no other reason except to show that you can

remove those lines and still boot without a problem. The example shown below uses cat
to list the new configuration file and lilo to process it.

```
[root]# cat lilo.conf
# global section
boot = /dev/hda3
prompt
timeout = 50
# default boot image
image = /boot/vmlinuz-2.2.5-15
    label = linux
    root = /dev/hda3
    read-only
    password = Wats?Watt?
    restricted
# additional boot images
other = /dev/hda1
    label = dos
    table = /dev/hda
[root]# lilo
Added linux *
Added dos
```

Invoking lilo, which is called the *mapper,* installs this configuration. Until it is run and
maps the new configuration options, they have no effect. After running lilo, reboot.
Note that you don't have to enter the password at the boot prompt, because the configuration includes the restrict option. However, if you attempt to boot the system in single-
user mode, you will be asked for the password.

Changing the Default Operating System

Another example of when and why you would modify the LILO configuration is to
change the default operating system. First, assume that a woefully misguided user wants
his desktop to boot Microsoft Windows by default and to boot Linux only when

requested. No problem! The first operating system listed in the `lilo.conf` file is used as the default.

Assume the sample `lilo.conf` shown above. All you have to do is cut the three lines beginning with `other = /dev/hda1` and paste them in before the line `image = /boot/vmlinuz-2.2.5-15`. For a change like this, however, don't use an editor. Use the administrative tool that comes with your distribution of Linux instead. On a Red Hat system, you use `linuxconf` from the X Windows interface. On a Caldera system, use the `lisa` utility. Both of these programs provide menu-driven tools for simple LILO configuration maintenance.

Booting Linux from DOS

A more complex example of LILO configuration is the rare occasion when Linux must be booted from a directory within the Windows directory structure. The reason this could be required is the 1024-cylinder limitation described earlier. Let's look at how the boot directory is created and how LILO is configured to boot from DOS.

WARNING   Use LOADLIN if you must boot from DOS. A mistake when moving the /boot directory from Linux to DOS could make it impossible to boot from the hard drive. It is provided here only as an example of what can be done. Do *not* attempt this example without a boot floppy capable of rescuing the system if something goes wrong.

First, you need to create and populate the boot directory. (Everything can be done from Linux.) To do so:

1. Boot Linux from the boot floppy created during the installation.
2. Mount the DOS partition under Linux.
3. Make an empty directory on the DOS partition.
4. Copy all of the files, including the kernel, from /boot to the new DOS directory.
5. Make /boot a logical link to the DOS directory.

Here is an example of this procedure:

```
# mkdir /dosc/linux
# cp /boot/* /dosc/linux
# rm -r /boot
# ln -s /dosc/linux /boot
```

In the example, the DOS partition is mounted on directory /dosc. A new directory named /dosc/linux is made. (From the perspective of DOS, this will appear as the directory C:\LINUX.) Next, all of /boot is copied to /dosc/linux. On most systems, this step will put a copy of the Linux kernel in /dosc/linux. If it doesn't on your system, copy the kernel to /dosc/linux/vmlinuz. The existing /boot directory is then removed and replaced with a logical link to the new directory /dosc/linux. Now lilo.conf is ready to be modified.

While this modification to the LILO configuration is rare, it is relatively simple. You need to do two things: install LILO in the MBR and tell LILO where the kernel file is located. For example, modify the lilo.conf file to tell the mapper to put LILO in the MBR: boot = /dev/hda. Assume that a listing of the /dosc/linux directory shows that the kernel is stored there under the name vmlinuz-2.2.5-15. You would make sure the image option points to /boot/vmlinuz-2.2.5-15. The link that you created means that you are really reading the kernel from /dosc/linux. After you re-run lilo, the system should be able to boot from the hard disk using LILO even if Microsoft Windows occupies all of the first 1024 cylinders of the drive. This is because the MBR is the first sector of the disk, and the kernel is located within the cylinders occupied by Windows.

The Linux Boot Prompt

The LILO process is modified through the lilo.conf file. The kernel boot process is modified through input to the boot prompt. As with the LILO append option, the boot prompt is used to pass parameters to the kernel. The difference, however, is that the boot prompt is used to manually enter kernel parameters while the append option is used to automate the process when the same parameters must be passed to the kernel for every boot. Use the boot prompt for special situations, such as repairing a system or getting an unruly piece of equipment running, or to debug input before it is stored in an append command in the lilo.conf file.

You rarely need to pass parameters to the kernel through the boot prompt. When you do, it is either to change the boot process or to help the system handle a piece of unknown hardware. Handling undetected hardware is the most common reason for entering data at the boot prompt during the initial installation.

Sometimes the system has trouble detecting hardware or properly detecting the hardware's configuration. You saw an example of an incorrect hard drive configuration in the case study at the end of Chapter 2; the system could not accurately determine the disk configuration from the BIOS. As you'll see in a continuation of that case study at the conclusion of this chapter, the system needs your input at the boot prompt to properly handle the disk drive.

A large number of the boot input statements define the characteristics of SCSI adapters and devices because there are twenty different SCSI host adapter device drivers that accept boot parameters. In most cases, the system detects the SCSI adapter configuration without a problem. But if it doesn't, booting the system may be impossible. An example of kernel parameters for one of these SCSI adapter device drivers illustrates the role of boot input for all of them:

```
Linux boot: linux aha152x=0x340,11,7
```

The string `Linux boot:` is, of course, the boot prompt. The keyword `linux` is the label assigned to the Linux kernel in the LILO configuration. Use the label to tell LILO which kernel should receive the parameter. All hardware parameters begin with a driver name. In this case, it is the aha152x driver for Adaptec 1520 series adapters. All hardware parameters begin with a driver name. The data after the equal sign is the information passed to the driver. In this case, it is the I/O port address, the IRQ, and the SCSI ID.

The reserve and ether Arguments

Another boot argument that is directly related to the configuration of device drivers is the `reserve` argument. `reserve` defines an area of I/O port address memory that is protected from *auto-probing*. To determine the configuration of their devices, most device drivers probe those regions of memory that can be legitimately used for their devices. For example, the 3COM EtherLink III Ethernet card by default is configured to use I/O port address 0x300, but it can be configured to use any of 21 different address settings from 0x200 to 0x3e0. If the 3c509 driver did not find the adapter installed at address 0x300, it could legitimately search all 21 base address regions. Normally, this is not a problem. On occasion, however, auto-probing can return the wrong configuration values. In extreme cases, poorly designed adapters can even hang the system when they are probed. I have never personally seen an adapter hang the system, but some years ago I had an Ethernet card that returned the wrong configuration. In that case, I combined the `reserve` argument with device driver input, as in this example:

```
Linux boot: linux reserve=0x210,16 ether=10,0x210,eth0
```

This boot input prevents device drivers from probing the 16 bytes starting at memory address 0x210. The second argument on this line passes parameters to the `ether` device driver. It tells that driver that the Ethernet adapter uses interrupt 10 and I/O port address 0x210. This specific adapter will be known as device `eth0`, which is the name of the first Ethernet device. Of course, you'll want to use the Ethernet adapter every time the system boots. Once you're sure this boot input fixes the Ethernet problem, store it as a kernel-specific option in the `lilo.conf` file. For example:

```
image = /boot/vmlinuz-2.2.5-15
    label = linux
    root = /dev/hda3
    read-only
    append = "reserve=0x210,16 ether=10,0x210,eth0"
```

The `ether` argument is also used to force the system to locate additional Ethernet adapters. By default, the system assumes that there is only one Ethernet adapter installed. Assume you have two Ethernet devices, `eth0` and `eth1`, installed. Use this boot input to force the system to probe for the second device:

```
ether=0,0,eth1
```

Old Ethernet cards are a major reason for boot prompt input. If you have an old card and experience a problem, read the Ethernet-HOWTO for configuration advice on your specific card. New PCI Ethernet cards do not usually require boot input. Most current Ethernet cards use loadable modules for device drivers. If your Ethernet card is not recognized during the boot, it may be that its module is not loaded. The first step is to check the module's configuration.

NOTE See the "Loadable Modules" section later in this chapter for information about managing modules and for specific examples of loadable modules used for Ethernet device drivers.

The reboot Argument

While hardware problems are the primary reason for using boot input, it also can be used to change the default behavior of the boot process. One argument that does this is `reboot`. The root user can reboot the system by entering **shutdown –r now** or **reboot** at the shell prompt, or it can be rebooted with the three-finger salute (Ctrl+Alt+Del). All of these have exactly the same effect as entering **halt** and cycling the power because, by default, the Linux system does a cold boot every time the system reboots.

Use `reboot=warm` at the boot prompt to change reboots to warm boots. I don't bother with this. It has no effect on many systems, and on a few it can actually hang the reboot. But some people like to have the option of cold booting with the power button and of warm booting with the three-finger salute.

The panic Argument

A potentially more useful argument that changes the boot behavior is panic. It is possible for the Linux kernel to crash from an internal error, called a *kernel panic*. If the system crashes from a kernel panic, it does not automatically reboot—it stops at the boot prompt waiting for instructions.

Normally, this is a good idea. The exception is an unattended server. If you have a system that does not have an operator in attendance and that remote users rely on, it might be better to have it try an automatic reboot after it crashes. To tell the system to wait 60 seconds and then reboot, pass it this command: panic=60.

> **NOTE** This might surprise Windows NT administrators, but I have never had a Linux system crash. This is partly because I perform frequent maintenance on the systems, so they are routinely rebooted. But I have one specialized system collecting network measurement data, and providing Web access to that data, that has run continuously for more than a year without a single problem.

The init and single Arguments

In a normal boot process, the kernel starts the /sbin/init program. Using the init argument, it is possible to tell the kernel to start another process instead of /sbin/init. For example, init=/bin/sh causes the system to run the shell program, which then can be used to repair the system if the /sbin/init program is corrupted.

Booting directly to the shell looks very much like booting to single-user mode with the single argument, but there are differences. init=/bin/sh does not rely on the init program. single, on the other hand, is passed directly to init so that init can perform selected initialization procedures before placing the system into single-user mode. In both of these cases, the person who boots the computer is given password-free access to the shell unless password and restrict are defined in the lilo.conf file as described in the previous section.

> **NOTE** This section has barely touched upon the very large number of arguments that can be entered at the boot prompt. See the "BootPrompt-HOWTO" document, by Paul Grotmaker, for the details of all of them. Most Linux systems include the HOWTO documents in /usr/doc.

Hardware Device Driver Initialization

When the system boots, several things happen. You have already seen the part that LILO plays in loading the operating system, but that is only the beginning. LILO causes the Linux kernel to load, and then things *really* begin to happen.

The kernel is the heart of Linux. It loads into memory and initializes the various hardware device drivers. Most of the possible boot prompt arguments are intended to help the kernel initialize hardware, and the messages the kernel displays during startup help you determine what hardware is installed in the system and if it is properly initialized.

If you're a speed-reader, you can catch all of the messages as they scroll by on the screen. If you're like the rest of us, use the dmesg command to display the kernel startup messages; combine it with the more command or with grep to examine the startup messages more effectively. more allows you to scroll through the messages one screenful at a time; grep permits you to search for something specific in the dmesg output. For example, combine dmesg and grep to locate kernel messages relating to the initialization of the Ethernet device eth0:

```
$ dmesg | grep eth0

loading device 'eth0'...

eth0: SMC Ultra at 0x340, 00 00 C0 4F 3E DD, IRQ 10 memory 0xc8000-
0xcbfff.
```

Reading the kernel messages helps you understand what occurs when the system starts up. Don't read these messages word for word—too many details will just bog you down. What you should do is look at the messages to gain a sense of how the system works. The following sections cover what you see when you read the kernel messages—and what it all means. Of course there are slight variations among the messages displayed on various systems, but the descriptions in the following section should give you a very good idea of what is going on as the kernel initializes the hardware on your system.

Kernel Version Number Display

The first thing the kernel displays is the kernel version number followed by information about when and where the kernel was compiled. The kernel version number is made up of three parts: the major number, the minor number, and the revision or patch level. For example, 2.2.5-15 is a valid kernel version number. The major (first) number changes very infrequently. After years of development, Linux is now at major number 2. The minor (middle) number changes when substantial changes are made to the kernel. Even numbers (0, 2, 4, and so on) are used for stable, production quality kernels. Odd numbers (1, 3, 5, and so on) indicate test kernels.

TIP   Only use a kernel that has an even minor number in your network server. The even number (2.2) in the example indicates a production-quality kernel.

The revision (final) number changes frequently, as indicated by the 5-15 in our example. When sufficient enhancements or fixes accumulate, a new revision is released. In the example, 5 is the revision number. Patches are also frequently released. The example is at patch level 15.

Console Initialization

After displaying the kernel revision and the processor megahertz (MHz) rating, the kernel initializes the console. The message displayed by the kernel looks something like this:

```
Console: colour VGA+ 80x25
```

The message on your system will probably contain the string 80x25. That's because the average console display is 80 characters by 25 lines. This can be changed by setting the vga option in the lilo.conf file. Caldera sets the console display to 80x30, but most administrators don't fiddle with this setting.

Speed Index and Memory Calculation

Next, the kernel calculates the speed index, which it displays as BogoMIPS (bogus MIPS). The more BogoMIPS, the faster your CPU.

The kernel also initializes memory and displays the amount of memory available on the system. If the kernel is unable to detect all of the memory installed in your system, try using the mem argument at the boot prompt. For example, mem=128M tells the kernel that the system has 128MB of memory.

CPU Check

Once the system's memory is initialized, the kernel checks a few things about the CPU. It starts by checking the floating point processor (FPU) and the hlt instruction. Some ancient PCs have a math co-processor, a 387 FPU, that causes systems to lock up. Some old 486 CPUs go to sleep and never wake up when they encounter a hlt instruction. Both of these things can cause the system to hang or lock up, so the kernel checks to see if your system has these problems. Only a very, very old system would. If you have such a system, bypass the FPU problem by entering **no387** at the boot prompt; avoid the hlt problem by entering **no-hlt** at the boot prompt. Again, this problem would only exist on very old computers.

The third CPU check relates to more current systems. The kernel checks for a bug in Pentium processors called the "F0 0F bug." If this bug is found, the kernel automatically installs a workaround to avoid the problem.

PCI Bus Initialization and Probing

After running its CPU checks, the kernel displays a few messages about initializing and probing the PCI bus. Normally, these messages tell you everything is fine. But on rare occasions, they are followed by a warning message telling you that you have an unknown PCI device, as illustrated below:

```
PCI: Probing PCI hardware.

Warning : Unknown PCI device (5333:8a01).
          Please read include/linux/pci.h
```

This warning indicates a PCI device that is so new, it is not yet supported by the Linux kernel. (I generated the message shown above by running an old kernel on new hardware that has an odd multifunction board.) If you get such a warning, you should first try to determine what hardware is causing it. It is probably a fancy new sound card or multifunction card that may be unnecessary for your network server. If you determine that the card that is causing the error is a necessary part of the system, make sure you have the latest production kernel. (See Chapter 15 for information on upgrading the kernel.)

Rarely is there any need to report a new PCI device. In the vast majority of cases, the kernel identifies the PCI hardware and moves on. But if even the latest kernel cannot recognize the hardware, you need to replace it with supported hardware and report the unrecognized hardware to the PCI support group at linux-pcisupport@cck.uni-kl.de. Send an exact description of the unidentified hardware. Be specific! Include chip-level identifiers if you know them. Send the exact warning message text along with a list of the contents of /proc/pci. A cat of /proc/pci is shown below:

```
PCI devices found:
 Bus 0, device  8, function 0:
  IDE interface: Winbond SL82C105 (rev 2).
   Medium devsel. Fast back-to-back capable. IRQ 14.
```

```
Master Capable. No bursts. Min Gnt=2.Max Lat=40.
I/O at 0xffa0.
Bus 0, device  7, function 0:
VGA compatible controller: Trident TG 9440 (rev 227).
Medium devsel. Fast back-to-back capable. IRQ 11.
Non-prefetchable 32 bit memory at 0xff800000.
Non-prefetchable 32 bit memory at 0xffbe0000.
Bus 0, device  4, function 0:
Non-VGA device: Intel 82378IB (rev 67).
Medium devsel. Master Capable. No bursts.
Bus 0, device  0, function 0:
Host bridge: Nexgen 82C501 (rev 0).
Medium devsel. Fast back-to-back capable.
Master Capable. No bursts.
```

TCP/IP Initialization

Next, the kernel components of TCP/IP are initialized. This includes the fundamental protocols, such as IP (Internet Protocol), and the network sockets interface. Sockets is the application protocol interface developed at Berkeley for BSD Unix. It provides a standard method for programs to talk to the network. The TCP/IP initialization messages from a Red Hat 6 system are:

```
Linux NET4.0 for Linux 2.2
Based upon Swansea University Computer Society NET3.039
NET4: Unix domain sockets 1.0 for Linux NET4.0.
NET4: Linux TCP/IP 1.0 for NET4.0
IP Protocols: ICMP, UDP, TCP, IGMP
Initializing RT netlink socket
```

Serial Port Initialization

The kernel then initializes the PS/2 mouse port, if one is used, and the serial ports. It displays the device name, I/O port address, and IRQ of each serial port. It also displays the model of Universal Asynchronous Receiver Transmitter (UART) that is used for the serial interface. Old systems used 8250 UARTs, which are inadequate for use with modern modems and a problem for systems that need to run PPP. As this example shows, current systems use the faster 16550 UARTS:

```
Detected PS/2 Mouse Port.

Serial driver version 4.27 with MANY_PORTS MULTIPORT SHARE_IRQ
enabled

ttyS00 at 0x03f8 (irq = 4) is a 16550A

ttyS02 at 0x03e8 (irq = 4) is a 16550A
```

Disk Drive Initialization

In addition to initializing serial ports, the kernel also initializes all of the disk drives. The following example is from a small system that has two IDE hard drives, one CD-ROM, and one floppy drive:

```
PIIX3: IDE controller on PCI bus 00 dev 39

PIIX3: not 100% native mode: will probe irqs later

    ide0: BM-DMA at 0xffa0-0xffa7, BIOS settings: hda:pio, hdb:pio

    ide1: BM-DMA at 0xffa8-0xffaf, BIOS settings: hdc:pio, hdd:pio

hda: Conner Peripherals 2113MB - CFA2161A, ATA DISK drive

hdb: WDC AC32100H, ATA DISK drive

hdc: TOSHIBA CD-ROM XM-5602B, ATAPI CDROM drive

ide2: ports already in use, skipping probe

ide0 at 0x1f0-0x1f7,0x3f6 on irq 14

ide1 at 0x170-0x177,0x376 on irq 15

hda: Conner Peripherals 2113MB - CFA2161A, 2015MB w/0kB Cache,
CHS=1023/64/63

hdb: WDC AC32100H, 2014MB w/128kB Cache, CHS=1023/64/63

hdc: ATAPI 8X CD-ROM drive, 256kB Cache

Uniform CDROM driver Revision: 2.54

FDC 0 is a post-1991 82077

md driver 0.90.0 MAX_MD_DEVS=256, MAX_REAL=12
```

These messages contain a tremendous amount of information that can help you feel more knowledgeable about the hardware in your system and that can help you resolve hardware problems. The kernel displays the name of each device and some interesting information about the device. For each hard drive, you're given:

- The device name. In the example there are two drives: hda and hdb.
- The hard drive manufacturer. The sample system has one Conner and Western Digital (WDC).
- The model number. The Conner is a CFA2161A and the Western Digital is an AC32100H.
- The capacity. The Conner stores 2015MB and the Western Digital holds 2014MB.
- The disk geometry, which is 1023 cylinders, 64 heads, and 63 sectors for both drives.

Likewise, the kernel tells you the device name of the CD-ROM and the fact that it uses an ATAPI interface. You're also given the device memory addresses, I/O port addresses, and IRQs of the IDE controllers. The device name (fd0) and capacity of the floppy drive is displayed along with the type of floppy disk controller being used (82077).

The kernel concludes its portion of the boot process by checking the partition table and then mounting the root partition. Once the root is mounted, the kernel starts the init program, which controls the rest of the startup.

Loading Linux Services—The init Process

The init process, which is process number one, is the mother of all processes. After the kernel initializes all of the devices, the init program runs and starts all of the software. The init program is configured by the /etc/inittab file. The inittab file that comes with Red Hat 6 is:

```
#
# inittab  This file tells INIT to set up
#       the system for each run-level.
#
# Author:  Miquel van Smoorenburg,
#       <miquels@drinkel.nl.mugnet.org>
#       Modified for RHS Linux by Marc Ewing
#       and Donnie Barnes
```

```
# The runlevels used by RHS are:
#  0 - halt (Do NOT set initdefault to this)
#  1 - Single user mode
#  2 - Multiuser, without NFS
#   (The same as 3, if you do not have networking)
#  3 - Full multiuser mode
#  4 - unused
#  5 - X11
#  6 - reboot (Do NOT set initdefault to this)
#
id:3:initdefault:

# System initialization.
si::sysinit:/etc/rc.d/rc.sysinit

l0:0:wait:/etc/rc.d/rc 0
l1:1:wait:/etc/rc.d/rc 1
l2:2:wait:/etc/rc.d/rc 2
l3:3:wait:/etc/rc.d/rc 3
l4:4:wait:/etc/rc.d/rc 4
l5:5:wait:/etc/rc.d/rc 5
l6:6:wait:/etc/rc.d/rc 6

# Things to run in every runlevel.
ud::once:/sbin/update

# Trap CTRL-ALT-DELETE
ca::ctrlaltdel:/sbin/shutdown -t3 -r now
```

```
# When the UPS indicates power has failed,

# schedule a shutdown in 2 minutes.

pf::powerfail:/sbin/shutdown -f -h +2 "Power Failure; System Shutting
Down"


# If power is restored before the shutdown, cancel it.

pr:12345:powerokwait:/sbin/shutdown -c "Power Restored; Shutdown
Cancelled"


# Run gettys in standard runlevels

1:12345:respawn:/sbin/mingetty tty1

2:2345:respawn:/sbin/mingetty tty2

3:2345:respawn:/sbin/mingetty tty3

4:2345:respawn:/sbin/mingetty tty4

5:2345:respawn:/sbin/mingetty tty5

6:2345:respawn:/sbin/mingetty tty6


# Run xdm in runlevel 5

# xdm is now a separate service
```

NOTE The comments in this sample file were edited slightly to better fit on a book page. They are a reduced version of the actual comments from the Red Hat 6 inittab file.

Understanding Runlevels

To understand the init process and the inittab file, you need to understand *runlevels*, which are used to indicate the state of the system when the init process is complete. There is nothing inherent in the system hardware that recognizes runlevels; they are purely a software construct. init and inittab are the only reasons why the runlevels affect the state of the system.

The Linux startup process is very similar to the startup process used by System V Unix. It is more complex than the initialization on a BSD Unix system, but it is also more flexible. Like System V, Linux defines several runlevels that run the full gamut of possible system states from not-running (halted) to running multiple processes for multiple users. The comments at the beginning of the sample `inittab` file describe the runlevels:

- Runlevel 0 causes `init` to shut down all running processes and halt the system.

- Runlevel 1 is used to put the system in single-user mode. Single-user mode is used by the system administrator to perform maintenance that cannot be done when users are logged in. This runlevel may also be indicated by the letter S instead of the number 1.

- Runlevel 2 is a special multiuser mode that supports multiple users but not support file sharing. I have never used this mode.

- Runlevel 3 is the most commonly used run mode. It is used to provide full multiuser support with the full range of services. It is the default mode used on most servers.

- Runlevel 4 is unused by the system. You can design your own system state and implement it through runlevel 4. Though I've never used this, the technical editor of this book used runlevel 4 to implement a special login program.

- Runlevel 5 initializes the system as a dedicated X Windows terminal. I don't think this is the best use for a powerful Linux system, but if you want to, you can use the system as a terminal by starting it in runlevel 5. Red Hat 6 no longer uses this to run a standalone `xdm` system, but Caldera 2.2 uses it as a way to launch the `kde` desktop environment at startup. In fact, Caldera 2.2 makes runlevel 5 the default runlevel, because it treats the `kde` X Windows desktop environment as the default user interface.

- Runlevel 6 causes `init` to shut down all running processes and reboot the system.

- Runlevels A, B, and C are special runlevels. Frankly, I have never used them or seen them used in a Linux `inittab` file.

All of the lines in the `inittab` file that begin with a sharp sign (#) are comments. A liberal dose of comments are needed to help you interpret the file, because the syntax of actual `inittab` configuration lines is terse and somewhat arcane. An `inittab` entry has this general format:

    label:*runlevel*:*action*:*process*

The *label* is a one- to four-character tag that identifies the entry. Some systems only support two-character labels. For this reason, most people limit all labels to two characters. The labels can be any arbitrary character string, but in practice, certain labels are commonly used. The label for a `getty` or other login process is usually the numeric suffix of the `tty` to which the process is attached. Other labels used in the Red Hat Linux distribution are:

- `id` for the line that defines the default run level used by `init`
- `si` for the system initialization process
- `ln` where *n* is a number from 1 to 6 that indicates the runlevel being initialized by this process
- `ud` for the update process
- `ca` for the process run when Ctrl+Alt+Del is pressed
- `pf` for the process run when the UPS indicates a power failure
- `pr` for the process run when power is restored by the UPS before the system is fully shut down
- `x` for the process run to turn the system into an X terminal

The *runlevel* field indicates the runlevels to which the entry applies. For example, if the field contains a 3, the process identified by the entry must be run for the system to initialize runlevel 3. More than one runlevel can be specified, as illustrated in the sample file by the `pr` entry. Entries that have an empty runlevel field are not involved in initializing specific runlevels. For example, an entry that is invoked by a special event, such as the three-finger salute (Ctrl+Alt+Del), does not have a value in the runlevel field.

The *action* field defines the conditions under which the process is run. Table 3.1 lists all of the valid action values and the meaning of each one.

Table 3.1   Valid Action Values

Action	Meaning
Boot	Runs when the system boots. Ignores runlevel.
Bootwait	Runs when the system boots, and `init` waits for the process to complete. Runlevels are ignored.
Ctrlaltdel	Runs when Ctrl+Alt+Del is pressed, which passes the SIGINT signal to `init`. Runlevels are ignored.
Initdefault	Doesn't execute a process. It sets the default runlevel.
Kbrequest	Runs when `init` receives a signal from the keyboard. This requires that a key combination be mapped to `KeyBoardSignal`. (See the documentation in `/usr/doc/kbd-0.95` for information on how keys are mapped.)

Table 3.1   Valid Action Values *(continued)*

Action	Meaning
Off	Disables the entry so the process is not run.
Once	Runs one time for every run level.
Ondemand	Runs when the system enters one of the special runlevels A, B, or C.
Powerfail	Runs when init receives the SIGPWR signal.
Powerokwait	Runs when init receives the SIGPWR signal and the file /etc/powerstatus contains the word OK.
Powerwait	Runs when init receives the SIGPWR signal, and init waits for the process to complete.
Respawn	Restarts the process whenever it terminates.
sysinit	Runs before any boot or bootwait processes.
wait	Runs the process upon entering the run mode and init waits for the process to complete.

The last field in an inittab entry is *process*. It contains the process that init executes. The process appears in the exact format that is used to execute the process from the command line. Therefore the process field starts with the name of the process that is to be executed and follows it with the arguments that will be passed to that process. For example, /sbin/shutdown -t3 -r now, which is the process executed when Ctrl+Alt+Del is pressed, is the same command that could be typed at the shell prompt to reboot the system.

Special Purpose Entries

Using what you have just learned about the syntax of the inittab file, take a closer look at the sample. You can ignore most of the file; more than half of it is comments. Many of the other lines are entries that are only used for special functions:

- The id entry defines the default runlevel, which is usually 3.
- The ud entry calls the /sbin/update process, which cleans up the I/O buffers before disk I/O starts in order to protect the integrity of the disks.
- The pf, pr, and ca entries are only invoked by special interrupts.
- The x entry is only used if the system is a dedicated X terminal.

> **WARNING**   Some administrators are tempted to change the ca entry to elimi-
> nate the ability to reboot the system with the three-finger salute. This is not a bad
> idea for server systems, but *don't* do it for desktop systems. Users need to have
> a method to force a graceful shutdown when things go wrong. If this is disabled,
> the user might resort to the power switch, which can result in lost data and other
> disk troubles.

These entries are of limited interest to a system administrator. The remaining 13 lines of
the inittab file are really composed of only three distinct entries. Six of these lines start,
and when necessary restart, the getty processes that provide virtual terminal services.
One example will explain them all:

```
3:2345:respawn:/sbin/mingetty tty3
```

The label field contains a 3, which is the numeric suffix of the device, tty3, to which the
process is attached. This getty is started for runlevels 2, 3, 4, and 5. When the process
terminates (for example, when a user terminates her connection to the device) the process
is immediately restarted by init.

The path name of the process that is to be started is /sbin/mingetty. Red Hat 6 uses
mingetty, which is a minimal version of getty specifically designed for virtual terminal
support. On a Caldera 2.2 system, the path name would be /sbin/getty with the VC
command-line option, which tells getty it is servicing a virtual terminal. The result, however, would be the same: to start a virtual terminal service process for tty3.

The remaining seven lines are the real heart of the sample inittab file—they invoke the
startup scripts. The first of these is the si entry:

```
si::sysinit:/etc/rc.d/rc.sysinit
```

This entry tells init to run the boot script located at /etc/rc.d/rc.sysinit to initialize
the system. This script, like all startup scripts, is an executable file that contains Linux
shell commands. Notice that the entry shows you the full path to the startup script. One
of the most common complaints about different Linux distributions is that the key files
are stored in different locations in the file system. Don't worry about memorizing these
differences—just look in the /etc/inittab file. It will tell you exactly where the startup
scripts are located.

The remaining six lines are used to invoke the startup scripts for each runlevel. Except for
the runlevel involved, each line is identical:

```
l3:3:wait:/etc/rc.d/rc 3
```

This line starts all of the processes and services needed to provide the full multiuser support defined by runlevel 3. The label is 13, which is symbolic of level 3. The runlevel is, of course, 3. init is directed to wait until the startup script terminates before going on to any other entries in the inittab file that relate to run level 3. init executes the script /etc/rc.d/rc and passes that script the command-line argument 3.

Startup Scripts

Anything that can be run from a shell prompt can be stored in a file and run as a shell script. System administrators use this capability to automate all kinds of processes; Linux uses this capability to automate the startup of system services. Two main types of scripts are used: the *system initialization* script and the *runlevel initialization* scripts.

System Initialization

The system initialization script runs first. On a Red Hat 6 system, this is a single script named /etc/rc.d/rc.sysinit. Caldera 1.3 used two scripts: /etc/rc.d/rc.modules and /etc/rc.d/rc.boot. On a Slackware 3.5 system, it is a script named /etc/rc.d/rc.S. In all cases, the scripts perform essentially the same tasks. For an example, I'll use the Red Hat rc.sysinit script.

The rc.sysinit script begins by initializing the swap space. When the swapon command successfully initializes the swap space, it displays a message like this:

```
adding Swap: 33260k swap-space (priority -1)
```

Likewise, if the command is not successful, an error is displayed. The swap space error message discussed in conjunction with the mkswap and swapon commands in Chapter 2 was a startup message displayed by the swapon command.

The next major task of the rc.sysinit script is to run the file system check. To do so, it uses the fsck command. The fsck command checks the structure and integrity of the Linux file system much like scandisk does for Microsoft Windows. If a file system error is encountered that fsck cannot simply repair, the boot process stops, and the system reboots in single-user mode. You then must run fsck manually and repair the disk problems yourself. When you finish the repairs, exit the single-user shell. The system will then attempt to restart the interrupted boot process from where it left off.

TIP   When I finish with fsck in these circumstances, I sync, halt, and cold boot the system. I like to start with a clean slate.

Next, the initialization script mounts the /proc file system and mounts the root file system as read-write. Recall that the root file system was initially mounted as read-only. After the fsck completes, the root is remounted as read-write. The rc.sysinit script finishes up by loading the loadable kernel modules.

Other initialization scripts may look different from Red Hat's, but they perform very similar functions. For example, a Caldera system begins by loading the loadable modules. It then activates the swap space, does the file system check, and remounts the root file system as read-write. The order is different, but the major functions are the same.

Runlevel Initialization

After the system initialization script is run, init runs a script for the specific runlevel. On both Red Hat and Caldera systems, this is done by running a control script and passing it the runlevel number. The control script, /etc/rc.d/rc, then runs all of the scripts that are appropriate for the runlevel. It does this by running the scripts that are stored in the directory /etc/rcn.d, where *n* is the specified runlevel. For example, if the rc script is passed a 3, it runs the scripts found in the directory /etc/rc.d/rc3.d. A listing of that directory from a Red Hat system shows that there are lots of scripts:

```
$ ls /etc/rc.d
init.d  rc.local  rc.sysinit  rc1.d  rc3.d  rc5.d
rc      rc.news   rc0.d       rc2.d  rc4.d  rc6.d
$ ls /etc/rc.d/rc3.d
K10xntpd        K30mcserv      S05apmd     S45pcmcia    S72autofs    S95innd
K15postgresql   K34yppasswdd   S10network  S50inet      S75keytable  S99linuxconf
K20bootparamd   K50snmpd       S11portmap  S55arpwatch  S80sendmail  S99local
K20rstatd       K55routed      S15netfs    S55named     S85gpm
K20rusersd      K60mars-nwe    S20random   S60lpd       S85httpd
K20rwalld       K75gated       S30syslog   S60nfs       S85sound
K20rwhod        K80nscd        S40atd      S65dhcpd     S90xfs
K25squid        K88ypserv      S40crond    S72amd       S91smb
```

The scripts that begin with a K are used to kill processes when exiting a specific runlevel. In the listing above, the K scripts would be used when terminating runlevel 3. The scripts that start with an S are used when starting runlevel 3. None of the items in rc3.d, however, is really a startup script. They are logical links to the real scripts, which are located in the /etc/rc.d/init.d directory. For example, S50inet is linked to init.d/inet. This raises the question of why the scripts are executed from the directory rc3.d instead of directly from init.d where they actual reside. The reasons are simple. The same scripts are needed for several different runlevels. Using logical links, the scripts can be stored in one place and still be accessed by every runlevel from the directory used by that runlevel. Additionally, the order in which the scripts are executed is controlled by the script name.

In other words, the scripts are executed in alphabetic order based on name. Thus S01network is executed before S80sendmail. This allows the system to control through simple naming convention the order in which scripts are executed. Different runlevels can execute the scripts in different orders while still allowing the real scripts in init.d to have simple, descriptive names.

A listing of the init.d directory shows the real script names:

```
$ ls init.d
amd        dhcpd     innd      named     postgresql sendmail  xfs
apmd       functions keytable  netfs     random     single    xntpd
arpwatch   gated     killall   network   routed     smb       ypbind
atd        gpm       linuxconf nfs       rstatd     snmpd     yppasswdd
autofs     halt      lpd       nscd      rusersd    sound     ypserv
bootparamd httpd     mars-nwe  pcmcia    rwalld     squid
crond      inet      mcserv    portmap   rwhod      syslog
```

Several of these scripts are clearly of interest to us as administrators of network servers:

- The httpd script starts the Web server.
- The inet script defines the TCP/IP configuration and starts the Internet daemon (inetd).
- The named script starts the DNS name server.
- The nfs script starts the NFS file server.
- sendmail starts the e-mail server.

It is useful to know where these services really start in case something goes wrong. All of these scripts may be important when troubleshooting a network problem.

Controlling Scripts

You can control which scripts are executed and the order in which they are executed. You could do this by directly changing the logical links in the runlevel directory, but that's not the best way. It's easier to control this through tksysv, the SYSV Runlevel Manager.

tksysv is available on both Red Hat and Caldera systems, and it is run under X Windows. Figure 3.2 shows the SYSV Runlevel Manager window.

Figure 3.2   The SYSV Runlevel Manager window

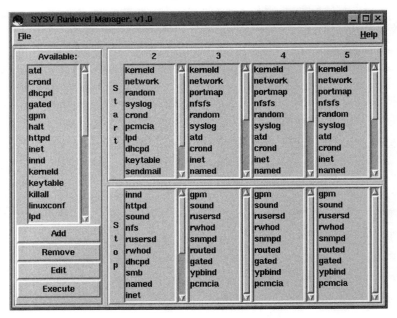

The SYSV Runlevel Manager lists all of the available startup scripts as well as the scripts that are currently being used by each runlevel. Each runlevel has a column of the display that is divided into Start and Stop scripts. These categories correspond to the S and K scripts in the directories. Using tksysv's simple visual interface, you can add scripts to a runlevel from the list of available scripts or delete scripts from a runlevel. You can even select a script from the list of available scripts and execute it in real time, though I don't recommend this.

The rc.local Script

In general, you do not directly edit boot scripts. The exception to this rule is the rc.local script located in the /etc/rc.d directory. It is the one customizable startup file, and it is reserved for your use; you can put anything you want in there. After the system initialization script and the runlevel scripts execute, the system executes rc.local. Since it is executed last, the values you set in the rc.local script are not overridden by another script.

If you add third-party software that needs to be started at boot time, put the code to start it in the `rc.local` script. Additionally, if something is not installed or configured correctly by the installation process, it can be manually configured in `rc.local`.

Loadable Modules

Loadable modules are pieces of object code that can be loaded into a running kernel. This is a very powerful feature. It allows Linux to add device drivers to a running Linux system in real time. This means that the system can boot a generic Linux kernel and then add the drivers needed for the hardware on your specific system. The hardware is immediately available without rebooting the system.

> **NOTE** Loadable modules span several of the topics discussed thus far. They play a role in the kernel, are a key part of the system initialization script, and are used to drive much of the hardware. This chapter introduces loadable modules because most are loaded during the boot process.

Usually you have very little involvement with loadable modules. In general, the system detects your hardware and determines the correct modules during the initial installation. But not always. Sometimes hardware is not detected during the installation, and other times new hardware is added to a running system. To handle these things, you need to know how to work with loadable modules.

Listing the Installed Modules

Use the `lsmod` command to check which modules are installed in your system. Here's an example:

```
# lsmod
Module              Pages              Used by
smc-ultra           1                  1 (autoclean)
8390                2      [smc-ultra] 0 (autoclean)
nls_iso8859_1       1                  1 (autoclean)
nls_cp437           1                  1 (autoclean)
vfat                4                  1 (autoclean)
```

Loadable modules perform a variety of tasks. Some modules are hardware device drivers, such as the smc-ultra module for the SMC Ultra Ethernet card. Other modules provide support for the wide array of file systems available in Linux, such as the ISO8859 file system used on CD-ROMs or the DOS FAT file system with long filename support (vfat).

Each entry in the listing produced by the lsmod command begins with the name of the module followed by the size of the module in memory pages. As the size field indicates, modules are small. Often they work together to get the job done. The interrelationships of modules are called *module dependencies*, which are an important part of properly managing modules. The listing tells you which modules depend on other modules. In our sample, the smc-ultra driver depends on the 8390 module. You can tell that from the 8390 entry but not from the smc-ultra entry. The 8390 entry lists the modules that depend on it under the heading "Used by."

All of the lines in this display end with the word autoclean. This means that a module can be removed from memory automatically if it is unused. All modules loaded by the system initialization script have the autoclean option set, but you can select different options by manually loading modules.

Manually Maintaining Modules

Modules can be manually loaded using the insmod command. This command is very straightforward—it's just the command and the module name. For example, to load the 3c509 device driver, enter **insmod 3c509**. This does not install the module with the autoclean option. If you want this driver removed from memory when it is not in use, add the –k option to the insmod command and enter **insmod –k 3c509**.

One limitation with the insmod command is that it does not understand module dependencies. If you used it to load the smc-ultra module, it would not automatically load the required 8390 module. For this reason, modprobe is a better command for manually loading modules. As with the insmod command, the syntax is simple. To load the smc-ultra drive, simply enter **modprobe smc-ultra**.

modprobe reads the module dependencies file that is produced by the depmod command. Whenever the kernel or the module libraries are updated, run depmod to produce a new file containing the module dependencies. The command depmod –a searches all of the standard modules libraries and creates the necessary file. After it is run, you can use modprobe to install any module and have the other modules it depends on automatically installed.

Use the rmmod command to remove unneeded modules. Again, the syntax is simple; rmmod appletalk removes the appletalk driver from your system.

These manual maintenance commands have limited utility on a running system, because the correct things are usually done by Linux without any prodding from you. For example, I booted a small system on my home network and immediately ran `lsmod`. I saw from this listing that I had `appletalk` and `ipx` installed, and I knew I didn't need either one. I typed in `rmmode appletalk`, but the message returned was "rmmod: module appletalk not loaded," because the system had already removed this unneeded module faster than I could type the command. Additionally, attempting to remove a command that is currently active returns the message "Device or resource busy." For these reasons, I have never actually used the `rmmod` command on an operational system.

Final Words

Well, that's it. You have taken your system from power up to full operation. You have gone from the ROM BIOS to the Linux loader to the kernel to the `init` process and, finally, to the boot scripts. All of these things play an important role in starting the system, and all of them can be configured by you.

Many operating systems hide the boot details from you, assuming that you will be frightened or confused by the messages. Linux hides nothing. It accepts the fact that ultimately you're in control of this process, and you can exercise as much or as little of that control as you want. You can modify kernel behavior with boot prompt input and control the behavior of the Linux loader through the `lilo.conf` file. You configure the process through the `inittab` file and control system services through the startup scripts. All of these configuration files are text files that are completely under your control.

Initial installation is usually completed in less than an hour, but when things go wrong, it can be one of the most challenging tasks for a system administrator, as the case studies illustrate. The information you have gained in this part of the book should make the task less of a challenge. Other than the `rc.local` file, you will rarely change the files discussed in this chapter. But when you do need to fix something, it is good to know where and when things happen in the boot process. Knowledge is a good thing, even if you only use it to ensure that your support contractors know what they are talking about.

The basic installation and planning covered in Part 1 of this book walked you through the creation of a running Linux system. In Part 2, *Internet Server Operations*, you'll turn that system into an operational Internet server by configuring the Internet services included in the basic Linux system. In the next chapter, *The Network Interface*, you'll begin that process by configuring the computer's network interface.

More Warts!

In Chapter 2, I installed Linux on a large disk by using expert mode in fdisk to change the number of cylinders in the disk geometry. I increased the cylinders from 1024, the system default, to 1244, the correct number for my large disk. Upon completing the installation, I rebooted the system. Everything appeared to work fine, but there was a subtle problem that was revealed when I entered the following few Linux commands:

```
# df
Filesystem          1024-blocks  Used Available Capacity Mounted on
/dev/hda3           6043889    883024  4691767    15%    /
/dev/hda1           3528376    200624  3327752     6%    /dosc
# fdisk
Using /dev/hda as default device!

Command (m for help): p

Disk /dev/hda: 255 heads, 63 sectors, 1024 cylinders
Units = cylinders of 16065 * 512 bytes

    Device Boot    Start      End    Blocks   Id  System
/dev/hda1              1      433   3538146    c  Win95 FAT32 (LBA)
/dev/hda2            434      442     72292+  82  Linux swap
/dev/hda3     *      443     1244   6381960   83  Linux native
Partition 3 has different physical/logical endings:
      phys=(1023, 254, 63)      logical=(1243, 254, 63)

Command (m for help): q
```

The df command showed that the Linux installation correctly partitioned and formatted the disk using the full 10BG of storage, and thus all 1244 cylinders. However, the fdisk printout showed that the system was still confused about the difference between the physical end and the logical end of the disk drive. The kernel provided fdisk with the wrong information, either because it was getting the wrong values from the BIOS or it was defaulting to maximum values that are inadequate for this disk drive.

To correct this, I provided the kernel with the correct disk geometry through the Linux boot prompt:

```
linux hda=1244,255,63
```

After the system rebooted with these kernel parameters, I reran the fdisk test to see how things were going:

```
# fdisk
Using /dev/hda as default device!
The number of cylinders for this disk is set to 1244.
This is larger than 1024, and may cause problems with:
1) software that runs at boot time (e.g., LILO)
2) booting and partitioning software from other OSs
   (e.g., DOS FDISK, OS/2 FDISK)

Command (m for help): p

Disk /dev/hda: 255 heads, 63 sectors, 1244 cylinders
Units = cylinders of 16065 * 512 bytes

   Device Boot    Start     End   Blocks    Id  System
/dev/hda1             1     433  3538146     c  Win95 FAT32 (LBA)
/dev/hda2           434     442    72292+   82  Linux swap
/dev/hda3     *     443    1244  6381960    83  Linux native

Command (m for help): q
```

fdisk warned me about potential booting and partitions problems, but I ignored this, because I won't be partitioning the disk again and I know it boots fine. The fdisk printout of the partitions then showed exactly what I wanted to see. The boot input corrected the problem, but I didn't want to have to manually enter kernel parameters at the boot prompt every time I rebooted. To automatically pass parameters to the kernel at every boot, I added the following append option to the Linux image definition in the /etc/lilo.conf file:

```
append = "hda=1244,255,63"
```

Note: I ran lilo to install the new lilo.conf configuration, and LILO indicated that it was successfully installed:

```
# lilo
Added linux *
Added dos
```

Now whenever I reboot, the system knows the correct disk geometry and uses the entire 1244 cylinders of our large disk drive.

24seven CASE STUDY

Part 2

Internet Server Operations

Topics Covered:

- Configuring the network interface with ifconfig and pppd
- Understanding the role of getty and login
- Configuring a PPP server and client
- Creating chat scripts
- Securing the rlogin command
- Understanding the Domain Name Service (DNS)
- Configuring the DNS resolver
- Configuring a DNS server with named
- Configuring sendmail with m4
- Understanding the sendmail.cf file
- Configuring an Apache Web server
- Configuring routing with route, routed, and gated
- Using Linux as an address-translation proxy server

4

The Network Interface

Nothing is more basic to network configuration than the interface the system uses to connect to the network. On most Linux servers, the network interface is an Ethernet card. Yet Linux systems are not limited to using Ethernet for network access. Another widely used network interface is the computer's serial port. Linux provides excellent support for serial-line communications, including a full range of tools to run TCP/IP over a serial line using Point-to-Point Protocol (PPP).

In Part 1 of this book, you installed Linux on your server. In Part 2 of the book, you'll configure the basic network services for your users. This chapter begins that discussion by looking at how network interfaces are installed and configured. It begins with the Ethernet interface, which is the most popular TCP/IP network interface. It then goes on to discuss how software is normally configured, as well as the commands you can use to modify the Ethernet configuration. Finally, this chapter covers how the serial interface is used for data communications and how PPP software is configured to turn the serial port into a TCP/IP network interface.

Configuring an Ethernet Interface

A Linux Ethernet interface is composed of both a hardware adapter card and a software driver. The hardware is an ISA or PCI adapter card. There are many possible brands and models of Ethernet cards. Select a card that is listed in "The Linux Hardware Compatibility HOWTO" by Patrick Reijnen (`sunsite.unc.edu/mdw/HOWTO/Hardware-HOWTO.html`). When you find a card that works well for you, stick with it until you have a good reason to change.

Loadable Ethernet Drivers

The Ethernet interface software is a kernel driver. The driver can be compiled into the kernel or can be loaded as a loadable module, which is the most common way to install an Ethernet driver. The loadable Ethernet drivers are found in the /lib/modules/*release*/net directory, where *release* is the kernel version number. A directory listing from a Red Hat 6 system shows the following:

```
$ ls /lib/modules/2.2.5-15/net

3c501.o       de4x5.o      ewrk3.o          ne.o            slhc.o
3c503.o       de600.o      fmv18x.o         ne2k-pci.o      slip.o
3c505.o       de620.o      hostess_sv11.o   ne3210.o        smc-ultra.o
3c507.o       depca.o      hp-plus.o        ni5010.o        smc-ultra32.o
3c509.o       dgrs.o       hp.o             ni52.o          smc9194.o
3c515.o       dlci.o       hp100.o          ni65.o          strip.o
3c59x.o       dummy.o      ibmtr.o          pcnet32.o       syncppp.o
82596.o       e2100.o      ipddp.o          plip.o          tlan.o
8390.o        eepro.o      ircomm.o         ppp.o           tulip.o
ac3200.o      eepro100.o   irda.o           ppp_deflate.o   via-rhine.o
acenic.o      eexpress.o   irda_deflate.o   rcpci.o         wanpipe.o
at1700.o      epic100.o    irlan.o          rtl8139.o       wavelan.o
bsd_comp.o    eql.o        irobex.o         sdla.o          wd.o
cops.o        es3210.o     lance.o          sdladrv.o       yellowfin.o
cosa.o        eth16i.o     lne390.o         shaper.o        z85230.o
cs89x0.o      ethertap.o   ltpc.o           sktr.o
```

All loadable network device drivers are listed here. A few, such as ppp.o and plip.o, are not for Ethernet devices. Most are easily identifiable as Ethernet drivers, such as the 3COM drivers, the SMC drivers, the NE2000 drivers, and the Ethernet Express drivers.

The Linux system detects the Ethernet hardware during the initial installation and installs the appropriate driver. Normally, this is a completely automatic process that requires no input from the system administrator, but not always. Sometimes Ethernet adapters are not detected by the initial installation. Other times the adapter is added after the initial installation, or an adapter has a non-standard configuration that must be communicated to the device driver. On even rarer occasions, the device driver itself is incorrect and needs to be replaced. When these things happen, users turn to you for help.

Manually Loading an Ethernet Device Driver

If the Ethernet adapter is not detected during the operating system installation, or if it is added after the system is installed, you can manually load the device driver using the mod-probe command described in Chapter 3, *The Boot Process*.

Most Linux distributions provide administrative tools for managing loadable modules. For example, Caldera gives you the lisa Kernel Module Manager. From the Kernel Module Manager menu, select Load Kernel Module, and then select the appropriate driver for your Ethernet adapter. Even if the system cannot automatically detect the card, manually selecting the loadable device driver means that you will be able to configure and use the Ethernet adapter.

Red Hat provides a button on the Control Panel labeled Kernel Daemon Configuration. Click it to start the Kernel Configurator shown in Figure 4.1. Use the Add button to add the appropriate Ethernet driver. After it is added, use the Restart Kerneld button to ensure that the kernel daemon reads the new configuration.

Figure 4.1   The Red Hat Kernel Configurator

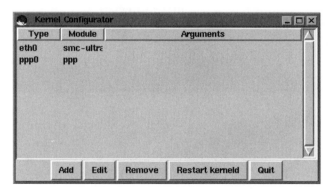

Configuring an Ethernet Device Driver

The Ethernet drivers expect the adapters to use the manufacturer's default configuration. Most drivers probe the card to discover the correct configuration, but this doesn't always work. When it doesn't, Ethernet adapter configuration parameters can be passed to the device driver through the boot prompt or by using the append command in the lilo .conf file. For example, the boot prompt input to tell the Ethernet driver that the adapter is using IRQ 10 and I/O port address 210 is:

```
linux ether=10,0x210,eth0
```

The same configuration parameters in an **append** command are:

```
append = "ether=10,0x210,eth0"
```

NOTE It is not necessary to pass configuration parameters to the driver if the card uses the manufacturer's default configuration, if the driver can detect the correct configuration, or if you use a PCI Ethernet adapter.

Compiling a New Device Driver

Configuration conflicts are primarily a problem with ISA adapters. A rare problem I have had with a PCI Ethernet adapter is a bad device driver. For a device driver to operate correctly, it must be compiled with the correct libraries for your kernel. Sometimes this means downloading the driver source code and compiling it yourself on your system.

The problem described in the "Not-So-Fast Ethernet" case study at the end of Chapter 1 was resolved by compiling a new device driver. Essentially, I broke one of my own rules by using the very latest hardware on my server. Before any Fast Ethernet cards made it to the hardware compatibility list, I did my best to guess what would work based on available drivers and the hardware used in available adapters. I guessed wrong and had to temporarily drop back to regular 10Mbps Ethernet. See the following "Fast at Last!" sidebar for the final solution to my Fast Ethernet problem.

Fast at Last!

Within a month after my failed attempt to force my Linux system onto the Fast Ethernet, the word came from one of the other Linux users that a Fast Ethernet driver was available for the adapter. He handed me a floppy disk that contained the driver source code in tar file format. The source code was from cesdis.gsfc.nasa.gov/linux/ drivers/, which is a great repository of Linux Ethernet driver software. I unpacked the source code with the tar command and compiled it with the GNU C compiler as follows:

```
# gcc -DMODULE -D__KERNEL__ -I/usr/src/linux/include/net -Wall
-Wstrict-prototypes -O6 -c tulip.c
tulip.c: In function `tulip_get_stats':
tulip.c:1909: warning: unused variable `i'
```

Fast at Last! *(continued)*

I ignored the warning message. (Heck, one warning wasn't going to stand between me and Fast Ethernet!) I copied the object file, `tulip.o`, to the `/lib/modules/2.0.30/` net directory. Now I was ready to use it. I entered the `modprobe tulip` command, and the card worked! This was a Slackware system, so I edited the `/etc/rc.d/rc.modules` file to uncomment the `modprobe tulip` command so that the card would be activated at every boot.

Once the adapter hardware and device driver are installed, the Ethernet interface can be used for a number of different network protocols. It can run NetWare protocols or, as described in Chapter 11, *File Sharing*, it can run NetBIOS Server Message Block (SMB) protocol. Both of these are useful, but the primary network protocol used on Linux systems is TCP/IP. In the next section, you'll configure the Ethernet interface for TCP/IP.

The `ifconfig` Command

The `ifconfig` command assigns TCP/IP configuration values to network interfaces. Many values can be set with this command, but only a few are really used. For example, the command to configure the interface on `robin.foobird.org` would be:

```
ifconfig eth0 172.16.5.4 netmask 255.255.255.0 \
    broadcast 172.16.5.255
```

The IP Address

The IP address is a software address specific to TCP/IP. Each device on the network has a unique address, even if the network is as large as the global Internet. In the above example, the `ifconfig` command assigns the IP address 172.16.5.4 to the Ethernet interface `eth0`. You must define an IP address for every interface, because the TCP/IP network is independent of the underlying hardware, which means that the IP address cannot be derived from the network hardware.

This approach has advantages and disadvantages, and is different from the address approach used by some other networks. NetBIOS uses the Ethernet hardware address as its address, and NetWare IPX incorporates the Ethernet address into the NetWare address. Using the address that is available in the hardware makes these systems simple to configure, because the system administrator does not need to be concerned about, or knowledgeable of, network addresses. But these systems are dependent on the underlying Ethernet, making it difficult or impossible to run them over global networks. TCP/IP is more difficult to configure, but it has the power to run a global network.

The netmask Argument   The IP address includes a network portion that is used to route the packet through the Internet and a host portion that is used to deliver the packet to a computer when it reaches the destination network. The netmask argument is used to define what bits in the IP address represent the network and what bits represent the host. If no netmask (network mask) is defined, the address is divided according to the old address class rules. In effect, these rules say that:

- If the first byte is less than 128, use the first 8 bits for the network and the next 24 bits for the host.

- If the value of the first byte is from 128 to 191, use the first 16 bits for the network and the last 16 bits for the host.

- If the value of the first byte is from 192 to 223, use the first 24 bits for the network and the last 8 bits for the host.

- Addresses with a first byte that is greater than 223 are not assigned to network hardware interfaces.

Except for the last one, these rules are used only if you fail to provide a netmask argument. Use netmask with the ifconfig command to define the address structure you want.

The old address classes did not provide enough flexibility for defining addresses. Three address classes proved inadequate to handle the huge number of addresses in the Internet and the incredible diversity of needs of the different networks connecting to the Internet. The solution is *classless IP addresses*. Classless addressing treats an IP address as 32 bits that can be divided between network and host portions in any way. The division of bits is controlled by a bit mask. If a bit is "on" in the mask (the bit is a one), the corresponding bit in the address is a network bit. If the bit is "off" (the bit is a zero), the corresponding bit in the address is a host bit. Here is our sample ifconfig command again:

```
ifconfig eth0 172.16.5.4 netmask 255.255.255.0 \
    broadcast 172.16.5.255
```

By the old class rules, the address 172.16.5.4 would define host 5.4 on network 172.16. The netmask argument 255.255.255.0 says that the first 24 bits of the address are the network portion and that only the last 8 bits are used to define the host. With this mask, the address is interpreted as host 4 on network 172.16.5.

Network Mask versus Subnet Mask

The netmask is sometimes called the *subnet mask*. However, there is a subtle difference between an address mask defined for classless addressing and a traditional subnet mask. The subnet mask is a network mask intended for local use. It is used to create additional networks within the structure of an address class and is only known within the local network. On the other hand, the address mask of a classless address is intended for global use and is distributed with the address via a routing protocol.

The difference is really one of intent. Do you intend to use the mask locally, or was this mask assigned to you with your IP address for global use? From the point of view of the individual network server, it makes no difference. The mask is defined in the same way on the `ifconfig` command. Except for the subtle distinction of the intended use of the mask, you can use the terms *address mask* and *subnet mask* pretty much interchangeably.

Internet Server Operations

PART 2

Even when the network I'm working with uses an IP address that conforms to the class rules, I don't allow the network mask to default to the class value. I always specifically define the network mask on the command line. Addressing is too important to leave to chance; I want to make sure I'm in control of it. For the same reason, I always define the broadcast address.

The Broadcast Address

The broadcast address is used to send a packet to every host on a network. The standard broadcast address is composed of the network address and a host address of 255. Given the `ifconfig` statement above, you would expect a default broadcast address of 172.16.5.255. Using the IP address of 172.16.5.4 and the netmask of 255.255.255.0, you get a network address of 172.16.5.0. Add to that the host address of 255, and you get 172.16.5.255. So why did I define the broadcast address instead of letting it default? Because you might be surprised by the default broadcast address.

You can check the configuration of an Ethernet interface by using the `ifconfig` command with only the interface name as a command-line argument. This does not change any configuration values; it displays the values that have already been set. Here is an example:

```
# ifconfig eth0 172.16.5.4 netmask 255.255.255.0
# ifconfig eth0
```

```
eth0 Link encap:Ethernet   HWaddr 00:60:97:90:37:51
     inet addr:172.16.5.4  Bcast:172.16.255.255
         Mask:255.255.255.0
     UP BROADCAST RUNNING MULTICAST  MTU:1500  Metric:1
     RX packets:319 errors:0 dropped:0 overruns:0
     TX packets:76 errors:0 dropped:0 overruns:0
     Interrupt:3 Base address:0x300
```

In this example, I configure the interface but do not define the broadcast address, expecting the default will be exactly what I want. Instead, the default appears to ignore my net-mask argument and creates a broadcast address that would be correct if I used the old address class rules. Be specific. There are several files and scripts involved in setting the network interface configuration during the boot. Unless you're specific about it, you might not get the configuration you want.

Configuring the Interface for Every Boot

The configuration values assigned by the ifconfig command do not survive the boot. To configure the interface every time the system boots, the ifconfig command must be stored in a startup file. Normally, this does not require any effort on your part. Configuring the network interface is a basic part of the Linux installation.

As you saw in Chapter 2, during installation, Linux detects the network interface and asks you to provide the address, address mask, broadcast address, and several other network-related parameters. The installation program stores these values on the disk where they are used later by the ifconfig command. Slackware stores the values in /etc/rc.d/rc.inet1; Caldera and Red Hat store the values in **/etc/sysconfig/network** and **/etc/sysconfig/network-scripts/ifcfg.**_interface_, where _interface_ is the name of the network interface, such as ifcfg.eth0. The startup scripts provided by these distributions then use the values to configure the interface.

However, if you want to manually configure the interface, you can directly configure it by storing the ifconfig command in the rc.local script. The rc.local script is the last startup script executed, so anything stored here will override the configuration done by the system. The following commands placed in rc.local would configure the network interface on robin in exactly the manner I wanted:

```
ifconfig eth0 172.16.5.4 netmask 255.255.255.0 \
    broadcast 172.16.5.255
route add -net 172.16.5.0 dev eth0
```

The ifconfig command provides the configuration that I have described. The second line says that the interface I have just configured is the route to the network to which it is connected. This line may be a slight surprise to readers who have worked on other Unix systems, which automatically create a route to the local network when the interface is configured by ifconfig. On those other systems, the route statement is not needed. On a Linux system, it is. The route command says to add a route to network 172.16.5.0 through the network device eth0. The Linux system has a route statement for every network interface.

> **NOTE**   The route command and routing are covered in more detail in Chapter 9, *Network Gateway Services.*

Despite this example, you generally don't edit any of the boot script files directly, nor do you manually configure the interface. Most system administrators use a network configuration tool to correct any problems with the network interface configuration.

Network Interface Configuration Tools

Most Linux distributions offer menu-driven or graphical configuration tools for the network interface. On a Slackware system, run netconfig to configure the interface. netconfig prompts for all of the information required by TCP/IP.

On a Caldera system, use lisa with the --net command-line argument. This displays a menu from which you choose Configure Network Access. Select Configure Network Card from the next menu and provide the various configuration values when prompted.

On a Red Hat system, the network interface is configured either through the Network Configuration tool found on the Control Panel or with the linuxconf toolkit. Figure 4.2 shows the linuxconf window after selecting the Basic Host Information item from the scroll menu. The interface in the figure has already been configured. The fields are self-explanatory.

In all of the aforementioned distributions, the designers of the configuration tools have made some decisions about what is needed and where it should be defined. One of the great things about Linux is that if you disagree with the tool design, or if you want to do something differently, you can go directly to the commands that the tools really use to get the job done.

Figure 4.2   Configuring the network interface with linuxconf

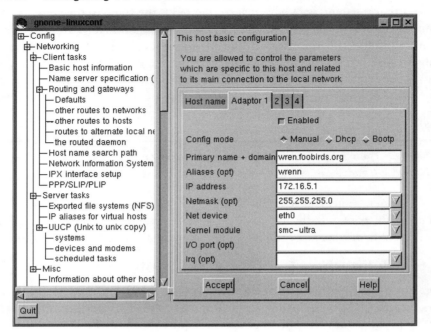

So far in this chapter, you have configured TCP/IP only on an Ethernet interface. This might lead you to believe that a Linux system requires TCP/IP and an Ethernet interface in order to communicate with other systems. That's not true. A Linux system can communicate without TCP/IP, and it can be configured to run TCP/IP without an Ethernet interface. The next section looks at both capabilities.

> **NOTE**   Clearly you want to use TCP/IP, and you want to use your Ethernet interface. The features examined in the next section do not replace TCP/IP and Ethernet. Instead, they are additional capabilities that permit you to use the computer's serial interface in ways that would not be possible on some other network server systems.

The Serial Interface

Most PC hardware comes with two serial ports. These ports are either a nine-pin connector or the traditional 25-pin RS-232 connector. In both cases, these connectors provide all of the signals you need to connect a terminal or a modem to the serial ports.

Figure 4.3 shows the RS-232 interface pin-out for the full 25-pin connector. The right-hand side of the figure illustrates the electrical handshake that takes place when a PC communicates with a modem by showing the pins that are actually used during an exchange of data. In telecommunications talk, the modem is called "data communications equipment" (DCE), and the PC is called "date terminal equipment" (DTE). The figure shows the exchange of signals between the DTE and the DCE.

Internet Server Operations

PART 2

Figure 4.3   The RS-232 hardware handshake

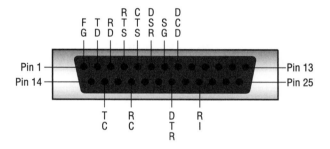

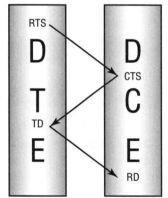

1	FG	Frame Ground	7	SG	Signal Ground
2	TD	Transmit Data	8	DCD	Data Carrier Detect
3	RD	Receive Data	15	TC	Transmit Clock
4	RTS	Request To Send	17	RC	Receive Clock
5	CTS	Clear To Send	20	DTR	Data Terminal Ready
6	DSR	Data Set Ready	22	RI	Ring Indicator

Only two of the interface pins are used to move data. Transmit Data (TD) is used to send data out of the computer, and Receive Data (RD) is used to read data into the computer. These are pins 2 and 3, respectively, on the RS-232 interface, as shown in the figure. A modem is able to directly connect to the computer, because it reads data from the TD pin that the computer writes to and writes data to the RD pin that the computer reads from.

A few other interface pins are used to set up and control the serial connection:

- Data Terminal Ready (DTR; pin 20) is used by the computer to signal that it is ready for the connection.
- Data Set Ready (DSR; pin 6) is used by the modem to signal that it is ready to connect.
- Data Carrier Detect (DCD; pin 8) is used by the modem to signal that it has a good connection to the computer at the remote end of the telephone line.
- Request To Send (RTS; pin 4) is used by the computer to indicate that it can accept and send data.
- Clear To Send (CTS; pin 5) is used by the modem to indicate that it can accept data.

Connecting a modem and a computer is straightforward, because they use the interface pins in complementary ways. However, you'll have a conflict if you attempt to connect two computers together, because they both want to use the same pins in the same way. For example, both will try to write to TD and read from RD. If you want to make a direct connection between two computers, buy a *null-modem cable*, also called a *direct connect cable*. The null-modem cable simply crosses some wires so that the two computers can communicate.

Connecting through the Serial Interface

Regardless of whether data comes through a modem or from a directly attached terminal, it is handled by the Linux system in the same way. Three programs handle the connection: init, getty, and login.

init is responsible for attaching the getty program to a serial port and for restarting the getty program whenever it terminates. You saw an example of this in the description of the inittab file in Chapter 3.

getty monitors the serial port. When getty detects a carrier signal on the port, it displays the "login:" prompt. It reads in the user's name and uses it to invoke login. For example if getty received "norman" in response to the login prompt, it would issue the command login norman.

login then prompts the user for a password and checks the password against the encrypted password in the /etc/passwd or /etc/shadow file. The Linux user is given up to three tries to enter the correct password. After the password is verified as correct, the UID and GID from the password file are assigned to the tty device, and the following environment variables are set:

HOME This variable defines the user's home directory. login takes the value from the /etc/passwd file.

SHELL This variable defines the user's login shell. `login` takes the value from the `/etc/passwd` file.

LOGNAME This variable defines the name by which the user is identified in the system log. `login` uses the username passed to it by `getty`.

PATH This variable defines the execution path. `login` defaults to a path of `/usr/local/bin:/bin:/usr/bin`.

MAIL This variable defines the path to the user's mail file. `login` uses the path `/var/mail/spool/`*username*, where *username* is the name passed to `login` by `getty`.

TERM This variable identifies the terminal type. `login` keeps the TERM environment variable set by `getty`. The value of TERM will be a valid terminal type from the `/etc/termcap` file.

Once these variables are set, `login` starts the shell identified in the user's `/etc/passwd` entry. The shell processes the initialization files that it finds in the user's home directory. These initialization files, such as `.bash_profile` and `.bashrc` for the `bash` shell, permit users to set their own environment variables; for example, to define a more complete execution path. Finally, the shell issues the command prompt to the user, and the user has full access to the system.

All of these processes and services happen automatically and require almost no configuration on your part. Beyond creating a user account for the user and configuring the modem to answer the telephone, there is nothing for the system administrator to do. The basic Linux system comes with the ability to support terminal connections through serial ports. If you have ever configured dial-up services on other PC operating systems, you'll appreciate what an advantage this is.

Of course, even on a Linux system, things don't always work smoothly. Linux comes with some terminal emulation programs such as `seyon` and `minicom` that can be used to troubleshoot your modem and your serial links.

> **NOTE** See Chapter 15, *Troubleshooting*, for information on troubleshooting with `minicom`.

The support for serial communications that is built into Linux is the foundation for running TCP/IP over a serial line. The next section covers just that.

Running TCP/IP over a Serial Port

Of much greater utility than the ability to connect a terminal to your server's serial port is the ability to run TCP/IP over a serial port. Doing so allows you to run TCP/IP over a telephone line with a modem. This is, of course, the way that most people connect to the Internet through a local ISP. But it is also a way for you to provide connectivity into the Internet or your enterprise network for a remote field office or for users working at home.

Point-to-Point Protocol (PPP) provides the framing mechanism for sending IP datagrams over a telephone line. PPP uses a three-layered architecture to accomplish this:

Data Link layer PPP uses High-level Data Link Control (HDLC) protocol to provide reliable data delivery over any type of serial line.

Link Control layer A Link Control Protocol (LCP) was specifically developed for PPP. It opens and closes connections, monitors link quality, and negotiates the link configuration parameters.

Network Control layer PPP is designed to carry a wide variety of network protocols. Protocols in this layer provide the control information that is necessary to customize the PPP link for the type of network traffic it is carrying. The network control protocol for TCP/IP is the Internet Protocol Control Protocol (IPCP).

Properly configuring a PPP service requires that all of these layers are correctly installed as well as that the serial port and modem over which the traffic passes are properly configured. The remainder of this chapter looks at how these things are done on a Linux system.

Installing PPP

The Physical layer provided by the serial device drive and the layers of the Point-to-Point Protocol are implemented in Linux as a combination of kernel drivers and a PPP daemon (pppd). The Physical layer protocols for the serial devices upon which PPP depends are installed in the kernel as device drivers. The HDLC Data Link layer protocol is also installed as a kernel module.

While the Physical layer and Data Link layer portions of PPP are provided by the kernel, the Link Control layer and the Network Control layer are provided by the PPP daemon. Thus the lower layers of PPP are implemented as kernel modules, and the upper layers are implemented as a daemon process. In order for PPP to function, all of these components must be properly installed.

NOTE   The serial device drivers are compiled into the Linux kernel, and therefore don't require you to install them.

The PPP Kernel Module

In Chapter 3, you saw the kernel messages that are displayed when the serial drivers are installed. Similarly, when PPP is compiled into the kernel, messages about PPP are displayed during startup, as in this example:

```
$ dmesg | grep PPP
PPP: version 2.2.0 (dynamic channel allocation)
PPP Dynamic channel allocation code copyright 1995 Caldera, Inc.
PPP line discipline registered.
```

If PPP is installed by your kernel, you're ready to run the PPP daemon. On most systems, however, the kernel component of PPP is not compiled in the kernel. If it isn't, you must install the loadable module ppp.o manually. To do so, use the commands covered in Chapter 3, and refer to the examples of installing an Ethernet driver earlier in this chapter. On our sample Red Hat system, either the Kernel Configurator shown in Figure 4.1 or the modprobe command could be used to install PPP. For example, modprobe ppp would load the ppp.o module required by PPP.

As explained in Chapter 3, different Linux distributions use different tools for maintaining the modules list. All, however, provide some means for you to specify that module ppp.o should be included in the kernel at startup.

The PPP Daemon

The PPP daemon is started by the pppd command. The command can be entered at the shell prompt, and it often is on client computers. On server systems, the command is usually stored in a shell script to run at boot time for dedicated servers or on demand for dial-up servers. Red Hat systems provide the /etc/sysconfig/network-scripts/ifup-ppp script to start the PPP daemon. However, the script is not usually edited directly. It is controlled through one of the configuration tools, such as linuxconf and kppp, described later in this chapter.

On other systems, you may find it more convenient to create your own custom pppd configuration. The syntax of the pppd command is:

```
pppd [tty-device] [speed] [options]
```

- *{tty-}device* is the name of the serial device over which the PPP protocol will operate. If no device is specified, the controlling terminal is the device that is used. As you'll see later, the ability to use the controlling terminal is very useful when you create a dial-up PPP server.
- *speed* is the transmission speed of the port written in bits per second.
- *options* are just that—command-line options.

There are an enormous number of pppd options. In addition to specifying options on the command line, there are three different files are available to store these options:

- /etc/ppp/options is used to store system-wide PPP options. This file is created and maintained by the system administrator.
- .ppprc, which each user can create and store in their home directory, is used to set personal PPP options.
- /etc/ppp/options.*device* sets PPP options for a specific serial device. For example, options.cua1 sets PPP options for /dev/cua1.

The files are read in the order listed above, which means that options in the last file read can override options in the first file read. Thus the order of precedence for options from all of these sources is:

1. Options defined on the command line have the highest priority.
2. Options defined in the options.*device* file have the next priority.
3. Options defined by the user in the .ppprc file have the next priority.
4. Options from the /etc/ppp/options file have the lowest priority.

Looking at this list, you might be concerned that the system-wide options you define in the /etc/ppp/options file can be overridden by the user with the .ppprc file. Don't be. Items that relate to system security cannot be overridden by the user. Additionally, you can always specify important options in the options.*device* file, which has the highest priority.

NOTE   There are more than 70 options available for the pppd command. If you want to read about all of them, see *Using and Managing PPP* by Andrew Sun (O'Reilly, 1999).

The following sections cover just those pppd options that you are most likely to use. By selecting the correct options, you can configure pppd for a dedicated line or for a dial-up line as either a PPP server or as a client.

Configuring a PPP Server

A Linux system can be used as a PPP server for both dedicated connections and dial-up connections. Configuring pppd for a dedicated line is the simplest configuration, and it provides a good example of the structure of the pppd command. A single line inserted in the rc.local startup file is all that is necessary to configure a PPP server for a dedicated line:

```
pppd /dev/ttyS1 115700 crtscts
```

This command starts the PPP daemon and attaches it to the serial device ttyS1. It sets the line speed for this dedicated line to 115700bps.

One option, crtscts, is also selected in this command. crtscts turns on Request To Send (RTS) and Clear To Send (CTS) hardware flow control. *Hardware flow control* uses the RTS and CTS pins in the serial interface to control the flow of data.

Always use hardware flow control with PPP. The alternative, software flow control, sends special characters in the data stream to control the flow of data. Software flow control, which is also called in-band flow control, at best wastes bandwidth doing something that could be done with hardware, and at worst sends control characters that can become confused with the actual data.

The pppd command for a client connected to a dedicated link would look the same as the one above except it would also have the defaultroute option:

```
pppd /dev/ttyS1 115700 crtscts defaultroute
```

defaultroute creates a default route that uses the remote PPP server as the default router. This assumes that this PPP link is our only link to the outside world, which is often the case. The sample pppd command shown above would be used to connect a small branch office into the enterprise network. If, however, there is already a default route defined, this option is ignored. This option is not used on the server end of the dedicated link, because the server is the client's router and therefore must already have another route to the outside world.

PPP configuration for a dedicated line is simple, because there are only two systems connected to the line—one at each end, a single server and a single client. The line is dedicated to this single purpose and therefore can be configured at startup and left unchanged for as long as the system is running. There is no need to configure the server to handle multiple clients.

Internet Server Operations

PART 2

However, PPP clients and server are not always connected to dedicated serial lines. It is more common for them to be connected via dial-up serial lines, and configuring a server for dial-up lines is more complex than configuring it for dedicated lines.

PPP Dial-Up Server Configuration

As you have already seen, Linux systems provide the software needed to support dial-up clients on a serial port. Creating a dial-up PPP server is simply an extension of this capability. The key is the /etc/passwd file. Use /etc/ppp/ppplogin as the login shell for dial-up PPP users, as in this example:

```
jane:x:522:100:Jane Resnick:/tmp:/etc/ppp/ppplogin
```

This looks exactly like any other /etc/passwd entry and functions in exactly the same way. The PPP user is prompted for a username—jane in this case—and a password. (Remember that the encrypted password is often stored in the /etc/shadow file.) After the user successfully logs in, she is assigned the home directory /tmp. The /tmp directory is commonly used for PPP users. The system then starts the user's login shell. In this case, the login shell is /etc/ppp/ppplogin, which is actually a shell script that starts the PPP server. Here is a sample ppplogin script:

```
#!/bin/sh
mesg -n
stty -echo
exec /sbin/pppd crtscts modem passive auth
```

Your ppplogin script will not necessarily look like this example; you create your own ppplogin script. The mesg and stty commands are primarily to show you that you can put whatever you think is necessary in the ppplogin script. The mesg -n line prevents users from sending messages to this terminal with programs such as talk and write. Clearly you don't want extraneous data being sent over the PPP connection.

The stty -echo command turns off character echo. When echo is on, the characters typed by the remote user are echoed back to the remote computer by the local computer. This was used on old teletype terminals so that the user could monitor the quality of the dial-up line. If the characters were garbled as they appeared on the screen, the user knew that they should disconnect and re-dial to get a clear line. Of course, those days are long gone. Echoing characters across a PPP line is never used.

The real purpose of the script is, of course, to start the PPP daemon, and that is exactly what the last line does. There are definite differences between the pppd command that you execute here and the one that you saw in the previous section for dedicated lines. First, this command does not specify a device name. That's intentional. When pppd is started without a device name, it attaches to the controlling terminal and runs in background mode. The controlling terminal is the terminal that `login` was servicing when it launched the `ppplogin` script. This permits you to use the same `ppplogin` script for every serial port. Likewise, this `pppd` command does not specify a line speed. In this case, the line speed is taken from the configuration of the serial port, again allowing you to use the same script for every serial port.

The remaining four items on the `pppd` command line are options:

- The `crtscts` option turns on hardware flow control, as discussed earlier.

- The `modem` option tells the PPP daemon to monitor the modem's Data Carrier Detect (DCD) indicator. By monitoring DCD, the local system can tell if the remote system drops the line. This is useful because it is not always possible for the remote system to gracefully close the connection.

- The `passive` option tells `pppd` to wait until it receives a valid Link Control Protocol (LCP) packet from the remote system. Normally, the PPP daemon attempts to initiate a connection by sending the appropriate LCP packets. If it doesn't receive a proper reply from the remote system, it drops the connection. Using `passive` gives the remote system time to initiate its own PPP daemon. With `passive` set, `pppd` holds the line open until the remote system sends an LCP packet.

- The `auth` option requires the remote system to authenticate itself. This is not the username and password authentication required by `login`, and it does not replace login security. PPP security is additional security designed to authenticate the user and the computer at the other end of the PPP connection.

PPP Security

PPP has two authentication protocols: Password Authentication Protocol (PAP) and Challenge Handshake Authentication Protocol (CHAP). PAP is a simple password security system. CHAP is a more advanced system that uses encrypted strings and secret keys for authentication. Authentication helps to prevent intruders from accessing your server through its serial ports.

PAP Security

Password Authentication Protocol is vulnerable to all of the attacks of any reusable password system. PAP is better than no security, but not by much. PAP sends the PPP client name and the password as clear text at the beginning of the connection setup. After this initial authentication, the client is not re-authenticated. While spying on a serial line is much more difficult than spying on an Ethernet, PAP clear-text passwords can still be stolen by someone spying on your network traffic. Additionally, an established session can be hijacked by a system spoofing addresses.

Because of these weaknesses, use PAP only when you must—for example, if you have to support a client that can only provide PAP authentication. Unfortunately, PAP is still very widely used and may be your only choice.

To configure PAP, make appropriate password entries in the /etc/pap-secrets file. A pap-secrets file might contain the following:

```
# Secrets for authentication using PAP
# client    server  secret                 IP addresses
crow        wren    Wherearethestrong?     172.16.5.5
wren        crow    Whoarethetrusted?      172.16.5.1
```

Given this configuration file, crow will send the PPP client name crow and the password Wherearethestrong? when asked for authentication by wren. wren will send the client name wren and the password Whoarethetrusted? when asked for authentication by crow. Both systems have the same entries in their pap-secrets files. These two entries provide authentication for both ends of the PPP connection.

The IP address field at the end of each entry defines the address from which the client name and the password are valid. Thus only the host at address 172.16.5.5 can use the client name crow and the password Wherearethestrong?. Even though this is a valid client name and password combination, if it comes from any other address, it will be rejected.

The auth option on the pppd command line forces the PPP daemon to require authentication. If it must, it will fall back to PAP, but first it will try to use CHAP.

CHAP Security

Challenge Handshake Authentication Protocol is the default authentication protocol used by PPP. CHAP is not vulnerable to the security attacks that threaten PAP. In fact, a PPP connection using CHAP is probably more secure than your local Ethernet connection. For one, CHAP does not send clear-text passwords. Instead, CHAP sends a string of characters called a *challenge string*. The system seeking authentication encrypts the challenge string with a secret key from the /etc/ppp/chap-secrets file and returns the encrypted string back to the servers. The secret key never travels across the network and therefore cannot be read off the network by a snooper.

Additionally, CHAP repeatedly re-authenticates the systems. Even if a thief steals the connection through address spoofing, he cannot keep the connection for long without responding correctly to the CHAP challenge.

CHAP is configured through the `chap-secrets` file. Entries in the `chap-secrets` file contain the following fields:

respondent This is the name of the computer that will respond to the CHAP challenge. Most documentation calls this the "client" field. However, PPP clients require authentication from servers in the same way that servers require authentication from clients. The first field defines the system that must respond to the challenge in order to be authenticated.

challenger This is the name of the system that will issue the CHAP challenge. Most documentation calls this the "server" field, but as noted earlier, servers are not the only systems that issue CHAP challenges. The second field contains the name of the computer that challenges the other system to authenticate itself.

secret This is the secret key that is used to encrypt and decrypt the challenge string. The challenger sends a challenge string to the system that is being authenticated. The respondent encrypts that string using the secret key and sends the encrypted string back to the challenger. Then the challenger decrypts the string with the secret key. If the decrypted string matches the original challenge string, the responding system is authenticated. Using this system, the secret key never travels across the network.

address This is an address written either as a numeric IP address or as a host name. If an address is defined, the respondent must use the specified IP address. Even if a system responds with the correct secret key, it will not be authenticated unless it is also the host at the correct IP address.

A sample `chap-secrets` file on `robin` might contain the following entries:

```
# cat chap-secrets
# Secrets for authentication using CHAP
# client    server   secret            IP addresses
robin       wren     Peopledon'tknowyou robin.foobirds.org
wren        robin    ,andtrustisajoke.  wren.foobirds.org
```

When `robin` is challenged by `wren`, it uses the secret key `Peopledon'tknowyou` to encrypt the challenge string. When `robin` challenges `wren`, it expects `wren` to use the secret key `,andtrustisajoke.`. It is very common for entries to come in pairs like this. After all, there are two ends to a PPP connection, and both systems require authentication to create a secure link. `wren` challenges `robin`, and `robin` challenges `wren`. When both computers are sure they are communicating with the correct remote system, the link is established. For this to work, of course, `wren` needs the same entries in its `chap-secrets` file.

For security reasons, it is very important to protect the /etc/ppp directory. Only the root user should be able to read or write the chap-secrets file or the pap-secrets file. Otherwise, the secret keys may be compromised. Additionally, only the root user should be allowed to write the options file. Otherwise, users would be able to define system-wide PPP options.

Finally, the scripts ip-up and ip-down should only be able to be written by the root user. pppd runs the ip-up script as soon as it makes the PPP connection, and it runs the ip-down script after it closes the connection. These scripts can perform privileged functions relating to the network connection. Thus, allowing anyone but the root user to modify these scripts compromises the security of your system.

PPP Client Configuration

Configuring a PPP client is as complex as configuring a server. The primary reason for this complexity is the fact that the client initiates the PPP connection. To do that, the client must be able to dial the server's phone number and perform any necessary login procedures. A pppd command for a client system might look like this:

```
pppd /dev/cua1 115700 connect "chat -v dial-server" \
        crtscts modem defaultroute
```

You have seen all but one of these options before. In fact, this command is identical to the PPP client configuration you created for the dedicated link except for the connect option. The connect option identifies the command used to set up the serial-line connection. In the sample, the command is enclosed in quotes because it contains whitespace characters. The complete command is chat -v dial-server.

The chat program is used to communicate with devices, such as modems, attached to a serial port. The -v option causes chat to log debugging information through syslogd. In the example, dial-server is the name of the script file that chat uses to control its interaction with the modem and the remote server.

chat Scripts

A chat script defines the steps that are necessary to successfully connect to a remote server. The script is a list of expect/send pairs. Each pair consists of a string that the local system expects to receive separated by whitespace from the response that it will send when the expected string is received. A sample script might contain the following:

```
$ cat dial-server
' ' ATZ
```

```
OK  ATDT301-555-1234
CONNECT \d\d\r
gin: karen
ord: TOga!toGA
```

The script contains instructions for the modem as well as the login for the remote server. The first line, expects nothing, which is what the empty string (' ') means, and sends a reset command to the modem. (ATZ is the standard Hayes reset command.) Next, the script expects the modem to send the string OK, and it responds with a Hayes dial command (ATDT). When the sample modem successfully connects to the remote modem, it displays the message CONNECT. In response to this, the script waits two seconds (\d\d) and then sends a carriage-return (\r).

Most systems don't really require anything like this, but it provides an example of a chat escape sequence. chat provides several escape sequences that can be used in the expect string or the response string. Table 4.1 lists these sequences and their meanings.

Table 4.1   Escape Sequences and Their Meanings

Escape Sequence	Meaning
\b	The backspace character
\c	Don't send a terminating carriage-return; used at the end of a send string
\d	Delay for one second
\K	A line break
\n	A newline character
\N	An ASCII null character
\p	Pause for 1/10 of a second
\q	Send the string, but don't record it in the log; used at the end of a send string

Table 4.1   Escape Sequences and Their Meanings *(continued)*

Escape Sequence	Meaning
\r	A carriage-return
\s	The space character
\t	The tab character
\\	The backslash
\ddd	The ASCII character with the octal value *ddd* (e.g., \177 is the DEL character)
^character	A control character (e.g., ^G is a Ctrl+G)

The last two lines of the sample script are the remote login. The script expects gin:, which are the last four characters of the "login:" prompt, and responds with the username karen. Next, ord:, which are the last four characters of the "Password:" prompt is expected, and T0ga!toGA is sent as a response. Once the login is complete, the remote system runs the ppplogin script, and the PPP connection is up and running.

> **NOTE**   chat is a very elementary scripting language. It is popular for setting up PPP connections, because most PPP connections do not require a complex script. If yours does, you may need to use a more powerful scripting language. Linux provides both dip and expect. To read more about dip, see *TCP/IP Network Administration* by Craig Hunt (O'Reilly, 1998). To read more about expect, see *Exploring Expect* by Don Libes (O'Reilly, 1997).

Configuring a PPP Client with linuxconf

So far, you have configured PPP by editing the configuration files with a text editor. It is also possible to configure a PPP client by using the linuxconf program under X Windows. To do so, select PPP/SLIP/PLIP from the linuxconf scroll-down menu. A window similar to the one shown in Figure 4.4 appears.

Figure 4.4 linuxconf PPP configuration window

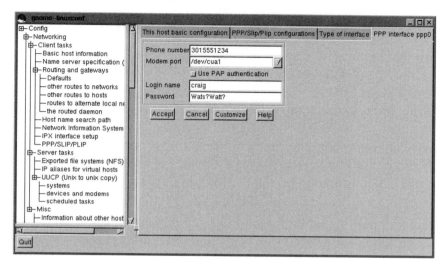

As shown in the figure, fill in the blanks to create a basic PPP configuration. Click the Customize button to get more configuration options, and the window in Figure 4.5 appears.

Figure 4.5 Customizing PPP with linuxconf

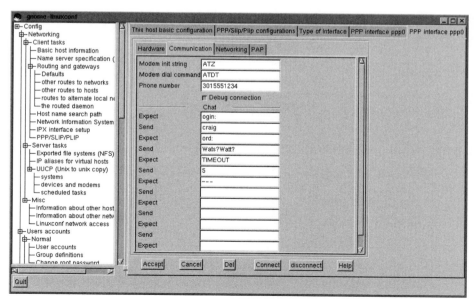

This window has four tabs for setting configuration values:

- Use the Hardware tab to set the baud rate, to select hardware flow control, and to specify `pppd` command-line options.
- The Communication tab defines the `chat` script, if one is required.
- Use the Networking tab to define static IP addresses or to change the size of the Maximum Receive Unit (MRU) and the Maximum Transmission Unit (MTU).
- The PAP tab holds the client name and password for PAP authentication.

> **NOTE** You can only select PAP authentication. This is the primary limitation of using `linuxconf` to define the PPP configuration—authentication is PAP or nothing.

Flow control, `chat` scripts, addresses, and PAP have been previously mentioned; only the Maximum Receive Unit and the Maximum Transmission Unit are new terms. These options let you set the number of bytes the system will send or accept in a single packet. The range supported by `pppd` is from 128 to 1500 bytes. These values are used to negotiate the packet size with the remote system; the largest size that is acceptable to both parties is used.

Adjust MRU and MTU to improve performance, but keep in mind that more is not always better. Buffer overflows from overly large packets can cause retransmissions that slow performance. If you have poor PPP link performance or see an error message such as "SILO Overflow," try reducing the size of the MRU and MTU until performance improves. Select the largest MRU and MTU that are consistent with good performance. On most systems MRU and MTU do not require tuning. The defaults work fine.

> **NOTE** These same values can be set on the pppd command line with the `mru` *size* argument and the `mtu` *size* argument, where *size* is the number of data bytes in the packet.

Configuring a PPP Client with kppp

Both Caldera 2.2 and Red Hat 6 offer a PPP configuration tool named kppp that is located in the KDE Internet menu. When you select this tool, a PPP login window appears. To configure a new PPP client, click the Setup button in that window. This opens the window shown in Figure 4.6.

Figure 4.6   The kppp Configuration window

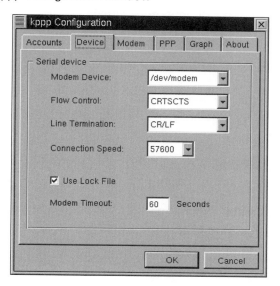

The kppp Configuration window contains six different tabs. The About tab, which provides copyright information, and the Graph tab, which is used to select display colors, are unimportant for the configuration. The meat of the configuration is set with the other four tabs:

PPP   Defines the behavior of the PPP window during and after a connection.

Modem   Sets the characteristics of the modem. Use this tab to:

- Define the commands used to control the modem; by default, these are the standard Hayes AT commands.

- Set the modem speaker volume.

- Set how long the modem should wait before redialing when it gets a busy signal.

- Indicate if the modem uses the CD pin to indicate if it has a connection to the remote system.

- Send the modem a Hayes ATI command query.

- Open a simple terminal that talks directly to the modem, which is useful for testing the modem and the connection before configuring PPP.

Device Sets the characteristics of the physical device. These include the device name, the port speed, the type of flow control used, and the characters used to terminate a line of data; these characters are normally a carriage-return (CR) and a line-feed (LF).

Accounts Allows you to select a current PPP configuration or define a new one. Click the New button on this tab to open the window shown in Figure 4.7.

Figure 4.7 The kppp New Account window

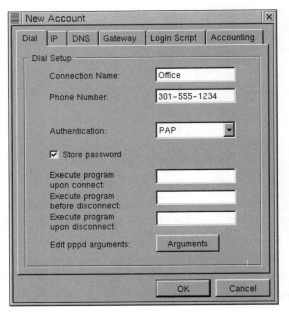

Use the New Account window to enter all of the information related to a specific PPP connection. This window has six tabs.

Dial Use this tab to:

- Select the authentication type.
- Specify the telephone number that PPP should dial to create the connection.
- Provide optional **pppd** command-line arguments.
- Identify scripts that should run before, during, or after the PPP connection.

IP Defines whether the system should use a dynamic address or a static address for this connection. If a static address is selected, the IP address and the address mask are entered in this tab.

DNS Defines the default domain name and the DNS server's IP address.

Gateway Specifies whether or not the remote system should be used as the default gateway and if the route through the PPP link should be the default route. If the remote server is not the default gateway, this tab can be used to enter the IP address of a gateway.

Login Script Use this tab to define a login script similar to the chat scripts described earlier.

Accounting Use this tab to track expenses if you live in a country that has usage charges.

Deciding whether or not to use tools like linuxconf and kppp to set up your PPP client is mostly a matter of personal taste. Some people prefer the graphic interface while others do not. Either way, the end result is the same, and the information you must provide is the same as well.

Final Words

A network server requires a network interface. On most servers, including Linux systems, this is an Ethernet interface. However, Linux systems also support a full range of network services through the serial port. Connect a terminal or modem to a Linux serial port, and it will support user logins. Run the Point-to-Point Protocol (PPP), and the serial port can be used to provide TCP/IP connections.

The same flexibility that Linux shows in the types of network connections it provides is seen in the full range of network services offered by a Linux system. In the next chapter, you'll start configuring some of these services with the basic Internet services: telnet, rlogin, and ftp.

Internet Server Operations

PART 2

5

Login Services

At this point, you've installed Linux and have a running network interface. Now you're going to configure the network services for your users. This chapter covers the services that permit users to log in to the server and run programs, which, in effect, creates an application server.

The term application server is poorly defined. Almost any service can be called an application; client/server applications are certainly applications, but this is not to what I am referring. In the context of this book, an *application server* must allow a user to log in and run an application directly on the server.

Unlike some commercial server operating systems, Linux offers this basic feature. The Telnet daemon (`telnetd`) and the remote login daemon (`rlogind`) allow users to log in and run applications directly on a Linux server. The other server that requires users to log in is the File Transfer Protocol (FTP) server. Most network servers provide an FTP server, and Linux is no exception.

The most remarkable thing about these services is that they require almost no configuration—they are installed and enabled during the basic Linux installation. All that you need to do is ensure that:

- The server daemons are started when they are needed
- The users have valid accounts to log in to the servers

In general, login servers won't provide service to people who don't complete a valid log in. There are two exceptions to this rule:

- FTP offers an anonymous log in that is available to people who don't have a valid user account.
- rlogin can be configured to grant service to trusted users who do not log in.

Both of these exceptions are covered in this chapter, which begins by looking at how telnetd, rlogind, ftpd, and various other network services are started when they are needed. Most are started by the Internet daemon (inetd).

Starting Services with inetd

Network services are started in two ways: by a boot script or by inetd. Chapter 1 discussed the tools, linuxconf and tksysv, that are used to control which services are started at boot time. Table 1.3 lists the large number of services that are started by the boot scripts. One of these is inetd, which is started by the /etc/init.d/inet script.

Despite the large number of services started by the boot scripts, most network services are started by inetd. Network services that are started at boot time continue to run whether or not they are needed, but inetd starts services only when they are actually needed.

NOTE Each startup technique has its own advantages. Starting services on demand saves the resources that are used when an unneeded service is left running. On the other hand, starting a daemon at boot time saves the overhead associated with repeated startups for a service that is in constant demand.

---

inetd is started at boot time and continues to run in the background as long as the system is running. It listens to the network ports and starts the appropriate service when data arrives on the port associated with the service. To understand this process, you need to understand a little about TCP/IP ports.

Protocol and Port Numbers

Data travel through a TCP/IP network in packets called *datagrams*. Each datagram is individually addressed with:

- The IP address of the host to which it should be delivered
- The protocol number of the transport protocol that should handle the packet once it is delivered to the host
- The port number of the service for which the data in the packet is bound

For data to be delivered correctly on a global scale, as it is in the Internet, the IP address must be globally unique, and the meaning of the protocol and port numbers must be well known to all systems in the network. Chapter 4 described how the IP address is assigned to the network interface during the installation. In the case of the IP address, you're the one responsible for making sure that it is unique. (In Chapter 15, *Troubleshooting*, you'll see what kinds of problems occur when the IP address isn't unique.) Protocol and port numbers are different. They are defined by Internet standards. Thus the protocol numbers and port numbers can be pre-defined in two files, /etc/protocols and /etc/services, that come with the Linux system.

The /etc/protocols File

Data from the network arrive at the computer as one stream. The stream may contain data packets from multiple sources bound for multiple applications. In telecommunications terminology, it is *multiplexed*. To deliver each packet to the correct application, it must be *de-multiplexed*. The first step in this process is for the Internet Protocol to pass the packet to the correct transport protocol. IP determines the correct protocol by means of the protocol number that is contained in the datagram packet header.

The /etc/protocols file identifies the protocol number of each transport protocol. The protocols file from a Red Hat 6 system contains the following:

```
# /etc/protocols:
# $Id: protocols,v 1.1 1995/02/24 01:09:41 imurdock Exp $
#
# Internet (IP) protocols
#
#       from: @(#)protocols      5.1 (Berkeley) 4/17/89
#
# Updated for NetBSD based on RFC 1340, Assigned Numbers (July 1992).


ip      0     IP            # internet protocol
icmp    1     ICMP          # internet control message protocol
igmp    2     IGMP          # Internet Group Management
ggp     3     GGP           # gateway-gateway protocol
```

Internet Server
Operations

PART 2

```
ipencap    4      IP-ENCAP        # IP encapsulated in IP
st         5      ST              # ST datagram mode
tcp        6      TCP             # transmission control protocol
egp        8      EGP             # exterior gateway protocol
pup        12     PUP             # PARC universal packet protocol
udp        17     UDP             # user datagram protocol
hmp        20     HMP             # host monitoring protocol
xns-idp    22     XNS-IDP         # Xerox NS IDP
rdp        27     RDP             # "reliable datagram" protocol
iso-tp4    29     ISO-TP4         # ISO Transport Protocol class 4
xtp        36     XTP             # Xpress Transfer Protocol
ddp        37     DDP             # Datagram Delivery Protocol
idpr-cmtp 39      IDPR-CMTP       # IDPR Control Message Transport
rspf       73     RSPF            # Radio Shortest Path First
vmtp       81     VMTP            # Versatile Message Transport
ospf       89     OSPFIGP         # Open Shortest Path First IGP
ipip       94     IPIP            # Yet Another IP encapsulation
encap      98     ENCAP           # Yet Another IP encapsulation
# End of protocols.
```

Some of the comments from this file were removed so that it would fit better on a book page, but other than this cosmetic difference, the protocols file on your Linux system, regardless of the distribution, will look essentially the same. In fact, you can find a similar file on any Unix or Windows NT system, because the protocol numbers are standardized. You will *never* need to edit this file.

Only two entries in this file are significant. One, tcp, defines the protocol number for Transmission Control Protocol—the TCP in TCP/IP. Its protocol number is 6. The other, udp, defines the protocol number for User Datagram Protocol as 17. TCP and UDP carry most of the information you are interested in.

The /etc/services File

The second stage of de-multiplexing the network data is to identify the application to which the data is addressed. The transport protocol does this using the port number from the transport protocol header.

The standard port numbers are identified in the /etc/services file. The port numbers for well-known services are assigned in Internet standards, so you never change the port number of an existing service. On rare occasions, you may need to add a new service to the file, but that is the only time you would edit this file.

There are not many transport protocols and only two that are of much interest, but there are a very large number of network services. For that reason, the following sample is only a small piece of the complete /etc/services file:

```
ftp-data        20/tcp
ftp             21/tcp
telnet          23/tcp
smtp            25/tcp          mail
time            37/tcp          timserver
time            37/udp          timserver
rlp             39/udp          resource
name            42/udp          nameserver
whois           43/tcp          nicname
domain          53/tcp
domain          53/udp
mtp             57/tcp                          # deprecated
bootps          67/udp                          # bootp server
bootpc          68/udp                          # bootp client
tftp            69/udp
gopher          70/tcp                          # gopher server
rje             77/tcp
finger          79/tcp
http            80/tcp
```

From the sample, you can tell that telnet uses port 23 and runs on top of the TCP transport protocol. Furthermore, you can tell that Domain Name Service (DNS), referred to as domain in the file, uses port 53 on both TCP and UDP. Each transport protocol has a complete set of port numbers, so a single port number, such as 53, can be assigned to a service for both UDP and TCP. In fact, it would be possible to assign a port number under UDP to one service and the same port number under TCP to a completely different service; however, in order to avoid confusion, this is never done.

inetd can monitor any port listed in the /etc/services file. Which protocol and port numbers are monitored by inetd are defined in the /etc/inetd.conf file. This, in turn, defines which services are started by inetd.

Configuring inetd

The inetd configuration is defined in the /etc/inetd.conf file. The file defines the ports that inetd monitors and the path names of the processes it starts when it detects network traffic on a port. Below are the active entries in the inetd.conf file that comes with Red Hat 6:

```
$ grep -v '^#' /etc/inetd.conf
ftp        stream  tcp nowait  root    /usr/sbin/tcpd       in.ftpd -l -a
telnet     stream  tcp nowait  root    /usr/sbin/tcpd       in.telnetd
shell      stream  tcp nowait  root    /usr/sbin/tcpd       in.rshd
login      stream  tcp nowait  root    /usr/sbin/tcpd       in.rlogind
talk       dgram   udp wait    root    /usr/sbin/tcpd       in.talkd
ntalk      dgram   udp wait    root    /usr/sbin/tcpd       in.ntalkd
imap       stream  tcp nowait  root    /usr/sbin/tcpd       imapd
finger     stream  tcp nowait  root    /usr/sbin/tcpd       in.fingerd
auth       stream  tcp nowait  nobody /usr/sbin/in.identd in.identd -l -e -o
linuxconf  stream  tcp wait    root    /bin/linuxconf       linuxconf -http
```

Every entry in the inetd.conf file defines a service that is started by inetd. Each entry is composed of seven fields:

Name The name of the service as listed in the /etc/services file. This name maps to the port number of the service.

Type The type of data delivery service used. There are only two common types: dgram for the datagram service provided by UDP and stream for the byte stream service provided by TCP.

Protocol The name of the protocol as defined in the /etc/protocols file. The name maps to a protocol number. All of the sample entries have either tcp or udp in this field.

Wait-status This is either wait or nowait. wait tells inetd to wait for the server to release the port before listening for more requests. nowait tells inetd to immediately begin listening for more connection requests on the port. wait is normally used for UDP, and nowait is normally used for TCP.

UID The username under which the service is run. Normally this is root, but for security reasons, some processes run under the user ID nobody.

Server This is the path name of the server program that inetd is to start. In the previous sample, the entries for linuxconf and auth are good examples. Both of these entries show the path to the appropriate server program. All of the other entries, however, share the same server path, /usr/sbin/tcpd. Clearly, this is not really the path to the ftp server, the telnet server, and every other server. In reality, tcpd is a security feature used by Linux. tcpd is called the Wrapper, and it is used to wrap security protection around network services. The details of how to use the Wrapper to improve security are covered in Chapter 14, *Security*. For now, it is sufficient to know that tcpd will start the correct server when it is called by inetd.

Arguments These are the command-line arguments that are passed to the server program. The first argument is always the name of the server program being executed. The argument list looks exactly as the command would look if it was being typed in at a shell prompt.

As you can see in the previous sample, inetd.conf comes pre-configured with several services active. The default file comes with an equal number of services inactive, as shown here:

```
$ grep '^#[a-z]' /etc/inetd.conf
#echo     stream  tcp     nowait   root     internal
#echo     dgram   udp     wait     root     internal
#discard  stream  tcp     nowait   root     internal
#discard  dgram   udp     wait     root     internal
#daytime  stream  tcp     nowait   root     internal
#daytime  dgram   udp     wait     root     internal
#chargen  stream  tcp     nowait   root     internal
#chargen  dgram   udp     wait     root     internal
#time     stream  tcp     nowait   root     internal
#time     dgram   udp     wait     root     internal
#exec     stream  tcp     nowait   root     /usr/sbin/tcpd    in.rexecd
#comsat   dgram   udp     wait     root     /usr/sbin/tcpd    in.comsat
#dtalk    stream  tcp     waut     nobody   /usr/sbin/tcpd    in.dtalkd
#pop-2    stream  tcp     nowait   root     /usr/sbin/tcpd    ipop2d
```

```
#pop-3    stream  tcp  nowait      root   /usr/sbin/tcpd     ipop3d
#uucp     stream  tcp  nowait      uucp   /usr/sbin/tcpd /usr/lib/uucp/uucico -l
#tftp     dgram   udp  wait        root   /usr/sbin/tcpd     in.tftpd
#bootps   dgram   udp  wait        root   /usr/sbin/tcpd     bootpd
#cfinger  stream  tcp  nowait      root   /usr/sbin/tcpd     in.cfingerd
#systat   stream  tcp  nowait      guest  /usr/sbin/tcpd     /bin/ps -auwwx
#netstat  stream  tcp  nowait      guest  /usr/sbin/tcpd     /bin/netstat  -f inet
#swat     stream  tcp  nowait.400  root   /usr/sbin/swat     swat
```

Comments in the inetd.conf file begin with a sharp sign (#). To disable a service, insert a sharp sign at the beginning of its entry. To enable a service, remove the sharp sign. For example, enable the BootP server by removing the sharp sign at the beginning of the bootps entry. Likewise, to disable the finger protocol, insert a sharp sign before the first character in the finger entry. This simple edit gives you complete control over the services provided by your Linux system.

WARNING Do not run services that you don't really use. Every network service is a potential hole for a security cracker to slither through. In this chapter, I use ftp, telnet, and login. Clearly, they should not be commented out of the configuration. But this chapter does not use gopher or pop-2. Those services could be commented out without harming my users.

Now that you know how telnetd, ftpd, and rlogind are started, let's look at how the user accounts they require are created. The next section reviews the variety of tools that are used to create user accounts on Linux systems.

Creating User Accounts

Each user who logs in to your Linux system is identified by a user account. The user account controls access to the system by defining the username and password that authenticate the user during the login. Once the user logs in to the system, the user account's user identifier (UID) and group identifier (GID) are used to control the user's privileges. These values, which are defined when you create a user account, control file system security and identify which users control what processes.

The user account is an essential part of a Linux system, and all Linux distributions provide tools for maintaining user accounts. This section examines several of these tools, but first take a look behind the scenes to see what these tools are doing for you.

The Steps to Creating a User Account

The tools that different Linux distributions offer to simplify the process of adding a user account may vary, but all of the tools ask for essentially the same information, because the underlying process of adding a user account is the same on all Linux systems. Adding a user account requires the following steps:

1. Edit the /etc/passwd file to define the username, UID, GID, home directory, and login shell for the user.

2. Run passwd to set a password for the user.

3. Run mkdir to create the user's new home directory.

4. Copy the default initialization files from /etc/skel to the user's home directory. The /etc/skel directory holds files such as .bashrc, which is used to initialize the bash environment. Your Linux system comes with a selection of files already in /etc/skel. If you want to provide additional or different initialization files for your users, simply add files to the /etc/skel directory, or edit the files that you find there.

5. Change the ownership of the user's home directory and the files it contains so that the user has full access to all of her files. For example, chown -r kathy:users /home/kathy.

Most of these steps involve building the user's home directory. However, much of the information about the user account is stored in the /etc/passwd file.

The passwd File

Every user on a Linux system has an entry in the /etc/passwd file. To see what accounts exist on your Linux system, just look inside that file. The passwd file from our sample Red Hat system contains the following entries:

```
# cat /etc/passwd
root:gvFVXCMgxYxFw:0:0:root:/root:/bin/bash
bin:*:1:1:bin:/bin:
daemon:*:2:2:daemon:/sbin:
adm:*:3:4:adm:/var/adm:
lp:*:4:7:lp:/var/spool/lpd:
sync:*:5:0:sync:/sbin:/bin/sync
```

```
shutdown:*:6:0:shutdown:/sbin:/sbin/shutdown
halt:*:7:0:halt:/sbin:/sbin/halt
mail:*:8:12:mail:/var/spool/mail:
news:*:9:13:news:/var/spool/news:
uucp:*:10:14:uucp:/var/spool/uucp:
operator:*:11:0:operator:/root:
games:*:12:100:games:/usr/games:
gopher:*:13:30:gopher:/usr/lib/gopher-data:
ftp:*:14:50:FTP User:/home/ftp:
nobody:*:99:99:Nobody:/:
craig:6VKY34PUexqs:500:100:Craig Hunt:/home/craig:/bin/bash
sara:niuh3ghdj73bd:501:100:Sara Henson:/home/sara:/bin/bash
kathy:wv1zqw:502:100:Kathy McCafferty:/home/craig:/bin/bash
david:94fddtUexqs:503:100:David Craig:/home/craig:/bin/bash
becky:tyebwo8bei:500:100:Rebecca Hunt:/home/craig:/bin/bash
```

Most of these accounts are included in the passwd file as part of the initial installation; only the last five entries are real user accounts added by the system administrator. The first entry is the root account for the system administrator, but most of the others are special accounts created for programs that need to control processes or that need to create and remove files.

Each /etc/passwd entry follows the *user:password:UID:GID:text_info:home:shell* format, where:

- *user* is the username. It should be no more than eight characters long and should not contain capital letters or special characters. kristin is a good username.

- *password* is the encrypted password of the user. Of course, you don't actually type an encrypted password here. The encrypted password is stored here by the passwd command. If you use the shadow password file, and most Linux distributions do, the encrypted password will not actually appear here. Instead, the password will be stored in /etc/shadow. See Chapter 14 for a description of the shadow password file.

- *UID* is the numeric user ID for this user account.

- *GID* is the numeric group ID of the primary group of this user.

- *text_info* is free-form text information about the user. At a minimum, you should have the user's first and last names. Some people like to include the user's telephone number and office room number. For historic reasons, this field is sometimes called the GECOS field.

- *home* is the user's home directory.

- *shell* is the login shell for this user.

Almost all of the information needed to create a user account appears in the passwd file. The next few sections examine some of this information in more detail.

Selecting a Login Shell

A *login shell* (or command shell) processes the command lines that are entered by the user. On a DOS system, this is COMMAND.COM. Linux provides a selection of several different login shells. Several shells are included in the distribution, and many more are available from ftp://sunsite.unc.edu/pub/linux/system/shells. Despite the variety of shells, most sites standardize on one or two; every user account I added to the sample passwd file listed above uses /bin/bash as the login shell.

The graphical tools such as linuxconf and lisa usually provide a list of possible shells. The Red Hat 6 linuxconf tool provides a drop-down box labeled Command Interpreter that gives you these shell selections:

/bin/sh This is the Bourne Shell, which is the original Unix shell. The Bourne Shell introduced many of the fundamental concepts of command shells, but as you can imagine given the great age of Unix, the original Bourne Shell is seriously out-of-date. Despite that, feel free to make this selection on a Red Hat 6 system, because there is no Bourne Shell stored at /bin/sh. Instead, it is a link to /bin/bash.

/bin/bash This is the Bourne Again Shell, which is the most popular shell on Linux systems. bash is the Bourne Shell with all of the modern enhancements such as command-line editing, command history, and filename completion that were introduced by newer shell programs.

/bin/bash2 This is yet another version of the Bourne Again Shell. It provides all of the features of bash.

/bin/ash This is the A Shell. ash is a very compact program, only about one-sixth the size of bash. ash has minimal features in keeping with its very small size.

/bin/bsh This is the B Shell, which is just a link to ash on a Red Hat 6 system.

/bin/csh This is the C Shell. csh is an early Unix shell with a command and scripting environment inspired by the C programming language. Though the original csh is now out-of-date, csh introduced important concepts, like command histories, that are still used today. On a Red Hat system, /bin/csh is a link to /bin/tcsh.

/bin/tcsh This is the Tenex C Shell, which is the enhanced csh. tcsh adds filename completion and command-line editing to the C shell.

/bin/ksh The is the Korn Shell, which is one of the most popular Unix shells and the one that first introduced command-line editing.

/bin/zsh The Z Shell most closely resembles the Korn Shell, but it also provides advanced features such as command completion and built-in spell checking.

This complete list of shells includes three shells that are just logical links, another one that is a minimal shell, and all of the most popular shells. Other Linux distributions have other lists. However, keep in mind that these lists are just suggestions; you don't have to select a shell from the list. You can type the path name of any shell installed on your system as the user's login shell.

If you do add other shells to your system, add their names to the /etc/shells file. The /etc/shells file is a list of valid shell names that is consulted by a number of programs, including linuxconf, to determine what shells are available on the system. A listing of the /etc/shells file on a Red Hat 6 system shows exactly the same shells as those listed above:

```
$ cat /etc/shells
/bin/bash
/bin/sh
/bin/ash
/bin/bsh
/bin/bash2
/bin/tcsh
/bin/csh
/bin/ksh
/bin/zsh
```

Understanding the User ID

The UID field is a unique numeric identifier for the user. The range of UID numbers is 0 to 32767. Numbers below 100 are reserved for special system accounts, such as uucp, news, mail, and so on. By definition, the root account is UID 0. Other than these restrictions, you can select any available number in the valid range.

On an isolated system, files are only available to users of that system. But on a network, files are available between systems through file sharing. The most popular file sharing technique on Unix and Linux systems is Network File System (NFS). NFS uses the same file security mechanisms as the Linux system—the UID and the GID—and can only work if the user IDs and group IDs assigned on the various systems on the network are coordinated. For example, if tyler was assigned UID 505 on crow and daniel was assigned 505 on robin, a potential conflict could exist. Mounting a file system from crow on robin would give daniel ownership privileges to files that really belonged to tyler! Because of this, care must be taken to develop a plan for assigning user IDs and group IDs across every system on your network.

> **NOTE**   NFS and the issue of properly assigning user IDs and group IDs in an NFS environment are covered in Chapter 11, *File Sharing*.

Understanding the Group ID

The GID field is used to identify the primary group to which the new user belongs. When you first install a Linux system, several groups are included, most of which are either administrative groups, such as adm and daemon, or groups belonging to specific services, such as news and mail. users is a catch-all group for all users.

When you use an administrative tool to create a user account, the tool assigns a group for the user if you don't select one. On some systems, such as Slackware, the system defaults to the group users. On a Red Hat system, the default is to create a brand new group that contains only the new user as a member. Neither approach is exactly right.

The group ID, like the user ID, is used for file system security. On Linux systems, there are three levels of file permissions: ownership privileges, group privileges, and world privileges. If everyone is included in the same group, as is the case when everyone is placed in the users group, then everyone has the same group privileges when attempting to access anyone's files. In effect, group privileges are no different from world privileges. This defeats the purpose of the group ID, which is to allow groups to share files while protecting those files from people who are not in the group.

Likewise, if a group is created that contains only one user, the purpose of the group ID is defeated—there is no point in having group privileges if there is no group. The owner of a file already has access privileges for the file based on the UID, so the GID is unnecessary when the group is one. Using this approach, group privileges are no different from ownership privileges.

To make the most effective use of group IDs, you need to create groups. You should have a plan for the group structure you will use on your network. This plan doesn't need to be complicated. Most network administrators use an organizational group structure where people in the same work group are members of the same GID. A more complex structure based on projects is also possible. Be careful, however, not to create a structure that requires lots of maintenance. Projects come and go, and you don't want to get into a situation where you are constantly changing groups and moving files for users.

> **NOTE**   For full NFS support, your group structure plan needs to be coordinated among the systems on your network. See Chapter 11 for information on planning and coordinating a group structure.

Creating New Groups   To create a group, add an entry for the new group in the /etc/ group file. Every group has one entry in the file, and all of the entries have the same format, name:password:gid:users, where:

- name is the name of the group.

- password is not used. Leave it blank.

- gid is the numeric group identifier. It is a number between 0 and 32767. GID 0 is used for the root group. Most administrators reserve the numbers below 100 for special groups.

- users is a list of users assigned to this group. The primary group of a user is assigned in the /etc/passwd file. This list is used to assign supplemental groups to a user.

Some examples from the /etc/groups file on a Red Hat system will help explain:

```
root::0:root
bin::1:root,bin,daemon
daemon::2:root,bin,daemon
mail::12:mail
news::13:news
uucp::14:uucp
users::100:kathy
popusers:x:231:kathy
slipusers:x:232:
kathy:x:501:
```

In a linuxconf example later in this chapter (refer to Figure 5.2), I create the user account kathy, leaving the Group box empty and allowing the system to create a default GID for kathy. By default, Red Hat creates a new group for the user using the username as the group name and using the first available number above 500 as the GID. That's where the kathy entry at the end of this file came from. Additionally, I used the Supplementary

Groups box to grant kathy membership in the users and the popusers groups. That's why kathy appears in the user list of both of those entries. Note that kathy is not in the user list of the group kathy. That is because it is her primary group, which is assigned in the /etc/passwd file.

You can create a new group by directly editing the /etc/groups file. Simply select an unused group name and an available GID number, and type the new entry directly into the file.

Alternatively, you can create a group by using the tools provided by your Linux distribution. The Red Hat system provides a graphical tool for creating groups as part of the linuxconf toolkit. The groupadd command is available for this purpose in several different distributions, including Red Hat. For example, to create a group for the sales department with a group name of sales and a GID of 890, enter **groupadd –g 890 sales**.

Regardless of how you create a group, the effect is the same. The new group is listed in the /etc/group file. In the same manner that there are several different ways to create a group, there are also several different tools for creating a user account.

Tools to Create User Accounts

All Linux distributions offer tools to help you create user accounts. Both Caldera and Red Hat have the useradd command. The following useradd command creates a user account with the username kathy, the UID 502, the GID 100, and the login shell /bin/bash:

```
# /usr/sbin/useradd -u 502 -g 100 -s /bin/bash kathy
```

This command creates the correct /etc/passwd entry, builds the new home directory (which by default is named /home/kathy), and copies the /etc/skel files to the new directory. It does everything except create the login password. To define the login password, run passwd kathy and define the user's initial password.

In addition to the text-based useradd command, both Caldera and Red Hat have fancier tools. Caldera provides a menu-driven interface using the Linux Installation and System Administration (lisa) tool. Run lisa with the --useradm option to jump right to the user administration menu. Select Add New Users from that menu and answer the prompts to build a new user account.

The linuxconf program found on Red Hat 6 systems provides an X Windows–based user administration tool.

Creating User Accounts with linuxconf

From the root user account run linuxconf at the shell prompt to start the application. linuxconf provides a very large number of configuration tools. Scroll down the list of tools until you get to User Accounts, and then select Normal ➤ User Accounts (see Figure 5.1). This display is a list of the accounts that have already been created on your system.

Figure 5.1 The linuxconf User Accounts window

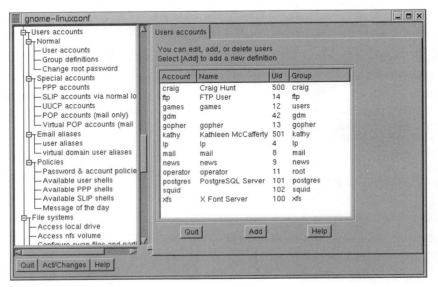

When you first install the system, you might be surprised by the number of user accounts that already exist. As you saw in the /etc/passwd example, most of these accounts are used by services that create and delete files as they run. As noted above, user accounts are used for file system security; any user or service that creates or deletes files needs a UID and a GID.

To edit or delete an account, simply click its entry in the list. This displays a detailed window that allows you to change any of the fields. The detailed window also contains a Del button that allows you to delete an entry.

To add a new user, simply click the Add button that appears at the bottom of the list of user accounts. Clicking the Add button opens the window shown in Figure 5.2. Fill in the blanks and click Accept to create a new user.

Figure 5.2   The linuxconf User Account Creation window

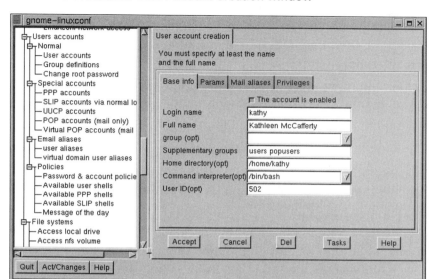

In Figure 5.2, I am creating a user account for Kathleen McCafferty. She will use the username kathy. Her home directory, which is the directory that she owns and the directory in which she will be placed at login, is /home/kathy. The Command Interpreter, /bin/bash, is her login shell. If no shell is selected, login provides a default shell. The default shell it uses is /bin/sh, which you know from the discussion above is merely a link to /bin/bash on a Red Hat 6 system.

In the Group field, there is a drop-down box that lists all of the groups currently available on the system. If you do not pick an initial group for the user, the Red Hat system will automatically create a new group that contains only the user and will assign that new group as the user's initial group. You saw this group in the listing of the /etc/groups file shown earlier. This behavior is specific to Red Hat systems. As noted above, some other systems default to the group users when no group is selected, while other systems force you to choose a group.

The User ID field is also optional. If no value is entered here, Red Hat will use the next available UID number above 500. I prefer to assign numbers according to a plan that has been coordinated across all of my servers, so I enter a specific UID in the box.

Using Slackware's adduser Command

To create a new user on a Slackware system, use adduser, which is a text-based tool. The following example adds the user kathy to a Slackware system:

```
# adduser
Login name for new user (8 characters or less) []: kathy
```

```
User id for kathy [ defaults to next available]: 501
Initial group for kathy [users]:
kathy's home directory [/home/kathy]:
kathy's shell [/bin/bash]:
kathy's account expiry date (MM/DD/YY) []:


OK, I'm about to make a new account. Here's what you entered so far:


New login name: kathy
New UID: 0
Initial group: users
Additional groups: [none]
Home directory: /home/kathy
Shell: /bin/bash
Expiry date: [no expiration]


This is it... if you want to bail out, hit Control-C.  Otherwise,
press ENTER to go ahead and make the account.


Making new account...


Changing the user information for kathy
Enter the new value, or press return for the default


        Full Name []: Kathy McCafferty
        Room Number []:
        Work Phone []:
        Home Phone []:
        Other []:
```

```
Changing password for kathy

Enter the new password. Use a combination of upper and lower case
letters and numbers.

New password:

Re-enter new password:

Password changed.

Done...
```

In the Slackware tool, default values are shown in square brackets. You can either accept the value offered by Slackware or enter your own.

The point of the linuxconf and adduser examples is not to show how you use these tools, but *why* you do and what you are really doing when you create a new account. The section "The Steps to Creating a User Account" tells you what is happening. Once you understand what is going on behind the scenes with the /etc/passwd file and the creation of the user's home directory, the operation of all of these tools becomes clear. The "why" has also been discussed: The user account is needed to identify the user for login and file system security. There are, however, two exceptions to the basic security model that you need to look at...

Understanding rlogin Security

The rlogin daemon is started by inetd. It requires that you create a user account for each user who will be accessing the system through its service. But in addition to these things that all login services have, rlogin has a unique security system that can pose problems.

rlogin uses a security system of trusted hosts instead of password authentication. Users on trusted hosts can access like-named user accounts on the local computer without providing a password because the trusted host has already authenticated the user, and user accounts with the same name are assumed to be owned by the same user. Thus a user logged in as sara on a trusted host is granted the same access as the user sara on the local host.

The hosts.equiv File

Trusted hosts are also called *equivalent hosts*, because users given access to a trusted host are given equivalent access to the local host. Use the hosts.equiv file to define the computers you trust.

By default, systems are not given trusted status. If no hosts.equiv file is present, no host is trusted. Not being granted trusted access does not mean that a user is denied access; it just means that the user must supply the correct password to gain access. Most administrators do not grant trust to any systems, because they want users to use passwords.

If you decide to make entries in the hosts.equiv file to grant trust, limit those entries to simple host names. The syntax of the hosts.equiv file allows for optional plus and minus signs, and for optional usernames. Don't use any of these optional values, because they make weak trusted-host security even weaker. As a result, be sure to avoid the following things:

- The plus sign (+) is used to indicate that a host or user is being given trust. However, the plus sign is unnecessary, because simply listing a host or user in the file grants trust. Furthermore, a plus sign can be dangerous: A plus sign without a following host name grants trust to all hosts—something you *never* want to do.

- The minus sign (-) is used to indicate that a user or host is explicitly denied trust. It is also unnecessary in this file, since simply not listing a host denies it trusted access. (As you'll see later, the minus sign is useful in the .rhosts file.)

- Using an optional username on a hosts.equiv entry should be avoided, because it grants the specified user password-free access to every account on the system, except the root account. Even without access to the root account, the user given access to every other account on the system can do a great deal of damage and can compromise all users' files. (The optional username is useful in the .rhosts file covered later.)

Given these guidelines, a reasonable hosts.equiv file is shown below:

```
robin
crow
owl
```

This file grants password-free access to the users on the three hosts that are identified by name.

The Problem with Trusted-Host Security

Clearly, the hosts.equiv file is a potential source of security problems. In addition to how the plus sign can allow the entire network into your computer, as mentioned earlier, the system relies on mapping computer addresses to computer names to verify trust, and computer addresses can be faked. For these reasons, most administrators do not grant trust to anyone. It is generally best to replace rsh and rlogin with secure shell (ssh).

> **NOTE** ssh, which is covered in Chapter 14, also offers trusted-host security using a file named shosts.equiv that uses exactly the same type of entries as hosts.equiv. However, the trusted-host security model works with ssh because ssh uses strong authentication so that addresses cannot be faked.

If you decide to use rlogin and the hosts.equiv file, use the following guidelines to reduce the security risk:

- Only grant trust to systems and users that you really do trust.
- Only grant trust if your computer is on an isolated network or if your network is protected from the outside world by a firewall that does not permit source routes.
- Only grant trust to hosts on your local network when you know and trust the person responsible for that host, and when you know the host is not available for public use.
- Always have a reason for conferring trusted status.
- Always err on the side of caution when granting trusted status.

The .rhosts File

The hosts.equiv file is used to grant trusted access to the entire system, and it is controlled by the system administrator. The .rhosts file, on the other hand, is used to control access to an individual user account, and each user can create their own. The .rhosts file grants or denies password-free access to an individual user's account. It is placed in the user's home directory and contains entries of exactly the same format as the entries in the hosts.equiv file.

> **NOTE** A filename that begins with a dot (.) indicates a hidden file that does not show up in a simple directory listing. Dot files, which usually define user configuration preferences, are included in the directory listing only if an –a option is used with the ls command, e.g., ls -a.

Individuals use the .rhosts file to simplify access to the different accounts they own. The optional minus sign and username that are avoided in the hosts.equiv file are the keys to a useful .rhosts file. For example, I have accounts on several different systems. In most cases, my username is craig. Sometimes, however, someone else has the craig account, and I'm given the account hunt. I want to be able to rlogin from any computer that I have an account on, but I don't want mistaken logins from the other Craig. The following .rhosts file is a way to address this problem:

```
crow hunt
crow -craig
```

Assume that my username on `crow` is `hunt` and that another user on `crow` has the username `craig`. Placing the `.rhosts` file shown above in my home directory on any other computer allows password-free access from my `hunt` account on `crow` while preventing password-free access from the other user's `craig` account on `crow`.

The preceding section mentioned that the `hosts.equiv` file does not grant password-free access to the root user account. However, a `.rhosts` file in the root user's home directory does grant password-free access to the root account. On our sample Red Hat system, the root user's home directory is `/root`. Thus a `/root/.rhosts` file would grant password-free root access.

WARNING   Granting password-free root access is a bad idea. The root account should be *very* tightly controlled.

The Anonymous FTP Service

One final topic before leaving the subject of remote login services: the FTP service. Like other services, to access the FTP server, a user must provide a username and a password. My sample user `kathy` could `ftp` to the local system and log in. The FTP server would set her default directory to/home/kathy, and she would be able to download and upload files to and from the system based on her normal file read and write permissions.

In addition to its standard service, `ftp` provides anonymous FTP, which allows anyone to login to the FTP server with the username **anonymous** and any password. Traditionally, the password used is your e-mail address. The purpose of this is, of course, to make certain files publicly available. All of the great Linux files available from `sunsite.unc.edu` are available through anonymous FTP.

Anonymous FTP is a great service, but it can present a security problem—and a big headache—if it is set up incorrectly. If you are familiar with setting it up on some Unix systems, you know how much is involved in doing it right.

On Linux, setting up anonymous FTP is very simple because Linux systems come with anonymous FTP already installed and configured. Look in the `/etc/passwd` file; you'll notice that the user account `ftp` is already there. Look in the `/home` directory; you'll find the anonymous FTP home directory `/home/ftp`. Finally, test the system with the command `ftp localhost`, and you should be able to log in as **anonymous**.

There is nothing to do to run anonymous FTP on your Linux server except to decide if you really want to. Properly set up, anonymous FTP is no more of a security risk than regular FTP. If you don't want to offer an FTP server at all, comment the `ftp` entry out of the `inetd.conf` file. If you specifically don't want anonymous FTP, comment the `ftp` entry out of the `/etc/passwd` file.

Final Words

Linux login services permit a user to connect to your server and run a program there. This simple, basic service is not even included with some network operating systems. Linux includes this and a full array of other basic Internet services. The Internet daemon (`inetd`) starts most of these services. A quick glance inside the `inetd.conf` file gives you an idea of the range of network services offered by Linux.

But even the extensive list you'll see there is not the whole story. Some of the most important network services are started independently of `inetd`. The next four chapters discuss four of these important services: Domain Name Service, `sendmail`, Web service, and routing. The discussion of these basic Internet services begins in Chapter 6, where you'll configure Domain Name Service (DNS).

Internet Server
Operations

PART 2

Rooting Out .rhosts

One of the greatest fears of administrators who permit the use of the rlogin and rsh commands is that a user will compromise the system with a poorly configured .rhosts file. Most security-conscious administrators simply eliminate the problem by commenting the r commands out of the inetd.conf file. But I have worked on networks where this is not an option for either technical or political reasons. A technical reason might be that r commands are embedded in some old scripts that no one has time to update. A political reason might be that a powerful user wants the commands, and the administrator lacks the clout to say the user cannot have them.

Regardless of the reason, I once worked at a site where the nets were stuck with the r commands, and the administrator wanted to periodically check the content of the users' .rhost files to make sure nothing was amiss. To do so, I used the find command to locate all of the .rhosts files stored on the system:

```
# find / -name .rhosts -print
/home/becky/.rhosts
/home/craig/.rhosts
/home/david/.rhosts
```

This told me who had an .rhosts file, but it did not tell me what was in it. I combined the find command with awk to automatically produce a script file that listed the contents of all .rhosts files. Here's an example:

```
# cat rhost.find
find / -name .rhosts -print | \
awk '{ print "echo Printing the contents of " $0 "; cat " $0 }' > prhosts
chmod 744 prhosts
./prhosts
```

This sample shell script, which I named rhost.find, uses find and awk to create another shell script named prhosts to display the contents of all of the .rhosts files found on the system. find locates the files and passes the name of each file to awk. awk embeds the name of each file in echo and cat commands that it stores in prhosts. The script then changes the mode of the prhosts file to "executable" and runs the prhosts script, which then gives me a listing of every .rhost file.

6

Linux Name Services

One of the most fundamental services on a TCP/IP network is *name service*. It is the service that translates host names into IP addresses. In Chapter 5, you configured `telnet` and `ftp`. Without name service, a user connecting to `crow` enters:

    telnet 172.16.5.5

With name service, that same command is:

    telnet crow

The result is the same. In either case, the user connects to the host at address 172.16.5.5. But most users prefer host names, because they are easier to remember and easier to use. This is particularly true in the global Internet. It is possible to guess that `www.sybex.com` is a valid name, but there is no intuitive way to guess the address, 206.100.29.83.

Linux systems use two techniques to convert host names to addresses: the host table and Domain Name Service (DNS). The `/etc/hosts` file is a table that maps names to addresses. It is a simple text file that is searched sequentially to match host names to IP addresses. Domain Name Service is a hierarchical, distributed database system with thousands of servers across the Internet handling name and address queries. DNS is far more important than the host table for the operation of the Internet, but both services play a role. This chapter's discussion of name services begins with a quick look at the host table.

The hosts File

Each entry in the /etc/hosts file contains an IP address and the names associated with that address. For example, the host table on crow might contain the following entries:

```
$ cat /etc/hosts
127.0.0.1               localhost localhost.localdomain
172.16.5.5              crow.foobirds.org crow
172.16.5.1              wren.foobirds.org wren
172.16.5.2              robin.foobirds.org robin
172.16.5.4              hawk.foobirds.org hawk
```

The first entry in this table assigns the name localhost to the address 127.0.0.1. (Every computer running TCP/IP assigns the loopback address to the host name localhost.) Network 127 is a special network address reserved for the loopback network, and host 127.0.0.1 is the loopback address reserved for the local host. The *loopback address* is a special convention that permits the local computer to address itself in exactly the same way that it addresses remote computers. This simplifies software, because the same code can be used to address any system, and, because the address is assigned to a software loopback interface (lo0), no traffic is sent to the physical network.

The second entry in the table is the entry for crow itself. The entry maps the address 172.16.5.5 to the name crow.foobirds.org and to the alias crow. Alias host names are primarily used to provide for shorter names, as in the example, but they are also used to provide generic names like mailhost, news, and www. Every networked computer with a permanent address has its own host name and address in its host table.

Every Linux system has a host table with the two entries just discussed, and most, like the system in the above example, have several additional entries for other key systems on the local network. This small table provides a backup for those times when DNS might not be running, such as during the boot process.

Understanding DNS

The limitations of the host table become obvious when it is used for a large number of hosts. The host table requires every computer to have a local copy of the table, and each copy must be complete, because only computers listed in the local host table can be accessed by name.

Consider today's Internet: It has millions of hosts. A host table with millions of entries is very inefficient to search and, more important, is impossible to maintain. Hosts are added to and deleted from the Internet every second. No system could maintain such a large and changeable table and distribute it to every computer on the network.

DNS solves these problems by eliminating the need for an all-inclusive, centrally maintained table and replacing it with a distributed, hierarchical database system. The current DNS database has millions of host entries distributed among tens of thousands of servers. Distributing the database in this way reduces the size of the database handled by any individual server, which in turn reduces the task of maintaining any individual piece of the database.

Additionally, DNS uses local caching to migrate information close to those who need it without sending unnecessary information. A local caching server starts with just the information it needs to locate the root of the hierarchical database. It then saves all of the answers to user queries that it receives and all of the supporting information learned in gaining those answers. In this way, it builds up an internal database of the information it needs to serve its users.

The DNS Hierarchy

The DNS hierarchy can be compared to the hierarchy of the Linux file system. Host names in individual domains parallel filenames in individual directories, and, like the root directory of the file system, DNS has a root domain.

In both the file system and the DNS system, the names of objects reveal the rooted hierarchical structure. Filenames move from the most general, the root (/), to the most specific, the individual file. Domain names start with the most specific, the host, and move to the most general, the root (.). A domain name that starts with a host and goes all the way to the root is called a *fully qualified domain name* (FQDN). For example, wren.foobirds.org is the FQDN of one of the systems on our sample network.

The top-level domains (TLDs), such as org, edu, jp, and com, are serviced by the root servers. The second-level domain, foobirds in the example, is the domain that has been officially assigned to your organization. When you're officially assigned a domain by your parent domain, a pointer is placed in the parent domain that points to your server as the server responsible for your domain. It is this delegation of authority that makes your domain part of the overall domain system. You will see how to delegate authority for subdomains later in this chapter.

> **NOTE** This book assumes that you already have an official domain name and IP address. If you don't and you need information on how to obtain a domain name or IP address, see *TCP/IP Network Administration* by Craig Hunt (O'Reilly, 1998).

You have complete freedom to create subdomains and host names within your domain. Organizations create subdomains for two basic reasons:

- To simplify the management of a large number of host names. This reason is easy to understand; it is exactly why DNS was created in the first place. Delegating pieces of the domain spreads the burden of maintaining the system to more people and computers so that no one person or computer is overwhelmed with work.

- To recognize the structure within the organization. This reason springs from a fact of organizational life. Some parts of the organization will want to control their own services no matter what.

Subdomains usually have either geographic or organizational names. `denver.foobirds.org` is an example of a geographic subdomain name while `sales.foobirds.org` is an example of an organizational name. One problem with naming a subdomain is that office locations change, and organizations reorganize. If the subdomain names you choose are too specific, you can bet that you will have to change them. Assume that your west coast office is in Santa Clara. You're better off naming the subdomain `west` or `westcoast` than you are calling it `santaclara`. If they move to a new building in San Jose, you don't want to have to change the subdomain name.

The analogy of the file system is a good one. Files are found by following a path from the root directory, through subordinate directories to the target directory. DNS information is located in a similar manner. Linux learns the location of the root file system during the boot process from the `root=` command that you place in the `lilo.conf` file. Similarly, your DNS server locates the root servers by reading a file, called the *hints file*, that contains the names and addresses of the root servers. (You will create that file later in this chapter.) Via queries, the server can find any host in the domain system by starting at the root and following pointers through the domains until it reaches the target domain.

Answering Queries

To answer a query for DNS information, the local name server must either have the answer to the query or know which name server does. No single system can have complete knowledge of all of the names in the Internet; servers know about their local domains and build up knowledge about other domains one query at a time.

Here's how it works. Assume you want the address of www.sybex.com. In effect, you are asking for the address record for www from the sybex.com database. A query for that address record comes to the local name server. If the server knows the address of www.sybex.com, it answers the query directly. If it doesn't know the answer, but it knows what server handles sybex.com, it queries that server. If it has no information at all, it queries a root server.

The root server does not directly answer the address query. Instead, it points your local server to a server that can answer queries for the sybex.com domain. It does this by sending your server a name server record that tells it the name of the server for the sybex.com domain and an address record that tells it the address of that server. Your local server then queries the sybex.com domain server and receives the address for www.sybex.com.

In this way, the local server learns the address of the host as well as the name and address of the servers for the domain. It caches these answers and will use them to directly answer queries about the sybex.com domain without again bothering the root servers.

The BIND Software

On all Linux systems, DNS is implemented with the Berkeley Internet Name Domain (BIND) software. Two versions of BIND are currently in widespread use:

- BIND 4 has been around for years and is found in previous releases of Linux.
- BIND 8 is the most recent version of BIND and is found on most new Linux distributions, such as Slackware 3.6, Caldera 2.2, and Red Hat 6. This chapter focuses on BIND 8.

NOTE If you are still running BIND 4, you should upgrade to BIND 8 for its enhanced security. Information about BIND 4 for earlier versions of Linux is included in Appendix B, *BIND Reference*.

BIND DNS is a client/server system. The client is called the *resolver*, and it forms the queries and sends them to the name server. Every computer on your network runs a resolver. Many systems, such as Microsoft Windows desktops, *only* run a resolver.

Under BIND, the resolver is not a distinct process. It is a library of software routines, called the *resolver code*, that is linked into any program that requires name service. The server side of BIND answers the queries that come from the resolver. The name server daemon is a distinct process called named. The configuration of named is much more complex than the configuration of the resolver, but there is no need to run named on every computer. (See "The named Configuration File" section later in this chapter for more on named and the named.conf file.)

Because all of the computers on your network, whether they are clients or servers, run the resolver, begin your DNS configuration by configuring the resolver.

Configuring the Resolver

The Linux resolver is configured by two files. One of these is host.conf, which was discussed at the end of this chapter. The host.conf file tells the resolver which name services to use and in what order to use them. The other configuration file, /etc/resolv.conf, configures the resolver for its interaction with the Domain Name Service. Every time a process that uses the resolver starts, it reads the resolv.conf file and caches the configuration for the life of the process. If the /etc/resolv.conf file is not found, a default configuration is used.

The default resolver configuration uses the hostname command to define the local domain. Everything after the first dot in the value returned by the hostname command is used as the default domain. For example, if hostname returns wren.foobirds.org, the default value for the local domain is foobirds.org.

The default configuration uses the local system as the name server. This means that you must run named if you don't create a resolv.conf file. Generally, I think you should create a resolv.conf file even if you do run named on the local host. There are two reasons for this. First, the resolv.conf file provides a means of documenting the configuration. Anyone can read the file and see the configuration you selected for the resolver. Second, the default values that work with one version of BIND may change with a future release. If you explicitly set the values you want, you don't have to worry about how default values change.

The Resolver Configuration Commands

resolv.conf is a text file that can contain the following commands:

> **nameserver** *address* The nameserver command defines the IP address of a name server the resolver should use. Up to three nameserver commands can be included in the configuration. The servers are queried in the order that they appear in the file until an answer is received or the resolver times out. When three name servers are listed, it takes 75 seconds for the resolver to time out. Normally, the first name server answers the query. The only time the second server is queried is if the first server is down or unreachable. The third server is only queried if both the first and second servers are down or unreachable. For this reason, I generally use only two nameserver entries. If no nameserver entry is found in the resolv.conf file, the name server running on the local host is used as the default.

domain *domainname* The domain command defines the local domain. The local domain is used to expand the host name in a query before it is sent to the name server. If the domain command is not used, the values defined in the search command are used. If neither command is found in the resolv.conf file, the value derived from the hostname command is used. No matter how the local domain value is set, it can be overridden for an individual user by setting the environment variable LOCALDOMAIN.

search *searchlist* The search command defines a list of domains that are used to expand a host name before it is sent to the name server. *searchlist* contains up to six domain names separated by whitespace. Each domain specified in the search list is searched in order until the query is answered. Unlike the domain command, which creates a default search list containing only the local domain, the search command creates an explicit search list containing every domain specified in *searchlist*.

options *option* The options command modifies the standard behavior of the resolver. There are currently two options available: debug to turn on debugging and ndots:*n* to change the number of dots used to determine when a host name doesn't need to be expanded before it is sent to the name server. The default value for ndots is 1, which means that a host name containing any dots at all is not expanded with the domain names from the search list. If you set *n* to 2 (ndots:2), a host name with one dot would be expanded, and a host name with two or more dots would not be expanded.

TIP Don't change the default setting of ndots. Studies have shown it to be the most efficient.

---

sortlist *addresslist* The sortlist command defines a list of network addresses that are preferred over other addresses. The *addresslist* is a list of address and mask pairs, for example, 172.16.5.0/255.255.255.0. The sortlist command is rarely used. To be of any use, it requires that the remote host has more than one address assigned to a single name, that the network path to one of those addresses is clearly superior to the others, and that you know exactly which path is superior. If you use a sortlist, the resolver reorders the addresses it receives from the name server to match the order you give in the address list. If the sortlist command is not specified, the addresses are used in the order they are received unless one of the addresses is from a network to which your computer is directly attached. By default, addresses from directly connected networks are preferred over other addresses.

A Sample `resolv.conf` File

Assume you're configuring a Linux workstation named `mute.swans.foobirds.org` (172.16.12.3) that does not run its own name server. A reasonable `resolv.conf` file might contain the following:

```
$ cat /etc/resolv.conf
search swans.foobirds.org foobirds.org
nameserver 172.16.12.1
nameserver 172.16.5.1
```

The configuration has two `nameserver` entries. The address of the first name server is 172.16.12.1. It's on the same subnet as `mute`. The other name server (172.16.5.1) is the main server for the `foobirds.org` domain. For efficiency sake, send queries to the server on the local subnet. For backup purposes, send queries to the main domain server when the local server is down.

The `search` command tells the resolver to expand host names first with the local subdomain `swans.foobirds.org` and then with the parent of that domain `foobirds.org`. This explicit list gives the workstation's users the behavior they have come to expect. In earlier versions of BIND, the default was to search the local domain and its parents. The default in BIND 8 is to search only the default domain. This explicit search list emulates the old behavior.

The Search List

Before leaving the subject of the resolver, additional discussion of when host names are expanded and how the search list is used is in order. Most administrators find everything about the resolver easy to understand except this.

The search list has only one purpose: to make things easier for users by allowing them to enter short host names. Queries to the name server must provide fully qualified domain names. The resolver uses the search list to turn the short host name entered by the user into the FQDN required by the name server.

Here's how this process works on a Linux system. If the user enters a name that contains one or more dots, the name is sent to the name server as is. It is only extended with a domain from the search list if it cannot be resolved as typed by the users. Therefore, `wren.foobirds.org` would not be extended.

If the user enters a name that does not contain any dots, the name is extended with a domain name from the search list and sent to the name server. If the name server cannot resolve the name, the resolver tries again using the next domain name in the search list and keeps on trying until the list of domain names is exhausted. If none of the domain names works, a final attempt is made by sending the name to the name server exactly as it was typed.

Assume you have the `resolv.conf` file shown above. The search list would contain `swans.foobirds.org` and `foobirds.org`. If the user entered the name `wren`, the resolver would extend it to `wren.swans.foobirds.org`. If the name server could not resolve the requested name, the resolver would try again with `wren.foobirds.org`. If that name could not be resolved, the resolver would make a final try sending just `wren`.

To have more than one domain in the search list, you must use the `search` command. The default value derived from the `hostname` command, the value entered by the `domain` command, and the value assigned to the LOCALDOMAIN environment variable all define just one domain—the local domain. The local domain then becomes the only value in the search list. In general, however, that is all you need. This permits the user to access computers that are in the local domain by host name alone, and for most users, this is sufficient.

> **NOTE**   The `domain` command and the `search` command are mutually exclusive. Whichever command appears last in the `resolv.conf` file is the one that defines the search list.

Configuring a Domain Name Server

There are three basic name server configurations:

- A *caching server* is a non-authoritative server. It gets all of its answers to name-server queries from other name servers.

- The *slave server* is considered an authoritative server, because it has a complete and accurate domain database that it transfers from the master server. It is also called the secondary server because it is the slave of the master, or primary, server.

- The *master server* is the primary server for the domain. It loads the domain information directly from a local disk file maintained by the domain administrator. The master server is considered authoritative for the domain, and its answers to queries are always considered to be accurate.

> **NOTE**   Most servers combine elements of more than one configuration. All servers cache answers, and many primary servers are secondary for some other domain. Mix and match these server configurations as needed for your network.

It is only necessary to run one master (or primary) server and one slave (or secondary) server for a domain. In all likelihood, however, you will run more than two servers. Many domain administrators create two official slave servers to increase reliability. To enhance performance, many network administrators place a caching server on each subnet or in each department.

TIP Create only one master server for your domain. It is the ultimate source of information about your domain. Create at least one slave server. It shares the workload and provides backup for the master server. (Many domain administrators create two official slave servers.) Use caching servers throughout your network to reduce the load on your master and secondary servers, and to reduce network traffic by placing name servers close to your users.

Up to five different types of files are required for a named configuration. All configurations require these three basic files:

named configuration file The named.conf configuration file defines basic parameters and points to the sources of domain database information, which can be local files or remote servers.

hints file The hints, or cache, file provides the names and addresses of the root servers that are used during startup.

local host file All configurations have a local domain database for resolving the loopback address to the host name localhost.

The other two files that are used to configure named are only used on the master server. These are the two files that define the domain database:

zone file The zone file defines most of the information. It is used to map host names to addresses, to identify the mail servers, and to provide a variety of other domain information.

reverse zone file The reverse zone file maps IP addresses to host names, which is exactly the opposite of what the domain file does.

NOTE A *zone* is the piece of the domain name space that is defined in a domain database file. A zone and a domain are not equivalent. For example, everything in the database file is in a single zone even if the file contains information about more than one domain.

To configure DNS, you need to understand how to configure all five configuration files. Let's start by looking at the named.conf file. It is used on every name server and defines the basic configuration.

The named Configuration File

In BIND 8, everything about the named configuration file changed: its name, the commands it contains, the structure of the commands, and the structure of the file. Even if you're familiar with configuring a domain name server, you should read this section.

BIND 8 provides three ways to insert a comment. A comment can be enclosed between /* and */, like a C language comment. It can begin with two slashes (//), like a C++ comment, or it can begin with a number sign (#), like a shell comment. However, a comment cannot begin with a semicolon (;) like comments did in previous versions of the BIND configuration file. The examples in this book use C++ style comments, but of course, you can use any of the three valid styles that you like.

The structure of the configuration commands is similar to the structure of the C programming language. A statement ends with a semicolon (;), literals are enclosed in quotes ("), and related items are grouped together inside curly braces ({}).

NOTE Complete syntax of each command is covered in Appendix B.

There are seven valid configuration statements for BIND 8.1.2. They are listed alphabetically in Table 6.1 with a short description of each command.

Table 6.1   named.conf Configuration Statements

Command	Usage
acl	Defines an access control list of IP addresses
include	Includes another file into the configuration file
key	Defines security keys for authentication
logging	Defines what will be logged and where it will be stored
options	Defines global configuration options and defaults
server	Defines a remote server's characteristics
zone	Defines a zone

The next few sections illustrate the function and format of some examples of the most commonly used commands.

The options Statement

Most named.conf files open with an options statement. Only one options statement can be used. The options statement defines global parameters that affect the way BIND operates. It also sets the defaults used by other statements in the configuration file. The most commonly used options statement defines the working directory for the server:

```
options {
        directory "/var/name";
};
```

The statement starts with the options command. The curly braces enclose a list of options, and the keyword directory defines the directory that named will read files from and write files to. The directory name is also used to complete any filename specified in the configuration file. The literal enclosed in quotes is the path name of the directory. Notice that both the directory clause and the options statement end with a semicolon.

TIP As you'll see when you read the section on the ndc tool later in this chapter, named can output several different files that are used to check the status of the name server. The options statement can be used to change the default path name of the output files. Don't do it. It gains you nothing and can confuse others who attempt to diagnose a name server problem on your system.

Several options can be set that affect all zones or all servers. In most cases, I prefer to set those values specifically for the zone or server that is being affected. The designers of BIND have set the defaults correctly for the vast majority of zones and servers. Zones and servers that need other values are exceptions and should be treated as such by defining the exceptional characteristics directly on the zone or server statement. You'll see examples of this in the zone statement.

One option that I have used on occasion is forwarders. The forwarders option causes the local server to forward to a specific list of servers all queries that it cannot resolve from its own cache. This builds a rich cache on the selected servers. The selected servers should be on your local network, because the point of building the rich cache is to reduce the number of queries sent over the wide area network. This is primarily useful if your WAN charges for usage like some ISDN networks.

A sample `forwarders` option is:

```
options {
        directory "/var/name";
        forward first;
        forwarders { 172.16.5.1; 172.16.12.1; };
};
```

The `forward first;` option says that the local server should try the forwarders before it tries to get an answer from any other external server. This is the default, so this option really didn't need to be specified. The other possible value is `forward only;`, which tells the server that it can only talk to the forwarders. Even if the forwarders are not responding, the local server is not allowed to find the answer itself when `forwarders only` is specified. The `forwarders` option lists the addresses of the servers to which queries are forwarded.

The zone Statement

The `zone` statements are the most important statements in the configuration file, and they constitute the bulk of the `named.conf` file. A `zone` statement performs the following critical configuration functions:

- It defines a zone that is serviced by this name server.
- It defines the type of name server that this server is for the zone. A server can be a master server or a slave server. And because this is defined on a per zone basis, the same server can be the master for some zones while being a slave for others.
- It defines the source of domain information for a zone. The domain database can be loaded from a local disk file or transferred from the master server.
- It defines special processing options for the zone.

A sample `zone` statement can illustrate all of these functions:

```
zone "foobirds.org" in {
        type master;
        file "foobirds.hosts";
        check-names fail;
        notify yes;
        also-notify { 172.16.80.3; };
};
```

Internet Server Operations

PART 2

The statement begins with the zone command. The name of the zone is written as a literal enclosed in quotes. The in keyword means that this zone contains IP addresses and Internet domain names. This is the default, so in is not really required. The curly braces enclose a list of options for this zone.

The type master; option says that this server is the master server for the foobirds.org domain. Other possible values are:

slave Identifies this as a slave server for the domain.

hints Identifies this as the hints file that is used to initialize the name server during startup. Every server has one hints zone.

stub Identifies this as a stub server. Stub servers are slave servers that only load the name server records from the master server's database. You won't use this value. It is primarily useful for non-recursive servers that want to refer a query to another server in the same way that root servers refer questions to other servers.

The file "foobirds.hosts"; option points to the file that contains the domain database information. For a master server, this is the file that is created by the domain administrator.

The last three options are in the example primarily to illustrate the available options. You probably won't use them. The check-names fail; option specifies what the server should do if it finds invalid host names in the zone file. The default is for a master server to abort loading the zone file and display an error message. (Since the default was chosen, this option wasn't actually needed.) Alternative values for this option are warn and ignore. warn displays a warning message and loads the zone anyway, which is the default for slave servers. ignore just ignores any errors.

The notify and also-notify options determine if the master server notifies slave servers when the zone information is updated. Slave servers periodically check the master zone file to see if it has been updated. With the notify yes; option, the master server sends a DNS NOTIFY message to the slave servers to cause them to immediately check the zone file. This is done to keep the master and slave databases tightly synchronized. The notify yes; option is the default, so it didn't need to be specified.

Normally, the DNS NOTIFY message is only sent to official name servers that are listed in the zone file. The also-notify { 172.16.80.3; }; option tells the master server to also notify 172.16.80.3. This system is not an official slave server, but it keeps a full copy of the zone database for some other purpose. See the case study "Phoney Slaves" at the end of this chapter for an example of when the also-notify option is used.

In most named.conf files, the zone statements are simpler than the example shown above. Let's look at some more realistic examples of name server configurations.

A Caching-Only Configuration

The caching-only configuration is the foundation of all server configurations, because all servers cache answers. The basic caching-only configuration created by Red Hat 6 during the Linux installation is used as the basis for all of the configurations created in this chapter. The name.conf file created by Red Hat is shown here:

```
$ cat /etc/named.conf
options {
        directory "/var/named";
};


//
// a caching only nameserver config
//
zone "." {
        type hint;
        file "named.ca";
};


zone "0.0.127.in-addr.arpa" {
        type master;
        file "named.local";
};
```

The options statement defines the default directory for named. In the sample file, it is /var/named. Both Red Hat and Caldera use this directory for named files. All subsequent file references in the named.conf file are relative to this directory.

The two zone statements in this caching-only configuration are found in all server configurations. The first zone statement defines the hints file that is used to help the name server locate the root servers during startup. The second zone statement makes the server the master for its own loopback address and points to the local host file. The hints file and the local host file, along with the named.conf file, are required for every server configuration.

The Hints File   The hints file contains information that named uses to initialize the cache. As indicated by the root domain (".") name on the zone statement, the hints the file contains are the names and addresses of the root name servers. The file helps the local server locate a root server during the startup. Once a root server is located, an authoritative list of root servers is downloaded from that server. The hints are not referred to again until the local server restarts.

The named.conf file points to the location of the hints file. The hints file can be given any filename. Commonly used names are named.ca, named.root, and root.cache. In the Red Hat 6 example, the hints file is called named.ca and is located in the /var/named directory. The hints file provided by the Red Hat installation contains the following server names and addresses:

```
.                       3600000   IN  NS  A.ROOT-SERVERS.NET.
A.ROOT-SERVERS.NET.     3600000       A   198.41.0.4
.                       3600000       NS  B.ROOT-SERVERS.NET.
B.ROOT-SERVERS.NET.     3600000       A   128.9.0.107
.                       3600000       NS  C.ROOT-SERVERS.NET.
C.ROOT-SERVERS.NET.     3600000       A   192.33.4.12
.                       3600000       NS  D.ROOT-SERVERS.NET.
D.ROOT-SERVERS.NET.     3600000       A   128.8.10.90
.                       3600000       NS  E.ROOT-SERVERS.NET.
E.ROOT-SERVERS.NET.     3600000       A   192.203.230.10
.                       3600000       NS  F.ROOT-SERVERS.NET.
F.ROOT-SERVERS.NET.     3600000       A   192.5.5.241
.                       3600000       NS  G.ROOT-SERVERS.NET.
G.ROOT-SERVERS.NET.     3600000       A   192.112.36.4
.                       3600000       NS  H.ROOT-SERVERS.NET.
H.ROOT-SERVERS.NET.     3600000       A   128.63.2.53
.                       3600000       NS  I.ROOT-SERVERS.NET.
```

```
I.ROOT-SERVERS.NET.   3600000      A    192.36.148.17
.                     3600000      NS   J.ROOT-SERVERS.NET.
J.ROOT-SERVERS.NET.   3600000      A    198.41.0.10
.                     3600000      NS   K.ROOT-SERVERS.NET.
K.ROOT-SERVERS.NET.   3600000      A    193.0.14.129
.                     3600000      NS   L.ROOT-SERVERS.NET.
L.ROOT-SERVERS.NET.   3600000      A    198.32.64.12
.                     3600000      NS   M.ROOT-SERVERS.NET.
M.ROOT-SERVERS.NET.   3600000      A    202.12.27.33
```

The hints file contains only name server (NS) and address (A) records. Each NS record identifies a name server for the root domain (.). The associated A record gives the IP address for each server. The structure of these database entries will become clear later in the chapter. For now, it is important to realize that you do not directly create or edit this file.

The sample file above is provided by the Linux installation. But even if your system doesn't provide a hints file, it is easy to get one. The official list of root servers is kept at the InterNIC. Download the file /domain/named.root from ftp.rs.internic.net via anonymous FTP. The file that is stored there is in the correct format for a Linux system, is ready to run, and can be downloaded directly to your hints file.

TIP Download the named.root file every few months to keep accurate root server information in your hints file.

The Local Host File Every name server is the master of its own loopback domain, which of course makes sense. The whole point of creating the loopback interface (1o0) is to reduce network traffic. Sending domain queries about the loopback address across the network would defeat that purpose.

The loopback domain is a reverse domain. It is used to map the loopback address 127.0.0.1 to the host name localhost. On our sample Red Hat system, the zone file for this domain is called named.local, which is the most common name for the local host file. The Red Hat installation provides the following file:

```
$ cat /var/named/named.local
@      IN     SOA     localhost. root.localhost.  (
                      1997022700 ; Serial
                      28800      ; Refresh
                      14400      ; Retry
                      3600000    ; Expire
                      86400 )    ; Minimum
       IN     NS      localhost.

1      IN     PTR     localhost.
```

Every Linux system that runs named has an essentially identical local host file. This one was created automatically by the Red Hat installation; if your system doesn't create one, you can copy this one. There is really no need to edit or change this file to run it on your system. At this point, the contents of the file don't need to be discussed, because they are always the same on every system. You will, however, see examples of all of these database records later in the chapter.

Most name servers are caching-only servers. For those servers, you:

- Configure the resolver. When running named on the local system, you can use the default resolver configuration.
- Create the named.conf file. You can copy the one shown above.
- Download the named.root from ftp.rs.internic.net and use it as the hints file.
- Create the named.local file. You can copy the one shown above.
- Reboot the system. named should start automatically. See "Running named" at the end of this chapter for more information on starting named.

This simple configuration works on most name servers, but not on all of them. The slave servers and the master server require more effort.

The Slave Server Configuration

Configuring a slave server is almost as simple as configuring a caching-only server. It uses the same three configuration files with only minor modifications to the named.conf file. Because of this, you can start with a caching-only configuration to test your system before you configure it as a slave server. Our sample slave server will be built by modifying the caching-only configuration shown above.

Assume that wren (172.16.5.1) is the master server for the foobirds.org domain and the 16.172.in-addr.arpa reverse domain. You want to configure robin as a slave server for those domains. To accomplish this, you add two new zone statements to the named.conf file on robin to create the following configuration:

```
$ cat /etc/named.conf
options {
        directory "/var/named";
};


// a slave server configuration
//
zone "." {
        type hint;
        file "named.ca";
};


zone "0.0.127.in-addr.arpa" {
        type master;
        file "named.local";
};


zone "foobirds.org" {
        type slave;
        file "foobirds.hosts";
        masters { 172.16.5.1; };
};


zone "16.172.in-addr.arpa" {
        type slave;
        file "172.16.reverse";
        masters { 172.16.5.1; };
};
```

The configuration file contains all of the statements you have already seen, because all servers use a hints file and a loopback domain database file. The two new zone statements declare zones for the domains foobirds.org and 0.16.172.in-addr.arpa. The type clause in each zone statement says that this is a slave server for the specified domain.

The file clause has a different purpose than those that you have seen before. In the previous examples, the file identified by the file clause was the source of the zone information. In this case, the file is the local storage for the zone information. The ultimate source for the information is the master server.

The masters clause identifies the master server. There can be more than one IP address provided in this clause, particularly if the master server is multi-homed and thus has more than one IP address. In most configurations, only one address is used, which is the address of the master server for the specified domain.

The slave server downloads the entire zone file from the master server. This process is called a "zone file transfer." When the file is downloaded, it is stored in the file identified by the file clause. You do not create or edit this file; it is created automatically by named. After the zone is downloaded, it loads directly from the local disk. The slave will not transfer the zone again until the master server updates the zone. Later in this chapter, you will see how the slave knows when the zone has been updated.

Configuring caching servers and slave servers doesn't seem very difficult, so what's the big deal about DNS configuration? The big deal is the master server, and that's what you're going to tackle next.

The Master Server Configuration

The named.conf file for a master server looks very much like the configuration file for a secondary server. In the example above, robin was the slave server for foobirds.org and 16.172.in-addr.arpa, and wren was the master server for those domains. The named .conf file for wren is:

```
$ cat /etc/named.conf
options {
        directory "/var/named";
};


// a master nameserver config
//
```

```
zone "." {
        type hint;
        file "named.ca";
};


zone "0.0.127.in-addr.arpa" {
        type master;
        file "named.local";
};


zone "foobirds.org" {
        type master;
        file "foobirds.hosts";
};


zone "16.172.in-addr.arpa" {
        type master;
        file "172.16.reverse";
};
```

The zone statements for the foobirds.org and 16.172.in-addr.arpa domains are exactly the same as the zone statement for the 0.0.127.in-addr.arpa domain, and they function the same way: The statements declare the zones, say that this is the master server for those zones, and identify the files that contain the database records for those zones.

So far, the configuration of the master server is exactly the same as any other server—you create a configuration file, a hints file, and a local host domain file. The difference comes from the fact that you must also create the real domain database files. The foobirds .hosts file and the 172.16.reverse file in our example can't be downloaded from a repository. You must create them, and in order to do so, you must understand the syntax and purpose of the database records.

DNS Database Records

The database records used in a zone file are called *standard resource records* or sometimes just "RRs." All resource records have the same basic format:

> [*name*] [*ttl*] IN *type data*

The *name* field identifies the domain object affected by this record. It could be an individual host or an entire domain. Unless the name is a fully qualified domain name, it is relative to the current directory.

A few special values can be used in the *name* field. These are:

A blank name refers to the last named object. The last value of the name field stays in force until a new value is specified.

@ An at sign refers to the current "origin." You can set the origin in the database file with the $ORIGIN command, but the real use of the at sign is to refer to the origin that the system derives from the zone command in the named.conf file.

* An asterisk is a wildcard character that can be used to match any character string.

The time-to-live (*ttl*) field defines the length of time in seconds that this resource record should be cached. This permits you to decide how long remote servers should store information from your domain. You can use a short TTL for volatile information and a long TTL for stable information. If no TTL value is specified, the default TTL value defined by the SOA record is used. (The SOA record is discussed in the next section.)

The *class* field is always IN, which is shown in the syntax above. There really are three possible values: HS for Hesiod servers, CH for Chaosnet servers, and IN for Internet servers. All of the information you deal with is for TCP/IP networks and Internet servers, so you will not use the other values.

The *type* field defines the type of resource record. The types used in this chapter, which are the most commonly used record types, are listed in Table 6.2.

Table 6.2   DNS Database Record Types

Record Name	Record Type	Function
Start of Authority	SOA	Marks the beginning of a zone's data and defines parameters that affect the entire zone.
Name Server	NS	Identifies a domain's name server.
Address	A	Maps a host name to an address.

Table 6.2   DNS Database Record Types *(continued)*

Record Name	Record Type	Function
Pointer	PTR	Maps an address to a host name.
Mail Exchanger	MX	Identifies the mail server for a domain.
Canonical Name	CNAME	Defines an alias for a host name.

The last field in the resource record is the *data* field, which holds the data that is specific to the type of resource record. For example, in an A record, this contains an address. The format and function of the data field is different for every record type.

Now that you know what records are available and what they look like, you're ready to put them together to create a database.

The Domain Database File

The domain database file contains most of the domain information. Its primary function is to convert host names to IP addresses, so A records predominate, but this file contains all of the database records except PTR records. Creating the domain database file is both the most challenging and rewarding part of building a name server.

In the foobirds.org domain, wren is the master server. Based on the named.conf file shown above, the domain database file is foobirds.hosts. It contains the following resource records:

```
;
;     The foobirds.org domain database
;
@   IN  SOA   wren.foobirds.org. sara.wren.foobirds.org. (
              1999022201 ; Serial
              21600      ; Refresh
              1800       ; Retry
              604800     ; Expire
              86400 )    ; Minimum
```

```
;   Define the nameservers
                    IN      NS      wren.foobirds.org.
                    IN      NS      falcon.foobirds.org.
                    IN      NS      bear.mammals.org.
;   Define the mail servers
                    IN      MX      10 wren.foobirds.org.
                    IN      MX      20 parrot.foobirds.org.
;
;       Define localhost
;
localhost   IN      A       127.0.0.1
;
;       Define the hosts in this zone
;
wren        IN      A       172.16.5.1
parrot      IN      A       172.16.5.3
crow        IN      A       172.16.5.5
hawk        IN      A       172.16.5.4
falcon      IN      A       172.16.5.20
puffin      IN      A       172.16.5.17
            IN      MX      5 wren.foobirds.org.
robin       IN      A       172.16.5.2
            IN      MX      5 wren.foobirds.org.
redbreast   IN      CNAME   robin.foobirds.org.
www         IN      CNAME   wren.foobirds.org.
news        IN      CNAME   parrot.foobirds.org.
;
;       Delegating sub-domains
;
swans       IN      NS      trumpeter.swans.foobirds.org.
            IN      NS      parrot.foobirds.org.
```

```
terns          IN     NS      arctic.terns.foobirds.org.
               IN     NS      trumpeter.swans.foobirds.org.
;
;     Glue records for subdomain servers
;
trumpeter.swans    IN     A       172.16.12.1
arctic.terns       IN     A       172.16.6.1
```

The SOA record All zone files begin with an SOA record. The @ in the name field of the SOA record refers to the current origin, which in this case is foobirds.org, because that is the value defined in the zone statement of the configuration file. Because it ties the domain name back to the named configuration file, the name field of the SOA record is usually an at sign.

> **NOTE** The data field of the SOA record is so long it normally spans several lines. The parentheses are continuation characters. After an opening parenthesis, all data on subsequent lines are considered part of the current record until a closing parenthesis.

The data field of the SOA record contains seven different components. The components of the data field in the sample SOA record contain the following values:

wren.foobirds.org This is the host name of the master server for this zone.

sara.wren.foobirds.org This is the e-mail address of the person responsible for this domain. Notice that the at sign (@) normally used between the username (sara) and the host name (wren.foobirds.org) is replaced with a dot (.).

1999022201 This is the serial number, a numeric value that tells the slave server that the zone file has been updated. To make this determination, the slave server periodically queries the master server for the SOA record. If the serial number in the master server's SOA record is greater than the serial number of the slave server's copy of the zone, the slave transfers the entire zone from the master. Otherwise, the slave assumes it has a current copy of the zone and skips the zone transfer. The serial number must be increased every time the domain is updated in order to keep the slave servers synchronized with the master.

21600 This is the length of the refresh cycle in seconds. Every refresh cycle, the slave server checks the serial number of the SOA record from the master server to determine if the zone needs to be transferred. A low refresh cycle keeps the servers tightly synchronized, but a very low value is not usually required, because the DNS NOTIFY message sent from the master server causes the slave to immediately check the serial number of the SOA record when the update occurs. A refresh cycle of

21600 seconds tells the slave server to check four times a day. This indicates that you have a stable database that does not change very frequently, which is often the case. Computers are added to the network periodically, but not usually on an hourly basis. When a new computer arrives, the host name and address are assigned before the system is added to the network, because the name and address are required to install and configure the system. Thus the domain information is disseminated to the slave servers before users begin to query for the address of the new system.

1800 This is the retry cycle. The retry cycle defines the length of time in seconds that the slave server should wait before asking again when the master server fails to respond to a request for the SOA record. Don't set the value too low—an hour (3600) or a half-hour (1800) are good retry values. If the server doesn't respond, it may be down. Quickly retrying a down server gains nothing and wastes network resources.

604800 This is the expiration time, the length of time in seconds that the slave server should continue to respond to queries even if it cannot update the zone file. The idea is that, at some point in time, out-of-date data is worse than no data. This should be a substantial amount of time. After all, the main purpose of a slave server is to provide backup for the master server. If the master server is down and the slave stops answering queries, the entire network is down instead of having just one server down. A disaster, such as a fire in the central computer facility, can take the master server down for a very long time. In the sample domain database file above, one week (604800) is used; an even more common value is one month (259200).

86400 This is the default time-to-live for this domain specified in seconds. The default TTL is used for any resource record that does not contain an explicit TTL. The sample sets the default TTL to one day, which is an average TTL. If the data in your domain is stable, you can set a high default TTL of several days and explicitly set a shorter TTL on those individual records that you expect to change.

All of the components of the data field of the SOA record set values that affect the entire domain. Several of these items affect remote servers. You decide how often slave servers check for updates and how long caching servers keep your data in their caches. The domain administrator is responsible for the design of the entire domain.

Defining the Name Servers   The NS records that follow the SOA record define the official name servers for the domain. Unless the `also-notify` option is used in the `zone` statement of the `named.conf` file, these are the only servers that receive a DNS NOTIFY message when the zone is updated.

Although they can appear anywhere in the file, the NS records often follow directly after the SOA record. When they do, the name field of each NS record can be blank. Because the name field is blank, the value of the last object named is used. In the example above, the last value to appear in the name field was the @ that referred to the foobirds.org domain defined in the named.conf file. Therefore, these NS records all define name servers for the foobirds.org domain.

The first two NS records point to the master server wren and the slave server robin that we configured earlier. The third server is external to our network. Name servers should have good network connections, and slave name servers should have a path to the Internet that is independent from the path used by the master server. This enables the slave server to fulfill it purpose as a backup server even when the network that the master server is connected to is down. Large organizations may have independent connections for both servers; small organizations usually do not. If possible, find a server that is external to your network to act as a slave server. Check with your Internet Service Provider (ISP). They may offer this as a service to their customers.

Defining the Mail Servers   The MX records define the mail servers for this domain. The name field is still blank, meaning that these records pertain to the last named object, which in this case is the entire domain. The first MX record says that wren is the mail server for the foobirds.org domain with a preference of 10. If mail is addressed to user@foobirds.org, the mail is directed to wren for delivery.

The second MX record identifies parrot as a mail server for foobirds.org with a preference of 20. The lower the preference number, the more preferred the server. This means that mail addressed to the foobirds.org domain is first sent to wren. Only if wren is unavailable is the mail sent to parrot. parrot acts as a backup for those times when wren is down or offline.

The MX records redirect mail addressed to the domain foobirds.org, but they do not redirect mail addressed to an individual host. Therefore, if mail is addressed to jay@hawk .foobirds.org, it is delivered directly to hawk; it is not sent to a mail server. This configuration permits people to use e-mail addresses of the form *user@domain* when they like, or to use direct delivery to an individual host when they want that. It is a very flexible configuration.

Some systems, however, may not be capable of handling direct delivery e-mail. An example is a Microsoft Windows system that doesn't run an SMTP mail program. Mail addressed to such a system would not be successfully delivered, and worse, would probably be reported to you as a network error! To prevent this, assign an MX record to the individual host to redirect its mail to a valid mail server.

There are two examples of this in the sample zone file. Look at the resource records for puffin and robin. The address record of each system is followed by an MX record that directs mail to wren. The MX records have a blank name field, but this time they don't refer to the domain. In both cases, the last value in the name field is the name from the preceding address record. It is this name that the MX record applies to. In one case it is puffin, and in the other it is robin. With these records, mail addressed to daniel@puffin .foobirds.org is delivered to daniel@wren.foobirds.org.

The MX record is only the first step in creating a mail server. The MX is necessary to tell the remote computer where it should send the mail, but for the mail server to successfully deliver the mail to the intended user, it must be properly configured.

NOTE   Chapter 7, *Configuring a Mail Server,* looks at how sendmail is config-ured to properly handle the mail.

Defining the Host Information   The bulk of the zone file is address records that map host names to IP addresses. The first one in our sample domain database file maps the name localhost.foobirds.org to the loopback address 127.0.0.1. The reason this entry is included in the database has something to do with the way that the resolver constructs queries. Remember that if a host name contains no dots, the resolver extends it with the local domain. So when a user enters telnet localhost, the resolver sends the name server a query for localhost.foobirds.org. Without this entry in the database, the resolver would make multiple queries before finally finding localhost in the /etc/hosts file. The localhost entry is followed by several address entries for individual hosts in the domain.

The only other unexplained records in this section are the CNAME records. The first CNAME record says that redbreast is a host name alias for robin. Aliases are used to map an obsolete name to a current name or to provide generic names like www and news. Aliases cannot be used in other resource records. Therefore, take care when placing CNAME records in the domain database. You have seen several examples of the fact that a blank name field refers to the previously named object. If the CNAME record is placed improperly, a record with a blank name field can illegally reference a nickname.

For example, the file contains these records for robin:

```
robin       IN     A       172.16.5.2
            IN     MX      5 wren.foobirds.org.
redbreast   IN     CNAME   robin.foobirds.org.
```

A mistake in placing these records could produce the following:

```
robin          IN     A        172.16.5.2
redbreast      IN     CNAME    robin.foobirds.org.
               IN     MX       5 wren.foobirds.org.
```

This would cause named to display the error "redbreast.foobirds.com has CNAME and other data (illegal)" because the MX record now refers to redbreast. Due to the potential for errors, many domain administrators put the CNAME records together in one section of the file instead of intermingling them with other resource records.

Delegating a Subdomain   The final six lines in the sample domain database file delegate the subdomains swans.foobirds.org and terns.foobirds.org. The root servers delegated the foobirds.org domain to you. You now have the authority to delegate any domains within the foobirds.org domain that you wish. In the example, two are delegated.

A domain does not officially exist until it is delegated by its parent domain. The administrator of trumpeter.swans.foobirds.org can configure the system as the master server for the swans domain and enter all of the necessary domain data. It doesn't matter, though, because no one will query the system for information about the domain. In fact, no computer in the outside world will even know that the swans domain exists. When you think of how the domain system works, you'll see why this is true.

The DNS system is a rooted hierarchical system. If a remote server has no information at all about the swans.foobirds.org domain, it asks a root server. The root server tells the remote server that wren and its slave servers know about foobirds.org. The remote server then asks wren. wren finds the answer to the query, either from its cache or by asking parrot or trumpeter, and replies with the answer along with the NS records for swans.foobirds.org and the IP addresses of trumpeter and parrot. Armed with the NS records and the IP addresses, the remote server can send other queries about the swans.foobirds.org domain directly to trumpeter.

The information path is from the root to wren and then to trumpeter. There is no way for the remote server to go directly to trumpeter or parrot for information until wren tells it where they are located. If the delegation did not exist in the foobirds.org domain, the path to the swans.foobirds.org domain would not exist.

> ***NOTE*** Notice that the root server sends the remote server to wren while wren looks up the answer for the remote server instead of just sending the remote server to trumpeter. The root servers are *non-recursive* servers: If they don't have an answer, they'll tell you who does, but they won't look it up for you. Most other servers are *recursive* servers: If they don't have the answer, they'll look it up for you.

The first four lines of the sample delegations are NS records.

```
swans      IN       NS       trumpeter.swans.foobirds.org.

           IN       NS       parrot.foobirds.org.

terns      IN       NS       arctic.terns.foobirds.org.

           IN       NS       trumpeter.swans.foobirds.org.
```

The first two say that trumpeter and parrot are authoritative servers for the swans.foobirds.org domain. The last two records say that arctic and trumpeter are authoritative servers for the terns.foobirds.org domain.

Two other records are part of the subdomain delegation. They are address records.

```
trumpeter.swans      IN       A       172.16.18.15

arctic.terns         IN       A       172.16.6.1
```

Both of these addresses are for name servers located in domains that are subordinate to the current domain. These address records are called *glue records* because they help to link all of the domains together. In order to connect to a name server, you must have its address. If the address for arctic was only available from arctic, there'd be a problem. For this reason, the address of a name server located in a subordinate domain is placed in the parent domain when the subordinate domain is delegated.

The Reverse Domain File

The reverse domain file maps IP addresses to host names. This is the reverse of what the domain database does when it maps host names to addresses.

But there is another reason this is called the reverse domain: All of the IP addresses are written in reverse. For example, in the reverse domain, the address 172.16.5.2 is written as 2.5.16.172.in-addr.arpa. The address is reversed to make it compatible with the structure of a domain name. An IP address is written from the most general to the most specific. It starts with a network address, moves through a subnet address, and ends with a host address. The host name is just the opposite. It starts with the host, moves through subdomain and domain, and ends with a top-level domain. To format an address like a host name, the host part of the address is written first, and the network is written last. The network address becomes the domain name, and the host address becomes a host name within the domain.

In our example, the network address 172.16.0.0 becomes the domain 16.172.in-addr.arpa. The zone file for this domain is shown below:

```
;         Address to host name mappings.
;
@    IN   SOA    wren.foobirds.org. sara.wren.foobirds.org. (
                 1999022702    ;   Serial
                 21600         ;   Refresh
                 1800          ;   Retry
                 604800        ;   Expire
                 86400 )       ; Minimum
            IN      NS      wren.foobirds.org.
            IN      NS      falcon.foobirds.org.
            IN      NS      bear.mammals.org.
1.5         IN      PTR     wren.foobirds.org.
2.5         IN      PTR     robin.foobirds.org.
3.5         IN      PTR     parrot.foobirds.org.
4.5         IN      PTR     hawk.foobirds.org.
5.5         IN      PTR     crow.foobirds.org.
17.5        IN      PTR     puffin.foobirds.org.
20.5        IN      PTR     falcon.foobirds.org.
1.12        IN      PTR     trumpeter.swans.foobirds.org.
1.6         IN      PTR     arctic.terns.foobirds.org.
6           IN      NS      arctic.terns.foobirds.org.
            IN      NS      falcon.foobirds.org.
```

Like other zone files, the reverse zone begins with an SOA record and a few NS records. They serve the same purpose and have the same fields as their counterparts in the domain database, which were explained above.

PTR records make up the bulk of the reverse domain, because they are used to translate addresses to host names. Look at the first PTR record. The name field contains 1.5. This is not a fully qualified name, so it is interpreted as relative to the current domain, giving us 1.5.16.172.in-addr.arpa as the value of the name field. The data field of a PTR record contains a host name. The host name in the data field is always fully qualified to prevent it from being interpreted as relative to the current domain. In the first PTR record, the data field is wren.foobirds.org, so a PTR query for 1.5.16.172.in-addr.arpa (172.16.5.1) returns the value wren.foobirds.org.

Delegating a Reverse Subdomain   The last two lines in the file are NS records that delegate the subdomain 6.16.172.in-addr.arpa to arctic and falcon. Subdomains can be created and delegated in the reverse domain exactly as they are in the host name space. However, limitations caused by the way that addresses are treated as host names in the reverse domain can make them more difficult to set up and to use than other subdomains.

The reverse domain treats the IP address as a host name composed of four pieces. The four bytes of the address become the four parts of the host name. However, addresses are really 32 contiguous bits, not four distinct bytes. In our sample network, we have delegated addresses on byte boundaries, so it's easy to assign reverse subdomains on the same boundary. What if we had only assigned the addresses 172.16.6.1 to 172.16.6.63 to arctic? The delegation shown above would send queries to arctic that it couldn't answer.

There are ways around this, but I find them cumbersome. A popular technique is to assign every possible address a CNAME that includes a new subdomain that takes into account the real domain structure, and then to delegate the new subdomain to the remote server. Assume we only want arctic to handle the addresses 172.16.6.1 to 172.16.6.63. We could enter 63 CNAME records in the reverse zone and two NS records as follows:

```
1.6      IN      CNAME     1.1-63.16.172.in-addr.arpa.
2.6      IN      CNAME     2.1-63.16.172.in-addr.arpa.

. . .

62.6     IN      CNAME     62.1-63.16.172.in-addr.arpa.
63.6     IN      CNAME     63.1-63.16.172.in-addr.arpa.
1-63     IN      NS        arctic.terns.foobirds.org.
         IN      NS        falcon.foobirds.org.
```

The first 63 records give the names 1.6.16.172.in-addr.arpa to 63.6.16.172.in-addr.arpa canonical names in the new 1-63 subdomain. The new subdomain is then delegated to arctic and falcon. If a query comes in for 2.6.16.172.in-addr.arpa, the resolver is told that the real name it is seeking is `2.1-63.16.172.in-addr.arpa` and that the servers for that name are `arctic` and `falcon`. This works, but it seems like a lot of typing to me. If possible, I prefer not to delegate reverse subdomains unless they occur on a byte boundary.

The reverse zone may seem like a lot of trouble for a little gain; after all, most of the action happens in the host name space. But keeping the reverse zone up-to-date is important. Several programs use the reverse domain to map IP addresses to names for status displays. `netstat` is a good example. As you'll see later in the chapter, some remote systems use reverse lookup to check on who is using a service and in extreme cases won't allow you to use the service if they can't find your system in the reverse domain.

Running named

`named` is started at boot time by one of the startup scripts. On a Slackware system, it is started by the `/etc/rc.d/rc.inet2` script. On Red Hat and Caldera systems, it is started by the `/etc/rc.d/init.d/named` script. Both of these scripts check that the `named` program and the `named.conf` file are available, and then they start `named`. To run `named`, create the configuration files and reboot.

If you can't—or don't want to—reboot, run `named` from the command line by typing **named &**. `named` is rarely started manually, because it automatically starts at every boot and because it does not need to be stopped and started to load a new configuration. Signals can be used to cause `named` to load a new configuration and to perform a number of other tasks.

named Signal Processing

`named` handles several different signals. The most commonly used, at least for me, is HUP. The HUP signal causes `named` to re-read the `named.conf` file and reload the name server database. Using HUP causes the reload to occur immediately. On a master server, this means that the local database files are reloaded into memory. On a slave server, this means that the slave immediately reloads its local disk copies and then sends a query to the master server for the SOA record to check if there is a new configuration.

The INT signal causes `named` to dump its cache to `named_dump.db`. The dump file contains all of the domain information that the local name server knows. Examine this file. You'll see a complete picture of the information the server has learned. Examining the cache is an interesting exercise for anyone who is new to DNS.

Use USR1 to turn on tracing. Each subsequent USR1 signal increases the level of tracing. Trace information is written to `named.run`. Tracing can also be enabled with the `-d` option on the named command line if the problem you are looking for occurs so early in the startup that the USR1 signal is not useful. The advantage of the USR1 signal is that it allows tracing to be turned on when a problem is suspected, without stopping and restarting named.

The opposite of the USR1 signal is the USR2 signal. It turns off tracing and closes the trace file. After issuing USR2, you can examine the file or remove it if it is getting too large.

There are some additional signals available, but only if they are compiled into BIND. The version of BIND that comes with Slackware, Caldera, and Red Hat does not have these signals compiled in. One of these signals that could become important is TERM. If named is compiled with dynamic updating enabled, the TERM signal saves data modified by dynamic updates back to the database files before the system is shut down. This will be important when tools are available that dynamically update the domain. Such tools are not currently available, but work on them is discussed in the DHCP section of Chapter 10.

The kill Command

The kill command is used to send a signal to a running process. As the name implies, by default it sends the kill signal. To use it to send a different signal, specify the signal on the command line. For example, specify -INT to send the INT signal. The process ID (PID) must be provided on the kill command line to ensure that the signal is sent to the correct process.

You can learn the process ID using the ps command. For example:

```
# ps ax | grep named
  271  ?  S     0:00 /usr/sbin/named
 7138  p0 S     0:00 grep named
```

In the case of named, you can learn the process ID by listing the named.pid file:

```
# cat /var/run/named.pid
271
```

Combining some of these commands, you can send a signal directly to named. For example, to reload the name server, you could enter the following command:

```
kill -HUP `cat /var/run/named.pid`
```

The cat /var/run/named.pid command that is enclosed in single quotes is processed by the shell first. On our sample system, this returns the PID 271. That is combined with the kill command and then is processed as kill -HUP 271. This works, but I find it easier to use the ndc command. With ndc, there is less to type and less to remember.

The ndc Tool

The name daemon control (ndc) tool allows you to send signals to named with much less fuss. You don't need to know the correct PID, and you don't need to remember the correct signal. For example, in the previous section, kill was used with the HUP signal to reload the name server. To do the same thing with ndc, you enter **ndc reload**. This command is simple and much more intuitive than the kill command. The valid ndc command-line arguments, as well as the signals that are equivalent to them, are listed in Table 6.3.

Table 6.3   ndc Commands

Argument	Signal	Function
status		Displays the status of named
dumpdb	INT	Dumps the cache to named_dump.db
reload	HUP	Reloads the name server
stats	IOT	Dumps statistics to named.stats
trace	USR1	Turns on tracing to named.run
notrace	USR2	Turns off tracing and closes named.run
querylog	WINCH	Toggles query logging, which logs each incoming query to syslog
start		Starts named
stop		Stops named

ndc has three arguments—status, start, and stop—that are not available as signals. status displays the named process status just like the ps command. start runs named if it is not currently running, and stop terminates named if it is running. ndc provides a simple, convenient way to interface with a running name server.

> **WARNING**   Tracing (trace) and query logging (querylog) can consume enormous amounts of disk space very quickly. Use them with caution.

Internet Server Operations

PART 2

Using the Host Table with DNS

You should always use DNS if you have a large network application. But even though you will be using DNS, you will have a host table. Which source of information should your system check first, DNS or the host table?

I usually configure my systems to use DNS first and to fall back to the host table only when DNS is not running. Your needs may be different. You may have special host aliases that are not included in the DNS database, or local systems that are known only to a small number of computers on your network and therefore are not registered in the official domain. In these cases, you want to check the host table before sending an unanswerable query to the DNS server.

There are two files involved in configuring the order in which name services are queried for information. The host.conf file is the most important for name service, because that's the file's primary focus. The nsswitch.conf file covers a wider range of administrative databases, including name service.

The host.conf File

The host.conf file defines several options that control how the /etc/hosts file is processed and how it interacts with DNS. To illustrate this, here's a sample host.conf file that contains every possible option:

```
# Define the order in which services are queried
order bind hosts nis
# Permit multiple addresses per host
multi on
# Verify reverse domain lookups
nospoof on
# Log "spoof" attempts
alert on
# Remove the local domain for host table lookups
trim foobirds.org
```

The order option defines the order in which the various name services are queried for a host name or an IP address. The three values shown in the example are the only three values available:

- bind stands for DNS. (As noted earlier, BIND is the name of the software package that implements DNS on Linux systems.)

- `hosts` stands for the `/etc/hosts` file.
- `nis` stands for the Network Information Service (NIS), which is a name service created by Sun Microsystems.

These services are tried in the order they are listed. Given the `order` command shown above, we try DNS first, then the `/etc/hosts` file, and finally NIS. The search stops as soon as a service answers the query.

The `multi` option determines whether or not multiple addresses can be assigned to the same host name in the `/etc/hosts` file. This option is enabled when `on` is specified and is disabled when `off` is specified. You may be wondering why you would want to do this. Well, assume that you have a single computer directly connected to a few different networks—this is called a *multi-homed host*. Each network requires an interface, and each interface requires a different IP address. Thus you have one host with multiple addresses. But also assume that this is your Web server and that you want everyone to refer to it by the host name `www` regardless of the network they connect in from. In this case, you have one host name associated with multiple addresses, which is just what the `multi` option was designed for. `multi` only affects host table lookups; it has no effect on DNS. DNS inherently supports multiple addresses.

As you've seen, Domain Name Service permits you to look up a host name and get an address as well as to look up an address and get a host name; names to addresses are in one database, and addresses to names are in another database. The `nospoof` option says that the values returned from both databases must match, or your system will reject the host name and return an error. For example, if the name `wren.foobirds.org` returns the address 172.16.5.1, but a lookup for the address 172.16.5.1 returns the host name `host0501.foobirds.org`, your system will reject the host as invalid. The `nospoof` option is used by people who want to accurately log the remote systems that are using their services. The keyword `on` enables the feature, and `off` disables it.

The `alert` option is related to the `nospoof` option. When `alert` is turned on, the system logs any of the host name/address mismatches described above. When `alert` is turned `off`, these events are not logged.

The `trim` option removes the local domain name before the name is looked up in the `/etc/hosts` file. This permits the system to match the host name alone even if the user enters the host name with the domain name. With this, the `/etc/hosts` file can be created without full domain names and still be useful. Given the `trim` command above, a query for `hawk.foobirds.org` would cause a host table query for `hawk`. Multiple `trim` commands can be included in the `host.conf` file to remove several different domains from host table queries. `trim` only affects host table lookups; it has no effect on DNS.

Real `host.conf` files don't actually use all of these commands. The `host.conf` file that comes with Red Hat 6 has only two lines:

```
# cat /etc/host.conf
order hosts,bind
multi on
```

The real heart of the `host.conf` file is the `order` command, which defines the order in which the name services are searched. Another file, `nsswitch.conf`, is sometimes used to define this exact same thing.

The `nsswitch.conf` File

The `nsswitch.conf` file handles much more than just the order of precedence between the host table and DNS. It defines the sources for several different system administration databases, because it is an outgrowth of the Network Information System (NIS). NIS makes it possible to centrally control and distribute a wide range of system administration files. Table 6.4 lists all of the administrative databases controlled by the `nsswitch.conf` file. Unless you run NIS on your network, the sources of all of these administrative databases, except for the `hosts` database, will be the local files.

Table 6.4   Databases Controlled by `nsswitch.conf`

Database	Holds
Aliases	E-mail aliases
Ethers	Ethernet addresses for Reverse ARP (RARP)
Group	Group IDs
Hosts	Host names and IP addresses
Netgroup	Network groups for NIS
Network	Network names and numbers
Passwd	User account information
Protocols	IP protocol numbers
Publickey	Keys for secure RPC (remote procedure call)
Rpc	RPC names and numbers

Table 6.4   Databases Controlled by `nsswitch.conf` *(continued)*

Database	Holds
Services	Network service port numbers
Shadow	User passwords

The `hosts` entry is the one we are interested in, because it indicates the source for host name and IP address information. In the following sample `nsswitch.conf` file, DNS is used as the primary source with the local file as the backup source. If DNS can successfully answer the query, it's finished. If DNS can't answer the query, the resolver tries the local file, which in this case is /etc/hosts.

```
# Sample for system that does not use NIS

passwd:     files
shadow:     files
group:      files

hosts:      dns files
aliases:    files

services:   files
networks:   files
protocols:  files
rpc:        files
ethers:     files
netgroup:   files
publickey:  files
```

This sample shows that each database is listed along with the source for that database. As you can see, only the `hosts` entry has more than one source—first DNS (`dns`) and then the local `hosts` file (`files`). To check the host table before DNS, simply reverse the order:

```
hosts: files dns
```

All of the other entries in the sample nsswitch.conf file point to local files as the source of information for those databases. You're already familiar with several of the local files: /etc/passwd, /etc/group, /etc/shadow, /etc/services, /etc/protocols, /etc/networks, and /etc/hosts. On most Linux systems, local files are used for all of these databases. Unless you run NIS, your nsswitch.conf file will probably look pretty much like the sample.

In addition to dns and files, there are three other possible source values. nis and nisplus are valid source values if you run NIS or NIS+ on your network. Also, compat is a valid source field value that might be of use if you run NIS. compat means that the source is a local file, but the local files should be read in a way that is compatible with the old SunOS 4.*x* system. Under SunOS 4.*x*, NIS data could be appended to a file by using a plus sign (+) as the last entry in a file. For example, if /etc/passwd ended with a +, the system should use the accounts in the password file plus every account in NIS. SunOS 4.*x* has been out of production for more than five years, and the nsswitch.conf file supercedes the old "plus syntax." However, some people still use it, and the compat function is there if you needed it. Of course, none of these source values is needed if you don't use NIS.

Final Words

Name service is a fundamental service of a Linux network. A name service converts text-based host names to the numeric IP address required by the network. In the same way that the services in Chapter 5 needed user IDs (UIDs) and group IDs (GIDs) to identify users, networks need IP addresses to identify computers. Domain Names Service (DNS) is the tool that maps host names to IP addresses for the network.

DNS is implemented on Linux systems with the Berkeley Internet Name Domain (BIND) software, which is the most widely used DNS software in the Internet. Linux is a fairly new operating system, but it benefits from the fact that it can run venerable software packages like BIND that have a very long history with many years of debugging and refinement. Linux developers wisely used these tried-and-true packages for the most critical network servers.

E-mail is another critical service that must be provided by every modern network, and Linux uses sendmail, which is the most widely used SMTP mail server software, to provide e-mail service. In the next chapter, you will configure an e-mail server using sendmail.

Phoney Slaves

The only true authoritative servers are the master and slave servers defined in the zone file. But there are occasions when it is worthwhile to pretend that your local server is a slave server. One such occasion is when it can save you money.

Our local telephone company charges by the minute for ISDN connections. A small branch office wanted to connect into the main office using an ISDN line, and they wanted to reduce the amount of per-minute charges caused by DNS queries. Even though each query lasted less than a second, it caused the ISDN line to connect and incur a minimum one-minute charge.

Most of the queries were for addresses within the local domain. Often they were for other computers on the branch office's local area network, but even these queries were being sent over the ISDN line to the name server at the main office. To reduce this traffic, we configured a server on the LAN as a slave server for the customer's domain. But that configuration only exists in the named.conf file of the local server. The master server did not add the branch office server to its list of official slave servers, and we did not want it to. We were careful to make sure that the server was not a real slave server, because we never want remote users sending queries to this server that can be resolved by the true authoritative servers. Even queries from the outside would cost us a minute of connect time!

Now the branch office slave server checks and downloads the entire domain from the master server twice a day. And since the full download takes less than a minute, it costs no more than any other query. Because a slave server has a full copy of the domain, the branch office server never had to forward a query for the local domain to the main office servers.

24seven **CASE STUDY**

7

Configuring a Mail Server

Electronic mail is still the most important user service on your network. The Web carries a greater volume of traffic, but e-mail is the service used for most person-to-person communication. And person-to-person communication is the real foundation of business. No network is complete without e-mail, and no network server operating system is worth its salt if it doesn't include full TCP/IP mail support.

Simple Mail Transport Protocol (SMTP) is the TCP/IP mail transport protocol. Linux provides full SMTP support through the sendmail program, though sendmail does more than just send and receive SMTP mail. sendmail provides mail aliases and acts as a "mail router," routing mail from all of the different user mail programs to the various mail delivery programs while ensuring that the mail is properly formatted for delivery.

This chapter looks at your role in configuring each of these functions. Configuring sendmail can be a large and complex task, but it doesn't have to be. Compared to some network server systems that require a second installation just to install the SMTP server software, Linux does a lot of the configuration for you, and for most sites, the default configuration works fine. This chapter will give you the information you need to make intelligent decisions about when and how to change the default configuration.

Using Mail Aliases

Mail aliases are defined in the `aliases` file. The location of the `aliases` file is set in the "Options" section of the `sendmail` configuration file. (You'll see this configuration file later in the chapter.) On Linux systems, the file is usually located in the `/etc` directory (`/etc/aliases`). The basic format of entries in the file is:

> `alias`: `recipient`

The `alias` is the username in the e-mail address, and `recipient` is the name to which the mail should be delivered. The `recipient` field can contain a username, another alias, or a full e-mail address containing both a username and a host name. Additionally, there can be multiple recipients for a single alias.

`sendmail` aliases perform important functions that are an essential part of creating a mail server. Mail aliases do the following:

Specify nicknames for individual users. Nicknames can be used to direct mail addressed to special names, such as postmaster or root, to the real users that do those jobs. When used in conjunction with the domain MX records covered in Chapter 6, aliases can be used to create a standard e-mail address structure for a domain.

Forward mail to other hosts. `sendmail` aliases automatically forward mail to the host address included as part of the recipient address.

Define mailing lists. An alias with multiple recipients is a mailing list.

The `aliases` file from a Red Hat 6 system with a few additions illustrates all of these uses:

```
#
#       @(#)aliases      8.2 (Berkeley) 3/5/94
#
#  Aliases in this file will NOT be expanded in the header from
#  Mail, but WILL be visible over networks or from /bin/mail.
#
#       >>>>>>>>>       The program "newaliases" must be run after
#       >> NOTE >>      this file is updated for any changes to
#       >>>>>>>>>       show through to sendmail.
#


# Basic system aliases -- these MUST be present.
```

```
MAILER-DAEMON:    postmaster
postmaster:       root


# General redirections for pseudo accounts.
bin:              root
daemon:           root
games:            root
ingres:           root
nobody:           root
system:           root
toor:             root
uucp:             root


# Well-known aliases.
manager:          root
dumper:           root
operator:         root
webmaster:        root


# trap decode to catch security attacks
decode:           root


# Person who should get root's mail
root:             staff


# System administrator mailing list
staff: kathy, craig, david@parrot, sara@hawk, becky@parrot
owner-staff: staff-request
staff-request: craig
```

```
# User aliases
norman.edwards:    norm
edwardsn: norm
norm: norm@hawk.foobirds.org
rebecca.hunt: becky@parrot
andy.wright: andy@falcon.foobirds.org
sara.henson: sara@hawk
kathy.McCafferty: kathy
kathleen.McCafferty: kathy
```

The Red Hat /etc/aliases file opens with several comment lines. Ignore the information about which mail programs display aliases in the headers of mail messages; it is not really significant. The comment that *is* significant is the one that tells you to run newaliases every time you update this file. sendmail does not read the /etc/aliases file directly. Instead, it reads a database file produced from this file by the newaliases command.

The next 15 lines define aliases for special names. All of these, except the webmaster alias that I added, come preconfigured in the Red Hat aliases file. The first two are aliases that people expect to find on any system running sendmail. Most of the others are aliases assigned to the daemon usernames that are found in the /etc/passwd file. No one can actually log in using the daemon usernames, so any mail that might be directed to these pseudo accounts is forwarded to a real user account. In the example, this mail is forwarded to the root user account.

Of course, you don't really want people logging in to the root account just to read mail, so the aliases file also has an alias for root. In the example, I edited the root entry to forward all mail addressed to root to staff, which is another alias. Notice how often aliases point to other aliases. Doing this is very useful, because it allows you to update one alias instead of many when the real user account that the mail is delivered to changes.

The staff alias is a mailing list. A *mailing list* is simply an alias with multiple recipients. In the example, several people are responsible for maintaining this mail server. Messages addressed to root are delivered to all of these people through the staff mailing list.

Two special aliases are associated with the mailing list. The owner-staff alias is a special alias used by sendmail for error messages relating to the staff mailing list. The format that sendmail requires for this special alias is owner-*list*, where *list* is the name of the mailing list. The other special alias, staff-request, is not required by sendmail, but it is expected by remote users. By convention, manual mailing list maintenance requests, such as being added to or deleted from a list, are sent to the alias *list*-request, where *list* is the name of the mailing list.

The last eight lines are user aliases I added to the file. These lines direct mail received at the mail server to the computers where the users read their mail. These aliases can be in a variety of formats to handle the various ways that e-mail is addressed to a user. The first three lines that forward mail to norm@hawk.foobirds.org all illustrate this. Assume that this /etc/aliases file is on wren and that the MX record in DNS says that wren is the mail exchanger for foobirds.org. Then mail addressed to norman.edwards@foobirds .org would actually be delivered to norm@hawk.foobirds.org. It is the combination of mail aliases and MX records that make possible the simplified mail addressing schemes used at so many organizations.

Defining Personal Mail Aliases

As the last eight lines in the Red Hat aliases file illustrate, one of the main functions of the alias file is to forward mail to other accounts or other computers. The aliases file defines mail forwarding for the entire system. The .forward file, which can be created in any user's home directory, defines mail forwarding for an individual user.

It is possible to use the .forward file to do something that can be done in the /etc/ aliases file. For example, if Norman Edwards had an account on a system but didn't really want to read his mail on that system, he could create the following .forward file:

```
norm@hawk.foobirds.org
```

This entry forwards all mail received in his account on the local system to the norm account at hawk.foobirds.org. However, if you want to permanently forward mail to another account, create an alias in the /etc/aliases file. Simple forwarding is not the primary use for the .forward file. A much more common use for the file is to invoke special mail processing before mail is delivered to your personal mail account. Chapter 13, *More Mail Services*, illustrates this when procmail and mail filtering are discussed.

Using sendmail to Receive Mail

sendmail runs in two different ways. When you send mail, a sendmail process starts, delivers your mail, and then terminates. To receive mail, sendmail runs as a persistent daemon process. The -bd option tells sendmail to run as a daemon and to listen to TCP port 25 for incoming mail. Use this option to accept incoming TCP/IP mail. Without it, your system will not collect inbound mail. As you'll see in Chapter 13, many systems do not collect inbound SMTP mail. Instead, they use protocols like POP and IMAP to move mail from the mailbox server to the mail reader. In general, mail servers run sendmail as

Internet Server Operations

PART 2

a daemon to collect inbound mail, and mail clients do not. Most of your systems are mail clients.

Most Linux systems, however, assume they are mail servers, so they come configured to run sendmail as a daemon. The code that runs the sendmail daemon in the Slackware Linux /etc/rc.d/rc.M startup script is very straightforward:

```
/usr/sbin/sendmail -bd -q 15m
```

The code runs sendmail with the –bd and -q options. In addition to listening for inbound mail, the sendmail daemon periodically checks to see if there is mail waiting to be delivered. It's possible that a sendmail process that was started to send a message was not able to successfully deliver the mail. In that case, the process writes the message to the mail queue and counts on the daemon to deliver it at a later time. The -q option tells the sendmail daemon how often to check the undelivered mail queue. In the Slackware example, the queue is processed every 15 minutes (-q 15m).

The code that Caldera and Red Hat use to start the sendmail daemon is found in the /etc/rc.d/init.d/sendmail script. It is more complex than the code used by Slackware, because Red Hat and Caldera use script variables read from an external file to set the command-line options. The file they read is /etc/sysconfig/sendmail, which normally contains these two lines:

```
DAEMON=yes
QUEUE=1h
```

If the variable DAEMON is equal to yes, sendmail is started with the –bd option. The QUEUE variable sets the time value of the –q option. In this case, it is one hour (1h), which is a value that I like even more than the 15 minutes used by Slackware.

WARNING   Don't set this time too low. Processing the queue too often can cause problems if the queue grows very large due to a delivery problem such as a network outage.

To control the daemon configuration, simply change the values in the /etc/sysconfig/sendmail file.

If you are configuring a mail client and don't want to run sendmail as a daemon, remove the code that starts sendmail from the startup script. Use a tool like tksysv to remove sendmail from the list of daemons started at boot time. If necessary, you can do this by directly editing the startup script or by setting DAEMON=no in the /etc/sysconfig/sendmail file, if your system uses that file.

It is not necessary to run `sendmail` as a daemon in order to send mail. Running `sendmail` with the –bd option is only required if your system directly receives SMTP mail. You can still send mail even if you don't run `sendmail` as a daemon.

The `sendmail` Configuration File

The file that defines the `sendmail` runtime configuration is `sendmail.cf`, which is a large, complex file divided into seven different sections. The section labels from the Red Hat `sendmail.cf` file provide an overview of the structure and the function of the file. The sections, each examined in detail in this chapter, are as follows:

Local Info This section defines the configuration information specific to the local host.

Options This section sets the options that define the `sendmail` environment.

Message Precedence This section defines the `sendmail` message precedence values.

Trusted Users This section defines the users who are allowed to change the sender address when they are sending mail.

Format of Headers This section defines the headers that `sendmail` inserts into mail.

Rewriting Rules This section holds the commands that rewrite e-mail addresses from user mail programs into the form required by the mail delivery programs.

Mailer Definitions This section defines the programs used to deliver the mail. The rewrite rules used by the mailers are also defined in this section.

NOTE All Linux `sendmail.cf` files have the same structure, because they are all created from the m4 macros (covered later in this chapter and in Appendix C) that come in the `sendmail` distribution.

The Local Info Section

Local Info, the first section in the `sendmail.cf` file, contains the host name, the names of any mail relay hosts, and the mail domain. It also contains the name that `sendmail` uses to identify itself when it returns error messages, as well as the version number of the `sendmail.cf` file.

The local information is defined by D commands that define macros, C commands that define class values, F commands that load class values from files, and K commands that define databases of information. Some sample lines lifted from the Local Info section of the Red Hat 6 `sendmail.cf` file are shown here:

```
# my name for error messages
DnMAILER-DAEMON
# operators that cannot be in local usernames
CO @ % !
# file containing names of hosts for which we receive email
Fw/etc/sendmail.cw
```

```
# Access list database (for spam stomping)
Kaccess hash -o /etc/mail/access
```

Lines that begin with # are comments. The first real command in the sample is a define macro (D) that defines the username that `sendmail` uses when sending error messages. The macro being defined is n. (Most macro names are only a single upper- or lowercase character.) The value assigned to n is MAILER-DAEMON.

The class command (C) assigns the values @, %, and ! to the class variable O. These three values are characters that cannot be used in local usernames, because they would screw up e-mail.

The file command (F) loads the values found in the file `/etc/sendmail.cw` into the class variable w. w which holds a list of valid host names for which the local computer will accept mail. Normally, if a system running `sendmail` receives mail addressed to another host name, it assumes the mail belongs to that host. If your system should accept the mail even if it appears to be addressed to another host, the name of that other host should be listed in the `/etc/sendmail.cw` file.

The last command defines an e-mail address database. The K command declares a database named "access." The database is in the hash format, which is a standard Unix database format. The file that contains the database is `/etc/mail/access`. All of this information, the internal name, the database type, and the file that holds the database, is defined by the K command.

NOTE The access database is used to control mail relaying and delivery. It's covered in detail in Chapter 13.

These four commands illustrate everything that is done in the Local Info section of the `sendmail.cf` file. This section is the most important section of the file from the standpoint of a system administrator trying to directly configure `sendmail.cf`, because it is probably the only part of the `sendmail.cf` file that you will ever customize.

The Options Section

Options define the `sendmail` environment. All of the option values are used directly by the `sendmail` program. There are nearly 100 options, but a few samples from the Red Hat `sendmail.cf` file can illustrate what options do:

```
# location of alias file
O AliasFile=/etc/aliases
# Forward file search path
O ForwardPath=$z/.forward.$w:$z/.forward
# timeouts (many of these)
O Timeout.queuereturn=5d
O Timeout.queuewarn=4h
```

These options all have something to do with `sendmail` functions that have already been discussed. The first option command (O) sets the location of the aliases file to `/etc/aliases`. The second option defines the location of the `.forward` file. Notice the `$z` and `$w` included in this option. These are macro values. The `$w` macro contains the computer's host name, indicating that it is possible to use the computer's host name as a filename extension on a `.forward` file. Given the fact that you already know the `.forward` file is found in the user's home directory, you can guess that the value of the `$z` macro is the user's home directory. (More about `sendmail` macros later.)

The last two options in the example relate to processing the queue of undelivered mail. The first of these options tells `sendmail` that if a piece of mail stays in the queue for five days (5d), it should be returned to the sender as undeliverable. The second of these options tells `sendmail` to send the user a warning message if a piece of mail has been undeliverable for four hours (4h).

This section requires no modifications. The options in the `sendmail.cf` file that comes with your Linux system are correctly defined for that system. I have never directly edited the options section of a Linux `sendmail.cf` file. In fact, the last time I edited an option was years ago, before the development of the m4 macros. In those days, it was sometimes necessary to move a `sendmail.cf` from one operating system to another. In those cases, it was necessary to edit the options to fit the new environment. That is not necessary now, because the m4 macros build a `sendmail.cf` customized for the target operating system.

Internet Server Operations

PART 2

The Message Precedence Section

Message Precedence is used to assign priority to messages entering the queue. By default, mail is considered "first-class mail" and is given a precedence of 0. The higher the precedence number, the greater the precedence of the message.

But don't get excited. Increasing priority is essentially meaningless. About the only useful thing you can do is select a negative precedence number, which indicates low-priority mail. Because error messages are not generated for mail with a negative precedence number, low priorities are useful for mass mailings. The precedence values from the Red Hat sendmail.cf are:

```
Pfirst-class=0
Pspecial-delivery=100
Plist=-30
Pbulk=-60
Pjunk=-100
```

Precedence values have very little importance. To request a precedence, mail must include a Precedence header, which it very rarely does. The five precedence values included in the sendmail.cf file that comes with your Linux system are more than you'll ever need.

NOTE   The Message Precedence section is not modified.

The Trusted Users Section

Trusted users are allowed to change the sender address when they are sending mail. Trusted users must be valid usernames from the /etc/passwd file. The trusted users defined in the sendmail.cf file that comes with your Linux system are root, uucp, and daemon:

```
Troot
Tdaemon
Tuucp
```

WARNING   Do not modify the Trusted Users list. Adding users to this list is a potential security problem.

The Format of Headers Section

Mail *headers* are those lines found at the beginning of a mail message that provide administrative information about the mail message, such as when and from where it was sent.

The Format of Headers section defines the headers that sendmail inserts into mail. The header definitions from the Red Hat sendmail.cf file are:

```
H?P?Return-Path: <$g>
HReceived: $?sfrom $s $.$?_($?s$|from $.$_)
        $.by $j ($v/$Z)$?r with $r$. id $i$?u
        for $u; $|;
        $.$b
H?D?Resent-Date: $a
H?D?Date: $a
H?F?Resent-From: $?x$x <$g>$|$g$.
H?F?From: $?x$x <$g>$|$g$.
H?x?Full-Name: $x
# HPosted-Date: $a
# H?l?Received-Date: $b
H?M?Resent-Message-Id: <$t.$i@$j>
H?M?Message-Id: <$t.$i@$j>
```

Each header line begins with the H command, which is optionally followed by header flags enclosed in question marks. The header flags control whether or not the header is inserted into mail bound for a specific mailer. If no flags are specified, the header is used for all mailers. If a flag is specified, the header is used only for a mailer that has the same flag set in the mailer's definition. (Mailer definitions are covered later in this chapter.) Header flags only control header insertion. If a header is received in the input, it is passed to the output, regardless of the flag settings.

Each line also contains a header name, a colon, and a header template. These fields define the structure of the actual header. Macros in the header template are expanded before the header is inserted into a message. Look at the first header in the sample. $g says to use the value stored in the g macro, which holds the sender's e-mail address. Assume the sender is David. After the macro expansion, the header might contain:

```
Return-Path: <david@wren.foobirds.com>
```

The sample headers provide an example of a conditional syntax that can be used in header templates and macro definitions. It is an if/else construct where $? is the "if," $| is the "else," and $. is the "endif." The example from above is:

```
H?F?Resent-From: $?x$x <$g>$|$g$.
```

This says that if ($?) macro x exists, use $x <$g> as the header template, else ($|) use $g as the template. Macro x contains the full name of the sender. Thus if it exists, the header is:

```
Resent-From: David Craig <david@wren.foobirds.org>
```

If x doesn't exist, the header is:

```
Resent-From: david@wren.foobirds.org
```

NOTE The headers provided in your system's sendmail.cf file are correct and sufficient for your installation. You'll never need to change them.

The Rewriting Rules Section

The Rewriting Rules section defines the rules used to parse e-mail addresses from user mail programs and rewrite them into the format required by the mail delivery programs. *Rewrite rules* match the input address against a pattern and, if a match is found, rewrite the address into a new format using the rules defined in the command.

Rewrite rules divide e-mail addresses into tokens for processing. A *token* is a string of characters delimited by an operator defined in the OperatorChars option. The operators also count as tokens. Based on this, you know that the address kathy@parrot contains three tokens: the string kathy, the operator @, and the string parrot.

The left-hand side of a rewrite rule contains a pattern defined by macro and literal values and by special symbols. The tokens from the input address are matched against the pattern. The macro and literal values are directly matched against values in the input address, and the special symbols match the remaining tokens. The tokens that match the special symbols in a pattern are identified numerically according to their relative position in the pattern that they match. Thus, the first token to match a special symbol is called $1, the second is $2, the third is $3, and so on. These tokens can then be used to create the rewritten address.

The right-hand side of a rewrite rule defines the format used to rewrite the address. It is also defined with literals, macro values, and special symbols.

An example will clarify how addresses are processed by rewrite rules. Assume the input address is:

```
kathy@parrot
```

Assume the current rewrite rule is:

```
R$+@$-    $1<@$2.$D>    user@host -> user<@host.domain>
```

The R is the rewrite command, $+@$- is the pattern against which the address is matched, and $1<@$2.$D> is the template used to rewrite the address. The remainder of the command line is a comment that is intended to clarify what the rule does.

The input address matches the pattern because:

- It contains one or more tokens before the literal @, which is what the special symbol $+ requires. The token that matches the special symbol is the string kathy. This token can now be referred to as $1, because it matched the first special symbol.

- It contains an @ that matches the pattern's literal @.

- It contains exactly one token after the @, which is what the $- requires. The token that matches this special symbol is the string parrot, which can now be referenced as $2, because it matched the second special symbol.

The template that rewrites the address contains the token $1, a literal <@, the token $2, a literal dot (.), the value stored in macro D, and the literal >. You know that $1 contains kathy and $2 contains parrot. Assume that the macro D was defined elsewhere in the sendmail.cf file as foobirds.org. Given these values, the input address is rewritten as:

```
kathy<@parrot.foobirds.org>
```

A rewrite rule may process the same address several times because, after being rewritten, the address is again compared against the pattern. If it still matches, it is rewritten again. The cycle of pattern matching and rewriting continues until the address no longer matches the pattern. After rewriting, the address is again compared to the pattern. This time it fails to match the pattern, because it no longer contains exactly one token after the literal @. In fact, it now has six tokens after the @: parrot, ., foobirds, ., org, and >. So no further processing is done by this rewrite rule, and the address is passed to the next rule in line.

Rulesets

Individual rewrite rules are grouped together in *rulesets,* so that related rewrite rules can be referenced by a single name or number. The S command marks the beginning of a ruleset and identifies it with a name or number. Therefore, the command S4 marks the beginning of ruleset 4, and SLocal_check_mail marks the beginning of the Local_check_ mail ruleset.

Five rulesets are called directly by sendmail to handle normal mail processing:

- Ruleset 3 is called first to prepare all addresses for processing by the other rulesets.

- Ruleset 0 is applied to the mail delivery address to convert it to the (mailer, host, user) triple, which contains the name of the mailer that will deliver the mail, the recipient host name, and the recipient username.

- Ruleset 1 is applied to all sender addresses.

- Ruleset 2 is applied to all recipient addresses.

- Ruleset 4 is called last to convert all addresses from internal address formats into external address formats.

There are three basic types of addresses: delivery addresses, sender addresses, and recipient addresses. A recipient address and a delivery address sound like the same thing, but there is a difference. As the mailing list alias illustrated, there can be many recipients for a piece of mail, but mail is delivered to only one person at a time. The recipient address of the one person to which the current piece of mail is being delivered is the delivery address. Different rulesets are used to process the different types of addresses.

Figure 7.1 shows the rulesets that handle each address type. The S and R symbols in Figure 7.1 represent rulesets that have numeric names, just like the other rulesets, but the S and R ruleset numbers are defined in the S and R fields of the mailer definition. Each mailer specifies its own S and R rulesets to process sender and recipient addresses just before the message is delivered.

Figure 7.1   sendmail rulesets

Rulesets

NOTE The rulesets provided in the sendmail.cf file that comes with your Linux system are adequate for delivering SMTP mail. It's unlikely you'll have to add to or change these rulesets.

The Mailer Definitions Section

The Mailer Definitions section defines the instructions used by sendmail to invoke the mail delivery programs. The specific rewrite rules associated with each individual mailer are also defined in this section. Mailer definitions begin with the mailer command (M).

Searching through the Mailer Definitions section of the Red Hat configuration file for lines that begin with M produces the following mailer definitions list:

```
Mprocmail,      P=/usr/bin/procmail, F=DFMSPhnu9, S=11/31, R=21/31,
T=DNS/RFC822/X-Unix, A=procmail -Y -m $h $f $u

Mlocal,         P=/usr/bin/procmail, F=lsDFMAw5:/|@qSPfhn9, S=10/30,
R=20/40, T=DNS/RFC822/X-Unix, A=procmail -Y -a $h -d $u

Mprog,          P=/usr/sbin/smrsh, F=lsDFMoqeu9, S=10/30, R=20/40,
D=$z:/, T=X-Unix, A=sh -c $u

Msmtp,          P=[IPC], F=mDFMuX, S=11/31, R=21, E=\r\n, L=990,
T=DNS/RFC822/SMTP, A=IPC $h

Mesmtp,         P=[IPC], F=mDFMuXa, S=11/31, R=21, E=\r\n, L=990,
T=DNS/RFC822/SMTP, A=IPC $h

Msmtp8,         P=[IPC], F=mDFMuX8, S=11/31, R=21, E=\r\n, L=990,
T=DNS/RFC822/SMTP, A=IPC $h

Mrelay,         P=[IPC], F=mDFMuXa8, S=11/31, R=61, E=\r\n, L=2040,
T=DNS/RFC822/SMTP, A=IPC $h
```

Internet Server Operations

PART 2

The Red Hat configuration contains seven mailer definitions. The first definition is for procmail. procmail (covered in Chapter 13), is an optional mailer found on most Linux systems. The first definition is used to invoke procmail with the –m command-line argument, which allows procmail to be used for mail filtering. The most interesting thing about this declaration is that the Red Hat configuration never makes use of it. This mailer is not invoked by any rewrite rule, either directly or through the mailertable database. If you're wondering how I know this and other details of this minor configuration glitch, see the upcoming "Nobody Is Perfect" sidebar.

The next two mailer definitions in the list are required by sendmail. The first of these defines a mailer for local mail delivery. This mailer must always be called "local." The second definition specifies a mailer, which is always called "prog," for delivering mail to programs. sendmail expects to find both of these mailers in the configuration and requires that they be given the names "local" and "prog." All other mailers can be named anything the system administrator wishes. However, in practice, that is not the case. Because the sendmail.cf files on all Linux systems are built from the same m4 macros, they all use the same mailer names.

The last four mailer commands define mailers for TCP/IP mail delivery. The first one, designed to deliver traditional 7-bit ASCII SMTP mail, is called smtp. The next mailer definition is for Extended SMTP mail and is called esmtp. The smtp8 mailer definition handles unencoded 8-bit SMTP data. Finally, relay is a mailer that relays TCP/IP mail through an external mail relay host. Examining any one of these mailer entries, such as the entry for the smtp mailer, explains the structure of all of them:

M   Beginning a line with an M indicates that the command is a mailer definition.

smtp Immediately following the M is the name of the mailer, which can be anything you wish. In this sample, the name is smtp.

P=[IPC] The P argument defines the path to the program used for this mailer. In this case, it is [IPC], which means this mail is delivered by sendmail. Other mailer definitions, such as local, have the full path of some external program in the field.

F=mDFMuX The F argument defines the sendmail flags for this mailer. Other than knowing that these are mailer flags, the meaning of each individual mailer flag is of little interest, because the flags are correctly set by the m4 macro that builds the mailer entry. In this example, m says that this mailer can send to multiple recipients at once; DFM says that Date, From, and Message-ID headers are needed; u says that uppercase should be preserved in host names and usernames; and X says that message lines beginning with a dot should have an extra dot prepended.

S=11/31 The S argument defines the S rulesets illustrated in Figure 7.1. The ruleset numbers can be different for every mailer, allowing different mailers to process e-mail addresses differently. In this case, the sender address in the mail "envelope" is processed through ruleset 11, and the sender address in the message is processed through ruleset 31. (You'll see more on this later when a sendmail configuration is tested.)

R=21 The R argument defines the R ruleset shown in Figure 7.1. This value can be different for every mailer to allow each mailer to handle addresses differently. The sample mailer processes all recipient addresses through ruleset 21.

E=\r\n The E argument defines how individual lines in a message are terminated. In this case, lines are terminated with a carriage return and a line feed.

L=990 The L argument defines the maximum line length for this mailer. This mailer can handle messages that contain individual lines up to 990 bytes long.

T=DNS/RFC822/SMTP The T argument defines the MIME types for messages handled by this mailer. This mailer uses DNS for host names, RFC822 e-mail addresses, and SMTP error codes.

A=IPC $h The A argument defines the command used to execute the mailer. In this case, the argument refers to an internal sendmail process. In other cases, the local mailer is a good example, the A argument is clearly a command line.

NOTE Don't worry too much about mailer definitions. It is good to know that they are there and how they are structured, but the configuration file that comes with your Linux system contains the correct mailer definitions to run sendmail in a TCP/IP network environment. You shouldn't need to modify any mailer definitions.

Nobody Is Perfect

The `sendmail.cf` file that comes with Red Hat 6 has an unused mailer declaration. This is not a problem. Because the mailer is unused, it has no effect on `sendmail` other than making the configuration slightly longer than it needs to be. So why point it out? The Caldera 1.3 `sendmail.cf` file doesn't have this glitch. Why not use it in the example? This reason is simple. I don't think hiding errors helps the reader. It gives the false impression that everything that comes from the vendor is perfect and that if you don't understand the configuration they give you, you must be at fault.

grep told me that the `procmail` mailer declaration was unused. Remember earlier that I said that ruleset 0 processes the delivery address and creates a triple containing the mailer name, the host name, and the username. If the `procmail` mailer name is used to deliver mail, it must appear somewhere in the configuration file as part of a delivery triple. A grep of `/etc/sendmail.cf` shows that in the Red Hat 6 configuration `procmail` does not appear in a delivery triple. Here is an example:

```
$ grep '^R' /etc/sendmail.cf | grep esmtp

R$* < @ [ $+ ] > $*      $#esmtp $@ [$2] $: $1 < @ [$2] > $3

R$* < @$* > $*           $#esmtp $@ $2 $: $1 < @ $2 > $3

$ grep '^R' /etc/sendmail.cf | grep procmail

$
```

To show what should happen, I check for the `esmtp` mailer. I select only rewrite rules and look for those containing the name of the mailer. `esmtp` is used twice in the configuration. The same check for `procmail` mailer shows that it is not used.

So why is it in the configuration? I can only make a guess: The person at Red Hat who created the configuration used the m4 macro MAILER(procmail) in the mistaken belief that it was necessary to do so in order to use the FEATURE(local_procmail) macro. It isn't. These macros are unrelated. The MAILER(procmail) macro only creates the mailer declaration you saw above. To use that mailer, you must either create your own rewrite rules that use it or use the FEATURE(mailertable) macro and create a mailertable that uses it. (There's a lot more about m4 macros later in this chapter, and you'll find a nice long list of them in Appendix C, *The m4 Macros for sendmail*.)

Configuring the `sendmail.cf` File

It's important to realize how rarely the `sendmail.cf` file needs to be modified on a typical Linux system. The configuration file that comes with your Linux system will work. Generally, you modify the `sendmail` configuration not because you need to, but because you want to. You modify it to improve the way things operate, not to get them to operate. To illustrate this, let's look at the default Red Hat configuration on the system `parrot` `.foobirds.org`.

Using the default configuration, the From address on outbound e-mail is `user@parrot` `.foobirds.org`. This is a valid address, but assume it's not exactly what you want. In the last chapter, MX records were defined for the domain. You want to hide the host name in outbound e-mail by using the address `user@foobirds.org`. To create the new configuration, you need to understand the purpose of class M and macro M, both of which are found in the Local Info section of the `sendmail.cf` file.

`sendmail` calls hiding the real host name *masquerading*. Thus the name of the macro used to rewrite the sender host address is M. Set M to the domain name to replace the name of the local host in outbound mail with the name of the domain. Class M defines other host names, not just the local host name, that also should be rewritten to the value of macro M. Class M is used on mail servers that need to rewrite sender addresses for their clients.

Checking the Red Hat `sendmail.cf` file on `parrot`, you find that no value is assigned to macro M, which means that masquerading is not being used. Further, you find that there is no class M declaration in the file. To masquerade the local host as `foobirds.org` and to masquerade the outbound mail from the clients `robin` and `puffin`, copy the `sendmail.cf` file to `test.cf` and then edit `test.cf`, changing the macro M declaration and adding a class M declaration:

```
# who I masquerade as (null for no masquerading)
DMfoobirds.org


# class M: host names that should be converted to $M
CMpuffin.foobirds.org robin.foobirds.org
```

Given the macro M and class M definitions shown above, `parrot` rewrites its own outbound mail to `user@foobirds.org` as well as rewriting mail from `user@puffin` `.foobirds.org` or `user@robin.foobirds.org` to `user@foobirds.org`. `parrot` is a mail server. While you might use macro M on any system, you won't use class M on any type of system except a mail server.

> **WARNING** A problem with using class M is that kathy@puffin.foobirds.org, kathy@robin.foobirds.org, and kathy@parrot.foobirds.org are all rewritten as kathy@foobirds.org. That's great if there really is only one kathy in the entire domain; otherwise, this may not be what you want. Coordinate usernames carefully across all systems. It simplifies the configuration of several different applications.

After setting a value for the M macro in the `test.cf` file, run a test to see if it works. Running sendmail with the test configuration does not affect the sendmail daemon that was started by the boot script. A separate instantiation of sendmail is used for the test.

Testing Your New Configuration

Test whether or not the change made to macro M in the configuration files modifies the rewrite process by directly testing the rewrite rulesets. First, you need to find out what rules are used to rewrite the address.

Use your knowledge of the flow of rulesets from Figure 7.1 to determine which rulesets to test. You know that ruleset 3 is applied to all addresses. It is followed by different rulesets, depending on whether the address is a delivery address, a sender address, or a recipient address. Furthermore, the rulesets used for sender and recipient addresses vary depending on the mailer that is used to deliver the mail. All addresses are then processed by ruleset 4.

There are two variables in determining the rulesets used to process an address: the type of address and the mailer through which it is processed. The three address types are delivery address, recipient address, and sender address. You know the address type, because you select the address being tested. In the example, the concern is the sender address.

There are two types of sender addresses: the sender address in the message header and the sender address in the "envelope." The message header address is the one on the From line sent with the mail. You probably see it in the mail headers when you view the message with your mail reader. The "envelope" address is the address used during the SMTP protocol interactions. The one that we're interested in is the one that remote users see in the mail—the header address.

Locating the Correct Mailer

The other variable that determines the rulesets used to process an address is the mailer. To find out which mailer delivers the mail, run sendmail with the -bv argument:

```
# sendmail -bv craig@wrotethebook.com
```

```
craig@wrotethebook.com... deliverable: mailer smtp, host
wrotethebook.com., user craig@wrotethebook.com
```

To see which mailer is used to deliver mail to remote sites, run sendmail with the –bv argument and give it a valid e-mail address for the remote site. In the example, the address craig@wrotethebook.com. sendmail displays the mail delivery triple returned by ruleset 0: the mailer, the host, and the user. From this, you know that the mailer is smtp.

Testing How Addresses Are Rewritten

To test the new configuration, run sendmail with the -bt option. sendmail displays a welcome message and waits for you to enter a test. A simple test is a list of ruleset numbers followed by an e-mail address. For example, entering **3,0 craig** at the prompt would process the e-mail address craig through the rulesets 3 and then 0, which should provide you with the mailer, host, user delivery triple for the address.

Because you know the mailer that you want to test, you can use the /try command at the prompt to process the sender From address for the smtp mailer. The following example illustrates the test. First, test the existing configuration to see how the address is processed by the default configuration:

```
# /usr/lib/sendmail -bt
ADDRESS TEST MODE (ruleset 3 NOT automatically invoked)
Enter <ruleset> <address>
> /tryflags HS
> /try smtp craig
Trying envelope sender address craig for mailer smtp
rewrite: ruleset  3   input: craig
rewrite: ruleset 96   input: craig
rewrite: ruleset 96 returns: craig
rewrite: ruleset  3 returns: craig
rewrite: ruleset  1   input: craig
rewrite: ruleset  1 returns: craig
rewrite: ruleset 11   input: craig
rewrite: ruleset 51   input: craig
rewrite: ruleset 51 returns: craig
rewrite: ruleset 61   input: craig
rewrite: ruleset 61 returns: craig < @ *LOCAL* >
rewrite: ruleset 93   input: craig < @ *LOCAL* >
```

```
rewrite: ruleset 93 returns: craig < @ parrot . foobirds . org . >
rewrite: ruleset 11 returns: craig < @ parrot . foobirds . org . >
rewrite: ruleset  4   input: craig < @ parrot . foobirds . org . >
rewrite: ruleset  4 returns: craig @ parrot . foobirds . org
Rcode = 0, addr = craig@parrot.foobirds.org
> ^D
```

Run sendmail -bt, which starts sendmail in test mode with the default configuration. This shows exactly how the standard configuration processes e-mail addresses. Specifically, it shows how local sender addresses are rewritten for outbound mail.

The /tryflags command defines the type of address to be processed. Four flags are available: S for sender, R for recipient, H for header, and E for envelope. By combining two of these flags,22 the /tryflags command says to process a header sender (HS) address.

The /try command tells sendmail to process the e-mail address craig through the mailer smtp. The address returned by ruleset 4, which is always the last ruleset to process an address, shows us the address that will be used on outbound mail after all of the rulesets have processed the address. With the default configuration, the input address craig is converted to craig@parrot.foobirds.org.

Next, run sendmail with the -C option to use the newly created test.cf configuration file. The –C option permits you to specify the sendmail configuration file on the command line:

```
# /usr/lib/sendmail -bt -Ctest.cf
ADDRESS TEST MODE (ruleset 3 NOT automatically invoked)
Enter <ruleset> <address>
> /tryflags HS
> /try smtp craig
Trying header sender address craig for mailer smtp
rewrite: ruleset  3   input: craig
rewrite: ruleset 96   input: craig
rewrite: ruleset 96 returns: craig
rewrite: ruleset  3 returns: craig
rewrite: ruleset  1   input: craig
rewrite: ruleset  1 returns: craig
```

```
rewrite: ruleset 31   input: craig
rewrite: ruleset 51   input: craig
rewrite: ruleset 51 returns: craig
rewrite: ruleset 61   input: craig
rewrite: ruleset 61 returns: craig < @ *LOCAL* >
rewrite: ruleset 93   input: craig < @ *LOCAL* >
rewrite: ruleset 93 returns: craig < @ foobirds . org . >
rewrite: ruleset 31 returns: craig < @ foobirds . org . >
rewrite: ruleset  4   input: craig < @ foobirds . org . >
rewrite: ruleset  4 returns: craig @ foobirds . org
Rcode = 0, addr = craig@foobirds.org
> exit
```

Running `sendmail -bt -Ctest.cf` starts `sendmail` in test mode and tells it to use the new configuration that is stored in `test.cf`. This test tells you that the value entered in the M macro is used to rewrite the sender address in the message header. You know this because the address returned from ruleset 4 is now `craig@foobirds.org`. This is just what you wanted.

Run additional tests (for example, `/try smtp kathy@robin.foobirds.org`) to see if client addresses are rewritten correctly. When you're confident that the configuration is correct and reliable, move the `test.cf` configuration file to `sendmail.cf` to make the new configuration available to `sendmail`.

If you are called upon to help someone configure `sendmail` on a system that doesn't already have the m4 source file installed, it may be easier to directly edit the `sendmail.cf` file, but only if the change is very small. If you can avoid it, don't make changes directly to the `sendmail.cf` file. If you really want to make major `sendmail` configuration changes, use m4 to build your configuration.

Using m4 to Configure `sendmail`

The `sendmail` distribution contains m4 source files that build the `sendmail.cf` file. Sample m4 source files probably are included with your Linux system. This section builds a custom `sendmail.cf` file using the m4 source files that come with a Caldera 1.3 system. If your Linux distribution doesn't include the m4 source files, you can download them from the Internet.

> **NOTE** See "Compiling sendmail" later in this chapter for details on download-
> ing and installing the latest sendmail distribution.

The sample configuration files are contained in the /usr/share/sendmail/cf/cf directory on a Caldera 1.3 system. Several of these are generic files pre-configured for different
operating systems. The Caldera system has generic configurations for BSD, Solaris,
SunOS, HP Unix, Ultrix, and, of course, Caldera. The Caldera configuration is named
generic-col1.2.mc. The directory also contains prototype files designed for use with
any operating system. Despite the fact that there is a Caldera source file, I prefer to modify
the tcpproto.mc file. The tcpproto.mc file is a prototype configuration for systems on a
TCP/IP network. It comes as part of the basic sendmail distribution and can be modified
for any Linux system, and frankly I find it a cleaner starting point than the vendor
configuration.

The m4 Macro Source File

The /usr/share/sendmail/cf/cf directory's prototype files contain m4 macro commands. In addition to lots of comments, the tcpproto.mc file contains the following macros:

```
VERSIONID(`@(#)tcpproto.mc    8.10 (Berkeley) 5/19/1998')

OSTYPE(unknown)

FEATURE(nouucp)

MAILER(local)

MAILER(smtp)
```

> **NOTE** These are the configuration macros. The file tcpproto.mc also contains
> divert and dnl commands. The divert(0) commands indicate which lines
> should be processed by m4, and the divert(-1) commands indicate what out-
> put should be discarded. The dnl option deletes everything up to the next new-
> line character. If dnl appears at the beginning of a line, the entire line is deleted.

The VERSIONID macro defines version-control information. This macro is optional and
is just ignored in this discussion.

The OSTYPE macro loads the m4 source file from the cf/ostype directory that defines the
operating system information. The cf/ostype directory contains more than 40 pre-
defined operating system macro files. Despite this, you will create your own OSTYPE file
for the sample configuration. The OSTYPE macro is required.

The FEATURE macro defines optional `sendmail` features. The `nouucp` feature in the `tcpproto.mc` prototype file means that no UUCP address processing code will be included in the `sendmail` configuration. I will add additional FEATURE macros to create a complete configuration.

The MAILER macros must be the last macros in the input file. The MAILER(local) macro adds the local mailer and the prog mailer to the configuration. The MAILER(smtp) macro adds mailers for SMTP, Extended SMTP, 8-bit SMTP, and relayed mail. All of these mailers were described earlier in the chapter and are all of the mailers needed for the configuration.

Creating a `sendmail.cf` for a Linux system from the `tcpproto.mc` prototype file could be as simple as changing the OSTYPE line from `unknown` to `linux` and then processing the file with the m4 command. The `sendmail.cf` file output by m4 would be ready for `sendmail`. In fact, it would be almost identical to the `linux.smtp.cf` configuration file delivered with Slackware Linux. However, this chapter undertakes a more ambitious configuration that is better suited to the Caldera sample system and that includes features to rewrite outbound e-mail addresses.

Creating an m4 OSTYPE File

Begin by creating a new operating system type, which in this example is called "caldera." This entails creating an m4 source file named `cf/ostype/caldera` that defines characteristics specific to OpenLinux 1.3. This is not as complex as it sounds. All OSTYPE files are built from m4 macros, and the longest m4 source file in the `cf/ostype` directory contains only eight macros. The `caldera.m4` file is even shorter:

```
define(`STATUS_FILE', `/var/log/sendmail.st')
define(`HELP_FILE', `/usr/share/sendmail/sendmail.hf')
FEATURE(local_procmail, `/usr/bin/procmail')
```

The first define macro tells `sendmail` that the status file is `/var/log/sendmail.st`. The second one defines the location of the help file as `/usr/share/sendmail/sendmail.hf`. The `/etc` directory is the default location for both of these files. File locations are the most common variable between different operating systems.

The last line is a FEATURE macro. It tells `sendmail` that this system uses `procmail` as the local mailer, and it defines the path to the `procmail` program.

The define macro is used to set the sendmail.cf macros and options that you saw earlier. As you'll recall, there are about 100 options alone, without even counting the sendmail.cf macros. Clearly, there must be a large number of define macros to set all of these values. Additionally, there are several other types of macros that can appear in an m4 source file, all of which are explained in Appendix C. Despite the large number of m4 macros, OSTYPE files are very short. The reason is that the default configuration values are correct for most systems, and m4 macros are only required to change a default value. For the new OSTYPE file, only three values are changed.

In addition to creating a new OSTYPE, the example uses m4 to create a custom configuration that converts *user@host* e-mail addresses into *firstname.lastname@domain* addresses. To do this, create a macro file with specific values for your domain.

Creating an m4 DOMAIN File

The DOMAIN macro points to a file in the cf/domain directory that contains information specific to your domain. This is a perfect place to put the commands that rewrite the host name to the domain name on outbound mail, so create a new DOMAIN macro file and call it foobirds.m4. Begin by changing to the cf/domain directory and copying the file generic.m4 to foobirds.m4 to act as a starting point for the configuration:

```
# cd /usr/share/sendmail/cf/domain
# cp generic.m4 foobirds.m4
# chmod 644 foobirds.m4
# tail -4 foobirds.m4
VERSIONID(`@(#)generic.m4        8.3 (Berkeley) 3/24/96')
define(`confFORWARD_PATH', `$z/.forward.$w:$z/.forward')dnl
FEATURE(redirect)dnl
FEATURE(use_cw_file)dnl
```

After copying generic.m4 to foobirds.m4, use the chmod command to set the file access permissions for the new file. By default, the files in the cf/domain directory are read-only. Make the file read and write for the owner, and read-only for the group and the world.

NOTE See Chapter 11, *File Sharing*, for information on Linux file permissions.

The tail command displays the last four lines in the newly created foobirds.m4 file. (All of the lines before this are of no interest for this discussion.) You have already seen the

VERSIONID macro. The first new line is the macro that defines confFORWARD_PATH, which tells sendmail where to look for the user's .forward file. The $z sendmail variable contains the path name of the user's home directory, and the $w variable contains the system's host name. Assuming the host name is parrot and the user is kathy, sendmail first looks for a .forward file at /home/kathy/.forward.parrot and then at /home/kathy/ .forward. This is an interesting example of what define macros can be used for, but it is unnecessary. $z/.forward.$w:$z/.forward is the default value for confFORWARD_ PATH. Therefore, delete this line from the file.

The FEATURE(redirect) macro adds support for the .REDIRECT pseudo-domain. The .REDIRECT pseudo-domain handles mail for people who no longer read mail at your site but who still get mail sent to an old address. After enabling this feature, add aliases for each obsolete mailing address in the form:

> *old-address*   *new-address*.REDIRECT

For example, assume that Jay Henson is no longer a valid e-mail user in your domain. His old username, jay, should no longer accept mail. His new mailing address is HensonJ @industry.com. Enter the following alias in the /etc/aliases file:

> jay   HensonJ@industry.com.REDIRECT

Now when mail is addressed to the jay account, the following error is returned to the sender telling them to try a new address for the recipient:

> 551 User not local; please try <HensonJ@industry.com>

This seems like a useful feature, so keep it in the configuration. The last line in the file also defines a useful feature. FEATURE(use_cw_file) is equivalent to the Fw/etc/sendmail .cw command in the sendmail.cf file. As described earlier, the sendmail.cw file provides a means for defining host aliases, which allow a mail server to accept mail addressed to other hosts.

To the lines taken from the generic.m4 file, add the following lines that perform the special address processing that you want.

> MASQUERADE_AS(foobirds.org)
>
> FEATURE(masquerade_envelope)
>
> FEATURE(genericstable)

The MASQUERADE_AS line tells sendmail to hide the real host name and display the name foobirds.org in its place in outbound e-mail addresses. This defines the sendmail M macro that was used earlier in the chapter. The M macro only masqueraded header sender addresses. To do this on "envelope" addresses as well as message header addresses, use the FEATURE(masquerade_envelope) macro. The last FEATURE macro tells sendmail to use the generic address conversion database to convert login usernames to the value found in the database. This allows much more freedom in rewriting outbound addresses than was possible by directly modifying the sendmail.cf file.

Building the m4 Configuration File

Now that the m4 source files have been created for the operating system and the domain, create a new m4 configuration file to use them. All of the m4 macros related to rewriting the outbound addresses are in the foobirds.m4 file. The macros that are specific to the Linux distribution are in the caldera.m4 file. You need to include those files in the configuration.

Begin by changing to the cf/cf directory and copying the tcpproto.mc file to linux.mc. Then change the file permission for linux.mc to 644 so that the file is writable by the owner.

Now modify the file to reflect the new configuration. To do that, change "unknown" in the OSTYPE macro to "caldera" and add a DOMAIN(foobirds) line to the linux.mc macro control file. The following tail command shows the macros in the edited file:

```
# tail -6 linux.mc
VERSIONID(`@(#)tcpproto.mc8.5 (Berkeley) 3/23/96')
OSTYPE(caldera)
DOMAIN(foobirds)
FEATURE(nouucp)
MAILER(local)
MAILER(smtp)
```

The next step is to process the linux.mc file through m4:

```
# m4 ../m4/cf.m4 linux.mc > linux.cf
```

The sample shows the m4 command format used to build a sendmail.cf file. The path name ../m4/cf.m4 is the path to the m4 source tree required to build a sendmail.cf file. The new macro control file is, of course, linux.mc. m4 reads the source files ../m4/cf.m4 and linux.mc, and it outputs the file linux.cf. The file output by the m4 command is in the correct format for a sendmail.cf file.

You created three files—cf/ostype/caldera.m4, cf/domain/foobirds.m4, and cf/cf/linux.mc—which together total less than 20 lines. These files create a sendmail.cf file that contains more than 850 lines. Most people find that the m4 macros are the best way to build a custom sendmail configuration.

Building a sendmail Database

The configuration you have just created should work just fine. It operates just like the sendmail.cf that was created earlier, including masquerading host names as foobirds .org. But you also want to convert the username part of outbound addresses from the login name to the user's real name written as *firstname.lastname*. To do that, create a database to convert the username part of outbound e-mail addresses. Build the database by creating a text file with the data you want and processing that file through the makemap command that comes with the sendmail distribution.

The genericstable database is the database that sendmail uses to convert outbound e-mail addresses. The format of the genericstable is very simple:

```
pat Pat.Stover
mandy Amanda.Jenkins
kathy Kathy.McCafferty
sara Sara.Henson
norm Norman.Edwards
craig Craig.Hunt
```

Every entry in the genericstable database has two fields: The first field is the key, and the second is the value returned by the key. In the sample database, the key is the login name, and the return value is the user's real name. Using this database, a query for "pat" will return the value "Pat.Stover."

Before the genericstable can be used by sendmail, it must be converted from a text file to a database with the makemap command, which is included in the sendmail distribution. Assume that the data shown above are stored in a file named usernames.txt. The following command would convert that file to a genericstable database:

```
# makemap hash genericstable < usernames.txt
```

The sample makemap command creates a hash type database, which is the most commonly used. makemap can also create dbm and btree databases.

After this genericstable database is created, login names on outbound mail are converted to full names. For example, the username mandy is converted to Amanda.Jenkins. Combining this with domain name masquerading rewrites outbound addresses into the *firstname.lastname@domain* format.

Testing the m4 Configuration

Test the new configuration you have just created with m4 macros in the same way that you test any sendmail configuration file. Use sendmail -bt exactly as it was used earlier in this chapter:

```
# /usr/lib/sendmail -bt -Clinux.cf
ADDRESS TEST MODE (ruleset 3 NOT automatically invoked)
Enter <ruleset> <address>
> /tryflags HS
> /try smtp craig
Trying header sender address craig for mailer smtp
rewrite: ruleset    3    input: craig
rewrite: ruleset   96    input: craig
rewrite: ruleset   96 returns: craig
rewrite: ruleset    3 returns: craig
rewrite: ruleset    1    input: craig
rewrite: ruleset    1 returns: craig
rewrite: ruleset   31    input: craig
rewrite: ruleset   51    input: craig
rewrite: ruleset   51 returns: craig
rewrite: ruleset   61    input: craig
rewrite: ruleset   61 returns: craig < @ *LOCAL* >
rewrite: ruleset   93    input: craig < @ *LOCAL* >
rewrite: ruleset    3    input: Craig . Hunt @ *LOCAL*
rewrite: ruleset   96    input: Craig . Hunt < @ *LOCAL* >
*LOCAL*: Name server timeout
rewrite: ruleset   96 returns: Craig . Hunt < @ *LOCAL* >
rewrite: ruleset    3 returns: Craig . Hunt < @ *LOCAL* >
rewrite: ruleset   93 returns: Craig . Hunt < @ foobirds . org . >
rewrite: ruleset   31 returns: Craig . Hunt < @ foobirds . org . >
rewrite: ruleset    4    input: Craig . Hunt < @ foobirds . org . >
rewrite: ruleset    4 returns: Craig . Hunt @ foobirds . org
```

```
        Rcode = 75, addr = Craig.Hunt@foobirds.org
        > ^D
```

This time when you process the sender address `craig` through the SMTP mailer, the address is rewritten to `craig.hunt@foobirds.org` using the genericstable database that you created. Again, after running several tests, copy `linux.cf` to `/etc/sendmail.cf`.

Of course, this entire configuration depends on your having the `m4` source files on the Caldera system. If your system doesn't have the `m4` source files, look at the next section to find out about downloading and installing the latest version of `sendmail`.

Compiling and Installing `sendmail`

Even if your Linux system comes with its own version of `sendmail`, obtaining the latest `sendmail` distribution provides useful documentation, including Eric Allman's excellent *"Sendmail Installation and Operation Guide."* The latest `sendmail` distribution is available via anonymous FTP from `ftp.sendmail.org`, where it is stored in the `pub/sendmail` directory. When you change to that directory, an information message is displayed that tells you about the latest version of `sendmail`. New releases of `sendmail` are constantly being created. The following examples are based on `sendmail` 8.9.3.

> **TIP** Remember that things will change for future releases, so always review the readme files and installation documents that come with new software before beginning an installation.

To compile `sendmail`, download the compressed `tar` file as a binary file and then uncompress and extract it with the `tar` command:

```
$ ftp ftp.sendmail.org
Connected to ftp.sendmail.org.
220 pub2.pa.vix.com FTP server ready.
Name (ftp.sendmail.org:craig): anonymous
331 Guest login ok, send your e-mail address as password.
Password:
230 Guest login ok, access restrictions apply.
Remote system type is UNIX.
Using binary mode to transfer files.
```

```
ftp> cd pub/sendmail

ftp> get sendmail.8.9.3.tar.gz

local: sendmail.8.9.3.tar.gz remote: sendmail.8.9.3.tar.gz

200 PORT command successful.

150 Opening BINARY mode data connection for sendmail.8.9.3.tar.gz
(1068290 bytes).

226 Transfer complete.

1068290 bytes received in 26 secs (40 Kbytes/sec)

ftp> quit

221-You have transferred 1068290 bytes in 1 files.

221-Thank you for using the FTP service on pub2.pa.vix.com.

221 Goodbye.

#  cp sendmail.8.9.3.tar.gz /usr/local/src

#  cd /usr/local/src

#  tar -zxvf sendmail.8.9.3.tar.gz
```

Next, change to the src directory in the sendmail directory created by the tar file, and use the Build script to compile the new version of sendmail:

```
# cd sendmail-8.9.3/src

# ./Build

Configuration: os=Linux, rel=2.0.36, rbase=2, rroot=2.0, arch=i686,
sfx=

Making in obj.Linux.2.0.36.i686

cc -O -I.   -DNEWDB     -c alias.c -o alias.o

cc -O -I.   -DNEWDB     -c arpadate.c -o arpadate.o

...

cc -O -I.   -DNEWDB     -c util.c -o util.o

cc -O -I.   -DNEWDB     -c version.c -o version.o

cc -o sendmail   alias.o arpadate.o clock.o collect.o conf.o
control.o convtime.o daemon.o deliver.o domain.o envelope.o err.o
headers.o macro.o main.o map.o mci.o mime.o parseaddr.o queue.o
readcf.o recipient.o safefile.o savemail.o snprintf.o srvrsmtp.o
stab.o stats.o sysexits.o trace.o udb.o usersmtp.o util.o version.o
-ldb -lresolv
```

Internet Server
Operations

PART 2

```
cp /dev/null sendmail.st
groff -Tascii -mandoc aliases.5 > aliases.0
groff -Tascii -mandoc mailq.1 > mailq.0
groff -Tascii -mandoc newaliases.1 > newaliases.0
groff -Tascii -mandoc sendmail.8 > sendmail.0
```

According to the documentation, this is all you need to do on most systems to compile sendmail. It certainly works on Red Hat 6 Linux systems, as this example illustrates.

Once sendmail compiles, it is installed by using the Build command with the install option:

```
# ./Build install
Configuration: os=Linux, rel=2.0.36, rbase=2, rroot=2.0, arch=i686,
sfx=
Making in obj.Linux.2.0.36.i686
install -c -o root -g kmem -m 4555 sendmail /usr/sbin
for i in /usr/bin/newaliases /usr/bin/mailq /usr/bin/hoststat /usr/
bin/purgestat
; do rm -f $i; ln -s /usr/sbin/sendmail $i; done
install -c -o root -g kmem -m 444 sendmail.hf \
    /usr/lib/sendmail.hf
install -c -o root -g kmem -m 644 sendmail.st \
    /etc/sendmail.st
install -c -o bin -g bin -m 444 sendmail.0 /usr/man/man8/sendmail.8
install -c -o bin -g bin -m 444 aliases.0 /usr/man/man5/aliases.5
install -c -o bin -g bin -m 444 mailq.0 /usr/man/man1/mailq.1
install -c -o bin -g bin -m 444 newaliases.0 /usr/man/man1/
newaliases.1
```

The Build command installs the executables in /usr/sbin and /usr/bin. It installs the help file (sendmail.hf) in /usr/lib and the status file (sendmail.st) in /etc. Notice that the help file and the status file are in different locations than they were in the Caldera example covered earlier. If the files are not in the locations you expect, you can do one of two things:

- Simply move the files to the locations that you desire.

- Change the sendmail configuration to point to these locations. These are the default locations expected by sendmail, so all you need to do is remove the define macros from the OSTYPE file that point to the "nonstandard" locations for these files. (See the "Creating an m4 OSTYPE File" section earlier in this chapter.)

Regardless of what you do, the location of the files and the configuration must agree.

One other thing that should be checked before declaring the installation complete is the sendmail.cf file. New versions of sendmail may add new configuration syntax that makes the older configuration files incompatible with the new release. sendmail uses the version (V) command inside the sendmail.cf file to indicate the level of the configuration syntax. The easiest way to check compatibility is to use sendmail to send a piece of test mail:

```
# /usr/sbin/sendmail -v -t

Warning: .cf file is out of date: sendmail 8.9.3 supports version 8,
.cf file is version 7

To: craig

From: root

Subject: Test

^D

craig... Connecting to local...

craig... Sent
```

Running sendmail with the –v option tells the program to provide verbose messages, which is just what you want when you're testing. The –t option tells sendmail that the mail will be typed in at the console. In this case, I type in a simple test message from root to craig. When you type in a message from the console, it must be terminated by a Control-D, which is what the ^D illustrates. The mail is delivered successfully, but sendmail complains about the version level of the configuration file.

This example shows that this configuration is not compatible with the new release. To solve this incompatibility, rerun m4 to rebuild your configuration. See "Building the m4 Configuration File" earlier in this chapter for an example of the m4 command that rebuilds your configuration.

You're all finished, and sendmail is now ready to run.

Final Words

sendmail is just the first step in building a fully functional mail server. Chapter 13 returns to this topic and looks at several other software systems that are used to provide service to e-mail clients.

The next chapter, *The Apache Web Server*, takes an in-depth look at a Web server configuration. Web service is as important to a corporate network service as e-mail is a user service.

8

The Apache Web Server

For most people, the World Wide Web has become synonymous with the Internet. No discussion of Internet servers is complete without mention of Web servers. Web services have become an essential part of every networked business— they are used to advertise products and offer services to external customers as well as to coordinate and disseminate information within the organization.

Linux systems make excellent Web servers. In fact, the free Apache server software that usually comes with Linux is the most widely used Web server in the world. This chapter describes how you can create your own Web server with Apache and Linux.

Installing Apache

The Apache Web server is included in most Linux distributions. Refer to Table 1.3 and you'll see it listed among the services included in the Red Hat distribution. However, you won't see it under the name Apache. The daemon that Apache installs to provide Web services is the Hypertext Transport Protocol daemon (httpd). You might be surprised to find it is already installed on your system and running. Try this little test:

```
$ ps ax | grep httpd
  321 ?  S    0:00 httpd
```

```
324   ?   S      0:00  httpd
325   ?   S      0:00  httpd
326   ?   S      0:00  httpd
329   ?   S      0:00  (httpd)
330   ?   S      0:00  (httpd)
331   ?   S      0:00  (httpd)
332   ?   S      0:00  (httpd)
333   ?   S      0:00  (httpd)
334   ?   S      0:00  (httpd)
335   ?   S      0:00  (httpd)
2539  p1  D      0:00  grep http
```

Use the process status (ps) command to check for all processes in the system and the grep command to display only those with the name httpd. Running this test on a freshly installed system, you'll discover that Apache is installed and running.

Start the Netscape Web browser and enter **localhost** in the Location box. Figure 8.1 shows the result. Not only is Apache installed and running, it is configured and responding with Web data. Users of desktop Linux systems are sometimes surprised to find out they are running a fully functional Web server.

If httpd is not running on your system, try using linuxconf or tksysv to add it to the boot process. Figure 8.2 shows tksysv running on a Red Hat system. Highlight httpd in the Available box, click Add, and then click Done in the next two dialog boxes to add it to the startup process. The next time you reboot, httpd will be running.

Figure 8.1   Apache installation Web page

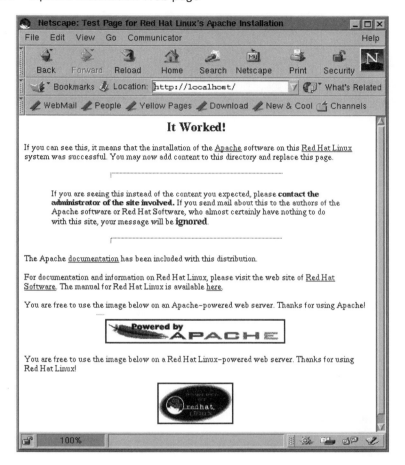

Figure 8.2 Enabling Apache with `tksysv`

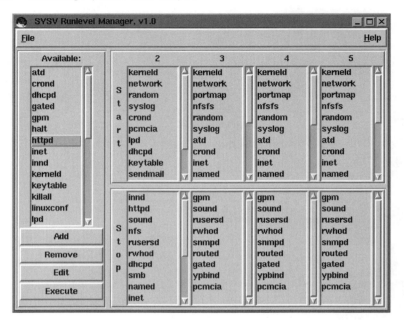

If `httpd` is not listed among the available software in the `tksysv` window, you need to install the Apache software package. Both Caldera and Red Hat use the Red Hat Package Manager (`rpm`) to manage the installation of optional software.

Using Package Manager

The Red Hat Package Manager is a tool that allows you to install the software you need, remove software you don't want, and check what software is installed in your system. `rpm` has many possible options, but most of these are for the developers who build the packages you want to install. For a network administrator, `rpm` comes down to three basic commands:

- `rpm -i` *package*: The –i option is used to install software.
- `rpm -e` *package*: The –e option is used to remove software.
- `rpm -q`: The –q option is used to list a software package already installed in the computer. Use –qa to list all installed packages.

To install a package with `rpm`, you must know its name. To find the full name of the Apache package, mount the Linux CD-ROM and look in the RPMS directory. Here is an example from a Red Hat 6 system:

```
$ cd /mnt/cdrom/RedHat/RPMS
$ ls *apache*
apache-1.3.6-7.i386.rpm
apache-devel-1.3.6-7.i386.rpm
```

This example assumes that the CD-ROM was mounted on `/mnt/cdrom`. It shows that two Apache software packages are included in the Red Hat distribution. One is the Web server software, and the other is a developer's toolkit. Install `apache-1.3.6-7.i386.rpm` with this command:

```
# rpm -i apache-1.3.6-7.i386.rpm
```

After installing the package, check that it is installed with another `rpm` command:

```
$ rpm -q apache
apache-1.3.6-7
```

Now you can use `linuxconf` or `tksysv` to add `httpd` to the list of daemons started at boot time.

Downloading Apache

If your Linux distribution does not include `httpd`, or if you want the latest release of the Apache software, download it from the Internet. Apache software is available at `www.apache.org` in both source and binary forms. Open your browser to the Apache Web page and select the Download link. Then select the Binaries link and the Linux link. This displays a list of pre-compiled `httpd` server daemons (see Figure 8.3).

Internet Server
Operations

PART 2

Figure 8.3   Linux binaries at the Apache Web site

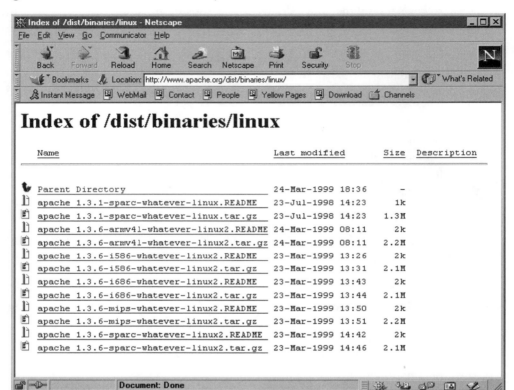

The binaries are listed by "machine type." Linux runs on several different platforms. Select the binary that is appropriate for your processors. Use the Linux uname command to find out exactly what machine type your server is. For example, a Pentium II system provides the following response:

```
$ uname -m
i686
```

Download the correct binary file to a working directory. Make a backup copy of the current daemon and move the new daemon to the proper execution path. For example, on a Red Hat system, move the daemon to /usr/sbin/httpd; on a Caldera system, move it to /usr/sbin/httpd.apache. Make sure to set the correct ownership and permissions for the file:

```
# mv /usr/sbin/httpd /usr/sbin/httpd.orig
# cp httpd /usr/sbin/httpd
```

```
# chown root:root /usr/sbin/httpd
# chmod 0755 /usr/sbin/httpd
```

The Apache software should be installed and ready to run with the configuration files from your current configuration.

Configuring the Apache Server

Normally, at this point in the discussion of server software, I say something like, "Installation is only the beginning. Now you must configure the software." That is not really the case for the Apache Web server running on Linux. It is configured and will run with only a little input from you. I suggest you edit the `httpd.conf` file and set the Web administrator's e-mail address in `ServerAdmin` and your server's host name in `ServerName`. Beyond that, the `httpd` configuration provided with your Linux distribution should be correct for that version of Linux.

However, the assumptions made by the distribution may not match the use you plan for your server. Red Hat assumes you will have a busy server. Caldera, which sells a Netscape product for their top-of-the-line Web servers, assumes that your Apache server will be lightly used. On a Caldera system, change the `MinSpareServers`, `MaxSpareServers`, and `MaxClients` options to dedicate more resources to the Web server. (This Caldera configuration is covered in an example below.)

Despite the fact that you may only change one or two options, you need to know how Apache is configured, what files the server requires, and where all the files are located. Given the importance of Web services for most networks, Apache is too essential for you to ignore. Apache is configured by three files:

   `httpd.conf` Defines configuration settings for the HTTP protocol and for the operation of the server. This includes defining what directory holds the three configuration files.

   `srm.conf` Configures how server requests are managed. This includes defining where HTTP documents and Common Gateway Interface (CGI) scripts are stored.

   `access.conf` Defines access control for the server and the information it provides.

All three files have a similar structure. They are all written as ASCII text files, comments begin with a #, and all of the files are well commented. Additionally, most of the commands in the files are written in the form of an option followed by the value being assigned to the option.

Internet Server Operations

PART 2

There is overlap in the function of the three files. You may think you know where a certain value should be set only to be surprised that it is in another file. To properly debug a misconfigured Web server, you need to understand all three files.

Analyzing the `httpd.conf` File

The `httpd.conf` file is stored in the `/etc/httpd/conf` directory on Red Hat systems and in the `/etc/httpd/apache/conf` directory on Caldera systems. To find where it is located on your system, look at the command that was used to start `httpd`. The location of the `httpd.conf` file is defined by the `-f` argument. The location of the other configuration files is defined in `httpd.conf`.

Of course, a very simple way to locate the file is with the `file` command:

```
# find / -name httpd.conf -print
/etc/httpd/apache/conf/httpd.conf
```

This command tells `find` to search every directory from the root (/) on down for a file named `httpd.conf` and to print out the result of the search.

TIP Use `find` any time you need to locate a file.

Once you find `httpd.conf`, print it out and read it. It is full of comments that explain the purpose of the configuration options.

TIP If you need additional information about an option, go to `www.apache.org` and look at the online documentation.

To examine the parameters in `httpd.conf`, I'll use those that are set in the default configuration on a Caldera 1.3 system as an example. All of the configuration options defined in the `httpd.conf` file begin with an uppercase letter. To print out just those lines that set options, use `grep` to display every line that begins with an uppercase letter (`[^A-Z]`). On a Caldera 1.3 system, `grep` displays 27 configuration options:

```
$ grep '^[A-Z]' httpd.conf
ServerType standalone
Port 80
HostnameLookups off
User nobody
Group #-1
```

```
ServerAdmin root

ServerRoot /etc/httpd/apache

ErrorLog /var/log/httpd/apache/error_log

TransferLog /var/log/httpd/apache/access_log

LogLevel warn

LogFormat "%h %l %u %t \"%r\" %>s %b \"%{Referer}i\" \"%{User-
Agent}i\"" combined

LogFormat "%h %l %u %t \"%r\" %>s %b" common

LogFormat "%{Referer}i -> %U" referer

LogFormat "%{User-agent}i" agent

CustomLog /var/log/httpd/apache/access_log common

PidFile /var/run/httpd.pid

ScoreBoardFile /var/log/httpd/apache/apache_status

ServerName localhost

UseCanonicalName on

Timeout 300

KeepAlive On

KeepAliveTimeout 15

MinSpareServers 1

MaxSpareServers 2

StartServers 5

MaxClients 15
```

In the following sections, these options are organized into related topics, and each command and the value it is set to are explained. Knowing the default configuration is very helpful when you're called upon to correct the configuration of someone else's system. However, before getting into the details of this Caldera configuration, take a look at the differences you'll see if you have a Red Hat 6 system.

Loading Dynamic Shared Objects

If you compare an httpd.conf file from Red Hat with one from Caldera, you may be surprised by how differently they appear. It is not the few differences in the values assigned to some configuration options that will catch your attention; it is the fact that there are many more lines in the Red Hat configuration. All of these additional lines spring from one difference: The Red Hat configuration uses Dynamic Shared Object (DSO) modules, and the Caldera configuration does not.

Apache is composed of many software modules. Like kernel modules, DSO modules can be compiled into Apache or loaded at runtime. The Caldera 1.3 configuration does not dynamically load any modules. Instead, it uses just those modules that are compiled into the daemon. Running httpd with the –1 command-line option lists all of the modules compiled into Apache. The following example is from a Caldera 1.3 system:

```
$ /usr/sbin/httpd.apache -l
Compiled-in modules:
  http_core.c
  mod_env.c
  mod_log_config.c
  mod_mime.c
  mod_negotiation.c
  mod_include.c
  mod_autoindex.c
  mod_dir.c
  mod_cgi.c
  mod_asis.c
  mod_imap.c
  mod_actions.c
  mod_userdir.c
  mod_alias.c
  mod_rewrite.c
  mod_access.c
  mod_auth.c
  mod_so.c
  mod_setenvif.c
```

> **NOTE** The Apache daemon is called `httpd.apache` on the Caldera system because Caldera also offers a Netscape Web server as an option. On other Linux systems, Apache is just called `httpd`.

Red Hat, on the other hand, uses many dynamically loaded modules. Two commands are used in the `httpd.conf` file to enable dynamically loaded modules. First, each module is identified by a `LoadModule` command. For example, to request the module that handles the user agent log file, enter this line in the `httpd.conf` file:

```
LoadModule agent_log_module    modules/mod_log_agent.so
```

The `LoadModule` command is followed by the module name and the path to the modules itself.

In addition to the `LoadModule` command, the Red Hat configuration identifies each module with an `AddModule` command. This adds the module name to the list of modules that are actually loaded at runtime. The module list includes all modules—those compiled into the server and those that are dynamically loaded. For example, to add the `agent_log_module` to the module list, add the following command to the `httpd.conf` file:

```
AddModule mod_log_agent.c
```

The `AddModule` command is followed by the source filename of the module being loaded. It is not the module name seen in the `LoadModule` command; it is the name of the source file that produced the object module, which is identical to the object filename except for the extension. In the `LoadModule` command, the object filename is `mod_log_agent.so`. Here the source filename is `mod_log_agent.c`. Executable modules, called *shared objects*, use the extension `.so`, and the C-language modules in the add list use the extension `.c`.

Table 8.1 lists the modules that Red Hat 6 identifies in its sample `httpd.conf` file with `AddModule` commands.

Table 8.1 DSO Modules Loaded in the Red Hat Configuration

Module	Purpose
mod_access	Specifies host- and domain-based access controls.
mod_actions	Maps a CGI script to a MIME file type.
mod_alias	Points to document directories outside the document tree.

Table 8.1 DSO Modules Loaded in the Red Hat Configuration *(continued)*

Module	Purpose
mod_asis	Defines file types returned without headers.
mod_auth	Enables user authentication.
mod_auth_anon	Enables anonymous logins.
mod_auth_db	Enables use of a DB authentication file.
mod_auth_dbm	Enables use of a DBM authentication file.
mod_autoindex	Enables automatic index generation.
mod_cern_meta	Enables compatibility with old CERN Web servers.
mod_cgi	Enables execution of CGI programs.
mod_digest	Enables MD5 authentication.
mod_dir	Controls formatting of directory listings.
mod_env	Allows CGI and SSI to inherit all shell environment variables.
mod_example	Provides examples of the Apache 1.2 API.
mod_expires	Sets the date for the Expires header.
mod_headers	Enables customized response headers.
mod_imap	Processes image map files.
mod_include	Processes SSI files.
mod_info	Enables use of the server-info handler.
mod_log_agent	Points to the agent log file.
mod_log_config	Enables use of custom log formats.
mod_log_referer	Points to the referer log, which logs information about remote sites that refer to your site.

Table 8.1   DSO Modules Loaded in the Red Hat Configuration *(continued)*

Module	Purpose
mod_mime	Provides support for MIME files.
mod_mime_magic	Determines the MIME type of a file from its content.
mod_mmap_static	Enables memory mapping of static documents.
mod_negotiation	Enables MIME content negotiation.
mod_proxy	Enables Web caching.
mod_rewrite	Enables URI-to-filename mapping.
mod_setenvif	Sets environment variables from client information.
mod_so	Provides runtime support for shared objects (DSO).
mod_speling	Automatically corrects minor spelling errors.
mod_status	Provides Web-based access to the server-info report.
mod_unique_id	Generates a unique request identifier for each request.
mod_userdir	Defines where users can create public Web pages.
mod_usertrack	Provides user tracking through a unique identifier called a cookie.

Internet Server Operations

PART 2

> **TIP**   If you decide to add modules to your configuration, read the modules documentation found in the manual/mod directory of the Apache distribution.

Beyond the differences in using the LoadModule and AddModule commands, Red Hat and Caldera httpd.conf files are largely the same. In the remainder of this section, the sample Caldera file is used to describe the content and function of the httpd.conf file.

Basic Configuration Options

ServerAdmin defines the e-mail address of the Web server administrator. In the Caldera configuration, this is set to root on the assumption that there is always a root account and that someone is responsible for reading the root account e-mail. You should change this to the full e-mail address of the real Web administrator. For example:

```
ServerAdmin pat@wren.foobirds.org
```

The ServerRoot option defines the directory that contains the httpd server files. On Red Hat and most other systems, this is /etc/httpd, but in Caldera 1.3, this points to /etc/httpd/apache. The conf directory under the ServerRoot contains the three configuration files.

ServerName defines the host name returned to clients when they read data from this server. In the default configuration listed above, this is set to localhost. Change this to provide a real host name. For example:

```
ServerName wren.foobirds.org
```

UseCanonicalName defines how httpd handles "self-referencing" URLs, which refer back to the server. When this is set to on, as it is in the Caldera example, the value in ServerName is used. If it is set to off, the value that came in the query from the client is used. If your site uses multiple host names, you may want to set this to off so that the user will see the name they expect in the reply.

The ServerType option defines how the server is started. If the server starts from a startup script at boot time, the option is set to standalone. If the server is run on demand by inetd, ServerType is set to inetd. Most of the time, Web servers are in high demand, so it is best to start them at boot time. It is possible, however, for a user to set up a small, rarely used Web site on a Linux desktop. In that case, running the server from inetd may be desirable.

Port defines the TCP port number used by the server. The standard number is 80. On occasion, private Web servers run on other port numbers. 8080 and 8000 are popular alternative ports for private Web sites. If you change the number, you must then tell your users the non-standard port number. For example, http://private.foobirds.org:8080 is a URL for a Web site running on TCP port 8080 on host private.foobirds.org.

When ServerType is set to inetd, it is usually desirable to set Port to something other than 80. The reason for this is that the ports under 1024 are "privileged" ports. If 80 is used, httpd must be run from inetd with the user ID root. This is a potential security problem, because an intruder might be able to exploit the Web site to get root access. Using port 80 is okay when ServerType is standalone, because the initial httpd process does not provide direct client service. Instead, it starts several other HTTP daemons to provide client services that do not run with root privilege.

Managing Child Processes

In the original Web server design, the server would fork processes to handle individual requests. This placed a heavy load on the CPU when the server was busy and impacted the responsiveness of the server. It was even possible for the entire system to be overwhelmed by HTTP daemon processes.

Apache uses another approach. A swarm of server processes starts at boot time. (The `ps` command at the beginning of the chapter shows several `httpd` processes running on a Linux system.) All of the processes in the swarm share the workload. If all of the persistent `httpd` processes become busy, spare processes are started to share the work.

Four options in the `httpd.conf` configuration file control how the child server process is managed. The options that control the management of these spare processes are:

MinSpareServers Defines the minimum number of idle server processes that must be maintained. In the Caldera configuration, this is set to 1. When the last idle process becomes busy, another process is created to maintain one idle process. The default value used in the Apache distribution is 5. The Caldera configuration assumes a lightly used server. For an average configuration, set the value back to 5.

MaxSpareServers Defines the maximum number of idle server processes that may be maintained. In the Caldera configuration, this is set to 2. The default value that ships with the Apache distribution is 10, though an extremely busy site might benefit from having this value set even higher.

StartServers Defines the number of persistent `httpd` processes started at boot time. In most configurations, this is set to 5.

MaxClients Defines the maximum number of clients to be serviced. Requests beyond the maximum number are queued until a server is available. Caldera set this to 15; the default set by Apache is 150. The Caldera setting is very low, so change to the Apache default if you expect to have a busy server.

The `User` and `Group` options define the UID and GID under which the swarm of `httpd` processes are run. When `httpd` starts at boot time, it runs as a root process, binds to port 80, and then forks a group of child processes that provide the actual Web services. The UID and GID defined in the file are assigned to these child processes. The UID and GID should provide the least possible system privilege to the Web server. On most Linux systems, this is the user `nobody` and the group `nobody`. An alternative to using `nobody` is to create a user ID and group ID just for `httpd`. If you do this, create the file permissions granted to the new user account very carefully. (See Chapter 11, *File Sharing*, for information on file system security.) The advantage of creating a special UID and GID for the Web server is that you can use group permission for added protection, and you won't be completely dependent on the world permission granted to `nobody`.

Performance Tuning Options

KeepAlive enables the use of persistent connections. Without the use of persistent connections, the client must make a new connection to the server for every link the client wants to explore. Because HTTP runs over TCP, every connection requires a connection setup. This adds time to every file retrieval. With persistent connections, the server waits to see if the client has additional requests before it closes the connection. Therefore, the client does not need to create a new connection to request a new document. The KeepAliveTimeout defines the number of seconds the server holds a persistent connection open waiting to see if the client has additional requests.

HostnameLookup tells httpd whether or not it should log host names as well as IP addresses. The advantage of enabling this is a more readable log. The disadvantage is that httpd has the added overhead of DNS name lookups. Setting this to off greatly enhances server performance.

Timeout defines the number of seconds the server waits for a transfer to complete. The value needs to be large enough to handle the size of the files your site sends and the low performance of the modem connections of your clients. But if it is set too high, the server will hold open connections for clients that may have gone offline. The sample has this set to five minutes (300 seconds).

Logging Options

Eight lines in our grep listing of active options deal with logging. ErrorLog defines the path of the error log file. The TransferLog option defines the path to the log where httpd writes information about server activity. Use the error log to detect failures and the transfer log to monitor activity and performance.

The LogLevel option defines what types of events are written to the error log. The Caldera configuration specifies that warnings and other more critical errors are to be written to the log, which I think is a good setting for an error log. However, you can choose any of these eight possible settings: debug, info, notice, warn, error, crit, alert, and emerg. The log levels are cumulative. debug provides debugging information and all other types of logging. warn provides warnings, errors, critical messages, alerts, and emergency messages. debug causes the file to grow at a very rapid rate. emerg keeps the file small but only notifies you of disasters. warn is a good compromise between enough detail and too much detail.

All of the LogFormat commands define the format of log file entries. The file these are written to is defined by the CutomLog entry. In the Caldera configuration, the custom entries are written to the same file as the TransferLog. This keeps all of the performance and monitoring information in the same file. Other options that are commented-out in the Caldera configuration could be used to create other log files:

```
#LockFile /var/log/httpd/apache/accept.lock
#CustomLog /var/log/httpd/apache/referer_log referer
#CustomLog /var/log/httpd/apache/agent_log agent
```

The lock file is used to control access to the logs if `httpd` was compiled with options that allow serialized file access. The `referer_log` stores the URL of the source page that linked to your Web server. This helps you determine what sites are pointing to your Web pages. Entries in the referer log are defined by this command:

```
LogFormat "%{Referer}i -> %U" referer
```

The `agent_log` identifies the browsers that are used to access your site. The "user agent" log is defined by this `LogFormat` statement:

```
LogFormat "%{User-agent}i" agent
```

Notice that a `LogFormat` statement and an associated `CustomLog` statement end with the same label. This label is an arbitrary name used to bind the format and the file together. The log files are described in greater detail later in the chapter.

The `PidFile` and `ScoreBoardFile` options both define the paths of files that relate to process status. The `PidFile` is the file in which `httpd` stores its process ID; the `ScoreBoardFile` is the file where `httpd` writes process status information.

Caching Options

Several options control the caching behavior of the server. A *cache* is a locally maintained copy of a remote server's Web page. Servers that cache Web pages are called *proxy servers*. When firewalls are used, direct Web access is often blocked. Users connect to the proxy server through the local network, and the proxy server is trusted to connect to the remote Web server. Proxy servers do not have to maintain cached copies of Web pages, but caching improves performance by reducing the amount of traffic sent over the WAN and by reducing the contention for popular Web sites.

The options that control caching behavior are:

    `CacheNegotiatedDocs` Defining this option allows proxy servers to cache Web pages from your server. By default, Apache asks proxy servers not to cache your server's Web pages. This option takes no command-line arguments.

    `ProxyRequests` Setting this option to on turns your server into a proxy server. By default, this is set to `off`.

CacheRoot Defines the directory where cached Web pages are written. To avoid making the directory writable by the user nobody, create a special user ID for httpd when you run a proxy server.

CacheSize Defines the maximum size of the cache in kilobytes. The default is 5, which is a very minimal size. Many system administrators consider 10MB a more reasonable setting.

CacheGcInterval Defines the time interval at which the server prunes the cache. It is defined in hours, and the default is 4. Given the defaults, every four hours, the server prunes the cache down to 5 kilobytes.

CacheMaxExpire Defines the maximum number of hours a document is held in the cache without requesting a fresh copy from the remote server. The default is 24 hours. With the default, a cached document can be up to a day out-of-date.

CacheLastModifiedFactor Defines the length of time a document is cached based on when it was last modified. The default factor is 0.1. Therefore, if a document is retrieved that was modified ten hours ago, it is only held in the cache for one hour before a fresh copy is requested. The assumption is that if a document changes frequently, the time of its last modification will be recent. Thus documents that change frequently are cached only a short period of time. Regardless, nothing is cached longer than CacheMaxExpire.

CacheDefaultExpire Defines a default cache expiration value for protocols that do not provide the value. The default is 1 hour.

NoCache Defines a list of the host names of servers whose pages you do not want to cache. If you know a server has constantly changing information, you don't want to cache information from that server, because your cache will always be out-of-date. Listing the name of that server on the NoCache command line means that queries are sent directly to the server, and responses from the server are not saved in the cache.

Multi-Homed Server Options

It is possible for a Web server to have more than one IP address. If it does, the system needs to know which address it should listen to for incoming server requests. There are two configuration options to handle this:

BindAddress Tells httpd which address should be used for server interactions. The default value is *, which means that the server should respond to Web service requests addressed to any of its valid IP addresses. If a specific address is used on the BindAddress command line, only requests addressed to that address are honored.

NOTE   BindAddress is not used to bind to addresses assigned to virtual hosts, which are described below.

Listen Tells httpd which additional addresses and ports should be monitored for Web service requests. Address and port pairs are separated by a colon. For example, to monitor port 8080 on IP address 172.16.64.52, enter **172.16.64.52:8080**. If a port is entered with no address, the address of the server is used. If the Listen command is not used, httpd only monitors the port defined by the Port command.

Defining Virtual Hosts

Some of the options commented-out of the sample httpd.conf file are used if your server hosts multiple Web sites. For example, to host Web sites for fish.edu and mammals.com on the wren.foobirds.org server, add the following lines to the httpd.conf file:

```
<VirtualHost www.fish.edu>

DocumentRoot /home/httpd/html/fish

ServerName www.fish.edu

</VirtualHost>

<VirtualHost www.mammals.com>

DocumentRoot /home/httpd/html/mammals

ServerName www.mammals.com

</VirtualHost>
```

Each VirtualHost option defines a host name alias your server responds to. For this to be valid, DNS must define the alias with a CNAME record. The example above requires CNAME records that assign wren.foobirds.org the aliases of www.fish.edu and www.mammals.com. When wren receives a server request addressed to one of these aliases, it uses the configuration parameters defined here to override its normal settings. Therefore, when it gets a request for www.fish.edu, it uses www.fish.edu as its ServerName value instead of its own server name and /home/httpd/html/fish as the DocumentRoot.

There are a couple of very interesting things about these commands. This is the first time we have seen section tags, which are the lines enclosed in angle brackets (< >). Section tags enclose options that are related to the item defined by the tags. All other section tags are found in the access.conf file, so you will see much more of them later.

Internet Server Operations

PART 2

Another interesting thing is that there are options defined here that don't normally occur in the `httpd.conf` file. Any valid configuration option, even those that normally occur in the other configuration files, can be placed within a `VirtualHost` declaration. The `DocumentRoot` option, which in this example points to the Web pages of the virtual host, is normally found in the `srm.conf` file.

Analyzing an `srm.conf` File

The `srm.conf` file provides the information needed to manage server requests. It points to the directories that contain the information offered by the server and to various items needed to format and present the information.

For example, both the Caldera and Red Hat configurations contain several `BrowserMatch` statements to present information in ways that are compatible with the different capabilities of different Web browsers. For example, a browser may only be able to handle HTTP 1.0 and not HTTP 1.1. In this case, `downgrade-1.0` is used on the `BrowserMatch` command line to ensure that the server properly formats responses for that browser.

> ***WARNING*** Don't fiddle with the BrowserMatch commands. They are already set to handle the limitations of different browsers.

This section discusses every configuration option used in the `srm.conf` file on our sample Caldera system. They all have something to do with managing what information is presented and how it is presented.

Defining Where Things Are Stored

The `DocumentRoot` option, which you saw above in the `VirtualHost` example, defines the directory that contains the Web server documents. For security reasons, this is not the same directory that holds the configuration files. The Caldera `DocumentRoot` is:

```
DocumentRoot /home/httpd/html
```

The `Alias` option and the `ScriptAlias` option both map a URL path to a directory on the server. For example:

```
Alias /icons/ /home/httpd/icons/
```
```
ScriptAlias /cgi-bin/ /home/httpd/cgi-bin/
```

The first line maps the URL path /icons/ to the directory /home/httpd/icons/. Thus a request for www.foobirds.org/icons/ is mapped to www.foobirds.org/home/httpd/icons/.

You may have several `Alias` commands to handle several different mappings, but you will have only one `ScriptAlias` command. The `ScriptAlias` command functions in exactly the same ways as the `Alias` command, except that the directory it points to contains executable CGI programs. Therefore, `httpd` grants this directory execution privileges. `ScriptAlias` is particularly important because it allows you to maintain executable Web scripts in a directory that is separate from the `DocumentRoot`. CGI scripts are the single biggest security threat to your server. Maintaining them separately allows you to provide tighter controls on who has access to the scripts.

The `UserDir` command enables personal user Web pages and points to the directory that contains the user pages. `UserDir` usually points to `public_html`. With this default setting, users create a directory named `public_html` in their home directories to hold their personal Web pages. When a request comes in for `www.foobirds.org/~sara`, it is mapped to `www.foobirds.org/home/sara/public_html`.

An alternative is to define a full path name such as on the `UserDir` command line `/home/userpages`. Then the administrator creates the directory and allows each user to store personal pages in subdirectories of this directory. A request for `www.foobirds.org/~sara` maps to `www.foobirds.org/home/homepages/sara`. The advantages of this approach are that it improves security and it makes it easier for you to monitor the content of user pages.

The `DirectoryIndex` option defines the name of the file that is retrieved if the client's request does not include a filename. Our sample system has the following values for this options:

```
DirectoryIndex index.html
```

Given the value defined for `DocumentRoot` and this value, if the server gets a request for `http://www.foobirds.org`, it gives the client the file `/home/httpd/html/index.html`. If it gets a request for `http://www.foobirds.org/songbirds/`, it gives the client the file `/home/httpd/html/songbirds/index.html`. The `DocumentRoot` is prepended to any request and the `DirectoryIndex` is appended to any request that doesn't end in a filename. If the file `index.html` is not found in the directory, `httpd` sends the client a listing of the directory. How that directory listing is formatted consumes the bulk of the `srm.conf` file.

Creating a Fancy Index

If the `FancyIndexing` option is set to on, `httpd` creates a directory list that includes graphics, links, and other fancy features. The following options define the graphics and features used in the fancy directory listing:

`IndexIgnore` Lists the files that should not be included in the directory listing. Files can be specified by name, by partial name, by extension, or by standard wildcard characters.

HeaderName Defines the name of a file that contains information to be displayed at the top of the directory listing.

ReadmeName Defines the name of a file that contains information to be displayed at the bottom of the directory listing.

AddIconByEncoding Defines the icon file used to represent a file based on the MIME encoding type of the file.

AddIconByType Defines the icon file used to represent a file based on the file's MIME file type.

AddIcon Defines the icon file used to represent a file based on the filename extension.

DefaultIcon Defines the icon file used to represent a file that has not been given an icon by any other option.

Defining File Types

MIME file types and file extensions play a major role in helping the server determine how a file should be handled. Specifying MIME options is also a major part of the srm.conf file. The options involved are:

DefaultType Defines the MIME type that is used when the server cannot determine the type of a file. By default, this is set to text/html. Thus, when a file has no file extension, the server assumes it is an HTML file.

AddEncoding Maps a MIME encoding type to a file extension. To map the gz extension to MIME encoding type **x-gzip,** Caldera includes the following line in the srm.conf file:

```
AddEncoding x-gzip gz
```

AddLanguage Maps a MIME language type to a file extension.

LanguagePriority Sets the language encoding in case the client does not specify a preference.

AddType Maps a MIME file type to a file extension.

AddHandler Maps a file handler to a file extension. A file handler is a program that knows how to process a file. The best example of this is cgi-script, which is the handler for CGI files.

Enabling Directory-Level Access Controls

The command `AccessFileName .htaccess` enables directory-level access control and states that the name of the access control file is `.htaccess`. If the server finds a file with this name in a directory from which it is retrieving information, it applies the access restrictions defined in the file before it releases the data. This command allows you to distribute access control to the individuals who create and manage the individual Web pages. The access control commands in the `.htaccess` file are the same as those in the `access.conf` file that defines system-wide access control.

Analyzing an `access.conf` File

The `access.conf` file defines access controls for your Web server. It can define access controls for all Web documents or for documents in individual directories. This file uses section labels just like those described above in the discussion of `VirtualHosts` in the `httpd.conf` file. `access.conf` uses section labels to associate related commands and to tie commands to specific objects, such as directories. A look at the configuration commands in the Caldera `access.conf` file shows this structure:

```
<Directory />
Options None
AllowOverride None
</Directory>
<Directory /home/httpd/html>
Options None
AllowOverride None
</Directory>
<Directory /home/httpd/cgi-bin>
AllowOverride None
Options ExecCGI
```

The `Directory` section labels enclosed commands that pertain to a specific directory. This configuration defines access controls for three directories: the root (/), /home/httpd/html, and /home/httpd/cgi-bin. The `Options` command specifies what server options are permitted for documents in the directory, and the `AllowOverride` command defines when the `.htaccess` file found in the directory is allowed to override the access control values set in `access.conf`.

Enabling Server Options

The Caldera example shows two possible values for the `Options` command. However, it has many other possible values:

`All` Permits the use of all server options.

`ExecCGI` Permits the execution of CGI scripts from this directory. This option is used in the example, but in this particular case, it is not actually required. The `ScriptAlias` command already defined /home/httpd/cgi-bin as the script directory. In the example, `Options` could be set to `None` for the /home/httpd/cgi-bin directory without undoing the effect of the `ScriptAlias` command. The `ExecCGI` option is really intended to allow CGI scripts to be executed from other directories. However, most configurations set this option for the `ScriptAlias` directory. It does no harm, and it provides another level of documentation that this directory contains executable scripts.

`FollowSymLinks` Permits the use of symbolic links. If this is allowed, the server treats a symbolic link as if it were a document in the directory.

`Includes` Permits the use of Server Side Includes (SSI). See the "Server Security" section later in this chapter for information about SSI.

`IncludesNOEXEC` Permits SSI that do not include `#exec` and `#include` commands.

`Indexes` Permits a server-generated listing of the directory if an `index.html` file is not found.

`MultiViews` Permits the document language to be negotiated. (See the `AddLanguage` and `LanguagePriority` commands discussed in the "Defining File Types" section earlier in this chapter.)

`None` Doesn't permit any server options. My personal favorite!

`SymLinksIfOwnerMatch` Permits the use of symbolic links if the target file of the link is owned by the same user ID as the link itself.

WARNING Use server options with care. All of them except `MultiView` cause potential security problems, and all of them use server resources.

Controlling Directory-Level Overrides

The `AllowOverride` command has many possible settings. In addition to the keyword `All`, which permits the `.htaccess` file to override everything defined in the configuration files, and `None`, which allows no overrides, individual commands can be permitted through `AllowOverride`. For example, to allow a directory to define its own file extension mapping, specify:

```
AllowOverride AddType
```

Notice that `AddType` is not really a command from the `access.conf` file. However, when this value is used on an `AllowOverride` command, `AddType` commands can be used in the directory's `.htaccess` file to define file extensions. `AllowOverride` can be used to permit just about anything in the configuration to be overridden by the `.htaccess` file.

Defining Access Controls

The basic configuration shown in the Caldera sample file is the most common, but it is not the only kind of configuration that can be set. The `access.conf` file also permits you to define host and user access controls. A few examples will make this capability clear:

```
<Directory /home/httpd/internal>
<Limit GET POST HEAD>
order deny,allow
deny from all
allow from foobirds.org
</Limit>
</Directory>
```

This example demonstrates the `Limit` command and label nesting. The `Directory` label identifies the directory for which access controls are being defined, and the `Limit` label defines the access methods that are being controlled. `GET`, `POST`, and `HEAD` are all of the access methods implemented in Apache. The `Limit` section encloses these specific access controls:

`order` Defines the order in which the access control rules are evaluated. `deny,allow` tells `httpd` to apply the `deny` rule first and then permit exceptions to that rule based on the `allow` rule. The example blocks access from everyone with the `deny` rule and then permit exceptions for systems that are part of the `foobirds.org` domain with the `allow` rule. These are the types of access rules used to protect an internal Web site.

`deny from` Identifies hosts that are not allowed to access Web documents found in this directory. The host can be identified by a full or partial host name or IP address. The keyword `all` blocks all hosts.

`allow from` Identifies hosts that are permitted to access documents. The host can be identified by a full or partial host name or IP address. The keyword `all` blocks all hosts.

Access controls can be specified without the `Limit` label, and commonly are. If the `Limit` label is not used, access controls are applied to all types of access.

Requiring User Authentication

The example above controls access on a host-by-host basis. It is also possible to control file access at the user and group level. An example with these additional levels of access control is:

```
<Directory /home/httpd/internal/accounting>
AuthUserFile /usr/local/etc/http.passwords
AuthGroupFile /usr/local/etc/http.groups
AuthType Basic
<Limit GET POST HEAD>
require hdqtrs rec bill pay
order deny,allow
deny from all
allow from foobirds.org
</Limit>
</Directory>
```

In this example, access is granted if the user belongs to a valid group and has a valid password. These groups and passwords have nothing to do with the groups and passwords used by `login`. The groups and passwords used here are specifically defined by you for use with the Web server. The files you create for this purpose are the ones pointed to by the `AuthUserFile` and `AuthGroupFile` entries.

You add a password to the Web server password file with the `htpasswd` command that comes with the Apache system. You add groups to the group file by editing the file with any text editor. The entries in the group file start with the group name followed by a colon and a list of users that belong to the group; for example, `hdqtrs: amanda pat craig kathy`.

The `require` command requires the user to enter the Web username and password. In the example above, access is limited to users who belong to one of the specified groups and who enter a valid password. Alternatively, the keyword `valid-user` could have been used on the `require` command line instead of a list of groups. If that were the case, any user with a valid password would have been given access, and the group file would have been ignored.

> **NOTE** Even if you do not use Web server groups, you should specify the `AuthGroupFile` entry when you use password authentication. If you don't want to create a dummy group file, simply point the entry to /dev/null.

The `order`, `deny`, and `allow` commands perform the same function in this example as they did in the previous one. Here we are adding password authentication to host authentication. However, host authentication is not a prerequisite for password authentication. If the `order`, `deny`, and `allow` commands were not in the example, any system on the Internet would be allowed to access the documents if the user on that system had the correct username and password.

All of these examples show us defining the access controls for a directory. That is the most common case. But it is possible to define access control for all directories on a server or for individual documents. To apply access controls to every document provided by the server, simply move the `Limit` section outside of the `Directory` section. The reason that the access controls only apply to a single directory is because the access controls are nested within the `Directory` sections. If the `Limit` section is defined as a stand-alone item in the `access.conf` file, the access controls it defines apply to every document on the server.

High-Performance User Authentication   If you have more than a few users who require password authentication to access your Web site, the performance of the standard password file will be inadequate. The standard authentication module, `mod_auth`, uses a flat file that must be searched sequentially to find the user's password. Searching a flat file of only a few hundred entries can be very time consuming.

An alternative is to store the passwords in an indexed database. Two modules, `mod_auth_dbm` and `mod_auth_db`, provide support for password databases. They are used in exactly the same way as the standard flat file authentication. The only differences are the commands used to define the database inside the `access.conf` file and the command used to add passwords to the password database. The `AuthUserFile` command used for the flat file is replaced by `AuthDBUserFile` for `mod_auth_db` or by `AuthDBMUserFile` for `mod_auth_dbm`. The example shown above rewritten to use a database file would be:

```
<Directory /home/httpd/internal/accounting>
AuthDBUserFile /usr/local/etc/http.passwords
AuthDBGroupFile /usr/local/etc/http.groups
AuthType Basic
```

```
<Limit GET POST HEAD>
require hdqtrs rec bill pay
order deny,allow
deny from all
allow from foobirds.org
</Limit>
</Directory>
```

The `htpasswd` file cannot be used to add passwords to this file. Instead, use the command `dbmmanage`. The format of the `dbmmanage` command is:

```
dbmmanage file command user password
```

Most of the fields in the `dbmmanage` command are self-explanatory. Usernames and passwords are exactly the contents you would expect for a password database. The *command* is the keyword that provides your directions to the `dbmmanage` command. The valid *command* values are:

> `add` Adds a username and password to the database. The provided password must already be encrypted.

> `adduser` Adds a username and password to the database. The provided password is provided as plain text and is encrypted by `dbmmanage`.

> `check` Checks if the username is in the database and if the passwords match.

> `delete` Removes an entry from the database.

> `import` Copies *username*:*password* entries from `stdin` to the database. The passwords must already be encrypted.

> `update` Changes the password for a user already in the database.

> `view` Displays the contents of the database.

To add the users `sara` and `jay` to the password database, enter these commands:

```
# cd /usr/local/etc
# dbmmanage http.password adduser sara
New password:
Re-type new password:
User sara added with password encrypted to 9jwUHif5Eu/M2
# dbmmanage http.password adduser jay
New password:
```

```
Re-type new password:

User jay added with password encrypted to MoiefJuxcM.OY

# dbmmanage http.password view

jay:MoiefJuxcM.OY

sara:9jwUHif5Eu/M2
```

Using an authentication database provides very dramatic performance improvements. Always use this feature if you have large Web site.

Setting Document-Level Access Controls

The Location directive is used to provide access control at the document level. It is used just like the Directory label, but instead of having a directory name on the command line, the Location label has a document name from a URL on the command line:

```
<Location /server-status>

SetHandler server-status

order deny,allow

deny from all

allow from foobirds.org

</Location>
```

If the Apache server gets a request for www.foobirds.org/server-status, it applies these access controls. /server-status is the name of a document, not the name of a directory. In fact, this is a special document that shows the server status and is constructed by a special handler. The access controls make the server status available to everyone in our domain, but deny it to all outsiders. In the next section, you'll see how the server-status page is used to monitor your Web server.

Managing Your Web Server

Despite the enormous number of options found in the three configuration files, configuration is not the biggest task you undertake when you run a Web server. Configuration usually requires no more than adjusting a few configuration options when the server is first installed.

On the other hand, monitoring your server's usage and performance and ensuring its reliability and security are daily tasks. But fear not—the Apache server provides some tools to simplify these tasks.

Internet Server Operations

PART 2

Monitoring Your Server

Apache provides tools to monitor the status of your server and logs that keep a history of how the system is used and how it performs over time. You have seen something about these in our discussion of the configuration files. One of these is the ScoreBoard file.

When Apache boots, it creates several persistent daemons. When demand is high, additional daemons are added to the daemon swarm. When demand is low, the additional daemons are killed. The status of the daemons is written to the scoreboard file and can be viewed with the httpd_monitor command.

httpd_monitor is included in the Apache distribution. If you're using Apache software that was included with the Linux distribution, it may not include this program. If it doesn't, you can find it in the support subdirectory of the Apache release available at www.apache.org. Running httpd_monitor displays the contents of the scoreboard file:

```
# httpd_monitor
sssss (0/5)
```

This display indicates that there are five daemons, none of which is currently active. The s indicates that a process is sleeping. Other possible status letters are active (r), starting (t), or dead (_). In the sample, all of the processes are sleeping.

A better monitor is the server-status monitor. To use this monitor, it must either be compiled into httpd or installed as a dynamically loadable module. These two lines from the Red Hat httpd.conf configuration file install the loadable module:

```
LoadModule status_module       modules/mod_status.so

...

AddModule mod_status.c
```

To get the maximum amount of information from the server-status display, add the ExtendedStatus option to your httpd.conf file. For example:

```
ExtendedStatus on
```

Enable the monitor in the srm.conf file by inserting the Location /server-status section. For example:

```
<Location /server-status>
SetHandler server-status
order deny,allow
deny from all
```

```
allow from foobirds.org
</Location>
```

Once the monitor is installed and enabled, you can access it from your browser at
`www.foobirds.org/server-status/?refresh=20`. The refresh value is not required, but
if you use it, the status display is automatically updated. In this example, I am asking for
a status update every 20 seconds. Figure 8.4 shows the status screen for our test server.

Figure 8.4   The Apache server-status display

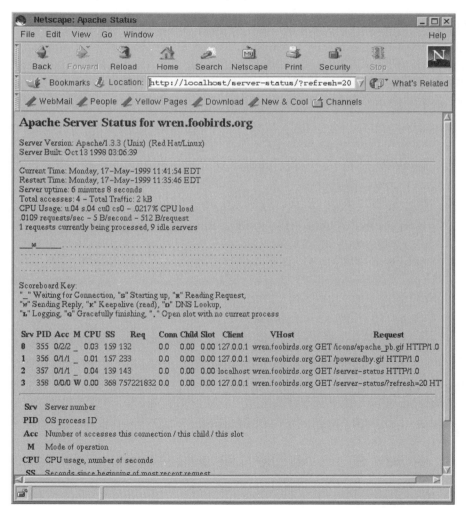

Internet Server
Operations

PART 2

Monitoring tells you about the real-time status of your server, but even more can be learned by looking at how your server is used over time. Logging provides that information.

Apache Log Files

Log files provide a great deal of information about your Web server. System failures which you know you want to track and correct are written to the file you defined with the ErrorLog option in the httpd.conf file. You define the level of errors being logged with the LogLevel option. Review the log at least once a day looking for problems. To keep a close eye on the file while you're logged in, use the tail command with the -f option:

```
$ tail -l 1 -f /var/log/httpd/apache/error_log
```

The tail -l 1 command prints the last record in the error file, and the -f option keeps the tail process running so that you will see any record as it is written to the file. This allows you to monitor the file in real time.

Just as important as errors, the logs provide information about who is using your server, how much it is being used, and how well it is servicing the users. Web servers are used to distribute information. If no one wants or uses the information, you need to know it.

Defining Log Formats

Apache log files conform to the Common Log Format (CLF). CLF is a standard used by all Web server vendors. Using this format means that the logs generated by Apache servers can be processed by any log analysis tool that also conforms to the standard. Several good tools are available:

- AccessWatch is available from http://netpressence.com/accesswatch at a cost of $40.
- Wusage is available from www.boutell.com for $75.
- wwwstat is available at www.ics.uci.edu/WebSoft/wwwstat at no cost.

All three tools analyze the Apache log and provide a series of graphic reports.

Apache logs can be customized to log just the information you want to track. The LogFormat command allows you to define exactly what information is logged. The format of a standard CLF entry is clearly defined by this LogFormat command from our sample httpd.conf file:

```
LogFormat "%h %l %u %t \"%r\" %>s %b" common
```

In this example, I am asking for exactly the information in a CLF entry:

%h Logs the client's host name.

%l Logs the name that the user used to login to the client. This would be a name from the client's passwd file. Many clients do not provide this information.

%u Logs the username used for Web server authentication. This is a name found in the AuthUser file you created on the server.

%t Logs the date and time.

%r Logs the first line of the request. The \" characters are just there to insert quotes in the output.

%>s Logs the status of the last request.

%b Logs the number of bytes sent.

If the server does not have a value for a field, it logs a dash in the field. For example, if the client does not provide a login name (and many do not), Apache inserts a dash in that field in the log entry.

The format is enclosed in quotes. The label common is not part of the format. It is an arbitrary string used to tie the LogFormat command to a CustomLog command. In the sample configuration, this particular LogFormat is tied to the file /var/log/httpd/apache/access_log defined by this command:

```
CustomLog /var/log/httpd/apache/access_log common
```

The label common binds the two commands together.

In addition to these standard fields, Apache can log the contents of any header records received or sent. For example, to log the value received from the client in the User-agent header, add the following to a LogFormat command:

```
%{User-agent}i
```

This works for any header. Simply replace User-agent with the name of the header. The i indicates this is an input header. To log an output header, use an o at the end of the description.

Using Conditional Logging

Apache also supports conditional logging, which allows you to identify fields that are logged only when certain conditions are met. The conditions that can be tested for are the status codes returned by the server. The status codes are:

200: OK The request is valid.

302: Found The requested document was found.

304: Not Modified The requested document has not been modified.

400: Bad Request The request is invalid.

401: Unauthorized The client or user is denied access.

403: Forbidden The requested access is not allowed.

404: Not Found The requested document does not exist.

500 Server Error There was an unspecified server error.

503: Out of Resources (Service Unavailable) The server has insufficient resources to honor the request.

501: Not Implemented The requested server feature is not available.

502: Bad Gateway The client specified an invalid gateway.

To make a field conditional, put a status code on the field in the LogFormat entry. For example, assume you only want to log the browser name if the browser requests a service that is not implemented in your server. Combine the Not Implemented (501) status code with User-agent header in this manner:

```
%501{User-agent}i
```

If this value appears in the LogFormat, the name of the browser is only logged when the status code is 501.

You can use multiple status codes. You can also use an exclamation point to specify that you only want to log a value when the status code is not a certain value; the exclamation point indicates "not." For example, to log the address of the site that referred the user to you Web page if the status code is not one of the good status codes, add the following to a LogFormat:

```
%!200,302,304{Referer}i
```

This particular conditional log entry is actually very useful. It tells you when a remote page has a stale link pointing to your Web site.

Put these features together with the common log format to create a more useful log entry:

```
LogFormat "%h %l %u %t \"%r\" %>s %b %{User-agent}i
%!200,302,304{Referrer}i" common
```

This entry provides all of the data of the CLF and thus can be analyzed by standard tools. But it also provides the browser name, and when the user requests a stale link, it provides the address of the remote site that references that link.

Server Security

Web servers are vulnerable to all of the normal security problems that are discussed in Chapter 14, *Security*. But they also have their own special security considerations. In addition to all of the normal threats, such as network break-ins and Denial of Service attacks, Web servers are responsible for protecting the integrity of the information disseminated by the server and for protecting the information sent by the client to the server.

Access to the server information is protected by access controls. As you saw in the `access.conf` configuration file, you can control access to your server at the host level and at the user level. Access control is important for protecting your internal and private Web pages, but most Web information is intended for dissemination to the world at large. For these global Web pages, you don't want to limit access in any way, but you do want to protect the integrity of the information on the pages.

One of the unique security risks for a Web server is having an intruder change the information on your Web pages. We have all heard of high-profile incidents where intruders get in and change the home page of some government agency, inserting comical or pornographic material. These attacks are not intended to do long-term harm to the server, but they are intended to embarrass the organization that runs the Web site.

Use Linux file permissions to protect the files and directories where you store Web documents. The server needs to read and execute these files, but it does not need write permissions.

NOTE   File permissions are discussed in Chapter 11.

The CGI and SSI Threat

Apache itself is very reliable and reasonably secure. The biggest threat to the security of your server is the code that you write for your server to execute. Two sources of these problems are Common Gateway Interface programs and Server Side Includes.

CGI   One of the biggest threats to server security is badly written CGI programs. Intruders exploit poor code by forcing buffer overflows or by passing shell commands through the program to the system. The only way to avoid this and still have the benefit of CGI programs, which can be written in C, Perl, Python, and other programming languages, is to be very careful about the code that you make available on your system. Here are some basic preventive measures to keep in mind:

- Personally review all programs included in the `cgi-bin` directory.
- Try to write programs that do not allow free-form user input.

Internet Server Operations

PART 2

- Use drop-down menus instead of keyboard input.
- Limit what comes in to your system from the user.

To make it easier to review all CGI scripts, keep them all in the `ScriptAlias` directory. Don't allow `ExecCGI` in any other directory unless you're positive no one can place a script there that you have not personally reviewed.

SSI   Server Side Includes is also called Server Parsed HTML, and the files often have the `.shtml` file extension. These files are processed by the server before they are sent to the client. These files can include other files or execute code from script files. If user input is used to dynamically modify the SSI file, it is vulnerable to the same type of attacks as CGI scripts.

SSI commands are embedded inside HTML comments. Therefore, each SSI command begins with `<!-` and concludes with `-->`. The SSI commands are listed in Table 8.2.

Table 8.2   Server Side Includes Commands

Command	Purpose
#config	Formats the display of file size and time.
#echo	Displays variables.
#exec	Executes a CGI script or a shell command.
#flastmod	Displays the date a document was last modified.
#fsize	Displays the size of a document.
#include	Inserts another file into the current document.

The most secure way to operate a server is to disallow all SSI processing. This is the default unless `All` or `Includes` is specified by an `Options` command in the `access.conf` file. A compromise setting is to allow SSI but to disallow the `#include` and `#exec` commands, which are the greatest security threat. Use `IncludesNOEXEC` on the `Options` command for this setting.

Client Security

In addition to protecting the security of your server, you are responsible for protecting the security of your clients. If you want to run an electronic commerce business, you must use a secure server that protects your customers' credit card information and other personal information.

Secure Apache servers use the Secure Sockets Layer (SSL) to encrypt protected sessions. To get these features, you need to purchase one of the servers that include SSL security.

TIP   Because of legal problems like U.S. export restrictions and licensing issues, encryption is a murky subject. It is certainly beyond the scope of this book. To find out more about secure Apache, U.S. readers should visit `www.us.apache.ssl` `.com` and investigate the Stronghold server. Readers outside of the U.S. and Canada should check out `www.algroup.co.uk/Apache-SSL`.

Creating Web Content

From my point of view, the worst part of creating a professional Web site is creating the content. Luckily, this is not a job assigned to the system administrator. The people who build professional Web sites are creative people with a good sense of design and an artistic eye. That's not me, and it is not most of the technical people I know. If it's not you either, the best approach to creating a Web site for your business is to hire someone who has the proper talent to do it, in the same way that your company hires professionals to produce its advertising campaigns. Web sites created by technical people who are more interested in mastering HTML than they are in layout and design often appear "amateurish" and thus hurt the reputation of your company.

Sometimes, however, you may be called upon to create a Web site for a church or school that cannot afford to hire a professional Web designer. In that case, you should find a decent Web-authoring tool to help you create the site.

There are many tools available for creating Web sites. For example, there are point-and-click tools like Netscape Communicator and Adobe Page Mill. There are also HTML editors such as ASHE, HoTMetaL Phonenix, and tkHTML. Additionally, text editors such as Adobe FrameMaker and WordPerfect permit you to save your work in HTML format.

HTML Resources

For more information on HTML and Web site creation, *Mastering Linux* by Arman Danesh (Sybex, 1999) contains a good description of HTML. Another fine book is *HTML: A Definitive Guide* by Bill Kennedy and Chuck Musciano (O'Reilly, 1998).

You can also find excellent information online. Tutorials on Web design, HTML, and pointers to many good HTML authoring tools are available by following the links from www.yahoo.com/computers_and_internet/information_and_documentation/data_formats/HTML to any number of excellent Web sites.

Final Words

Web services are an essential part of any organization's Internet server. Linux is an excellent platform for a Web server using the Apache software that is included in the distribution. Apache is the most popular Web server on the Internet. With Linux, it can effectively support a large organization's Web site.

Thus far, this book has illustrated some of the things, such as `sendmail`, DNS, and Web service, that Linux does best. The next chapter concludes the Internet server operations part of this book with a look at how Linux can be used to create a low-cost Internet router. While Linux may not create the most powerful router, it is certainly one of the most cost effective.

9

Network Gateway Services

A computer can only communicate directly with computers with which it shares a physical connection. Given this fact, the computer on your desk should only be able to communicate with computers that are electrically connected to the network cable that connects to your system. So how does it communicate with a computer on the other side of the world? There are two primary techniques: circuit switching and packet switching.

Circuit switching is the technique used by the voice telephone network. When you pick up the telephone, you get a dial tone. At this point, you have an electrical connection to the telephone switch at the local telephone company's central office. As you dial the telephone number, you provide the switch with the information it needs to make additional connections. Using this information, the switch connects your inbound port to an outbound port. If the number you are calling is serviced by the local switch, it sets up a connection between the port your telephone is attached to and the port connected to the phone you're calling. If the number you are calling is remotely located, the local switch sets up a connection to the next switch down the line. Each switch connects to the next switch in line until the switch servicing the remote phone is reached. This creates a circuit from your phone to the remote phone, wherever it is located, which is dedicated to your use until you hang up the phone.

When your computer runs PPP, it uses the telephone system to create a circuit between itself and the remote server.

Packet switching is the technique used by most data networks. Every packet in the network contains an address that tells the switch where the packet is bound. When the packet arrives at a switch, the switch reads the address and determines how the packet should be forwarded. If the switch has a physical connection to the destination node, it delivers the packet itself. Otherwise, it forwards the packet to the next switch in the path toward the destination node. Each packet is handled separately. No end-to-end connection is established.

In the circuit-switched model, the connection is between your phone and the phone at the remote end. In the packet-switched system, the connection is between your host and the local router. Figure 9.1 illustrates that packet switches use hop-by-hop routes versus the end-to-end connections used by circuit switches.

Figure 9.1   Circuit switching versus packet switching

Circuit Switching

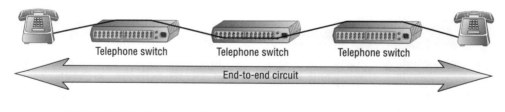

Packet Switching

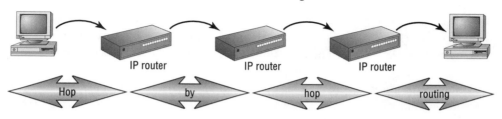

NOTE Whether you configure your system as a host or as an IP router, it will not have end-to-end knowledge of the routes through the network. It will only know about local routers.

The Internet—and all TCP/IP networks—are packet-switched networks. An IP packet switch is called a *gateway* or an *IP router*. Routers interconnect networks, moving data from one network to another until the destination network is reached. At that point, direct delivery is made to the destination host. This is illustrated in Figure 9.2.

Figure 9.2   Routing through networks

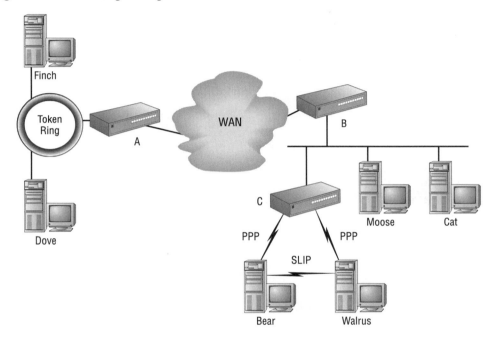

In the figure, an IP datagram from finch to walrus would first go to router A, then to router B, then to router C, and finally to walrus. Notice that IP routers can interconnect different types of physical networks. And, as this chapter demonstrates, any Linux system can be configured to be an IP router.

Understanding Routing

Routing turns TCP/IP networks into an internet and is an essential function of the Internet Protocol (IP). Even a Linux system, which has the Transport layer and the Application layer sitting above the IP layer, makes routing decisions in the IP layer. When the IP layer receives a packet, it evaluates the destination address in the header of the packet as follows:

- If the destination address is the address of the local computer, IP evaluates the protocol number and passes the packet up to the appropriate transport protocol. (See the discussion of protocol numbers in Chapter 5, *Login Services*.)

- If the destination address is on a directly connected network, IP delivers the packet to the destination host.

- If the destination is on a remote network, IP forwards the datagram to a local router. The router that the packet is sent to must share a physical network with the local system. It is the responsibility of that router to then forward the packet on to the next router and so on, hop by hop, until the packet reaches its destination.

Based on this list of possible decisions, IP will either directly deliver the packet or forward it to a router for additional processing. From Chapter 5, you know how IP uses the protocol number and the port number to deliver data to the correct application within the local host. But you may not yet know how IP delivers data across a network. To deliver a packet to another host on a directly attached network, IP must use the Physical-layer addressing of that network. To do this, it must convert IP addresses to Physical-layer addresses.

Converting IP Addresses to Ethernet Addresses

As Figure 9.2 illustrates, IP can run over many different types of networks. The IP address is a logical address. The address means something to the logical IP network, but it doesn't mean anything to the physical networks over which IP must transport the data. To send data over a physical network, IP must convert the IP address to an address understood by the network. The most common example of this is the conversion from an IP address to an Ethernet address. The protocol that performs this conversion is the Address Resolution Protocol (ARP).

NOTE   The ARP protocol is included with your Linux system and is installed by default as part of the TCP/IP network software. You don't have to do anything to activate ARP, and it should run without problems.

The ARP protocol dynamically builds a table that maps IP addresses to Ethernet addresses. It does this using the broadcast facilities of the Ethernet. When ARP receives a request to convert an IP address to an Ethernet address, it checks to see if it has the mapping for that address in the ARP table. If the mapping is there, it uses it. If it isn't in the table, ARP sends a broadcast to the Ethernet asking who owns the IP address. When a computer sees an ARP broadcast for its IP address, it responds with its Ethernet address. ARP then adds that response to the table.

Use the arp command to examine the contents of the ARP table on your Linux system. Use the –a command-line option to view the entire table:

```
$ arp -a
bluejay (172.16.55.1) at 00:00:C0:4F:3E:DD [ether] on eth0
duck (172.16.55.11) at 00:10:4B:87:D4:A8 [ether] on eth0
raven (172.16.55.251) at 08:00:20:82:D5:1D [ether] on eth0
gw50 (172.16.50.254) at 00:00:0C:43:8D:FB [ether] on eth1
```

The arp command lists the host name, IP address, and Ethernet address of every system currently stored in the ARP table. The keyword ether enclosed in square brackets indicates the hardware type. This will always be ether. There are other hardware values, but they are for obscure networks like ARCnet. Most of the entries in the example are for the network connected to network interface eth0.

However, a router has more than one network interface, so it is possible to see an arp display with more than one Ethernet interface indicated. The last line in the display shows this. gw50 is reached through interface eth1.

You can also use the arp command to check for the table entry of an individual host:

```
$ arp bluejay
Address  HWtype  HWaddress          Flags Mask    Iface
bluejay  ether   00:00:C0:4F:3E:DD  C               eth0
```

NOTE   It is possible to enter the arp command looking for a specific host and to receive the response "no entry." This does not necessarily indicate a problem. Try sending a ping to the host first in order to prime the cache. Then enter the arp command. You should see the correct table entry.

This example contains much the same information as you saw in the first example. Again, there's the hardware type, the Ethernet address, the network interface name, and the host name. (If you prefer the IP address to the host name, use the –n option on the arp command line.) There are two fields, however, that you didn't see in the previous listing: the Flags field and the Mask field.

The Flags field can contain three possible values:

C This flag indicates that this is a complete entry. To be valid, an entry must be complete. Therefore, this flag should always be set.

M This flag says that this entry was manually entered as a permanent entry. ARP table entries are normally dynamic. They are learned from the computers on the network, and they are only held in the ARP table for a few minutes. However, the system administrator can place static entries in the table. These entries stay in the table as long as the system is running. See Chapter 15, *Troubleshooting*, for information on using a permanent entry to troubleshoot an address assignment problem.

P This flag means that the entry will be published. In other words, if this computer receives an ARP broadcast for the IP address in this entry, the local host will respond with the Ethernet address even though the IP address does not really belong to the local host. This is called *proxy ARP*. It is used to help systems that cannot respond for themselves. See the "Proxy ARP" sidebar for an example of when this is used.

The Mask field contains an optional network mask if one is used. By default, the mask is 255.255.255.255, which says that the entire IP address is matched to the Ethernet address. Other masks are rarely used. Solaris Unix systems use the mask 240.0.0.0 to map multicast addresses to the Ethernet broadcast address.

WARNING The only time I have heard of using an optional mask value on a Linux system is to publish a single Ethernet address for an entire subnet. In that case, the mask required for the specific subnet is used. However, *don't* do this. Subnets should be connected through routing, not through proxy ARP.

Proxy ARP

A host that connects to an Ethernet through a PPP link cannot respond to an ARP request. ARP requests are sent via Ethernet broadcasts, and the telephone lines over which PPP runs don't understand Ethernet broadcasts. To address this problem, you can use proxy ARP.

Assume that two telecommuters connect to subnet 172.16.55.0 through PPP links to bluejay. Both have been assigned addresses on subnet 172.16.55.0: killdeer (172.16.55.8) and meadowlark (172.16.55.23). bluejay is configured to provide proxy ARP for both systems with the following commands:

```
# arp -s killdeer 00:00:C0:4F:3E:DD pub

# arp -s meadowlark 00:00:C0:4F:3E:DD pub

# arp killdeer
```

Proxy ARP *(continued)*

```
Address      HWtype  HWaddress            Flags Mask    Iface

killdeer     ether   00:00:C0:4F:3E:DD    CMP           eth0

# arp meadowlark

Address      HWtype  HWaddress            Flags Mask    Iface

meadowlark   ether   00:00:C0:4F:3E:DD    CMP           eth0
```

The –s command-line argument tells arp that this is a static entry, and the pub argument says that this entry will be published. Notice that the same Ethernet address is used for both killdeer and meadowlark, and that the address is the Ethernet address of bluejay. bluejay responds to ARP requests with its own Ethernet address so that it receives packets bound for killdeer and meadowlark. Because bluejay is configured to forward packets, when it receives packets for these systems, it sends those packets to the correct host through the appropriate PPP link.

The IP address must be converted to a Physical-layer address for all types of external data delivery, whether the system is making a direct delivery or forwarding a packet for further processing. A traditional host will only accept packets from the network that are addressed to the host. It will not accept packets addressed to other hosts or forward those packets on. Routers, on the other hand, do exactly that. To get this behavior, you must enable forwarding on a router.

Enabling IP Packet Forwarding

When a computer forwards a packet that it has received from the network on to a remote system, it is called *IP forwarding*. All Linux systems can be configured to forward IP packets. In general, hosts do not forward datagrams, but routers must.

To use a Linux system as a router, enable IP forwarding. On Red Hat and Caldera systems, forwarding can be enabled in the /etc/sysconfig/networks file:

```
$ cat /etc/sysconfig/network
NETWORKING=yes
FORWARD_IPV4=false
HOSTNAME=pecan.nuts.com
```

```
DOMAINNAME=nuts.com

GATEWAY=172.16.12.254

GATEWAYDEV=eth0
```

The commands in this file require very little explanation. From this file, you know that networking is enabled (NETWORKING). You can also see the host name (HOSTNAME), the domain name (DOMAINNAME), and the name of the network interface (GATEWAYDEV).

The two remaining commands both deal with routing. One defines the default gateway (GATEWAY). (You'll learn more about the default gateway later in this chapter.) The other command tells the system whether or not it should forward IP datagrams. FORWARD_IPV4=false tells the system that it should not forward datagrams. If the variable is set to true, the system forwards IP packets.

On Linux systems that don't use the /etc/sysconfig/network configuration file, forwarding can be enabled by setting the correct value in the /proc/sys/net/ip4/ip_forward file. If the file contains a 0, forwarding is disabled. If it contains a 1, forwarding is enabled. (A cat of the ip_forward file will show you the current setting of your system.) Use the echo command to write a 1 to the file to enable forwarding:

```
echo "1" /proc/sys/net/ipv4/ip_forward
```

If you intend to run your Linux system as a router, stow this command in the rc.local file to enable forwarding every time the system boots.

Regardless of whether the system is a router or a host, it can only make final delivery if it is on the same network as the destination host. In all other cases, the system must send the packet on to a router. The routing table tells the local system which router the packet should be sent to.

The Linux Routing Table

Chapter 4, *The Network Interface*, described the structure of an IP address, explaining that it is composed of a network portion and a host portion. Routing is network-oriented; IP makes its decision on whether to directly deliver the packet or forward the packet to a router based on the network portion of the address. When the decision is made to forward the packet to a router, IP looks in the routing table to determine which router should handle the packet.

The Linux routing table is displayed by entering the route command with no command-line arguments. Because I prefer to look at network numbers instead of host names when analyzing a routing table, I use the –n option, which prevents route from converting IP addresses to host names for the routing table display. Here is an example:

```
$ route -n
Kernel IP routing table
Destination Gateway       Genmask       Flags Metric Ref Use Iface
172.16.55.0 0.0.0.0       255.255.255.0 U     0      0   38  eth0
172.16.50.0 172.16.55.36  255.255.255.0 UG    0      0   8   eth0
127.0.0.0   0.0.0.0       255.0.0.0     U     0      0   1   lo
default     172.16.55.254 0.0.0.0       UG    1      0   17  eth0
```

The routing table listing contains the following fields:

Destination The destination network (or host). Normally this is a network, but as you'll see in the Flags field discussion, it is possible to have a host-specific route.

Gateway The gateway for the specified destination. If this field contains all zeros (0.0.0.0) or an asterisk (*), it means that the destination network is directly connected to this computer and that the "gateway" to that network is the computer's network interface.

Genmask The bit mask applied to addresses to see if they match the destination address.

Flags The flags describe certain characteristics of this route. The possible flag values are:

U This route is up and operational.

H This is a route to a specific host. None of the routes in the example is host-specific routes, which are rarely used.

G This route uses an external gateway. The system's network interfaces provide routes to directly connected networks. All other routes use external gateways. Directly connected networks do not have the G flag set; all other routes do.

D This route was added because of an ICMP Redirect Message. When a system learns of a route via an ICMP Redirect, it adds the route to its routing table so that additional packets bound for that destination will not need to be redirected. The system uses the D flag to mark these routes.

Metric This is the routing cost for this interface. Normally, this field is zero for routes to directly connected networks. Routes to external gateways often have a metric of 1, though that is not always the case. The metric is an arbitrary value that you set. The higher the metric, the more "expensive"—and therefore the less preferred—the route. I'll talk more about routing metrics in the "Routing Protocols" section later in this chapter.

Ref Shows the number of times the route has been referenced to establish a connection.

Use shows the number of packets transmitted via this route.

Iface The name of the network interface used by this route. For Ethernet network interfaces, the names will be eth0, eth1, eth2, and so on. For PPP network interfaces, the names will be ppp0, ppp1, ppp2, and so on.

With this knowledge of how the routing table is displayed, take a look at each line in the sample table:

- The first line defines the connection of this host to the local Ethernet. From this entry, you can tell that the host is connected to subnet 172.16.55.0 and that it connects to that subnet directly through interface eth0.

- The second line is a static route added by the network administrator. It tells you that 172.16.55.36 is the gateway to subnet 172.16.50.0.

- The third line defines the loopback network and states that the gateway to the loopback network is the interface lo0.

- The last line defines the default route, which identifies the default gateway. If the destination of a packet does not match a specific route in the routing table, the packet is sent to the default gateway. In our sample system, specific routes exist for networks 172.16.55.0, 172.16.50.0, and 127.0.0.0. All other destinations are sent to the default router.

Notice that both of the external gateways are connected to local Ethernet 172.15.55.0. If they weren't, the local system could not communicate with them and thus could not communicate with the outside world.

Routes enter the routing table in one of two ways: either the system administrator enters them as static routes, or they are added to the table by a routing protocol as dynamic routes. The next few sections look at both techniques for defining network routes.

Defining Static Routes

Static routes are defined on every Linux system that connects to a TCP/IP network. You saw an example of this in the "Configuring the Interface for Every Boot" section of Chapter 4, where the static route required by the network interface was defined. A minimal routing table has a route for the loopback address and a route for the network interface.

Every Linux system has at least these two static routes. These two routes from the sample routing table shown above are:

```
172.16.55.0 0.0.0.0    255.255.255.0  U   0    0    38 eth0
127.0.0.0   0.0.0.0    255.0.0.0      U   0    0    1 lo
```

To create these routes, enter these two commands:

```
route add -net 172.16.55.0 netmask 255.255.255.0 dev eth0
route add -net 127.0.0.0   netmask 255.0.0.0     dev lo0
```

You will not need to enter these commands yourself. They are stored in one of the startup scripts that come with your Linux system. On a Slackware system, you'll find these commands in the rc.inet1 script. On Caldera and Red Hat systems, they are in the /etc/sysconfig/network-scripts/ifup script. In all of those scripts, the actual network address is replaced by the script variable ${NETWORK}, the address mask is replaced by ${NETMASK}, and the actual interface name is replaced by the variable ${DEVICE}. However, the purpose and function of the route commands are the same.

The route Command

All static routes are defined by the route command. It allows anyone to display the routing table and allows the root user to add and delete routes in the table. The system administrator added this static route to the sample routing table we looked at earlier:

```
172.16.50.0 172.16.55.36 255.255.255.0 UG 0 0 8 eth0
```

This route statement creates the route:

```
route add -net 172.16.50.0 netmask 255.255.255.0 gw 172.16.55.36
```

Examining this command shows almost everything you need to know about the route command syntax. All route commands start with an option that defines the "action" of the route command, which is either add or delete. All of the sample commands add routes to the routing table. To change a route, first delete it, and then add it back in with the necessary corrections.

The -net option tells route that you are adding a network route. The alternative is -host for a host-specific route, but this is rarely used, because most routes are network routes.

The -net option is followed by the destination address and by the network mask that is used to determine the network portion and the host portion of the address. The network mask must be preceded by the keyword netmask.

Internet Server Operations

PART 2

> **WARNING**   Always use the netmask keyword. If you don't, the address is inter-
> preted using the natural mask, which means that the address is interpreted
> according to the old address class rules. Be specific. Define the mask yourself.

All of our sample route commands end with either an external gateway or a local device
name. When an external gateway is used, it is defined by the gw option and the IP address
of the gateway. When the interface device name is used, it is usually preceded by the keyword dev, though this is not required. The network interface name must be included on
a route statement that defines the connection of the device to the local network. On other
route statements, the interface name is optional. Use the device name on all route statements when you have more than one interface to ensure that the route uses the interface
that you intend.

Defining the Default Route

Thus far, all of the routes from the sample routing table have been discussed except for
the default route. The sample table contains a default route that specifies 172.16.55.254
as the default router:

```
default    172.16.55.254 0.0.0.0    UG 1 0 17 eth0
```

Enter the following command to define that route:

```
route add default gw 172.16.55.254
```

This command looks similar to the previous route command except that the keyword
default is used in place of the destination network. It is the presence of this keyword that
defines the default route.

Most Linux systems connected to a TCP/IP internet have a static default route. Because
it is so common, it is unlikely that you will need to enter a route command to define it.
All Linux installations that I have worked with ask you for the address of the default
router during the initial installation. Provide it at that time. Slackware stores the default
gateway in the rc.inet1 script file; Caldera and Red Hat store it in the /etc/sysconfig/
network file, as you saw earlier.

For most Linux servers, all you need to do is define the default route, because most servers
are hosts that depend on a single external router for routing service. On occasion, however, a Linux server may be used as the router for a small network. When it is, you may
need to run a routing protocol, as discussed next.

Using Dynamic Routing

Static routing tables are the most efficient when there are a limited number of routers. If the network has only one router, the correct configuration is to use a static default route. Use dynamic routing protocols when the routing environment of a network is changeable or complex, for example, when there are multiple routers that can reach the same destinations.

Routing Protocols

Routing and routing protocols are not the same thing. All Linux systems make routing decisions, but very few systems run routing protocols. Routing protocols perform two functions: They select the "best" route to a destination, and they communicate that route to other routers on the network. Thus a *routing protocol* is a program for defining routes and for disseminating routes.

There are several different routing protocols, and considering the fact that Linux systems are not usually used as routers, a surprising number of these protocols are available for Linux systems. Protocols are differentiated by the metric they use for determining the best route and by the technique they use for distributing routing information.

Routing protocols are divided into interior protocols and exterior protocols. *Interior protocols* are used inside of a routing domain. *Exterior protocols* are used to exchange routing information between routing domains. Within your enterprise network, you'll use an interior routing protocol. It is possible that you will use an exterior routing protocol between your network and your ISP, but even that is unlikely. Most corporate networks are located within the ISP's routing domain and therefore use an interior routing protocol to talk to the ISP. Following is an overview of the three interior protocols—Routing Information Protocol (RIP), Routing Information Protocol Version 2 (RIPv2), and Open Shortest Path First (OSPF)—and the one exterior protocol, Border Gateway Protocol (BGP).

Border Gateway Protocol

BGP is the only exterior routing protocol in widespread use. BGP supports *policy-based routing*, which allows you to define organizational or political reasons for choosing a route. The routing metrics used within different routing domains cannot be directly compared. You cannot know exactly how the metrics are determined within another routing domain. You may not even know what interior routing protocols they use. Instead of trusting the technical process used to select the routes, you trust the organization that advertises the routes. You may do this because of the reputation of the organization, or because you have a business agreement with them to trust their routes. This is the basis of policy-based routing.

BGP is a *path-vector protocol*. The path vector provides an end-to-end list of every routing domain along the route, which allows you to decide whether or not you trust the advertisements that come from those domains.

You will not run BGP unless you are told to run it by your ISP. Exterior protocols are only used externally, and for them to be used successfully, both parties must agree to use the protocol. If your ISP requires you to use BGP, you can be sure they will know how it should be configured. The protocols that you use on your own network are the interior routing protocols.

Routing Information Protocol

RIP is the most commonly used interior routing protocol. It is included as part of the operating system with all Linux and Unix systems, as well as in the Windows NT RRAS package. RIP is already installed in your system, and it is easy to configure and run.

RIP defines the "best" route as being the lowest-cost route, which is the one with the lowest routing metric. The *routing metric* is an arbitrary number from 1 to 15 that represents the number of gateways that traffic must pass through to reach the destination. RIP calls each router a "hop" and the metric a "hop count." The best route to a destination is the one that passes through the fewest routers. This technique for determining the best route is called a *distance-vector algorithm*.

When RIP starts, it broadcasts a request for routing information. A router running RIP responds to the request by sending an update packet that contains the destination addresses and associated metrics from its routing table. In addition to responding to requests, routers that run RIP issue update packets every 30 seconds. If a router stops issuing updates for 180 seconds, the other routers on the network assume it is dead and delete any routes that go through that router.

RIP processes an update packet in the following manner:

- If the packet contains new routes that are not in the routing table, they are added.
- If the packet contains routes that are lower cost than the same routes in the existing routing table, the old routes are deleted, and the new routes are used. The cost of a new route is determined by adding the cost of reaching the router that sent the update to the cost metric included in the update packet.
- If the packet contains routes that have a cost of 15, those routes are deleted from the routing table if the update came from the gateway used for those routes. For example, if your routing table contains a route to subnet 172.16.50.0 through gateway 172.16.55.36 and it receives a RIP update from 172.16.55.36 with a cost of 15 for the route to 172.16.50.0, your system deletes the route.

RIP has been around for a long time, and it shows its age. Very large networks cannot use RIP, because the longest route it allows is 15 hops. This should be large enough for your network, but is insufficient for large national networks. Additionally, it can take a long time for the routing table to reflect the current state of the network, because RIP waits 180 seconds before discarding routes from an inactive router. This can be worsened by the "count to infinity" problem. (Not familiar with "counting to infinity"? See the upcoming sidebar.) More important than either of these problems is the fact that RIP is not equipped to handle network bit masks, which makes it incompatible with many current networks.

Counting to Infinity

A problem with the original RIP design is something known as "counting to infinity." Let's use Figure 9.2 to illustrate this problem.

Router B advertises finch as being two hops away, because it reaches finch through A. C advertises finch as being three hops away, because it reaches it through B. Assume that router A crashes. B no longer gets updates from A, so it doesn't think it can reach finch through A. However, it does see an update from C saying that finch is three hops away. So B updates its routing table and now advertises finch as being four hops away. Because C reaches finch through B, it updates its routing table and advertises finch as being five hops away. B then sees the update from C and changes its routing table. This goes on and on until we reach infinity. Luckily, infinity is only 15 for a RIP hop count.

RIP addresses this problem in three ways: "split horizon," "poison reverse," and "triggered updates." The split horizon rule says that a router never advertises a route on the network from which it learned the route. Therefore, C would not advertise that it could reach finch to B, because it learned the route from B.

Poison reverse takes this one step further. It says that a router should advertise an infinite distance for a route on the network from which it learned the route. Thus C would tell B that it cannot reach finch by advertising a hop count of 15 for the route to finch.

With triggered updates, changes to the routing table are immediately advertised instead of waiting the normal 30-second interval between RIP updates. Therefore, even when a count-to-infinity problem does occur, it only takes as long as it takes for the routers to exchange 15 packets. Without triggered updates, counting to infinity can take several minutes.

Counting to Infinity *(continued)*

Split horizon, poison reverse, and triggered updates have effectively eliminated the count-to-infinity problem in RIP. However, they do not address the other problems with RIP. To address those problems, the new routing protocols described next have been developed.

RIP Version 2

RIPv2 enhances the original RIP packet with the addition of a network mask field and a "next hop address" field. The network mask is the bit mask that is used to determine the destination network. Sending the mask with the destination address in the routing update is an essential component of classless IP addresses.

The key difference between a network mask and a subnet mask is the scope of the address. Subnet masks are only known locally, but network masks must be known globally. To make them globally available, they must be distributed to other systems. The routing protocol is used to do this, and RIPv2 adds this capability to RIP.

The "next hop address" field provides the address of the gateway. In RIP, only the destination address and the metric are provided. The gateway is always assumed to be the router that sends out the update. The next hop address field specifically provides the address of the gateway, which allows the system that sends the update to be different from the gateway that will handle the route. Thus, RIPv2-capable systems can provide updates for routers that don't run RIPv2. If the next hop address is 0.0.0.0, the router that sends the update is assumed to be the gateway for the route.

In addition to these enhancements that address the biggest problem with RIP, RIPv2 adds a few nice features:

- RIPv2 is completely compatible with RIP because the RIP packet format is unchanged. All of the features of RIPv2 are implemented in unused fields of the original RIP packet. RIP and RIPv2 routers can coexist on a single network without a problem.
- RIPv2 uses multicasting instead of broadcasting to reduce the load on systems that do not want RIPv2 updates.
- RIPv2 provides an authentication scheme that prevents routing updates from a misconfigured host from accidentally being accepted as valid.

Despite its improvements, RIPv2 is still RIP. Therefore, it uses the same distance-vector algorithm for determining the best route, and it limits the diameter of the network to 15 hops. OSPF, a different type of interior protocol, was developed for very large national networks.

Open Shortest Path First Protocol

OSPF is very different than RIP. A router running RIP sends information about the entire network to its neighbors. A router running OSPF floods information about its neighbors to the entire network. *Flooding* means that the router sends the update out of every network port, and that every router that receives the update also sends it out of every port except the one it receives it on. Flooding rapidly disseminates routing information to the entire network.

OSPF is called a *link-state protocol* because it creates a graph of the state of all of the links in the network. Every OSPF router creates its graph using the information about all of the routers and their neighbors that flooding distributes throughout the network. Each graph is unique, because every router creates the graph with itself as the root of the tree. The graph is built using the Dijkstra Shortest Path First algorithm, hence the name of the protocol. The algorithm builds the graph in this manner:

1. The system starts by installing itself as the root of the graph with a cost of 0.

2. The system installs the neighbors of the system that was just added to the graph. The cost of reaching those neighbors is calculated as the cost of reaching the system just installed plus the cost that system advertises for reaching the neighbors.

3. The system selects the lowest-cost path for each destination. It repeats steps 2 and 3 for every system for which it has information.

Clearly, building a link-state graph for a large network every time a route changes creates a lot of overhead for the router. For this reason, OSPF divides the routing domain up into smaller, more manageable pieces. The entire routing domain is called an *autonomous system*, and the pieces are called *areas*. A special area, called the *backbone area*, is defined to interconnect all of the areas in the autonomous system. Routers within an area only have knowledge of their area and therefore only create a graph of the systems in that area.

OSPF is a much more complex system than RIP, but OSPF is better suited for large networks. However, it is unlikely that you will need to use OSPF on a network that uses Linux servers for routers. Most Linux systems that run a routing protocol run RIP.

Running RIP with routed

Every Linux system includes the routing daemon `routed`, an implementation of RIP. To run RIP, simply enter `routed`.

`routed` requires no command-line arguments and no configuration file. The routing daemon listens to the RIP updates on the network to build a functioning routing table. If the computer is a router, i.e., the computer has more than one network interface, the routing daemon broadcasts its own updates. If the computer has only one network interface, it is considered a host, and the routing daemon does not broadcast routing updates.

Command-line options can be used to change this default behavior regardless of the number of network interfaces installed in the computer. Use –s to force the daemon to broadcast RIP updates; specify –q to stop it from broadcasting update packets. The –q argument is more useful than the –s argument. Sometimes you don't want a computer with multiple network interfaces broadcasting routes. However, I have never configured a host with only one network interface to broadcast RIP updates.

routed does not require configuration, but it is possible to use the /etc/gateways file to pass supplemental routing information to the routing daemon.

The /etc/gateways File

routed broadcasts a RIP request immediately on startup and uses the information in the RIP updates it receives to build a table. The entire reason for running a routing protocol is to use the information from that protocol to build the routing table. On the surface, adding static routes to a dynamic table doesn't seem to make much sense, and generally there is no reason to do so. But it is possible that there are routers on your network that can't or won't provide RIP updates and that must be added to the table manually. The /etc/gateways file provides that capability in case you need it.

routed reads the /etc/gateways file during startup and adds the routes defined there to the routing table. The sample entries from a gateways file are enough to illustrate its purpose because all entries in the file have the same basic format. Here are two sample entries:

```
$ cat /etc/gateways
net 0.0.0.0 gateway 172.16.55.254 metric 1 active
net 172.16.50.0 gateway 172.16.55.36 metric 1 passive
```

All entries start with the keyword net or host to indicate whether this is a host-specific route or a network route. The keyword is followed by the destination address. (The destination 0.0.0.0 is a special address that stands for the default route.) The destination address is followed by keyword gateway and the IP address of the external gateway used to reach the destination.

Next comes the keyword metric and the cost assigned to this route. Normally, external gateways are given a cost of 1, but this is arbitrary, so you can assign a higher value if you want. Assigning a higher metric, however, only makes sense if you have two routes to the same destination and you want to prefer one of those routes over the other.

All entries end with the keyword active or passive. An active router is expected to participate in the exchange of routing updates. If it fails to respond to routing requests and does not periodically broadcast RIP updates, it is removed from the routing table. This is the normal behavior expected of any RIP router.

A `passive` router does not participate in the exchange of RIP updates. Perhaps the system runs a different routing protocol. Regardless of the reason, it is not required to participate and is installed in the routing table as a permanent, static route.

The first line in our example creates an active default route. This default route is used during the RIP startup period, but once RIP is up and running, this default router is expected to be an active participant in the routing protocol. If you use a default route when running a routing protocol, use an active default route. A static default route can defeat the purpose of a dynamic routing protocol by not allowing the protocol to update the route when network conditions change.

The second line creates a static route to subnet 172.16.50.0 through router 172.16.55.36. Because this is a passive route, 172.16.55.36 does not need to run RIP. The only reason to create such a route would be that 17216.55.36 does not run RIP.

`routed` is adequate for many small networks. It requires no installation and very little configuration. However, it is not suitable for all networks. In particular, it does not support classless IP addresses. If you need a routing protocol that supports classless IP addresses, run the gateway daemon.

Using gated

The gateway daemon (`gated`) is a software package that combines many of the most advanced routing protocols. `gated` provides Linux systems with access to interior and exterior routing protocols that normally only run on dedicated routing hardware, such as CISCO routers. `gated` allows your system to run multiple routing protocols and to combine the routes learned from those protocols. To support multiple protocols, and in particular exterior routing protocols, `gated` provides a way for you to define routing policies that specify what routing you will accept and what routes you will advertise.

When running multiple protocols, it is possible for your system to receive routes to the same destination from different routing protocols. Each protocol uses its own metric for selecting the best route. `gated` must compare these incompatible metrics and select the best route. It does this using a *preference value*. A `gated` preference value is an arbitrary number between 0 and 255 that indicates if one source of routing information is preferred over another. The sources of information can be different routing protocols, different interfaces, different routers, and different routing domains. The lower the preference number, the more preferred the source. The default preferences used for routing protocols are shown in Table 9.1.

Given the preference values in Table 9.1, a route through a network interface to a directly connected network is the most preferred, and a route learned from EGP, an obsolete exterior routing protocol, is the least preferred. Most of the routing sources listed in the table

Table 9.1 Default gated Preference Values

Route Source	Preference Value
Direct route	0
OSPF	10
Internally-generated default	20
ICMP redirect	30
Static route	60
Hello protocol	90
RIP	100
OSPF ASE	150
BGP	170
EGP	200

have been mentioned before in this text. Two have not. Hello is an old interior routing protocol that chooses routes based on packet delay. It is rarely used. OSPF ASE routes were learned by OSPF from an external autonomous system. ASE means "autonomous system external." Because the ASE routes come from another routing domain, the metrics in those routes do not receive the same level of trust as the metrics in interior routes. In fact, the three lowest-preference routing sources, EGP, BGP, and OSPF ASE, all get the routes from external routing domains.

You can modify these default preferences when you configure gated, but I have never needed to. The defaults have worked well for all of my configurations. This is because I don't recommend using a general-purpose system like Linux for extremely complicated and demanding routing situations. Instead, use dedicated router hardware. For less demanding applications, such as providing the gateway to a single subnet, Linux with gated is an excellent choice.

Installing gated

The gated software is part of some Linux distributions. Red Hat includes it. Use tksysv or linuxconf to check if gated was installed during the initial system installation. If it was, you can use tksysv or linuxconf to enable it. Figure 9.3 shows a system with the gated package installed. In the Service Control window, locate gated and click Enabled, and then Accept. Activate the change when you exit linuxconf, and the service is ready to run.

Figure 9.3   Enabling the gated daemon with linuxconf

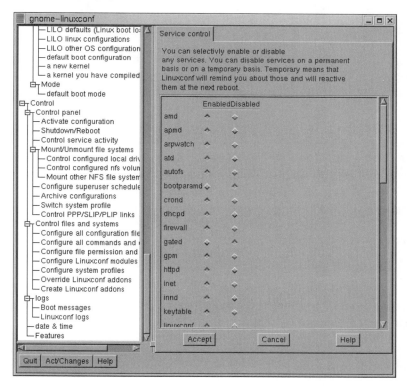

If the gated package was not installed during the initial installation, use the Red Hat Package Manager (RPM) to install the software from the CD-ROM. gnorpm is the X Windows tool used with Red Hat 6 for installing RPM software. Run gnorpm from the System menu. Figure 9.4 shows gnorpm after gated is installed.

Internet Server Operations

PART 2

Figure 9.4 Installing gated with gnorpm

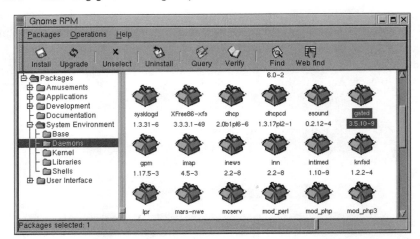

> **TIP** If you don't have gated software, it's easy to obtain from the Internet at www.gated.org. You can download a pre-compiled Linux gated binary directly from the Web site. If you prefer, you can download the source tree as a compressed tar file and compile your own version of gated.

No matter how it is installed, gated is configured through the /etc/gated.conf file.

The gated.conf File

At startup, gated reads the gated.conf file. The file contains configuration statements that tell gated which routing protocols should be run and how they should be configured. There are several types of configuration statements:

- Options statements
- Interface statements
- Definition statements
- Protocol statements
- Static statements
- Control statements
- Aggregate statements

Not all of these statements are required for a configuration, but when they are used, the statements must appear in the order listed above.

These statements can be divided into two groups: statements you probably won't use and statements you might use. Among the statements you're unlikely to use are the options statements, the static statements, the control statements, and the aggregate statements:

- The options statements set parameters such as nosend (don't send any routing information) and noresolv (don't use DNS) that are only used for special configurations.

- The static statements define the static routes that should be included in the routing table. Generally, when you run a routing protocol, you don't need to define static routes.

- The control statements are used to define the routing policy. They are primarily used when passing routing between routing domains. While it is unlikely you will be using Linux for this, I give an example of this later, because it is one of the key features of gated.

- The aggregate statements are used to aggregate routes within regional and national networks to reduce the number of routes exchanged between national networks. If you run a national network, please don't run it on a PC!

The statements that you are more likely to use in a Linux gated configuration are definition statements, interface statements, and protocol statements:

- The definition statements define invalid destination addresses, the autonomous system number for exterior routing protocols and the router IP address for BGP and OSPF. You'll see some examples of definition statements later.

- The interface statements are used to define the characteristics of your router's network interfaces. You will see this statement in our sample configuration.

- The protocol statements are the heart of the gated.conf file. Every routing protocol available in gated has a protocol statement. Use the protocol statement to configure the routing protocol for your network.

gated is a complex system that can handle many different routing configurations. The configuration language has a multitude of options. Details of the language are covered in the online manual at www.gated.org and in printed form in *TCP/IP Network Administration* by Craig Hunt (O'Reilly, 1998).

Routers running on Linux systems, however, don't require all of these configuration options. The best way to understand the gated configuration commands is to look at a few reasonable Linux configurations.

Running RIPv2

First, let's assume that you have a host on a network that needs to run RIPv2. This system is not a router, but because it is on a network segment with more than one router, you

Internet Server Operations

PART 2

decide to configure it to listen to the RIPv2 updates that the routers are broadcasting.
Here is the sample configuration:

```
#  enable rip, don't broadcast updates,
#  listen for RIP-2 updates on the multicast address,
#  check that the updates are authentic.
#
rip yes {
        nobroadcast ;
        interface 172.16.60.2
            version 2
            multicast
            authentication simple "EZDozIt" ;


    } ;
```

The comments at the beginning of the configuration file help to explain the configuration.
Other than these comments, the entire file is one protocol statement. All of the lines
enclosed inside the curly braces ({}) are part of the RIP protocol statement.

The statement begins with `rip yes`, which enables the RIP protocol. The `nobroadcast`
clause tells the system not to send RIP update packets; it will just listen to the packets provided by the routers. If your system is a router instead of a host, delete this clause, and it
will send updates.

The `interface` clause defines the interface the routing protocol should use and the characteristics of the interface. In this case, you identify the interface by its IP address. Hosts
have only one interface. If this was a router that ran RIPv2 on all interfaces, you could
provide a comma-separated list of all interface IP addresses or the keyword `all` to indicate that all interfaces should be used.

The `interface` clause also contains some parameters that are specific to RIPv2. The
parameter `version 2` explicitly tells `gated` to run RIPv2. The keyword `multicast` says to
listen for updates on the RIPv2 multicast address. Finally, the `authentication` parameter
defines the type of RIPv2 router authentication that will be used. In this case, you use
`simple` password authentication. The password is EZDozIt.

This example provides a RIPv2 host configuration that could be used on any system with only slight modifications. Our sample host receives its RIP updates from local routers. In the next section, you'll configure one of these routers.

Running OSPF

In this sample, a router is configured to send RIPv2 packets on one subnet, the one that it shares with our sample host, and OSPF link-state advertisements on another subnet that it shares with other routers. Here's the router configuration:

```
#  Don't time-out subnet 60
interfaces {
    interface 172.16.60.1 passive ;
} ;
# Define the OSPF router id
routerid 172.16.1.9 ;
# Enable RIP-2; announce OSPF routes to
# subnet 60 with a cost of 5.
rip yes {
    broadcast ;
    defaultmetric 5 ;
    interface 172.16.60.1
        version 2
        multicast
        authentication simple "EZDozIt" ;
} ;
# Enable OSPF; subnet 1 is the backbone area;
# use password authentication.
ospf yes {
    backbone {
        authtype simple ;
        interface 172.16.1.9 {
            priority 5 ;
```

Internet Server Operations

PART 2

```
                        authkey "UcantrustME" ;
                    } ;
            } ;
    } ;
```

The configuration begins with an `interface` statement. It tells the system that the systems on subnet 60 may not provide RIPv2 updates. Normally, if no routing information is received on an interface, the interface is marked as inactive and assumed to be "down." This statement ensures that the interface is not assumed to be "down" just because the hosts on the subnet do not advertise RIPv2 updates. Unlike the interface clause you saw above, this statement is not subordinate to a protocol statement.

The `routerid` definition statement defines the address that will be used to identify this router for OSPF. Routers have more than one network interface and therefore more than one IP address. To ensure that the correct address is used in the OSPF link-state advertisements, specifically define the OSPF `routerid`.

The next statement is a protocol statement that enables RIPv2. Except for two differences, it is identical to the statement used earlier to enable RIPv2 for the host. The first difference is that the router will advertise RIPv2 routes, as indicated by the `broadcast` keyword. The second difference is that you define the RIP metric used to advertise routes learned from other protocols, which can be any valid RIP metric value. This router learns routes from OSPF that do not have a valid RIP metric. The `defaultmetric` clause tells `gated` to use a cost of 5 to advertise those routes in RIP updates. This clause is required to make the routes learn from OSPF available to the RIPv2 system. Without it, the OSPF routes are considered "unreachable" by the RIPv2 systems.

The final protocol statement in the sample `gated.conf` file enables OSPF. Remember that OSPF divides the autonomous system into areas. Every OSPF router must connect to some area. As mentioned earlier, the area that interconnects all other areas within the routing domain is called the backbone area. This router connects to the backbone area as indicated by the keyword `backbone`. If the router was not connected to the backbone, the area it was connected to would be defined here. For example: `area 1`. The number that identifies the area is the number that you define when you design the area hierarchy of your OSPF routing domain.

The OSPF protocol is also using simple password authentication, as indicated by the `authtype simple` ; clause. The `interface` clause identifies the interface over which OSPF runs and the protocol characteristics related to that interface. The `authkey "UcantrustME"` ; clause defines the password used to authenticate OSPF routers in this area.

The `priority 5 ;` clause defines the priority number this system uses when the area elects a designated router. The larger the priority number, the less likely the router will be elected the designated router. Give your most powerful router the lowest priority number.

A designated router is used to reduce the size of the link-state database and thus the complexity of calculating the Dijkstra graph of the area. The designated router treats all other routers in the area as neighbors, but all other routers treat only the designated router as a neighbor.

To understand how this reduces the size of the link-state database, think of a network of five routers. Without a designated router, all five routers advertise four neighbors for a total of 20 neighbors in the database. With a designated router, only that router advertises four neighbors. The other four routers advertise one neighbor for a total of eight neighbors in the database.

A simple OSPF configuration, such as the one shown in the example above, should be adequate for any Linux system that needs to run OSPF. Much of the configuration information will come from the network designer who defines your routing hierarchy. The area you connect to, the type of authentication used, the authentication password, and the priority number of your system are all design decisions that will be made before your network even begins to run OSPF.

As a final example of running `gated`, let's configure a Linux system to run an exterior gateway protocol.

Running BGP

In this section, a router is configured to connect the OSPF backbone area described above to an external autonomous system using BGP. The configuration for this router is:

```
# Defines our AS number for BGP
autonomoussystem 249;


# Defines the OSPF router id
routerid 172.16.1.5;


# Disable RIP
rip no;


# Enable BGP
```

```
bgp yes {
   preference 50 ;
   group type external peeras 164 {
        peer 26.6.0.103 ;
        peer 26.20.0.72 ;
        };
};


# Enable OSPF; subnet 1 is the backbone area;
# use password authentication.
ospf yes {
     backbone {
         authtype simple ;
         interface 172.16.1.5 {
             priority 10 ;
             authkey "UcantrustME" ;
             } ;
          } ;
};


# Announce routes learned from OSPF and route
# to directly connected network via BGP tp AS 164
export proto bgp as 164 {
     proto direct ;
     proto ospf ;
};


# Announce routes learned via BGP from
# AS number 164 to our OSPF area.
```

```
export proto ospfase type 2  {
     proto bgp as 164  {
          all ;
          };
     };
```

BGP exchanges routing information between autonomous systems. The definition statements at the beginning of this file define the autonomous system number (ASN) for BGP and the router identifier for OSPF. The `autonomoussystem` statement says that the ASN of our autonomous system is 249. The ASN is required for BGP.

> **NOTE**   To exchange routing data between official routing domains, you need an official ASN; you can't just make one up, and you can't use the ones in this example— they are the official ASNs of two governemnt networks I work on. For information on filing the paperwork to apply for your own official ASN, go to www.iana.org and follow the links to the appropriate registry for your part of the world. If you use BGP to link together independent networks within a single autonomous system, and the routing data stay within that autonomous system, use one of the ASN numbers reserved for private use. The numbers reserved for private use are 64512 to 65534.

The first protocol statement in the sample configuration disables RIP. This router does not run RIP. On one side it connects to the OSPF backbone area, and on the other side it connects to an external routing domain with BGP.

The second protocol statement enables OSPF. There is nothing new here; it looks almost identical to the OSPF protocol statement you have already seen. Notice, however, that I have given this router a higher priority number. Given the work it will be doing to handle BGP, I don't want it also to have the burden of being the designated router for OSPF.

The next protocol statement enables BGP. For purposes of illustration, I set the preference for routes learned from BGP to 50. Normally, they have a preference of 170. It's unlikely you would ever want to make routes learned from an external domain this highly preferred, but this illustrates that the default preferences defined by `gated` can be overridden in the configuration file.

The `group` clause defines the characteristics of a group of BGP peers. The IP address of each peer is identified within the `group` clause by a `peer` clause.

One of the characteristics defined by the `group` clause is the type of BGP session to establish with the peers. In the example, BGP is used as a classic exterior gateway protocol, thus the `type external` parameter. BGP can be used for other purposes. As noted in the discussion of ASN numbers, it is possible to use BGP to distribute routes within a routing domain instead of between routing domains. When it is used in this way, BGP is referred to as *internal BGP* (IBGP). Here is the `group` clause from the sample file:

```
group type external peeras 164
```

This says that BGP will run as an exterior routing protocol and that the ASN of the external autonomous system with which it will communicate is 164.

On the other hand, assume that you have a large, far-flung enterprise internet. Within that enterprise network are several networks that run OSPF as an interior routing protocol and have their own independent connections to the global Internet. You could use internal BGP to move routing information between the individual networks that make up our enterprise network. An example of the `group` statement for such a configuration is:

```
group type igp peeras 64550 proto ospf
```

This says that BGP will run as an internal gateway protocol, that the ASN 64550 will be used within your enterprise network, and that the routers you are exchanging updates with learn their routes through OSPF.

The sample configuration concludes with two control statements: the `export` statements that define the routing policy. The first statement defines which internal routes are advertised to the external world. It tells `gated` to export to the autonomous system identified by ASN 164 all direct routes and all routes that the local router learns from OSPF.

The final `export` statement defines the routes that `gated` accepts from the external world and advertises on the internal network. The first line of this statement is:

```
export proto ospfase type 2
```

This tells `gated` to advertise the routes via the OSPF protocol as autonomous system external (ASE) routes, which means the routes are clearly marked as routes learned from an external source. The `type 2` parameter indicates that the routes come from a protocol that does not use a metric that is directly comparable to the OSPF metric. The alternative is `type 1`, which means that the metrics are directly comparable. However, BGP is a path-vector protocol, not a link-state protocol, and its metrics are not directly comparable to those used by OSPF. You know the routes were learned from BGP by looking at the rest of the export statement:

```
proto bgp as 164 {
    all ;
    }
```

This says that the routes being exported were received via BGP and that they come from the autonomous routing domain identified by ASN 164. Furthermore, the keyword `all` in this clause says that `gated` should accept all routes from that autonomous system. Instead of the keyword `all`, you can use specific addresses to accept only specific routes or the keyword `restrict` to block all routes.

> **NOTE** These discussions of OSPF and BGP show that routing can be a very complex topic. If you need to use a routing protocol that is more complicated than RIPv2, read more about it and design your routing architecture before you try to configure a system. I suggest *Internet Routing Architectures* by Bassam Halabi (Cisco, 1999) and *IP Routing Fundamentals* by Mark Sportack (Cisco, 1999) for additional information about routing protocols.

Network Address Translation

Network Address Translation (NAT) is an extension of routing that allows the router to modify the addresses in the packets it forwards. Traditional routers examine addresses, but they don't change them. NAT boxes convert the IP addresses used on the local network to "official" IP addresses. This allows you to use a private network number and still have Internet access. The private network numbers defined in RFC 1918 are:

- Network 10.0.0.0
- Networks 172.16.0.0 to 172.31.0.0 (Network 172.16.0.0 is used for the examples in this book)
- Networks 192.168.0.0 to 192.168.255.0

Private network numbers are popular, and for some good reasons:

- Using a private network number reduces paperwork. You don't have to ask anyone's permission to use these addresses. No applications, no fees. Just do it.
- The addresses are yours. If you change ISPs, there is no need to renumber the hosts on the network. You may need to change the configuration of the NAT box, but that is probably easier than changing the configuration of all of your desktop systems.
- You conserve IP addresses. Having more addresses than you really need can make designing a network much easier, but you don't want more than you need if you're wasting valuable IP addresses. When you use private addresses, you don't waste any IP addresses. These addresses are re-useable, and the same addresses you're using are probably being used by dozens of other networks around the world.
- Private IP addresses eliminate address spoofing. *Spoofing* is a security attack in which someone at a remote location pretends to be on your local network by using

one of your network addresses. These addresses cannot be forwarded through the Internet, so spoofing one of these addresses won't do the attacker much good.

Private network numbers are explicitly defined for private use. They cannot be routed through the Internet, because any number of private networks might be using the same addresses. Before packets originating from a host that uses a private IP address can be forwarded to an external network, the source address in the packet must be converted to a valid Internet address.

Weigh all of the factors before you decide to use NAT. Network address translation has some problems:

- It places additional overhead on the router, which reduces the router's performance.
- It doesn't work well with all protocols. TCP/IP protocols were not designed with NAT in mind.
- It interferes with end-to-end authentication schemes that authenticate the source address.

Address translation is implemented in two ways: as a NAT box or as a proxy server. A *NAT box* is a router that has a group of valid addresses available. It maps the addresses from the local network to the addresses in its address pool. A *proxy server* is a firewall that maps all of the addresses from the local network to its own address and differentiates the systems by using port numbers. A NAT box does a many-to-many mapping, and a proxy server does a many-to-one mapping, but both perform the same service. Linux implements IP address translation as a proxy server.

Configuring a Linux Proxy Server

Linux includes IP address translation as part of the firewall software that comes with the system. Firewalls and how to configure a Linux server as a firewall are discussed in Chapter 14, *Security*. This chapter looks at the one aspect of the firewall software that allows you to translate addresses.

Despite the fact that address translation is included in the firewall software, it is not specifically a security feature. A very common use for address translation is to connect a small network to the Internet. Assume that you have a small office network that connects to the Internet through a local ISP. Further, assume that the ISP assigns the office only one IP address even though you have four computers on the your network. Using a Linux proxy server, all four computers can communicate with the Internet with only one valid IP address.

To use a Linux system as a proxy server, it must be configured to forward packets like a router, and several features must be configured in the kernel. The kernel must be configured for the firewall software (CONFIG_IP_FORWARD) and (CONFIG_FIREWALL), and it must be configured for address translation (CONFIG_IP_MASQUERADE). These things are kernel configuration options that may already be enabled for your kernel.

NOTE Refer to Chapter 15 for a description of how to configure and compile the kernel.

Once the proxy service is enabled in the Linux kernel, it can be configured using the ipchains command.

Address Masquerading

The IP firewall administration (ipchains) command is used to configure and manage a Linux firewall. (The command is used for exactly that purpose in Chapter 14.) You can also use it to configure the address translation features of a Linux proxy server.

Assume the address of the small office network that you want to connect through a proxy server is 192.168.16.0. Placing these three ipchains commands in the rc.local startup script of the proxy server will do the job:

```
# ipchains -P forward DENY
# ipchains -A forward -p tcp -s 198.168.16.0/24 -j MASQ
# ipchains -A forward -p udp -s 198.168.16.0/24 -j MASQ
```

The first line defines the default policy of the proxy server. The –P option says this is the default policy for an address filter rule chain, and forward tells us the name of the rule chain. The forward rule chain is the set of rules used to process packets being forwarded through the proxy server. The policy specified by the keyword DENY is that all packets will be blocked at the firewall unless they are specifically permitted by some other filter rule. This rule prevents having packets leak from the local network, which uses the private network address 192.168.16.0, onto the Internet. Sending packets that have private network addresses on the network violates Internet standards.

The second line adds (–A) a filter rule to the forward rule chain. This rule says that TCP packets (–p tcp) with a source address from network 192.168.16.0 (–S 192.168.16.0/24) should be sent to the MASQ code (-j MASQ) for processing. MASQ does the address translation. The name MASQ comes from the fact that address translation is also called *IP masquerading*. MASQ causes the firewall to act as a proxy server by replacing the source address on outbound packets with its the server's IP address.

The third line does exactly the same thing for UDP packets (–p udp) that the second line does for TCP packets.

Once the rules are installed, the proxy server fills the role of a router for the small network: It forwards packets and connects the network to the outside world. The performance of a proxy server limits its use to small networks, but in appropriate situations, it can be invaluable.

Final Words

This chapter concludes the Internet server operations part of this book. All of the services needed for an Internet server have been covered: remote login, file transfer, sendmail, Web service, and routing.

The next chapter begins Part Three, *Departmental Server Operations*, where the services needed on a departmental server are examined. To begin, Chapter 10 covers the BOOTP and DHCP servers that simplify the configuration of desktop computers.

Routing Servers

I worked on a network that had 12 local Novell NetWare networks among a total of 50 subnets. All of the other subnets were native TCP/IP networks and so was the organization's backbone network. The Novell servers acted as TCP/IP routers connecting the NetWare networks to the TCP/IP backbone.

The company decided to replace the aging Novell servers with new departmental servers. However, some of the divisions that used Novell—Personnel and Accounting, in particular—resisted the idea of having their data flow across the same building network as that used by other less sensitive departments.

A departmental server that could act as a router was the solution, because data directed to computers within the department stay on the departmental network, and only packets addressed to the outside world are forwarded to the shared network. Linux was selected for the job because it makes a perfect departmental server and can act as a router.

The routing configuration for these systems was very simple. Each server had two Ethernet cards installed—one connected to each network. IP forwarding was enabled in each system, and a simple, static routing table was created that contained the necessary routes for each network interface and a default route pointing to the default router on the shared network. These simple Linux routers used the Internet features described in this part of the book, as well as the departmental server features that are described in the next chapter, to meet the company's needs.

24seven **CASE STUDY**

Part 3

Departmental Server Operations

Topics Covered:

- Configuring a DHCP server, client, and relay agent
- Understanding the BootP service
- Understanding Linux file permissions
- Configuring an NFS server and client
- Using mount, fstab, and automounter to access file systems
- Understanding NetBIOS
- Configuring a NetBIOS SMB server or client with Samba
- Installing, configuring, and sharing printers
- Creating a mailbox server with POP or IMAP
- Controlling spam e-mail
- Filtering e-mail with procmail

10

Desktop Configuration Servers

TCP/IP is able to link the world together into a global Internet because it does not depend on any one physical network technology. It can run over the modem attached to a PC or over the fiber-optic network attached to a super computer. It does this by creating a logical network on top of the physical networks that is independent of the specific characteristic of any one network.

However, this flexibility comes at the price of complexity. It is more difficult to configure a computer to run TCP/IP than it is to configure it for some other networks.

You're a technical person—that's why you run the network. Configuring TCP/IP may seem very simple to you, but it can be a daunting task for the average user setting up a PC. If your network is small, you can manually configure all of the desktop systems yourself. On a large network, manual configuration becomes an impossible task. Even on a small network, fixing the configuration every time a user upgrades is a thankless and boring job. The solution is the topic of this chapter: creating a server that does this job for you.

Understanding Configuration Protocols

Protocol developers have worked to reduce the burden of manual system configuring for a long time. Some of the documents that define the configuration protocols are 15 years old. Surprisingly, these protocols have only come into widespread use in the past few years. This is partly because the early users of the Internet were technical people who liked to configure their own systems and partly because of the tremendous growth in the number of systems running TCP/IP that has occurred in recent years. Microsoft also deserves some credit for pushing hard to get people to use *Dynamic Host Configuration Protocol* (DHCP), which is the best of the configuration protocols. This section examines DHCP as well as the other configuration protocols used to configure desktop systems.

Bootstrap Protocol

Bootstrap Protocol (BootP) was the first comprehensive configuration protocol. It can provide all of the information commonly used to configure TCP/IP—from the client's IP address to what print server the client should use. The BootP protocol is designed to deliver this information to the client, even though the client doesn't have an IP address.

Here's how it works. The BootP client broadcasts a BOOTREQUEST packet to UDP port 67 using a special IP broadcast address of 255.255.255.255 that is called the *limited broadcast address*. The broadcast address assigned in Chapter 4, *The Network Interface*, with the ifconfig command was made up of the network address with a host field of all ones, for example 172.16.55.255. Clearly, a BootP client that doesn't know the IP network address couldn't use such a broadcast address, which is why the limited broadcast address is used.

> **NOTE** Unless specially configured to do so, routers do not forward the limited broadcast address. For this reason, configuration servers are traditionally departmental servers, with one server placed on each subnet.

The client puts all of the information it knows about itself in the BOOTREQUEST packet, which might only be its Physical layer address. When a BootP server receives a packet on port 67, it creates a BOOTREPLY packet by filling in as much of the missing configuration information as it can. The server then broadcasts the packet back to the network using UDP port 68. The client listens on port 68. When it receives a packet on the port that contains its Physical-layer address, it uses the information from the packet to configure TCP/IP.

Dynamic Host Configuration Protocol

BootP is simple and effective. So effective, in fact, that it became the basis for Dynamic Host Configuration Protocol. DHCP operates over the same UDP ports, 67 and 68, as BootP. It provides all of the services of BootP as well as some important extensions.

DHCP is designed to provide all possible TCP/IP configuration parameters to its clients. DHCP includes every parameter that was defined in the "Requirements for

Internet Hosts" RFC, which means that everything necessary for TCP/IP can be configured from the DHCP server. There is absolutely no reason to go to the user's desktop to configure TCP/IP.

The other, and probably more important, extension is that DHCP permits IP addresses to be dynamically assigned. Manually configuring a system with `ifconfig` permanently assigns an address to the interface. The address assigned to a host through BootP is also a permanent assignment. Both of these techniques are *static*—the address is permanently assigned and cannot be used for any other host. With DHCP, an address is "leased" to the host for a specific period of time. When the time expires, the host must either renew the lease or return the address to the server so that it can be assigned to another system.

The advantages of dynamic address assignment are:

- You don't need to create a custom configuration for each host. On a BootP server, you must create a configuration for every client, because you are responsible for assigning each system a unique IP address. With a DHCP server, the server is responsible for the address assignments. You'll see examples of both of these when you configure a DHCP server and a BootP server later in this chapter.

- You make more effective use of scarce IP addresses. When a salesperson is out on the road for a week, the PC sitting on his desk is not wasting an IP address.

Dynamic address assignment, like everything else, is not perfect. Servers cannot get their addresses from DHCP. DNS does not know about addresses that are assigned through DHCP, which means that remote computers cannot look up the address of a system that gets its address from DHCP. Therefore, a system using a dynamically assigned address cannot offer services to other systems.

So DHCP does have its shortcomings, but they're not fatal flaws. First, skilled technical people who don't have any trouble doing a TCP/IP configuration run most servers. Second, the number of servers on your network is small compared to the total number of systems, and therefore the burden of server configuration is correspondingly small. Finally, the bulk of the systems on your network are probably PCs running Microsoft Windows. These systems can't offer TCP/IP services to remote users, so no one has to look up the IP address of one of these systems. Windows clients are perfect candidates for dynamic address assignment.

People are working on the problem of coordinating addresses between DHCP and DNS. The next version of BIND should have an implementation of *Dynamic DNS*, which allows DHCP servers to update the DNS database information to reflect dynamic address assignments. Allowing remote systems to change DNS is a security concern. For this reason, the work on Dynamic DNS is progressing in a slow and careful manner. Meanwhile,

DHCP works fine for most of your systems and can dramatically decrease your configuration workload.

Reverse Address Resolution Protocol

Before leaving the topic of configuration protocols, I should quickly mention *Reverse Address Resolution Protocol* (RARP). As the name implies, it is the reverse of ARP. Instead of asking for an Ethernet address in response to an IP addresses, this protocol broadcasts an Ethernet address and asks for an IP address in response.

A RARP server uses the /etc/ethers file to map Ethernet addresses to IP addresses. It then sends the IP address from the ethers file to the client system. A sample /etc/ethers file is shown here:

```
00:00:C0:4F:3E:DD bluejay
00:10:4B:87:D4:A8 duck
08:00:20:82:D5:1D raven
00:00:0C:43:8D:FB osprey
```

Each line in the file contains an Ethernet address followed by a host name or IP address. Host names are most commonly used, but they must be valid names that map to IP addresses.

I mention this protocol because the nsswitch.conf file covered in Chapter 6, *Linux Name Services*, includes /etc/ethers as a part of the NIS service, which might make you curious about it. However, you should *not* use RARP. RARP only provides the client with an IP address. No other configuration information is provided. Much better configuration servers are available as part of Linux, including DHCP, which is the right configuration server for your network.

Installing the DHCP Server

Many Linux distributions include the DHCP daemon (dhcpd). Refer to Table 1.3 and you'll see it listed among the services offered in Red Hat 6. dhcpd is the server side of DHCP and is only required on the DHCP server. The clients do not run dhcpd.

NOTE   Information on configuring a DHCP client is provided later in the chapter.

Use linuxconf or tksysv to ensure that the DHCP daemon is started at boot time. If these programs do not list dhcpd as one of the available services, install the DHCP package using the rpm command or gnorpm (the X Windows tool used with Red Hat 6 for installing RPM software). If you use gnorpm, DHCP can be found in the System Environment/ Daemons path on Red Hat 6 systems.

NOTE For an example of using gnorpm to install a software package, see the "Installing gated" section in Chapter 9, *Network Gateway Services*.

Of course, it is possible that your Linux system does not come with the DHCP software or that you want a more recent version than the one that comes with your system. In either case, you can download and compile dhcpd yourself.

Compiling dhcpd

The source code for dhcpd is available at www.isc.org or via anonymous FTP at ftp.isc.org/isc/dhcp. The latest production release at the time of this writing is dhcp-2.0. (Red Hat 6 includes dhcp-2.0b1p6-6.) The latest beta release is dhcp-3 .0b1p10, which is not widely used for production. To upgrade to a newer release, download and use tar to extract the file:

```
# cd /usr/local/src
# ftp ftp.isc.org
Connected to isrv4.pa.vix.com.
220 isrv4.pa.vix.com FTP server July 14 1999 ready.
Name (ftp.isc.org:craig): anonymous
331 Guest login ok, send your complete e-mail address as password.
Password:
230 Guest login ok, access restrictions apply.
ftp> get isc/dhcp/dhcp-2.0.tar.gz
local: dhcp-2.0.tar.gz remote: dhcp-2.0.tar.gz
200 PORT command successful.
150 Opening BINARY mode data connection for
    dhcp-2.0.tar.gz (284789 bytes)
226 Transfer complete.
284789 bytes received in 21.6 secs (13 Kbytes/sec)
ftp> quit
221 Goodbye.
# tar -zxvf dhcp-2.0.tar.gz
```

Change to the newly created directory, dhcp-2.0 in the example, and run the configure script located there. configure determines the type of system you're running and creates the correct Makefile for that system.

Next, type **make** to compile the daemon:

```
# cd dhcp-2.0
# ./configure
System Type: linux
# make
```

TIP On Linux systems, dhcpd should compile without errors. Of course, things may change with future releases. If you get errors, send mail to the dhcp-server @fugue.com mailing list, describing your configuration and the exact problem you have. The list is read by most of the people using dhcpd, and someone may have already solved your problem. To join the mailing list, go to www.fugue.com/ dhcp/lists and fill out the "Add Me" form.

Finally, copy the daemon and the man pages to the correct directories with the make install command. Before running make install, you may want to remove the old version of dhcpd from the system. On a Caldera 1.3 system using dhcpd-1.0p12, enter **rpm –uninstall dhcpd-1.0p12** to remove it.

To remove an old package on a Red Hat 6 system, run gnorpm. In the gnorpm window, open the System Environment and the Daemons folders, highlight dhcp, and click Uninstall (see Figure 10.1).

Figure 10.1 Uninstalling dhcp with gnorpm

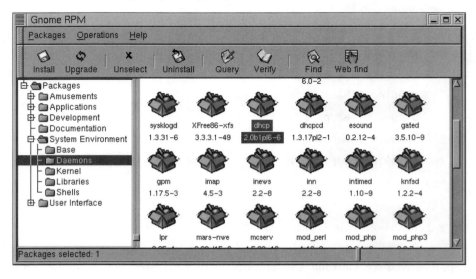

Customizing dhcpd for Linux

Given the straightforward nature of compiling dhcpd for Linux, you may be wondering why it deserves its own section in this chapter. Well, that's because it's not as simple as it looks. Installing dhcpd may not be all that is required to get it running on your Linux system. There are a few potential problems that need to be addressed by system-specific configurations.

If you provide service to Microsoft Windows DHCP clients, you may encounter problems with the limited broadcast address. If it appears that Microsoft Windows clients do not see DHCP messages from the server while other types of clients do, you need to define a specific route for the limited broadcast address on your Linux server. To do so, first add the name all-ones to the /etc/hosts table:

```
255.255.255.255 all-ones
```

Then add a route for the limited broadcast address:

```
route add -host all-ones dev eth0
```

To re-install the special route after each boot, add the route statement to the rc.local startup script.

> **NOTE** For the versions of the kernel that require it, Caldera and Red Hat already have the code to add the limited broadcast route in the /etc/rc.d/init.d/dhcpd script used to start dhcpd.

In addition to the limited broadcast problem, there are some problems that relate to specific Linux kernels.

Multiple network interfaces Use a Linux kernel that is version 2.0.31 or higher if you have more than one network interface. dhcpd cannot use multiple interfaces with older Linux kernels.

SO_ATTACH_FILTER undeclared This error may occur when compiling dhcpd under Linux 2.2. If it occurs, the symbolic link /usr/include/asm is broken. That link should point to the Linux asm headers. For example, on our Red Hat system, the link is:

```
lrwxrwxrwx 1 root root 26 Apr 9 18:23 asm -> ../src/linux/include/
asm
```

Protocol not configured To run under Linux 2.1 and 2.2, dhcpd needs the CONFIG_PACKET and CONF_FILTER options configured in the kernel. If the message "Set CONFIG_PACKET=y and CONFIG_FILTER=y in your kernel configuration" is displayed during the dhcpd build, you need to reconfigure the kernel and enable these options. See Chapter 15, *Troubleshooting*, for information on configuring the kernel.

IP BootP agent Linux 2.1 will run dhcpd only if the BootP agent is enabled. (The BootP agent is part of dhcpd.) Check to see if /proc/sys/net/ipv4/ip_bootp_agent exists. If it does, check to see if it contains a 1. If it doesn't exist or it doesn't contain a 1, insert the following line into the rc.local startup script to write a 1 to the ip_bootp_agent file:

```
echo 1 > /proc/sys/net/ipv4/ip_bootp_agent
```

As the Linux kernel versions change and new releases of dhcpd are issued, the list of problems will change. The information needed to complete the installation is covered in the README file that comes with the dhcpd distribution. Read it carefully before you try to run dhcpd.

Initializing the dhcpd.leases File

dhcpd stores a database of the address leases it has assigned in the dhcpd.leases file. The file must exist for dhcpd to boot. When the server is first installed, create an empty dhcpd.leases file to ensure that the daemon starts correctly.

dhcpd writes database entries into the file as ASCII text. If you're curious, you can view the file to see what leases have been assigned. Entries in the file have the following format:

```
lease address {statements}
```

Each lease begins with the keyword lease and the IP address that is assigned by the lease. This is followed by a group of statements that define the characteristics of the lease. Possible values that might appear in the list of statements are:

start *date* Defines the start time of the lease. *date* contains the year, month, day, hour, minute, and second.

end *date* Defines the time when the lease will end. *date* contains the year, month, day, hour, minute, and second.

hardware ethernet *address* Specifies the client's Ethernet address.

uid *client-identifier* Specifies the client's DHCP identifier if one was used by the client when it obtained the lease.

client-hostname "*name*" Specifies the client's host name if the client provided one using the client-hostname option when it requested an address.

hostname "*name*" Specifies the host name of a Microsoft Windows client that provided a host name using the hostname option when it requested an address.

abandoned Identifies this as an abandoned lease. If the server has trouble assigning an address, it marks it "abandoned" until it runs short of available addresses and needs to try this one again.

You don't need to be concerned about these commands. When you create the file, you create it empty. Once you create it, you can forget about it, since dhcpd maintains the file. The file that does require your input, however, is the dhcpd.conf file used to configure the server.

Configuring the DHCP Server

Once dhcpd is installed, it must be configured. The DHCP daemon is configured through the dhcpd.conf file. The file can contain an extensive list of configuration commands that provide direction to the server and configuration information to the clients.

A DHCP server provides service to individual hosts through static address assignment and to entire subnets of hosts through dynamic address assignment. The dhcpd configuration language includes host and subnet statements that identify the systems being serviced.

A host statement might contain the following:

```
host osprey {
    hardware ethernet 00:00:0C:43:8D:FB ;
    fixed-address 172.16.70.8 ; }
```

This statement defines the host name, Ethernet address, and IP address of the client. When configured in this way, dhcpd provides the same service as a BootP server. It matches the client's Ethernet address against the configuration entry and returns a static IP address to the client.

The format of the subnet statement is:

```
subnet 172.16.70.0 netmask 255.255.255.0 {
    range 172.16.70.100 172.16.70.250 ; }
```

The subnet statement declares that the system is providing DHCP service to network 172.16.70.0. Furthermore, it says that the server is providing dynamic addressing and that the range of addresses available for dynamic allocation is from 172.16.70.100 to 172.16.70.250. The range clause defines the scope of addresses available for dynamic assignment. It is always associated with a subnet statement, and the range of addresses defined in the clause must fall within the address space of the subnet.

Controlling Server and Protocol Operations

Configuration parameters and options can be associated with individual host and subnet statements. The group statement can be used to apply parameters and options to a group of host or subnet statements. Additionally, configuration parameters and options can be specified that apply to every system and network defined in the configuration file. With this flexibility, the dhcpd configuration language allows you create every conceivable configuration.

The configuration language includes several things that control the operation of the DHCP server and the DHCP protocol. First are the allow and deny statements that control how dhcpd handles certain client requests. Each statement begins with either the command allow or deny followed by a keyword that describes the request that is being allowed or denied. The three possible keywords are:

unknown-clients Configuration requests from clients for which the server does not have a specific host entry can be allowed or denied. By default, unknown clients are allowed. If they are denied, some of the dynamic capabilities of DHCP are lost.

bootp The server can be directed to handle configuration requests from BootP clients or to ignore them. By default, BootP clients are allowed so that all clients, BootP and DHCP, can be handled by a single server.

booting The deny booting statement is used within a host statement to tell the server that it should not handle configuration requests from a specific client. The default is to handle a client's configuration request, which means that it is not necessary to use the allow booting statement.

The authoritative or not authoritative statements tell the server whether or not the configuration information it has is known to be accurate. By default, a DHCP server is authoritative, and the configuration information it provides is accurate. If for some reason a DHCP server is configured by someone who does not have authority over the network configuration, the not authoritative statement can be used to limit the amount of authority the server asserts over the clients. Frankly, I think that only authoritative DHCP servers should be set up—and only by the network administrator.

In addition to the various statements described above, there are several configuration parameters that control server and protocol operation. These parameters are:

always-reply-rfc1048 *flag* Some older BootP devices may only be able to accept responses formatted according to RFC 1048. If that is the case, use this option in a host statement to send responses to a specific BootP client in the old format.

boot-unknown-clients *flag* If *flag* is false, only clients that have a host statement in the configuration file are assigned addresses. By default, *flag* is true, and addresses are dynamically assigned to any client on a valid subnet.

default-lease-time *seconds* Defines the length of time given an address lease if the client does not request a specific lease length.

dynamic-bootp-lease-cutoff *date* Defines a termination date for addresses assigned to BootP clients. By default, dhcpd assigns permanent addresses to BootP clients. This parameter changes that behavior, but it cannot change the way that BootP clients work. If the lease runs out, a BootP client will not know that its address is invalid.

dynamic-bootp-lease-length *seconds* Defines the maximum length of an address lease for a BootP client. Because BootP clients do not renew address leases, a client that does not boot frequently enough will lose its lease.

filename "*file*" Defines the path name of the boot file for diskless clients.

fixed-address *address*[, *address*...] Assigns a permanent IP address to a host as part of a host statement. More than one address can be supplied for a client that boots on more than one subnet.

get-lease-hostnames *flag* If *flag* is true, dhcpd does a reverse lookup for every dynamically-assigned address and sends the host name it gets from DNS to the client. This process can add lots of overhead for the server on a big network. By default, *flag* is false, and no lookups are done.

hardware ethernet *address* Defines the client's Ethernet address. The hardware parameter must be part of a host statement, which uses the Ethernet address to tie the host information to a specific client. The Ethernet address is the only way for a BootP client to be recognized. DHCP clients can use other values in addition to the Ethernet address to identify themselves.

max-lease-time *seconds* Defines the maximum length of a lease, regardless of the lease length requested by the client.

next-server *name* Defines the host name of the server from which the boot file is to be loaded. This is only significant for diskless devices that boot from a server.

range [dynamic-bootp] *low-address* [*high-address*] Defines the scope of addresses available for dynamic assignment. The argument dynamic-bootp tells dhcpd to assign dynamic addresses to BootP clients as well as DHCP clients. Because BootP clients do not understand address leases, they are normally not given dynamic addresses.

Departmental
Server Operations

PART 3

`server-identifier` Defines the IP address of the server that is sent to clients. By default, the address of the server's network interface is used. Only set this value if, for some reason, the server gets the wrong address from its configuration.

`server-name "name"` Defines the host name of the DHCP server.

`use-host-decl-names flag` Tells dhcpd to send the name provided on the host statement to the client as its host name.

`use-lease-addr-for-default-route flag` Sends the client its own address as the default route instead of sending the true default route. This forces the client to use ARP for all addresses, which means that the real router must be configured as a proxy ARP server.

These statements and parameters provide configuration information to the server, defining how the server operates. However, most of the information in the configuration file is information for the client. The next section looks at the configuration options that provide configuration information to the clients.

dhcpd Configuration Options

The dhcpd option statements cover all DHCP configuration options defined in the RFCs. Furthermore, any new option that might be defined in the future can be included in the dhcpd configuration by using the decimal option code assigned to it in the RFC that describes the option. An option name in the form option-*nnn*—where *nnn* is the decimal option code—can be used to add any new option to the dhcpd.conf file. For example, assume that you want to assign the string "yes" to a new DHCP configuration option that has an option code of 142. You could add the following to your configuration file:

```
option option-142 "yes"
```

The statement begins with the keyword option, which is followed by the name of the option and the value assigned to the option. In the example, the name is option-142, and the value is yes.

The standard options are listed below. In an attempt to make this huge list more manageable, I divided it into six sections: Basic Options, Tuning Options, Routing Options, NetBIOS Options, Diskless Client Options, and Other Server Options.

Basic Options

The basic options define such things as the address, the subnet mask, and the default router. The following list also includes the servers that I think you are most likely to use, such as DNS servers and print servers.

`option broadcast-address address` Defines the broadcast address.

`option dhcp-client-identifier string` Defines the string used to identify DHCP clients in lieu of the hardware address.

option `domain-name` *domain* Defines the domain name.

option `domain-name-servers` *address-list* Lists the addresses of the DNS name servers.

option `host-name` *host* Defines the client's host name.

option `lpr-servers` *address-list* Lists the addresses of the print servers.

option `nntp-server` *address-list* Lists the addresses of the Network News Transfer Protocol (NNTP) servers. These are the servers from which the client gets news service.

option `ntp-servers` *address-list* Lists the addresses of the Network Time Protocol (NTP) servers.

option `pop-server` *address-list* Lists the addresses of the POP3 mailbox servers.

option `routers` *address-list* Defines the default router.

option `smtp-server` *address-list* Lists the addresses of the SMTP e-mail servers.

option `subnet-mask` *mask* Defines the subnet mask. If this option is not defined, the network mask from the `subnet` statement is used.

option `time-offset` *seconds* Defines the offset from Coordinated Universal Time of this time zone.

Tuning Options

The following list identifies the options that are used to tune the TCP/IP protocol.

option `all-subnets-local` 0 | 1 Specifies if all subnets use the same MTU. 1 means that they all do, and 0 means that some subnets have smaller MTUs.

option `arp-cache-timeout` *seconds* Defines how long entries are cached by ARP.

option `default-ip-ttl` *ttl* Defines the default time-to-live (TTL) for outgoing datagrams. Possible values are 1 to 255.

option `default-tcp-ttl` *ttl* Defines the default TTL value for TCP segments. Possible values are 1 to 255.

option `ieee802-3-encapsulation` 0 | 1 0 tells the client to use Ethernet II (DIX) Ethernet encapsulation, and 1 tells the client to use IEEE 802.3 encapsulation.

option `interface-mtu` *bytes* Defines the Maximum Transmission Unit.

option `mask-supplier` 0 | 1 Specifies if the client should respond to ICMP subnet mask requests. 0 means no, and 1 means yes. Use 0; don't configure clients to respond to subnet mask requests.

option `max-dgram-reassembly` *bytes*   Defines the largest datagram the client must reassemble. It cannot be less than 576 bytes.

option `path-mtu-aging-timeout` *seconds*   Sets the number of seconds for timing out RFC 1191 Path MTU values.

option `path-mtu-plateau-table` *bytes*[, ...]   Defines a table of MTU sizes for RFC 1191 Path MTU Discovery. The minimum MTU value is 68.

option `perform-mask-discovery` 0 | 1   0 enables ICMP mask discovery, and 1 disables it. Because the DHCP server provides the correct subnet mask, ICMP mask discovery is rarely used on networks that have a DHCP server.

option `tcp-keepalive-garbage` 0 | 1   Specifies if the TCP keepalive messages should include an octet of garbage for compatibility with older implementations. 0 means don't send a garbage octet, and 1 means send it. Keepalives are generally discouraged.

option `tcp-keepalive-interval` *seconds*   Defines the number of seconds TCP should wait before sending a keepalive message. Zero (0) means that TCP should not generate keepalive messages. Keepalive messages are generally discouraged.

option `trailer-encapsulation` 0 | 1   0 means the client should not use trailer encapsulation, and 1 means the client should use trailer encapsulation.

Routing Options

The following options all relate to routing. Except for defining the default route, everything related to routing is covered here. The default route is listed under "Basic Options."

option `ip-forwarding` 0 | 1   0 tells the client to disable IP forwarding, and 1 says to enable it.

option `non-local-source-routing` 0 | 1   0 tells the client to disable non-local source routing, and 1 says to enable it. 0 is more secure. Source routes are a potential security problem that can allow intruders to route data off of the local network.

option `policy-filter` *address mask*[, ...]   Lists the only valid destination/mask pairs for incoming source routes. Any source-routed datagram whose next-hop address does not match one of the filters is discarded by the client.

option `router-discovery` 0 | 1   1 means the client should locate routers with the RFC 1256 Router Discovery mechanism, and 0 means it shouldn't. Because the DHCP server provides the correct list of routers, router discovery is rarely used on networks that have a DHCP server.

option `router-solicitation-address` *address*   Defines the address to which the client should send RFC 1256 Router Discovery requests.

option `static-routes` *destination gateway*[,...]   Defines a lists of static routes for the client.

NetBIOS Options

The following options configure NetBIOS over TCP/IP.

`option netbios-dd-server` *address-list* Lists the addresses of the NetBIOS datagram distribution servers (NBDDs).

`option netbios-name-servers` *address-list* Lists the IP addresses of the NetBIOS name servers (NBNSs).

`option netbios-node-type` *type* Defines the NetBIOS node type of the client. A type of 1 is a NetBIOS B-node; 2 is a P-node; 4 is an M-node; and 8 is an H-node.

`option netbios-scope` *string* Defines the NetBIOS over TCP/IP scope parameter.

NOTE To understand these values, see the discussion of NetBIOS in Chapter 11, *File Sharing*.

Diskless Client Options

DHCP can be used to boot diskless clients, such as X terminals. This list contains the options that pertain to diskless clients.

`option bootfile-name` *string* Defines the path to the client's boot file.

`option boot-size` *blocks* Defines the number of 512-octet blocks in the boot file.

`option merit-dump` *path* Defines the path name of the file the client should dump core to in the event of a crash.

`option root-path` *path* Defines the path name of the client's root disk.

`option swap-server` *address* Defines the IP address of the client's swap server.

Other Server Options

The most commonly used network servers are covered in the "Basic Options" list, but there are several other network servers available. Options relating to those servers are listed here.

`option cookie-servers` *address-list* Lists the addresses of the cookie servers.

`option finger-server` *address-list* Lists the `finger` servers available to the client. `finger` servers are used at sites that block `finger` traffic at the firewall.

`option font-servers` *address-list* Lists the X Windows font servers.

`option ien116-name-servers` *address-list* Lists the IEN 116 name servers. IEN 116 is an obsolete name service.

`option impress-servers` *address-list* Lists the addresses of the Image Impress servers.

option `irc-server` *address-list*   Lists the addresses of the Internet Relay Chat (IRC) servers.

option `log-servers` *address-list*   Lists the MIT-LCS UDP log servers.

option `mobile-ip-home-agent` *address-list*   Lists the Mobile IP agents this server should use.

option `nis-domain` *name*;   Defines the name of the local Network Information Services (NIS) domain.

option `nis-servers` *address-list*   Lists the addresses of the NIS servers.

option `resource-location-servers` *address-list*   Lists the addresses of the Resource Location servers.

option `streettalk-directory-assistance-server` *address-list*   Lists the addresses of the StreetTalk Directory servers.

option `streettalk-server` *address-list*   Lists the addresses of the StreetTalk servers.

option `tftp-server-name` *string*   Oddly enough, *string* should be the host name of the DHCP server, because some clients use this option instead of `server-name` to identify the DHCP server.

option `time-servers` *address-list*   Lists the time servers.

option `www-server` *address-list*   Lists the Web servers available to the client. This is primarily useful for defining proxy Web servers that a client must use.

option `x-display-manager` *address-list*   Lists the X Windows display manager servers.

These six lists comprise quite a slew of possible options, most of which you will never use—not because the options are unimportant, but because the default values most systems configure for these options are correct. However, this large set of configuration options permits you to control the complete TCP/IP system configuration from the DHCP server. Options, parameters, `group` statements, `host` statements, and `subnet` statements are combined together in the dhcpd.conf file to create the server and the client configurations. The next section examines a configuration file in detail.

Creating a dhcpd.conf File

dhcpd reads its configuration from the /etc/dhcpd.conf file. The dhcpd.conf file identifies the clients to the server and defines the configuration that the server provides each client. The sample dhcpd.conf file shown here dynamically assigns IP addresses to the DHCP clients on a subnet and supports a few BootP clients that require static addresses:

```
# Define global values that apply to all systems.
max-lease-time 604800;
default-lease-time 86400;
option subnet-mask 255.255.255.0;
option domain "foobirds.org";
option domain-name-servers 172.16.55.1, 172.16.5.1;
option pop-server 172.16.18.1;


# Define the dynamic address range for the subnet.
subnet  172.16.55.0 netmask 255.255.255.0 {
    option routers 172.16.55.1;
    option broadcast-address 172.16.55.255;
    range 172.16.55.64 172.16.55.192;
    range 172.16.55.200 172.16.55.250;
}


# Use host statements for clients that get static addresses
group {
    use-host-decl-names true;
    host kestrel {
        hardware ethernet 00:80:c7:aa:a8:04;
        fixed-address 172.16.55.4;
    }
    host ibis {
        hardware ethernet 00:00:c0:a1:5e:10;
        fixed-address 172.16.55.16;
    }
```

The file begins with the parameters and options that apply to all of the subnets and clients served. The first two lines define how dhcpd should handle dynamic address assignments. These are:

max-lease-time Specifies the longest address lease that dhcpd is allowed to grant, regardless of the lease length requested by the client. In the example, this parameter is one week.

default-lease-time Defines the address lease time used when a client does not request a specific address lease length. In the example above, the default lease is set to one day (86400 seconds).

The meaning of the next four lines is easy to see. These options define the subnet mask, domain name, domain server addresses, and POP server address used by all clients.

The network that dhcpd serves is identified by an address and an address mask in the subnet statement. dhcpd only provides configuration services to clients that are attached to this network or identified directly by host statements. The options and parameters in the subnet statement only apply to the subnet and its clients. In the example, the options define the subnet's default router and the broadcast address.

> **NOTE** Every dhcpd.conf has at least one subnet statement.

The two addresses in the range parameter define the scope of addresses that are available for dynamic address allocation. The first address is the lowest address that can be automatically assigned, and the second address is the highest address that can be assigned. The subnet statement in the example has two range parameters to create two separate groups of dynamic addresses. This illustrates that you can define a noncontiguous dynamic address space with multiple range statements.

> **NOTE** If a range parameter is defined in a subnet statement, any DHCP client on the subnet that requests an address is granted one as long as addresses are available. If a range parameter is not defined, dynamic addressing is not enabled.

The configuration concludes with a group of host statements. The group statement that encloses the host statements applies the use-host-decl-name configuration parameter to all of the hosts. With this parameter set, the client at Ethernet address 00:80:c7:aa:a8:04 receives the host name kestrel as part of its configuration information. Without this parameter, the client is sent an IP address but is not sent a host name. The Ethernet address contained in each host statement is the key used to identify the client and to determine which client receives what configuration information.

In the example, the host statements define the host name and IP address of individual clients. The clients are assigned permanent addresses, so they do not need to understand address leases, and they can run either DHCP or BootP. In addition to providing the information from the host statement to the clients, dhcpd sends them the subnet mask, domain name, DNS server addresses, and print server address defined in the global section of the configuration file.

Using the dhcpd.conf file, you can define any configuration information needed by any host or subnet your system serves. Note, however, that the largest unit served by a DHCP server is a subnet. To serve an enterprise network from a single server, you need to install DHCP relay servers.

Configuring a dhcrelay Server

The DHCP relay agent (dhcrelay) is provided as part of the dhcpd distribution that can be downloaded from www.isc.org. Version 1 of dhcpd does not provide this feature, but newer versions, such as the release provided with Red Hat 6, do provide dhcrelay.

The relay agent listens for DHCP boot requests and forwards those requests to a DHCP server. The relay agent must be attached to the same subnet as the DHCP client, because the request from the client uses the limited broadcast address. However, the relay does not need to share a subnet with the server, because it uses the server's IP address to send the request directly to the server. The server then sends the DHCP reply packet back to the relay. The relay is responsible for broadcasting the reply packet on the local subnet so that the client can retrieve it.

Use the dhcrelay command to run a DHCP relay. A simple dhcrelay command is:

```
dhcrelay -q 172.16.70.3
```

The –q option tells dhcrelay not to print out network configuration information when it starts. Normally it does. In this example, I am placing this command in the rc.local startup script and am not interested in having the configuration print out during the boot.

The IP address on the command line is the address of the DHCP server. When dhcrelay receives a DHCP request on the local network, it sends that request to 172.16.70.3. To use more than one DHCP server, specify multiple servers on the command line as follows:

```
dhcrelay -q 172.16.70.3 172.16.90.4
```

dhcrelay sends the request to all of the servers listed on the command line.

On occasion, the DHCP relay service is provided by a Linux system that is also acting as a router for a small network. In that case, the router has more than one interface and should be configured to provide DHCP relay service for the correct interface. For example, assume you have a small router with two Ethernet interfaces, eth0 and eth1. eth0 is connected to a backbone network with other routers. eth1 is connected to a local subnet that has DHCP clients and that needs DHCP relay service. The dhcrelay command for this situation might be:

```
dhcrelay -i eth1 172.16.70.3
```

This command tells dhcrelay to only listen for DHCP requests on interface eth1. When it receives any, it forwards them to 172.16.70.3.

The placement of DHCP servers and relays and the coordination between all of these systems is an important part of planning a DHCP service. See the case study, "Architecting a Configuration Service," at the end of this chapter for an example of planning the DHCP service for an actual network.

Configuring a DHCP Client

Not every Linux system is a server. It is also possible to configure a Linux desktop system as a DHCP client. The current dhcpd distribution provides dhclient, which is a DHCP client that runs under Linux. Some Linux systems ship with the DHCP Client daemon (dhcpcd), and Red Hat 6 provides a client tool named pump. This section discusses all of these Linux DHCP clients, beginning with dhclient, because it is a component of the software package used to create the DHCP server.

Running dhclient Software

Older versions of dhcpd do not include the dhclient software. If your Linux system doesn't have the client, follow the instructions shown above for downloading and compiling dhcpd. The latest versions of dhcpd include the client software.

Once the client software is installed, it is run using the command dhclient. The command does not require any command-line arguments. However, the command should be run very early in the boot process, because other boot processes may depend on the network, and the network is unavailable until the client has run and configured it. It is not sufficient to place this command in the rc.local file. Look at a Caldera or a Red Hat system. The script that starts the network is S01network, the very first script run after sysinit. This is the script that will be replaced by the script you create to run dhclient.

When dhclient starts, it reads two files: the configuration file dhclient.conf and the lease file dhclient.leases. You create the configuration file; the lease file is created by dhclient and is used to preserve information about IP address leases.

The dhclient.leases File

The dhclient.leases file contains a history of the address leases granted to the client. dhclient uses this information for address renewal and to speed the boot process. The leases are stored in a format that dhclient calls *lease declarations* that looks like the commands in the configuration file. The format of these entries is:

```
lease { lease-description [ ... lease-description ] }
```

The lease declaration begins with the lease keyword followed by one or more lease descriptions. If more than one command is used to describe a lease, they are enclosed in curly braces. The following commands are possible in a lease description:

bootp Means that the lease was acquired from a BootP server rather than a DHCP server.

expire *date* Defines when dhclient must stop using the address lease if it has not renewed it. date in all of these commands is year, month, day, hour, minute, and second.

filename "*path*" Defines the filename of the boot file for diskless clients.

fixed-address *address* Defines the address assigned by the lease. Despite the name fixed-address, this command is found in all lease statements, even those that assign dynamic addresses.

interface "*name*" Identifies the interface on which the lease is valid.

option *option-name value* Defines the value of a configuration option supplied by the server.

rebind *date* Defines when dhclient should connect to a new server if it has not renewed the address lease.

renew *date* Defines when dhclient should renew the address lease.

server-name "*hostname*" Defines the name of the boot server for diskless clients.

Using this information, you can read the dhclient.leases file to see what leases are active and when they expire. The lease declaration can also be used in the dhclient .conf file to manually define an address lease your system can fall back on if no server provides a valid lease. The next section looks at creating a dhclient.conf file.

The dhclient.conf Configuration File

The first—and most important—thing to know about the dhclient.conf file is that you can create an empty one, and dhclient will probably work fine. The dhclient.conf file allows you to change the default settings of the DHCP client. On most networks, this is unnecessary. However, the capability exists if you need to use it.

The manual page for dhclient.conf provides an example of a very complex client configuration. The following sample is a somewhat simplified version of that dhclient.conf file:

```
# Set the protocol timers
timeout 60;
retry 60;
select-timeout 5;
reboot 10;


# Define configuration parameters for eth0
interface "eth0" {
    send host-name "sparrow.foobirds.org";
    send dhcp-client-identifier 1:0:a0:24:ab:fb:9c;
    send dhcp-lease-time 28800;
    supersede domain-name "foobirds.org";
    prepend domain-name-servers 127.0.0.1;
    request subnet-mask, broadcast-address, routers,
            domain-name-servers;
    require subnet-mask, routers;
}


# Define a static address for emergencies
alias {
    interface "eth0";
    fixed-address 172.16.5.23;
    option subnet-mask 255.255.255.255;
}
```

Protocol Timers   The first four lines of the sample file set values for the protocol timers used by `dhclient`:

> `timeout`   Sets the maximum number of seconds `dhclient` waits for a server to respond. If a server does not provide the client with an offer of an address lease within the timeout period, the client attempts to use any lease in the `dhclient .leases` file that has not expired or any static address defined in the `dhclient.conf` file. The value set in the sample file, 60 seconds, is the default, so this command was not really required.

> `retry`   Sets the number of minutes `dhclient` waits before it tries again after it failed to get a response from a server. The default is 5 minutes. In the example, it is set to 2 minutes.

> `select-timeout`   Sets the number of seconds the client waits after receiving information from a server to see if another server responds. More than one server may exist on a network. The servers may be configured differently and may provide different levels of configuration information to the client, so sometimes it's worthwhile to "wait for a better offer." By default, the client does not wait. It takes the first offer. In the example, `dhclient` is configured to wait 2 seconds.

> `reboot`   Sets the number of seconds the client tries to reacquire the address it used during the last boot. The system assumes that the client will reattach to the same subnet and that the address it was last using is still available for it to use. Normally, these are very good assumptions, and making them speeds the reboot process. This didn't need to be specified in the configuration because it was set to 10 seconds, which is the default.

The `interface` Declaration   Next comes the `interface` declaration. The `interface` declaration is used to define parameters that only relate to a specific interface. It is intended for use on computers that have more than one interface to allow you to configure each interface in a unique way. In the example, there is only one interface, so the command is not required. However, it does no harm, and it illustrates the use of the `interface` declaration. The curly braces enclose all of the parameters that relate to the specified interface.

`send` Statements   The first three items associated with the interface declaration are `send` statements, which tell `dhclient` to fill in values for the specified configuration options before sending the request packet to the server. Any of the options listed in the "dhcpd Configuration Options" section of this chapter plus the `option dhcp-lease-time` can be used in a `send` statement. Of course, only certain options make any sense when used in this way. Generally, the `send` statement is used to help the server identify the client. That's what's happening in the sample file with the `host-name` option and the dhcp-client-identifier option. The dhcp-lease-time option defines the length of the address lease requested by the client. If this option is not specified, dhclient defaults to requesting a two-hour lease. In the example, eight hours (28800 seconds) are requested.

The supersede, prepend, request, and require Commands   A supersede command defines a value for a configuration option that is used instead of the value provided by the server. In the example, the domain-name option is defined with a value of foobirds.org. Regardless of the domain-name value provided by the DHCP server, the computer uses foobirds.org as a domain name.

The prepend command also affects the value provided for a configuration option. The value specified on the command line is inserted at the beginning of the list of values assigned to the option. The prepend command can only be used for configuration options that accept a list of values. In the example, the command is used to place the local host at the beginning of the list of name servers.

The request command defines the configuration options that dhclient requests from the server. These are requested in addition to an IP address. Any valid configuration option name can be listed. In the example, the subnet mask, the broadcast address, the default router, and the DNS servers are requested.

The require statement defines the configuration options that the client requires from a DHCP server. If the server does not provide this information, the client will not use any of the configuration information provided by the server. In the example, a subnet mask and a default router are required. As the curly brace indicates, this is the last command in the interface declaration.

The alias Declaration   The configuration file ends with an alias declaration, which defines a static address that is used by the client if it does not receive a valid address lease from a server. The example file shows all of the elements of an alias declaration:

- An interface statement to define the interface being assigned an address
- A fixed-address option to define the address
- A subnet-mask configuration option to define the address mask

Other Configuration Commands   This sample configuration is much more complex than any configuration you will ever create, but even a complex example like the one you saw earlier does not cover all of the configuration commands available for dhclient. Following are the other configuration commands you can use:

append {*option-list*}   Adds values to the end of the list of values provided by the server. This statement can only be used for options that allow more than one value.

The append command is essentially the opposite of the prepend command described earlier.

backoff-cutoff *time* Defines the maximum amount of time that the client is allowed to back off on configuration requests. The default is two minutes. A randomized exponential back-off algorithm prevents clients from all trying to configure themselves at the same time. This value prevents the client from backing off for an excessive amount of time.

default {*option-list*} Sets values for options that are used if the server does not supply the values. If the server provides a value, it is used; otherwise, the value defined here is used. For example, to make sure the client has a subnet mask, even if one is not provided by the server, you might enter:

    default subnet-mask 255.255.255.0;

initial-interval *time* Sets the time interval that is multiplied by a random number between zero and one to determine the amount of time the client backs off between attempts to reach a server. The time between attempts is doubled on each failed attempt. If it exceeds the backoff-cutoff amount, it is set to that amount. The default time interval is 10 seconds.

media "*media setup*" [, ...] Defines media configuration parameters for network interfaces which aren't capable of sensing the media type unaided.

reject *address* DHCP offers from the server at the specified address are ignored.

script "*path*" Identifies the dhclient configuration script file. This is a script that configures the local system's network interface with the values learned from the DHCP server. For more information, see the manual page for dhclient-script.

Looking at this large configuration language and the complex example, you may be wondering why you would do this. After all, this is at least as challenging as statically configuring TCP/IP with ifconfig. The reason is primarily for mobility. A computer consultant may need to move a Linux laptop from network to network in the course of a business day. A tool like dhclient eliminates the need to manually reconfigure the system every time it is attached to a new network.

The philosophy of dhclient is very different from that of the DHCP client provided with Microsoft Windows, which assumes that Windows users run DHCP because they don't know how to, or don't want to, manually configure TCP/IP. dhclient assumes that the people running a Linux desktop are sophisticated users who can easily configure TCP/IP and who want more than basic configuration from a DHCP client. However, there are times when you may want only basic configuration for your Linux desktop. For example, the policy of your network may require that every desktop uses DHCP. For those situations, Linux provides two simpler DHCP clients: dhcpcd and pump.

Using the dhcpcd Client

The DHCP Client daemon (dhcpcd) requests boot assistance from any DHCP server and stores the configuration information it receives in the following files in the /etc/dhcpc directory:

resolv.conf This is a standard resolv.conf file created by dhcpcd from the domain name and DNS server list received from the DHCP server.

hostinfo-eth0 This file contains the address lease information and other configuration options received from the server.

dhcpcd-cache.eth0 This file contains the previous address lease information to be used for address renewal.

Notice that two of the filenames end with the device name eth0. This is the default. If your system boots through another device, such as eth1, the dhcpcd command needs to be modified. To configure interface eth1, change the command to read:

```
dhcpcd -c net-script eth1
```

The −c option on the command line invokes the script that configures the system with the information that dhcpcd gathers. The script is system specific. If you want to manually install dhcpcd yourself, you need to write your own script. However, that is not usually necessary, because distributions that provide dhcpcd generally provide the correct script with the software.

Using the pump DHCP Client

During the initial installation of Linux in Chapter 2, *Basic Installation*, the network was configured with a static address. To use DHCP on the sample Red Hat 6 system, you would select DHCP instead of Static Address from the Select Boot Protocol menu during the installation. Once DHCP is selected, Red Hat does not prompt for any network information; it relies on pump to obtain the information from a DHCP server.

The pump command is very simple: pump −i eth0 configures interface eth0 with the information received from the DHCP server. Red Hat runs the pump command from the /sbin/ifup script. While pump normally runs from a startup script, it is possible to manually enter the command in order to check the status, release the address lease, or renew the lease. The possible pump command-line options are listed in Table 10.1.

Table 10.1   pump Command-Line Options

Command Option	Purpose
--interface=*device*	Identifies the device being configured.
--kill	Kills the pump daemon.
--lease=*hours*	Requests a specific lease time in hours.
--lookup-hostname	Causes pump to look up the host name via DNS.
--release	Releases the address assigned to the interface.
--renew	Requests a lease renewal.
--status	Displays the interface status.
--help	Displays a help message for the pump command.
--usage	Displays the syntax of the pump command.

Using the options in Table 10.1, you could query the status of an interface configured by pump by entering **pump –i eth0 --status**.

To use DHCP for a simple, automatic configuration, use pump or dhcpcd. If you need to create a custom configuration, use dhclient. All of these packages work well to configure a DHCP client.

I recommend DHCP, but you may not be in charge of the decision. It is possible that your network has a large and established population of systems that use BootP. I recommend that you use dhcpd to service them so that you are positioned to migrate to DHCP when those systems finally upgrade. However, if you're forced to run BootP instead of DHCP, Linux also makes an excellent platform for a BootP server.

Installing a BootP Server

Some Linux distributions include the BootP Server daemon (bootpd), though it is less common than it once was. Neither Caldera nor Red Hat provides it in their current distributions. The reason for this is simple: Most people use dhcpd to service their BootP clients. If you absolutely must use bootpd, download the bootpd-2.4.tar.gz file from metalab.unc.edu where it is stored in the pub/linux/system/network/boot.net directory. Extract the source code with tar, change to the newly created bootpd-2.4 directory, and enter **make linux**. This should compile the bootp daemon.

The bootpd command is started by inetd. Make sure the following line is in the inetd.conf file:

```
bootps dgram udp wait root /usr/sbin/tcpd bootpdI
```

Also make sure that the following entries are in the /etc/services file:

```
bootps          67/tcp                        #BootP server
bootps          67/udp
```

bootpd is started from inetd because the type of clients that use BootP do not reboot frequently, and therefore most of the time bootpd is idle. Microsoft Windows systems are not BootP clients; BootP clients are Unix systems, network devices, and X terminals. Some of these devices are completely dependent on BootP for their configuration because they have no local disk storage, and generally, when they are turned on, they are left on until they crash.

bootpd is less popular than dhcpd both because BootP is an outdated protocol and bootpd is difficult to configure. bootpd has a terse, arcane configuration language that is difficult to read and write.

Configuring bootpd

The BootP server configuration is stored in the /etc/bootptab file. Each bootpd configuration parameter is identified by a tag that is two characters long. Table 10.2 lists the bootpd configuration parameter tags and what they represent.

Table 10.2   bootpd Configuration Parameter Tags

Tag	Configuration Information
bf	Displays the name of the boot file.
bs	Defines the boot file size.
cs	Lists the cookie servers.
df	Defines the dump file path name.
dn	Defines the domain name.

Table 10.2   bootpd Configuration Parameter Tags *(continued)*

Tag	Configuration Information
ds	Lists the domain name servers.
ef	Defines the vendor extension file path name.
gw	Lists the default gateway.
ha	Defines the hardware address.
hd	Defines the boot file directory.
hn	Tells bootpd to send the host name.
ht	Defines the hardware type.
im	Lists the Impress servers.
ip	Defines the client's address.
lg	Lists the log servers.
lp	Lists the print servers.
ns	Lists the IEN-116 name servers.
nt	Lists the Network Time Protocol servers.
ra	Lists the reply address.
rl	Lists the resource location servers.
sa	Identifies the TFTP server.
sm	Defines the subnet mask.
sw	Identifies the swap server.
T*n*	Defines vendor extension *n*.
tc	Invokes a template.
td	Defines the secure TFTP directory.

Departmental Server Operations

PART 3

Table 10.2   bootpd Configuration Parameter Tags *(continued)*

Tag	Configuration Information
to	Defines the time zone offset.
ts	Lists time servers.
vm	Defines the vendor magic cookie selector.
yd	Defines the NIS domain name.
ys	Identifies the NIS server.

Like the dhcpd.conf file, the bootptab file begins with global parameters used by all clients. Here's an example:

```
defaults:\
      :hd=/usr/boot:
      :dn=foobirds.org:ds=172.16.55.1 172.16.50.5:\
      :sm=255.255.255.0:\
      :hn:
defaults-64:\
      :lp=172.16.64.6:\
      :gw=172.16.64.254:
grackle:\
      :tc=defaults:\
      :bf=null:\
      :tc=defaults-64:\
      :ht=1:ha=0080c7aaa804:\
      :ip=172.16.64.4:
flicker:\
      :tc=defaults:\
      :bf=null:\
      :tc=defaults-64:\
```

```
:ht=1:ha=0000c0a15e10:\
:ip=172.16.64.16:
```

The first two entries in the example are called *templates* because these entries don't actually define specific clients. Instead, they define values that can be used in the client entries. The one named `defaults` defines global values for the entire enterprise network, and the one named `defaults-64` defines configuration values for subnet 64. The remaining entries are entries for specific clients.

The client definitions use the `tc` tag to incorporate the information defined in a template into the client entry. `:tc=defaults:\` includes the values defined in the `defaults` template, and `:tc=defaults-64:\` incorporates the parameters defined in the `defaults-64` template.

TIP To find out more about the bootptab configuration syntax, see the bootptab manual page.

BootP Gateway

Both clients in the example above are on the same subnet. One server on each subnet is a common configuration. It reduces server load, improves performance, and eliminates the need to pass BootP information through a router, which requires a special configuration.

An alternative to a BootP server on each subnet is the BootP gateway program (`bootpgw`), which eliminates the need to create a special router configuration by relaying BootP traffic between networks. The BootP gateway program is included in the BootP `tar` file. After extracting and compiling the source code from the `tar` file, change the `bootps` entry in the `inetd.conf` to run `bootpgw` instead of `bootpd`:

```
bootps dgram udp wait root /usr/sbin/tcpd bootpgw 172.16.64.8
```

The IP address on the `bootpgw` command line is the address of the remote BootP server. In the example, the address is 172.16.64.8. No other configuration is required for `bootpgw`.

Final Words

Configuring TCP/IP is complex for users who do not understand the technical aspects of networking. Centralizing the configuration on a server makes it simpler for users to connect their PCs to the network, and it makes it simpler for you to support your network.

The configuration service is the foundation service of a departmental network. It allows you to control the configuration of every system in your department. This simplifies the task of running a departmental network, and it allows you to point your clients to your other servers.

In the next chapter the most fundamental of the other departmental services is configured. File sharing is the service that created the original demand for departmental networks.

Architecting a Configuration Service

A conflict exists between centralizing control to reduce configuration errors and improving booting efficiency and redundancy by placing the configuration servers close to the clients. The centralized solution places one large DHCP server in the central facility and a relay server on each subnet; the distributed solution uses no central server and places a DHCP server on every subnet. Real-life solutions combine elements of both.

I worked with an enterprise network composed of about 60 subnets. About 40 of the subnets were located at the sprawling headquarters facility. The remaining networks were located about 1500 miles away at a large production facility. The two sites were connected directly by a private leased circuit.

Clearly, the remote production facility could not depend on headquarters for configuration services. The company was forced to accept some level of distribution. Their computer services group offered two types of network support. For one level of support, they handled everything from setup to maintenance, and they used an internal billing mechanism to recover the cost of support from their internal customers. The other level of support allowed an organization to run its own subnet. The organization was assigned a subnet number and was connected to the rest of the enterprise through a router run by the services group. This service was much less expensive. These two support models offered freedom when the organization could handle it and support when the organization wanted and needed it.

Pleased with their support model, the company decided to replicate this service model in their configuration server architecture. Every organization that ran its own subnet was encouraged to buy and install its own DHCP server, because those organizations handled their own maintenance and had the best idea of their own requirements. Every subnet that was under central support was given a DHCP server. These servers were not quite central servers, and they were not quite distributed servers. Each server was co-located with one of the routers run by the central services group. The DHCP server was then directly connected to each of the subnets coming into the router.

The 36 subnets that were under central support were covered by 10 Linux servers. Here's a sample configuration from one of those servers:

```
# Define global values that apply to all systems.
option subnet-mask 255.255.255.0;
option domain "foobirds.org";
option domain-name-servers 172.16.55.1, 172.16.12.3;

# Identify the subnets
subnet  172.16.42.0 netmask 255.255.255.0 {
    option routers 172.16.42.254;
```

```
        option broadcast-address 172.16.41.255;
        range 172.16.42.50 172.16.42.250;
    }
    subnet  172.16.52.0 netmask 255.255.255.0 {
        option routers 172.16.52.254;
        option broadcast-address 172.16.52.255;
        range 172.16.52.50 172.16.52.250;
    }
    subnet  172.16.62.0 netmask 255.255.255.0 {
        option routers 172.16.62.254;
        option broadcast-address 172.16.62.255;
        range 172.16.62.50 172.16.62.250;
    }
    subnet  172.16.72.0 netmask 255.255.255.0 {
        option routers 172.16.72.254;
        option broadcast-address 172.16.72.255;
        range 172.16.72.50 172.16.72.250;
    }
```

No DHCP relay servers were required for this configuration. Sharing space with the routers made it possible to directly connect centrally maintained servers to every subnet. These "area" servers provided the advantages of central control with the speed and redundancy of distributed servers.

11

File Sharing

The ability to share information by sharing files is the fundamental service of a departmental network. Linux is a perfect system for this service, because it provides a wide range of different file-sharing mechanisms that integrate Microsoft Windows clients, Unix clients, and other clients that are not compatible with either of these into a single, cohesive network.

Compared to servers that see the world as all Microsoft or all Unix, Linux servers increase your flexibility for designing the right network. Linux does this by providing three distinct models of file sharing:

The mainframe model Allows clients to log in to the server and share files directly through the Linux file system. This model works with any client system that can emulate a terminal. Any system with a `telnet` or `rlogin` client has access to files on the server.

The Unix network model Allows clients to share files across the network with the Network File System (NFS). NFS is the most popular file-sharing software on Unix networks.

The Microsoft network model Allows clients to use the Server Message Block (SMB) protocol to share files across the network. SMB is the NetBIOS protocol used by Microsoft LanManager and Windows NT systems to provide file-sharing services to Microsoft Windows clients.

This chapter examines all three file-sharing techniques, beginning with the mainframe model that uses the basic capabilities of the Linux file system.

The Linux File System

telnet and rlogin permit users to log in to the server and work together there on shared files. Using FTP, files developed elsewhere can be placed on the server when users want to permit shared access. As you saw in Chapter 5, *Login Services*, all that is required for this type of access is a user account for each user and the telnetd, ftpd, and rlogind daemons in the inetd.conf file.

Linux File Permissions

File sharing is controlled through the file permissions that exist in the Linux file system. When the user's account is created, every Linux user is assigned a user ID (UID) and a group ID (GID), which are used to identify the user for file access. Every file is also given a UID and GID. By default, these are the UID and GID of the person who creates it, though that can be changed. Permissions are granted based on matching the UIDs and GIDs of the file and the user as follows:

Owner permissions The permissions granted to the user who has the same UID and GID as the file.

Group permissions The permissions granted to users who have the same GID as the file.

World permissions The permissions granted to all other users, those who have neither the UID nor the GID of the file.

Each of these groups can be granted any combination of three possible permissions:

Read permission The contents of the file may be examined.

Write permission The contents of the file may be modified.

Execute permission The program contained in the file may be executed.

Use the –l option with the ls command to view the ownership and permissions assigned to a file:

```
$ ls -l
total 1641
-rw-r--r--  1 craig  users    8255 May 17 14:09 fig2-1.gif
-rw-r--r--  1 craig  users    8206 May 17 14:10 fig2-2.gif
-rw-r--r--  1 craig  users   16328 May 16 22:04 fig3-2.gif
-rw-r--r--  1 craig  users    3832 May 16 22:13 fig4-1.gif
-rw-r--r--  1 craig  users   16741 May 16 22:18 fig4-2.gif
```

```
-rw-r--r--  1 craig   users    14350 May 16 22:24 fig4-4.gif
-rw-r--r--  1 craig   users    22737 May 16 22:27 fig4-5.gif
-rw-r--r--  1 craig   users    14316 May 16 22:34 fig5-1.gif
-rw-r--r--  1 craig   users    15739 May 16 22:35 fig5-2.gif
-rw-r--r--  1 craig   users    21528 May  1 20:46 fig8-1.gif
-rw-r--r--  1 craig   users    16479 May  1 21:18 fig8-2.gif
-rw-r--r--  1 craig   users    22295 May 17 11:43 fig8-4.gif
-rw-r--r--  1 craig   users    16482 Apr 24 19:50 fig9-3.gif
-rw-r--r--  1 craig   users    11756 Apr 24 19:54 fig9-4.gif
```

Each line in the long format directory listing begins with the file permissions. The first 10 characters are the same for every file in the example above: –rw-r--r--. The very first character indicates if this is a directory (d), a link (1), or a file (-). In the example, all of the entries are files.

The next nine characters are divided into three groups of three to define the permissions for the owner of the file, for the members of the group to which this file is assigned, and for all other users. An r in the permission field indicates read permission, a w indicates write, and an x indicates execute.

In the sample, the owner is granted read and write permissions (rw-), and everyone else— members of the group as well as other users of the system—are granted only read access (r--).

The permissions can be viewed as three 3-bit numbers. r is 4 (binary 100), w is 2 (binary 010), and x is 1 (binary 001). Thus the permission granted to the owner in the sample is 6 (rw-), and the permissions granted to the group and to the world are 4 (r--) for a file permission setting of 644.

Changing File Permissions

Use the chmod (Change Mode) command to change the permissions for a file. For example:

```
$ chmod 777 test.pl
$ ls -l test.pl
-rwxrwxrwx  1 craig   users   16513 May 18 14:22 test.pl
```

In this example, the permission is changed to 777, which grants read, write, and execute permissions to the owner, to the group, and to the world. The ls –l command illustrates what this full array of permissions looks like in a directory listing. It is unlikely, however, that you will want to grant such liberal permissions. It is more likely that you will want to offer less than the 644 you saw earlier, particularly if you don't want everyone who logs in to the system to be able to read your private files. To prevent those outside your group from reading your report before it is released, you might use the following setting:

```
$ chmod 640 report.txt
$ ls -l report.txt
-rw-r-----  1 craig  users  16513 May 18 14:22 report.txt
```

This setting permits the owner to read and write the file and the other members of the group to read the file, but it blocks general users from accessing the file at all. This is better, but it is still not enough. The problem is that the group to which this file is assigned is too broad.

Hidden Bits

So far, this discussion of file permissions is limited to user file permissions. Read, write, and execute are types of permission granted to various classes of users. There are also some permissions that are used to granted special privileges to executable files. These permissions are:

- Sticky bit, which permits the program to remain in memory after execution. The Sticky bit is an artifact of an earlier age; programs don't really need to stay in memory anymore. A more common use for the Sticky bit is to use it with directories instead of files. When used with a directory, users may only delete files for which they have specific write permission, even if they have directory write permission.

- SetGID, which permits the program to set the group ID it runs under on execution.

- SetUID, which permits the program to set the user ID it runs under on execution.

These three permissions create another group of three permission bits. The Sticky bit is set by the value 1 (binary 001), the SetGID permission is set by value 2 (binary 010), and the SetUID permission is set by value 4 (binary 100). All are set by placing a fourth digit at the beginning of the file permission value. Therefore, to grant a file SetUID permission, read, write, and execute permissions for the owner and the group, and execute permission for the world, you would use the value 4771 with the chmod command. 4 sets the SetUID permission, the first 7 sets the owner permission, the second 7 sets the group permission, and the 1 sets the world permission.

Hidden Bits *(continued)*

I call these permissions *hidden bits* because they don't appear to have a place in the three-character display (rwx) shown above. But that's not really true. ls shows all of these permissions as alternate values in the execution bit:

- If the Sticky bit is set, an uppercase letter "T" appears in the world execute permission field.

- If both world execute and the Sticky bit are set, a lowercase letter "t" appears in the world execute permission field.

- If SetGID is set, an uppercase letter "S" appears in the group execute permission field.

- If both group execute and the Sticky bit are set, a lowercase letter "s" appears in the group execute permission field.

- If SetUID is set, an uppercase letter "S" appears in the owner execute permission field.

- If both owner execute and the Sticky bit are set, a lowercase letter "s" appears in the owner execute permission field.

Be careful granting programs SetUID and SetGID permissions. If these programs are owned by the root user, they can have a great deal of power over the system. If the programs are incorrectly written, they can be exploited by an intruder and compromise your entire system.

The chgrp Command

The ls -l command lists the username of the file owner and the group name assigned to the file. In all of the examples shown above, the user is craig, and the group is users. By default, the file is assigned the owner's primary GID, which is the GID assigned to the user in the /etc/passwd file. This might not be what you want, particularly if access to the files should be limited to a group that logs in to the system to jointly work on the file. Use the chgrp command to change the group of a file:

```
$ chgrp rnd report.txt
$ ls -l report.txt
-rw-r----- 1 craig  rnd 16513 May 18 14:22 report.txt
```

In this example, the group of the `report.txt` file is changed to `rnd`. Now `craig` has read and write permissions for this file, and anyone in the group `rnd` has read permission. All other users have no access at all.

> **NOTE** `craig`, who is the owner of the file, must be a member of the `rnd` group to change the file to that group. Unless you're the root user, you cannot change a file to a group of which you're not a member.

This is a good example of how files are shared using the "mainframe model." Anyone in the `rnd` group can copy the `report.txt` file to their home directory where they can modify the copy by adding their comments and changes. The person in charge of the report can then look at the comments and changes using a command such as `diff` and decide what should be included in the final copy. Only the person in charge of the report can actually write to the master copy.

Sharing files by logging in to the server can work with any client system. It doesn't even require a client computer; a terminal will work just fine. But most users have powerful desktop computers that have the software tools that they like best. A better way to share files lets users work with the files on their desktop systems with the applications they like. Both Unix and Microsoft Windows offer such a service. For Unix systems, Network File System is the service that provides this type of file sharing.

Understanding NFS

The *Network File System* (NFS), originally developed by Sun Microsystems, allows directories and files to be shared across a network. Through NFS, users and programs access files located on remote systems as if they were local files.

NFS is a client/server system. The client uses the remote directories as if they were part of its local file system; the server makes the directories available for use. Attaching a remote directory to the local file system is called *mounting* a directory. Offering to share a directory is called *exporting*.

NFS is a remote procedure call (RPC) protocol that runs on top of UDP and IP. A *remote procedure call* is simply a system call that is processed by a remote server. When a program makes an I/O call for an NFS file, the call is intercepted by the NFS file system and sent over the network to the remote server for processing.

The daemons that process the NFS requests on the server are not assigned standard UDP port numbers. Instead, they are dynamically assigned port numbers by the RPC portmapper. There are a couple of versions of the portmapper used on Linux systems. On some systems, the program is `rpc.portmap`. On Red Hat systems, the program is `portmap` and is started by the script `/etc/rc.d/init.d/portmap`.

TIP You should not need to worry about starting the portmapper. It should be running on your system by default. If you tend to worry anyway, just use `ps ax | grep portmap` to double-check.

Use the `rpcinfo` command to view the port numbers that portmapper has assigned to various RPC services:

```
# rpcinfo -p
   program vers proto   port
    100000    2   tcp    111  rpcbind
    100000    2   udp    111  rpcbind
    100024    1   udp   1006  status
    100024    1   tcp   1008  status
    100011    1   udp   1017  rquotad
    100011    2   udp   1017  rquotad
    100005    1   udp    603  mountd
    100005    1   tcp    605  mountd
    100005    2   udp    608  mountd
    100005    2   tcp    610  mountd
    100003    2   udp   2049  nfs
    100021    1   udp   1026  nlockmgr
    100021    1   tcp   1024  nlockmgr
    300019    1   tcp    645  amd
    300019    1   udp    646  amd
```

Departmental
Server Operations

PART 3

Port number 111, rpcbind, is the portmapper's own port number. All of the other port numbers in this listing from a Red Hat 6 server are assigned to NFS daemons. If other RPC services, such as NIS, were running on this server, portmapper would also list those services in response to the rpcinfo command. In this case, only NFS is running. The various NFS daemons, in the order that they appear in the listing, are as follows:

status The status monitor reports crashes and reboots to the lock manager so that file locks can be properly reset if an NFS client reboots without gracefully terminating its NFS connection. Two copies of rpc.statd are running to monitor both TCP and UDP traffic.

rquotad The remote quota server, rpc.rquotad, enforces file system quotas for NFS mounted file systems. File system quotas control the amount of disk storage an individual user can consume. This daemon extends that feature to NFS users.

mountd The mount daemon processes the client's file system mount requests. rpc.mountd is the program that checks whether or not a file system is being exported and whether or not the client making the request is allowed to mount the requested file system.

nfs The rpc.nfsd program handles the user-level interface to the NFS kernel module (nfsd.o). The real work of NFS file I/O is handled in the kernel module.

nlockmgr The NFS lock manager handles file-lock requests from clients. File locking is used to prevent file corruption when it is possible that multiple sources may attempt to write a file at the same time. Read-only files do not require file locking.

amd The automounter daemon handles automatic NFS mount requests. See the section on automounter later in this chapter for more information.

NOTE These daemons are part of the kernel NFS implementation that was released as part of the Linux 2.2 kernel. If you have an older system with a user-level implementation of NFS, you will see a different list of daemons, though an NFS daemon to handle file I/O, and a mount daemon to handle mount requests will certainly be included.

Installing NFS

As shown above, the Network File System includes several different daemons and services to perform client and server functions and to provide advanced features such as automatic file-system mounting. Table 1.3 lists four NFS-related services that are available in the

Red Hat 6 distribution. Each of these services has a corresponding startup script in the /etc/rc.d/init.d directory:

nfs This script starts most of the NFS daemons listed above. It also processes the exports file and clears the lock file. The exports file and the exportfs command that is used to process it are covered later in this chapter.

netfs This script mounts the NFS file systems listed in the /etc/fstab file. Red Hat also uses this script to mount SMB file systems. Most other Linux systems don't use a separate script for this purpose, instead relying on the mount -a command to mount everything in the fstab file. (SMB, the mount command, and fstab are covered later in this chapter.)

amd This script starts the automounter daemon (amd) that automatically mounts files when the files are accessed.

autofs This script starts the automounter file system (automount) that automatically mounts files when they are needed and dismounts them when they are not in use. autofs and amd are two different implementations of the Sun Microsystems automounter.

NFS is included in your Linux distribution. To install and run it on your system, select the necessary services during the initial installation. If your Linux system is already running, NFS may well be installed. Check the process status to see if the necessary daemons are running:

```
# ps ax | grep nfs
  442 ?        SW      0:00 [nfsd]
  443 ?        SW      0:00 [nfsd]
  444 ?        SW      0:00 [nfsd]
  445 ?        SW      0:00 [nfsd]
  446 ?        SW      0:00 [nfsd]
  447 ?        SW      0:00 [nfsd]
  448 ?        SW      0:00 [nfsd]
  449 ?        SW      0:00 [nfsd]
# ps ax | grep mountd
  427 ?        SW      0:00 [rpc.mountd]
```

Departmental
Server Operations

PART 3

TIP   In this example, eight copies of the user-level nfsd server process are running to support user connections. By default, the rpc.nfsd command starts only one process. Starting additional processes is a command-line option. In the Red Hat nfs script, this command-line option is set by the RPCNFSDCOUNT script variable. To change the number of nfsd processes running, change the number assigned to that variable. Normally, eight nfsd processes are enough to provide very good service. If your server is extremely busy, you can try increasing this number to improve performance.

If the server daemons are not running, make sure the NFS software is installed on your system. Use rpm -qa | grep nfs to check this. Here is an example of a Red Hat system with the kernel NFS system installed:

```
# rpm -qa | grep nfs
knfsd-1.2.2-4
knfsd-clients-1.2.2-4
```

NOTE   Because the knfsd code is kernel-level code, it must also be configured in the kernel. The CONFIG_NFS_FS option must be enabled for kernel-level NFS. See Chapter 15, *Troubleshooting*, for a discussion of kernel configuration.

If the NFS software is not installed or the scripts are not running, you can use rpm or gnorpm to install the software, and tksysv or linuxconf to enable the startup scripts. (All of these commands are covered elsewhere in this book.) You don't have to reboot to start these services. Once the software is installed and the scripts are enabled on a Red Hat 6 system, you can enter nfs start to manually start the daemons:

```
# /etc/rc.d/init.d/nfs start
Starting NFS services:                            [  OK  ]
Starting NFS statd:                               [  OK  ]
Starting NFS quotas:                              [  OK  ]
Starting NFS mountd:                              [  OK  ]
Starting NFS daemon:                              [  OK  ]
```

If everything is installed and the startup scripts have been run, but the daemons are still not running, it may be because you haven't yet configured the server. Some startup scripts check to see if the /etc/exports configuration file exists before starting the daemons. Your next task is to create this file.

Configuring an NFS Server

The /etc/exports file is the NFS server configuration file. It controls which files and directories are exported, which hosts can access them, and what kind of access is allowed. The general format of entries in the /etc/exports file is:

    directory [host(option)]...

The *directory* variable is the full path name of the directory or file being exported. If the directory is not followed by a host or an option, all hosts are granted read/write access to the directory.

The *host* variable is the name of the client granted access to the exported directory. If no host value is specified, the directory is exported to everyone. Valid host values are:

- Individual host names such as parrot.foobirds.org.
- Domain wildcards such as *foobirds.org for every host in the foobirds.org domain.
- IP address/address mask pairs such as 172.16.5.0/255.255.255.0 for every host with an address that begins with 172.16.5.
- Net groups such as @group1.

NOTE I never use net groups. They are a Sun NIS construct, and I never use NIS. If you want to find out more about net groups, see the netgroup manual page.

The *option* variable defines the type of access being granted. If the *option* is specified without a host name, the access is granted to all clients. Otherwise, the access is granted only to the host that is named. The two most common options are:

ro Specifies that clients may only read from the directory. Writing to the directory is not permitted.

rw Grants full read and write access to the directory. Read/write access is the default permission used when no option is included in the exports file entry.

In addition to these two options, there are other, less commonly used options. Here are some of them:

insecure Allows client requests from ports greater than 1024. By default, the server runs with secure set, which only accepts requests from port numbers below 1024. Only a process running as root can bind to a port less than 1024. Setting insecure allows any user to create a program that can directly access your server without going through the nfsd daemon. I never use the insecure setting.

noaccess Makes everything in the specified directory inaccessible to the client. This is used to export file systems while excluding access to certain directories. I never use this setting, for I don't believe in exporting file systems that contain material you don't want your clients to see. Instead, I try to be much more selective in what I export, and I try to limit exported file systems to those that clients really need.

link_relative Prepends the necessary number of directories to all links to make them relative to the root. By default, the system is configured to link_absolute, which means that links are used as written. I have never used link_relative, and the documentation says it has "subtle, perhaps questionable, semantics." I take that as a warning.

> **NOTE** In addition to the options listed here, there are several that relate to UIDs and GIDs, which are described in the upoming "Mapping User IDs and Group IDs" section of this chapter.

Given the syntax described above, a realistic sample /etc/exports file might contain these entries:

```
/usr            172.16.5.0/255.255.255.0(ro)

/home           172.16.5.0/255.255.255.0(rw)

/usr/man        flicker(rw) parrot(rw)

/usr/doc        flicker(rw) parrot(rw)

/usr/local      hawk(rw)

/home/sales     *.sales.foobirds.org(rw)
```

The first entry in this file grants read-only access to the /usr directory to every client on the local subnet. In the example, the subnet is defined with an IP address and an address mask, which allows you to grant access to everyone on the local network without also granting access to everyone in the local domain or without trying to list all of the hosts on the local network. The /usr directory contains documentation and executables that could be of interest to any Linux client. Read permission is all that is required to access those useful files.

The second line in the example grants read and write access to the /home directory. Again, the access is given to every host on the local subnet. Perhaps the /home directory is being exported to give users NFS access to their home directories on the server. To make full use of their directories, the users require read and write permissions.

The next three lines all grant individual hosts read and write access to specific directories within the /usr directory. These entries do not affect the first line of the file. The /usr directory is still exported as read-only to all local clients. These additional entries were added so that the people who maintain the documentation in /usr/doc and /usr/man can modify the documentation directly from their desktop systems, and so the people who maintain the executables in /usr/local can do it from their desktops.

The last line in the file exports the /home/sales directory to every host in the sales .foobirds.org subdomain. In this case, the /home/sales directory is probably used by the sales division to share files. As this shows, it is possible for the server to share directories with computers in other domains or networks.

Even though specific hosts have been granted read/write access to some of these directories, the access granted to individual users of those systems is controlled by standard Linux user, group, and world file permissions based on the user's UID and GID. Essentially, NFS trusts that a remote host has authenticated its users and assigned them valid UIDs and GIDs, which is similar to the trusted host security model used by rlogin that was discussed in Chapter 5. Exporting files grants the client system's users the same access to the files they would have if they directly logged in to the server.

For example, assume that the server exporting these files is wren. Further, assume that user craig has accounts on both wren and eagle, and that both systems assign him UID 501 and GID 206. Everything works fine! But what happens if hawk has a user named david and assigns him UID 501 and GID 206? The david account now has the same access to Craig's files as the craig account. That might not be what you intended. The case study at the end of this chapter talks about the importance of coordinating UIDs and GIDs across an NFS domain. Linux also provides some tools to ease this problem.

Mapping User IDs and Group IDs

User IDs and group IDs are as fundamental to NFS as they are to any other part of the Linux file system. But unlike the UID and GID you assign when creating new user accounts, you may not have any control over the UIDs and GIDs assigned by your NFS clients. NFS provides several tools to help you deal with the possible problems that arise because of this.

One of the most obvious problems with a trusted-host security model is dealing with the root account. It is very unlikely that you want people with root access to your clients to also have root access to your server. By default, NFS prevents this with the root_squash setting, which maps requests that contain the root UID and GID to the nobody UID and GID. Thus if someone is logged in to a client as root, they are only granted world permissions on the server. You can undo this with the no_root_squash setting, but I don't recommend it. The no_root_squash setting opens more holes for intruders to exploit, which is never a good thing.

You can extend the number of UIDs and GIDs that are mapped to nobody with the squash_uids, squash_gids, and all_squash settings. all_squash maps every user of a client system to the user nobody. squash_uids and squash_gids map only the UIDs or GID that you specify. A sample /etc/exports illustrates this:

```
/pub            (ro,all_squash)
/usr/local/pub (squash_uids=0-50,squash_gids=0-50)
```

The first entry exports the /pub directory to every client. It grants every client read-only access to the directory and limits every user of those clients to the world permissions granted to nobody, meaning that the only files the users can read are those that have world read permission.

The second entry exports a directory, /usr/local/pub, to every client. This directory is exported with read/write permission, which is the default. The squash_uid and squash_gid commands prevent users from accessing the directory with one of the non-user accounts that are assigned low UIDs and GIDs. For example, on our Red Hat system, UID 10 is assigned to uucp. Attempting to write a file as uucp would cause the file to be written with the owner mapped to nobody. Thus the user uucp would only be able to write to the /usr/local/pub directory if that directory had world write permission.

It is also possible to map every user from a client to a specific user ID or group ID. The anonuid and anongid options provide this capability. These options are most useful when the client has only one user and the client does not assign that user a UID or GID.

The perfect example of this is a Microsoft Windows PC running NFS. PCs generally have only one user and they don't use UIDs or GIDs. To map the user of a PC to a valid user ID and group ID, enter a line like this in the /etc/exports file:

```
/home/kristin  robin(all_squash,anonuid=1001,anongid=1001)
```

Here, the host name of Kristin's PC is robin. The entry grants that client read/write access to the directory /home/kristin. The all_squash option maps every request from that client to a specific user ID, but this time, instead of nobody, it maps to the UID and the GID defined by the anonuid and anongid options. Of course, for this to work correctly, 1001:1001 should be the UID and GID pair assigned to kristin in the /etc/passwd file.

A single mapping is sufficient for a PC, but it might not handle all of the mapping needed for a Unix client. Unix clients assign their users UIDs and GIDs. If these differ from the UIDs and GIDs assigned to those same users on the Linux server, you might have problems.

Use the `map_static` option to point to a file that maps the UIDs and GIDs for a specific client. For example:

```
/export/shrike shrike(map_static=/etc/nfs/shrike.map)
```

This entry in the `/etc/exports` file says that the `/export/shrike` directory is exported to the client `shrike` with read/write permission. The `map_static` option points to a file on the server named `/etc/nfs/shrike.map` that maps the UIDs and GIDs used on shrike to those used on the server. The `shrike.map` file might contain the following entries:

```
# UID/GID mapping for client shrike
# remote    local   comment
uid 0-50     -      #squash these
gid 0-50     -      #squash these
uid 100-200 1000    #map 100-200 to 1000-1100
gid 100-200 500     #map 100-200 to 1000-1100
uid 501     2001    #map individual user
gid 501     2001    #map individual user
```

The first two lines in the file map the low user IDs and group IDs that are usually reserved for non-user accounts to the user nobody. The next two lines map all of the user IDs and group IDs in the range of 100 to 200 on the client to corresponding numbers in the range of 1000 to 1100 on the server. In other words, 105 on the client maps to 1005 on the server. This is the most common type of entry. On most systems, existing UIDs and GIDs have been assigned sequentially. Often, several systems have assigned the UIDs and GIDs sequentially from 101 to different users in a completely uncoordinated manner. This entry maps the users on `shrike` to UIDs and GIDs starting at 1000. Another file might map the 100 to 200 entries of another client to UIDs and GIDs starting at 2000. A third file might map yet another client to 3000. These are the entries that allow the server to coordinate UIDs and GIDs where no coordination exists. The last two lines map an individual user's UID and GID. This is less commonly required, but it is possible.

There are two more techniques for mapping UIDs and GIDs. The `map_daemon` option tells the server to query the map daemon `rpc.ugidd` running on the client. This, of course, requires the client to install and run the daemon. I stay away from techniques that require more software on the clients. Generally, there are many clients and few servers, and keeping software updated on many clients is harder than keeping it updated on a few servers. However, if you're interested in this technique, see the `rpc.ugidd` manual page.

The other option, `map_nis`, tells the server to query the NIS server for the UID/GID mapping. I don't use NIS, but if you're interested in this, see the NIS documentation.

Departmental
Server Operations

PART 3

> **NOTE** This discussion of UID/GID mapping may make NFS seem more complex than it is. Coordination among the system administrators and perhaps some minimal mapping files are generally sufficient to handle the mapping problem.

The exportfs Command

After defining the directories you want to export in the /etc/exports file, run the exportfs command to process the exports file and to build /var/lib/nfs/xtab. The xtab file contains information about the currently exported directories, and it is the file that mountd reads when processing client mount requests. To process all of the entries in the /etc/exports file, run exportfs with the –a command-line option:

```
# exportfs -a
```

This command, which exports everything in the exports file, is normally run during the boot from a startup script.

It is possible, however, to user the exportfs command on a running system. If you edit the /etc/exports file and want the changes to take effect without rebooting the system, use the –r argument:

```
# exportfs -r
```

This –r option causes exportfs to synchronize the contents of the exports file and the xtab file. Items that have been added to the exports file are added to the xtab file, and items that have been deleted are removed from xtab.

You can even use the exportfs command to export a directory that is not listed in the /etc/exports file. For example, assume that you wanted to temporarily export the /usr/local directory to the client falcon with read/write permission. You could enter this command:

```
# exportfs falcon:/usr/local -o rw
```

After the client has completed its work with the temporarily exported file system, the directory can be removed from the export list with the –u option. This command would end the export and prevent falcon from mounting the /usr/local directory:

```
# exportfs -u falcon:/usr/local
```

In fact, the –u option can be combined with the –a option to completely shut down all exports without terminating the NFS daemons:

```
# exportfs -ua
```

Despite all of its features, however, `exportfs` generally is not used to export individual directories. Usually, it is used with either the –a or the –r options to process all of the entries found in the /etc/exports file. For example, the Red Hat `nfs` script runs `exportfs -r` before starting the daemons.

Once the daemons are running and the `exports` file has been processed by `exportfs`, the clients can mount and use the file systems offered by your server. The next section looks at how a Linux system is configured as an NFS client.

Configuring an NFS Client

To configure an NFS client, you need to know the host name of the server and the directories it exports. The name of the server is usually very well advertised—no one creates a server unless they want to have clients. The network administrator will tell you which systems are NFS servers.

The Linux `showmount` command lists the directories that a server exports and the clients permitted to mount those directories. For example, a `showmount -e` query to `wren` produces the following output:

```
$ showmount --exports wren
Export list for wren:
/home/sales    *.sales.foobirds.org
/usr           172.16.5.0/255.255.255.0
/home          172.16.5.0/255.255.255.0
/usr/doc       flicker.foobirds.org,parrot.foobirds.org
/usr/man       flicker.foobirds.org,parrot.foobirds.org
/usr/local     hawk.foobirds.org
```

The `showmount` command lists the NFS directories exported by `wren`, and which clients are allowed to mount those directories. You can mount any of the directories offered by `wren` if you are on one of the approved clients.

The mount Command

Before you can use an NFS directory, you must attach it to the local file system with the `mount` command. The `mount` command can be as simple or as complex as it needs to be to get the job done.

At it simplest, `mount` identifies the remote file system you want to access and the local directory through which you will access it. The remote file system is identified by the server name paired with all or part of a directory exported by the server. The local directory is just that, the name of an empty directory you created to mount the remote NFS directory. The local directory is called the *mount point*. Putting this all together, you could mount the directories exported by wren with the following commands:

```
# mount wren:/usr/local/bin /usr/local/bin
# mount wren:/usr/man /usr/man
# mount wren:/usr/doc /usr/doc
```

These examples assume that empty /usr/local/bin, /usr/man, and /usr/doc directories existed on the client before the mount commands were issued. It wouldn't make sense to mount a remote directory full of manual pages over an existing /usr/man directory unless that directory was empty. The purpose for creating central repositories for man pages and documentation is to save storage on client system. You can only do that if the directories on the client are actually empty.

A simple mount command works under most circumstances, but when needed, options can be added to the mount command line with the –o argument. Table 11.1 lists the mount command options that apply to all types of file systems.

Table 11.1   Linux mount Command Options

Option	Purpose
async	Use asynchronous file I/O.
atime	Update the inode access time for every access.
auto	Mount when -a option is used.
defaults	Set rw, suid, dev, exec, auto, nouser, and async.
dev	Allow character devices, and block special devices on the file system.
exec	Permit execution of files from the file system.
noatime	Don't update inode access time.
noauto	Don't mount with the -a option.
nodev	Don't allow character devices, and block special devices on the file system.
noexec	Don't allow execution of files from the file system.

Table 11.1   Linux mount Command Options *(continued)*

Option	Purpose
nosuid	Don't allow programs stored on the file system to run setuid or setgid.
nouser	Only root can mount the file system.
remount	Remount a mounted file system with new options.
ro	Mount the file system read-only.
rw	Mount the file system read/write.
suid	Allow programs to run setuid or setgid.
sync	Use synchronous file system I/O.
user	Permit ordinary users to mount the file system.

NOTE   Despite the length of this list, you will see even more NFS mount options in the next section. In general, you don't have to worry about setting options, because the default values are usually correct. However, these options are there if you need them.

Assume you want to mount the /usr/local/bin directory, but for security reasons you don't want to allow any of the programs stored there to run with setuid or setgid permission. You could enter the following mount command:

```
# mount -o nosuid wren:/usr/local/bin /usr/local/bin
```

The umount Command

The opposite of the mount command is the umount command, which is used to remove a mounted directory from the local file system. There are no options associated with the umount command. A file system can be dismounted using either the remote file system name or the local mount point directory on the umount command line, so to dismount the /usr/local/bin directory, enter either the remote name:

```
# umount wren:/usr/local.bin
```

or the local name:

```
#umount /usr/local/bin
```

Using `fstab` to Mount NFS Directories

A mount command with the -a flag set causes Linux to mount all file systems listed in
/etc/fstab. Most Linux systems include a mount -a command in the startup to re-mount
the NFS file systems after a system boot. The Red Hat 6 netfs script is a little different.
Because the script is designed to mount only network file systems, it adds the –t nfs argument to the mount -a command to limit the mount to all file systems in fstab that have
a file system type of NFS.

> **NOTE**   The general structure and content of the fstab file is covered in Chapter 3,
> *The Boot Process*.

NFS entries in the fstab file are exactly like those described in Chapter 3 except for the
type field, which contains the keyword nfs, and the enormous number of possible NFS
mount options. Any of the Linux mount command-line options listed in Table 11.1, as well
as all of those listed in Table 11.2, can be used in an NFS entry in the fstab file.

Table 11.2   More mount Options

Option	Function
acdirmax=n	Sets the maximum cache time for directory attributes. Defaults to 60 seconds.
acdirmin=n	Sets the minimum cache time for directory attributes. Defaults to 30 seconds.
acregmax=n	Sets the maximum cache time for file attributes. Defaults to 60 seconds.
acregmin=n	Sets the minimum cache time for file attributes. Defaults to 3 seconds.
actimeo=n	Sets all cache times to the same value.
bg	Does retries in background mode.
fg	Does retries in foreground mode.

Table 11.2   More mount Options *(continued)*

Option	Function
hard	Retries indefinitely until the server responds.
intr	Allows a keyboard interrupt to kill a process.
mounthost=*name*	Sets the name of the server running mountd.
mountport=*n*	Sets the port number of mountd.
mountprog=*n*	Uses an alternate RPC program number for mountd on the remote server.
mountvers=*n*	Uses an alternate RPC version number for the mountd on the remote server.
namlen=*n*	Sets the maximum length of a filename for the remote file system. Defaults to 255 bytes.
nfsprog=*n*	Uses an alternate RPC program number for nfsd on the remote server.
nfsvers=*n*	Uses an alternate RPC version number for nfsd on the remote server.
noac	Disables all caching.
nocto	Does not retrieve attributes when creating a file.
port=*n*	Sets the NFS server port number. 2049 is the default.
posix	Runs in a POSIX-compatible mode.
retrans=*n*	Sets the number of retransmissions before a major timeout occurs. The default is 3.
retry=*n*	Sets the amount of time to retry mount. Defaults to 10000 minutes.
rsize=*n*	Sets the size of the read buffer. The default is 1024 bytes.
soft	Allows the access to time out if the server doesn't respond.

Departmental
Server Operations

PART 3

Table 11.2   More mount Options *(continued)*

Option	Function
tcp	Runs over TCP instead of UDP.
timeo=*n*	Sets the length of time before an access times out. Must be used with soft.
udp	Runs over UDP. This is the default.
wsize=*n*	Sets the write buffer size. The default value is currently 1024 bytes.

I have never used most of these options. The key options that I do use are those that can improve NFS performance, such as tuning the buffer size. The default of 1024 works well for rsize and wsize, but increasing the buffer size can improve performance. I find that 4096 works well on most Pentium-class systems for both rsize and wsize.

If you have an unreliable server, you may want to change the hard failure setting to soft, or at least add the intr option. That way if the server fails, it will not cause your client system to hang on a hard failure, or if it does, you can escape with a keyboard interrupt.

> **NOTE**   All of the options mentioned here can be used on the mount command line with the –o argument. Additionally, all of the options mentioned earlier in the mount command section can also be used in the fstab file. I divided the list of options to show where certain options are most commonly used and to make the list more manageable.

Understanding what to put in the fstab file for an NFS entry can be confusing with all of these options. An easy way to learn what should be in an fstab entry is to mount the file system and then display its entry in the mtab file. The mtab file stores information about currently mounted file systems. The entries in mtab are very similar to those in the fstab file. Simply mount a file and print mtab. Then you'll know what you should enter in fstab. For example:

```
# mount owl:/home/jane /home/owl
# cat /etc/mtab
/dev/hdb1 / ext2 rw 0 0
none /proc proc rw 0 0
owl:/home/jane /home/owl nfs rw 0 0
```

Based on this, you would add the following entry to the fstab file to mount the /home/owl directory at each boot:

```
owl:/home/jane /home/owl nfs rw 0 0
```

The fstab file is used to automatically re-mount file systems at boot time. The automounter automatically mounts NFS file systems only when they are actually needed.

The Automounter

There are two automounter implementations available for Linux: the automounter daemon (amd) and the automounter file system (autofs). Both are configured in a similar manner, and both are given mount points and map files that define the characteristics of the files systems mounted on those mount points. Although its mount points can be defined in /etc/amd.conf, amd mount points and map files are often defined on the command line:

```
amd -a /amd /mnt/wren /etc/nfs/wren.map
```

This command line tells amd that its working directory, where the real physical mounts are made, is /amd. The mount point for the user directory is /mnt/wren. Like any NFS mount point, this directory must already exist. The map file that defines the file system mounted on /mnt/wren is /etc/nfs/wren.map.

I rarely use amd. I use autofs because the syntax and structure more closely resemble the original Sun implementation. This makes it easier to move configuration files between systems and to use Sun skills to implement a Linux server.

> **TIP** If you want to learn more about amd, see the amd and amd.conf manual pages.

For autofs, the mount points are usually not defined on the automount command line. Instead, autofs mount points are defined in the auto.master file, which lists all of the maps that are used to define the autofs file system. The format of entries in the auto.master file is:

```
mount-point    map-name        options
```

The *options* are standard mount command options. Generally, they are not defined here. Most administrators put options in the map file. Most auto.master entries contain only a mount point and a map file. To reproduce the amd configuration shown above, the autofs auto.master file would contain:

```
/mnt/wren        /etc/nfs/wren.map
```

This entry tells automount to mount the file system defined in the map file /etc/nfs/ wren.map at /mnt/wren whenever any user refers to this directory. On Red Hat systems, the automount command is started by the /etc/rc.d/init.d/autofs script. Run autofs reload to load automounter after you change the file.

> **NOTE**   In addition to using autofs to load the automounter configuration, you can run autofs start to start the automount and autofs stop to shut down.

The map file contains the information needed to mount the correct NFS file system. The format of a map file entry is:

```
key       options    filesystem
```

For NFS entries, the key is a subdirectory name. automount (and amd) can mount more than NFS file systems, so the first field is called the key, as opposed to the subdirectory, to indicate that it is not limited to a subdirectory name. The *options* are the standard mount command options, and *filesystem* is the path name of the file system being mounted. The map file for our example contains:

```
doc       -ro        wren:/usr/doc

man       -ro        wren:/usr/man
```

This tells the automounter to mount wren:/usr/doc with read-only permission if any user tries to access /mnt/wren/doc and to mount wren:/usr/man read-only if anyone accesses /mnt/wren/man.

Automounting Home Directories

So far you've seen automounter handle some simple NFS examples, but it can do much more. For instance, it can automatically mount the home directory of any user based on a single entry in the map file. Assume you have this entry in the auto.master file:

```
/home/owl        /etc/nfs/home.map
```

With this entry, any request for a subdirectory in /home/owl will cause the automounter to check /etc/nfs/home.map for a directory to mount.

Assume the entry in home.map is:

```
*                owl:/home/&
```

This entry can mount any home directory found in the /home directory exported by owl to a like-named mount point on the local host. The * is a wildcard character that tells automounter to match anything the user types in. The & is another wildcard character, which is replaced by the value typed in by the user. For instance, if the user tries to access /home/owl/daniel, automounter mounts owl:/home/daniel. If the user enters /home/owl/kristin, it mounts owl:/home/kristin. When constructing a path to the remote file system, automounter uses whatever value the user enters as the "key." This is a very useful feature, particularly when users log in to multiple systems and need access to their home directories from those systems.

Automounting Physical Devices

Probably the most widely used feature of the automounter has nothing to do with NFS. The automounter can mount any type of file system, even physical devices. It can automatically mount a CD-ROM or floppy drive when it is needed. This means it is not necessary for a user to mount a removable device, like a CD-ROM, before using it.

On a Red Hat system, which uses automount, the following entry is included in the /etc/auto.master file:

```
/misc    /etc/auto.misc   --timeout 60
```

Any request for a subdirectory in /misc causes the automounter to mount the file systems defined in /etc/auto.misc. (The timeout for these devices is set to 60 seconds.) The auto.misc map contains the following significant entry:

```
cd               -fstype=iso9660,ro      :/dev/cdrom
```

If a user accesses /misc/cd, automounter mounts /dev/cdrom on that mount point. Notice that the file system path does not include a host name; i.e., the path starts with a colon. When the host name is blank, the device is located on the local host. The fstype option defines the standard CD-ROM file system type.

On a Caldera 1.3 system, this feature is implemented using amd. When I said earlier that I don't really use amd, it wasn't strictly the truth. I don't *configure* amd. But if it is already configured to automatically mount CD-ROM drives and floppies, as it is in Caldera 1.3, I make use of it. The amd command line started during the Caldera boot contains the mount point /auto and the map file for that mount point /etc/amd.localdev. To access a CD-ROM without manually entering a mount command, simply access the directory /auto/cdrom. For floppies, the directory is /auto/floppy. amd automatically mounts the correct device to the requested directory.

NFS is a useful server for your Unix and Linux clients. But on most networks, the majority of clients are Microsoft Windows PCs. Those clients can be made to run NFS with optional client software. However, a better and more natural file-sharing service for Microsoft Windows PCs is provided by Samba. Samba is an implementation of the NetBIOS Server Message Block (SMB) protocols for Linux.

Departmental
Server Operations

PART 3

Understanding SMB and NetBIOS

Microsoft Windows printer- and file-sharing applications are based on NetBIOS (Network Basic Input Output System). The BIOS defines the applications interface used to request DOS I/O services. NetBIOS extends this with calls that support I/O over a network. Developed fifteen years ago for the PC Network product by Sytek, the NetBIOS API outlived the original product to become part of Windows for Workgroups, LAN Manager, and Windows NT.

Originally, NetBIOS was a monolithic protocol that took data all the way from the application to the physical network. NetBIOS has changed over time into a layered protocol. Its layers include the NetBIOS API, the SMB protocol, and the NetBIOS Frame (NBF) protocol.

Today, NetBIOS runs over TCP/IP, which allows NetBIOS applications to run over large internets. It does this by encapsulating the NetBIOS messages inside TCP/IP datagrams. The protocol that does this is NetBIOS over TCP/IP (NBT), which is defined by RFCs 1001 and 1002.

NBT requires some method for mapping NetBIOS computer names, which are the addresses of a NetBIOS network, to the IP addresses of a TCP/IP network. There are three methods:

IP broadcast A packet containing a NetBIOS computer name is broadcast, and when a host sees its own name in such a broadcast, it returns its IP address to the source of the broadcast.

lmhosts file A file that maps NetBIOS computer names to IP addresses.

NetBIOS name server (NBNS) A NBNS maps NetBIOS names to IP addresses for its clients. The Samba nmbd daemon can provide this service.

The systems on a NBT network are classified according to the way they resolve NetBIOS names to IP addresses. There are four possible classifications:

b-node A system that resolves addresses through broadcasts is a *broadcast-node* (b-node). Broadcasting is only effective on a physical network that supports broadcasts and is usually limited to a single subnet.

p-node A system that directly queries an NBNS name server to resolve addresses is a *point-to-point*-node (p-node).

m-node A system that first uses broadcast address resolution and then falls back to an NBNS server is a *mixed-node* (m-node). Using a "dual approach" eliminates the complete dependence on an NBNS server that is the weakness of the p-node solution. The problem with m-node is that it uses the least desirable broadcast approach first. In practice, m-nodes are very rarely used.

h-node A system that first attempts to resolve the address using the NBNS server, then falls back to using broadcasts, and if all else fails looks for a local lmhosts file is a *hybrid-node* (h-node). h-node is the method used by most systems.

NetBIOS Name Service

Even though installing the Samba software has not yet been discussed, this is probably a good place to discuss the NetBIOS Name Server daemon (nmbd) and how it is configured. nmbd is the part of the basic Samba software distribution that turns your Linux server into an NBNS server. nmbd can handle queries from LanManager clients, and it can be configured to act as a WINS server.

> **NOTE** The Microsoft implementation of NetBIOS name service is Windows Internet Name Service (WINS). Samba is compatible with WINS and can be used as a WINS server.

nmbd WINS configuration options are defined in the smb.conf file, which is covered in detail later. The options that relate to running WINS are:

wins support Set to yes or no. This option determines whether or not nmbd runs as a WINS server. no is the default, so by default, nmbd provides browsing controls but does not provide WINS service.

dns proxy Set to yes or no. This option tells nmbd to use DNS to resolve WINS queries that it cannot resolve any other way. This is only significant if nmbd is running as a WINS server. The default is yes. DNS can only help with NetBIOS name resolution if NetBIOS names and DNS host names are the same.

win server Set to the IP address of an external WINS server. This option is only useful if you're *not* running a WINS server on your Linux system. This option tells Samba the address of the external WINS server to which it should send NetBIOS name queries.

wins proxy Set to yes or no. The default is no. When set to yes, nmbd resolves broadcast NetBIOS name queries by turning them into unicast queries and sending them directly to the WINS server. If wins support = yes is set, these queries are handled by nmbd itself. If instead wins server is set, these queries are sent to the external server. The wins proxy option is only needed if clients don't know the address of the server or don't understand the WINS protocol.

Provide your clients the NetBIOS name server's address through DHCP.

To define the address of the NBNS server, enter the following line in the dhcpd .conf file:

```
option netbios-name-servers 172.16.5.1 ;
```

> **NOTE** See the "NetBIOS Options" section in Chapter 10, *Desktop Configuration Servers*, for the DHCP options that define a client's NetBIOS configuration.)

The NetBIOS name server is generally started at boot time with the following command:

```
nmbd -D -H /etc/lmhosts
```

When started with the –D option, nmbd runs continuously listening for NetBIOS name service requests on port 137. The server answers requests using registration data collected from its clients, the NetBIOS name-to-address mappings it has learned from other servers, and the mappings defined in the /etc/lmhosts file. The –H option points to the lmhosts file. You can call this file anything you wish, but the traditional name is lmhosts.

The lmhosts file is there so that you can manually provide address mapping for the server when it is necessary, though it usually isn't. Most WINS servers do not need a lmhosts file, because the servers learn address mappings dynamically from clients and other servers. NetBIOS names are self-registered; clients register their NetBIOS names with the server when they boot. The addresses and names are stored in the WINS database, wins.dat. lmhosts is only a small part of the total database.

The lmhosts Files

The lmhosts file contains static-name-to-address mappings. The file is similar to the hosts file described in Chapter 6, *Linux Name Services*. Each entry begins with an IP address that is followed by a host name. However, this time the host name is the NetBIOS name. Here is a sample lmhosts file:

```
$ cat /etc/lmhosts
172.16.5.5      crow
172.16.5.1      wren
172.16.5.2      robin
172.16.5.4      hawk
```

Given this lmhosts file, the NetBIOS name robin maps to the IP address 172.16.5.2. Notice that these NetBIOS names are the same as the TCP/IP host names assigned to these clients. You should always use the same host names for your systems for both NetBIOS and TCP/IP. Doing otherwise limits your configuration choices and creates confusion.

NetBIOS name service is an essential part of a NetBIOS network, but the real point of creating such a network is to share files and other network resources. The remainder of this chapter discusses installing and configuring Samba to do just that.

Installing Samba

Samba services are implemented as two daemons. The SMB daemon (`smbd`), the heart of Samba, provides the file- and printer-sharing services. The NetBIOS Name Server daemon (`nmbd`) provides NetBIOS-to-IP-address name service.

You can download Samba software from the Internet if you need it. Go to `www.samba.org` to select your nearest download site, and then download the file `samba-latest.tar.gz` from that site. Unzip and untar the source tree into a working directory. Change to that directory, run `./configure`, and then run `make` and `make install`. This will install the latest version of Samba in `/usr/local/samba`. However, compiling your own copy of Samba should not be necessary on a Linux system.

Samba is included in most Linux distributions and can be installed during the initial system installation. Samba is listed as `smb` in Table 1.3, which lists the services offered by Red Hat 6. Selecting `smb` installs the Samba package and causes the `/etc/rc.d/init.d/smb` script to run at boot time, which starts both `smbd` and `nmbd`. Use the `ps` command to see if those daemons are already running on your system:

```
# ps ax | grep mbd
  342  ?  S    0:00 (smbd)
  351  ?  S    0:00 nmbd -D
```

If the daemons aren't running, use `rpm` or `gnorpm` to make sure you have installed the software.

NOTE   If you use gnorpm, the path to the Samba package on a Red Hat 6 system is System Environment/Daemons.

If the software is installed and the daemons aren't running, use `linuxconf` or `tksysv` to make sure that the proper scripts run at startup time. As you saw above, the script on a Red Hat system is `smb`. Even if the software is installed and the scripts are being run, the daemons may not be running. That is because most systems do not start the daemons unless a Samba server configuration file exists.

In the `ps` test shown above, the `smbd` and `nmbd` daemons are running. Since Red Hat systems won't run the daemons unless an `smb.conf` file exists, that is a pretty good hint that the Red Hat system comes with Samba pre-configured.

I used a Windows 95 client system to test this. On the Windows client, I double-clicked the Network Neighborhood and then the Entire Network icon. This opened the Entire Network window shown in Figure 11.1.

Departmental
Server Operations

PART 3

Figure 11.1   Browsing the Microsoft Network

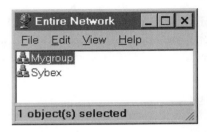

The first thing I noticed is that in addition to the Sybex workgroup I expected to see, there was a new workgroup named Mygroup. Double-clicking the Mygroup icon displayed an icon labeled with the host name of the Linux server, in this case wren. Double-clicking the wren icon opened the dialog box shown in Figure 11.2.

Figure 11.2   Samba's Enter Network Password dialog box

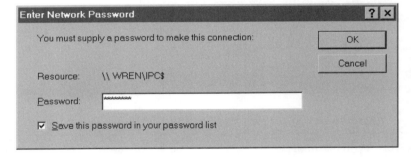

This box requests a password before I can browse the shares offered by wren. The password I entered is the one defined in the /etc/passwd file, which is the same password I use to directly log in to wren.foobirds.org. When I entered the password and clicked OK, a directory window opened that contained only one file folder, which was named craig. Double-clicking this folder opened the window shown in Figure 11.3.

Figure 11.3   A home directory share

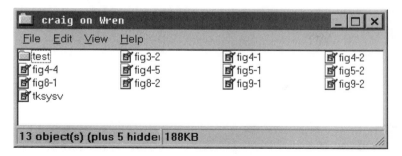

Wait a minute—this is my home directory on wren! I didn't know that I could access this directory so easily. Without any configuration input from me, I can access my Linux home directory from my Microsoft Windows PC. Let's look at the Samba server configuration on our Red Hat system to see how this happened.

Configuring a Samba Server

The Samba server is configured by the smb.conf file. Look in the startup script to see where smbd expects to find the configuration file. On a Red Hat system, it is /etc/smb.conf. On a Caldera system, it is /etc/samba.d/smb.conf, and the default used in most Samba documentation is /usr/local/samba/lib/smb.conf. Use find or check the startup script so you know where it is on your system.

The smb.conf file is divided into sections. Except for the global section, which defines configuration parameters for the entire server, the sections are named after shares. A *share* is a resource offered by the server to the clients. In the context of this chapter, it is a file system that is offered by the server for the clients to use for file sharing. A share can also be a shared printer, but I won't talk about that now, because printer sharing is the topic for Chapter 12, *Printer Services*.

The best way to learn about the smb.conf file is to look at one. Minus the lines that deal with sharing printers, the Red Hat smb.conf file contains the following active lines:

```
[global]
    workgroup = MYGROUP
    server string = Samba Server
    log file = /var/log/samba/log.%m
    max log size = 50
```

```
        security = user
        dns proxy = no
    [homes]
        comment = Home Directories
        browsable = no
        writable = yes
```

The smb.conf Variables

Reading an smb.conf file can be confusing if you don't understand the variables found in the file. Table 11.3 lists each variable and the value it carries.

Table 11.3   smb.conf Variables

Variable	Meaning
%a	Client machine architecture
%d	Server process ID
%g	GID of the username assigned to the client
%G	GID of the username requested by the client
%h	DNS host name of the server
%H	Home directory of the username assigned to the client
%I	IP address of the client
%L	NetBIOS name of the server
%m	NetBIOS name of the client
%M	DNS host name of the client
%N	NIS server, if NIS is supported
%p	NIS home directory, if NIS is supported
%P	The root directory of the current service

Table 11.3 smb.conf Variables *(continued)*

Variable	Meaning
%R	The protocol negotiated during connection
%S	The name of the current service
%T	The date and time
%u	The username assigned to the client
%U	The username requested by the client
%v	The Samba version number

Variables provide flexibility because each variable is replaced in the configuration by a value obtained from the system. This allows the same configuration statement to be interpreted differently in different situations. Here is an example from the file listing shown above:

```
log file = /var/log/samba/log.%m
```

In this example, the %m variable is replaced by the NetBIOS name of the client, so a different log file is created for each client with a file extension that is the client's NetBIOS name.

Variables provide flexibility. If the NetBIOS name of the client is crow, the log file is named /var/log/samba/log.crow. If the client's NetBIOS name is robin, the log file is /var/log/samba/log.robin. If you have a small enough client base, this is a good configuration.

The smb.conf Global Section

The Red Hat sample configuration file contains two sections: *global* and *homes*. The global section defines several parameters that affect the entire server:

workgroup Defines the workgroup of which this server is a member. A workgroup is a hierarchical grouping of hosts. It organizes network resources in the same way that directories organize file resources, and it is used for the same reason: Grouping computers into workgroups helps a user locate related systems. Workgroups are not used for security. Hosts that are not in the workgroup are still allowed to share files with systems that are. Replace the MYGROUP name in the example with a meaningful workgroup name of 15 characters or less.

`server string` Defines the descriptive comment for this server. The string is displayed by the `net view` command on DOS clients, so it provides an opportunity for you to describe the server. Change the string in the example to something meaningful for your system.

`log file` Defines the location of the log file. The most interesting thing about this entry is that it contains an `smb.conf` variable.

`max log size` Defines the maximum size of a log file in kilobytes. The default is 5MB, or 5000KB. In the sample configuration, this is reduced to 50KB, probably because a separate log is being created for each client. If the maximum size is exceeded, `smbd` closes the log and renames it with the extension `.old`.

`security` Defines the type of security used. In Samba, there are four possible settings:

`share` Requests share-level security. This is the lowest level of security. Essentially, if you configure some resource as shared, it is shared with everyone. It is possible to associate a password with a share, but the password is the same for everyone who wants to use that share.

`user` Requests user-level security. Every user is required to enter a username and an associated password. By default, this is the username and password defined in `/etc/passwd` that the user would use to log in to the Linux server. The default values for passwords can be changed. See the upcoming "Samba Passwords" sidebar for more details.

`server` Defines server-level security. This is similar to user-level security, but an external server is used to authenticate the username and password. The external server must be defined by the `password server` option.

`domain` Defines domain-level security. In this scheme, the Linux server joins a Windows NT domain and uses the Windows NT domain controller as the server that approves usernames and passwords. Use the `password server` option to point to the Windows NT Primary Domain Controller (PDC). Log in to the PDC and create an account for the Linux system. Finally, add these lines to the global section on the Linux system:

```
domain master = no
local master = no
preferred master = no
ostype = 0
```

dns proxy Specifies whether or not nmbd should forward unresolved NBNS queries to DNS. (See the previous section for details.)

In addition to these options, several other parameters are commonly used in the global section; they are shown in Table 11.4.

Table 11.4   Other Global Section Parameters

Option	Purpose
auto services	Defines a list of shares that are automatically visible to all users browsing the system.
deadtime	Defines the timeout for inactive connections.
debug level	Sets the level of messages written to the log.
lock directory	Defines the path of the directory where wins.dat, status files, and lock files are stored.
message command	Defines how smbd handles WinPopup messages.
name resolve order	Defines the order in which services are queried to resolve NetBIOS names. Possible values are lmhosts, hosts, wins, and bcast.
netbios aliases	Defines other names the server will answer to.
netbios name	Defines the server's NetBIOS name.
protocol	Defines the highest protocol Samba will request during connection setup. Don't use this!
smbrun	Defines the path to the smbrun program that executes shell commands for smbd.
syslog	Maps debug levels to syslog levels.
syslog only	Uses syslog instead of Samba log files.
time server	Tells the server to advertise itself as a Windows time server.

Samba Passwords

The encrypt passwords option can be set to encrypt passwords before they are sent across the network. This makes the server more compatible with Windows NT clients, and it makes it harder for intruders to sniff passwords from the network. However, if encrypted passwords are used, the Samba server must maintain two password files: passwd and smbpasswd. Use the smb passwd file option to point to the location of the smbpasswd file. Use the mksmbpasswd.sh script to build the smbpasswd file from the passwd file, and then use the unix password sync and the passwd program options in the smb.conf file to help keep the password databases synchronized.

By default, Samba uses clear-text passwords, so none of this synchronization is required. Only one database, /etc/passwd, is used. However, this is not compatible with many Windows NT and Windows 98 clients because recent versions of Microsoft software require encrypted passwords. To force those clients to use clear-text passwords, you must edit the Registry of every client. For Windows 98, the Registry setting is:

    [HKLM\System\CurrentControlSet\Services\VxD\VNETSUP]

    "EnablePlainTextPasswords"=dword:00000001

On Windows NT, the setting is:

    [HKLM\System\CurrentControlSet\Services\Rdr\Parameters]

    "EnablePlainTextPasswords"=dword:00000001

Personally, I would rather maintain two databases on a server than edit the Registry on every Windows NT client. For this reason, I think encrypted passwords are less of a headache.

As the Red Hat sample configuration demonstrates, your server will run without tuning all of these parameters. My advice is not to fiddle with parameters on a running system. I believe in the old adage "If it ain't broke, don't fix it." About the only option in Table 11.4 that I routinely add to the configuration is netbios name. The correct value is taken from Linux server's host name, but I like to document the name in the file to help others who may need to read my configuration file.

The `smb.conf` Homes Section

The homes section is a special share section. It tells `smbd` to permit users to access their home directories through SMB. Unlike other share sections, which you will see later, this section does not tell `smbd` the specific path of the directory being shared. Instead, `smbd` uses the home directory from the `/etc/passwd` file based on the username of the user requesting the share. It is this special section that makes my home directory on `wren` available to me on my PC.

The homes section from the Red Hat example is:

```
[homes]
    comment = Home Directories
    browsable = no
    writable = yes
```

The configuration parameters defined in this homes section are:

`comment` Provides a description of the share that is displayed in the comment field of the Network Neighborhood window when this share is viewed on a Microsoft Windows system.

`browsable` Specifies whether or not all users may browse the contents of this share. `no` means that only users with specific permission, i.e., the correct user ID, are allowed to browse this share. `yes` means all users, regardless of UID, can browse the share. This parameter only controls browsing; actual access to the contents of the share is controlled by standard Linux file permissions.

`writable` Specifies whether or not files can be written to this share. If `yes`, the share can be written to. If `no`, the share is read-only. This parameter defines the actions permitted by Samba. Actual permission to write to the directory defined by the share is still controlled by standard Linux file permissions.

Both the global and homes sections described are included in the sample Red Hat configuration. Having a firm understanding of those elements, you're ready to create your own share section in the `smb.conf` file.

Sharing a Directory through Samba

To share a directory through Samba, create a share section in `smb.conf` that describes the directory and the conditions under which you are willing to share it. To share the `/home/sales` directory used in the NFS examples and a new directory named `/usr/doc/pcdocs`, you might add the following two share sections to the sample `smb.conf` file.

```
[pcdocs]
    comment = PC Documentation
    path = /usr/doc/pcdocs
```

```
        browsable = yes
        writable = no
        public = yes


[sales]
        comment = Sales Department Shared Directory
        path = /home/sales
        browsable = no
        writable = yes
        create mode = 0750
        hosts allow = sales.foobirds.org
```

Each share section is labeled with a meaningful name. This name is displayed as a folder in the Network Neighborhood window on client PCs. Each section contains some commands you have already seen and a few new commands. The first new command is path, which defines the path of the directory being offered by this share.

The pcdocs share also contains the command public. public allows anyone to access the share, even if they don't have a valid username or password. These public users are granted "guest account" access to the share. On a Linux system, this usually means they run as user nobody and group nobody and are limited to world permissions.

Setting File and Directory Permissions

The sales share is being offered as a writable share. The create mode command controls the permissions used when a client writes a file to the /home/sales directory. In the sample above, it is specified that files will be created with read/write/execute for the owner, read/execute for the group, and no permissions for the world (750). A related command, directory mode, defines the permission used when a client creates a directory within a share. For example:

```
    directory mode = 0744
```

This sets the permissions for new directories to read/write/execute for the owner, read/execute for the group, and read/execute for the world (744). This is a reasonable setting that allows cd and ls to work as expected.

WARNING I usually stick with the defaults, but if you want to try the directory mode command, remember that directories *must* have the world execute bit set in order for the change directory (cd) command to work properly.

Limiting Access to a Share

The sales share section also contains a `hosts allow` command, which defines the clients that are allowed to access this share. Even if a user has the correct username and password, they are only allowed to access this share from the specified hosts. By default, all hosts are granted access, and specific access is controlled by the username and password.

Normally, I define the hosts in a `hosts allow` command by IP addresses. If host names are used, the Samba server must be able to resolve the host names to IP addresses, which normally means that fully qualified domain names should be used. The hosts identified in this example are identical to those listed in the NFS example to illustrate that Samba can also control access with domain wildcards.

There are several different ways to define individual hosts or groups of hosts in the `hosts allow` command. As the name of the command implies, it uses the same syntax as the `hosts.allow` file discussed in Chapter 14, *Security*. Some examples of how it can be used in the `smb.conf` file are:

> `hosts allow = 172.16.5.0/255.255.255.0` Allows every host on network 172.16.5.0 access to the share.

> `hosts allow = 172.16. EXCEPT 172.16.99.0/255.255.255.0` Allows every host on network 172.16.0.0 to have access to the share except for those hosts on subnet 172.16.99.0. 172.16 might be your enterprise network, and 172.16.99 might be an untrusted subnet where you have publicly accessible computers.

In addition to the `hosts allow` command, there is a `hosts deny` command that defines computers that are explicitly denied access to the share. Its syntax is similar to that of the `hosts allow` command.

Two other variations on this theme are the `hosts equiv` and `use rhosts` commands. These commands tell `smbd` to use the `hosts.equiv` file or the `.rhosts` file to determine who is granted access to the share. (These two files are described in Chapter 5.) Most security people discourage the use of these files because they permit password-free access to the files in the share.

Combining these two new share sections with the section that came with the Red Hat configuration creates a server that does everything you want. It provides access to user home directories. It provides access to public directories used to offer online documentation or other publicly shared resources. And it offers private directories that are only accessible to members of the selected group. This provides everything that NFS did in a manner that is much simpler for Microsoft Windows clients to use.

Of course, you're not limited to serving only Windows clients. Linux systems can also be Samba clients.

Using a Linux Samba Client

While Linux systems can be used as SMB clients, I don't recommend it if you have Linux servers. I find NFS to be a more natural way to share files between Linux systems, and features like autofs and mounting from fstab make integrating NFS into a Linux client very seamless. But not all servers are Linux servers. It is possible that you will need to configure a Linux system as a client to a Windows NT server or even as a peer to a Windows 9x desktop. For those situations, you need to use the Samba client tools.

Using smbclient

The smbclient program is a tool for transferring files with a system offering an SMB share. It is particularly useful for transferring files with Windows 9x systems that do not have FTP server software. smbclient acts like an FTP tool for SMB share files. An example will illustrate:

```
$ smbclient //goose/c -W sybex
Added interface ip=172.16.12.3 bcast=172.16.12.255
nmask=255.255.255.0
start lmhosts: Can't open lmhosts file /etc/lmhosts. Error was No
such file or directory
Server time is Mon May 24 21:49:14 1999
Timezone is UTC-4.0
Password:
security=share
smb: \> cd craig
smb: \craig\> ls
  .                 D        0  Sat Apr 10 10:22:22 1999
  ..                D        0  Sat Apr 10 10:22:22 1999
  GOOD1.DOC         A   147024  Sun Apr  4 21:11:20 1999
  BESTYET.DOC       A   217036  Mon Apr  5 18:47:22 1999
  sybex             D        0  Sat Apr 10 10:23:34 1999

  32943 blocks of size 32768. 6115 blocks available

smb: \craig\> prompt
prompting is now off
smb: \craig\> mget *.DOC
```

```
getting file \craig\GOOD1.DOC of size 147024 bytes as GOOD1.DOC
(222.947 kb/s) (average 222.947 kb/s)

getting file \craig\BESTYET.DOC of size 217036 bytes as BESTYET.DOC
(388.898 kb/s) (average 299.014 kb/s)

smb: \craig\> quit
```

The `smbclient` tool is invoked by the `smbclient` command. The share that you're accessing is described on the command line using the Microsoft Universal Naming Convention (UNC). The UNC format is *//server/sharename*, where *server* is the NetBIOS name of the server and *sharename* is the name of the share.

If a share password is required, which might be the case if the server uses only share-level security, it follows the UNC on the command line. In the example above, share-level security is used, but the password is not provided on the command line, so the server will prompt the user for it.

Use the –U command option and provide the username and password separated by a % if the server uses user-level security. If a workgroup name is required, provide it with the –W option.

Once usernames and passwords have been provided, files are sent and retrieved using exactly the same commands that you use with FTP. If you can use FTP, you can use `smbclient`. In the example above, I changed to the `craig` subdirectory of the share (`cd`), turned off prompting (`prompt`), and got all of the files that have a `.doc` extension from the server to the client (`mget`).

The `smbclient` is the workhorse of the Samba client tools. It is not very elegant, but it is the basis for several other client tools that are shell scripts that use `smbclient` to get the work done. A more graceful way to integrate SMB server files into the Linux file system is with `smbfs`.

Using `smbmount`

The SMB file system (`smbfs`) allows you to mount SMB shares and use them as if they were part of the Linux file system. Shares are mounted using the `smbmount` command and dismounted using the `smbumount` command. To mount the share shown above in the `smbclient` example, enter:

```
smbmount //crow/user/tyler /home/tyler/crow –U tyler –P Wats?Watt?
```

The `smbmount` command starts with the name of the share. The share name is followed by a standard Linux mount point. The mount point is the location within the Linux file system at which the share is mounted. In the example, this is followed by the username (`-U`) and password (`-P`) required by the SMB server.

Once it is mounted, the share has essentially the same look and feel of any Linux directory, and most standard Linux commands can be used to manipulate the files in the share directory. Of course, not everything is the same. Some features of the Linux file system are not available from all SMB servers. For example, a Windows *9x* system offering a share does not have file-level security, nor does it understand Linux UIDs and GIDs. smbfs does its best to "fake it." It uses the UID and GID in force when smbmount was started. You can override these defaults with the −u and −g command-line options. For example:

```
smbmount //crow/user/tyler /home/tyler/crow -U tyler -P Wats?Watt? -u
689 -g 100
```

This command is the same as the one above, except that it tells smbfs to use the UID 689, presumably the UID assigned to tyler, and the GID 100, which is the GID of users.

To dismount an SMB share, use the smbumount command with the path of the mount point:

```
smbumount /home/tyler/crow
```

smbfs makes using SMB shares on a Linux client much easier than accessing those shares through smbclient.

Final Words

File sharing is the foundation application of departmental networks. Linux servers make excellent platforms for a file server—Linux is fast and very stable, and it provides a wider choice of file services than most other server operating systems.

Files can be shared in three different ways:

- Through direct login. Users wishing to share files can directly log in to a Linux server, regardless of the capability of their desktop systems. Files can then be shared using the Linux file system.
- Through Network File System. NFS is the leading file-sharing protocol of Unix systems. Linux systems come with a full range of NFS server and client software.
- Through Server Message Block protocols. SMB is the file-sharing protocol used by Microsoft Windows systems. A Linux system can act as an SMB server or client to share files with Microsoft Windows systems.

In the next chapter, you'll configure Linux as a departmental print server. Again, you will see that Linux has the ability to integrate both Unix and Windows clients on a single network.

Coordinating UIDs and GIDs

When files are shared across a network, the systems need to identify users in a consistent and coordinated manner. For this reason, WINS was developed to provide a central place for clients to register and resolve NetBIOS names. NFS includes a number of tools for mapping UIDs and GIDs. Clearly, resolving user identity is an important issue in a file-sharing network. The bigger the network, the bigger the problem.

I worked with an organization with 5000 employees composed of eight different operating units that had 50 different subnets. Many of the subnets had their own network administrators and ran their own NFS services. The decision was made to create a unified NFS system that spanned the entire enterprise. For this system to permit true file sharing required that UIDs and GIDs be coordinated across the enterprise.

First, is file sharing across an enterprise really a good idea? True file sharing is when people cooperate to produce the end product. You don't really want 5000 people contributing to your report, so true file sharing across a very large organization is not usually what you want.

What most enterprise networks want is file dissemination. They want to make a finished product available to everyone in the organization. The Web is a good vehicle for this when the product is information, and NFS is a good choice when the product is an executable program.

Second, do you really need to coordinate UIDs and GIDs if what you want to do is disseminate information? Not really. The user nobody has world permission. Items being disseminated to the entire enterprise can be given world read and execute permissions.

Well, if enterprise file sharing wasn't really what the organization wanted, did anything good come from this project? Yes! A plan to assign UIDs and GIDs in a sensible, coordinated manner. The central services held all of the UIDs and GIDs above 20,000 in order to assign them to every employee. Every existing employee was assigned a UID and a GID, and every new employee is assigned one when they come on board. Further, each operating unit was given 1000 UIDs and GIDs to use as they see fit.

What began as a way to centralize services became a benefit to all of the independent subnet administrators. When a user from another organization is added to a subnet's NFS server, there is no worry about mapping or conflicts, because a central authority coordinates UIDs and GIDs for the whole organization. In the end, enterprise-wide file sharing was not as important as enterprise-wide cooperation and coordination.

12

Printer Services

Printer servers allow everyone on a network to share printers. Linux printer servers offer two techniques for sharing printers. The traditional Unix network technique uses the Line Printer daemon (lpr) command and an lpd server. This approach is best suited for serving Linux and Unix clients. The other technique uses a Samba server to share printers with Microsoft Windows clients. This chapter covers both techniques. But before you can use any technique to share a printer with your clients, you must install and configure the printer on your server.

Installing Printers

As noted in Chapter 2, printer installation is often part of the basic Linux system installation and configuration. I generally wait until I have the system running before trying to configure the printer, while many other administrators prefer to configure the printer during the initial installation.

In truth, installing the printer during or after the initial installation is essentially the same procedure. To install a printer, you must know the type of printer and its capabilities. Figure 12.1, which is from the initial Red Hat installation, illustrates the type of questions you're expected to answer.

Figure 12.1   Configuring a printer during the initial installation

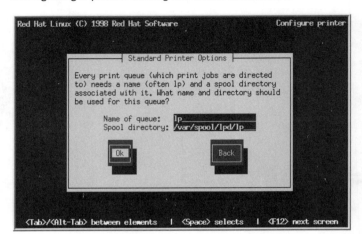

The meanings of the different fields in this window become clear later in the chapter when you look at an actual printer installation. This figure illustrates that the questions you're asked during the initial installation are identical to those you're asked if you install a printer after the system is running. Despite the fact that the process is almost identical, I still prefer to put this off until the system is running. There are a few reasons for this:

- First, the printer is not an essential component needed to boot the system. I prefer to put off non-essentials until the system is running.

- Second, installing a printer is not always as easy as you think it is going to be. A problem during the initial installation can be much more difficult to recover from than a problem that occurs after the system is running.

- Finally, more configuration tools are available after the basic system is installed and the system has booted. I use the X Windows printer configuration tools.

X Tools for Configuring Printers

The Red Hat PrintTool is a graphical printer configuration tool available as part of the Red Hat Control Panel and as one of the Admin tools in the Caldera Looking Glass desktop environment. To launch this tool on a Red Hat system, click the Printer Configuration icon in the Control Panel.

The first time you run PrintTool, no printer queues are listed because you haven't configured any yet. Click the Add button to start defining your printer. The Add A Printer Entry window shown in Figure 12.2 appears.

Figure 12.2   Selecting a printer

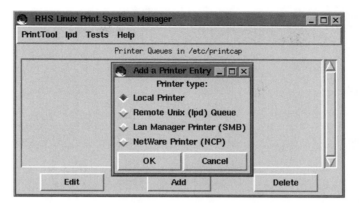

This window gives you four choices of how the system will communicate with the printer:

Local Printer   This printer is directly attached to one of the physical ports of the Linux system. If your system is a printer server, you'll have at least one printer directly attached to the computer.

Remote Unix (lpd) Queue   The lpr command is used to communicate with this printer. This configuration selects the client side of lpd printer sharing. The server for the remote printer doesn't really need to be a Unix system. Many different systems provide lpd servers. In this chapter, you configure your Linux system to be an lpd server.

Lan Manager Printer (SMB)   The SMB protocol is used to communicate with this printer. This setting selects the client side of SMB printer sharing, which allows your Linux system to use the printers shared by Microsoft Windows systems. Of course, SMB servers don't have to be Microsoft Windows systems, as you saw in Chapter 11, *File Sharing*. Later in this chapter, you'll configure your Linux system to be an SMB printer server.

NetWare Printer (NCP)   The Novell NetWare Core Protocol (NCP) is used to communicate with this printer. This setting selects the client side of NetWare printer sharing, which allows the Linux system to use printers offered by Novell servers.

In the example, I select Local Printer, which is the normal selection for a printer server. Selecting Local Printer causes the PrintTool to try to detect possible parallel printer ports. It displays a message describing which printer ports it believes are active. On my sample system, PrintTool lists three printer ports with one, lp1, active.

Departmental
Server Operations

PART 3

Printer Port Names

Linux defines three parallel printer ports, as this `ls` demonstrates:

```
$ ls -l /dev/lp*

crw-rw----  1 root   daemon   6, 0 May  5  1998 /dev/lp0

crw-rw----  1 root   daemon   6, 1 May  5  1998 /dev/lp1

crw-rw----  1 root   daemon   6, 2 May  5  1998 /dev/lp2
```

The Linux device names for the parallel ports are /dev/lp0, /dev/lp1, and /dev/lp2. The numbers listed just before the dates are the device's major and minor numbers. The major number (6) stands for the parallel port driver. The minor number (0, 1, or 2) indicates which addressable device this is for that driver. The three parallel port device numbers on this system are 60 for lp0, 61 for lp1, and 62 for lpt2.

Don't try to compare DOS port names with Linux port names. This is often done, but I think it adds more confusion than benefit. There are two DOS printer ports and three Linux printer ports. lp1 is assigned I/O port address 0x378, which is the same as DOS port LPT1, but lp0 is the first printer port just like LPT1. Which Linux port is LPT1? Who cares?! This is Linux, not DOS. DOS is dead—long live Linux!

Figure 12.3 A PrintTool local printer entry

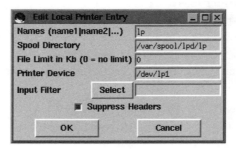

Look familiar? Some of these fields are the same as those you saw in Figure 12.1, though here there are more. This figure shows five different configuration fields. All but one are already filled in by the PrintTool. You can edit the fields that PrintTool has filled in, but usually you don't need to; the values inserted by PrintTool should work fine. However, frequently you will need to provide a value for the fifth field, Input Filter, that PrintTool left blank.

The fields in Figure 12.3 are:

Names Defines the printer name. The first printer will be automatically assigned the name `lp`. At least one printer on the system must be named `lp`. If you have more than one printer on the server, assign `lp` to the "default" printer. You can assign multiple names to a printer by separating the names with a vertical bar. For example, `hp|lj|lp` assigns the names `hp`, `lj`, and `lp` to the same printer.

Spool Directory Specifies the path to the directory where print jobs are stored. The spool directory holds print jobs until the printer can print them. By default, the spool directories are located in `/var/spool/lpd`. Normally, individual spool directories are given the same name as the printer that services them. In the example, the printer name is `lp`, so the spool directory name is `/var/spool/lpd/lp`.

File Limit Defines the maximum size of print files that will be accepted into the spool directory. The default is no limit. To set a limit, enter the number of kilobytes in this field.

Printer Device Defines the port to which the local printer is attached. As you'll see later, only local printers ask for this field.

Input Filter Defines the program used to prepare the print file. Every type of printer has its own command language and data format language. For example, some printers use Adobe's PostScript, and others use HP's Printer Control Language (PCL). A program is required to convert the Linux print file to the appropriate form for the printer. If you're familiar with installing a printer under Microsoft Windows, you may have been wondering when you tell the system what type of printer you have and what driver it should use. Well, this is when. The Linux input print filter is functionally equivalent to the Microsoft Windows print driver. The PrintTool does not provide a default value for the filter. To set the correct value, click the Select button. The window shown in Figure 12.4 appears.

Departmental
Server Operations

PART 3

Figure 12.4   Selecting a print filter

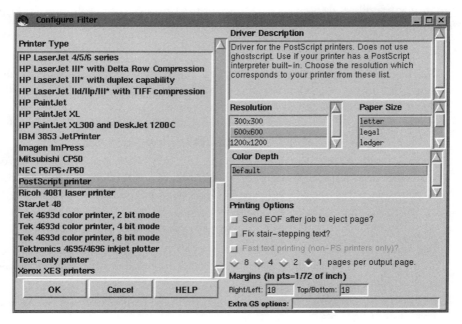

Use the scroll bar to view the list of printer filters. The PrintTool provides more than 50 different printer selections. Select your printer and then set any of the optional configuration parameters that you need on the right side of the window. For the example, I chose PostScript, which should work with any PostScript printer, and set the resolution for the printer to 600×600 and the paper size to Letter. The choices here are not always obvious if you don't have the documentation for the printer. I suggest that you go to the printer manufacturer's Web page and get the spec sheet for your printer if you don't have any other documentation. In the example, I use 600×600, because the documentation says it is the correct setting for my HP LaserJet PostScript printer.

TIP   It's a very good idea to use one of the printers for which the system has built-in support. Trying to make a printer work that is not compatible with your system is a lot of work for very little reward. I highly recommend that you use a printer from the filter list. If you're buying a printer, I recommend a PostScript printer. They work with every Linux tool in a seamless manner.

That's it. Click OK twice, and the new printer should be added to the list in the PrintTool. Select Restart lpd from the lpd menu in the PrintTool, and your new printer should be ready to go. Test the printer by selecting a test from the Tests menu. Generally, I test a printer with both the ASCII and the PostScript test pages.

Configuring Remote Printers

Remote printers require slightly different configurations than local printers. Figure 12.5 shows two configuration windows, one for a remote Unix printer (on the left) and one for a remote SMB printer (on the right).

Figure 12.5   Configuring remote printers

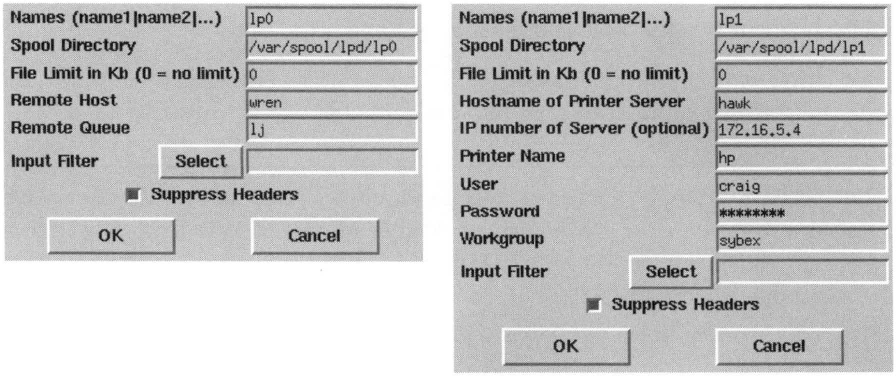

Four of the fields in the entry for the remote Unix printer are identical to those used in the local printer (shown in Figure 12.3). The difference is that instead of a single line to define a physical device port, this entry has two fields to define the remote computer and the printer on that computer. The Remote Host field contains the host name of the printer server; the name must be written in a form that your system can resolve to an IP address. The Remote Queue field contains the name of the remote printer as it is defined on the remote server. Note that this doesn't need to be the same as the name that you use in the Name field. Name is your local name for the printer; Remote Queue is the remote server's local name for the printer.

The SMB printer entry has five fields in place of the single physical port field used for local printers. These five fields are:

> **Hostname of Printer Server**   Defines the NetBIOS name of the printer server. In the sample, the NetBIOS name of the server is hawk.
>
> **IP number of Server**   Specifies the IP address of the server. This is identified as optional in the configuration window because it is only needed if the NetBIOS name cannot be resolved to an IP address through the NetBIOS name server or the lmhosts file.

Printer Name Defines the SMB share name of the printer. This is the name that the remote server advertises for the printer, which is the same name you see when you browse the remote server.

User Specifies your SMB username on the remote server. This is only needed if the server requires user-level security to access its printers.

Password Specifies the password required by the remote server to access its printers. This is combined with the username for user-level security, but it may be required even when the User field is not for printers that have share-level security.

Workgroup Specifies the name of the workgroup to which the print server belongs. In the example, the workgroup is named sybex.

Both of these remote printers have a blank Input Filter field. Usually the filter is handled by the remote server. Most of the time this field is blank on the client system.

TIP Clearly, in order to successfully configure a printer, you need to know what type of printer you have, what its capabilities are, and how it is connected to the system. Gather this information *before* you start the configuration process. While none of this is difficult, it is not obvious unless you have the right information on hand.

Understanding `printcap`

The `/etc/printcap` file defines the printers and their characteristics. Understanding a `printcap` file is the most difficult part of configuring a Linux printer server. There are an enormous number of possible configuration parameters, and the syntax of the parameters is terse and arcane.

Generally, you use a tool like the one described above to configure a printer. You don't directly edit the `printcap` file. However, a system administrator should understand the content of the file well enough to read it and know what it is doing. To do that, you need a basic understanding of the file structure and the configuration parameter syntax.

The file contains one entry for each active printer. Printer entries can span multiple lines by beginning the continuation lines with a vertical bar (|) or a colon (:). Ending a line with a backslash (\) also indicates that the following line is a continuation line. Every field in a printer entry, other than the printer name, begins and ends with a colon.

Each printer entry starts with a printer name. Multiple printer names can be used if they are separated by vertical bar characters. One printer must have the name lp.

Every active line in the printcap file begins with either a printer name, a vertical bar, or a colon. Comments begin with a number sign (#). Blank lines and leading blank characters are ignored.

printcap Parameters

The configuration parameters used in a printcap file define the printer characteristics that lpd needs to know in order to communicate with the printer. The syntax of the parameters varies slightly depending on the type of value they are assigned. There are three types of parameters:

Boolean All printcap boolean values default to false. Specifying a boolean enables its function. Booleans are specified simply by entering the parameter name in the file. For example, :ab: tells lpd to always print banners.

Numeric Some parameters are assigned numeric values. The syntax of numeric parameters separates the value from the parameter name with a #. For example, :mx#1000: sets the maximum size for an acceptable print file to 1MB.

String Some parameters use string values. The syntax of string parameters separates the value from the parameter name with an =. For example, :rp=laser: defines the name of a remote printer as laser.

A glance at the man page shows that there are an enormous number of printcap parameters. Thankfully, you'll never need to use most of them. Most printer definitions are fairly simple, and most printcap files are small. Servers usually have only one or two directly attached printers; any other printers defined in the printcap are probably remote printers.

A Sample printcap

Below is the printcap file that is the result of the three printers defined in the PrintTool examples from the previous section:

```
# #
# This printcap is being created with printtool v.3.27
# Any changes made here manually will be lost if printtool
# is run later on.
# The presence of this header means that no printcap
# existed when printtool was run.
#
```

Departmental
Server Operations

PART 3

```
##PRINTTOOL3## LOCAL POSTSCRIPT 600x600 letter
lp:\
        :sd=/var/spool/lpd/lp:\
        :mx#0:\
        :sh:\
        :lp=/dev/lp1:\
        :if=/var/spool/lpd/lp/filter:
##PRINTTOOL3## REMOTE
lp0:\
        :sd=/var/spool/lpd/lp0:\
        :mx#0:\
        :sh:\
        :rm=wren:\
        :rp=lj:
##PRINTTOOL3## SMB
lp1:\
        :sd=/var/spool/lpd/lp1:\
        :mx#0:\
        :sh:\
        :af=/var/spool/lpd/lp1/acct:\
        :lp=/dev/null:\
        :if=/usr/lib/rhs/rhs-printfilters//smbprint:
```

The first printer, which has the printer name lp, is the one directly attached to the parallel port. Most of the configuration parameters are easily traced back to the fields in the Print-Tool configuration window. The parameters are:

sd Defines the path to the spool directory.

mx Defines the maximum acceptable size for a print file. Setting this to 0 means that there is no limit on the size of print jobs.

sh Specifies whether or not headers or banner pages are printed. This is the "suppress headers" boolean. By default, it is false, meaning that headers are not suppressed. In other words, headers are printed by default. PrintTool, however, sets the boolean to true. (Simply specifying a boolean sets it to true.) This means that headers and banner pages are not printed between print jobs. This setting is fine for a small server, but you might want to comment out this boolean if you have several users so that an identifying banner page is printed for each print job.

lp Defines the device name for the printer. For a local printer, this is the port to which the printer is attached.

if Defines the input filter for this printer.

The second printer in this file (lp0) is a remote printer. The remote machine to which the printer is attached is defined by the rm parameter, and the name of the remote printer on that machine is defined by the rp parameter. In the example, the remote host is wren, and the remote printer name is lj. Most of the real configuration work for this printer takes place on a remote system. Even though this is a remote printer, it has a local spool directory. Print files are written to the local spool directory where they are queued for delivery to the remote system.

The third printer, known as lp1, is the remote SMB printer. This is the most unique definition. lpd naturally handles local printers and remote lpd printers. Remote SMB printers require a little more effort. The real work for this type of printer is handled by the smbprint program, which is invoked as the printer's input filter with the if parameter. (smbprint is covered in detail later in this chapter.) The device name, which is defined by the lp parameter, is /dev/null. In this case, you don't actually want any output from the input filter to go to a local printer, so it is sent to the bit-bucket. The real output is sent directly by smbprint to the remote server. The af parameter defines a file to which accounting information is written.

Writing a printcap from scratch is unnecessary. To create the printcap entry, select a printer that is documented to work with your Linux system and use a printer configuration tool. Use the printcap manual page to help you read and update the printcap if you need to make any changes. Once the printer is configured and running locally, it is ready to share with others.

Sharing Printers with lpd

The Line Printer daemon (lpd) provides printer services for local and remote users. It is an essential service that is started at boot time from a startup script. On both Red Hat and Caldera systems, lpd is started by the /etc/rc.d/init.d/lpd script that is generally included in the startup by default. If it isn't included in your server's startup, you can add the script using linuxconf or tksysv.

You can use the lpd script to stop, start, or reload the Line Printer daemon. Since the printcap file is only read by lpd during its startup, the reload option is useful to incorporate changes if you edit the printcap file. Here is an example of using the reload command with the startup script:

```
# /etc/rc.d/init.d/lpd reload
Shutting down lpd: lpd
Starting lpd: lpd
```

Line Printer Daemon Security

The Line Printer daemon uses trusted-host security, and it can use the same security file as the rlogin command. (See Chapter 5 for information about rlogin trusted-host security.) All of the users on a host listed in the server's hosts.equiv file are permitted to use the server's printers. To restrict access to only those remote users who have accounts on the server, include the :rs: boolean in the printer description in the printcap file. When :rs: is specified, only users who are logged in to like-named accounts on a trusted host are granted access to the printer. This parameter is applied on a printer-by-printer basis, so it is possible to restrict access to one printer while permitting access to another printer on the same system.

A problem with using the hosts.equiv file for printer access is that the file also grants password-free login access. You probably want to share your printer without granting any other access to your server. To accommodate this, lpd also uses the /etc/hosts.lpd file for security. A trusted host defined in that file is only given access to printers, and the :rs: parameter works with this host just as it does with a host defined in the hosts.equiv file.

The syntax of the hosts.lpd file is exactly the same as the syntax of the hosts.equiv file. A hosts.lpd file might contain:

```
owl
robin
crow
```

This example shows a file that restricts printer access to the clients owl, robin, and crow.

Using lpr

Use the Line Printer Remote (lpr) program to send print jobs to the Line Printer daemon. There are several lpr command-line arguments, but the command usually identifies the printer and the file to be printed, as in this example:

```
% lpr -Plj sample.txt
```

This command sends a file called `sample.txt` to a printer called `lp0`. The printer can be local or remote; it doesn't matter as long as the printer is defined in the `printcap` file and thus known to `lpd`. Assuming the `printcap` shown earlier, `lp0` is a remote printer.

Managing lpd

The Line Printer Control (`lpc`) program is a tool for controlling the printers and administering the print queue on `lpd` printer servers. Table 12.1 lists the `lpc` commands, their syntax, and their meanings.

Table 12.1   lpc Commands

Command	Usage
abort *printer*	Kills a printer daemon.
clean *printer*	Removes all files from a print queue.
disable *printer*	Turns off spooling to a print queue.
down *printer message*	Ends spooling and printing, and outputs a message.
enable *printer*	Enables spooling to a print queue.
exit	Exits from lpc.
help *command*	Displays a description of each command.
restart *printer*	Starts a new printer daemon.
start *printer*	Enables printing and spooling.
status *printer*	Displays the status of printers and queues.
stop *printer*	Stops a printer after the current job ends.
topq *printer job# user*	Moves print jobs to the top of the queue.
up *printer*	Enables spooling and printing.

In all of the commands except `topq`, the printer name is optional. If it is not specified, the default printer is used. The `topq` command also takes a job number or a username to identify the print job that you want to move to the top of the queue. Moving a job to the top of the queue means that it will be the next job printed. The only other command options are the *message* that can be added to the down command and the *command* that can be added to the help command. *message* is a text message sent out to notify users that the printer is going down. *command* is the name of an lpc command for which you want help information.

lpc can be invoked interactively. The following example shows the printer lp being restarted:

```
% lpc
lpc> status all
lp:
    queuing is enabled
    printing is enabled
    2 entries in spool area
    no daemon present
lw:
    queuing is enabled
    printing is enabled
    no entries
    no daemon present
dj:
    queuing is enabled
    printing is enabled
    no entries
    no daemon present
lpc> restart lp
lp:
    no daemon to abort
lp:
    daemon started
lpc> exit
```

Note that the keyword all is used in place of a printer name in the sample status command. all can be used to refer to all printers in any lpc command that accepts a printer name as an optional parameter.

The status and restart commands used in the example can be used by anyone. Most other lpc commands can only be used by the root user. For example, the following command moves the print jobs belonging to user tyler to the top of the queue for printer lp:

```
# lpc topq lp tyler
lp:
        moved cfA405owl
```

While lpc is primarily for the system administrator, there are other commands primarily for the users. The lpq command displays a list of jobs queued for a printer. Command-line arguments permit the user to select which printer queue is displayed and to limit the display from that queue to a specific user's jobs or even to a specific job. Here's an example of displaying the queue for the printer lp:

```
% lpq -Plp
Rank    Owner       Job  Files                 Total Size
1st     tyler       405  ...                   5876 bytes
2nd     daniel      401  ...                   12118 bytes
3rd     daniel      404  ...                   12118 bytes
```

A queued print job can be removed by the owner of the job with the lprm command. Assume that daniel wants to remove print job number 404 shown in the example above. He enters the following command:

```
% lprm -Plaser 404
dfA404robin dequeued
```

Sharing Printers with Samba

Chapter 11 shows how a Linux server can be an SMB server by using the Samba software package, and it shows how Samba is used to share files. What Chapter 11 doesn't show is that Samba can also be used to share printers with SMB clients. Here, you see how that's done.

First, of course, you need to make sure that Samba is installed in your system. (See Chapter 11 for those details.) Once Samba is installed, shared printers are configured through the smb.conf file.

Departmental
Server Operations

PART 3

Defining Printers in the `smb.conf` File

The best way to understand the SMB configuration file is to look at one that works. Red Hat systems come with a pre-configured `smb.conf` file that includes support for sharing printers. The active lines in the Red Hat `smb.conf` file are:

```
[global]
    workgroup = MYGROUP
    server string = Samba Server
    printcap name = /etc/printcap
    load printers = yes
    log file = /var/log/samba/log.%m
    max log size = 50
    security = user
    socket options = TCP_NODELAY
    dns proxy = no
[homes]
    comment = Home Directories
    browsable = no
    writable = yes
[printers]
    comment = All Printers
    path = /var/spool/samba
    browsable = no
    guest ok = no
    writable = no
    printable = yes
```

You saw many of these lines in Chapter 11, so you already know to change the `workgroup` option to the correct workgroup name for your network and to change the `server string` to something meaningful that describes your server. Some of these lines, however, were not covered in that chapter. All of the new lines deal with sharing printers. Two of the new lines are in the global section:

`printcap name` Defines the location of the `printcap` file. As you'll see in a minute, the `printcap` file is used to identify the printers that are available to share. The default path is `/etc/printcap`.

load printers Tells smbd whether or not it should offer all of the printers in the printcap file as shared printers. The default is yes, which tells Samba to share all of the printers defined in the printcap file. no means don't not read the printcap file at all. If no is specified, all shared printers must be defined individually.

Both of these lines are used to prepare the server to automatically share the printers defined in the printcap file. In addition to these two new lines, there is an entirely new section labeled "printers." It also deals with automatically sharing printers.

The Printers Share Section

The printers section performs a similar function to the homes section, which makes every home directory available to the appropriate user. The printers section is defined to make every printer available to your clients. The Red Hat printers share section is:

```
[printers]
    comment = All Printers
    path = /var/spool/samba
    browsable = no
    guest ok = no
    writable = no
    printable = yes
```

You know the comment, browsable, writable, and path options from Chapter 11. Here, however, path does not define the path of a shared file. Instead, it defines the path of the spool directory for the SMB shared printers. But which printers are shared? Based on the two options defined in the global section, all printers that are defined in the printcap file.

There are two lines in this section that you have not seen before. The first is printable, which identifies this share as a printer. The default for this option is no, meaning that by default, shares are considered to be file shares instead of printer shares. When you create a printer share, you must set this option to yes. Enabling printable permits clients to write printer files to the spool directory defined by the path option. This appears to contradict the writable command that says clients cannot write to the share. The writable option is there to say that no one can write a file to the spool that is not a print file. Because print files are created by clients in the spool directory, you may want to add a create mode command that limits the permissions of the files created. I use create mode = 0700.

The other new line, guest ok, defines whether or not guest accounts are permitted access to the resource. This is exactly the same as the public option discussed in Chapter 11, so these two options are used interchangeably. no means that the user nobody cannot send a print job to the printer. A user must have a valid user account to use the printer. This is designed to prevent guest users from abusing the printer, but it is also useful to have a valid username for sorting out print jobs if you use banner pages and accounting on your server.

Generally, this section is all you need to make every printer on the server available to all of your clients. You can use the host allow command described in Chapter 11 to restrict access to printers in the same way that you restrict access to files, but in general, a printer server offers all of its printers to all of its clients.

smb.conf Printer Configuration Options

If you don't want to share every printer defined in the printcap file, you can remove the printers section, set the load printers option to no, and add individual share sections for just those printers that you do want to share. Individual share sections can be created for each printer in the same way that they are created for file sharing.

In addition to the printer configuration options described above, you can use any relevant options described in Chapter 11 and any of the options listed in Table 12.2.

Table 12.2   More smb.conf Printer Options

Option	Use
lpq cache	Defines how long lpq information is cached.
lpq command	Specifies the path to the lpq command.
lprm command	Specifies the path to the lprm command.
min page space	Defines the minimum amount of free space that must remain in the spool directory. Samba will not accept print jobs if free space drops below the minimum. By default, there is no minimum.
postscript	Forces Samba to interpret print files as PostScript files in order to print files that start with a Ctrl+D.
printer	Defines the name of a specific shared printer.
printing	Defines the printing system used on the server. Linux uses bsd or lprng, which is a variant of bsd. Possible values are aix, bsd, hpux, lprng, plp, qnx, softq, and sysv.

An smb.conf file with a share section for a specific printer might contain the following:

```
[global]
    workgroup = SYBEX
    server string = Author's Printer server
    load printers = no
    security = user
[homes]
    comment = Home Directories
    browsable = no
    writable = yes
[hp5m]
    comment = PostScript Laser Printer
    path = /var/spool/samba
    browsable = no
    public = no
    writable = no
    create mode = 0700
    printable = yes
    printer = lp
```

In this case, no printers section is included. Instead, a share dsection named hp5m is added that shares printer lp. The printer name (lp) must be found in the printcap file for this to work. The printcap name is allowed to default to /etc/printcap.

Using an SMB Printer

A Linux system can be an SMB client as easily as it can be an SMB server. A Linux user can print to a remote SMB printer with a standard lpr command if the SMB printer is properly defined in the printcap file. I used the Red Hat PrintTool earlier in the chapter to define a remote SMB printer. The PrintTool screen used to create that printer is shown in Figure 12.6.

Departmental
Server Operations

PART 3

Figure 12.6   Defining an SMB printer with PrintTool

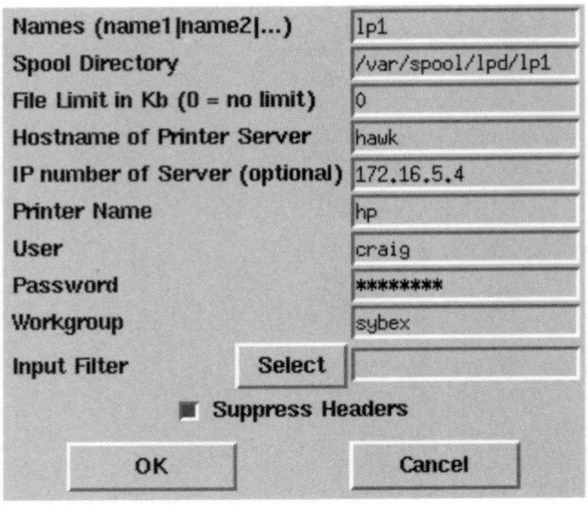

Names (name1|name2|...)	lp1
Spool Directory	/var/spool/lpd/lp1
File Limit in Kb (0 = no limit)	0
Hostname of Printer Server	hawk
IP number of Server (optional)	172.16.5.4
Printer Name	hp
User	craig
Password	********
Workgroup	sybex
Input Filter	Select

☑ Suppress Headers

[OK]   [Cancel]

The PrintTool input in Figure 12.6 created this `printcap` entry:

```
lp1:\
        :sd=/var/spool/lpd/lp1:\
        :mx#0:\
        :sh:\
        :af=/var/spool/lpd/lp1/acct:\
        :lp=/dev/null:\
        :if=/usr/lib/rhs/rhs-printfilters//smbprint:
```

The key to making this entry work is the input filter (`if`) used for this printer. `smbprint` is a script file that uses `smbclient` to print to the remote system.

The additional information entered in the PrintTool window is used to configure the `smbprint` script. That information is stored in the `.config` file in the spool directory of the SMB printer. A glance at the `sd` parameter in the `printcap` file tells the path of the spool directory, and a `cat` command shows the contents of the `.config` file:

```
# cat /var/spool/lpd/lp1/.config
share='\\hawk\hp'
hostip=172.16.5.4
user=craig
password='Wats?Watt?'
workgroup='sybex'
```

The .config file contains five entries, which must occur in exactly the order shown. If no value is provided for an entry, the entry still appears in the file but with a null entry, e.g., password=' '. The five entries are:

share Defines the share name, which is the NetBIOS name of the remote server combined with the share name of the remote printer.

hostip Specifies the numeric IP address of the remote server.

user Defines the user's login name on the remote server.

password Defines the password required by the remote server for access to the printer.

workgroup Identifies the workgroup to which the print server belongs.

If the printcap is properly configured and the .config file contains the necessary information, a user on our Linux system should be able to print to the printer on hawk by entering **% lpr –Plp1 sample.txt**. I think this is the easiest way to use a remote SMB printer from a Linux system.

However, you can also use a remote printer directly through the smbclient software. Using smbclient to access shared files was discussed in Chapter 11, and printing with smbclient is very similar. Use smbclient in the same way to connect to the share, except this time the share is a remote printer. For example:

```
smbclient //hawk/hp –U craig%Wats?Watt? –W SYBEX
```

After connecting to the printer share, use the same put command that you use to transfer a file to the server. When smbclient transfers a file to a printable share, the file is printed. For example, to print the file sample.txt on the hp printer after connecting to that printer with the smbclient command, enter the following:

```
smb:> put sample.txt
```

> **NOTE** The smbclient also has a print command that functions in the same way as the put command. put is generally preferred.

Final Words

File and printer sharing are the basic services of a departmental network. Linux is an excellent platform for providing these network services, because it can provide the native services expected by Unix clients in addition to the same services in the native format expected by Microsoft Windows clients. Other departmental servers do not do as effective a job of integrating all of your clients together into a single network.

Another service that Linux excels at is e-mail. The next chapter concludes the section on departmental servers with a discussion of departmental mail services.

Departmental
Server Operations

PART 3

13

More Mail Services

A departmental mail server usually acts as a mailbox server that holds mail for its clients until they are ready to download it for their readers. The mailbox service supports mobile users and systems that do not receive mail in real time. Linux offers two techniques for creating a mailbox server: Post Office Protocol (POP), which is the traditional mailbox protocol, and Internet Message Access Protocol (IMAP), which is growing in popularity. In this chapter, you will use both protocols to configure a Linux system to act as a department mailbox server.

In addition to the essential mailbox services, Linux systems offer some additional mail services that you may want to use. These include spam filters and tools that are designed to help you limit the amount of unwanted junk mail that bombards your users.

Understanding POP and IMAP

A host turns into a mailbox server when it runs either the POP or the IMAP daemon. Most Linux systems run both. Unless you do something to prevent it, such as choosing the Select Individual Packages option during a Red Hat 6 installation and then specifically "un-selecting" POP and IMAP, both POP and IMAP are installed by default during the initial installation.

Neither of these daemons requires any configuration. All users who have a valid user account on the system are allowed to download mail via POP or IMAP.

Adding a POP User with linuxconf

One concern with granting a mailbox user a valid user account on the server is that the user is able to directly log in to the server. This may be exactly what you want. Many administrators allow users to log in and read mail directly on the server with one of the local Linux mail readers, such as pine. The advantage of this is that a mobile user can read mail without waiting for the entire mailbox to be transferred over a slow modem line.

For other administrators, allowing users to directly log in to the server is exactly what they do *not* want. These administrators are concerned that the user will have access to other shell commands and services beyond the mailbox service they want to provide.

linuxconf provides a solution for both types of administrators. Figure 13.1 shows the creation of a POP user account with linuxconf. This is a special account with limited functionality specifically designed for use with a mailbox server.

Figure 13.1   Creating a POP user account

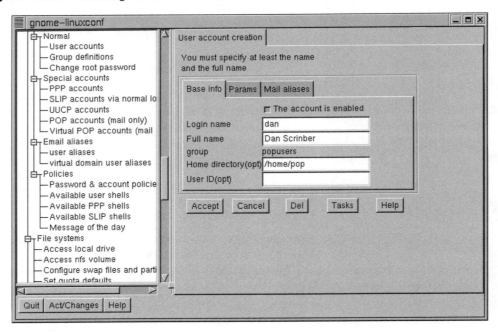

From the scrolling menu on the left, select POP Accounts (Mail Only), which opens the User Account Creation window on the right. In this window, enter the username, full name, and home directory for the POP user to create the desired account. Click the Accept button and enter a password for the user.

The account created in Figure 13.1 inserted the following entry in the /etc/passwd file:

```
$ grep dan /etc/passwd
dan:8eAvrnfm4E:503:231:Dan Scribner:/home/pop:/bin/false
```

Notice that the dan entry looks just like any other passwd entry except for the login shell. Instead of a valid login shell, dan is assigned /bin/false, which means that dan cannot directly log in to the server.

The account created in Figure 13.1 is limited to mailbox access. Despite being called a POP account by linuxconf, it works equally well for both POP and IMAP. If instead you want to create an account that allows the user to choose between mailbox access and reading the mail directly on the server, use linuxconf to create a normal user account as described in Chapter 5, *Login Services*.

The POP Protocol

There are two versions of POP: POP2 and POP3. The POP protocols verify the user's login name and password and move the user's mail from the server to the user's local mail reader. Both protocols perform the same basic functions, but they are incompatible. POP2 uses port 109, and POP3 uses port 110. Linux systems come with both versions of POP, but most of your clients will use POP3.

POP3 is defined in RFC 1725. It is a simple request/response protocol: The client sends a command to the server, and the server responds to the command. Table 13.1 shows the set of POP3 commands defined in RFC 1725.

Table 13.1   POP3 Commands

Command	Function
USER *username*	The username required for the login.
PASS *password*	The user's password required for the login.
STAT	Requests the number of unread messages/bytes.
RETR *m*	Retrieves message number *m*.

Table 13.1   POP3 Commands *(continued)*

Command	Function
DELE *m*	Deletes message number *m*.
LAST	Requests the number of the last message accessed.
LIST [*m*]	Requests the size of message *m* or of all messages.
RSET	Undeletes all messages and resets the message number to 1.
TOP *m* *n*	Prints the headers and the first *n* lines of message number *m*.
NOOP	Does nothing.
QUIT	Ends the POP3 session.

Using your knowledge of the protocol and the configuration, you can `telnet` to the POP port and test if your server responds. The `telnet` test shown here proves that the daemon is available, installed, and ready to run:

```
% telnet localhost pop-3
Trying 127.0.0.1 ...
Connected to localhost.
Escape character is '^]'.
+OK POP3 almond Server (Version 1.004) ready
quit
+OK POP3 almond Server (Version 1.001) shutdown
Connection closed by foreign host.
```

If POP is not ready to run, the `telnet` test returns an error. This example shows what happens when the POP ports are not configured in the /etc/services file:

```
$ telnet localhost pop-3
pop-3: bad port number
```

Check the /etc/services file to see the actual POP ports. On a Red Hat 6 system, you'll see the following POP2 and POP3 ports:

```
$ grep 'pop.[2,3]' /etc/services
```

```
pop-2        109/tcp      postoffice    # POP version 2
pop-2        109/udp
pop-3        110/tcp                     # POP version 3
pop-3        110/udp
```

I've never really had a problem with the ports not being defined, but I have had a different problem indicated by this `telnet` test:

```
$ telnet localhost pop-3
Trying 127.0.0.1...
telnet:Unable to connect to remote host:Connection refused
```

The POP daemon is started by `inetd`. The error shown above means that the POP daemon is not properly configured in the `inetd.conf` file and that `inetd` is not starting the daemon. This happens on a Red Hat 6 system because the POP entries are commented-out of the `inetd.conf` file:

```
$ grep 'pop.[2,3]' /etc/inetd.conf
#pop-2 stream  tcp  nowait  root  /usr/sbin/tcpd ipop2d
#pop-3 stream  tcp  nowait  root  /usr/sbin/tcpd ipop3d
```

Remove the # from the start of each entry to run POP on a Red Hat 6 system. Most Linux systems, including earlier releases of Red Hat, come with POP ready to run. Most Linux systems also come with IMAP ready to run.

The IMAP Protocol

Internet Message Access Protocol (IMAP) is an alternative to POP. It provides the same basic service as POP and adds features to support mailbox synchronization. *Mailbox synchronization* is the ability to read individual mail messages on a client or directly on the server while keeping the mailbox on both systems completely up-to-date.

On an average POP server, the entire contents of the mailbox is moved to the client and either deleted from the server or retained as if never read. Deletion of individual messages on the client is not reflected on the server, because all of the messages are treated as a single unit that is either deleted or retained after the initial transfer of data to the client. IMAP provides the ability to manipulate individual messages on the client or the server and to have those changes reflected in the mailboxes of both systems.

Like the POP protocol, IMAP is also a request/response protocol with a small set of commands. Table 13.2 lists the basic set of IMAP commands from version 4 of the IMAP protocol.

Table 13.2 IMAP4 Commands

Command	Use
CAPABILITY	Lists the features supported by the server.
NOOP	Literally means "No Operation," but sometimes used as a way to poll for new messages or message status updates.
LOGOUT	Closes the connection.
AUTHENTICATE	Requests an alternative authentication method.
LOGIN	Opens the connection and provides the username and password for plain-text authentication.
SELECT	Opens a mailbox.
EXAMINE	Opens a mailbox as read-only.
CREATE	Creates a new mailbox.
DELETE	Removes a mailbox.
RENAME	Changes the name of a mailbox.
SUBSCRIBE	Adds a mailbox to the list of active mailboxes.
UNSUBSCRIBE	Deletes a mailbox name from the list of active mailboxes.
LIST	Displays the requested mailbox names from the complete set of all available mailboxes.
LSUB	Displays the requested mailbox names from the set of active mailboxes.
STATUS	Requests the status of a mailbox.
APPEND	Adds a message to the end of the specified mailbox.
CHECK	Forces a checkpoint of the current mailbox.
CLOSE	Closes the mailbox and removes all messages marked for deletion.

Table 13.2   IMAP4 Commands *(continued)*

Command	Use
EXPUNGE	Removes from the current mailbox all messages that are marked for deletion.
SEARCH	Displays all messages in the mailbox that match the specified search criteria.
FETCH	Retrieves a message from the mailbox.
STORE	Modifies a message in the mailbox.
COPY	Copies the specified messages to the end of the selected mailbox.
UID	Searches for or fetches messages based on the message's unique identifier.

This command set is more complex than the one used by POP because IMAP does more. The protocol is designed to remotely maintain mailboxes that are stored on the server, and the protocol commands clearly illustrate the "mailbox" orientation of IMAP. Despite the increased complexity of the protocol, it is still possible to run a simple test of your IMAP server using `telnet` and a small number of the IMAP commands:

```
$ telnet localhost imap
Trying 127.0.0.1...
Connected to localhost.
Escape character is '^]'.
* OK localhost IMAP4rev1 v12.250 server ready
A0001 LOGOUT
* BYE wren.foobirds.org IMAP4rev1 server terminating connection
A0001 OK LOGOUT completed
Connection closed by foreign host.
```

NOTE   The command in this example is preceded by the string A0001. This is a *tag*, which is a unique identifier generated by the client for each command. When you manually type in commands for a test, you are the source of the tags.

Departmental
Server Operations

PART 3

The test above shows that imapd is up and running. However, a test on a freshly installed Red Hat 6 system returns the "Unable to connect" error. Again, the reason is that imap is commented-out of the inetd.conf file:

```
$ grep imapd /etc/inetd.conf
#imap  stream  tcp  nowait  root  /usr/sbin/tcpd imapd
```

Remove the # at the beginning of the imapd entry in the inetd.conf file to enable IMAP. Then rerun the telnet test, which tells you the version of IMAP running on your server. The next section describes how to get a newer version of IMAP if you need one.

Compiling IMAP

IMAP is not a new protocol (it is about as old as POP3). Despite its age, IMAP is not completely standardized. There have been four distinct versions of IMAP: IMAP, IMAP2, IMAP3, and the current version, IMAP4 Rev1. New RFCs about IMAP are still being issued. There are currently more than a dozen. The fear that IMAP is still in flux and that it is difficult to implement has discouraged some vendors, so it is not as widely implemented as POP. However, Linux distributions do include imapd.

The amount of change and development going on with IMAP means that you may not have the latest version of the daemon. The IMAP source code can be obtained via anonymous FTP from ftp.cac.washington.edu.

Download /imap/imap.tar.Z and uncompress and restore it using the tar command. This creates a new directory that contains the source code and the Makefile needed to build IMAP. The name of the directory tells you the current release level of the software. At this writing, it is imap-4.5. Read the Makefile carefully—it supports many different operating systems. There are two possible selections for Linux. Use the three-character OS type lnx for Linux systems that use the /etc/passwd file, or use slx on the make command line for systems that use the shadow password file. For example:

```
# make slx
```

It should compile without error and produce three daemons: ipop2d, ipop3d, and imapd. Use whereis or find to check where your system expects to find the IMAP daemon. Then copy the new imapd to that location. (On a Red Hat 6 system, imapd is stored in /usr/sbin.) Make sure that the permissions for the imapd file are the same file permissions given to the previous version of the daemon. The following example shows all of these steps:

```
# tar -Zxvf imap.tar.Z
# cd imap.4.5
```

```
# make slx
# mv /usr/sbin/imapd /usr/sbin.imapd.orig
# cp imapd/imapd /usr/sbin/imapd
# chmod 755 /usr/sbin/imapd
```

Rerun the `telnet localhost` imap test to make sure your new daemon is responding to clients.

The University of Washington package provides implementations of POP2 and POP3, as well as IMAP. POP2 and POP3 have not changed for a long time, so it is unlikely you will want to use these to replace the corresponding daemons on your system.

Using POP or IMAP from a Client

You're responsible for giving the user the correct information to configure his mail agent. The user needs to know:

- The host name of the mail server
- The username and password required by the mail server
- Whether POP or IMAP should be used

Figure 13.2 shows a user configuring this information for the Netscape Communicator.

Figure 13.2   Configuring the mail client

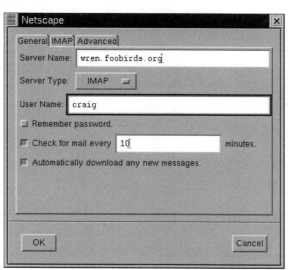

This particular window permits the user to select POP3, IMAP, or something called *Movemail* from the Server Type list. By now, the meaning of POP3 and IMAP is obvious, but Movemail is something new. Movemail simply copies mail from the system's mail spool directory to the user's Netscape mail directory. Movemail only works when the local computer is also the mail server. Of course, with a Linux computer, this is possible.

Notice also that the configuration window allows you to name two different computers for outbound mail and inbound mail. It is possible for the departmental mailbox server and the server that forwards mail to the outside world to be two different computers.

Stopping Spam E-Mail

SPAM is a world-famous canned luncheon meat from Hormel Food. *Internet spam* isn't—it's junk e-mail. Spam e-mails are the unsolicited advertisements you receive trying to sell you a college diploma, pheromones that women can't resist, or pornography if those pheromones don't work. I'm sure you know what I mean, because everyone attached to the Internet gets tons of this stuff.

One of your tasks as the administrator of a mail server is to reduce the amount of junk mail moving through the network. The techniques used for that task are the topic of this section.

Spam, Spam, Spam, Spam, and Spam

In a classic Monty Python comedy skit, John Cleese plays a waiter reciting a menu. In the beginning, the menu has one SPAM selection, but with each recitation of the menu, more and more of the items become SPAM, until he finally describes the menu as "Spam, spam, spam, spam, and spam."

Similarly, e-mail spam replicates itself through every possible mailing list until you find yourself with a mailbox full of exactly the same message repeated over and over again. It is this mindless repetition that gives spam e-mail its name.

Don't Be a Spam Source

Your first duty in the spam war is to make sure that your system is not a source of spam. Your system can be a source of locally generated spam, or it can be a relay for spam generated elsewhere. You need to respond to both possibilities.

Defining an Acceptable Use Policy

To prevent locally generated spam, you need to make sure that everyone using your server knows that sending unsolicited advertisements from your server is not allowed. I have to admit that the idea of such a thing is alien to me. The government agencies and large businesses that I work with would fire *anyone* who misused corporate property in any way, let alone run a private advertising firm on a corporate server!

But your situation may be different. You may be offering a community service on your system. In that case, you need a written Acceptable Use Policy (AUP) that tells people what type of use is allowed and what isn't.

> **TIP** If you're not sure what an AUP should look like, ask your ISP or check a national ISP. A copy of the UUNET Acceptable Use Policy is available at www.us.uu.net/support/usepolicy/, or check out the Sprintlink acceptable use policy at www.sprint.net/acceptableuse.htm.

Running the Identification Daemon

Running the auth server (identd) also helps to discourage home-grown spammers. The identification daemon monitors port 113. If it gets a request from a remote system, it tells that system the name of the user running the current connection process to that system. This allows remote mail servers to put a real username on the Received: header in incoming e-mail. Linux provides this service by default, as the following grep of /etc/services and inetd.conf shows:

```
$ grep ^auth /etc/services
auth   113/tcp   ident   # User Verification
$ grep ^auth /etc/inetd.conf
auth stream tcp nowait nobody /usr/sbin/in.identd in.identd -l -e -o
```

Properly Configuring Mail Relaying

In addition to discouraging local users from generating spam, you need to discourage remote users from using your server as a tool for distributing spam. Nobody likes spammers, and the spammers know it. They do their best to hide the true source of the spam by relaying their junk mail through other people's servers. If your mail server allows relaying, spammers can make use of it.

To discourage spam, the default configuration of sendmail 8.9 properly handles local mail, but does not relay messages for any outside sources. This is just the opposite of earlier versions of sendmail that relayed all mail by default. If your system runs an older version of sendmail, you should upgrade to 8.9 to get the full range of anti-spam tools.

Blocking all relaying works in most cases because most systems that run `sendmail` are not mail servers—they're desktop Linux and Unix systems dedicated to a single user. Because the user's mail originates on the system that is running `sendmail`, the mail is handled as local mail, and relaying is not required.

Blocking all relaying doesn't work if the system is a mail server. Most of the mail a mail server delivers originates on its clients—these might be Microsoft Windows PCs that don't run their own `sendmail` program. Blocking relaying at the server causes the client to get an error like this when trying to deliver mail:

To create a mail server, you must allow some level of relaying. Use the following `sendmail` features to relax the relay restrictions just enough to get the job done:

FEATURE(`'promiscuous_relay'`) Tells `sendmail` to relay mail from all sources.

FEATURE(`'relay_entire_domain'`) Tells `sendmail` to relay mail from any local domain, i.e. any domain defined in class M. (Don't remember the `sendmail` classes? Shame on you! You'll have to read Chapter 7, *Configuring a Mail Server*, again.)

FEATURE(`'relay_based_on_MX'`) Tells `sendmail` to relay mail for any host for which the local host is the MX server.

FEATURE(`'relay_local_from'`) Tells `sendmail` to relay mail that contains the local domain in the MAIL FROM: header.

FEATURE(`'accept_unresolvable_domains'`) Tells `sendmail` to accept mail from a host even if it can not be found in DNS or the host table. Normally, mail from hosts that do not exist in the domain name system is rejected.

Red Hat 6 uses `sendmail` 8.9.3, which blocks relaying by default. To turn this system into a mail server, create a new configuration file that allows the appropriate level of relaying. For example, you could create the following variation on the `foobirds.m4` DOMAIN file used in Chapter 7:

```
VERSIONID(`@(#)generic.m4     8.3 (Berkeley) 3/24/96')
define(`confFORWARD_PATH', `$z/.forward.$w:$z/.forward')dnl
FEATURE('relay_entire_domain')
```

```
FEATURE(redirect)dnl
FEATURE(use_cw_file)dnl
MASQUERADE_AS(foobirds.org)
FEATURE(masquerade_envelope)
FEATURE(genericstable)
```

This file contains all of the same features described in Chapter 7 plus the relay_entire_ domain feature. This additional feature permits you to use the M class as a way to identify those hosts whose mail the server should relay.

> **WARNING**   Be careful that you don't weaken the configuration so much you become a spam source! All of the features listed above weaken the barrier to mail relaying, but some are worse than others. promiscuous_relay should not be used because it turns the system into a potential spam relay. Avoid the relay_ local_from feature, because it is very easy for spammers to write anything they want in the MAIL FROM: header, including your local domain name. Additionally, accept_unresolvable_domains should not be used unless it is absolutely required. It is intended for when your mail server really can't resolve domain names. You may need this on a laptop Linux system that does not always have access to a DNS server, but otherwise I wouldn't use it.

Using sendmail to Block Spam

The world will be grateful that your server is not a source for junk mail, but your users will only be happy if they are not the target for spam. sendmail 8.9 provides two techniques for blocking incoming spam: one uses a DNS-based service to block spam sources; the other uses a local database that you create. The first is easy and convenient; the second gives you greater control. This section examines both techniques to help you decide which is right for you.

Using the Realtime Blackhole List

The simplest way to block spam is to let someone else do it. sendmail allows you to use the Realtime Blockhole List (RBL) that comes from the Mail Abuse Prevention System (MAPS).

NOTE Visit the Web site at `maps.vix.com/rbl` to find out more about the MAPS system.

Using the RBL is very easy because the system is implemented through DNS. Every Linux system can issue DNS queries, so this is a very effective way to distribute information. Of course, a program can only make use of the information if it understands it. `sendmail` does. If you want to use the RBL to block spam, add the following feature to your `sendmail` configuration:

```
FEATURE('rbl')
```

With this feature enabled, mail from every site listed in the RBL is rejected.

While this is simple, it isn't perfect, because you can't choose which sites listed in the RBL are rejected. It's an all or nothing proposition. In fact, that's what makes it as easy as turning a light switch on or off. The RBL enforces a very stern policy. Any site that relays spam—which could be *your* site if you don't upgrade to `sendmail` 8.9—is listed in the RBL. If the site stops relaying spam, it is removed from the list after about a month. This means that you might be blocked from receiving e-mail from a friendly site just because the administrator at that site forgot to turn off relaying.

As usual, the choice is between simplicity and flexibility. For spam filtering, most small sites should choose simplicity. If your site is small, you probably have only a few other sites with which you exchange mail. The likelihood of any of those sites appearing in the RBL is very slim. However, if you run the mail server for a large site that exchanges mail with many other sites, simplicity may not be a choice. You may need to define your own e-mail access list to prevent the RBL from blocking mail that you want. `sendmail` allows you to do that.

Understanding the Access Database

The `sendmail` access database defines e-mail sources using e-mail addresses, domain names, and IP network numbers along with the action that `sendmail` should take when it receives mail from the specified source. For example:

```
spammer@bigisp.com        REJECT

wespamu.com               REJECT

172.18                    REJECT
```

This database tells `sendmail` to reject any mail from the e-mail address `spammer@big.isp.com`, from any host in the domain `wespamu.com`, and from any computer whose IP address begins with network number 172.18. Each entry in the database begins with the source of the mail followed by a keyword that tells `sendmail` what action to take. Table 13.3 lists the valid keywords and the actions they cause.

Table 13.3   Access Database Actions

Keyword	Action
DISCARD	Drops any message received from the specified source.
OK	Absolutely accepts messages from the specified source.
REJECT	Issues an error message and drops any mail from or to the specified address.
RELAY	Relays mail coming from or bound to the specified address.
Error message	Returns the specified error message to the source address.

An extension to the database shown above illustrates how these actions are used:

```
spammer@bigisp.com      REJECT
wespamu.com             REJECT
172.18                  DISCARD
friendly.org            OK
129.6                   RELAY
weselljunk.com          550 Junk mail is not accepted
```

The REJECT commands cause sendmail to return an error message to the source and then discard the mail. The DISCARD command drops the mail without sending any message back to the source. Most anti-spam authorities discourage silently discarding mail because they feel it does not discourage the spammer. For all he knows, you received the mail, so he just keeps sending more junk.

The OK command causes sendmail to accept mail from friendly.org regardless of other conditions. For example, if mail arrives from a host name that includes the friendly.org domain and cannot be resolved by DNS, sendmail accepts that mail even though the accept_unresolvable_domains feature has not been enabled. To do this, you must, of course, fully trust friendly.org.

The RELAY command causes sendmail to relay mail for network 129.6, even though basic relaying is not enabled on the system. Like the OK command, using the RELAY command means that you fully trust every host on network 129.6.

TIP If you don't have anything else in your database, you probably want an entry like this one for your own network. As discussed above, sendmail 8.9 blocks all mail relaying, even mail from your clients. I use the access database and an entry like 172.16.5 RELAY to enable relaying for every host attached to my local network. I like this technique because it doesn't rely on host names, which are easy to spoof, and it can be as tightly controlled as I want through the access database.

Creating Your Own Access Database

Formatting the entries in the access database is the easy part. Deciding exactly what to put in the database is harder. Luckily, there are organizations on the Internet, like the Mail Abuse Prevention System, that collect information about spammers that you can use to help you build your access database. The best known sites are www.arachnoid.com/lutusp/antispam/spammers.txt, www.wsrcc.com/spam/spamdomains.txt, www.mindspring.com/cgi-bin/spamlist.pl, and www.e-scrub.com/cgi-bin/blacklists.cgi.

Are all of the organizations listed at these sites really active spammers? Probably not. But you can use these lists as a starting point for building your own access database. See the case study at the end of this chapter for an example of how these lists are used to create an access database.

Of course, in addition to extracting data from lists of spammers, you can enter your own entries directly into the access list using your favorite editor. Once you build your access list, convert it into a database using the makemap commnand that comes with sendmail:

```
makemap hash /etc/mail/access < /etc/mail/access.text
```

I generally use an editor and makemap to create the database, but you can use linuxconf to build the database for you. Figure 13.3 shows an anti-spam filter being created with linuxconf.

Figure 13.3   Using linuxconf to create the access database

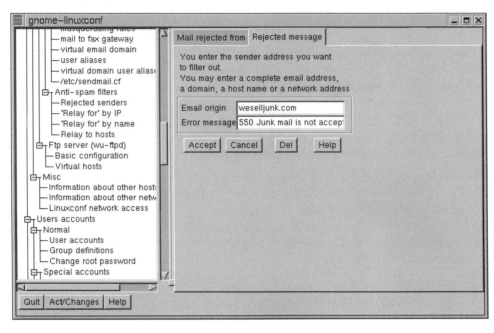

On the left-hand side of the window, select one of the items from the linuxconf Anti-Spam Filters menu. There are four possible selections:

Rejected senders   This selection creates a true spam filter. The selection opens the Mail Rejected From tab. Click Add to open the Rejected Message tab shown in Figure 13.3. This tab is where you define the anti-spam rule, including both the source of the e-mail and the error message that will be sent to that source. The figure shows that mail from weselljunk.com will be rejected with the error message "550 Junk mail is not accepted." This is the only linuxconf menu selection that blocks e-mail. The other three selections are used to loosen the mail relaying restrictions so that you can create a mail server.

'Relay for' by IP   Use this selection to define a host or network for which the server should relay mail. The host or network must be identified by IP number. This enables mail relaying for your clients.

'Relay for' by name   Use this selection to define a host or domain for which the server should relay mail. The host or network must be identified by name. This enables mail relaying for your clients.

Relay to hosts This selection identifies remote hosts to which the server will relay mail. A possible use is to identify an external mail server that your system relays mail through, for example your corporate mail server.

When you click the Act/Changes button, which stands for Activate Changes, the linuxconf tool will build the access database file for you. If you build your access list manually with a text editor, like I do, you must also manually build the database.

Using the Access Database in sendmail

After building the database, you also need to let sendmail know that you have an access database and that you want to use it. Use the access_db feature to do that.

Assume that you're using the configuration that was created in Chapter 7. There you created three files: an OSTYPE file for the Caldera system, a DOMAIN file for the specifics of the foobirds.org domain, and a linux.mc file to bring all of the files together into a single configuration. Because the access database doesn't really have anything to do with the operating system and is specific to our server, let's add the necessary feature to the foobirds.m4 DOMAIN file:

```
VERSIONID(`@(#)generic.m4        8.3 (Berkeley) 3/24/96')
define(`confFORWARD_PATH', `$z/.forward.$w:$z/.forward')dnl
FEATURE('access_db', 'hash -o /etc/mail/access')
FEATURE(redirect)dnl
FEATURE(use_cw_file)dnl
MASQUERADE_AS(foobirds.org)
FEATURE(masquerade_envelope)
FEATURE(genericstable)
```

This is the same foobirds.m4 file described in Chapter 7 with one addition. The first FEATURE listed in this file invokes the access database and describes where it is located. As described in Chapter 7, the foobirds.m4 macro file is referenced in the macro control file linux.mc. Process the control file with the m4 command to produce a sendmail.cf file that uses the new database:

```
# m4 ../m4/cf.m4 linux.mc > sendmail.cf
```

After you create and install the new `sendmail.cf` file with `m4`, your new access database is in force and blocking spammers. If you need even more control over the process, you can define your own anti-spam `sendmail` rewrite rules.

Using Anti-Spam Rewrite Rules

Most administrators think of `sendmail` rewrite rules as a way to modify addresses on outbound e-mail that originates on the local system in the user's mailer. The anti-spam rulesets allow you to process the addresses and headers from incoming mail. `sendmail` 8.9 provides three anti-spam rulesets for your personal rules:

`Local_check_relay` A ruleset where you can define rules for handling mail that is being relayed

`Local_check_rcpt` A ruleset where you can define rules to process inbound mail based on the recipient address

`Local_check_mail` A ruleset where you can define rules to process inbound mail based on the sender address

Assume that you have been receiving junk mail that is trying to masquerade as local mail by using a From address that contains only a username. Further, assume that you have configured your mail server so that the From address of local mail always includes the host name. You could use `Local_check_mail` to check the sender address as follows:

```
SLocal_check_mail
# Check for user@host
R$+@$+    $@$#OK
R$*       $#error $: 550 Invalid From address
```

The first line in this example is an S command that defines the ruleset named `Local_ check_mail`. The first R command matches the incoming address against the pattern $+ @ $+, which looks for one or more tokens ($+), a literal at-sign (@), and one or more tokens. Any address in the form of *user@host* matches this pattern. The transformation says that if the address matches the pattern, exit the ruleset ($@) and return the mailer name $#OK to the calling ruleset. $#OK is a phony mailer used to indicate that the address is valid.

The second R command matches every address that failed to match the first rule. For all of these addresses, the rule returns the mailer name $#error and the text of an error message. The $#error mailer is a special mailer that returns the mail to the sender along with an error message. An alternative to this would be the $#discard mailer, which silently discards the mail. Most administrators prefer to return an error message.

Departmental
Server Operations

PART 3

In addition to these rulesets, you can call a ruleset from a header definition to check the format of the headers your system receives. Sometimes spammers use malformed headers that indicate the mail is spam. Assume you're getting spammed by someone who forgets to create a valid-looking Message-ID header. You could use code like the following:

```
LOCAL_RULESETS
HMessage-Id: $>100


S100
R$+@$+           $@ $#OK
R$*              $#error $: 550 Invalid Header
```

The LOCAL_RULESETS section contains an H command for the sendmail.cf file. Unlike the H commands you saw in Chapter 7, this one doesn't contain a header format. Instead, it uses the $> syntax to call a ruleset to process the header. This example calls ruleset 100 because that is the name of the new ruleset I defined.

The S100 command is the first line of ruleset 100. This ruleset is essentially identical to the one described in the previous example. It checks to make sure that the Message-ID header contains both a unique message identifier and a host name in the form *identifier@host*. All other formats are rejected as errors.

I don't recommend that you use either of these rewrite rule examples in your configuration. I simply created them to illustrate how these rulesets are used. Frankly, I don't develop rewrite rules to fight spam. First, rewrite rules can be complex and difficult to develop. I don't want the cure to be worse than the disease. Second, the format of spam mail is constantly changing. The rule I write today may be useless tomorrow. I think it is better to rely on the RBL, the access database, and the ability of the user's mailer to filter mail.

Filtering Out Spam at the Mailer

Despite your best efforts, spam and other unwanted mail *will* get to your users. This is partly because you can't block all of the spam and partly because not all unwanted e-mail is spam. Sometimes a user just doesn't want to look at some legitimate e-mail simply because of personal preference. In this case, the mail needs to be filtered at the user's mail reader. Most mail readers provide this capability.

Using the elm Filter

The elm mailer comes with a filtering tool aptly named filter. Even if you don't use elm, you can use the filter program to process incoming mail.

The `filter` program is invoked with the `.forward` file covered in Chapter 7 during the discussion of `sendmail` aliases). Its primary purpose is to provide each user with a way to specify personal mail forwarding. One of the best features of `.forward` is that it can forward mail to a program, which is the feature used to send mail to the `filter` program.

To process your mail through the `filter` program, put the following line in `.forward`:

```
| "exec /usr/local/bin/filter -o ~/filter.errors"
```

The `filter` program reads its configuration from the `filter-rules` file in the `.elm` directory in the user's home directory. Therefore, if the home directory of the user running `filter` is /home/sara, `filter` looks for a file named /home/sara/.elm/filter-rules. If the user doesn't really run `elm`, they need to create a `.elm` directory to hold the configuration file.

The `filter-rules` file contains the direction for filtering the mail. It is written as a series of "if" statements. If the incoming mail matches the condition defined by the statement, it is processed in the manner that the statement directs. A sample `filter-rules` file illustrates how this works:

```
if (from = "*.gov") then Save ~/Mail/clients
if (from = "neil@sybex.com") then Save ~/Mail/editors
if (from = "emily@sybex.com") then Save ~/Mail/editors
if (from = "*.wespamu.com") then Delete
```

This set of filters routes the mail received from different sources to different mailboxes. Mail from government consulting clients is routed to the `clients` mailbox; mail from Sybex editors is routed to the `editors` mailbox. The first three rules route mail to different mailboxes. The last rule discards unwanted mail; everything from `wespamu.com` is deleted.

All of the lines in the `filter-rules` file have the same basic format:

```
if (condition) then action
```

The `condition` can test the contents of the From:, To:, Subject:, and Sender: headers. The content string, which is enclosed in quotes, can be a partial string and can use wildcard characters to match more than a single case—`*.gov` is an example of this. The `action` can delete the message, save it in a mail folder, forward it to another address, or pass it to another program for further processing.

`filter` is easy to use and available on all Linux systems. However, there are many equally useful systems, and user's tend to use the filtering mechanism that comes with the mail reader they use.

Filtering with Netscape

Many users use Netscape to read their e-mail. You can, of course, use the `filter` program or `procmail`, which is discussed next, to filter your mail even if you then read the mail with the Netscape mail reader. However, Netscape provides its own mail filter capability, which is particularly suited to those who prefer a graphical interface.

From the Edit menu in the Netscape Messenger window, select Mail Filters to open the Filter Rules window shown in Figure 13.4.

Figure 13.4 Defining Netscape filter rules

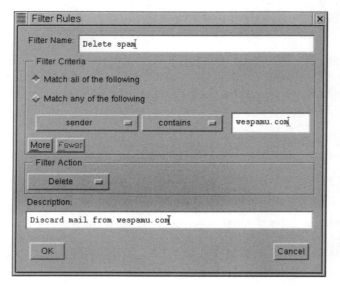

In many ways, these rules are very similar to those used in the `filter` program. Again, you are constructing if/then statements, but this time a graphics template is used to do it. Figure 13.4 shows the same rule that was applied to `wespamu.com` in the `filter` example: If the sender name contains the string `wespamu.com`, then delete the message.

The first drop-down list in the Filter Criteria section of the Filter Rules dialog box defines the item in the mail that is being tested. In Figure 13.4, `sender` is selected, which filters based on the sender's e-mail address. The drop-down list also allows you to match on:

    `subject` Filters mail based on the content of the Subject: header.

    `body` Filters mail based on the content of the message body.

date Filters mail based on the date the mail was created. Selecting this value changes the list of available conditional tests to is, isn't, is before, and is after.

priority Filters mail based on its priority. Selecting this item changes the list of available conditional tests to is, isn't, is higher than, and is lower than. It also causes a new drop-down box to appear that contains the possible priority selections. These are lowest, low, normal, high, and highest.

status Filters mail based on whether or not it has been read or replied to. Selecting this item changes the list of available conditional tests to is and isn't, and causes a new drop-down box to appear that contains the selections read and replied.

to Filters mail based on the e-mail addresses in any of the To: headers.

CC Filters mail based on the e-mail addresses in any of CC: headers.

to or CC Filters mail based on any recipient addresses. Every e-mail address in every To: or CC: header is checked.

age in days Filters mail based on how old it is in days. Selecting this value changes the list of available conditional tests to is, is greater than, and is less than.

In addition to all of these standard matches, you can select the Customize Headers item from the end of the first drop-down box to specify any header that you want to match against. The Customize Header selection opens a box from which you choose a previously defined header or you click the New button to enter a header name. Any valid header name can be used. If the header is encountered in the incoming mail, its content is matched against the filter.

The second drop-down box defines the conditional test. In Figure 13.4, contains is selected. This means the filter checks to see if the sender address contains the string defined in the next box, which is wesapmu.com in the figure. Depending on the conditional test selected, the value that is tested against can be a full or partial value; contains permits a partial value to match. The other choices that are available when the sender address is being tested are:

doesn't contain The test evaluates to true, and the action is taken if the tested field does not contain the specified value.

is The test evaluates to true, and the action is taken if the tested field is equal to the specified value.

isn't The test evaluates to true, and the action is taken if the tested field is not equal to the specified value.

begins with The test evaluates to true, and the action is taken if the string at the beginning of the tested field exactly matches the specified value.

ends with The test evaluates to true, and the action is taken if the string at the end of the tested field exactly matches the specified value.

This list of conditional tests is available for the sender address, the subject header, the to address, and the CC address. All conditional tests except begins with and ends with are available for testing the content of the message body, and all except is and isn't are available when testing to or CC. As noted, when other values are tested, they generate their own list of valid conditionals.

The last drop-down box in the Filter Rules dialog box selects the filter action. In the example, the action is Delete. Other available actions are:

move to folder Mail that matches the filter is routed to a specific mailbox. If this action is selected, two additional items appear in the window. One is a drop-down list that allows you to select the mailbox to which the mail is sent. The other is labeled New Folder and permits you to define a new mailbox to receive the mail.

change priority The priority of mail that matches the filter is changed to the priority you select. Selecting this action causes a drop-down box to appear that contains the possible priority selections. This box is identical to the one that appears if priority is selected as the item being tested in the first drop-down box.

mark read Mail that matches the filter is marked as "read."

ignore thread Mail that matches the filter is part of a thread that is ignored. A *thread* is related mail or news postings on the same topic.

watch thread Mail that matches the filter is part of a thread that is being monitored.

A filter can contain multiple rules. Click the More button to add additional rules. Use the Match All Of The Following check box to filter mail only if it matches every rule defined for the filter, or use the Match Any Of The Following checkbox to filter mail if it matches any rule in the filter.

In addition to defining the rules, you must give each filter a name, and you can optionally give it a description. Once defined to your satisfaction, click OK, and the rule is enabled.

Managing Mail with procmail

As mentioned in Chapter 7, procmail is the default local mail delivery program for Linux systems. procmail provides the most powerful and complex e-mail filtering system available for Linux. procmail filters are defined by the user in the .procmailrc file. Additionally, the system administrator can define system-wide filters in the /etc/procmailrc file. The format of both files is the same, but it is much more common for procmail filtering to be defined by the user than by the system administrator.

The .procmailrc file contains two type of entries: environment variable assignments and mail filtering rules, which procmail calls *recipes*. *Environment variable assignments* are straightforward and look just like these assignments would in a shell initialization script like .bashrc. For example, HOME=/home/craig is a valid environment variable assignment. Assignment statements are rarely needed because the variables usually have the correct values for your system.

NOTE See the procmailrc manual page for the full listing of the more than 30 environment variables.

The real substance of a .procmailrc file is the recipes. The syntax of each recipe is:

:0 [*flags*] [:[*lockfile*]]

[* *condition*]

action

Every recipe begins with :0, which differentiates it from an assignment statement. The :0 is optionally followed by flags that change how the filter is processed. Table 13.4 lists all of the flags and their meanings.

Table 13.4   procmail Recipe Flags

Flag	Meaning
A	Execute this recipe if the preceding recipe evaluated to true.
a	This has the same meaning as the A flag, except that the preceding recipe must also have successfully completed execution.
b	Pass the body of the message on to the destination. This is the default.
B	Filter the message body.
c	Create a carbon copy of this mail.
D	Tests are case sensitive. By default, case is ignored.
e	Execute this recipe if the execution of the preceding recipe returned an error.
E	Execute this recipe if the preceding recipe was not executed.
f	Pass the data through an external filter program.

Departmental
Server Operations

PART 3

Table 13.4 procmail Recipe Flags *(continued)*

Flag	Meaning
H	Filter the message headers. This is the default.
h	Pass the message header on to the destination. This is the default.
I	Ignore write errors for this recipe.
r	Write the mail out as is without ensuring it is properly formatted.
w	Check the exit code of the external filter program.
W	This is the same as the w flag, except no error message is printed.

An optional *lockfile* can be identified to prevent multiple copies of procmail from writing to the same mailbox at the same time. This can happen on a busy system causing some pretty strange-looking mail. The *lockfile* name is preceded by a colon. If the colon is used and no name is specified, a default name created from the mailbox name and the extension .lock is used for the lockfile.

The conditional test is optional. If no *condition* is provided, the recipe acts as if the *condition* is true, which means that the *action* is taken. If a condition is specified, it must begin with an asterisk (*). The condition is written as a regular expression. If the value defined by the regular expression is found in the mail, the condition evaluates to true, and the action is taken. To take an action when mail does *not* contain the specified value, put an exclamation point in front of the regular expression. Here are some examples of valid conditional tests:

```
* ^From.*neil@sybex.com
* !^Subject: Chapter
```

The first conditional checks to see if the mail contains a line that begins with (^) the literal string From followed by any number of characters (.*) and the literal string neil@sybex .com. The second conditional matches all mail that does not (!) contain a line that begins with the string Subject: Chapter. If multiple conditions are defined for one recipe, each condition appears on a separate line.

NOTE To learn more about regular expressions, see *Mastering Regular Expressions* by Jeffrey Friedl, (O'Reilly, 1997).

While there may be multiple conditions in a recipe, there can be only one action. The action can direct the mail to a file, forward it to another e-mail address, send it to a program, or define additional recipes to process the message. If the action is an additional recipe, it begins with :0. If the action directs the mail to an e-mail address, it begins with an exclamation point (!), and if it directs it to a program, it begins with a vertical bar (|). If the action directs the mail to a file, just the name of the file is specified.

A Sample .procmailrc File Using the information described above, you might create a .procmailrc file such as this one:

```
MAILDIR=$HOME/mail

:0 c

backup

:0:

* ^From.*@sybex.com

editors

:0 c

* ^From.*rdenn

* ^Subject:.*NT

!robert@bobsnet.org

    :0 A

    ntbook

:0

* ^From.*@wespamu.com

/dev/null

:0 B

* .*pheromones

| awk -f spamscript > spam-suspects
```

This sample .procmailrc file begins with an environment variable assignments statement. The statement assigns a value to the variable MAILDIR, and it uses the value of the HOME variable. Thus, it illustrates both assigning a variable and using a variable. Frankly, the statement is just there to illustrate how variables are used. It was not really needed for this file.

The first recipe in the file is:

```
:0 c

backup
```

It makes a carbon copy of the mail and stores it in a mailbox named `backup`. This recipe came straight from the `.procmailrc` documentation where it is suggested as a way to ensure that no mail is lost when you're first debugging the `.procmailrc` file. After all of the recipes work as you want them to, remove this recipe from the file so that you don't continue to keep two copies of every piece of mail.

The second recipe is:

```
:0:

* ^From.*@sybex.com

editors
```

This recipe puts all the mail that contains a line that begins with (`^`) the literal `From`, any number of characters (`.*`), and the literal `@sybex.com` into the mailbox named `editors`. The most interesting thing in this recipe is the first line. Notice the `:0:` value. From the syntax, you know that the second colon precedes the name of the lockfile. In this case, no lock filename is provided, so the name defaults to `editors.lock`.

The third recipe is:

```
:0 c

* ^From.*rdenn

* ^Subject:.*NT

!robert@bobsnet.org

    :0 A

    ntbook
```

This recipe searches for mail that is from someone named `rdenn` and that has a subject of `NT`. A carbon copy is made of the mail and is sent to `robert@bobsnet.org`. The other copy of the mail is stored in the `ntbook` mailbox.

The fourth recipe is:

```
:0

* ^From.*@wespamu.com

/dev/null
```

This recipe shows how spam mail is deleted using `procmail`. All mail from `wespamu.com` is deleted by sending it to `/dev/null`, the null device.

The final recipe is:

```
:0 B
*  .*pheromones
| gawk -f spamscript > spam-suspects
```

This recipe illustrates how mail is passed to an external program for processing. All messages that contain the word "pheromones" anywhere in the message body are passed to gawk for processing. In this example, gawk runs a program file named spamscript that extracts information from the mail and stores it in a file named spam-suspects. You can imagine that the administrator of this system created an awk program named spamscript to extract all of the e-mail addresses from suspected spam.

This range of recipes illustrates the power and flexibility of procmail. Despite the obscure syntax of a .procmailrc file, it may be the best tool for filtering e-mail.

Final Words

This chapter concludes Part 3, *Departmental Server Operations*. In this part of the book, configuration services, file sharing, printer sharing, and mail services have all been covered. Add these to the login services, name services, Web services, and routing covered in Part 2, and you have a complete network server.

The final part of the book, *Security and Troubleshooting*, examines those tasks that are necessary to keep that complete server running in tip-top shape. Part 4 begins with a chapter on security, which is particularly critical for a network server, because connecting to a network greatly increases the security threats to your server.

Departmental
Server Operations

PART 3

An Asexual Network

A company that received complaints about advertisements with explicit sexual content wanted to block as much of this material as possible. Simply taking every site from a spammer list that had the word "sex" in the site name was a place to start. These commands were used to create an access.txt file from the spammer lists:

```
# grep sex spammers.txt > temp.txt
# grep sex spamdomains.txt >> temp.txt
# sort -u temp.txt > sorted.txt
# rm temp.txt
# awk sorted.txt { print $1, REJECT } > access.txt
# rm sorted.txt
```

In the example, grep extracts all of the lines containing the word "sex" from some spammer lists and stores the matching lines in a file named temp.txt. sort with the –u command-line option eliminates duplicates, placing the sorted entries in sorted.txt. awk then extracts the domain name from each entry in the file and appends the keyword REJECT to each entry. This creates valid access database entries that are stored in access.txt.

Other lists were manually searched for spammers accused of distributing sexually explicit material, and complaints from users were used to extend the access database. In the process of blocking spam, this was only a start, but hey, you have to start somewhere.

Part 4

Security and Troubleshooting

Topics Covered:

- Finding information about the latest security problems and fixes
- Using the built-in Linux Wrapper program to improve security
- Using the built-in firewall features of Linux
- Improving Linux password security
- Monitoring your server for security problems
- Analyzing network trouble reports
- The basic Linux troubleshooting tools
- Looking for configuration errors
- Testing routing
- Testing Domain Name Service
- Analyzing network traffic

14

Security

Good security is good system administration. Security is a fundamental part of running a reliable network server. Undoubtedly, your server will be attacked and compromised by people on the network. Your job is to reduce the number of successful attacks, to limit the amount of damage done, and to quickly recover from the attack. This chapter will help you do your job.

This is a book about Linux network servers, so it focuses on network security threats. Despite this emphasis, you should remember that network security is only part of the overall security of your system:

- Physical security is required to protect the server hardware and to prevent unauthorized access to the system console.

- File system security, which is described in Chapter 11, *File Sharing*, is necessary to protect the data on the server.

The focus of this chapter on network security is not meant to downplay the importance of physical and file system security, but security threats originating from the network are a major source of Linux server problems. This chapter describes those threats and tells you how to face them.

Understanding the Threats

Connecting your server to a network gives it access—and makes it vulnerable—to every-one on the network. The larger the network, the larger the threat. When you connect your system to a network, you should assess the security threat that the network connection creates. To make this assessment, you need to consider the potential harm to your orga-nization from a successful security attack.

The impact of a security attack depends on what system and what information are com-promised. The loss of a key server affects many users, while the loss of a desktop client may affect only one user. Likewise, unauthorized access to a file containing plans for the office party cannot be compared to unauthorized access to your corporate strategic plan. Your efforts should be directed toward protecting things that are important; however, every system requires some level of protection. A break-in on a small, insignificant system can end up compromising your entire network.

The Basic Threats

There are three basic threats to the information stored on your network:

Threats to the secrecy of data   These are the unauthorized disclosures of sensitive data that can be caused by setting the wrong file permissions, by having someone improperly gain root privileges, or by having the data stolen directly off the wire.

Threats to the integrity of data   These are the unauthorized modifications of data that can be caused by using the wrong file permissions or by someone improperly gaining root privileges. This is a common threat to Web servers where intruders change data in obvious and embarrassing ways. But a more insidious threat is the possibility of subtle modifications to data that are designed to undermine the repu-tation of an organization. Once a system has suffered an unauthorized access, all files on the system are suspect.

Threats to the availability of data   These attacks deny legitimate access to the data. If files are improperly protected or an intruder gains root access, files can be deleted. Vandals can also launch a Denial of Service (DOS) attack to overwhelm your server blocking access to your data when you need it.

The network threats that lead to these data problems are:

Unauthorized access   This is any time that someone who should not have login access to your system is able to log in.

Denial of Service   Any attack that is designed not to gain access to your system but to prevent you from using your system.

All networked systems are vulnerable to these attacks. Luckily, Linux provides a range of tools to help you reduce the threat.

A Reality Check

Legend has it that network threats come from sophisticated code hackers who have a deep understanding of networks and operating systems. These legendary characters are motivated by espionage or a desire to force unresponsive computer corporations to improve their software. I wish it were true! If it were, these people would have no interest in attacking my Linux system.

Unfortunately, the reality is that most attacks come from unskilled people running canned attack scripts. The scripts have become so simple to use they are now called "kiddie scripts." The people who run these scripts are not interested in espionage, but they don't mind causing a little mayhem! Additionally, if they were truly rebels against the corporate system working to improve the security of operating system software, they would be writing new Linux code. After all, Linux is open source code; no one can claim that a corporate monolith is keeping the code hidden.

Given this, you might guess that Linux is not a target for security attacks. You would guess wrong. Unfortunately, Linux is one of the most popular targets for attack. A recent study by Peter Mell of NIST showed that attack scripts for Linux are as popular as scripts for Windows NT, and that these two systems are the most popular operating systems for attack scripts.

Clearly, open source code is no protection from attack. The people who run attack scripts are not motivated to "fix" the system—they are just looking for easy targets. Your job is to make sure that your system isn't an easy target.

Look at it this way. The bad news is you don't have to be important to be a target of security attacks. The good news is the guy at the other end of the attack isn't a network guru. If you can track the vulnerabilities exploited by the "kiddie scripts" and close those holes as they appear, your system will be reasonably secure.

Keeping Informed

To secure a system, you need to know its vulnerabilities. Your goal should be to stay as well informed about Linux's vulnerabilities as the vandals are. Frankly, you won't be able to. *You* have a life and responsibilities, so the vandals who have nothing better to do will get ahead of you and may compromise your system. Despite the difficulty, you should do your best to keep up-to-date about security problems.

There are several good sources of information about known security vulnerabilities:

- General information about security vulnerabilities is available on the Web at www.geek-girl.com/bugtraq.
- A good site for security advisories is www.10pht.com.

Security and Troubleshooting

PART 4

- A good site for Linux software updates and security hole announcements is www.freshmeat.com.

- Visit www.cert.org to view the Computer Emergency Response Team (CERT) advisories about known security problems. The advisories usually include fixes if any are available.

Track all of the problems that pertain to Linux, Unix, and Unix applications—all of these could affect your Linux server. Figure 14.1 shows me checking the advisories at geek-girl.com.

Figure 14.1   Searching the Bugtraq Archives at geek-girl.com

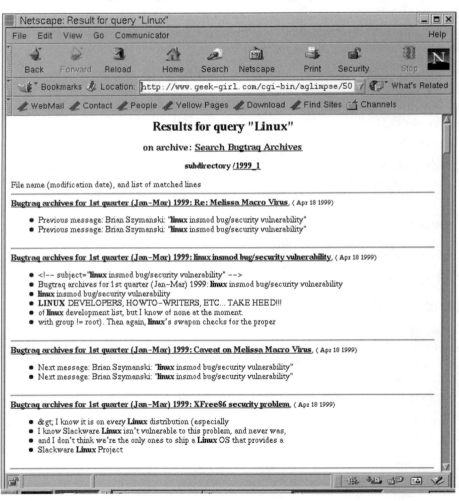

Figure 14.1 is the result of searching the Bugtraq Archives for the string "Linux." Some of the bug reports on this page describe a reported problem with the insmod command that might cause a security problem. Clicking a link takes you to the bug report so that you can read it and evaluate if this bug is a threat to your system.

In addition to visiting the sites that report bug and security problems, I suggest that you visit the Web sites that provide attack scripts. Two such sites are www.rootshell.com and www.insecure.org. These sites give you access to the same scripts that intruders use to attack your system. You can make sure that your system is not vulnerable to the old attacks and evaluate the new scripts as they are released to understand the vulnerabilities they exploit. In addition to providing scripts, these sites give information about what is currently going on in the network security world.

Figure 14.2   The Exploits report at rootshell.com

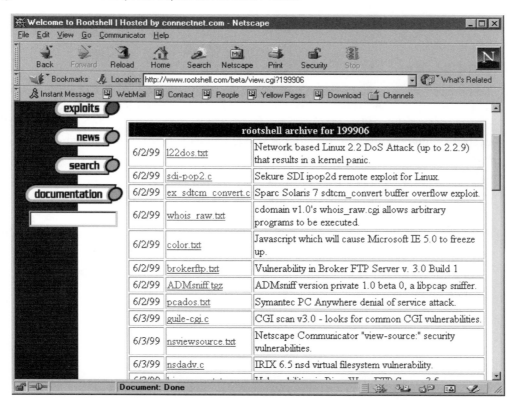

Figure 14.2 shows the Exploits report from www.rootshell.com as it existed in June, 1999. Not everything in the report relates to Linux, but a quick scan down the list lets you know what articles affect your server.

Closing the Holes

Most intruders enter systems through well-known holes in the system software. The most important thing you can do to improve the security of your system is close the holes by installing security updates as soon as they become available.

Vulnerabilities are not limited to the Linux kernel itself. In fact, most of the vulnerabilities that are exploited occur in the network software that runs on your Linux system. In 1998, the two pieces of software that were attacked the most were sendmail, listed in 11 exploits, and IMAP, listed in eight exploits. Both of these packages run on Linux systems. Clearly, it is not enough to keep the Linux operating system up-to-date. You must keep all software packages updated.

Finding the Latest Software

To update software, you need to need to know what software needs to be updated and where to find it. Security advisories, such as those found at CERT, usually describe the problem and tell you the solution; often they point you to the appropriate software fix. Even the vulnerability reports found at places like geek-girl.com sometimes include fixes, as shown in Figure 14.3.

The vulnerability report shown in Figure 14.3 includes links to the software updates that fix the reported problem. Clicking a link retrieves the fix that can then be installed. Since these fixes are Linux software packages that use the RPM format, typing in the rpm command shown in the report would download and install the fix with a single command.

Unfortunately, the fix is not always included in a vulnerability report, and you may need to look for it yourself. On a Red Hat 6 system, all you need to do is click the Red Hat Errata icon on the desktop to go to the location at the Red Hat Web site where security problems and fixes are listed.

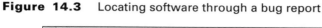

Figure 14.3   Locating software through a bug report

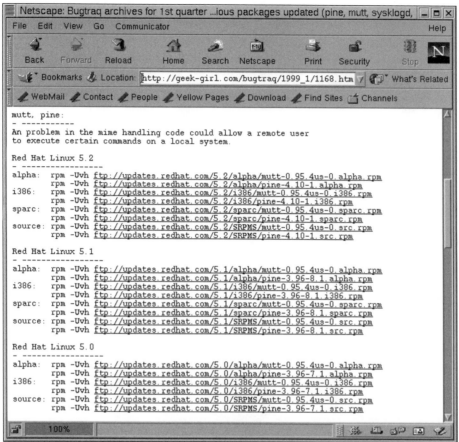

Figure 14.4 shows a security report on the Red Hat Web site. The report describes the problem and provides a link to the software update. If you're looking for a specific fix, you can search through the advisories on the Web page. The big advantage of this is that you will often find fixes for bugs that you have never heard of. On the downside, sometimes you find out that a bug you have heard of has not yet been fixed. Nevertheless, you should take all of the bug fixes that are offered and periodically check back to see if the bug you're concerned about does get fixed.

Figure 14.4 A Red Hat security advisory

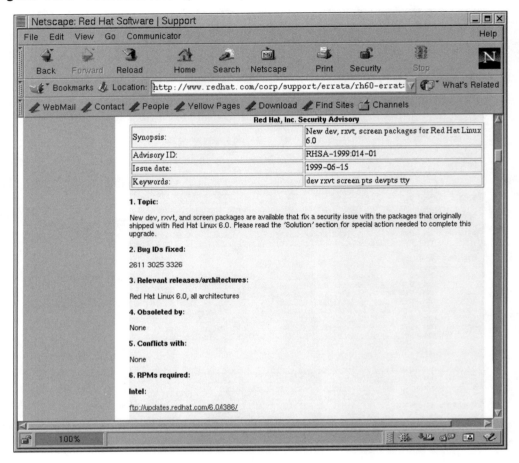

TIP Frequently, administrators complain that the authors of software don't fix bugs, but I find that a much more common problem is that system administrators don't use the bug fixes that are out there. Set aside a time each month to download and install the fixes provided by your software vendor. Make it part of your routine.

Removing Unneeded Software

Reduce the burden of keeping software updated by removing all of the software you don't really need. Earlier, I pointed out that `sendmail` and IMAP were attacked in many different exploits over the last year. Why was `sendmail` the leading target? In part, it is the fact that it is a large and complex system that lends itself to different types of attacks, but it is also that `sendmail` runs everywhere. Many, many systems on *every* major network run `sendmail`, and the SMTP port that `sendmail` monitors is often allowed to pass through firewalls. Intruders look for easy targets, and with so many copies of `sendmail` running on desktop Unix and Linux clients, they are bound to find one that is misconfigured or out-of-date.

However, there is no need to run so many copies of `sendmail`. A Linux client doesn't need to run a `sendmail` daemon. It can be configured to relay mail to a departmental server that is running `sendmail` for outbound mail and to collect its mail from a mailbox server for inbound mail. Simply reducing the number of copies of a software package that you run on your network reduces the chances for a configuration error that is exploited by an intruder.

I'm not trying to pick on `sendmail`. I could repeat this same argument about IMAP and dozens of other software packages. In fact, most network daemons fall into this category—clients don't need them. There are two simple ways to block access to unneeded daemons:

> **Comment unneeded daemons out of the /etc/inetd.conf file.** Most network services are started by `inetd`, which only starts services listed in the `inetd.conf` file. Removing a service from the file prevents outsiders from using the specified network service, but it does not block the desktop client from using the service on outbound connections. Thus if `ftp` is deleted from `inetd.conf`, the user can still `ftp` to remote sites, but no one from a remote site can use `ftp` to log in to the user's desktop.

> **Remove scripts that launch unneeded daemons from the startup.** Some network service daemons, such as `sendmail` and `named`, are started at boot time. Use `tksysv` or `linuxconf` to remove unneeded daemons from the startup. For example, a Red Hat desktop client does not need to run the `httpd` startup script if it is not a Web server. The client will still be able to use a Web browser even if the `httpd` script is not run at startup.

Network daemons are not the only unneeded software, and clients are not the only targets. Unneeded software on a server can also open a hole for an intruder. If you have a dedicated DNS server, it needs to run `named`, but it doesn't require the `sendmail` daemon. Likewise, if you're running a dedicated mailbox server, it doesn't need to have a C compiler installed. (You can do your compiles on your desktop system and move the finished product to the server.)

> ***TIP***   Everything you have on your server is a potential tool for an intruder. Think hard about what you really need for the server to do its job.

There are two ways to limit the software installed on a server. First, when you do the initial Linux installation, don't install what you don't need. During the initial installation, you select the software packages that are installed and the daemons that are loaded. Choose carefully based on your plan for the system you're installing.

The other way to limit the software on a system is to remove it after it is installed. For example, to remove IMAP from a system with rpm, you could enter **rpm –e imap-4.5-3**.

In addition to installing the latest software and removing unneeded software, you should limit access to the software and services running on your system to just those systems that you actually want to serve. Linux makes this simple by providing two powerful access control mechanisms: Wrapper and ipchains.

Controlling Access with Wrapper

The Wrapper daemon, named tcpd, is executed by inetd. It is an integral part of most Linux distributions. Using Wrapper on a Linux system is easier than it is on many other systems, because the entries in the inetd.conf file already point to the tcpd program.

> ***NOTE***   Don't remember the format of the inetd.conf file? It's explained in Chapter 5, *Login Services*.

The following entries are from the inetd.conf file on a Red Hat 6 system:

```
ftp    stream tcp  nowait root /usr/sbin/tcpd in.ftpd -l -a

telnet stream tcp  nowait root /usr/sbin/tcpd in.telnetd

shell  stream tcp  nowait root /usr/sbin/tcpd in.rshd

login  stream tcp  nowait root /usr/sbin/tcpd in.rlogind

talk   dgram  udp  wait   root /usr/sbin/tcpd in.talkd

ntalk  dgram  udp  wait   root /usr/sbin/tcpd in.ntalkd

imap   stream tcp  nowait root /usr/sbin/tcpd imapd

finger stream tcp  nowait root /usr/sbin/tcpd in.fingerd
```

As this sample shows, the path to `tcpd` is used in place of the path of each network service daemon. Therefore, when `inetd` receives a request for a service, it starts `tcpd`. `tcpd` then logs the service request, checks the access control information, and, if permitted, starts the real daemon to handle the request.

The Wrapper package performs two basic functions: It logs requests for Internet services, and it provides an access control mechanism for those services. Logging requests for specific network services is a useful monitoring function, especially if you are looking for possible intruders.

Tracking Remote Access

The Wrapper uses the `authpriv` facility of `syslogd` to log its messages. Look in the `/etc/syslog.conf` file to find out where your system logs `authpriv` messages. On a Red Hat 6 system, these messages are logged to `/var/log/secure`, a sample of which is shown here:

```
# cat /var/log/secure
Jun  9 08:09 owl login: ROOT LOGIN ON tty1
Jun  9 08:48 owl login: LOGIN ON tty1 BY craig
Jun 11 00:48 owl in.telnetd[950]: connect from 172.19.50.52
Jun 11 00:48 owl login: LOGIN ON 1 BY craig FROM beaver.mammals.com
Jun 12 01:11 owl in.telnetd[3467]: connect from 127.0.0.1
Jun 12 01:11 owl login: LOGIN ON 2 BY craig FROM localhost
Jun 12 01:19 owl imapd[3489]: connect from 127.0.0.1
Jun 14 10:23 owl in.telnetd[2090]: connect from 172.19.24.1
Jun 14 10:23 owl login: LOGIN ON 1 BY craig FROM cat.mammals.com
Jun 15 14:30:06 owl in.ftpd[10201]: connect from sr1.sybex.com
Jun 16 05:27 owl in.rshd[6434]: connect from 172.19.60.22
Jun 17 20:20 owl login: ROOT LOGIN ON tty1
Jun 17 14:54 owl in.telnetd[1388]: connect from 172.19.50.52
Jun 17 14:54 owl login: LOGIN ON 2 BY craig FROM beaver.mammals.com
Jun 18 14:28:44 owl in.ftpd[10190]: refused connect from 172.25.98.2
```

This sample `/var/log/secure` file shows that not everything in this log comes from `tcpd`. It also contains messages for `login`. Combining the two messages can provide some useful insight.

The logins on June 9 are from the system console. The first message from `tcpd` is the `telnet` connection on June 11. The message tells you that someone used `telnet` to connect to `owl` from IP address 172.19.50.52. The `login` message that follows tells you that the person logged in as `craig` and that the host name associated with the remote IP address is `beaver.mammals.com`. If this is what you expect, there is nothing to be concerned about.

In this particular file, the message that caught my attention occurred on June 16. `tcpd` reports that on that date, someone accessed the system through remote shell (`rshd`) from IP address 172.19.60.22. The remote shell can be used to remotely execute commands on your system, so it can be a powerful tool for intruders. If you don't recognize the IP address or if you don't understand why someone at that address would be running a remote shell to your system, you should be very concerned.

Of less concern is the message from June 18 that shows a failed attempt to connect to `ftp`. This bears watching if it occurs frequently, but it is not yet a problem, because the connection was refused based on Wrapper's access control configuration.

If logging were all it did, Wrapper would be a useful package. But the real power of Wrapper is its ability to control access to network services.

tcpd Access Control Files

Two files define access controls for `tcpd`:

- The `hosts.allow` file lists the hosts that are allowed to access the system's services.
- The `hosts.deny` file lists the hosts that are denied service.

If these files are not found, `tcpd` allows every host to have access and simply logs the access request.

When the files are present, `tcpd` reads the `hosts.allow` file first and then reads the `hosts.deny` file. It stops as soon as it finds a match for the host and the service in question. Therefore, access granted by `hosts.allow` cannot be overridden by `hosts.deny`. For this reason, I usually start by inserting an entry in `hosts.deny` that denies all access to all systems. Then I put entries in the `hosts.allow` file that permit access to just those systems that I really want to provide services to. The format of entries in both files is the same:

services : *clients* [: *shell-command*]

services is a comma-separated list of network services or the keyword ALL. ALL is used to indicate all network services. Otherwise, each individual service is identified by its process name, which is the name that immediately follows the path to `tcpd` in the `inetd.conf` file. For example, the process name in the following `inetd.conf` entry is `imapd`:

```
imap stream tcp nowait root /usr/sbin/tcpd imapd
```

clients is a comma-separated list of host names, domain names, Internet addresses, network numbers, and the keyword LOCAL. Alternatively, it can be the keyword ALL. ALL matches all host names and addresses; LOCAL matches all host names that do not include a domain name part. A host name matches an individual host. An IP address can be defined by itself to match a specific host or with an address mask to match a range of addresses. A domain name starts with a dot (.) and matches every host within that domain. A network number ends with a dot and matches every IP address within the network address space.

shell-command is an optional shell command that tcpd executes when a match occurs. If a match occurs, tcpd logs the access, grants or denies access to the service, and then passes the shell command to the shell for execution.

A few examples can illustrate the variety of valid ways in which *services* and *clients* can be described in a Wrapper access-control entry. First, here's something simple from an imaginary hosts.allow file:

```
ALL : LOCAL, .foobirds.org
in.ftpd,in.telnetd : sr1.sybex.com
```

The keyword ALL in the *services* field indicates that the first rule applies to all network services. In the *clients* field, the keyword LOCAL indicates that all host names without a domain part are acceptable, and .foobirds.org matches all host names in that domain. By itself, LOCAL would match wren, but not wren.foobirds.org. Combining these two tests in a single rule allows every system in the local domain to use all of the network services. The second rule grants ftp and telnet access to users on the remote system sr1.sybex.com.

The syntax of a standard Wrapper access-control file can be a little more complicated than the example above. A hosts.allow file might contain:

```
imapd, ipopd3 : 172.5.4.
ALL EXCEPT imapd, ipopd3 : ALL
```

The first entry says that every host whose IP address begins with 172.5.4 is granted access to the IMAP and POP services. The second line says that all services except IMAP and POP are granted to all hosts. These entries would limit mailbox service to a single subnet while providing all other services to anyone who requested them. The EXCEPT keyword is used to except items from an all-encompassing list. It can also be used on the *clients* side of an access rule. For example:

```
ALL: .foobirds.org EXCEPT crow.foobirds.org
```

If this appeared in a `hosts.allow` file, it would permit every system in the `foobirds.org` domain to have access to all services except for the host `crow.foobirds.org`. The assumption is that `crow.foobirds.org` is not trusted for some reason—perhaps users outside of the domain are allowed to log in to `crow`.

The final syntax variation uses the at sign (@) to narrow the definition of *services* or *clients*. Here are two examples:

```
in.telnetd@172.16.7.2 : 172.16.7.0/255.255.255.0

in.rshd : KNOWN@robin.foobirds.org
```

When the @ appears in the services side of a rule, it indicates that the server has more than one IP address and that the rule being defined applies only to one of those addresses. Examples of systems with more than one address are multi-homed hosts and routers. If your server is also the router that connects your local network to outside networks, you may want to provide services on the interface connected to the local network while not providing those services on the interface connected to the outside world. The @ syntax lets you do that. If the first line in this example appeared in a `hosts.allow` file, it would permit access to the `telnet` daemon through the network interface that has the address 172.16.7.2 by any client with an address that begins with 172.16.7.

The purpose of the @ when it appears on the *clients* side of the rule is completely different. On the *clients* side, the @ indicates that a username is required from the client as part of the access control test. This means that the client must run an IDENT server. You can test for a specific username, but it's more common to use one of three possible keywords:

KNOWN The result of the test is KNOWN when the client returns a username in response to the query.

UNKNOWN The result of the test is UNKNOWN when the client does not run the IDENT server and thus fails to respond to the query.

ALL This setting requires the client to return a username. It is equivalent to using KNOWN but is less commonly used.

Defining an Optional Shell Command

The shell command allows you to define additional processing that is triggered by a match in the access control list. In all practical examples, this feature is used in the `hosts.deny` file to gather more information about the intruder or to provide immediate notification to the system administrator about a potential security attack. For example:

```
in.rshd : ALL : (safe_finger -l @%h | /usr/sbin/mail -s %d - %h root) &
```

In this example from a hosts.deny file, all systems are denied access to rshd. After logging the attempted access and blocking it, tcpd sends the safe_finger command to the shell for execution. All versions of finger, including safe_finger, query the remote host to find out who is logged in to that host. This information can be useful when tracking down an attacker. The result of the safe_finger command is mailed to the root account. The ampersand (&) at the end of the line causes the shell commands to run in the background. This is important; without it, tcpd would sit and wait for these programs to complete before returning to its own work.

NOTE The safe_finger program is provided with Wrapper. It is specially modified to be less vulnerable to attack than the standard finger program.

There are some variables, such as %h and %d, used in the example above. These Wrapper variables, listed in Table 14.1, allow you to take values for the incoming connection and use them in the shell process.

Table 14.1   Wrapper Variables

Variable	Value
%a	The client's IP address.
%A	The server's IP address.
%c	All available client information, including the username when available.
%d	The network service daemon process name.
%h	The client's host name. If the host name is unavailable, the IP address is used.
%H	The server's host name.
%n	The client's host name. If the host name is unavailable, the keyword UNKNOWN is used. If a DNS lookup of the client's host name and IP address do not match, the keyword PARANOID is used.
%N	The server's host name.
%p	The network service daemon process ID (PID).
%s	All available server information, including the username when available.

Security and Troubleshooting

PART 4

Table 14.1 Wrapper Variables *(continued)*

Variable	Value
%u	The client username or the keyword UNKNOWN if the username is unavailable.
%%	The percent character (%).

Using information from Table 14.1, you can figure out exactly what the sample shell command is doing. Assume that the attempted access to `in.rshd` came from the host `bad.worse.org`. The command passed to the shell would be:

```
safe_finger -l @bad.worse.org |
    /usr/sbin/mail -s in.rshd-bad.worse.org root
```

With all of the possible rules that can be defined with the standard Wrapper access control syntax, I have never encountered a situation when I couldn't define the rule I needed. But if you do, it is possible to use an extended version of the Wrapper access control language.

Optional Access Control Language Extensions

If you compile your own version of Wrapper with PROCESS_OPTIONS enabled in the Makefile, the syntax of the Wrapper access control language is changed and extended.

> **NOTE** To compile your own version of Wrapper, you will need the source code. Get Wrapper from `ciac.llnl.gov` by following the Tools link and then the Access Control link.

After compiling Wrapper with PROCESS_OPTIONS, the command syntax is no longer limited to three fields. The new syntax is:

```
services : clients : option : option …
```

The *services* field and the *clients* field are defined in exactly the same way as they were in the original Wrapper syntax. The *option* field is new and so is the fact that multiple options are allowed for each rule. There are several possible options:

`allow` Grants the requested service. This option must appear at the end of a rule.

`deny` Denies the requested service. This option must appear at the end of a rule.

`spawn` *shell-command* Executes the shell command as a child process.

twist *shell-command* Executes the shell command instead of the requested service.

keepalive Sends keepalive messages to the client. If the client does not respond, the connection is closed.

linger *seconds* Specifies how long to try to deliver data after the server closes the connection.

rfc931 [*timeout*] Uses the IDENT protocol to look up the client username. *timeout* defines how many seconds the server should wait for the client's response. The default timeout period is specified as a compiler option.

banners *path* Displays the contents of a message file to the client. *path* is the name of a directory that contains the banner files. The file displayed is the file that has the same name as the network daemon process.

nice [*number*] Sets the nice value for the network service process. The Linux kernel uses the nice value to calculate a scheduling priority. The default value is 10.

umask *mask* Sets a umask value for files created by the process. The documentation only shows the command with a umask value of 022, which prevents files from being created with group and world write permission, but this option should accept any valid umask value. The value defined by umask turns off bits in the default file mode, which is usually 0666, to produce the new permission. Thus, removing the bits defined by 022 from 0666 produces a file permission of 0644.

user *user*[.*group*] Runs the network service process with the specified user ID and group ID regardless of what is defined in inetd.conf. The documentation only shows the command in the form user nobody and user nobody.kmem, but it should accept any valid username and group name.

setenv *name value* Sets an environment variable for the process runtime environment.

A few examples based on the samples shown earlier will illustrate the differences in the new syntax. Using the new syntax, a hosts.allow file might contain:

```
ALL : LOCAL, .foobirds.org : ALLOW
in.ftpd,in.telnetd : sr1.sybex.com : ALLOW
ALL : ALL : DENY
```

With the new syntax, there is no need to have two files. The options ALLOW and DENY permit everything to be listed in a single file. The function of the first two lines is identical to the first host.allow example described earlier. The third line is the same as having the line ALL : ALL in the hosts.deny file. Everything done with the basic syntax can be done in a single file with the extended syntax.

Using the ALLOW and DENY options, this command:

```
ALL: .foobirds.org EXCEPT crow.foobirds.org
```

can be rewritten as:

```
ALL: .foobirds.org : ALLOW

ALL: crow.foobirds.org : DENY
```

The shell command example using the original syntax is almost identical in the new syntax:

```
in.rshd : ALL: spawn (safe_finger -l @%h | /usr/sbin/mail -s %d - %h
root) & : DENY
```

A more interesting variation on the shell command theme comes from using the twist option. Instead of passing a command to the shell for execution, the twist command executes a program for the client—but not the program the client expects. For example:

```
in.ftpd : ALL: twist /bin/echo 421 FTP not allowed from %h : DENY
```

In this case, when the remote system attempts to start the FTP daemon, echo is started instead. The echo program then sends the message to the remote system and terminates the connection.

Remember, even with the extended syntax, Wrapper can only protect services started by inetd or services like portmapper that read the hosts.allow and hosts.deny files on their own. This does not provide security for any other service. To control access to those other services, you need to use the Linux IP firewall (ipfw).

Realistic Wrapper Rules

The most important thing you can do to secure your system is to keep the software up-to-date. This is essentially a passive activity—you depend on the software developer for the update. A more active approach to security is access control—it is something you can do even before problems are detected. The two basic tools for access control are the inetd.conf file and the Wrapper program. The rules you use to configure these things are very simple:

- Don't run any services you don't need to run.

- Don't provide service to anyone to whom you don't need to provide service.

Realistic Wrapper Rules *(continued)*

These rules lead to the following simple Wrapper configuration that I put on my servers immediately after the installing the system software. First, to prevent access from everyone in the outside world, I make this entry in the /etc/hosts.deny file:

```
ALL : ALL
```

Next, I make an entry in /etc/hosts.allow to permit access to the necessary services by my clients in the local domain:

```
ALL : LOCAL, .foobirds.org
```

This example assumes that the local domain is foobirds.org and that I want to provide all services to this domain. This is often the case, because I don't install unneeded software, or I block that software completely by commenting it out of the inetd.conf file. Therefore, all of the software left running on the server is intended to serve my clients.

I find using this simple configuration to be effective against many attacks. Attack scripts look for simple targets and are often discouraged by the first sign of resistance. Of course, a skilled and determined attacker can find their way around any defense. Luckily, most of us don't really attract attacks from highly skilled people.

Controlling Access with `ipfw`

Everyone thinks they know what a firewall is until you get down to the details. In a large sense, a firewall is a system that protects the local network from the big, bad global network. It is the sentinel through which all network traffic must pass before it can enter or exit the local network. In its simplest incarnation, a firewall is a filtering router that screens out unwanted traffic. And at its most complex, it is an entire network with multiple routers and multiple servers.

Linux provides an excellent, low-cost choice for a firewall for a small network. To create a Linux firewall, use the routing capabilities of Linux combined with the filtering features of `ipfw` to create a filtering router.

Maintaining Firewall Rules with `ipchains`

The Linux kernel categorizes firewall traffic into three groups and applies different filter rules to each category of traffic. These are:

Input firewall Incoming traffic is tested against the input firewall rules before it is accepted.

Output firewall Outbound traffic is tested against the output firewall rules before it is sent.

Forwarding firewall Traffic that is being forwarded through the Linux system is tested against the rules for the forwarding firewall.

NOTE   In addition to the three standard categories, the Linux 2.2 kernel allows user-defined categories.

The Linux kernel maintains a list of rules for each of these categories. These lists of rules are called *chains* and are maintained by the ipchains command. Use the following options with the ipchains command to create or delete user-defined chains, add rules to a chain, delete rules from a chain, and change the order of the rules in the chain:

-A Appends rules to the end of a chain.

-C Checks a packet against the rules in a chain. Use this for testing user-defined and built-in chains.

-D Deletes selected rules from a chain.

-F Removes all of the rules from a chain.

-I Inserts rules into a chain. A rule number is defined to specify where in the chain of rules the new rule is inserted. For example, to insert a rule at the head of the chain, assign it rule number 1.

-L Lists all rules in a chain. If no chain is specified, all rules in all chains are listed.

-M Defines address masquerading parameters or lists current settings. See Chapter 9, *Network Gateway Services*, for a description of IP masquerading.

-N Creates a user-defined chain with the specified name.

-P Sets the default policy for a chain.

-R Replaces a rule in a chain.

-S Sets timeout values for IP masquerading.

-X Deletes the specified user-defined chain.

-Z Resets the packet and byte counters in all chains to zero.

Firewall rules are composed of a filter against which the packets are matched and the action taken when a packet matches the filter. The action can either be a standard policy or a jump to a user-defined rule chain for additional processing. The standard policies are:

accept Lets the packet pass through the firewall.

reject Discards the packet and return an ICMP host unreachable error message back to the sender.

deny Silently discards the packet. No error is returned to the sender.

masq Masquerade packets to make it appear as if they came from the local host. This policy is covered in Chapter 9.

redirect Regardless of the destination of the packet, delivers it to a port on the local host.

return In a user-defined rule chain, this means to return to the chain that called this chain. In one of the three kernel chains, this means to exit the chain and use the default policy for the chain.

Use the parameters that come with the ipchains command to construct filters that match the protocol used, the source or destination address, or the network interface used for the packet. The ipchain parameters are:

-p *protocol* Defines the protocol to which the rule applies. *protocol* can be any numeric value from the /etc/protocols file or one of the keywords: tcp, udp, icmp, or all.

-s *address*[/*mask*] [*port*[:*port*]] Defines the packet source to which the rule applies. *address* can be a host name, a network name, or an IP address with an optional addresss mask. *port* can be a name or number from the /etc/services file or a numeric ICMP message type. A range of ports can be specified using the format *port*:*port*. If no specific *port* value is specified, all ports are assumed.

-d *address*[/*mask*] [*port*[:*port*]] Defines the packet destination to which the rule applies. The address and port are defined using the same rules as those used to define these values for the packet source.

--destination-port[*port*[:*port*]] Defines the destination port to which the rule applies. This filters all traffic bound for a specific port. The *port* is defined using the same rules as those used to define these values for the packet source.

--icmp-type *type* Defines the ICMP type to which the rule applies. *type* can be any valid ICMP message type number or name. The valid ICMP message names can be listed by typing **ipchains –h icmp**. There are more than 30 valid message type names.

-j *target* Identifies a standard policy to handle the packet or a user-defined chain to which control should be passed.

-i *name* Defines the name of the interface to which the rule applies. A partial interface name can be used by ending it with a +; for example, eth+ would match all Ethernet interfaces that begin with eth.

-f Indicates that the rule only refers to second and subsequent fragments of fragmented packets.

-b Indicates a rule that matches the IP packet in both directions. Thus, if the source is host A and the destination is host B, using the –b option will also match the packets when the source is host B and the destination is host A.

-v Causes the command to produce verbose output.

-n Causes the command to produce numeric output; i.e., IP addresses are not converted to host names.

-l Causes the Linux kernel to log the IP header fields of packets that match the rule.

 -o [*maxsize*] Used by firewall code developers to copy the number of bytes defined by *maxsize* from the IP packet to a user process. Only valid when the kernel has been compiled with CONFIG_IP_FIRE-WALL_NETLINK.

-m *value* Marks packets with a 32-bit unsigned value which might be used by kernel code hacker. This is not currently used.

-t *andmask xormask* Modifies the Type-of-Service (TOS) field in the IP header by ANDing the TOS field with first mask and XORing the result of with the second mask.

-x Displays the exact value of the packet and byte counters instead of rounding to the nearest thousand, million, or billion.

-y Matches TCP packets where the SYN bit is set, and the ACK and FIN bits are cleared. Such packets are used to initiate a TCP connection.

Sample ipchains Commands

Putting this all together creates a filtering router that can protect your networks. Assume you have a Linux router attached to an internal network with the address 172.16.5.254 and to an external network with the address 192.198.6.5. Here is an example of some ipchains commands you might use on that system:

```
ipchains −A input −i eth1 −s 172.16.0.0/16 −j reject

ipchains −A input −d 172.16.5.1 25 −j accept

ipchains −A input −d 172.16.5.6 80 −j accept
```

```
ipchains -A input -d 172.16.5.4 110 -j accept

ipchains -A input -d 172.16.0.0/16 -syn -j reject
```

The `-A input` arguments say that these rules should be appended to the input rule chain. The first rule says that if packets arrive on the external network interface (`eth1` in the example) that have source addresses indicating that they came from your internal network (172.16 in the example), then somebody is trying to spoof you, and the packets should be discarded.

The next three rules are basically identical. They accept packets if the destination and port are the correct destination and port for a specific server. For example, port 25 is SMTP, 172.16.5.1 is the e-mail server, port 80 is the HTTP port, 172.16.5.6 is the Web server, port 110 is the POP port, and 172.16.5.4 is the mailbox server. You accept these inbound connections because they are destined for the correct systems. The last rule rejects all other inbound TCP connections. It says that if any packets that have the SYN bit set, — arrive at the router,—meaning that they are initiating a connection—those packets are rejected.

These examples illustrate the power of the filtering features built into Linux 2.2. Very similar features are available in earlier Linux kernels where they are configured using the `ipfwadm` command. In addition to these built-in features, Linux can run third-party firewall packages.

TIP   See the Firewall-HOWTO document in the `/usr/doc/HOWTO` directory for information about third-party firewall software that can run under Linux.

Improving Authentication

Linux uses traditional Unix passwords. The passwords are no more than eight characters long and are transmitted across the network as clear text. Traditionally, the passwords are stored in the `/etc/passwd` file, which is world readable. All of these things are security problems.

Limiting passwords to eight characters limits a user's choices. If you're using Red Hat 6, select MD5 Passwords during the installation or run `authconfig` after the system is running to enable the use of long passwords. (See Chapter 2, *Basic Installation*, for a description of this feature.) Regardless of how long a password can be, the user can pick a bad one. A bad password is one that is easy to guess. See the following sidebar for some advice you can give your users to help them pick good passwords.

Password Dos and Don'ts

- Do use a mixture of numbers, special characters, and mixed-case letters.

- Do use at least eight characters.

- Do use a seemingly random selection of letters and numbers that is easy to remember, such as the first letter of each word from a line in a book, song, or poem.

- Don't use the name of a person or a thing.

- Don't use any English, or foreign language, word or abbreviation.

- Don't use any information associated with the account, such as the login name, the user's initials, phone number, social security number, job title, or room number.

- Don't use keyboard sequences, e.g., qwerty.

- Don't use any of the above things spelled backward, in caps, or otherwise disguised.

- Don't use an all numeric password.

- Don't use a sample password, no matter how good, that you've gotten from a book that discusses computer security.

Linux prevents users from picking the worse kinds of passwords by applying many of the rules listed in the sidebar to reject as bad. Passwords are chosen with the `passwd` command. Linux tests the password entered by the user at the `passwd` prompt in several different ways. Here is an example of Red Hat 6 blocking the selection of some bad passwords:

```
$ passwd
Changing password for craig
(current) UNIX password:
New UNIX password:
BAD PASSWORD: it is derived from your password entry
New UNIX password:
```

```
BAD PASSWORD: it is too simplistic/systematic

New UNIX password:

BAD PASSWORD: it is too short

passwd: Authentication token manipulation error
```

Linux does its best to make sure you use a good password, but no matter how good a password is, it is useless if someone steals it. Because the passwords are transmitted over the network as clear text, they are very easy to steal.

Two packages that can prevent thieves from stealing passwords off of the wire are described later in this section. However, passwords do not have to be stolen off of the wire. If passwords are stored in the /etc/passwd file, the entire file can be read by anyone on the system and subjected to a "dictionary attack." In a dictionary attack, a large selection of possible passwords are encrypted using the same method of encryption that is used for passwords, and the result of the encryption is compared to the passwords stored in the /etc/passwd file. When the encrypted values match, you know the original password because you know the string you used to create the encrypted value.

There is no well-known method for reversing the encryption of passwords stored in the passwd file to obtain the original password. But if passwords are poorly chosen, they are susceptible to a dictionary attack. The first line of defense against this problem is to store the encrypted passwords in a file that is not world readable.

Shadow Passwords

The shadow password file, /etc/shadow, can only be read by root. It grants no world or group file permissions. It is designed to prevent ordinary users from reading the encrypted passwords and subjecting them to a dictionary attack. In Chapter 2, this feature was enabled by selecting Shadow Passwords during the Red Hat 6 installation.

In addition to improved password security, the shadow password file provides the system administrator with some password management features. The shadow password file contains encrypted passwords and the information needed to manage them. The format of a shadow password file entry is:

username:*password*:*changed*:*min*:*max*:*warn*:*inactive*:*close*:*reserved*

In this entry:

- *username* is the login username.
- *password* is the encrypted password.
- *changed* is the date that the password was last changed written as the number of days from January 1, 1970 to the date of the change.

- *min* is the minimum number of days the user must keep a new password before it can be changed.
- *max* is the maximum number of days the user is allowed to keep a password before it must be changed.
- *warn* is the number of days before the password expires that the user is warned.
- *inactive* is the number of days after the password expires before the account is locked. Once the account is locked, the user is not able to log in and change his password.
- *close* is the date on which the account will be closed.
- *reserved* is a field reserved for the system's use.

An excerpt from the shadow password file on a Red Hat 6 system is shown below:

```
root:$1$kjhwqfeiluhivnbmv.:10750:0:99999:7:-1:-1:134538444
bin:*:10750:0:99999:7:::
daemon:*:10750:0:99999:7:::
adm:*:10750:0:99999:7:::
uucp:*:10750:0:99999:7:::
xfs:!!:10750:0:99999:7:::
gdm:!!:10750:0:99999:7:::
postgres:!!!:10750:0:99999:7:::
squid:!!!:10750:0:99999:7:::
craig:$1$obuoguhg.5LV/He0:10751:-1:99999:-1:-1:-1:135495028
kathy:$1$iugioufdjhbhjbih:10751:-1:99999:-1:-1:-1:135496088
sara:$1$piuhihblhjbhtyjjt:10751:-1:99999:-1:-1:-1:135497800
david:$1$kjiojhjhjkhvjhvuviuvug:-1:99999:-1:-1:-1:135498997
rebecca:$1$ihiohuhuhhfhjH:10751:-1:99999:-1:-1:-1:135499870
```

The encrypted password only appears in this file. Every *password* field in the /etc/passwd file contains an x, which tells the system to look in the shadow file for the real password. Every *password* field in the /etc/shadow file contains either an encrypted password, ! !, or *. If the *password* field contains ! !, it means that the account has a valid login shell but the account is locked so that no one can log in through the account. If the *password* field contains *, it indicates this is a system account, such as daemon or uucp, that does not have a login shell and therefore is not a login account.

Password Aging

In addition to protecting the password, the shadow file supports *password aging* which defines a lifetime for each password and notifies the user to change the password when it reaches the end of its life. If it is not changed, the user is blocked from using her account. The *changed*, *max*, and *warn* fields tell the system when the password was changed, how long it should be kept, and when to warn the user to change it.

When the password is changed, it must be used for the number of days defined by the *min* field before it can be changed again, which prevents the user from changing his favorite password to a temporary password and then immediately back to the favorite. This reduces one of the most common tricks used to avoid really changing passwords.

The *inactive* and *close* fields help eliminate unused accounts. The *inactive* field gives the user some number of days to log in and set a new password after the password expires. If the user does not log in before the specified number of days has elapsed, it indicates that the account is unused, and the account is locked to prevent the user logging in.

The *close* field lets you create a user account that has a specified "life." When the date stored in the *close* field is reached, the user account is disabled even if it is still active. The expiration date is stored as the number of days since January 1, 1970.

On a Red Hat 6 system, the /etc/shadow file is not edited directly. It is modified by using the linuxconf tool. Figure 14.5 shows this configuration window.

Security and
Troubleshooting

PART 4

Figure 14.5   Defining password parameters with `linuxconf`

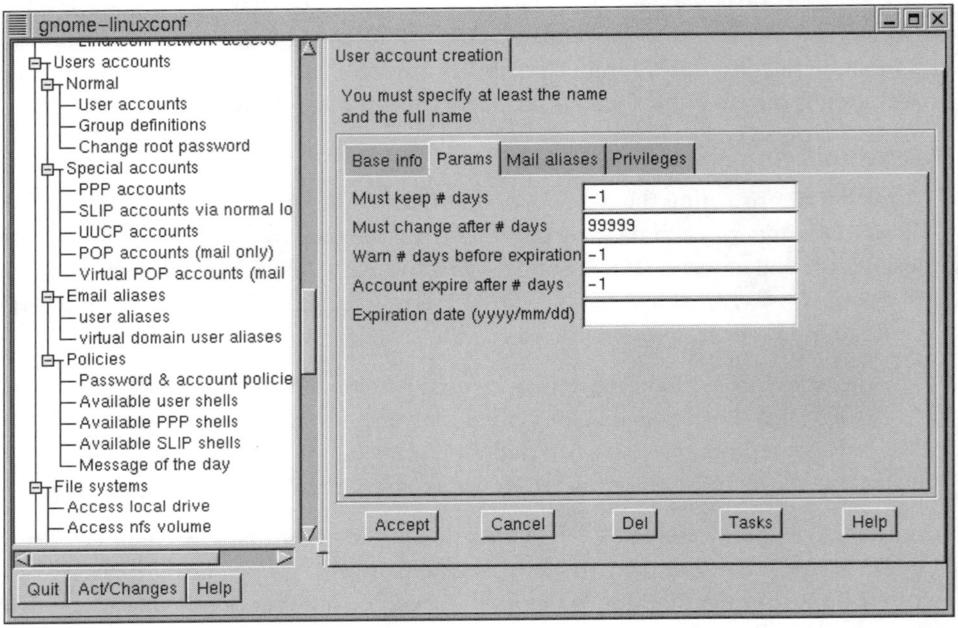

The various boxes in this configuration window can be directly mapped to fields in the shadow password file:

Must keep # days This sets the value for `min`. The value shown in Figure 14.5 is –1. This is the default value, which means that no minimum value is set, and the user is not forced to keep a password she doesn't like.

Must change after # days This sets the value for *max*. The example forces the user to change passwords every 90 days. The default value set by the Red Hat 6 system is 99999 days, which means the user will never be forced to change her password.

Warn # days before expiration This sets the value for *warn*. The example warns the user seven days before the password expires. The default value is –1, which means no warning is sent. This default setting makes sense because the other default values are configured so that the password never expires.

Account expires after # days This sets the value for *inactive*. The example set this to 30 days. By default it is set to –1, meaning that an inactive account will never be locked.

Expiration date (yyyy/mm/dd) This sets the value for *close*. No value is set in the example, and no value is set by default. Generally, this is used instead of the other values for short-term user accounts. For most accounts, this field is not used.

For most sites, the default values, which do not implement password aging, are fine. Password aging has only a marginal value for increasing system security. It is primarily used to remind users about security and to make sure that unused accounts do not go unnoticed.

The shadow password file protects the passwords that are stored on your system from a dictionary attack. However, it does not prevent the passwords from being stolen off the wire when they are transmitted. Several optional tools exist to protect passwords as they pass across the network.

One-Time Passwords

As I said earlier, choosing good passwords and protecting your password file are useless if a thief steals your password from the network. Clear-text, reusable passwords that travel over a network simply aren't secure. All security experts know this, so several alternatives to reusable passwords have been created. One of my favorites is *one-time password*, which is just what it sounds like—you use it once and throw it away. These passwords are desirable because they cannot be reused. Anyone who steals a one-time password is stealing useless garbage.

One-time Passwords In Everything (OPIE) is free, one-time passwords software for Linux. OPIE is available from `ciac.llnl.gov`. Follow the link to Tools and then to Authentication Tools. OPIE is source code delivered in a compressed `tar` file `opie-2.32.tar.gz`. To install OPIE:

1. Use `tar` to extract the file.
2. Change to the new `opie-2.32` directory.
3. Run `./configure`.
4. Run `make`.
5. Run `make install`.

Security and Troubleshooting

PART 4

Installing OPIE replaces login, su, and ftpd with its own versions of these programs that accept both traditional passwords and OPIE one-time "password phrases"—a string of six short "words," which may or may not be real words.

The OPIE Transition Mechanism

OPIE can be configured to accept either traditional reusable passwords or OPIE password phrases. Users like this feature because they can use convenient reusable passwords for console local logins where there is no danger of having the password stolen and one-time passwords for remote logins. Yet the problem with this feature is that it opens up a very big security hole by making it possible for people to forget what they are doing and use a reusable password in the wrong situation.

Sometimes, however, you need to use this feature to overcome the resistance to one-time passwords. To enable this feature, run configure with --enable-access-file when you build the OPIE software, which permits you to use the /etc/opieaccess file. In this file, list the hosts from which reusable passwords are allowed. For example:

```
permit   127.0.0.1      255.255.255.255

deny     172.16.5.25    255.255.255.255

permit   172.16.5.0     255.255.255.0
```

The first field can either permit access with reusable passwords or explicitly deny it. By default, every system not mentioned in the /etc/accessopie file is denied reusable password access. The second field is the address. The third field is the address mask which allows you to specify entire networks with a single line.

Selecting Your Secret Password

The list of one-time password phrases is generated by a program named opiekey. To uniquely identify yourself to that program, you need a secret password. Use opiepassword to select that secret password.

For example, assume I'm new to OPIE and want to generate a list of password phrases before going on a trip. First, I log in to the OPIE server's console with my traditional reusable password and run opiepasswd to select a secret OPIE password, which must be at least 10 characters long. opiepasswd accepts the secret password and displays the first password phrase, which is DUG AHOYEMILSAMJOTBERN:

```
$ opiepasswd -c

Updating craig:

Reminder - Only use this method from the console; NEVER from remote.
If you are using telnet, xterm, or a dial-in, type ^C now or exit
with no password. Then run opiepasswd without the -c parameter.

Using MD5 to compute responses.

Enter old secret pass phrase: OJ1CCFftNt

Enter new secret pass phrase: N'pim.c,.na.o

Again new secret pass phrase: N'pim.c,.na.o

ID CRAIG OPIE key is 499 P18318

DUG AHOY EMIL SAM JOT BERN
```

NOTE Running opiepasswd from the console is the most secure method. If it is not run from the console, you must have a copy of the opiekey software with you to generate the correct responses needed to enter your old and new secret passwords, because clear-text passwords are only accepted from the console.

Creating Additional Password Phrases

One password phrase, of course, is not enough. To generate additional password phrases, run opiekey. The second-to-last line output by the opiepasswd command contains important information. It displays the initial sequence number (499) and the seed (p18318). Along with the secret password, these values are required by opiekey to generate the OPIE password phrases.

opiekey takes the login sequence number, the user's seed, and the user's secret password as input and outputs the correct password phrases. Use the -n argument to request several passwords. Print them out or write them down, and you're ready to go on the road. The following example requests five password phrases from opiekey:

```
$ opiekey -n 5 499 p18318

Using MD5 algorithm to compute response.

Reminder: Don't use opiekey from telnet or dial-in sessions.
```

```
Enter secret pass phrase: N'pim.c,.na.o
495: NERO BORN ABET HELL YANG WISE
496: VERB JUKE BRAN LAWN NAIR WOOL
497: POE MOOR HAVE UN DRAB MONT
498: SACK WAND WAKE AURA SNUG HOOD
499: DUG AHOY EMIL SAM JOT BERN
```

NOTE Login sequence numbers count down from 499 and cannot be reused. When the sequence number gets down to 10, re-run opiepasswd and select a new secret password in order to reset the sequence number to 499.

The opiekey command line requests five password phrases (-n 5) starting from sequence number 499. The seed (p18318) is provided on the command line. opiekey prompts for the secret password you defined with the opiepasswd command. The sequence number, the seed, and the secret password are then used to generate the password phrases, and opiekey prints out the number you requested in sequence number order.

To log in, you must use the password phrase that goes with the sequence number displayed by login. For example:

```
login: craig
otp-md5 496 p18318
Response or Password: VERB JUKE BRAN LAWN NAIR WOOL
```

A system running OPIE displays a line indicating that the one-time passwords are being generated with the MD5 algorithm (otp-md5), that this is login sequence number 496 and that the seed used for the one-time passwords is p18318. The correct response is the six short "words" for login number 496 from the list of password phrases. That response cannot be used again to log in to the system.

I may be the only person who will ever tell you "I like one-time passwords." But I do like them. I particularly like their portability. I don't need any special software on the client, just a list of passwords in my wallet that I can use anywhere. If you have opiekey software on the client system, you can produce one-time passwords one at a time. But why would you? If you control the software on both the client and on the server, use secure shell. It is a better authentication tool than OPIE. Use OPIE for those times when you need complete freedom to log in from any system. Use secure shell when you want a really good remote login tool.

Secure Shell

The secure shell (ssh2) program provides remote access with strong authentication and public key session encryption. Secure shell is both secure and easy to use.

The secure shell software is available at www.cs.hut.fi/ssh. To install the software:

1. Download the compressed tar file, which is currently ssh-2.0.13.tar.gz.

2. Run tar to create the ssh-2.0.13 directory.

3. Change to the directory and run the configure command to build the correct Makefile.

4. Run make and make install to build and install the secure shell components:

   sshd2 This daemon process services incoming secure shell connections.

   ssh2 This user command is used to securely log in to a remote system. This command creates the outgoing connections that are handled by the remote sshd2.

   scp This secure copy command performs the same function as remote copy (rcp).

   ssh-keygen2 This program generates the secure shell encryption keys.

NOTE In addition to installing these software components, the make install command generates the host keys that secure shell uses to authenticate the host and encrypt the session. With these keys, the system is immediately ready to communicate securely.

When a secure shell client and server connect, they exchange keys. The keys are compared to the known keys they have stored in the /etc/ssh2/knownhosts directory and in the .ssh2/knownhosts directory under the user's home directory. If the key is not found in one of these locations, the user is asked to verify that the new key should be accepted. If the key is found or is accepted by the user, the host key is used to encrypt a randomly generated session key. The session key is then used by both systems to encrypt the remainder of the session. If no special authentication has been configured, the user is prompted for a password; there is no need to worry about password thieves, because the password is encrypted before it is sent. The following example illustrates how a login looks with the default configuration:

```
> ssh parrot
Host key not found from the list of known hosts.
Are you sure you want to continue connecting (yes/no)? yes
Host 'parrot' added to the list of known hosts.
craig's password: Watts?Watt?
```

Security and Troubleshooting

PART 4

The client user is not limited to simple password authentication. By default, the server configuration is set to accept password authentication and public key authentication. If users wish to use public key authentication, they must create their own private and public keys.

Creating User Keys

The ssh-keygen2 program generates the public and private encryption keys used for public key authentication. Simply invoke the ssh-keygen2 command and enter a *passphrase*, which is your secret password, when prompted. Here is an example:

```
$ ssh-keygen2
Generating 1024-bit dsa key pair
   6 Oo.oOo.oOoo.
Key generated.
1024-bit dsa, craig@parrot.foobirds.org, Wed Jun 23 1999 13:50:48 -
0400
Passphrase : Who are the trusted?
Again      : Who are the trusted?
Private key saved to /home/craig/.ssh2/id_dsa_1024_a
Public key saved to /home/craig/.ssh2/id_dsa_1024_a.pub
```

> **NOTE** A passphrase can literally be a phrase, because blanks are allowed. The example uses a line from a song. Though a random collection of words may be more secure, the passphrase must be easy to remember. If you forget it, no one will be able to recover it for you.

Two keys are created: id_dsa_1024_a is the private key, which must be protected, and id_dsa_1024_a.pub is the public key, which is distributed to remote sites for encrypting the session. After the keys are created on the client system, copy the public key to the .ssh2 directory in the users' home directory on the server. Now when users log in to the server, they're prompted for the passphrase.

The default configuration provides simple and secure communication and complete protection from password thieves. There are, however, configuration options for both the server and the client that allow you to customize secure shell for your environment.

Configuring sshd2

Very little configuration is required to get secure shell running, but a great deal of configuration is possible. Many of the software packages discussed in this book fit this pattern: There are a great many configuration options, but the default values for those options work in almost every case and rarely need to be changed. sshd2 fits this pattern. Without configuration, it will work just fine, but there are configuration options that you can use to modify it for your particular site.

sshd2 is configured by the /etc/sshd2/sshd2_config file. The configuration values in this file are keyword value pairs. There are more than 30 possible configuration values. Those that are implemented in secure shell release 2.0.13 are listed in Table 14.2.

Table 14.2   sshd2 Configuration Parameters

Keyword	Purpose
AllowedAuthentications	Defines a comma-separated list of acceptable authentication methods. Possible values are password, publickey, and hostbased. The default is password,publickey.
AllowHosts	Specifies hosts from which logins are allowed. The * and ? wildcards can be used.
AllowSHosts	Specifies which host names are valid in .shosts, .rhosts, hosts.equiv, and shosts.equiv entries.
AuthorizationFile	Specifies the name of the user's authorization file.
CheckMail	Tells sshd2 whether or not it should notify the user about new mail at login.
Ciphers	Defines a comma-separated list of the acceptable session encryption techniques. Possible values are des, 3des, blowfish, idea, arcfour, twofish, any, anystd, anycipher, anystdcipher, and none.
DenyHosts	Specifies hosts from which login is not allowed. The * and ? wildcards can be used.

Security and
Troubleshooting

PART 4

Table 14.2 sshd2 Configuration Parameters *(continued)*

Keyword	Purpose
DenySHosts	Specifies the host names that are not valid in the .shosts, .rhosts, hosts.equiv, and shosts.equiv files.
ForwardAgent	Specifies whether the connection to the authentication agent will be forwarded to the remote server.
ForwardX11	Specifies whether X11 connections will be redirected over the secure channel.
HostKeyFile	Identifies the file containing the private host key. The default is /etc/ssh2/hostkey.
IgnoreRhosts	Specifies that .rhosts and .shosts files are not used in hostbased authentication.
KeepAlive	Specifies whether or not the system should send keepalives.
ListenAddress	Specifies the IP address of the interface that sshd2 should service.
LoginGraceTime	Defines the timeout for a login. The default is 600 seconds.
MaxConnections	Defines the maximum number of concurrent connections sshd2 will service.
NoDelay	Defines whether or not sshd2 should use the TCP_NODELAY socket option.
PasswordGuesses	Specifies the number of password tries a user is allowed. The default is 3.
PermitEmptyPasswords	Specifies whether or not sshd2 allows login to accounts with empty password strings.

Table 14.2   sshd2 Configuration Parameters *(continued)*

Keyword	Purpose
PermitRootLogin	Specifies whether or not sshd2 accepts logins to the root account. The default is yes. Other values are no, which disables root logins through sshd2, and nopwd, which disables password authenticated root logins.
Port	Defines the port number used by sshd2. The default is port 22.
PrintMotd	Specifies whether or not sshd2 should print the message of the day at login. The default is yes.
PublicHostKeyFile	Identifies the file containing the public host key. The default is /etc/ssh2/hostkey.pub.
RandomSeedFile	Specifies the name of the random seed file.
RequiredAuthentications	Specifies which authentication methods must be used. This must be a subset of the values defined for AllowAuthentications.
QuietMode	Limits logging to only fatal errors.
Ssh1Compatibility	Specifies whether or not sshd2 needs to support older SSH1 clients.
Sshd1Path	Provides the path to sshd1 daemon, which supports SSH1 clients.
UserConfigDirectory	Defines the path to the user's configuration files.
UserKnownHosts	Specifies whether or not the user's knownhosts directory is searched for public keys for hostbased authentication.
VerboseMode	Causes sshd2 to print debugging messages.

Security and
Troubleshooting

PART 4

An example of using the /etc/sshd2/sshd2_config file to increase security might be to limit the remote clients that are allowed to connect to the server. To limit clients to only those hosts in the sybex.com domain and the nist.gov domain, the following entry could be added to the sshd2_config file:

```
AllowHosts *.sybex.com *.nist.gov
```

Configuring the ssh2 Client

Each user can customize the secure shell client using the ssh2_config file, which is located in the .ssh2 directory of the user's home directory. There are more than 25 configuration options available for the ssh2_config file. Those that are implemented in secure shell release 2.0.13 are listed in Table 14.3.

Table 14.3   ssh2 Client Configuration Options

Option	Usage
AuthorizationFile	Specifies the name of the user's authorization file.
Ciphers	Defines the acceptable session encryption techniques. Possible values are des, 3des, blowfish, idea, arcfour, twofish, any, anystd, anycipher, anystdcipher, and none.
Compression	Specifies whether or not compression should be used.
DontReadStdin	Tell ssh2 not to read standard input (stdin).
EscapeChar	Defines the escape character. The default is a tilde (~).
ForwardAgent	Specifies whether or not the connection to the authentication agent is forwarded to the remote machine.
ForwardX11	Specifies whether or not X11 connections are automatically redirected over the secure channel.
GoBackground	Specifies whether or not ssh2 runs in the background.

Table 14.3   ssh2 Client Configuration Options *(continued)*

Option	Usage
Host	Specifies the host name of the remote server. The default is to use the host name from the ssh2 command line.
IdentityFile	Defines the name of the user's identification file.
KeepAlive	Specifies whether or not ssh2 should transmit keepalives.
LocalForward	Connects a local port to a port on the remote system via the secure channel. The value provided to this command is "port:remotehost:remoteport". The quotes are required.
NoDelay	Specifies whether or not ssh2 should use the TCP_NODELAY socket option.
PasswordPrompt	Defines the password prompt displayed to the user.
Port	Defines the port number used to connect to the remote host. The default is 22.
QuietMode	Suppresses all messages except fatal errors.
RandomSeedFile	Specifies the name of the user's random seed file.
RemoteForward	Connects a port on the remote machine to a local port via the secure channel. The value provided to the command is "port:remotehost:remoteport". The quotes are required.
Ssh1AgentCompatibility	Specifies how SSH1 connections are forwarded. Possible values are: none–don't forward SSH1 connections; traditional–forward exactly as an old SSH1 connection; or ssh2–forward as an SSH2 connection.
Ssh1Compatibility	Specifies whether or not to use SSH1 compatibility mode.

Security and
Troubleshooting

PART 4

Table 14.3 ssh2 Client Configuration Options *(continued)*

Option	Usage
Ssh1Path	Specifies the path to the ssh1 client.
User	Specifies the username for the login.
VerboseMode	Causes ssh2 to print debugging messages

Secure shell is an excellent way to have secure communications between to systems across the Internet. However, it does require that both systems have the secure shell software installed. When you control both ends of the link, this is not a problem. For example, when I travel with my Linux laptop, I always use secure shell. But there are times when you must log in from a system that is not under your control. For those occasions, one-time passwords, as provided by OPIE, are still essential.

Monitoring Your System

Monitoring your system is an essential part of security. It helps you discover what attacks are being launched against your system so that you can concentrate on plugging popular holes. Monitoring also lets you know when someone has successfully penetrated your defenses.

Some basic Linux commands can help you learn what constitutes normal activity on your system so that you know when things are out of the ordinary:

- Use the who command to find out who's logged in and what they're doing.
- Use the last command to find out when people normally log in.
- Use the log files, such as /var/log/secure, to monitor access to network services and to monitor failed login attempts.
- Use ps to find out what processes are normally running.
- Develop a feel for your system. Intruders often change that feel.

Security Monitoring Tools

In addition to using simple commands to learn about your system, you should use some of the tools that have been specifically designed to detect the holes that intruders exploit and the changes they make to your system. There are several, and many of them are available at `ciac.llnl.gov`; follow the Tools link and then the System Monitoring Tools link. Some of these tools are:

COPS The Computer Oracle and Password System is a security scanner that checks the system for several possible configuration errors. It is a classic tool, but is old and somewhat outdated.

ISS The Internet Security Scanner checks the system for known security weaknesses, with an emphasis on network security.

Tiger The Tiger package is a group of shell scripts and C programs that scan configuration files and file systems looking for security problems. It is more up-to-date than COPS and very easy to use.

Tripwire The Tripwire package maps the file system and digitally signs files. The digital signatures are later used to detect if anyone has altered a critical file.

Pick one of the tools (I think Tiger is the easiest to use), run it, and use the report as a guide to possible security holes. Then use your own judgment to determine how much of a threat the reported holes actually are.

I find the security reports from the scanners to be primarily useful as a pointer to possible security problems. However, they can't replace your own judgment about what is right for your system.

To me, Tripwire is more useful than the scanners. Intruders often change files to provide themselves a backdoor into your system. Tripwire can be very useful in detecting these file changes.

A common complaint about security scanners is that they are out-of-date. It is very difficult for the security scanners to stay up-to-date because systems and problems change very rapidly. But even though these programs are dated, old security holes can be exploited just as effectively as new ones, so it is worth running a scanner at least once. A more up-to-date source of security holes may be the attack scripts used by intruders.

Attacking Your Own Server

Attack scripts automate the most common security attacks. This makes them simple, effective tests of the security of your system. If an attack script can successfully penetrate your system's defenses, intruders can get into your system.

WARNING Not all attack scripts are designed to be system friendly. *Never* run them against your real server, and *never* run them on a real network.

Security and
Troubleshooting

PART 4

Run attack scripts offline against a test system. Use them against a new Linux release or upgraded software before installing it on your real server. Here's how:

1. Install the new Linux release on a test system. This is not the real server; it is just an old PC that you use for tests.

2. Install the attack scripts on the laptop system you use as a network diagnostic tool. (You'll hear more about using a laptop as a diagnostic tool in Chapter 15, *Trouble-shooting*.)

3. Assign both systems private network numbers and interconnect them with a piece of Ethernet cable so that neither system is attached to a real network.

4. Launch each attack script from the laptop and record all of the vulnerabilities the scripts reports. These are the same vulnerabilities that would be seen by a real network attacker.

5. Before installing the Linux upgrade on the real server, locate fixes for as many of the reported problems as possible.

6. Upgrade the server and install the security fixes all in the same weekend.

Attack scripts are available at `www.rootshell.com`. Current scripts that could be used for this procedure are `nmap`, `queso`, `strobe`, and `netcat`.

Final Words

Attaching your server to a network increases the risk of security problems, and security problems are the greatest risk to the stability and reliability of your system. The most difficult task of running a 24seven service is keeping the system up and running 24 hours a day, seven days a week. Linux makes that possible, because it is rock solid. So solid, in fact, that whenever a Linux system crashes, I suspect an outside force, such as a security intruder.

However, security breaches are not the only threats to the reliability and stability of your Linux server. The next chapter describes the other kinds of network problems that can appear and what you can do to troubleshoot those problems.

It Really *Is* Scary Out There!

Many network administrators don't understand how bad the network neighborhood is. The people who run the enterprise firewall protect most of us from ever seeing the break-in attempts. I *do* see them, because one of the networks I administer is outside of the firewall. On average, that network is probed by network intruders more than once a week!

I actually had occasion to use a break-in to my advantage. I needed to schedule a major server upgrade. This happened to be a Solaris upgrade on one of the test servers. I had the upgrade software sitting on my desk for nine months, but every time I scheduled the upgrade, my boss would cancel it in favor of something that was "higher priority." Frankly, I think that system administrator training, which is what the test server was used for, is high priority, but the boss is the boss.

I teach a workshop at the Networld+Interop conference, which offers a large group of network computers that can be used to check e-mail or to log in to your office computer. I prefer to use my own laptop, but on occasion I have used one of the conference systems and logged in with an OPIE password. This time was different. Just before leaving for the Atlanta airport, I sat down at one of the conference systems and logged in to the test server back at the office using a standard, clear-text password, knowing full well that sending a reusable password over the Internet wasn't smart. I then caught my plane to Dulles airport.

The next morning—elapsed time from the suicidal login was about 10 hours—I sat down at the console of the test server to check the system security. I didn't get far. The first command I tried was last to check who had logged in to the system and from where. The last command failed, complaining that the wtmp file was corrupted. This is a dead giveaway that someone had logged on to the system and had done a poor job of covering their tracks.

System administrators are usually too busy to spare the time to chase an intruder, so I rarely waste time analyzing a break-in. Besides, the cause of this one was obviously a stolen password. I dumped the system to tape, wrote a report on the probable cause of the break-in, and sent the tapes and the report to the security group. When an interesting problem occurs, the security group, not the system administrator, does the analysis. The system administrator's job is to quickly restore the server. Recovering a server after a break-in is extremely high priority.

Suddenly, upgrading the Solaris software on the test server became my most important job. Upon doing so, not only did I receive a thank you from my boss for recovering the server system so quickly, but I was able to get the upgrade software off my desk.

24*seven* CASE STUDY

15

Troubleshooting

It is better to avoid trouble than it is to fix things after trouble arises. Because avoiding trouble is one of the primary motivations for good security, some of the techniques described in Chapter 14—such as keeping the system software and your knowledge of potential problems up-to-date—apply equally well, whether the threat is a security intruder or a bug that crashes your favorite application. The bug fixes posted at the vendor's site are not always about security, but they are almost always of interest to you.

TIP There is a difference between fixing bugs and enhancing the system. Fix bugs that you have detected on your server or that you know are a direct threat to your server. Avoid installing things just to get a new feature—reliability is more important than new features for a server. Try out the latest bells and whistles on your desktop system, and debug them before you move them to the server.

Despite your best efforts, things *will* go wrong. It's inevitable. No matter how great your knowledge, you will make mistakes, and no matter how hard you try to avoid them, problems will appear. Networking your system only adds to this potential, because mistakes made by someone far away can negatively impact your users.

The heart of your Linux system is the kernel. Therefore, keeping the kernel updated is an essential part of keeping the system software up-to-date. This chapter begins by looking at how you can avoid trouble by keeping your Linux kernel current. It then goes on to examine several basic Linux commands that can help you analyze and solve network problems.

This chapter examines several basic Linux commands that can help you analyze and solve network problems. But before getting to these, let's look at how to build an updated Linux kernel.

Configuring the Linux Kernel

The Linux kernel is a C program compiled and installed by make. Use make xconfig to customize the kernel configuration and create the Makefile needed to compile the kernel for your system. There are a huge number of kernel configuration options. make xconfig provides a nice X Windows interface that allows you to go directly to those parts of the configuration that you want to modify. The ability to ignore those configuration options you don't need and jump directly to those you do need is very useful.

Protecting Your Existing Kernel

Before you start to build a new kernel you must protect the existing kernel. If something goes wrong, you want to be able to fall back to a kernel that you know is good. Protecting the kernel involves three things: protecting the current source tree, protecting the current bootable kernel, and protecting the module library.

Protecting the Kernel Source

The standard Linux kernel source directory is /usr/src/linux. This directory name is usually a link to the real kernel source tree. The real source directory is identified by a name that includes the kernel revision number, as shown in this Red Hat 6 example:

```
$ ls -l /usr/src
total 4380
lrwxrwxrwx   1 root  root  11    Jun 8 16:58 linux -> linux-2.2.5
drwxr-xr-x  17 root  root  1024  Jun 8 16:58 linux-2.2.5
drwxr-xr-x   7 root  root  1024  Jun 8 17:01 redhat
```

On this sample system, the linux link points to the linux-2.2.5 source directory.

To begin the upgrade, place the new source tree in the /usr/src directory and assign it a unique name. For example, assume you want to upgrade the Red Hat system to kernel 2.2.9. Download the kernel source file linux-2.2.9.tar.gz from sunsite.unc.edu into the /usr/src directory. Simply extracting the new kernel from the tar file will create a linux subdirectory, which is not really what you want. You need to temporarily get rid of the linux link, extract the tar file, and change the name of the directory it creates to linux-2.2.9. Then reinstall the linux link to point to the new directory. Here's an example:

```
# rm linux
rm: remove `linux'? y
# tar -zxvf linux-2.2.9.tar.gz
# mv linux linux-2.2.9
# ln -s linux-2.2.9 linux
# rm linux-2.2.9.tar.gz
rm: remove `linux-2.2.9.tar.gz'? y
# ls -l
total 13561
lrwxrwxrwx  1 root root 11   Jul  7 16:24 linux -> linux-2.2.9
drwxr-xr-x 17 root root 1024 Jun 22 07:23 linux-2.2.5
drwxr-xr-x 14 1046 1046 1024 May 13 19:41 linux-2.2.9
drwxr-xr-x  7 root root 1024 Jun 22 07:31 redhat
```

The ls command in the example shows that after these steps are complete, the new source tree exists and is called linux-2.2.9, the linux link points to the new directory, and the old directory linux-2.2.5 still exists in case it is needed as a backup.

Protecting the Bootable Kernel

In addition to backing up the source directory, you need to make a backup copy of the executable kernel before proceeding. Making a backup copy of the kernel is easy and can be done in two different ways. The first and most preferred method is to use a unique name for each bootable kernel file that provides information about the release level of the kernel. On the sample Red Hat 6 system, the lilo.conf file boots a kernel named vmluniz-2.2.5. Naming the new kernel vmlinuz-2.2.9 in the example would avoid overwriting the old kernel and thus would keep the old kernel as a backup. This is the approach described in the "Compiling and Installing the Kernel" section later in this chapter.

However, if you prefer to use the same name for all kernels, e.g., `vmlinuz`, use the `cp` command to copy the current kernel to a backup file with a name like `vmlinuz.old`. Here's an example:

```
# cp /boot/vmlinuz /boot/vmlinuz.old
```

A backup copy of the kernel won't do any good unless it can be used during the boot. To be useful, it must be added to the `lilo.conf` file. In the following sample `lilo.conf` file, a new image command was added to load the old kernel in case of problems:

```
boot=/dev/hda
map=/boot/map
install=/boot/boot.b
prompt
timeout=50
# Normal Linux boot
image=/boot/vmlinuz
        label=linux
        root=/dev/hdb1
        read-only
# Emergency Linux boot
image=/boot/vmlinuz.old
        label=safe
        root=/dev/hdb1
        read-only
# DOS boot
other=/dev/hda1
        label=dos
        table=/dev/hda
```

With this `lilo.conf` file, you can enter **safe** at the boot prompt to boot the old kernel that you know is good. Of course, this would only be used if the new kernel does not boot correctly.

NOTE Don't remember the commands and structure of the `lilo.conf` file? Review Chapter 3, *The Boot Process*.

Protecting the Module Library

Loadable modules must be compatible with the kernel that is using them. Modules are re-compiled along with the kernel that will load them. If you are forced to drop back to an earlier version of the kernel, you need to make sure that you keep the modules required for that kernel. Generally, this is not a problem because the kernel-build process gives the new module library a unique name based on the release number. However, you may be compiling a kernel that has the same release number as the current kernel—not to upgrade but to create a more efficient kernel customized for your system. In this case, you may want to make a backup copy of the current module library just to ensure that all of the modules are there if you need to fall back.

> **TIP** Usually, I don't bother with backing up the module library, because I always upgrade when I build a custom kernel. New kernels are constantly being released. I find that by the time I'm ready to customize the kernel of a new distribution, a new kernel is available. Using a new kernel release means that I don't have a conflict with module library names.

Now that you have everything backed up, it's safe to proceed with configuring and compiling a new kernel.

Configuring the Kernel with `xconfig`

To start the kernel configuration process, change to the `/usr/src/linux` directory and run `make xconfig`, which opens the window shown in Figure 15.1.

Figure 15.1   The Kernel Configuration window

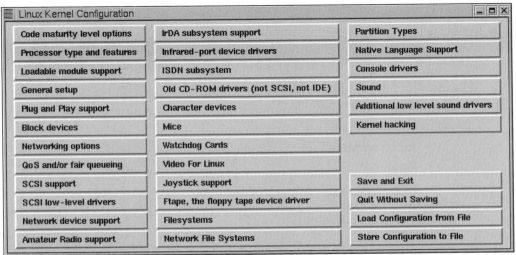

The Kernel Configuration window displays 30 buttons that represent different configuration categories. (These buttons are described in detail in the upcoming "Understanding the Kernel Configuration Categories" section.) Click a button to view and set the configuration options in that category. Figure 15.2 shows the window that appears if the Network Device Support button is selected.

Figure 15.2 Network device support configuration options

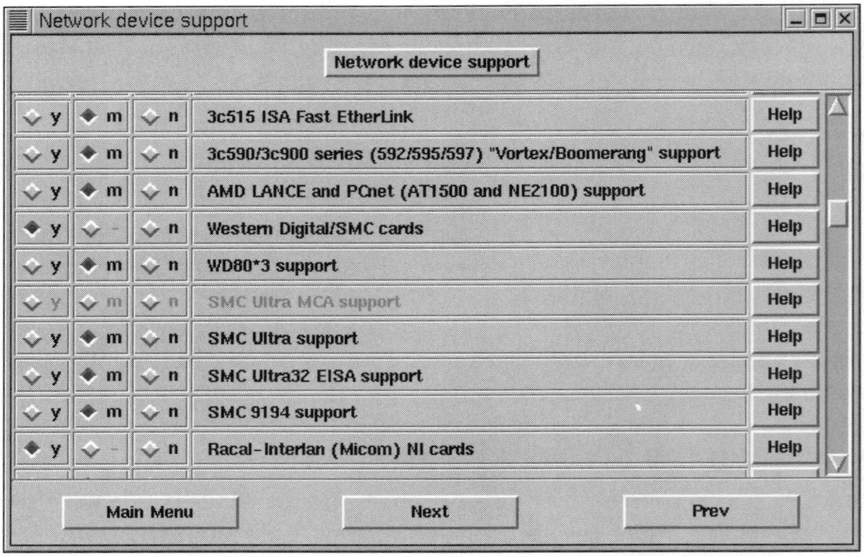

The Network Device Support window lists all of the network device drivers that can be compiled into or loaded by the kernel. You have three standard choices for most configuration options:

y Compiles the option into the new kernel.

m Causes the option to be loaded as a loadable module by the kernel. Not every option is available as a loadable module. Notice the Western Digital/SMC cards option. When a configuration question must be answered yes or no, the module selection is not available.

n Tells the kernel not to use the configuration option.

In addition to these standard selections, some options offer a drop-down list of configuration keywords. An example of this is the Processor Type And Features configuration option. Figure 15.3 shows the drop-down list of processor types available in this option window. The five possible selections are:

386 Select 386 for Intel, Cyrix, and AMD 386 CPUs, for Cyrix and TI 486/DLC CPUs, and for UMC 486SX-S CPUs.

486/Cx486 Select 486 for Intel, IBM, Cyrix, and AMD 486 CPUs, for AMD and Cyrix 5x86 CPUs, for NexGen Nx586 CPUs, and for UMC U5D and U5S CPUs.

586/K5/5x86/6x86 Select 586 for generic Pentium-class CPUs.

Pentium/K6/TSC Select Pentium for Intel Pentium and Pentium MMX CPUs and for AMD K5, K6, and K6-3D CPUs.

PPro/6x86MX Select PPro for the Intel Pentium Pro, Pentium II, and Pentium III CPUs and for Cyrix, IBM, and National Semiconductor 6x86MX and MII CPUs.

Figure 15.3   Selecting processor types and features

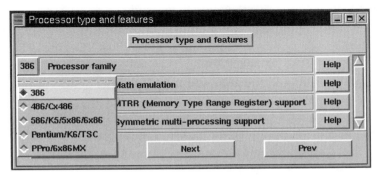

NOTE This processor list is limited to PC processors because this book is focused on PC architectures. But this is only a partial list of the possible processors that Linux can run on, because Linux runs on a variety of hardware architectures in addition to PCs.

Each configuration option also has a Help button. Clicking the Help button provides additional information about the option and advice about when the option should be set. Even if you think you know what the option is about, you should read the description displayed by the Help button before you change any option from its default setting.

Understanding the Kernel Configuration Categories

Now that you know what is displayed when you select a configuration category, let's look at what the categories mean. More than half of the kernel configuration categories configure hardware subsystems and devices. This is not surprising given the kernel's role in initializing hardware. The remaining categories cover options for configuring the kernel architecture and optional features, such as networking and network file systems, that require kernel support.

The 30 configuration categories (shown in Figure 15.1) are:

Code maturity level options Specifies whether or not you want the option to include experimental code in the kernel. For operational servers, this is set to No.

Processor type and features Allows you to select the processor type, as described above, and to set support for processor features. Say Yes to math emulation and to memory type range register support; these features will not interfere with normal operation and will only be used if needed. Unless you have a server with more than one CPU, say No to symmetric multi-processing support.

Loadable module support The options in this category are used to enable support for loadable modules. Every option here should be set to Yes.

General setup This category has more than 25 different configuration options, including specifying support for networking and the PCI bus. Unless you have odd hardware or software requirements, the defaults should be correct.

Plug and Play support Specifies whether or not your system should support automatic configuration of Plug-and-Play devices and if you want to support intelligent parallel port devices. Common settings are to say Yes for Plug and Play and to use a loadable module for intelligent parallel port devices.

Block devices Defines the block device support for the kernel. Block devices include disk drives and CD-ROM drives. The default settings enable support for a wide range of possible devices through loadable modules. The options that are disabled tend to be for odd hardware that is not really appropriate for an operational server. Before changing the block device settings, read the ide.txt file in /usr/src/linux/ Documentation.

Networking options Defines the networking support for the kernel. There are more than 50 network configuration options. By default, the options are configured for a server and do not need to be modified. If you plan to run your system as a router, you should carefully examine the options that relate to the IP: Advanced Router option. Selecting that option provides several selections that tune the kernel for routing, as opposed to the normal state, which is to have the kernel tuned for a host computer.

QoS and/or fair queueing Specifies options that change the way network packets are handled by the server. This option should be set to No for an operational server. The optional packet handlers require special software to administer them.

SCSI support Enables support for SCSI devices. Most operational servers use SCSI devices for disk and tape support, so these options should be set to Yes.

SCSI low-level drivers Defines which SCSI interfaces are supported. Most of these are configured as loadable modules.

Network device support Defines which network interface cards are supported. Most network interfaces are configured as loadable modules. (This window was shown in Figure 15.2.)

Amateur Radio support Defines whether or not the kernel should have support for an amateur radio network connection. Set this to No for all operational servers.

IrDA subsystem support Defines whether or not the kernel should have support for the Infrared Data Association's infrared wireless network. If you use an infrared wireless network in your office, enable the support here; otherwise, this should be set to No. Before attempting to use this option, read the irda.txt file in the /usr/src/ Documentation directory and the IR-HOWTO. You will also need optional software to manage the IrDA service.

Infrared-port device drivers Specifies which infrared devices will be supported by the kernel.

ISDN subsystem Defines the Integrated Services Digital Network (ISDN) support for the kernel. ISDN is an optional digital telephone service that can be purchased in many parts of the world. If it is possible that you will be using it on your system, you can configure the ISDN options as loadable modules.

Old CD-ROM drivers (not SCSI, not IDE) Specifies what nonstandard CD-ROM devices should be supported by the kernel. Operational servers do not use old, nonstandard devices of any kind. Unless you use a nonstandard CD-ROM, you can say No to this option.

Character devices Defines which character devices are supported by the kernel. Character devices include terminals, serial ports, PS/2 mice, and parallel ports. Most of these devices are necessary and thus are compiled into the kernel or supported as loadable modules.

Mice Defines the mice supported by the kernel. Support for PS/2 is compiled into the kernel, and all other mice are normally enabled as loadable modules.

Watchdog Cards Specifies the watchdog timer hardware that will be supported by the kernel. Watchdog timer hardware can be used to shut down or reboot the system if certain conditions are meet, such as a heat sensor triggering or the watchdog software failing to update the /dev/watchdog device at a specified interval. Watchdog Timer Support must be selected in Character Devices before these cards can be used.

Video for Linux Specifies the audio and video capture devices that will be supported by the kernel. For most servers, these devices are not needed, but they are required by desktop systems for a range of applications, such as video conferencing. Most of these devices can be specified as loadable modules.

Security and
Troubleshooting

PART 4

Joystick support Defines the joystick support provided by the kernel. Most servers do not have joysticks.

Ftape, the floppy tape device driver Defines the support for IDE tape drives, which are called floppy tapes. These devices can be supported by loadable modules.

Filesystems Specifies the file system types that will be supported by the kernel. There are a large number of possible file systems, most of which can be supported as loadable modules.

Network File Systems Specifies the kernel support for network-based file systems, including Coda, NFS, Novell NetWare, and Microsoft SMB protocols. These network file services can be supported as loadable modules. A Linux network server may require all of these.

Partition Types Adds support for accessing native BSD, Macintosh, SunOS, Solaris, and UnixWare file systems to the kernel. An operational server does not dual-boot and does not share disk space with other operating systems. Support for these partition types is not needed on a server.

Native Language Support Provides support for a wide variety of languages. All of these languages are available as loadable modules.

Console drivers Defines the hardware support for the console monitor. This should specify the correct settings for your monitor and adapter card.

Sound Defines the hardware support for the sound card. Operational servers don't use sound cards, but your desktop system will. Use this window to enable support for sound and to set the card configuration.

Additional low-level sound drivers Defines several more sound cards that are supported by the Linux kernel.

Kernel hacking Enables kernel debugging that allows certain keyboard sequences to control the kernel. This feature is intended for kernel developers, not system administrators, so on an operational server, I set this to No.

For a production system, avoid using any experimental code in the kernel. You should also avoid any hardware you don't need. It is not necessary, however, to say "no" to unneeded hardware. If the hardware driver is a loadable module, it will not be loaded unless it is actually needed.

Compiling and Installing the Kernel

After selecting the configuration options you want, compile the kernel. To do so:

1. Run `make dep ; make clean` to build the dependencies and clean up the odds and ends.

2. Use `make zImage` to build a compressed kernel.

3. The loadable modules used by the kernel also need to be compiled, so run `make modules` to build the modules.

4. Run `make modules_install` to put the modules in the correct directory.

5. Copy the kernel from the `/usr/src/linux/arch/i386/boot` directory, where it is stored under the name `zImage`, to the `/boot` directory.

6. Give the kernel the name defined in your `lilo.conf` file.

TIP It's a good idea to name the kernel image file with the release number. For example, a kernel produced from the `linux-2.2.9` source tree would be named `vmlinuz-2.2.9`.

7. Double-check the `lilo.conf` file and then run `lilo` to build the new boot map. For example, in the following sample, I call the new kernel `vmlinuz-2.2.9` and the old one `vmlinuz-2.2.5`:

```
[root]# cat /etc/lilo.conf
boot=/dev/hda
map=/boot/map
install=/boot/boot.b
prompt
timeout=50
# Normal Linux boot
image=/boot/vmlinuz-2.2.9
        label=linux
        root=/dev/hdb1
        read-only
# Emergency Linux boot
image=/boot/vmlinuz-2.2.5
        label=safe
        root=/dev/hdb1
        read-only
# DOS boot
other=/dev/hda1
        label=dos
        table=/dev/hda
```

```
[root]# /sbin/lilo
Added linux *
Added safe
Added dos
```

The new kernel is now ready to run. Reboot the system and put the new kernel in action. If anything goes wrong during the boot, drop back and boot the safe kernel. Once you're comfortable with the new kernel, say after a month, you can remove the old source tree, module library, and kernel if you need the disk space.

Troubleshooting a Network Server

Even though you're liberal about fixing known bugs and conservative about installing unneeded software, problems will occur. Many of these problems will be detected and reported by your users before you know anything is wrong. Tracking down those reported problems is as much an art as a science.

The art of troubleshooting is your intuition about the state of your server and the network and your insight into the accuracy of the user's problem report. I don't say this to demean the intelligence of the user reporting the problem, because I'm as guilty of providing inaccurate trouble reports as the next guy. When under stress, I have completely misunderstood very clear instructions and reported a problem when the only real problem was my lack of time to carefully read the instructions. Thus you cannot assume too much from the trouble report, and you need to be methodical in applying your own knowledge to the problem. Here are some suggestions:

- Duplicate the problem yourself and then have the user duplicate the problem while you walk him through it. This often eliminates problems that spring from user confusion.

- Avoid oversimplification. The problem is not always a confused user. In a networked server, the problem can occur in any part of the network hardware or software, from your system to the remote system.

- Divide a complex problem into pieces and test the individual pieces to isolate the problem.

The science of troubleshooting is your knowledge of how your server and the network operate, and the tools that are available to conduct empirical tests of the server and the network. Your knowledge helps you focus on the proper area for testing and helps you select the proper tools for testing that area. Here are some guidelines to help you make those decisions:

- If the problem occurs on outbound connections, it is probably unrelated to any of the network daemons running on your server. Use `ifconfig` to check the configuration of the network interface, `ping` to test the basic connectivity, and `traceroute` to test the route to the remote server. Talk with the administrator of the remote server to ensure they are running the service requested by the user and that it is properly configured.

- If the problem occurs on inbound connections, make sure your system is running the required daemon either through `inetd.conf` or through a startup script. Connect to the daemon from the local host to make sure it is running. If the daemon is running, ensure that it is properly configured. Check to make sure that the remote system is allowed access to the service by Wrapper and `ipfw`.

- If the problem occurs only on one client, concentrate on testing that client. If the problem happens for many clients, concentrate on the network and the server.

Diagnostic Tools

Troubleshooting may require both hardware and software tools. You may not think of yourself as a hardware person, but a small kit of hardware tools is useful to have on hand. A simple cable tester and a LAN maintenance toolkit with every hand tool you'll ever need can be bought at most places that sell LAN equipment. Add to those tools a dual-boot laptop, and you'll have all of the troubleshooting hardware you'll need.

A laptop is my favorite piece of test equipment. I configure the laptop to dual-boot Microsoft Windows and Linux. When a user reports a problem that I can't resolve sitting at my desk, I take my laptop to the user's office, plug it directly into her Ethernet cable, and run my tests from there. This quickly tells me if the problem exists in the user's computer or in the network.

> **TIP**   I use a dual-boot system so that I have access to the great tools available on the Linux system but can demonstrate Microsoft Windows connectivity for the user. I find that many Microsoft Windows users don't believe the network is running unless I can show it running with Windows.

Linux includes a large array of simple software tools that can help you isolate a problem through testing. I believe these software tools are sufficient to address any enterprise network problem. In addition to the tools like `sendmail -bt` and `lsmod` that were covered earlier, the tools I use and recommend are:

`ifconfig` Use this to display the network interface's configuration, characteristics, and statistics.

`arp` and `arpwatch` Use these to monitor the mapping of IP addresses to Ethernet addresses.

`ping` Use this to test basic network connectivity.

`traceroute` Use this to test routing and trace the network path end to end.

`netstat` Use this to display the status of ports and active connections.

`nslookup`, `dig`, and `host` Use these to test Domain Name Service. `nslookup` is a powerful interactive tool that comes with the BIND software. `dig` and `host` are similar tools that can be used inside of shell scripts.

`tcpdump` Use this to analyze network packets.

In the following sections, all of these software tools provided by Linux are examined.

Checking the Network Interface

Configuration errors, including those that allow security breaches, are often the cause of problems on mature systems. You cannot eliminate these problems simply by configuring your system correctly. When you're on a network, the configuration errors made by the administrator at the remote end of the network may affect your users. Additionally, you may be the expert called upon to help users correct the configuration errors they make setting up their desktop systems.

> **WARNING** I specifically said "mature systems" because the desire to have the latest thing, even though it is not quite ready for prime time, can be an even bigger cause of problems. Beta software should be avoided for a production server unless its use is absolutely necessary.

Checking the configuration of a network server can mean reading configuration files as well as actively running tests. Red Hat and Caldera systems store the basic network interface configuration in files in `/etc/sysconfig`. To check the configuration of Ethernet interface `eth0` on a Red Hat system, you could list the `/etc/sysconfig/network` file and the `/etc/sysconfig/network-scripts/ifcfg-eth0` file as shown here:

```
$ cat /etc/sysconfig/network
NETWORKING=yes
FORWARD_IPV4=false
HOSTNAME=parrot.foobirds.org
DOMAINNAME=foobirds.org
```

```
GATEWAY=172.16.12.254

GATEWAYDEV=eth0

$ cat /etc/sysconfig/network-scripts/ifcfg-eth0

DEVICE=eth0

IPADDR=172.16.12.3

NETMASK=255.255.255.0

NETWORK=172.16.12.0

BROADCAST=172.16.12.255

ONBOOT=yes
```

The meaning of the entries in these files is obvious. If the value assigned in each entry is correct, the configuration of the interface should be correct. But I never quite trust this type of indirect evidence. I prefer to ask the interface itself what it thinks its configuration is by using the ifconfig command. The ifconfig command is an alternative to reading the configuration files.

> **NOTE** In Chapter 4, *The Network Interface*, the ifconfig command was used to define the network configuration. Here it is used to display the interface configuration.

Checking an Ethernet Interface

Enter the ifconfig command with the interface name and no other command-line arguments to display the current configuration. This example shows the configuration of eth0 on a Linux system:

```
$ ifconfig eth0
eth0 Link encap:Ethernet   HWaddr 00:00:C0:9A:D0:DB
        inet addr:172.16.55.105   Bcast:172.16.55.255
           Mask:255.255.255.0
        UP BROADCAST RUNNING PROMISC MULTICAST MTU:1500      Metric:1
        RX packets:157916883 errors:30 dropped:125 overruns:0   frame:30
        TX packets:104108 errors:28 dropped:0 overruns:0     carrier:28
        collisions:35531 txqueuelen:100
        Interrupt:10 Base address:0x1400
```

Security and Troubleshooting

PART 4

The first line displayed by `ifconfig` lists the interface name (`eth0`), the link protocol (`Ethernet`), and the hardware address (`00:00:C0:9A:D0:DB`). Of these, the first two are obvious, but the hardware address is a nice bit of information to have for tracking down Physical-layer network problems. (More on this when I discuss using `arp` to debug address assignment problems.)

The second line displays the IP configuration. It contains the IP address, the broadcast address, and the network mask assigned to the interface. These values should be exactly what you expect. As illustrated in Chapter 4, sometimes these values are not what you expect, which can be the cause of a network problem. Check these when the network problem seems to be localized to a single, recently configured computer.

The third line of the display lists the flags that are set for this interface. The flags define the interface characteristics. In the example, the following values are set:

UP The interface is enabled. The interface should always be UP when the system is running. Use the `ifconfig` command to manually mark the interface DOWN only when changing a configuration value, such as the IP address. After making the change, re-enable the interface with the new configuration value by marking it UP. Here is an example of these steps:

```
# ifconfig eth0 down
# ifconfig eth0 172.16.5.9 up
```

BROADCAST The interface supports broadcasts. Some physical networks, such as Ethernet, provide built-in support for broadcasting packets.

RUNNING The interface is operational. The interface must be RUNNING at all times. If it isn't, the driver for this interface may not be properly installed.

PROMISC The interface is set to promiscuous mode. Normally, an Ethernet interface only passes packets that contain the local host's Ethernet address or the Ethernet broadcast address up to the IP layer for processing. Promiscuous mode means that the interface accepts all packets and sends them all up to IP for processing. This feature is required by the `tcpdump` tool (which is covered later in the chapter). If you don't intend to run `tcpdump`, this feature should not be used. To turn it off, enter the following `ifconfig` commands:

```
# ifconfig eth0 down
# ifconfig eth0 -promisc up
```

MUTLICAST The interface supports multicasts. Ethernet emulates multicasting by using its built-in broadcast facility.

MTU The maximum transmission unit used by this interface. In the example, it is 1500 bytes, which is the standard for Ethernet.

Metric The routing cost associated with this interface. In the example, it is 1, which is the normal cost associated with all network interfaces.

The next three lines output by the ifconfig command contain network statistics. The first of these lines provides statistics for received packets:

```
RX packets:157916883 errors:30 dropped:125 overruns:0    frame:30
```

This line provides the total number of packets received, the number of received packets that contained an error, the number of packets dropped by the interface, the number of times an input buffer overrun occurred, and the number of framing error occurrences. A high percentage of drops and overruns can indicate that your server is so overloaded with work it is not able to properly service the input packet buffer. A high percentage of framing errors and corrupted packets (errors) can indicate a physical network problem. In the example, all of the receive errors were caused by framing errors. If all of the error counts are low, as they are in this example, physical network problems are not indicated.

The other two lines of statistics relate to the transmitted packets:

```
TX packets:104108 errors:28 dropped:0 overruns:0 carrier:28

collisions:35531 txqueuelen:100
```

The first of these lines starts with the total number of packets transmitted. Displayed next are the number of transmitted packets that contained an error, the number of packets dropped by the interface, the number of times an output buffer overrun occurred, and the number of times the carrier signal was unavailable for a transmission. In the example, all of the output errors were caused by a lack of carrier. The collisions field indicates the number of times a transmission resulted in a collision. (See the upcoming sidebar for more information on Ethernet collisions.) The txquelen field is not really a statistic; it simply displays the maximum size of the transmit queue.

The last line displayed by ifconfig provides the configuration settings used for the Ethernet adapter card. These values must match the configuration actually set on the adapter card. See "Adapter Card Configuration" in Chapter 1, *Getting Started*, for information about these values.

Security and
Troubleshooting

PART 4

Understanding Ethernet Collisions

On a shared Ethernet, it's normal to have a high number in the collision field. Ethernet uses a technique called Carrier Sense Multiple Access with Collision Detection (CSMACD) to share the cable among many hosts.

The best model for understanding how CSMACD works is a human conversation. To speak during a lively conversation, you wait for a lull in the discussion—that lull is the human equivalent to a carrier signal. When you sense the lull, you begin to speak— that's the transmission. If someone begins speaking just before you do, you hear them speaking and you stop—that's the collision detection. After giving the person their say, you speak again.

In CSMACD, a collision is when two or more Ethernet nodes attempt to transmit at the same time. Collisions only become a problem when there is so much traffic on a shared network that the collisions inhibit throughput. The collision rate is determined by calculating the collisions as a percentage of the total packets transmitted. In the example shown above, 35,531 collisions occurred for 104,108 transmissions, which gives a collision rate of about 3 percent. That's a heavily used network. If the collision rate reaches 5 percent, you should segment the network by moving from shared hubs to Ethernet switches. Allocating dedicated switch ports to your busy servers should dramatically reduce the collision rate.

Resolving Address Conflicts

Most common interface configuration problems are easy to detect because they cause a hard failure. For example, a bad subnet address causes a failure every time the user attempts to contact a system on another subnet.

However, a bad IP address can be a more subtle problem. If the IP address is grossly misconfigured, i.e., the network portion of the address is incorrect, the system will have a hard failure that is easy to detect. But if the host portion of the address is incorrect, the problem may go undetected for a long period of time.

Let me explain. Assume a PC user is assigned the address 172.16.12.13 but accidentally enters the address as 172.16.12.31. This is a valid address; it's just not the correct one for the PC. Everything works fine until the Linux system that is really assigned 172.16.12.31 comes online, which might be a long time on a small network. Once the real owner of the address joins the network, problems emerge, but they are not necessarily hard failures, and they may not even affect the PC that misappropriated the address. The problems are intermittent because sometimes the PC answers the ARP request first, and sometimes the Linux system answers first. Therefore, some computers have the PC mapped to the address in their ARP tables, while others have the Linux system in their tables. To further complicate matters, as ARP table entries time out and are re-mapped, the mix of which computers have which system mapped to the address constantly changes.

Using **arp** to Check for Address Conflicts

The arp command can be used to view and, if necessary, to change the contents of the ARP table. If you suspect a problem with the ARP table, display the contents of the table immediately after the problem occurs.

> **NOTE** An ARP problem is indicated when the wrong host responds to a request or when an error message about duplicate IP addresses is displayed. Act quickly, because the ARP table is refreshed every few minutes so the evidence of the problem may be lost.

The –a command-line argument displays all of the entries in the table. The command displays the host name, IP address, and Ethernet address of every system listed in the ARP table. It also displays the Ethernet interface through which the information was learned. The following example was produced on a Red Hat Linux system:

```
$ arp -a
is1 (172.16.55.251) at 08:00:20:82:D5:1D [ether] on eth0
dog (172.16.55.178) at 08:00:20:9A:4F:25 [ether] on eth0
warthog (172.16.55.33) at 08:00:20:87:B7:6E [ether] on eth0
fs1 (172.16.55.250) at 08:00:20:8D:19:7B [ether] on eth0
sloth (172.16.55.36) at 08:00:20:71:97:06 [ether] on eth0
crow (172.16.55.183) at 08:00:20:82:DA:43 [ether] on eth0
snipe (172.16.55.1) at 0A:00:20:18:48:31 [ether] on eth0
duck (172.16.55.110) at 08:00:5A:09:C3:46 [ether] on eth0
? (172.16.55.216) at 08:00:4E:34:70:92 [ether] on eth0
rabbit (172.16.55.181) at 00:20:AF:16:95:B0 [ether] on eth0
deer (172.16.55.145) at 08:00:69:0A:47:2E [ether] on eth0
```

If you know the Ethernet addresses of the hosts on your network and the IP addresses that are supposed to be assigned to those hosts, it is easy to detect the error in this list. If you don't have that information, you need to do some research.

Suppose that rabbit is the system you're having problems communicating with and that you suspect an ARP table problem. You can focus on that single host and ignore the other entries in the table. From the console of rabbit, it is easy enough to use ifconfig to obtain the correct Ethernet address. You can then delete the bad ARP entry and place the correct Ethernet address in the client's ARP table as follows:

```
# arp -d rabbit
# arp -s rabbit 00:00:C0:DD:DA:B1
```

This would temporarily fix things for the one client, but it is not a solution. The real problem is locating the culprit at 00:20:AF:16:95:B0 that is passing itself off as rabbit. Without a list of the Ethernet addresses on your network, you must enlist the help of your users to check the Ethernet addresses of their computers looking for the address in question. Clearly having a map of the IP addresses and Ethernet addresses on your network is important. arpwatch can help you build that map.

Building an Ethernet List with arpwatch

The arpwatch command is included with Red Hat 6. It monitors ARP activity, dynamically builds a map of Ethernet and IP address assignments, and sends informative messages about ARP to the root user. The dynamically constructed database of Ethernet/IP address mappings is stored in arp.dat. On Red Hat systems, that file is found in /var/arpwatch. An excerpt from an arp.dat file is shown here:

```
$ head -15 /var/arpwatch/arp.dat
8:0:20:22:fd:51    172.16.55.59     928927150    dopey
0:0:c0:9a:d0:db    172.16.55.59     928894146    dopey
0:0:c:43:8d:fb     172.16.55.254    930939507
0:e0:29:0:be:b9    172.16.55.173    930939632    goat
0:60:97:5b:69:62   172.16.55.182    930939614    herbivore
8:0:20:82:da:43    172.16.55.183    930939633    crow
0:e0:29:0:bd:93    172.16.55.19     930939652    dingo
0:10:4b:87:de:49   172.16.55.119    930865112    dot
0:10:4b:87:e0:77   172.16.55.34     930937149    owl
0:aa:0:a3:55:cb    172.16.55.34     929662402    owl
```

```
0:a0:24:8d:ea:d1  172.16.55.26     929509418    donkey
0:a0:24:d6:26:c0  172.16.55.185    930938674    shrike
0:e0:29:5:8e:83   172.16.55.29     930939527    pike
8:0:20:71:97:6    172.16.55.36     930939649    sloth
a:0:20:18:48:31   172.16.55.1      930939610    snipe
```

Entries in the `arp.dat` file contain four fields: the Ethernet address, the IP address, a time stamp, and the host name. If the host name cannot be determined, the fourth field is blank, as it is in one line of the sample file.

Simply looking at this file can tell you some interesting things. First and foremost, it is good to know what Ethernet address goes with what IP address. As you saw above, this can be useful for debugging certain types of address problems. Second, a quick look at this file can tell you if possible address conflicts already exist. Look at the entries for dopey and owl in the sample file. These entries show two different Ethernet addresses attempting to use the same IP address. I'm dopey, so I know the reason that two systems have used that IP address is because I move dopey from one hardware platform to another. However, I don't know why two Ethernet cards have duplicated the address of owl. That situation needs to be watched.

Keeping a Watch on arp

You don't have to read the `arp.dat` file to find out when new Ethernet-to-IP-address mappings are added or to find out if two Ethernet addresses are using the same IP address. `arpwatch` monitors ARP activity and automatically e-mails reports to the root user when something significant occurs.

`arpwatch` has five message types it mails to root:

Changed ethernet address The IP address is using a different Ethernet address than the one previously stored in the `arp.dat` database. This could simply mean that the IP address has been legitimately moved to a new system, or that a new Ethernet card has replaced the old card in the system. However, if combined with other evidence (see the next message type), this could indicate a duplicate IP address problem.

Flip flop The IP address has reverted back to the Ethernet address it was using previously. Multiple flip flop messages clearly indicate that a single IP address is moving between two different Ethernet addresses. Unless you personally know the cause, investigate flip flop messages.

New activity An old Ethernet/IP address pairing that has been unused for six months or more is now back in use. I have never received this message; on my network, nothing sits unused for six months.

Security and
Troubleshooting

PART 4

New station A new Ethernet/IP address pairing has just been detected. In an earlier example, I pointed out an error from a user mistakenly entering 172.16.12.31 instead of 172.16.12.13. As soon as that system came online, an e-mail message would be sent to the root user account of the server as shown below:

```
From: arpwatch@wren.foobirds.org (Arpwatch)
To: root@wren.foobirds.org
Subject: new station (?)


          hostname: ?
        ip address: 172.16.12.31
  ethernet address: 0:10:4b:87:f7:e1
   ethernet vendor: 3Com 3C905-TX PCI
         timestamp: Friday, June 18, 1999 19:33:22
```

If you had just given a user the address 172.16.121.13 and received this e-mail message, the user's error would be obvious. Notice that arpwatch was unable to provide a host name in this message; this is because 172.16.12.31 does not have a name assigned yet. If the user had used the correct address, the name associated with that address would have appeared in the message.

Reused old ethernet address An IP address is paired with an Ethernet address that is at least three generations old. This means that the arp.dat file has at least three Ethernet addresses mapped to the same IP addresses. I have never had this message on a network that uses static address assignments.

In the sample arp.dat file shown above, there are two Ethernet addresses assigned to owl. That duplicate address assignment produced the three e-mail messages shown below:

```
Subject:changed ethernet address (owl.foobirds.org)
    Date:Thu, 17 Jun 1999 03:41:31 -0400
    From:arpwatch@wren.foobirds.org (Arpwatch)
     To:root@wren.foobirds.org


          hostname: owl.foobirds.org
        ip address: 172.16.55.34
  ethernet address: 0:10:4b:87:e0:77
   ethernet vendor: 3Com 3C905-TX PCI
```

```
       old ethernet address: 0:aa:0:a3:55:cb
        old ethernet vendor: Intel
                  timestamp: Thursday, June 17, 1999 3:41:31
         previous timestamp: Thursday, June 17, 1999 2:58:21
                      delta: 43 minutes


Subject:flip flop (owl.foobirds.org)
   Date:Thu, 17 Jun 1999 19:33:22 -0400
   From:arpwatch@wren.foobirds.org (Arpwatch)
     To:root@wren.foobirds.org


                   hostname: owl.foobirds.org
                 ip address: 172.16.55.34
           ethernet address: 0:aa:0:a3:55:cb
            ethernet vendor: Intel
       old ethernet address: 0:10:4b:87:e0:77
        old ethernet vendor: 3Com 3C905-TX PCI
                  timestamp: Thursday, June 17, 1999 19:33:22
         previous timestamp: Thursday, June 17, 1999 19:31:19
                      delta: 2 minutes


Subject:flip flop (owl.foobirds.org)
   Date:Thu, 17 Jun 1999 19:33:22 -0400
   From:arpwatch@wren.foobirds.org (Arpwatch)
     To:root@wren.foobirds.org


                   hostname: owl.foobirds.org
                 ip address: 172.16.55.34
           ethernet address: 0:10:4b:87:e0:77
            ethernet vendor: 3Com 3C905-TX PCI
```

```
     old ethernet address: 0:aa:0:a3:55:cb
      old ethernet vendor: Intel
               timestamp: Thursday, June 17, 1999 19:33:22
      previous timestamp: Thursday, June 17, 1999 19:33:22
                   delta: 0 seconds
```

The changed ethernet address message shows when the new Ethernet address first became associated with owl. This is followed by two flip flop messages that show that owl is alternating between two Ethernet addresses. The second flip flop message has a delta of zero seconds. The delta tells you how much time elapsed between the change of Ethernet addresses. A delta of zero seconds indicates that two systems with two different Ethernet addresses responded to the same ARP request. This tells you that you definitely have a duplicate address problem.

arpwatch is a powerful tool for resolving duplicate address problems and is useful for documenting the Ethernet/IP address mappings on your network. However, Ethernet is not the only network over which TCP/IP runs. Occasionally, you may also be called upon to debug a PPP link running over a modem connection.

Checking a PPP Interface

Troubleshooting a PPP connection can be complex because of the added layers of hardware and software involved. In addition to the TCP/IP software, the connection uses PPP software and a scripting language, like chat or dip, to establish the connection. The hardware uses a serial port, a serial device driver, and an external modem, which also has its own command language. To fully test a PPP connection, you need to check all of these things.

Chapter 4 describes PPP configuration and the design of login scripts. As pointed out there, both chat and dip can be run with a –v option to monitor the progress of the script. When used with dip, -v echoes each line of the script to the controlling terminal as it is executed. When used with chat, -v sends the script errors to syslogd. To monitor the execution of a chat script in real time, use the –V option and the pppd –detach option. For example:

```
# pppd /dev/ttyS1 56700 connect "chat –V –f my-script" \
      -detach crtscts modem defaultroute
```

The –V option associated with the chat command sends a line-by-line execution trace of the script to stderr. The –detach parameter associated with the pppd command leaves the controlling terminal attached, which means that stderr will be displayed on the terminal. Thus you can watch and debug your chat script in real time.

Testing the Link Hardware

To test a PPP link, separate the hardware from the software by testing the port, the driver, and the modem with a tool that doesn't depend on PPP. Any terminal emulator will do the job. One emulator that is available on most systems is minicom.

As the root user, run minicom with the –s option to display the configuration menu. Use the menu to make sure everything is configured the way it should be to test the modem and the link. There are several selections in the mincom configuration menu, but for the purpose of testing the PPP link hardware, only the Serial Port Setup selection is meaningful. Most Linux systems have only one modem port, /dev/ttyS1, which is often linked to the device name /dev/modem. A PPP server, however, may have several ports. Use the Serial Port Setup menu selection to ensure that minicom is configured to use the same port at the same speed that is used to run PPP. It wouldn't help much to test the wrong serial port!

> **WARNING** You must configure minicom before your users will be able to use it. Otherwise, they will get this error: "There is no global configuration file /etc/minirc.dfl. Ask your sysadm to create one (with minicom -s)."

Once minicom is configured, entering the minicom command should connect you directly to the modem. From there you can use modem commands to dial the telephone number and directly connect to the PPP server at the remote location. Here is an example:

```
Welcome to minicom 1.82


OPTIONS: History Buffer, F-key Macros, Search History Buffer, I18n
Compiled on Mar 21 1999, 21:10:56.


Press CTRL-A Z for help on special keys


AT S7=45 S0=0 L1 V1 X4 &c1 E1 Q0
OK
atz
OK
atdt3015551234
CONNECT 28800 V42bis
^M
```

```
Enter username> craig
Enter user password> Watts?Watt?
                Welcome to the PPP Modem Pool


PORT-2> show us
03 Jul 1999  09:05:44
Port    Username            Status          Service


  1     dave                PPP
  2     craig               Executing Cmd


PORT-2> logout


Xyplex Logged out port 2 at 03 Jul 1999  09:06:48
NO CARRIER
^A




CTRL-A Z for help | 38400 8N1 | NOR | Minicom 1.82   | VT102 |
Offline

x
```

This example contains lots of output from minicom, the modem, and the remote server. Mixed in with that is a little bit of user input, which is indicated by bold type. The first thing in the example is welcoming information from minicom followed by a modem initialization command (AT) issued by minicom. The response (OK) to that command tells you that the modem is operational.

Ever doubtful, I issue my own modem reset command (atz) to which the modem responds. Next, I dial the telephone number of the remote PPP server with the atdt command. The server answers. I log in and run a command. When convinced that everything is running fine, I log out of the server and close minicom by typing Ctrl+A followed by **x**. This test tells me:

- That I have the correct port
- That the port is operational

- That I have the correct line speed
- That the modem is operational
- That the phone line is operational
- That the remote modem is correctly configured
- That the remote server is operational
- That I have the correct login for the remote server

Failures in a terminal emulator test focuses further testing on these possible PPP problem areas:

- If the modem fails to respond to commands, the problem must be somewhere between your system and the modem. You should check that the port is correct and defined in /dev, that the modem cable works, and that the modem itself works.
- If the local modem works but it is unable to connect to the remote modem, double-check the phone number, and check with the remote system administrator to make sure the modems are compatibly configured.
- If the modems display a "connect" message but the remote server does not respond, the configuration problem is either between the remote system and its modem or between the two end systems. Again, call the remote system administrator and check the configuration.
- If the login fails, double-check the username and password.
- If all of this succeeds and the PPP connection is still not made, the problem lies in the PPP configuration of the two end systems. It is possible that the connection is failing because of parameter disagreements or because the authentication is failing. Again, this must be worked out with the remote system administrator.

The next section of this chapter moves the testing up from the physical interface. Once the interface is debugged and operational, the focus of testing is on the flow of IP datagrams across the network.

Testing the Connection

The ping tool is used to test the network connection between your system and some remote host. ping is both simple and powerful. Its power lies in the fact that it does not depend on the application configuration of either end system. ping uses the ICMP Echo message, which tests the connection from the local IP layer to the remote IP layer. A ping test separates the network from the application. Any tool that helps you divide a network problem into separate pieces so that those pieces can be tested individually is extremely useful.

The Message of a Successful ping

A successful ping test tells you that the remote system is reachable. This means that the interface configuration of both the local and the remote system must be correct, that the routing configuration of both systems must be correct, and that the network hardware is operational end to end. A successful test eliminates a lot of potential problems allowing you to concentrate your testing.

For example, assume a user reported that she was unable to use ftp to connect to dog.mammals.org. You could run a ping test:

```
# ping dog.mammals.org
PING dog.mammals.org (172.32.30.2): 56 data bytes
64 bytes from 172.32.30.2: icmp_seq=0 ttl=32 time=1.0 ms
64 bytes from 172.32.30.2: icmp_seq=1 ttl=32 time=0.7 ms
64 bytes from 172.32.30.2: icmp_seq=2 ttl=32 time=0.7 ms
64 bytes from 172.32.30.2: icmp_seq=3 ttl=32 time=0.7 ms
^C
--- 172.32.30.2 ping statistics ---
4 packets transmitted, 4 packets received, 0% packet loss
round-trip min/avg/max = 0.7/0.7/1.0 ms
```

This test shows that the connection to dog.mammals.org is running perfectly. The summary line says that every packet transmitted was successfully echoed back and that none was lost. The sequence numbers (icmp_seq) tells you that every packet was received in sequence, and the round-trip times tell you that you have a fast connection to the remote site. A high packet loss, packets arriving out of sequence, or high round-trip times could indicate a congested network or a bad connection. But none of those things is happening in this example. Clearly, the user's problem lies elsewhere.

After verifying that the user's report about not being able to log in with ftp is true, check with the remote system administrator to see if they allow ftp access and are actually running the ftp daemon. Sometimes services are blocked at the server or at the firewall for security reasons and the user does not know it.

The Message of a Failed ping

A failed ping test can also tell you a lot:

```
# ping 172.16.2.2
PING 172.16.2.2 (172.16.2.2): 56 data bytes
```

```
ping: sendto: Network is unreachable

ping: wrote 172.16.2.2 64 chars, ret=-1

ping: sendto: Network is unreachable

^C

--- 172.16.2.2 ping statistics ---

3 packets transmitted, 0 packets received, 100% packet loss
```

Again, the test directs you to focus your troubleshooting efforts on certain layers of the network. A failure indicates you should focus on the network hardware, the interface configuration, and lower-layer network services. The error message further helps refine that focus.

The specific text of ping error messages vary slightly, but the messages fall into three main categories:

Network unreachable This indicates that the local host does not have a valid route to the remote computer. (The next section looks at some tools that can help you try to track down a routing problem.) A related message that you might see in a ping test is ICMP Redirect, which is not really an error. An ICMP Redirect means that you have the wrong route in your routing table for this destination and that the local router is correcting your routing table.

No answer This indicates that the remote host did not respond to the ICMP Echo packets. With the Linux ping command, an error message saying "No answer" is not displayed. Instead, when the ping is terminated the summary line says "100% packet loss," which means exactly the same thing. "No answer" can be caused by many things. Any interruption of service anywhere on the network from your host to the remote system can cause this problem. This error means that no IP packets can successfully travel from your host to the remote host. Look for network errors.

Unknown host This indicates that name service was not able to resolve the host name into an address. Possibly the user gave you the wrong host name or the DNS is misconfigured. Later in the chapter, tools for testing DNS servers are discussed.

Security and Troubleshooting

PART 4

NOTE   I consider ping one of the best test tools available to the system administrator. Unfortunately, some sites block ICMP Echo messages at their firewalls or drop them at their routers. This is bad Internet citizenship. The Internet works best when everyone works together. Unfortunately, some people just don't get it. Interfering with ICMP Echo limits the effectiveness of one of the simplest and best test tools.

The results of the ping test guide you in the next phase of testing. ping directs you to focus on routing, DNS, or the application as the cause of the problem. Linux provides tools to test all of these things. The next section discusses the tools that let you test routing.

Testing Routing

When a routing problem is indicated, the first thing to do is examine the routing table to make sure that the necessary routes for the local interface and the default route are defined. Use the route command with the –n option to display the table:

```
# route -n
Kernel IP routing table
Destination Gateway     Genmask         Flags Metric Ref Use Iface
172.16.12.3 0.0.0.0     255.255.255.255 UH    0      0   0 eth0
172.16.12.0 0.0.0.0     255.255.255.0   U     0      0   0 eth0
127.0.0.0   0.0.0.0     255.0.0.0       U     0      0   0 lo
0.0.0.0     172.16.12.2 0.0.0.0         UG    0      0   0 eth0
```

The various fields in the routing table listing are described in Chapter 9, *Network Gateway Services*. For this check, however, the details aren't important. You just want to make sure that the route to the remote host exists in your routing table—either a specific route to the network that the host is attached to or a default route. (The default route has a destination of 0.0.0.0.) If you built the routing table from static routing entries, this will probably be a default route. If the table was built dynamically by a routing protocol, it might be very large and contain a specific route for the remote network. Regardless of how it got there, you need to make sure your system has the necessary route.

NOTE   In the case of a large routing table, use grep with the route command to search for a default route or a specific route.

Using traceroute

Once you're sure that your system has the proper routes, use the traceroute command to test the route end to end. traceroute traces the route of UDP packets through the network and lists every router between your computer and the remote hosts. It does this by sending out UDP packets with small time-to-live (TTL) values and invalid port numbers to force ICMP errors and to record the sources of those errors.

Here's how it works. The TTL field is intended to ensure that packets do not loop through the network forever. Every router that handles a datagram subtracts 1 from the datagram's TTL. If the TTL reaches 0, the router discards the datagram and sends an ICMP Time Exceeded error message back to the source of the packet. Normally, the TTL is set to 255 when a datagram is created. This guarantees that the datagram can reach any point in the Internet while preventing the packet from circling the world forever.

traceroute sends out three UDP packets with a TTL of 1, followed by three packets with a TTL of 2, followed by three packets with a TTL of 3, and so on up to a TTL of 30. (You can change the maximum TTL from 30 to some other value with the –m command-line option.) Each group of three packets is intended to trigger an error message somewhere along the path. The three packets with a TTL of 1 will trigger ICMP Time Exceeded errors at the first router, those with a TTL of 2 will trigger the errors at the second router, and so on until the final destination is reached. traceroute captures the error messages that come back from the routers, extracts the router's address from the error messages, and prints out a list of router addresses as a trace.

To detect when the end of the trace is reached, traceroute uses an invalid port number. This causes the host at the remote end to return an ICMP Unreachable Port error. When traceroute receives this error message, it prints out the address of the remote system that sent the error and terminates the trace. Putting all of these error messages together, traceroute produces a trace like this one:

```
$ traceroute terp.umd.edu
traceroute to terp.umd.edu (128.8.10.90), 30 hops max,
    40 byte packets
 1  172.16.55.254 (172.16.55.254) 1.424ms 3.187ms 1.295ms
 2  fgw225.chcc.org (172.16.2.232) 1.156ms 1.983ms 1.374ms
 3  igw225.chcc.org (172.16.5.254) 4.703ms 3.754ms 3.080ms
 4  Hssi2-1-0.GW1.TCO1.ALTER.NET (137.39.34.161)  9.511ms
    14.801ms   13.224ms
 5  115.ATM2-0.XR1.TCO1.ALTER.NET (146.188.160.34) 7.955ms
    8.788ms   11.569ms
 6  193.ATM3-0.XR1.DCA1.ALTER.NET (146.188.160.101) 7.794ms
    8.894ms   12.435ms
 7  195.ATM1-0-0.BR1.DCA1.ALTER.NET (146.188.160.225)
    13.934ms   13.076ms   14.229ms
```

Security and Troubleshooting

PART 4

```
 8   dca5-core1-s3-0-0.atlas.digex.net (209.116.159.97)
     87.888ms   100.783ms   96.771ms
 9   dca5-core3-pos1-1.atlas.digex.net (165.117.51.102)
     112.287ms   117.283ms 111.309ms
10   dca6-core1-pos4-3.atlas.digex.net (165.117.51.2)
     106.369ms   *   99.697ms
11   dca1-core10-pos1-2.atlas.digex.net (165.117.51.189)
     106.123ms   113.786ms 107.322ms
12   dca1-core5-pos5-0-0.atlas.digex.net (165.117.59.2)
     111.850ms   *   110.117ms
13   dca1-core2-fa6-0-0.atlas.digex.net (165.117.16.2)
     115.335ms   99.689ms   87.126ms
14   209.49.104.194 (209.49.104.194)   110.538ms   116.827ms
     106.463ms
15   1.atm1-0-0.csc0gw.net.umd.edu (128.8.0.223)   105.528ms
     105.439ms   107.240ms
16   d.root-servers.net (128.8.10.90)   118.430ms   105.404ms
     101.596 ms
```

This example shows a trace from my desktop system to a system at the University of Maryland. Each line indicates a hop along the path to the destination. The round-trip travel time of each packet is also printed. Note that there are three packets sent to each hop along the path. If a packet is lost, i.e., if no error is returned for the packet, an asterisk (*) is printed instead of a round-trip time. If a series of three asterisks is printed on several lines, it indicates that the trace was unable to reach the remote end. The last router that responds is probably the last router that can be reached along the path.

TIP   One row of asterisks is not enough to tell you there is a problem, because some routers don't return ICMP errors. I let four or five lines of asterisks print out before I believe there is a remote routing problem.

In theory, every router that handles a traceroute packet will respond with an error, and an accurate trace of the route will be produced. Reality is a little different. Some routers silently discard the packets and return no error. Sometimes different packets take different routes. If you examine the output of a traceroute command too closely or take it too much to heart, you'll be making a mistake. Use `traceroute` as a guide to where potential problems exist, but don't assume it is completely accurate. Check if the trace reached the remote site, and if it didn't, check where it stopped. Those are the most meaningful things you can get from a `traceroute`.

TIP   Routing is a two-way street. If possible, have the administrator of the remote system test the route from the remote server back to your system.

Analyzing Network Protocols

Linux provides some test tools for checking the state of TCP/IP protocol connections or examining the protocol interactions as they take place on the wire. System administrators often wonder why they would want to do this. The basic TCP/IP protocols have been in use for 15 years and don't require any debugging. Even if your system uses some new protocol that does have a bug, it is unlikely that as a system administrator you have the time or inclination to try to debug a protocol.

These things are true, but these tools have uses beyond debugging a protocol. The most important role for protocol analysis is as a tool to gain more information and insight about a network problem. Discovering that a connection terminates during the parameter negotiation can steer you toward checking the configuration, or discovering that a connection hangs without a clean termination can point you to a malfunctioning wrap-up script. Protocol analysis may be the last tool you use, but there are times that it is very helpful.

Checking Socket Status with `netstat`

`netstat` is a command that can be used to check on a wide variety of network information, such as the status of network connections, the contents of the routing table, what masqueraded connections are supported by the system, and what multicast groups the system has joined. The most important of these is the status of network connections, which is the default `netstat` display. To limit that display to TCP/IP network connections, use the `--inet` command-line option:

```
$ netstat -n --inet
Active Internet connections (w/o servers)
Proto R-Q S-Q Local Address Foreign Address    State
tcp     1   0 robin:1967    www.sybex.com:80   CLOSE_WAIT
tcp     1   0 robin:1966    www.sybex.com:80   CLOSE_WAIT
```

```
tcp    1    0 robin:1964    www.sybex.com:80   CLOSE_WAIT
tcp    1    0 robin:1963    www.sybex.com:80   CLOSE_WAIT
tcp    0  126 robin:23      phoebe:1449             ESTABLISHED
```

This command lists the currently active IP connections. Each line displays the transport protocol being used, the number of packets in the send and receive queues, the local address including port number, the remote address including port number, and the status of the connection. In the example above, the first three lines describe outbound connections to well-known port number 80. From Chapter 8, *Web Servers*, you know that 80 is the Web server port. So those are outbound Web connections. The last line in the sample shows an inbound connection to port 23—the telnet port.

The State field on each line indicates the TCP protocol state for that connection. Table 15.1 lists the possible TCP protocol states that netstat can display.

Table 15.1   TCP Protocol States

State	Meaning
CLOSED	The socket is completely closed.
CLOSE_WAIT	The remote end is shut down, but the local socket is not yet closed.
CLOSING	Both ends of the connection are shut down, but the local system still has data to send.
ESTABLISHED	The connection is established.
FIN_WAIT1	The local end of the connection is shutting down.
FIN_WAIT2	The socket is waiting for the remote end of the connection to shut down.
LAST_ACK	The protocol is waiting for the final acknowledgment on a closed socket.
LISTEN	The socket is listening for incoming connections.
SYN_RECV	A connection request has been received.

Table 15.1   TCP Protocol States *(continued)*

State	Meaning
SYN_SENT	A connection attempt is underway.
TIME_WAIT	The socket is closed but waiting to clear remaining packets from the network.
UNKNOWN	netstat cannot determine the state of the socket.

In the example above, the inbound telnet connection has a state of ESTABLISHED, meaning it is a healthy, active connection. The three outbound connections are all sitting in CLOSE_WAIT. All of these connections are directed at the same remote Web server. The probable cause for this is a user with a browser open to the remote server that is not actively requesting data. Perhaps the user is reading the data; perhaps the user is out to lunch. In either case, the user has left the browser running. This is normal and causes not harm other than consuming a port number. When the user closes the browser, these ports will close.

With the –a option, netstat can be used to display all sockets, not just those that are active, and it does not have to limit the display to IP sockets. The example below is an excerpt of the full socket listing from a Linux system. This listing is only about half of the number of lines actually displayed. To see the full listing, enter the netstat command on your own Linux system.

```
# netstat -a
Active Internet connections (servers and established)
Proto R-Q S-Q Local Address   Foreign Address State
tcp    0   2 parrot:telnet   robin:1027      ESTABLISHED
tcp    0   0 *:netbios-ssn      *:*          LISTEN
tcp    0   0 *:www              *:*          LISTEN
tcp    0   0 *:smtp             *:*          LISTEN
tcp    0   0 *:1024             *:*          LISTEN
tcp    0   0 *:printer          *:*          LISTEN
tcp    0   0 *:imap2            *:*          LISTEN
tcp    0   0 *:login            *:*          LISTEN
```

tcp	0	0	*:shell	*:*	LISTEN
tcp	0	0	*:telnet	*:*	LISTEN
tcp	0	0	*:ftp	*:*	LISTEN
udp	0	0	parrot:netbios-dgm	*:*	
udp	0	0	parrot:netbios-ns	*:*	
udp	0	0	*:netbios-dgm	*:*	
udp	0	0	*:netbios-ns	*:*	
udp	0	0	*:1024	*:*	
udp	0	0	*:talk	*:*	
raw	0	0	*:icmp	*:*	7
raw	0	0	*:tcp	*:*	7

Active UNIX domain sockets (servers and established)

Proto	RefCnt	Flags	Type	State	I-Node	Path
unix	1	[ ]	STREAM	CONNECTED	415	@00000019
unix	1	[ ]	STREAM	CONNECTED	888	@0000003e
unix	0	[ACC]	STREAM	LISTENING	519	/dev/printer
unix	0	[ACC]	STREAM	LISTENING	725	/dev/gpmctl
unix	0	[ACC]	STREAM	LISTENING	395	/dev/log
unix	1	[ ]	STREAM	CONNECTED	889	/dev/log

The first line in this listing shows an active inbound telnet connection just like the one seen earlier. The next several lines all have the status LISTEN. These are the TCP services that this system offers. If the list of services produced by netstat on your server does not match the services that you think your system offers, you need to check the server's configuration. The asterisks in the address fields mean that any address is accepted.

Next comes the UDP services offered by the system. UDP is a connectionless protocol, so it does not maintain connection state. For all UDP entries, the State field is empty. Again, these services should match the services you think you're offering.

For network testing, you can ignore the rest of the listing. It contains two entries for *raw sockets*, which are sockets that communicate directly to IP without using a transport protocol, and several entries for Unix sockets. The Unix sockets define sockets-based I/O for Linux devices and are not related to the TCP/IP network.

Use `netstat` to check the socket status when inbound or outbound connections appear to hang. An example of how all this `netstat` information can be used to diagnose a problem is shown in the case study at the end of this chapter.

Watching the Protocols with `tcpdump`

`tcpdump` reads every packet from the Ethernet and compares it to a filter you define. If it matches the filter, the packet header is displayed on your terminal, which permits you to monitor traffic in real time. For example:

```
# tcpdump host 172.16.5.1 and 172.16.24.1
tcpdump: listening on eth0
10:46:11.576386 phoebe.1027 > wren.telnet: S
    400405049:400405049(0) win 32120
    <mss 1460> (DF)
10:46:11.578991 wren.telnet > phoebe.1027: S
    1252511948:1252511948(0) ack 400405050 win 32120
    <mss 1460> (DF)
10:46:11.773727 phoebe.1027 > wren.telnet: .
    ack 1 win 32120 <nop> (DF)
```

This example shows a successful TCP three-way handshake between `wren` and `phoebe`. TCP is a connection-oriented protocol. Before TCP data can be sent, the connection must be established with a three-way handshake. First, the system requesting the connection sends a *synchronize sequence numbers* (SYN) packet to the destination host. The packet contains the sequence numbers that will be used by the source as well as other parameters such as the transmission window size (`win`) and the maximum segment length (`mss`). If the destination system will accept the connection, it sends a SYN (`S`) acknowledgment (`ack`) packet that includes the sequence numbers the destination will be using. Finally, the source sends a packet acknowledging the packet received from the destination, and the connection is underway.

Each TCP packet displayed by `tcpdump` begins with a time stamp followed by the source and destination address. From the first line of the example, you can tell that `phoebe` is the source of the connection and is attempting to connect to the `telnet` port of `wren`.

Next, the flag field of the TCP header is displayed. In the example, the first two packets have a flag value of S, which means the SYN bit is set. That setting indicates that this is a connection request and that the computers are synchronizing sequence numbers. (The first packet is the SYN packet, and the second packet is the SYN ACK packet.) The next fields in the first two packets are the sequence numbers being used. (400405049 in the case of phoebe and 1252511948 in the case of wren.) The example also indicates that phoebe has requested a windows size of 32120 bytes, a maximum segment size of 1460 bytes, and that its packets not be fragmented (DF).

> **NOTE** Clearly, the details of this display don't make much sense unless you have a detailed understanding of the TCP/IP protocols. To further complicate matters, other protocols will produce other display formats, because they have different header formats. If you really want to tackle the details of such a display, you should read *Internetworking with TCP/IP: Principles, Protocols and Architecture* by Douglas Comer (Prentice-Hall, 1995).

The example shows only the first three packet headers. Immediately after the handshake, many packets are exchanged. If the example really stopped after the three-way handshake, the connection would be a failure. A failure at this point in the connection indicates that the remote system does not offer the requested service. Perhaps the service is not installed or it is blocked for security reasons. Regardless, a failure at this point clearly shows that the remote system does not allow connections to the requested port.

A test designed to debug a real protocol problem might involve hundreds or even thousands of packets. Attempting to debug a complex protocol problem requires a great deal of technical skill, which most system administrators have, and a great deal of time, which no system administrator has. Ignore the details and look for gross failures that might indicate where the network problem occurs.

tcpdump Filters

In the tcpdump example, the filter is host 172.16.5.1 and 172.16.24.1, which captures all traffic going to or coming from these two IP addresses. A wide variety of tcpdump filters can be defined. Table 15.2 lists the basic IP filters that are available for tcpdump.

Table 15.2 tcpdump Packet Filters

Filter	Captures Packets...
dst host | net | port *value*	Destined for the specified host, network, or port.
src host | net | port *value*	From the specified host, network, or port.
host *host*	To or from the specified host.

Table 15.2   tcpdump Packet Filters *(continued)*

Filter	Captures Packets...
`net address [/len	mask mask]`	To or from the specified network. An optional address mask can be defined either as a bit length or a dotted decimal mask.
`port port`	To or from the specified port.
`ip proto protocol`	Of the specified protocol type. Valid protocols are `icmp`, `igrp`, udp, nd, or tcp.
`ip broadcast	multicast`	That are either IP broadcast packets or IP multicast packets.

TIP   With these filters, you should be able to capture any packets you need to debug a network problem. But my advice is to keep it simple. Designing complex filters and analyzing large packet dumps can take more time then other, simpler methods of attacking a problem.

Testing Services

At the top of the protocol stack are the applications and services that the user needs. Most errors are reported when a user attempts to use a service and the attempt fails. To be complete, testing needs to include the services.

Usually a service can be tested directly. To test a Web server, connect to the server with your browser. To test an FTP server, use the `ftp` command to connect to that server. These are user-oriented services, so they come with user-oriented commands that you can use for your testing.

Some services, however, are intended to provide service to a remote computer instead of a remote user. Directly testing these services is slightly more difficult but often possible by using `telnet` to connect directly to the server port. You have already seen multiple examples of this in earlier chapters. Refer back to the examples of testing `imapd` and the POP daemon in Chapter 13, *More Mail Services*.

If ping tests succeed but tests involving a specific service fail, the problem is in the configuration of the service at either the client or server end. Client configuration is usually simple and easy to check but the server configuration can be very complex. Some complex services, such as sendmail and DNS, include their own test programs. Chapter 7, *Configuring a Mail Server*, provides detailed examples of using sendmail –bt to test your local sendmail configuration. The next section of this chapter looks at the tools that are available to test a DNS configuration.

Testing DNS with nslookup

nslookup is a test tool that comes with the BIND software. It is an interactive program that allows you to query a DNS server for any type of resource record and to directly view the server's response. This is useful for checking your own servers, but even more important, it can be used to *directly* query remote servers. Notice the emphasis on the word directly. Using nslookup, it is possible to directly connect to a remote server to see how that server responds to queries without going through your local name server. This is important because it eliminates the possibility that errors in your local server's configuration are affecting the results. Any test program that allows you to separate local problems from remote problems is worth its weight in gold.

To illustrate what I mean, here's an example of how to use nslookup:

```
% nslookup
Default Server:  wren.foobirds.org
Address:  172.16.5.1

> set type=NS
> mammals.org.
Server:  wren.foobirds.org
Address:  172.16.5.1

mammals.org           nameserver = goat.mammals.org
mammals.org           nameserver = shark.fish.org
mammals.org           nameserver = whale.mammals.org
goat.mammals.org    inet address = 172.32.3.2
shark.fish.org      inet address = 172.30.8.2
whale.mammals.org   inet address = 172.32.3.1
```

Begin by entering the `nslookup` command with no arguments. This starts `nslookup` in interactive mode, which is the best way to use it to debug a server problem. When `nslookup` starts, it is using your local server as indicated by the Default Server message. You need the name server (NS) records to locate the name servers for the remote domain you wish to test, so set the query type to NS and then enter the domain name you want to query. In the example, the domain name is `mammals.org`, and the local name server returns all of the NS records for that domain, which identify three servers: `goat` and `whale` in the `mammals.org` domain and `shark.fish.org`.

Now that you know the authoritative servers, connect to one of them to run the next phase of the test:

```
> server goat.mammals.org
Default Server:  goat.mammals.org
Address:  172.32.3.2

> set type=ANY
> dolphin.mammals.org
Server:  goat.mammals.org
Address:  172.32.3.2

dolphin.mammals.org   inet address = 172.32.3.8

> exit
```

To connect directly to the remote server, use the `server` command. In the example, I chose to connect to `goat`. Then set the query to the type of resource records you're interested in. This can be the keyword ANY for all available resource records or any of the standard resource record types—address records (A), mail exchange records (MX), start of authority records (SOA), and so on. (See Table 6.2 in Chapter 6, *Linux Name Services*, for the possible DNS record types.) The ANY query is particularly useful, because it provides all of the information available from the name server.

A successful test tells you that the remote server is responding and can resolve the desired host name. If the test fails completely, the user may have the wrong host name. If the test works but your local server is having trouble with the host name, the problem could be in your local server or one of the other remote servers.

Security and Troubleshooting

PART 4

Sometimes remote severs get out of synchronization, so querying all of the authoritative remote servers is worthwhile when you have intermittent problems resolving a host name. For example, assume you're having intermittent problems resolving the host name dolphin.mammals.org. You could begin with the identical test shown above, but instead of entering **exit** after testing the first remote server, you could switch to another server and rerun the test:

```
> server shark.fish.org
Default Server:  shark.fish.org
Address:  172.30.8.2
> dolphin.mammals.org
Server:  shark.fish.org
Address:  172.30.8.2


*** shark.fish.org can't find dolphin.mammals.org:
    Non-existent domain
```

In this case, the second authoritative server disagrees with the first. goat resolves the query for dolphin to an address, but shark can't. The most likely cause for this problem is that the servers have two different copies of the zone file. As in the following example, check the SOA records on each system to see if the serial numbers are different:

```
> set type=SOA
> mammals.org.
Server:  shark.fish.org
Address:  172.30.8.2


mammals.org        origin = goat.mammals.org
   mail addr = amanda.goat.mammals.org
   serial=10164, refresh=43200, retry=3600, expire=3600000,
   min=2592000
> server goat.mammals.org
Default Server:  goat.mammals.org
Address:  172.32.3.2
```

```
> mammals.org.
Server:  goat.mammals.org
Address:  172.32.3.2

mammals.org          origin = goat.mammals.org
    mail addr = amanda.goat.mammals.org
    serial=10164, refresh=43200, retry=3600, expire=3600000,
    min=2592000


> exit
```

In this example, the serial numbers are the same. This is bad news. If the serial numbers were different, the problem might be a temporary one that would be resolved as soon as the slave server updated the zone from the master server. The fact that the serial numbers are the same but the contents of the zone files are different is a major problem that must be addressed by the remote domain administrator. Luckily, the SOA record tells you who that is. Send mail to amanda@goat.mammals.org and report the problem. She needs to get this fixed!

I like the interactive nature of nslookup because it allows me to work through a problem adjusting my next test based on the results of previous tests. The disadvantage of such a system is that it is difficult to script for repetitive tests. However, Linux provides two more DNS test tools that are suitable for scripting: host and dig.

Testing DNS with host

The host command is a very simple tool for looking up an IP address. The format of the host command is:

```
host [options] domain-name [server]
```

Only the host command and the domain name of the remote host are needed to look up an IP address. To look up different resource record types, specify the desired record type (mx, soa, ns, etc.) with the –t argument in the *options* field. To pass the query to a specific server, identify the server in the *server* field. If no server is specified, the local server is used.

Here is an example of the host command in action:

```
$ host -t any dolphin.mammals.org goat.mammals.org
Using domain server 172.32.3.2:
```

```
dolphin.mammals.org has address 172.32.3.8
$ host -t any dolphin.mammals.org shark.fish.org
Using domain server 172.30.8.2:
Host not found.
```

This is the same test that was run above using `nslookup`. Two different servers, `goat` and `shark`, are queried for any type of DNS records relating to `dolphin`. `goat` replies with an address record, and `shark` replies with an error.

The `host` command is simple to use, to script, and to understand. However, it is best suited to simple queries. In the example above, you discovered that the two servers give different answers. Therefore, your next step is to query each server for the zone's SOA record. Each time a query is made, the `host` command is retyped with the −t option and the name of the server. For multi-step queries, `nslookup` is easier.

Testing DNS with `dig`

`dig` is another DNS test command very similar to `host`. It has the same strengths and weaknesses, but is both more powerful and more complex. The basic format of a `dig` command is:

```
dig [@server] domain-name [type]
```

If a server is defined, the name of the server must be preceded by an `@`. If a server is not specified on the command line, the local server is used. The type of resource record being requested is identified using a standard record type or the keyword `any`, and if a resource record type is not specified, the `dig` command fetches address records. For example, to query the server `goat` for any records pertaining to `dolphin`, enter:

```
$ dig @goat.mammals.org dolphin.mammals.org any
```

One of my favorite `dig` features is its ability to make reverse domain queries simple. Remember that when IP addresses are mapped back to domain names, they are first reversed to make the structure compatible with domain names, and then the domain name `in-addr.arpa` is appended to the end of the reversed address. To do a reverse lookup with `nslookup`, you first set the query type to PTR and then manually enter the reversed and expanded address. With `dig`, you just use the −x option as shown here:

```
$ dig -x 172.16.55.105
; <<>> DiG 8.2 <<>> -x
;; res options: init recurs defnam dnsrch
```

```
;; got answer:

;; ->>HEADER<<- opcode: QUERY, status: NOERROR, id: 6

;; flags: qr aa rd ra; QUERY: 1, ANSWER: 1, AUTHORITY: 2, ADDITIONAL:
5

;; QUERY SECTION:

;;        105.55.16.172.in-addr.arpa, type = ANY, class = IN

;; ANSWER SECTION:

105.55.16.172.in-addr.arpa.   8H IN PTR   rail.foobirds.org.

;; AUTHORITY SECTION:

55.16.172.in-addr.arpa.   8H IN NS        dove.foobirds.org.

55.16.172.in-addr.arpa.   8H IN NS        hawk.foobirds.org.

;; ADDITIONAL SECTION:

dove.foobirds.org.            19h7m19s IN A    172.16.2.2

hawk.foobirds.org.            16m17s IN A      172.16.16.1

;; Total query time: 2 msec

;; FROM: rail.foobirds.org to SERVER: default -- 172.16.5.1

;; WHEN: Tue Jun 29 16:07:30 1999

;; MSG SIZE  sent: 43  rcvd: 213
```

This example shows something else about dig—it is very talkative. It displays everything that is exchanged between the DNS client and the server. The meat of the response is the answer section buried in the middle of the display, which says that the address 172.16.55.105 is assigned to rail.foobirds.org. The other parts of the display are:

- The query section, which displays the query sent to the server
- The authority section, which gives a list of the authoritative name servers for the domain that was queried
- The additional section, which provides the addresses of the authoritative servers

dig, host, and nslookup are a powerful trio of tools for testing and debugging domain name service. When the error message is Unknown Host, a Linux system is well equipped to tackle the problem.

Security and Troubleshooting

PART 4

Final Words

This final part of *Linux Network Servers 24seven* has examined some of the ongoing tasks that are necessary for maintaining a reliable operational server. This book has focused on building a Linux server from the ground up that would be suitable for a 24seven operational environment. Starting from selecting the hardware and software and moving on to installing Linux and configuring the network interface, you have seen how to lay the foundation for a reliable operational server. This book has described how the basic Internet services of routing, name service, e-mail service, and Web service are configured, maintained, and secured. Further, you have learned that a Linux system provides configuration services and file and printer sharing that are compatible with all types of clients, making Linux the operating system that can integrate your departmental network and thus simplify maintenance.

When configured and maintained by a well-informed computer professional, Linux is an excellent platform for an Internet or a departmental server. You provide the professional expertise, and this book has provided the information.

We're Under Attack, but It's Friendly Fire

A while back, I noticed strange symptoms on my campus e-mail server. The CPU utilization was very high. The mail queue was taking forever to process, and several users were having trouble downloading their mail. Nothing really appeared to be wrong with the network until I entered the netstat command, which showed hundreds of connections in SYN_RECV state—the classic symptom of a SYN flooding Denial of Service attack!

All of these connection attempts were originating from the same system on our internal network. I changed the router to block connections from that specific system and immediately the mail server began to recover. I called the administrator of the offending system and told him I thought an intruder had broken into his computer.

That, however, was not the case. The offending computer was an experimental, massively parallel computer with hundreds of processors. A mistake in the experimental software caused the system to simultaneously start hundreds of connection requests whenever the system tried to connect to a remote host. I told the experimenters not to point their test software at the campus mail server! They moved the test system off of the live network, and we lived happily ever after. Using netstat to discover the problem and route filtering to block the offender, the initial problem was solved in just a few minutes.

24seven **CASE STUDY**

Part 5

Appendices

Topics Covered:

- Configuring X Windows using XF86Setup, xf86config, and Xconfigurator

- The syntax and structure of both the new and the old BIND configuration commands

- The syntax and function of the m4 macros that may be used to construct a sendmail configuration file

X Windows Configuration

Configuring X Windows is a basic Linux configuration task. However, it wasn't covered in Chapter 2, and there are some good reasons for that intentional omission:

- I believe very firmly that separable tasks should be tackled separately. X Windows doesn't have to be done during the initial setup, so it shouldn't be done at that time.

- X Windows is not required to boot a Linux system. Therefore, Linux can be installed and booted before X Windows is installed, which allows the basic installation to be debugged before the complication of X Windows is added and allows you to have access to all of the tools of a running Linux system to help you install X Windows.

- Sometimes you should skip installing X Windows entirely. Not every server needs X Windows. I oppose putting unneeded software on a system.

- X Windows configuration can be complex, and it is not appropriate to guess the required values. (Incorrect sync rates can harm a monitor.) Therefore, you don't want to be hunting around for the monitor's technical manual while the system is waiting, unbooted, for your input.

All of this means that X Windows configuration should wait until *after* you have booted the basic Linux system. Given this, I'm deeply disturbed by the trend in Red Hat 6 and Caldera 2.2 to force you to configure X Windows during the initial installation. Linux is about choices. The installation program should ask you if you want to configure X and let you choose when to do it. At least Red Hat 6 allows you to decide if you want to automatically start X Windows at boot time. I say "no" and then reconfigure X after the system boots. Caldera 2.2 does not even give you that option. Hopefully, future releases of these distributions will get back on track and let the system administrator decide how and when to configure the system.

In this appendix, "X Windows" means the XFree86 implementation of X Windows. It is the only version covered. This appendix covers three different tools for configuring XFree86 X Windows. The structure of the XFree86 configuration file is also covered.

Using XF86Setup

XF86Setup is a graphical program for configuring X Windows. Type **XF86Setup** at the command prompt, and an introductory window is displayed. At the top of the window are six buttons to open the windows used to configure different aspects of the X Windows system.

The Mouse Window

The Mouse window, shown in Figure A.1, configures the mouse. Select the correct mouse protocol, such as Intellimouse or MouseMan. The mouse protocol used by your mouse can often be determined by reading the label on the bottom of the mouse.

Next, select the device port to which the mouse is attached, e.g., /dev/ttyS0. If the port is a serial port, you can set the baud rate, though this is rarely required. Most serial mice operate at 1200 baud. Some older Logitech serial mice can benefit from setting the baud rate to 9600 and adjusting the sample rate. For other serial mice, modifying the baud rate and sample rate is meaningless.

Test the mouse buttons in the white area to the right of the screen. The white area is a stylized three-button mouse. The numbers at the bottom of this area track the movement of the mouse. The three boxes at the top darken when the corresponding mouse button is pressed. If pressing the middle button on a three-button mouse darkens the two outside buttons instead of the middle button, use the ChordMiddle option.

Figure A.1   Configuring a mouse with XF86Setup

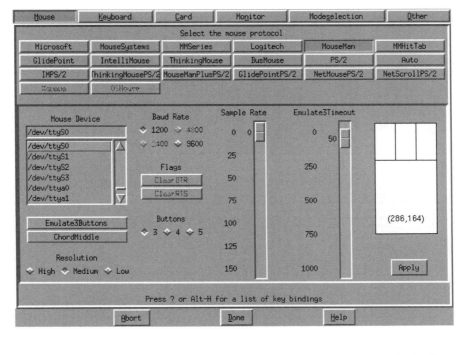

If you have a two-button mouse, select the Emulate3Buttons option, which allows you to emulate a middle button by simultaneously pressing the right and left mouse buttons. The Emulate3Timeout slider controls the speed with which the buttons must be clicked to be interpreted as the middle button. If you have trouble pressing the buttons simultaneously, move the slider down to increase the timeout value.

The Keyboard Window

Use the Keyboard window (see Figure A.2) to select the type of keyboard installed on your system and to define optional mappings for special keys.

Figure A.2 Configuring the keyboard with XF86Setup

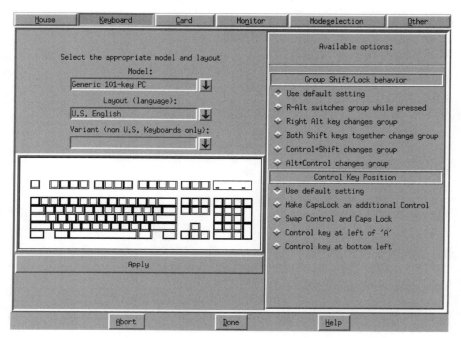

The Card Window

Use the Card window to configure your video adapter card. At a minimum, you must know the make and model of the video adapter card as well as the amount of video RAM the card uses. If you know those basic things, click the Card List button in the card window and select your video card from the list displayed. Figure A.3 shows what the card window looks like after the 4MB Matrox Millennium card was selected from the card list.

Selecting a pre-configured card is the easiest way to get the system running. It is possible, however, to manually configure the video adapter by selecting values in the card window. X Windows offers accelerated servers designed for specific video chipsets. If you have previously installed an accelerated server, you can select it from the line of server buttons near the top of the window and then select the appropriate Chipset, RamDAC, and ClockChip for the server. To do this requires very detailed knowledge of the hardware configuration of the video card.

Figure A.3   Configuring a video card with XF86Setup

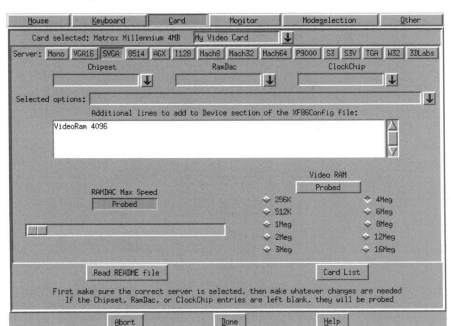

The Monitor Window

Use the Monitor window to set the horizontal and vertical sync rate of the monitor attached to your system. Figure A.4 shows the monitor window after it has been configured for a specific monitor.

Be very careful to use sync rates that the monitor can support, because using the wrong sync rates can damage the monitor hardware. The correct sync rates are printed in the monitor's technical manual. If you don't have the manual, visit the monitor manufacturer's Web site. Most manufacturers now provide monitor spec sheets online.

All modern computer monitors are "multi-sync" monitors, which means that they can operate at a range of frequencies. There are some industry standard frequencies that are found on most monitors as factory pre-set video modes. If you are careful not to exceed the upper limit of the monitor's capabilities, you can safely select one of these standard values from the list at the center of the window. Therefore, even if you don't know the exact horizontal and vertical sync range of the monitor, you can configure it as long as you know the monitor's maximum performance.

Appendices

PART 5

Figure A.4 Configuring the monitor with XF86Setup

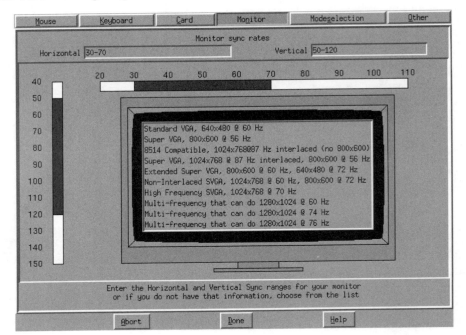

The Modeselection Window

The Modeselection window lists various screen resolutions and color depths. Screen resolutions are defined in pixels, such as 800×600 and 1280×1024, which is the format most computer users are familiar with. Colors are defined as bit-planes per pixel: 8bpp, 16bpp, 24bpp, and 32bpp. These settings give color ranges from 256 colors to more than 16 million colors. (Some graphics applications require at least 16bpp of color to run properly.) High resolutions with high color depth consume a large amount of video memory. Select a default video mode you're sure your video adapter can support.

The Other Window

The Other window lists six optional server settings:

Allow server to be killed with hotkey sequence This allows you to escape from a malfunctioning X Windows server by pressing Ctrl+Alt+Backspace. This is a very desirable option.

Allow video mode switching This allows you to switch between different video modes by pressing the Ctrl+Alt++ keys simultaneously. If you select multiple modes in the Modeselection window, use this feature to switch between them.

Don't trap signals This option prevents the server from trapping signal when shutting down.

Allow video mode changes from other hosts This allows remote systems to change the resolution of your monitor.

Allow changes to keyboard and mouse settings from other hosts This allows remote computers to change the configuration of your mouse and keyboard.

The first two options are enabled by default, and the last three options are disabled. These are the correct settings for most systems.

Using xf86config

I generally configure systems with XF86Setup. However, because it is a graphical program, it depends on creating a minimum resolution connection with the video card and monitor. If it has trouble doing that, it may not be able to run on your system. An alternative is to use the text-based configuration tool xf86config, which does not require a graphical interface.

> **NOTE** A complete xf86config example is shown in the following sections. The text displayed by xf86config has been edited slightly to fit on the book page, but it is essentially identical to what you will see if you run xf86config.

Welcome to xf86config

Enter **xf86config** at the command prompt to start the configuration process. The program opens by displaying a page of introductory material:

```
This program will create a basic XF86Config file, based on

menu selections you make.


The XF86Config file usually resides in /usr/X11R6/lib/X11

or /etc/X11. A sample XF86Config file is supplied with

XFree86; it is configured for a standard VGA card and

monitor with 640x480 resolution. This program will ask for

a pathname when it is ready to write the file.
```

You can either take the sample XF86Config as a base and edit it for your configuration, or let this program produce a base XF86Config file for your configuration and fine-tune it. Refer to /usr/X11R6/lib/X11/doc/README.Config for a detailed overview of the configuration process.

For accelerated servers (including accelerated drivers in the SVGA server), there are many chipset and card-specific options and settings. This program does not know about these. On some configurations some of these settings must be specified. Refer to the server man pages and chipset specific READMEs.

Before continuing with this program, make sure you know the chipset and amount of video memory on your video card. SuperProbe can help with this. It is also helpful if you know what server you want to run.

Press enter to continue, or ctrl-c to abort. ^M

The most interesting elements of this induction are the pointers to additional documentation, to the location of the X Windows configuration file, and to the SuperProbe tool. SuperProbe is useful if you don't have complete information about the video adapter card. If you want to run SuperProbe, exit xf86config by pressing Ctrl+C, and then run SuperProbe. Otherwise, read the introduction and press Enter.

Configuring the Mouse

Next, xf86config asks a series of questions to configure the mouse:

First specify a mouse protocol type. Choose one from the following list:

1. Microsoft compatible (2-button protocol)
2. Mouse Systems (3-button protocol)

3. Bus Mouse

4. PS/2 Mouse

5. Logitech Mouse (serial, old type, Logitech protocol)

6. Logitech MouseMan (Microsoft compatible)

7. MM Series

8. MM HitTablet

9. Microsoft IntelliMouse

10. Acecad tablet

If you have a two-button mouse, it is most likely of type
1, and if you have a three-button mouse, it can probably
support both protocol 1 and 2. There are two main varieties
of the latter type: mice with a switch to select the
protocol, and mice that default to 1 and require a button
to be held at boot-time to select protocol 2. Some mice can
be convinced to do 2 by sending a special sequence to the
serial port (see the ClearDTR/ClearRTS options).

Enter a protocol number: **6**

You have selected a Logitech MouseMan type mouse. You might
want to enable ChordMiddle which could cause the third
button to work.

Answer the following question with either 'y' or 'n'.
Do you want to enable ChordMiddle? **y**

If your mouse has only two buttons, it is recommended that
you enable Emulate3Buttons.

Appendices

PART 5

```
Answer the following question with either 'y' or 'n'.
Do you want to enable Emulate3Buttons? n


Now give the full device name that the mouse is connected
to, for example /dev/tty00. Just pressing enter will use
the default, /dev/mouse.


Mouse device: ^M
```

To configure the mouse, select a mouse protocol. In the example, I selected the Mouse-Man protocol by entering the number **6** and, because the Logitech MouseMan is a three-button mouse that requires the ChordMiddle feature, I answered Yes to the ChordMiddle question. Emulate3Buttons is only needed on two-button mice, so the Emulate3Buttons question is answered with a No in the example.

Conclude the mouse configuration by entering the name of the device port to which the mouse is attached. Usually the special device name /dev/mouse is already set as a link to the real port. Pressing Enter, as was done in the example, defaults to /dev/mouse. If that link is not set on your system, enter the real device name.

Configuring the Keyboard

Now xf86config asks you to configure the keyboard:

```
Beginning with XFree86 3.1.2D, you can use the new X11R6.1
XKEYBOARD extension to manage the keyboard layout. If you
answer 'n' to the following question, the server will use
the old method, and you have to adjust your keyboard layout
with xmodmap.


Answer the following question with either 'y' or 'n'.
Do you want to use XKB? n


If you want your keyboard to generate non-ASCII characters
in X, because you want to be able to enter language
specific characters, you can set the left Alt key to Meta,
```

and the right Alt key to ModeShift.

Answer the following question with either 'y' or 'n'.

Do you want to enable these bindings for the Alt keys? **n**

These questions allow you to specify special keyboard mappings. For a standard server configuration, you can safely answer No to these questions.

Configuring the Monitor

In the next section, xf86config asks you to configure the monitor. To do this, you need accurate technical information about the capabilities of your monitor. xf86config provides its own warning about this part of the configuration:

Now we want to set the specifications of the monitor. The

two critical parameters are the vertical refresh rate,

which is the rate at which the the whole screen is

refreshed, and most importantly the horizontal sync rate,

which is the rate at which scanlines are displayed.

The valid range for horizontal sync and vertical sync

should be documented in the manual of your monitor. If in

doubt, check the monitor

database/usr/X11R6/lib/X11/doc/Monitors to see if your

monitor is there.

Press enter to continue, or ctrl-c to abort.^M

Read the warning and press Enter to continue with the monitor configuration. The system now asks for the monitors horizontal sync range:

You must indicate the horizontal sync range of your

monitor. You can either select one of the predefined ranges

below that correspond to industry-standard monitor types,

or give a specific range.

It is VERY IMPORTANT that you do not specify a monitor type with a horizontal sync range that is beyond the capabilities of your monitor. If in doubt, choose a conservative setting.

```
 hsync in kHz; monitor type with characteristic modes
 1 31.5; Standard VGA, 640x480 @ 60 Hz
 2 31.5 - 35.1; Super VGA, 800x600 @ 56 Hz
 3 31.5, 35.5; 8514 Compatible, 1024x768 @ 87 Hz
   interlaced (no 800x600)
 4 31.5, 35.15, 35.5; Super VGA, 1024x768 @ 87 Hz
   interlaced, 800x600 @ 56 Hz
 5 31.5 - 37.9; Extended Super VGA, 800x600 @ 60 Hz,
   640x480 @ 72 Hz
 6 31.5 - 48.5; Non-Interlaced SVGA, 1024x768 @ 60 Hz,
   800x600 @ 72 Hz
 7 31.5 - 57.0; High Frequency SVGA, 1024x768 @ 70 Hz
 8 31.5 - 64.3; Monitor that can do 1280x1024 @ 60 Hz
 9 31.5 - 79.0; Monitor that can do 1280x1024 @ 74 Hz
10 31.5 - 82.0; Monitor that can do 1280x1024 @ 76 Hz
11 Enter your own horizontal sync range
```

Enter your choice (1-11): **11**

Please enter the horizontal sync range of your monitor, in the format used in the table of monitor types above. You can either specify one or more continuous ranges (e.g. 15-25, 30-50), or one or more fixed sync frequencies.

Horizontal sync range: **30-70**

The first element of the monitor configuration is the horizontal sync rate. If you don't know the monitor sync rate, carefully select an industry-standard sync rate based on your knowledge of the display capabilities of the monitor. If you do know the monitor's horizontal sync rate, choose "Enter your own horizontal sync range" and then use the sync rate information from the monitor's technical manual or its online spec sheet to enter the correct values. In the example, a horizontal sync rate of 30KHZ through 70KHZ is entered.

Next, enter the vertical sync rate:

```
You must indicate the vertical sync range of your monitor.
You can either select one of the predefined ranges below
that correspond to industry-standard monitor types, or give
a specific range. For interlaced modes, the number that
counts is the high one (e.g. 87 Hz rather than 43 Hz).


 1 50-70
 2 50-90
 3 50-100
 4 40-150
 5 Enter your own vertical sync range


Enter your choice: 5


Vertical sync range: 50-120


You must now enter a few identification/description
strings, namely an identifier, a vendor name, and a model
name. Just pressing enter will fill in default names.


The strings are free-form, spaces are allowed.
Enter an identifier for your monitor definition: Console
Enter the vendor name of your monitor: Mag Innovision
Enter the model name of your monitor: 720V2
```

Again, you can select from an industry standard range or enter your own values based on the documentation you have for the monitor. In the example, a vertical sync range of 50KHZ to 120KHZ is entered.

Finish this section by entering description information about the monitor. Anything or nothing can be entered here, but it is best to use something descriptive.

Configuring the Video Card

Next, xf86config prompts you to configure the video adapter card:

```
Now we must configure video card specific settings. At this
point you can choose to make a selection out of a database
of video card definitions. Because there can be variation
in Ramdacs and clock generators even between cards of the
same model, it is not sensible to blindly copy the settings
(e.g. a Device section). For this reason, after you make a
selection, you will still be asked about the components of
the card, with the settings from the chosen database entry
presented as a strong hint.


The database entries include information about the chipset,
what server to run, the Ramdac and ClockChip, and comments
that will be included in the Device section. However, a lot
of definitions only hint about what server to run (based on
the chipset the card uses) and are untested.


If you can't find your card in the database, there's
nothing to worry about. You should only choose a database
entry that is exactly the same model as your card; choosing
one that looks similar is just a bad idea (e.g. a GemStone
Snail 64 may be as different from a GemStone Snail 64+ in
terms of hardware as can be).


Do you want to look at the card database? y
```

Saying Yes to the preceding question causes xf86config to display a very long list of video adapter cards. Page though the listings by pressing Enter. Following is what the listing looks like after paging through more than 300 video adapter entries:

```
324 Matrox Millennium 2MB              mga2064w

325 Matrox Millennium 4MB              mga2064w

326 Matrox Millennium 8MB              mga2064w

327 Matrox Millennium G200 16MB        mgag200

328 Matrox Millennium G200 4MB         mgag200

329 Matrox Millennium G200 8MB         mgag200

330 Matrox Millennium G200 SD 16MB     mgag200

331 Matrox Millennium G200 SD 4MB      mgag200

332 Matrox Millennium G200 SD 8MB      mgag200

333 Matrox Millennium II 16MB          mga2164w

334 Matrox Millennium II 4MB           mga2164w

335 Matrox Millennium II 8MB           mga2164w

336 Matrox Mystique                    mga1064sg

337 Matrox Mystique G200 16MB          mgag200

338 Matrox Mystique G200 4MB           mgag200

339 Matrox Mystique G200 8MB           mgag200

340 Matrox Productiva G100 4MB         mgag100

341 Matrox Productiva G100 8MB         mgag100


Enter a number to choose the corresponding card definition.
Press enter for the next page, q to continue configuration.
324
Your selected card definition:


Identifier: Matrox Millennium 2MB
Chipset:  mga2064w
Server:   XF86_SVGA
Do NOT probe clocks or use any Clocks line.


Press enter to continue, or ctrl-c to abort.^M
```

Appendices

PART 5

Select the appropriate card from the list. In the example, the 2MB Matrox Millennium is selected. xf86config displays the specifics of the card definition. Remember what it says about the server, the clock chip, and clock probing. This information comes in handy later in the configuration.

Configuring the Server for the Video Card

Now that you've selected the appropriate video card for your system, you must select the X Windows server and define the link to that server. To do so, use the information found in the video card definition displayed above to answer the following questions:

```
Now you must determine which server to run. Refer to the
manpages and other documentation. The following servers are
available (they may not all be installed on your system):


1 The XF86_Mono server. This a monochrome server that
  should work on any VGA-compatible card, in 640x480
  (more on some SVGA chipsets).
2 The XF86_VGA16 server. This is a 16-color VGA server
  that should work on any VGA-compatible card.
3 The XF86_SVGA server. This is a 256 color SVGA server
  that supports a number of SVGA chipsets. On some
  chipsets it is accelerated or supports higher color
  depths.
4 The accelerated servers. These include XF86_S3,
  XF86_Mach32, XF86_Mach8, XF86_8514, XF86_P9000,
  XF86_AGX, XF86_W32, XF86_Mach64, XF86_I128 and
  XF86_S3V.


These four server types correspond to the four different
"Screen" sections in XF86Config (vga2, vga16, svga, accel).


5 Choose the server from the card definition, XF86_SVGA.
```

```
Which one of these screen types do you intend to run by
default (1-5)? 5


The server to run is selected by changing the symbolic link
'X'. For example, 'rm /usr/X11R6/bin/X; ln -s
/usr/X11R6/bin/XF86_SVGA /usr/X11R6/bin/X' selects the SVGA
server.


Answer the following question with either 'y' or 'n'.
Do you want me to set the symbolic link? y
```

Five possible server selections are offered. Four of these are the four different server types; the fifth is the server recommended for your card. Unless you know the details of configuring the card and the server, selecting the recommended server is the safest bet. That is exactly what happens in the example when 5 is entered for the default server selection.

Finally, you need to set a link to the appropriate server. Answer Yes when xf86config asks if it should create the link.

Defining the Amount of Video Card Memory

In this next section of the configuration, simply enter the amount of video RAM used by the video adapter card, and enter a descriptive name for the card. If you don't enter a name, the name from the card listing is used.

```
Now you must give information about your video card. This
will be used for the "Device" section of your video card in
XF86Config.


You must indicate how much video memory you have. It is
probably a good idea to use the same approximate amount as
that detected by the server you intend to use. If you
encounter problems that are due to the used server
not supporting the amount memory you have (e.g. ATI Mach64
is limited to 1024K with the SVGA server), specify the
maximum amount supported by the server.
```

```
How much video memory do you have on your video card:


1 256K

2 512K

3 1024K

4 2048K

5 4096K

6 Other


Enter your choice: 4


You must now enter a few identification/description
strings, namely an identifier, a vendor name, and a model
name. Just pressing enter will fill in default names
(possibly from a card definition).


Your card definition is Matrox Millennium 2MB.


The strings are free-form, spaces are allowed.
Enter an identifier for your video card definition: ^M
The strings are free-form, spaces are allowed.
Enter an identifier for your video card definition: ^M
You can simply press enter here if you have a generic card,
or want to describe your card with one string.
Enter the vendor name of your video card: ^M
Enter the model (board) name of your video card:
```

Setting the RamDac and ClockChip for the Video Card

Depending on the card you select, you may be asked to specify the correct RamDac hardware and ClockChip hardware for your video adapter. Use the card definition displayed by xf86config as a guide for this part of the configuration. In the example, when I selected the Matrox Millennium card, `xf86config` printed "Do NOT probe clocks or use any Clocks line." That advice is useful for answering the questions in this part of the configuration:

```
Especially for accelerated servers, Ramdac, Dacspeed and
ClockChip settings or special options may be required in
the Device section.


A Clockchip line in the Device section forces the detection
of a programmable clock device. With a clockchip enabled,
any required clock can be programmed without requiring
probing of clocks or a Clocks line. Most cards don't have a
programmable clock chip. Choose from the following list:


 1 Chrontel 8391                        ch8391
 2 ICD2061A and compatibles (ICS9161A, DCS2824)  icd2061a
 3 ICS2595                              ics2595
 4 ICS5342 (similar to SDAC, but not completely
   compatible)  ics5342
 5 ICS5341                              ics5341
 6 S3 GenDAC (86C708) and ICS5300 (autodetected) s3gendac
 7 S3 SDAC (86C716)                     s3_sdac
 8 STG 1703 (autodetected)              stg1703
 9 Sierra SC11412                       sc11412
10 TI 3025 (autodetected)               ti3025
11 TI 3026 (autodetected)               ti3026
12 IBM RGB 51x/52x (autodetected)        ibm_rgb5xx


Just press enter if you don't want a Clockchip setting.
What Clockchip setting do you want (1-12)? ^M
```

No clock chip is selected by pressing Enter in response to the clock chip question—just as the configuration suggested.

Now the system asks you if you want it to probe the clock line:

```
For most modern configurations, a Clocks line is neither
required or desirable. However for some older hardware it
can be useful since it prevents the slow and nasty sounding
clock probing at server start-up. Probed clocks are
displayed at server startup, along with other server
and hardware configuration info. You can save this
information in a file by running 'X -probeonly
2>output_file'. Be warned that clock probing is inherently
imprecise; some clocks may be slightly too high (varies per
run).

At this point I can run X -probeonly, and try to extract
the clock information from the output. It is recommended
that you do this yourself and if a set of clocks is shown
then you add a clocks line (note that the list of clocks
may be split over multiple Clocks lines) to your Device
section afterwards. Be aware that a clocks line is not
appropriate for most modern hardware thathas programmable
clocks.

You must be root to be able to run X -probeonly now.

The card definition says to NOT probe clocks.
Do you want me to run 'X -probeonly' now? n
```

In this example, the clock line is not probed, because the description of the video card said that it should not be probed.

Selecting the Video Display Modes

Next, xf86config asks you to select the default resolution and the number of colors for the video display.

For each depth, a list of modes (resolutions) is defined.
The default resolution that the server will start-up with
will be the first listed mode that can be supported by the
monitor and card. Currently it is set to:

```
"640x480" "800x600" "1024x768" "1280x1024" for 8bpp
"640x480" "800x600" "1024x768" for 16bpp
"640x480" "800x600" for 24bpp
"640x480" "800x600" for 32bpp
```

Note that 16, 24 and 32bpp are only supported on a few
configurations. Modes that cannot be supported due to
monitor or clock constraints will be automatically skipped
by the server.

```
1 Change the modes for 8pp (256 colors)
2 Change the modes for 16bpp (32K/64K colors)
3 Change the modes for 24bpp (24-bit color, packed pixel)
4 Change the modes for 32bpp (24-bit color)
5 The modes are OK, continue.
```

    Enter your choice: **5**

In this example, **5** is selected, which provides all of the listed video modes that can be supported on the video hardware.

Finishing xf86config

Finally, the configuration is written out to the XF86Config file:

```
I am going to write the XF86Config file now. Make sure you
don't accidently overwrite a previously configured one.

Shall I write it to /etc/X11/XF86Config? y
```

File has been written. Take a look at it before running
'startx'. Note that the XF86Config file must be in one of
the directories searched by the server (e.g.
/usr/X11R6/lib/X11) in order to be used. Within the server
press ctrl, alt and '+' simultaneously to cycle video
resolutions. Pressing ctrl, alt and backspace
simultaneously immediately exits the server (use if
the monitor doesn't sync for a particular mode).

For further configuration, refer to
/usr/X11R6/lib/X11/doc/README.Config.

Using Xconfigurator

Xconfigurator is the program that Red Hat uses during the initial installation to install
X Windows. It is very similar to xf86config except that it provides a menu-driven graphical interface, and it handles more of the configuration automatically. It can be run at any
time by typing **Xconfigurator** at the shell prompt. When Xconfigurator starts, it displays an introductory window very similar to the introduction provided by xf86config.

Xconfigurator then automatically probes the system to detect the video card installed.
Figure A.5 shows the result of such a probe. If the correct video card is located, just
click OK.

Figure A.5 Xconfigurator video card probe

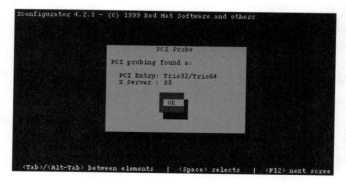

Xconfigurator then requests the monitor configuration. The nice thing about configuring a monitor with Xconfigurator is that it has a very long list of pre-configured monitors. All you need to do is select your monitor from the list. Unlike the other configuration tools, you don't need to have the monitor's technical manual on hand—as long as the monitor is in the Xconfigurator list. Figure A.6 shows a monitor being selected.

Figure A.6   Configuring a monitor with Xconfigurator

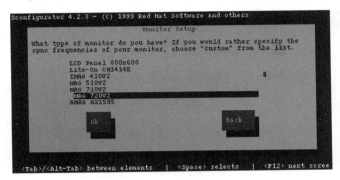

After you select the monitor, Xconfigurator does another round of probing using both the video card and monitor information. The screen will blink several times, and then Xconfigurator will display the optimal video setting as shown in Figure A.7.

Figure A.7   Probing for video modes

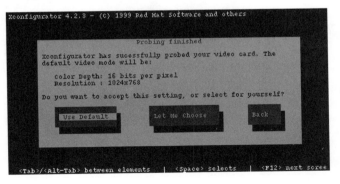

Click the Use Default button, and `Xconfigurator` will test the new server and write the new configuration file. If you prefer to manually create your own configuration, click Let Me Choose. You will then walk through a series of menus that cover the same configuration information that was requested by `XF86Setup` and by `xf86config`. Figure A.8 shows a few of those configuration menus.

Figure A.8 Xconfigurator manual configuration options

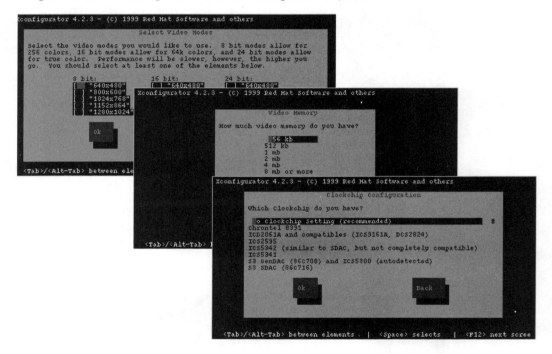

NOTE Some of the menu windows shown in Figure A.8 are reached by pressing the Back button after pressing Let Me Choose. The Back button allows you to move backward through the configuration that `Xconfigurator` created when it probed the hardware.

Regardless of whether you create the configuration with XF86Setup, xf86config, or Xconfigurator, the configuration is stored in the XF86Config file. All of these tools are designed for one purpose: to make it easier for you to create that file.

Understanding the XF86Config File

The XFree86 configuration file is XF86Config. It is generally located in either the /etc directory, the /etc/X11 directory, or the /usr/X11R6/lib/X11 directory. The configuration file is composed of up to nine different sections:

- The Files section defines the paths to the fonts, to the color database, and to the dynamic modules library.
- The Modules section is only used if the X configuration requires the use of dynamic modules. If it does, the modules are specified here with Load statements.
- The ServerFlags section defines X server options, such as allowing the configuration to be modified from remote computers.
- The Keyboard section defines the type of keyboard used and any special key mappings.
- The Pointer section configures the mouse. The mouse protocol and options such as ChordMiddle are defined here.
- The Monitor section defines the monitor configuration. Horizontal and vertical sync rates are defined here along with standard video modes.
- The Device section identifies the video adapter being used. The video RAM, RamDac, and ClockChip are defined here.
- The Screen section identifies the video server and ties it back to the video adapter and and the monitor. The selected color depth and screen resolutions are defined here.
- The XInput section defines optional input devices, such as a Summa Sketch pad. This section is only used if you have special graphics input devices.

From the description of these various sections, it is easy to see how the input you provide is used to create the configuration file and where the input is used in the configuration. Not everything in the XF86Config file comes from your input, but a large part of it does.

Appendices

PART 5

BIND Reference

There are two versions of the Berkeley Internet Name Domain (BIND) software in widespread use. Current versions of Linux ship with BIND 8; previous versions of Linux shipped with BIND 4. The DNS database files used by the different versions of BIND are the same.

The most apparent changes in the two versions of BIND are in the configuration files. First, the name of the file has changed. The configuration file for BIND 4 is called `named.boot` while the configuration file for BIND 8 is called `named.conf`. Second, the commands used to configure a BIND 4 system are completely different than the commands used to configure BIND 8.

NOTE   If you already have BIND 4 running and you upgrade to BIND 8, you can convert an existing `named.boot` file to the new `named.conf` format by using `named-bootconf.pl`, which is part of the BIND 8 distribution.

This appendix provides a reference to the syntax and structure of both the new and the old BIND configuration commands. It is a reference, not a tutorial. (See Chapter 6, *Linux Name Services*, for a tutorial on configuring a Linux DNS server and for realistic examples of the configuration commands that you will actually use.) Most of the commands shown here are not required for an average installation; some of these commands are only useful for root domain servers. Use this appendix to help you read unfamiliar commands in either type of configuration file. Use Chapter 6 to help you create your own configuration file.

The syntax of the BIND configuration commands is described with these conventions:

bold Indicates something must be typed as shown.

italic Indicates that you provide your own value for the specified field.

Square brackets [ ] Indicates that the item is optional.

vertical bar | Indicates that you choose one keyword or the other.

> **NOTE** My source for much of this information is the online documentation at the www.isc.org Web site. Visit that Web site for the latest information.

BIND 8 named.conf Commands

The named.conf file is used to configure BIND 8. The file defines the BIND 8 operational environment and points to the sources of DNS database information. The file is composed of four basic configuration statements: options, logging, zone, and server. In addition to these configuration commands, an include statement can be used. It causes an external file to be loaded into the named.conf file. The external file can contain any or all of the four basic configuration statements.

The options Statement

The options statement defines global options that affect the operation of BIND and the DNS protocol. The syntax of the options command is:

```
options {
    [ directory pathname; ]
    [ named-xfer pathname; ]
    [ dump-file pathname; ]
    [ memstatistics-file pathname; ]
    [ pid-file pathname; ]
    [ statistics-file pathname; ]
    [ auth-nxdomain yes|no; ]
    [ deallocate-on-exit yes|no; ]
```

```
    [ fake-iquery yes|no; ]
    [ fetch-glue yes|no; ]
    [ host-statistics yes|no; ]
    [ multiple-cnames yes|no; ]
    [ notify yes|no; ]
    [ recursion yes|no; ]
    [ forward only|first; ]
    [ forwarders { address-list; }; ]
    [ check-names master|slave|response  warn|fail|ignore; ]
    [ allow-query { address_match_list }; ]
    [ allow-transfer { address_match_list }; ]
    [ listen-on [ port ip_port ] { address_match_list }; ]
    [ query-source [address ip_addr|*] [port ip_port|*] ; ]
    [ max-transfer-time-in number; ]
    [ transfer-format one-answer|many-answers; ]
    [ transfers-in number; ]
    [ transfers-out number; ]
    [ transfers-per-ns number; ]
    [ coresize size; ]
    [ datasize size; ]
    [ files size; ]
    [ stacksize size; ]
    [ cleaning-interval number; ]
    [ interface-interval number; ]
    [ statistics-interval number; ]
    [ topology { address_match_list }; ]
};
```

There are only a few types of values provided to the options. The path name provided to the directory option must be an absolute path from the root. All other path values can be relative to the value provided for the directory option or absolute paths from the root.

Some values are fairly obvious. *ip_port* is an IP port number; *number* is just that, a number; and *size* is the size of a file in bytes, which can be abbreviated with K for kilobyte or M for megabytes (e.g., 5M is 5 million bytes).

ip_addr is a single IP address. An *address-list* is a list of IP addresses separated by semicolons. An *address_match_list* is a list of addresses that can include an IP address written in standard dotted decimal notation with an optional address mask prefix. For example, 172.16.0.0/16 matches every address where the first 16-bits are 172.16. An exclamation point (!) before an address means "don't match" the value. Therefore, placing an exclamation point in front of our sample address would indicate to match everything *except* addresses where the first 16-bits are 172.16. An address_match_list can also include special keywords:

any Match every possible address.

none Match no address.

localhost Match every address assigned to the local host.

localnet Match every address where the network portion of the address is the same as the network portion of any address assigned to the local hosts.

Each configuration option is described in Table B.1.

Table B.1   BIND 8 Configuration Options

Option	Meaning
directory	The path of the working directory from which the server reads and writes files.
named-xfer	The path to the named-xfer program.
dump-file	The file where the database is dumped if named receives a SIGINT signal. The default is named_dump.db.
memstatistics-file	The file where memory usage statistics are written if deallocate-on-exit is set. The default is named.memstats.
pid-file	The file where the process ID is stored.
statistics-file	The file where statistics are written when named receives a SIGILL signal. The default is named.stats.

Table B.1   BIND 8 Configuration Options *(continued)*

Option	Meaning
auth-nxdomain	yes causes the server to respond as an authoritative server. The default is yes.
deallocate-on-exit	yes is used to detect memory leaks. The default is no.
fake-iquery	yes causes the server to respond to inverse queries with a fake reply instead of an error. The default is no.
fetch-glue	yes causes the server to fetch all of the glue records for a response. The default is yes.
host-statistics	yes causes the server to keep statistics on every host. The default is no.
multiple-cnames	yes allows multiple CNAME records for a domain name. The default is no.
notify	yes causes the server to send DNS NOTIFY messages when a zone is updated. The default is yes.
recursion	yes causes the server to recursively seek answers to queries. The default is yes.
forward	first causes the server to first query the servers listed in the forwarders option and then look for the answer itself. only causes the server to only query the servers listed in the forwarders option.
forwarders	Lists the IP addresses of the servers to which queries are forwarded. The default is not to use forwarding.
check-names	Checks host names for compliance with the RFC specifications. You can select to check names when the master server loads the zone (master), when the slave transfers the zone (slave), or when a response is processed (response). If an error is detected, you can choose to ignore it (ignore), send a warning to the administrator about it (warn), or reject the bad name (fail).

Table B.1   BIND 8 Configuration Options *(continued)*

Option	Meaning
allow-query	Queries will only be accepted from hosts in the address list. The default is to accept queries from all hosts.
allow-transfer	Only hosts in the address list are allowed to receive zone transfers. The default is to allow transfers to all hosts.
listen-on	Defines the interfaces and ports on which the server provides name service. By default, the server listens to the standard port (53) on all installed interfaces.
query-source	Defines the address and port used to query other servers.
max-transfer-time-in	Sets the maximum amount of time the server waits for an inbound transfer to complete. The default is 120 minutes (2 hours).
transfer-format	one-answer transfers one resource record per message. many-answers transfers as many resource records as possible in each message. For compatibility with older systems, the default is one-answer.
transfers-in	Sets the maximum number of concurrent inbound zone transfers. The default value is 10.
transfers-out	Limits the number of concurrent outbound zone transfers.
transfers-per-ns	Limits the number of concurrent inbound zone transfers from any single name server. The default value is 2.
coresize	Sets the maximum size of a core dump file.
datasize	Limits the amount of data memory the server may use.
files	Limits the number of files the server may have open concurrently. The default is unlimited.
stacksize	Limits the amount of stack memory the server may use.

Table B.1   BIND 8 Configuration Options *(continued)*

Option	Meaning
cleaning-interval	Sets the time interval for the server to remove expired resource records from the cache. The default is 60 minutes.
interface-interval	Sets the time interval for the server to scan the network interface list looking for new interfaces or interfaces that have been removed. The default is 60 minutes.
statistics-interval	Sets the time interval for the server to log statistics. The default is every 60 minutes.
topology	Forces the server to prefer certain remote name servers over others. Normally, the server prefers the remote name server that is topologically closest to itself.

The logging Statement

The logging statement defines the logging options for the server. The syntax of the command is shown here:

```
logging {
    [ channel channel_name {
        ( file pathname
            [ versions number|unlimited ]
            [ size size ]
        |syslog (kern|user|mail|daemon|auth|syslog|lpr
                    |news|uucp|cron|authpriv|ftp
                    |local0|local1|local2|local3
                    |local4|local5|local6|local7)
        |null;)

        [ severity critical|error|warning|notice
                    |info|debug [level]|dynamic; ]
```

```
        [ print-category yes|no; ]
        [ print-severity yes|no; ]
        [ print-time yes|no; ]
      }; ]

      [ category category_name {
        channel_name; [ channel_name; ... ]
      }; ]
      ...
   };
```

The logging statement can include two different types of subordinate clauses: the channel clause and the category clause. The channel clause defines how logging messages are handled. Messages are written to a file (file), sent to syslog (syslog), or discarded (null). If a file is used, you can specify how many old versions are retained (version), how large the log file is allowed to grow (size), and the severity of the messages written to the log file (severity). You can also specify that the time (print-time), category (print-category), and severity (print-severity) of the message be included in the log.

The category clause defines the category of messages sent to the channel. Thus the category clause defines what is logged, and the channel clause defines where it is logged. The logging categories are listed in Table B.2.

Table B.2   BIND 8 Logging Categories

Category	Type of Messages Logged
cname	Messages recording CNAME references.
config	Messages about configuration file processing.
db	Messages that log database operations.
default	Various types of messages. This is the default if nothing is specified.
eventlib	Messages containing debugging data from the event system.

Table B.2   BIND 8 Logging Categories *(continued)*

Category	Type of Messages Logged
insist	Messages that report internal consistency check failures.
lame-servers	Messages about lame server delegations.
load	Messages about loading the zone.
maintenance	Messages reporting maintenance events.
ncache	Messages about negative caching.
notify	Messages tracing the NOTIFY protocol.
os	Messages reporting operating system problems.
packet	Messages containing dumps of all of the packets sent and received.
panic	Messages generated by a fault that causes the server to shut down.
parser	Messages about configuration command processing.
queries	Messages about every DNS query received.
response-checks	Messages reporting the results of response checking.
security	Messages concerning the application of security criteria. These are most meaningful if allow-update, allow-query, and allow-transfer options are in use.
statistics	Messages containing server statistics.
update	Messages concerning dynamic updates.
xfer-in	Messages recording inbound zone transfers.
xfer-out	Messages recording outbound zone transfers.

Appendices

PART 5

The zone Statement

The zone statement identifies the zone being served and defines the source of domain database information. There are three variants of the zone statement: one for the master server, one for the slave servers, and a special one for the root cache zone. The syntax of each variant is shown here:

```
zone domain_name [ in|hs|hesiod|chaos ] {
  type master;
  file pathname;
  [ check-names warn|fail|ignore; ]
  [ allow-update { address_match_list }; ]
  [ allow-query { address_match_list }; ]
  [ allow-transfer { address_match_list }; ]
  [ notify yes|no; ]
  [ also-notify { address-list };
};

zone domain_name [ in|hs|hesiod|chaos ] {
  type slave|stub;
  [ file pathname; ]
  masters { address-list };
  [ check-names warn|fail|ignore; ]
  [ allow-update { address_match_list }; ]
  [ allow-query { address_match_list }; ]
  [ allow-transfer { address_match_list }; ]
  [ max-transfer-time-in number; ]
  [ notify yes|no; ]
  [ also-notify { address-list };
};

zone "." [ in|hs|hesiod|chaos ] {
  type hint;
```

```
    file pathname;
    [ check-names warn|fail|ignore; ]
};
```

The zone statement starts with the keyword zone followed by the name of the domain. For the root cache, the domain name is always ".". This is then followed by the data class. This is always in for Internet DNS service, which is the default if no value is supplied.

The type option defines whether this is a master server, a slave server, or the hints file for the root cache. A stub server is a slave server that only loads the NS records instead of the entire domain.

The file option for a master server points to the source file from which the zone is loaded. For the slave server, it points to the file to which the zone is written. In the root cache statement, the file option points to the hints file used to initialize the cache.

check-names, allow-query, allow-transfer, and notify were all covered in the section on the options statement. Except for the scope of the options, they function the same here. When specified in a zone statement, these options only apply to the specific zone. When specified in the options statement, they apply to all zones. The specific settings for a zone override the global settings of the options statement.

There are a few options that haven't been discussed yet:

allow-update Identifies the hosts that are allowed to dynamically update the zone. By default, no remote system is allowed to modify the zone.

max-transfer-time-in Defines the maximum amount of time the slave server waits for a zone transfer to complete.

also-notify Defines a list of additional servers that will receive a NOTIFY message when the zone is updated. By default, all servers listed on the NS records in the zone are notified. This list is in addition to those servers.

The server Statement

The server statement defines the characteristics of a remote server. Here is the syntax of the server statement:

```
server address {
    [ bogus yes|no; ]
    [ transfers number; ]
    [ transfer-format one-answer|many-answers; ]
    [ keys { key_id [key_id ... ] }; ]
};
```

Appendices

PART 5

`transfers` and `transfer-format` were covered in the section on the `options` statement. Here they apply to just this remote server. This is particularly useful for the `transfers-format` command. You can globally set this to the more efficient `many-answers` format in the `options` statement and then use individual `server` statements to fall back to the more compatible `one-answer` setting for servers that cannot handle the newer format.

The other options included in the `server` statement are:

> `bogus yes` prevents the local server from sending queries to this server. The default is `no`, which permits queries to the remote server.

> `keys` Specifies the key used by the remote host for encryption. This is not yet implemented in BIND, so currently the `keys` option is ignored.

BIND 4 `named.boot` Commands

For older systems running BIND 4, the `/etc/named.boot` file defines the name server configuration and the location of the name server database information. If you're using BIND 4 on a Linux system, you should consider upgrading to BIND 8. If you're installing a new system, you should always use the latest stable release. The material in this section is intended to help you read and debug existing BIND 4 configurations.

`named.boot` contains the following types of records:

> `directory path` Defines a default directory used for all subsequent file references.

> `primary domain file` Declares the local name server as the primary master server for the domain. The server loads the DNS database from the specified file.

> `secondary domain address-list file` Declares the local server a secondary slave server for the domain. The address list contains the IP address of at least one authoritative server for this domain. The master server should be listed. The local server will try each server in the list until it successfully loads the name server database. The local server transfers the zone file and stores it in the file identified by `file`.

> `cache . file` Points to the file that initializes the root cache.

> `stub domain address-list file` Declares the local server is a stub server for the domain. The zone information is loaded from one of the listed servers and stored in the specified file.

> `forwarders address-list` Lists the servers where a query is sent when the local server can't resolve the query from its own cache. The listed servers are tried in order until one responds to the query.

> `slave` Forces the local server to use only the servers listed on the forwarders command line. A server that has a slave command in its configuration does not attempt

to contact the authoritative servers for a domain, even if the forwarding servers do not respond to its query.

`sortlist` *network network* ... Causes the server to prefer addresses from the listed networks over addresses from other networks.

`xfrnets address[&mask]` ... Limits zone transfers to hosts with the specified address.

`include` *file* Inserts the contents of a file at the location that the command appears in the boot file.

`bogusns` *address-list* Prevents queries from being sent to the name servers specified in the address list.

`limit` *name value* Sets process limits for the parameter defined by *name*. There can be multiple `limit` commands in a boot file, one for each parameter limit that is being set. There are four possible parameter names:

> `datasize` Sets the process data size quota.

> `transfers-in` Sets the maximum number of inbound zone transfers.

> `transfers-out` Sets the maximum number of outbound zone transfers.

> `transfers-per-ns` Sets the maximum number of simultaneous zone transfers allowed from any one remote name server.

`options` *option option*... Enables optional features. The *option* keywords are booleans, so simply specifying an option's name on the command line enables the option. By default, the options are turned off. The options are:

> `query-log` Logs all queries via `syslogd`.

> `forward-only` Sends all queries to the forwarders exactly as if the `slave` command was used.

> `fake-iquery` Responds to inverse queries with a fake reply rather than an error.

> `no-recursion` Only answers queries for data in a zone for which this server is authoritative.

> `no-fetch-glue` Does not locate missing glue records to complete a query response.

`check-names` *source action* Check host names for compliance to the standards defined in RFC 952. *source* can be:

- primary for the master server
- secondary for the slave server

- `response` for a message received during recursive search

action can be:

- `fail` to reject the data
- `warn` to send a warning to the log file
- `ignore` to process the data as if no error occurred

`max-fetch` *value* Performs the same function as `limit transfers-in`.

`domain` *name* Defines the default domain exactly as the `domain` command used in the `resolv.conf` file does. This is an obsolete command.

The m4 Macros for sendmail

This appendix is a quick reference guide to the m4 macros that you might use to construct a sendmail configuration file. (See Chapter 7, *Configuring a Mail Server*, for a tutorial on how m4 macros are used.) This appendix describes the syntax and function of the macros; the information is accurate as of the day of publication. For the most current and accurate description of these macros, see the "SENDMAIL Installation and Operation Guide," by Eric Allman, which comes with the sendmail distribution, and the readme file in the cf directory.

Most of the macros in the .mc file point to other m4 source files. The macro names, OSTYPE, DOMAIN, FEATURE, MAILER, HACKS, and SITECONFIG, are all names of subdirectories within the sendmail/cf directory. The value passed to each of these macros is the name of a file within the specified directory. For example, the command OSTYPE(linux) tells m4 to load the file linux.m4 from the ostype directory and process the m4 source code found there. The .m4 source files pointed to by the OSTYPE, DOMAIN, FEATURE, and MAILER commands are built primarily from define and FEATURE macros.

There are two macros in the .mc file that don't point to .m4 files: the VERSIONID macro and the define macro. The VERSIONID macro, described in Chapter 7, specifies the version number of the `.mc` source file. The define macro is used to set specific configuration values. This appendix contains an extensive list of define macros.

The macro commands HACK, SITECONFIG, LOCAL_RULE_n, and LOCAL_CONFIG are rarely used in a macro configuration file. I will cover them very quickly. Likewise, for the sake of simplicity, I'll skip UUCP configuration because UUCP has limited utility on a modern network and will focus instead on SMTP. In this appendix, I concentrate on the define, FEATURE, OSTYPE, DOMAIN, and MAILER macros.

The macro configuration file (`.mc`) and the `m4` source files (`.m4`) can contain any of the commands documented below. In fact, pretty much any macro can appear in any file. To bring some order out of this chaos, I have organized the appendix to first cover the define and FEATURE macros used to build most `.m4` files. Then I cover the OSTYPE, DOMAIN, and MAILER macro commands in the order in which they are most likely to appear in the `.mc` file. Finally, I conclude with the rarely used HACK, SITECONFIG, LOCAL_RULE_n, and LOCAL_CONFIG macros.

define

define sets a value for a `sendmail.cf` macro, option, or class. Most "defines" are done in the `m4` source files that are called by the `.mc` file, not in the `.mc` file itself. Because many define parameters are equivalent to options, macros, and classes, the command

    define(`confMAILER_NAME', `MAILER_DAEMON')

placed in an `m4` source file has the same effect as

    DnMAILER_DAEMON

placed directly in the `sendmail.cf` file.

Many of the available configuration parameters are shown below. Most correspond to `sendmail` options, macros, or classes. In the parameter description list, the name of the corresponding option, macro, or class is shown enclosed in square brackets ([]). Macro names begin with a dollar sign ($j), class names begin with a dollar sign and an equal sign ($=w), and options are shown with long option names (`SingleThreadDelivery`).

The list of define parameters is quite long. However, because most of the parameters default to a reasonable value, they do not have to be explicitly set in the `m4` source file. The default value of each parameter is shown in the listing below (unless there is no default).

confALIAS_WAIT Sets the amount of time to wait for alias file rebuild. Defaults to 10m. [`AliasWait`] confALLOW_BOGUS_HELO Defines special characters that are not normally allowed in DNS host names that will be allowed in the host name on a HELO command line. [AllowBogusHELO]

confAUTO_REBUILD Automatically rebuilds the alias file if True. Defaults to False. [AutoRebuildAliases]

confBIND_OPTS Sets DNS resolver options. Defaults to undefined. [ResolverOptions]

confBLANK_SUB Defines the character used to replace unquoted blank characters in e-mail addresses. [BlankSub]

confCF_VERSION Sets the configuration file's version number. [$Z]

confCHECKPOINT_INTERVAL Checkpoints the queue files after this number of queued items are processed. Default is 10. [CheckpointInterval]

confCHECK_ALIASES Looks up every alias during alias file build. Default is False. [CheckAliases]

confCOLON_OK_IN_ADDR Treats colons as regular characters in addresses. Default is False. [ColonOkInAddr]

confCONNECTION_RATE_THROTTLE Sets the maximum number of connections permitted per second. [ConnectionRateThrottle]

confCON_EXPENSIVE Holds mail bound for mailers that have the e flag set until the next queue run. Defaults to False. [HoldExpensive]

confCOPY_ERRORS_TO Sets the address that receives copies of error messages. [PostmasterCopy]

confCR_FILE Points to the file that lists the hosts for which this server will relay mail. Defaults to /etc/mail/relay-domains. [$=R]

confCT_FILE Defines the file of trusted usernames. Defaults to /etc/sendmail.ct. [$=t]

confCW_FILE Points to the file of local host aliases. Defaults to /etc/sendmail.cw. [$=w]

confDAEMON_OPTIONS Sets SMTP daemon options. [DaemonPortOptions]

confDEF_CHAR_SET Defines the default character set for unlabeled 8-bit MIME data. Defaults to unknown-8bit. [DefaultCharSet]

confDEF_USER_ID Defines the user ID and group ID used by sendmail. Defaults to 1:1. [DefaultUser]

confDELIVERY_MODE Sets the default delivery mode. Defaults to background. [DeliveryMode] confDIAL_DELAY Sets the time delay before retrying a "dial on demand" connection. Defaults to 0s, which means "don't retry." [DialDelay]

confDOMAIN_NAME Defines the full host name. [$j]

confDONT_BLAME_SENDMAIL Doesn't perform file security checks if True. Defaults to False. Don't use this option. It is a threat to the security of your server. [DontBlameSendmail]

confDONT_EXPAND_CNAMES Doesn't convert nicknames to canonical names if True. Defaults to False, which means "do convert." [DontExpandCnames]

confDONT_INIT_GROUPS Disables the initgroups(3) routine if True. Defaults to False, which means "use the initgroups(3) routine." [DontInitGroups]

confDONT_PROBE_INTERFACES Doesn't automatically accept the addresses of the server's network interfaces as valid addresses if True. Defaults to False. [DontProbeInterface]

confDONT_PRUNE_ROUTES Doesn't prune route addresses to the minimum possible if True. Defaults to False. [DontPruneRoutes]

confDOUBLE_BOUNCE_ADDRESS When errors occur sending an error message, sends the second error message to this address. Defaults to postmaster. [DoubleBounceAddress]

confEIGHT_BIT_HANDLING Defines how 8-bit data is handled. Defaults to pass8. [EightBitMode]

confERROR_MESSAGE Points to a file containing a message that is prepended to error messages. [ErrorHeader]

confERROR_MODE Defines how errors are handled. Defaults to print. [ErrorMode]

confFALLBACK_MX Defines a backup MX host. [FallbackMXhost]

confFORWARD_PATH Defines places to search for .forward files. Defaults to $z/.forward.$w:$z/.forward. [ForwardPath]

confFROM_HEADER Defines the From: header format. Defaults to $?x$x <$g>$|g..

confFROM_LINE Defines the format of the Unix From line. Defaults to From $g $d. [UnixFromLine]

confHOSTS_FILE Defines the path to the host names file. Defaults to /etc/hosts. [HostsFile]

confHOST_STATUS_DIRECTORY Defines the directory in which the host status is saved. [HostStatusDirectory]

confIGNORE_DOTS Ignores dots in incoming messages if True. Defaults to False. [IgnoreDots]

confLOCAL_MAILER Defines the mailer used for local connections. Defaults to local.

confLOG_LEVEL Defines the level of detail for the log file. Defaults to 9. [LogLevel]

confMAILER_NAME Defines the sender name used on error messages. Defaults to MAILER-DAEMON. [$n]

confMATCH_GECOS Matches the e-mail username to the GECOS field. This match is not done if this parameter is not set. [MatchGECOS]

confMAX_DAEMON_CHILDREN Refuses connections when this number of children is reached. By default, connections are never refused. [MaxDaemonChildren]

confMAX_HOP Defines the counter used to determine mail loops. Defaults to 25. [MaxHopCount]

confMAX_MESSAGE_SIZE Sets the maximum size for a message the server will accept. By default, no limit is set. [MaxMessageSize]

confMAX_QUEUE_RUN_SIZE Defines the maximum number of entries processed in a queue run. Defaults to 0, which means no limit. [MaxQueueRunSize]

confMAX_RCPTS_PER_MESSAGE Defines the maximum number of recipients allowed for a piece of mail. [MaxQueueRunSize]

confMCI_CACHE_SIZE Sets the number of open connections that can be cached. Defaults to 2. [ConnectionCacheSize]

confMCI_CACHE_TIMEOUT Sets the amount of time inactive open connections are held in the cache. Defaults to 5m. [ConnectionCacheTimeout]

confME_TOO Sends a copy to the sender if True. Defaults to False. [MeToo]

confMIME_FORMAT_ERRORS Sends MIME-encapsulated error messages if True. Defaults to True. [SendMimeErrors]

confMIN_FREE_BLOCKS Sets the minimum number of blocks that must be available on the disk to accept mail. Defaults to 100. [MinFreeBlocks]

confMIN_QUEUE_AGE Sets the minimum time a job must be queued. Defaults to 0. [MinQueueAge]

confNO_RCPT_ACTION Defines handling for mail with no recipient headers: do nothing (none); add a To: header (add-to); add an Apparently-To: header (add-apparently-to); add a Bcc: header (add-bcc); add a To: undisclosed-recipients header (add-to-undisclosed). Defaults to none. [NoRecipientAction] confOLD_STYLE_HEADERS Treats headers without special characters as old style if True. Defaults to True. [OldStyleHeaders]

confOPERATORS Defines the address operator characters. Defaults to .:%@!^/[]+. [OperatorChars]

confPRIVACY_FLAGS Sets flags that restrict the use of some mail commands. Defaults to authwarnings. [PrivacyOptions]

confQUEUE_FACTOR Defines a value used to calculate when a loaded system should queue mail instead of attempting delivery. Defaults to 600000. [QueueFactor]

confQUEUE_LA Sends mail directly to the queue when this load average is reached. Defaults to 8. [QueueLA]

confQUEUE_SORT_ORDER Sorts queue by Priority or Host order. Defaults to Priority. [QueueSortOrder]

confRECEIVED_HEADER Defines the Received: header format. Defaults to $?sfrom $s $.$?_($?s$|from $.$_) $.by $j ($v/$Z)$?r with r. id i?u for u.; $b.

confREFUSE_LA Defines the load average at which incoming connections are refused. Defaults to 12. [RefuseLA]

confREJECT_MSG Defines the message displayed when mail is rejected because of the access control database. Defaults to 550 Access denied.

confRELAY_MAILER Defines the default mailer name for relaying. Defaults to relay.

confRUN_AS_USER Runs as this user to read and deliver mail. By default, this is not used. [RunAsUser]

confSAFE_FILE_ENV Chroot() to this directory before writing files. By default this is not done. [SafeFileEnvironment]

confSAFE_QUEUE Creates a queue file then attempts delivery. This is not done unless this parameter is specified. [SuperSafe]

confSAVE_FROM_LINES Does not discard Unix From lines. They are discarded if this is not set. [SaveFromLine]

confSEPARATE_PROC Delivers messages with separate processes if True. Defaults to False. [ForkEachJob]

confSERVICE_SWITCH_FILE Defines the path to the service switch file. Defaults to /etc/service.switch. [ServiceSwitchFile]

confSEVEN_BIT_INPUT Forces input to seven bits if True. Defaults to False. [SevenBitInput] confSINGLE_LINE_FROM_HEADER Forces a multiline From: line to a single line when True. Defaults to False. [SingleLineFromHeader]

confSINGLE_THREAD_DELIVERY Forces single-threaded mail delivery when True and HostStatusDirectory is defined. Defaults to False. [SingleThreadDelivery]

confSMTP_LOGIN_MSG Defines the SMTP greeting message. Defaults to $j Sendmail $v/$Z; $b. [SmtpGreetingMessage]

confSMTP_MAILER Defines the mailer used for SMTP connections; must be smtp, smtp8, or esmtp. Defaults to esmtp.

confTEMP_FILE_MODE Sets the file mode used for temporary files. Defaults to 0600. [TempFileMode]

confTIME_ZONE Sets the time zone from the system (USE_SYSTEM) or the TZ variable (USE_TZ). Defaults to USE_SYSTEM. [TimeZoneSpec]

confTO_COMMAND Sets the maximum time to wait for a command. Defaults to 1h. [Timeout.command]

confTO_CONNECT Sets the maximum time to wait for a connect. [Timeout.connect]

confTO_DATABLOCK Sets the maximum time to wait for a block during DATA phase. Defaults to 1h. [Timeout.datablock]

confTO_DATAFINAL Sets the maximum time to wait for a response to the terminating ".". Defaults to 1h. [Timeout.datafinal]

confTO_DATAINIT Sets the maximum time to wait for a DATA command response. Defaults to 5m. [Timeout.datainit]

confTO_FILEOPEN Sets the maximum time to wait for a file open. Defaults to 60s. [Timeout.fileopen]

confTO_HELO Sets the maximum time to wait for a HELO or EHLO response. Defaults to 5m. [Timeout.helo]

confTO_HOSTSTATUS Sets the timer for stale host status information. Defaults to 30m. [Timeout.hoststatus]

confTO_ICONNECT Sets the maximum time to wait for the very first connect attempt to a host. [Timeout.iconnect]

confTO_IDENT Sets the maximum time to wait for an IDENT query response. Defaults to 30s. [Timeout.ident]

confTO_INITIAL Sets the maximum time to wait for the initial connect response. Defaults to 5m. [Timeout.initial]

confTO_MAIL Sets the maximum time to wait for a MAIL command response. Defaults to 10m. [Timeout.mail] confTO_MISC Sets the maximum time to wait for other SMTP command responses. Defaults to 2m. [Timeout.misc]

confTO_QUEUERETURN_NONURGENT Sets the "Undeliverable mail" timeout for low-priority messages. [Timeout.queuereturn.non-urgent]

confTO_QUEUERETURN_NORMAL Sets the "Undeliverable mail" timeout for normal-priority messages. [Timeout.queuereturn.normal]

confTO_QUEUERETURN_URGENT Sets the "Undeliverable mail" timeout for urgent-priority messages. [Timeout.queuereturn.urgent]

confTO_QUEUERETURN Sets the time until a message is returned from the queue as undeliverable. Defaults to 5d. [Timeout.queuereturn]

confTO_QUEUEWARN_NONURGENT Sets the time until a "still queued" warning is sent for low priority messages. [Timeout.queuewarn.non-urgent]

confTO_QUEUEWARN_NORMAL Sets the time until a "still queued" warning is sent for normal priority messages. [Timeout.queuewarn.normal]

confTO_QUEUEWARN_URGENT Sets the time until a "still queued" warning is sent for urgent priority messages. [Timeout.queuewarn.urgent]

confTO_QUEUEWARN Sets the time until a "still queued" warning is sent about a message. Defaults to 4h. [Timeout.queuewarn]

confTO_QUIT Sets the maximum time to wait for a QUIT command response. Defaults to 2m. [Timeout.quit]

confTO_RCPT Sets the maximum time to wait for a RCPT command response. Defaults to 1h. [Timeout.rcpt]

confTO_RSET Sets the maximum time to wait for a RSET command response. Defaults to 5m. [Timeout.rset]

confTRUSTED_USERS Defines trusted usernames to add to root, uucp, and daemon.

confTRY_NULL_MX_LIST Connects to the remote host directly if the MX points to the local host and this is set to True. Defaults to False. [TryNullMXList]

confUNSAFE_GROUP_WRITES Doesn't reference programs or files from group-writable :include: and .forward files if True. Defaults to False. [UnsafeGroupWrites]

confUSERDB_SPEC Defines the path of the user database file. [UserDatabaseSpec]

confUSE_ERRORS_TO Delivers errors using the Errors-To: header if True. Defaults to False. [UserErrorsTo]

confUUCP_MAILER Defines the default UUCP mailer. Defaults to uucp-old.

confWORK_CLASS_FACTOR Defines the factor used to favor high-priority jobs. Defaults to 1800. [ClassFactor] confWORK_RECIPIENT_FACTOR Defines the factor used to lower the priority of a job for each additional recipient. Defaults to 30000. [RecipientFactor]

confWORK_TIME_FACTOR Defines the factor used to lower the priority of a job for each delivery attempt. Defaults to 90000. [RetryFactor]

define macros are the most common macros in the m4 source files. The next most commonly used macro is the FEATURE macro.

FEATURE

The FEATURE macro processes m4 source code from the cf/feature directory. Source files in that directory define optional sendmail features that you may wish to include in your configuration. The syntax of the FEATURE macro is:

FEATURE(*name*, [*argument*])

The argument is optional. If an argument is passed to the source file, the argument is used by the source file to generate code for the sendmail.cf file. For example:

    FEATURE(mailertable, dbm /usr/lib/mailertable)

generates the code for accessing the mailertable and defines that table as being a dbm database located in the file /usr/lib/mailertable.

The available features and their purposes are listed in Table C.1.

Table C.1   Optional sendmail Features

Name	Purpose
accept_unqualified_senders	Allows network mail from addresses that do not include a valid host name.
accept_unresolvable_domains	Accepts mail from hosts that are unknown to DNS.
access_db	Enables the use of the access database.
allmasquerade	Also masquerades recipient addresses.
always_add_domain	Adds the local host name to all locally delivered mail.

Appendices

PART 5

Table C.1   Optional `sendmail` Features *(continued)*

Name	Purpose
bestmx_is_local	Accepts as local, mail addressed to a host that lists the local system as its MX server.
bitdomain	Uses a table to map bitnet hosts to Internet addresses.
blacklist_recipients	Filters incoming mail based on values set in the access database.
domaintable	Uses a domain table for domain name mapping.
genericstable	Uses a table to rewrite local addresses.
limited_masquerade	Lists only masquerade hosts in $=M.
local_lmtp	Uses mail.local with LMTP support.
local_procmail	Uses procmail as the local mailer.
loose_relay_check	Disables validity checks for addresses that use the % hack.
mailertable	Routes mail using a mailer table.
masquerade_entire_domain	Masquerades all hosts within the masquerading domains.
nocanonify	Doesn't convert names with $[... $] syntax.
nodns	Doesn't include DNS support.
nouucp	Doesn't include UUCP address processing.
nullclient	Forwards all mail to a central server.
promiscuous_relay	Relays mail from any site to any site.

Table C.1 Optional sendmail Features *(continued)*

rbl	Enables use of the Realtime Blackhole List server.
Name	**Purpose**
redirect	Supports the .REDIRECT pseudo-domain.
relay_based_on_MX	Relays mail for any site whose MX points to this server.
relay_entire_domain	Relays mail for any host in your domain.
relay_host_only	Only relays mail for hosts listed in the access database.
relay_local_from	Relays mail if the source is a local host.
smrsh	Uses smrsh as the prog mailer.
stickyhost	Treats "user" differently than "user@local.host".
use_ct_file	Loads $=t from /etc/sendmail.ct.
use_cw_file	Loads $=w from /etc/sendmail.cw.
uucpdomain	Uses a table to map UUCP hosts to Internet addresses.
virtusertable	Maps virtual domain names to real mail addresses.

The use_cw_file and the use_ct_file features are equivalent to Fw/etc/sendmail.cw and Fw/etc/sendmail.ct commands in the sendmail.cf file.

> ***NOTE*** See Chapter 7 for descriptions of host aliases ($=w) and trusted users ($=t). The redirect feature is also covered in Chapter 7.

Several FEATURE macros remove unneeded lines from the sendmail.cf file. nouucp removes the code that handles UUCP addresses for systems that do not have access to

UUCP networks, and nodns removes the code for DNS lookups for systems that do not have access to DNS. nocanonify disables the code that converts nicknames and IP addresses into host names. Finally, the nullclient feature strips everything out of the configuration except for the ability to forward mail to a single mail server via a local SMTP link. The name of that mail server is provided as the argument on the nullclient command line, e.g., FEATURE(nullclient, big.isp.net) forwards all mail to big.isp.net without any local mail processing.

Several features relate to mail relaying and masquerading. They are stickyhost, allmasquerade, limited_masquerade, and masquerade_entire_domain. (All of these features are covered in the DOMAIN section later in this appendix.)

Several of the features define databases that are used to perform special address processing. All of these features accept an optional argument that defines the database. (See the sample mailertable command at the beginning of this section for an example of defining the database with the optional argument.) If the optional argument is not provided, the database description always defaults to hash -o /etc/*filename*, where *filename* matches the name of the feature. For example, mailertable defaults to the definition hash -o /etc/mailertable. The database features are:

mailertable Maps host and domain names to specific mailer:host pairs. The mailer, host, user triple is returned by ruleset 0 based on the delivery address. The mailertable allows you to define the mailer and the host of the delivery triple based on the domain name in the delivery address. If the host or domain name in the delivery addresses matches a key field in the mailertable database, it returns the mailer and host for that address. The format of a mailertable entry is:

 domain-name *mailer*:*host*

where *domain-name* is either a full host name (host plus domain) or a domain name. If a domain name is used, it must start with a dot (.), and it will match every host in the specified domain.

domaintable Converts an old domain name to a new domain name. The old name is the key, and the new name is the value returned for the key.

bitdomain Converts a Bitnet host name to an Internet host name. The Bitnet name is the key, and the Internet host name is the value returned. The bitdomain program that comes with the sendmail distribution can be used to build this database. Bitnet is obsolete.

uucpdomain Converts a UUCP name to an Internet host name. The key is the UUCP host name, and the value returned is the Internet host name. This is useful if you still have users who address e-mail using old UUCP addresses.

genericstable Converts a sender e-mail address. The key to the database is either a username or a full e-mail address (username and hostname). The value returned by the database is the new e-mail address. genericstable converts the same addresses as those processed for masquerading, and the features that affect masquerading affect the genericstable conversion in exactly the same way. (See Chapter 7 for an example of using the genericstable, and see the DOMAIN section of this appendix for information on masquerading.) If you use the genericstable and you don't use masquerading, use generics_domain and generics_domain_file to get the same functions normally provided by masquerade_domain and masquerade_domain_file.

virtusertable Aliases incoming e-mail addresses. Essentially, this is an extended alias database for aliasing addresses that are not local to this host. The key to the database is a full e-mail address or a domain name. The value returned by the database is the recipient address to which the mail is delivered. If a domain name is used as a key, it must begin with an at sign (@). Mail addressed to any user in the specified domain is sent to the recipient defined by the virtusertable database. Any host name used as a key in the virtusertable database must also be defined in class w.

Some features are important in the fight against spam because they help you control what mail your server will deliver or forward on for delivery. These are accept_unqualified_senders, accept_unresolvable_domains, access_db, blacklist_recipients, and rbl. All of these are covered in the section on controlling spam in Chapter 13, *More Mail Services*.

Two of the remaining FEATURE commands relate to domains. The always_add_domain macro makes sendmail add the local host name to all locally delivered mail, even to those pieces of mail that would normally have just a username as an address. The bestmx_is_local feature accepts mail addressed to a host that lists the local host as its preferred MX server as if the mail was local mail. If this feature is not used, mail bound for a remote host is sent directly to the remote host even if its MX record lists the local host as its preferred MX server. The bestmx_is_local feature should not be used if you use a wildcard MX record for your domain.

The last two features are used to select optional programs for the local and the prog mailers. local_procmail selects procmail as the local mailer. Provide the path to procmail as the argument in the FEATURE command. The smrsh feature selects the SendMail Restricted SHell (smrsh) as the prog mailer. smrsh provides improved security over /bin/sh, which is often used as the prog mailer. Provide the path to smrsh as the argument in the FEATURE command.

Appendices

PART 5

The FEATURE commands discussed in this section and the define macros discussed previously are used to build the m4 source files. The next few sections of this appendix describe the purpose and structure of the OSTYPE, DOMAIN, and MAILER source files.

OSTYPE

OSTYPE points to the m4 source file that contains the operating system *n* specific information for this configuration. This required file is examined in detail in Chapter 7.

While all m4 macros can be used in OSTYPE source files, Table C.2 lists the define parameters most frequently associated with the OSTYPE file and the function of each parameter. If the parameter has a default value, it is shown enclosed in square brackets after the parameter's functional description.

Table C.2   OSTYPE defines

Parameter	Function
ALIAS_FILE	Name of the alias file. [/etc/aliases]
confEBINDIR	Directory for smrsh and LMTP executables. [/usr/libexec]
CYRUS_BB_MAILER_ARGS	cyrusbb mailer arguments. [deliver -e -m $u]
CYRUS_BB_MAILER_FLAGS	Flags added to lsDFMnP for the cyrusbb mailer.
CYRUS_MAILER_ARGS	cyrus mailer arguments. [deliver -e -m $h -- $u]
CYRUS_MAILER_FLAGS	Flags added to lsDFMnP for the cyrus mailer. [A5@]
CYRUS_MAILER_MAX	Maximum size message for the cyrus mailer.
CYRUS_MAILER_PATH	Path to the cyrus mailer. [/usr/cyrus/bin/deliver]

Table C.2 OSTYPE defines *(continued)*

Parameter	Function
CYRUS_MAILER_USER	User and group used to the cyrus mailer. [cyrus:mail]
ESMTP_MAILER_ARGS	esmtp mailer arguments. [IPC $h]
FAX_MAILER_ARGS	FAX mailer arguments. [mailfax $u $h $f]
Parameter	**Function**
FAX_MAILER_MAX	Maximum size of a FAX. [100000]
FAX_MAILER_PATH	Path to the FAX program. [/usr/local/lib/fax/mailfax]
HELP_FILE	Name of the help file. [/usr/lib/sendmail.hf]
LOCAL_MAILER_ARGS	Arguments for local mail delivery. [mail -d $u]
LOCAL_MAILER_CHARSET	Character set for local 8-bit MIME mail.
LOCAL_MAILER_FLAGS	Local mailer flags added to lsDFM. [rmn]
LOCAL_MAILER_MAX	Maximum size of local mail.
LOCAL_MAILER_PATH	The local mail delivery program. [/bin/mail]
LOCAL_SHELL_ARGS	Arguments for the prog mail. [sh -c $u]
LOCAL_SHELL_DIR	Directory that the shell should run. [$z:/]
LOCAL_SHELL_FLAGS	Flags added to lsDFM for the shell mailer. [eu]
LOCAL_SHELL_PATH	Shell used to deliver piped e-mail. [/bin/sh]
MAIL11_MAILER_ARGS	mail11 mailer arguments. [mail11 $g $x $h $u]
MAIL11_MAILER_FLAGS	Flags for the mail11 mailer. [nsFx]

Appendices

PART 5

Table C.2 OSTYPE defines *(continued)*

MAIL11_MAILER_PATH	Path to the mail11 mailer. [/usr/etc/mail11]
PH_MAILER_ARGS	phquery mailer arguments. [phquery -- $u]
Parameter	**Function**
PH_MAILER_FLAGS	Flags for the phquery mailer. [ehmu]
PH_MAILER_PATH	Path to the phquery program. [/usr/local/etc/phquery]
POP_MAILER_ARGS	POP mailer arguments. [pop $u]
POP_MAILER_FLAGS	Flags added to lsDFM for the POP mailer. [Penu]
POP_MAILER_PATH	Path of the POP mailer. [/usr/lib/mh/spop]
PROCMAIL_MAILER_ARGS	procmail mailer arguments. [procmail -m $h $f $u]
PROCMAIL_MAILER_FLAGS	Flags added to DFMmn for the procmail mailer. [Shu]
PROCMAIL_MAILER_MAX	Maximum size message for the procmail mailer.
PROCMAIL_MAILER_PATH	Path to the procmail program. [/usr/local/bin/procmail]
QUEUE_DIR	Directory containing queue files. [/var/spool/mqueue]
RELAY_MAILER_ARGS	relay mailer arguments. [IPC $h]
SMTP8_MAILER_ARGS	smtp8 mailer arguments. [IPC $h]
SMTP_MAILER_ARGS	smtp mailer arguments. [IPC $h]
SMTP_MAILER_CHARSET	Character set for SMTP 8-bit MIME mail.

Table C.2   OSTYPE defines *(continued)*

SMTP_MAILER_FLAGS	Flags added to mDFMUX for all SMTP mailers.
SMTP_MAILER_MAX	Maximum size of messages for all SMTP mailers.

Parameter	Function
STATUS_FILE	Name of the status file. [/etc/sendmail.st]
USENET_MAILER_ARGS	Arguments for the usenet mailer. [-m -h -n]
USENET_MAILER_FLAGS	usenet mailer flags. [rlsDFMmn]
USENET_MAILER_MAX	Maximum size of usenet mail messages. [100000]
USENET_MAILER_PATH	Program used for news. [/usr/lib/news/inews]
UUCP_MAILER_ARGS	UUCP mailer arguments. [uux - -r -z -a$g -gC $h!rmail ($u)]
UUCP_MAILER_CHARSET	Character set for UUCP 8-bit MIME mail.
UUCP_MAILER_FLAGS	Flags added to DFMhuU for the UUCP mailer.
UUCP_MAILER_MAX	Maximum size for UUCP messages. [100000]
UUCP_MAILER_PATH	Path to the UUCP mail program. [/usr/bin/uux]

DOMAIN

DOMAIN points to the m4 source file that contains configuration information specific to your domain. Chapter 7 provides a detailed example of creating a domain source file and then calling that file with the DOMAIN macro.

Table C.3 lists the define macros that commonly appear in DOMAIN source files. All of these define mail relay hosts. The value provided for each parameter is either a host name, i.e. the name of a mail relay server, or a *mailer:hostname* pair where *mailer* is an internal mailer name and *hostname* is the name of the mail relay server. If only a host name is used, the mailer defaults to relay, which is the name of the SMTP relay mailer.

Table C.3   Mail Relay defines

Parameter	Function
UUCP_RELAY	Server for UUCP-addressed e-mail.
BITNET_RELAY	Server for BITNET-addressed e-mail.
DECNET_RELAY	Server for DECNET-addressed e-mail.
FAX_RELAY	Server for mail to the .FAX pseudo-domain. The fax mailer overrides this value.
LOCAL_RELAY	Server for unqualified names. This is obsolete.
LUSER_RELAY	Server for apparently local names that really aren't local.
MAIL_HUB	Server for all incoming mail.
SMART_HOST	Server for all outgoing mail.

The precedence of the relays defined by these parameters is from the most specific to the least specific. If both the UUCP_RELAY and the SMART_HOST relay are defined, the UUCP_RELAY is used for outgoing UUCP mail even though the SMART_HOST relay is defined as handling "all" outgoing mail. If you define both LOCAL_RELAY and MAIL_HUB, you must also use the FEATURE(stickyhost) command to get the expected behavior. When the stickyhost feature is specified, LOCAL_RELAY handles all local addresses that do not have a host part, and MAIL_HUB handles all local addresses that do have a host part. If stickyhost is not specified and both relays are defined, the LOCAL_RELAY is ignored and MAIL_HUB handles all local addresses.

In addition to the defines shown in Table C.3, macros that relate to masquerading and relaying also appear in the DOMAIN source file. The macros are:

LOCAL_USER(*usernames*) Defines local usernames that should not be relayed even if LOCAL_RELAY or MAIL_HUB are defined. This command is the same as adding usernames to class L in the sendmail.cf file.

MASQUERADE_AS(*host.domain*) Converts the host portion of the sender address on outgoing mail to the specified domain name. Sender addresses that have no host name or that have a host name found in the w class are converted. This has the same effect as the M macro in the sendmail.cf file. See examples of MASQUERADE_AS and macro M in Chapter 7.

MASQUERADE_DOMAIN(*otherhost.domain*) Converts the host portion of the sender address on outgoing mail to the domain name defined by the MASQUERADE_AS command, if the host portion of the sender address matches the value defined here. This command must be used in conjunction with MASQUERADE_AS. Its effect is the same as adding host names to class M in the sendmail.cf file. See Chapter 7.

MASQUERADE_DOMAIN_FILE(*filename*) Loads class M host names from the specified file. This can be used in place of multiple MASQUERADE_DOMAIN commands. Its effect is the same as using the FMfilename command in the sendmail.cf file.

EXPOSED_USER(*username*) Disables masquerading when the user portion of the sender address matches *username*. Some usernames, such as root, occur on many systems and therefore are not unique across a domain. For those usernames, converting the host portion of the address makes it impossible to sort out where the message really came from and makes replies impossible. This command prevents the MASQUERADE_AS command from having an effect on the sender addresses for specific users. This is the same as setting the values in class E in the sendmail.cf file.

There are also several features that affect relaying and masquerading. I have already discussed FEATURE(stickyhost). Others are:

FEATURE(masquerade_envelope) Causes envelope addresses to be masqueraded in the same way that sender addresses are masqueraded. See Chapter 7 for an example of this command.

FEATURE(allmasquerade) Causes recipient addresses to be masqueraded in the same way that sender addresses are masqueraded. Thus, if the host portion of the recipient address matches the requirements of the MASQUERADE_AS command, it is converted. Don't use this feature unless you are positive that every alias known to the local system is also known to the mail server that handles mail for the masquerade domain.

FEATURE(limited_masquerade) Limits masquerading to those hosts defined in class M. The hosts defined in class w are not masqueraded.

FEATURE(masquerade_entire_domain) Causes MASQUERADE_DOMAIN to be interpreted as referring to all hosts within an entire domain. If this feature is not used, only an address that exactly matches the value defined by MASQUERADE_DOMAIN is converted. If this feature is used, then all addresses that end with the value defined by MASQUERADE_DOMAIN are converted. For example, assume MASQUERADE_ AS(foobirds.org) and MASQUERADE_DOMAIN(swans.foobirds.org) are defined. If FEATURE(masquerade_entire_domain) is set, every host name in the swans .foobirds.org domain is converted to foobirds.org on outgoing e-mail. Otherwise, only a host named swans.foobirds.org is converted.

Some features define how the server handles mail if it is the mail relay server. These features, which are also described in Chapter 13, are:

promiscuous_relay Relays from any site to any site. Normally, sendmail does not relay mail. Using this feature is a bad idea because it makes you a possible relay server for spammers.

relay_entire_domain Relays from any domain defined in class M to any site.

relay_hosts_only Relays mail from any host defined in the access database or class R.

relay_based_on_MX Relays mail from any site for which your system is the MX server.

relay_local_from Relays mail with a sender address that contains your local domain name.

WARNING   Mail relays can be abused by spammers and spoofers. Use them with caution.

MAILER

MAILER points to an m4 source file that contains the configuration commands that define a sendmail mailer. A least one MAILER command must appear in the configuration file. Generally more than one MAILER command is used.

It is possible that you will need to customize a file location in an OSTYPE file or that you will need to define domain specific information in a DOMAIN file, but unless you develop your own mail delivery program you will not need to create a MAILER source file. Instead, you will need to invoke one or more existing files in your macro configuration file.

Table C.4 lists each MAILER value and its function. These are invoked using the MAILER(value) command in the macro configuration (.mc) file.

Table C.4 MAILER Values

Name	Function
local	The local and prog mailers.
smtp	All SMTP mailers: smtp, esmtp, smtp8, and relay.
Name	Function
uucp	All UUCP mailers: uucp-old (uucp) and uucp-new (suucp).
usenet	Usenet news support.
fax	FAX support using FlexFAX software.
pop	Post Office Protocol (POP) support.
procmail	An interface for procmail.
mail11	The DECnet mail11 mailer.
phquery	The phquery program for CSO phone book.
cyrus	The cyrus and cyrusbb mailers.

Your macro configuration file should have a MAILER(local) and a MAILER(smtp) entry. Selecting local and smtp provides everything you need for a standard TCP/IP installation. None of the remaining mailers is widely used. The other mailers are:

uucp Provides UUCP mail support for systems directly connected to UUCP networks. The uucp-old mailer supports standard UUCP mail and the uucp-new mailer is used for remote sites that can handle multiple recipients in one transfer. Specify MAILER(uucp) after the MAILER(smtp) entry if your system has both TCP/IP and UUCP connections.

usenet Sends local mail that contains .usenet in the recipient name to the program inews. Use a user mail agent that supports Usenet news. Don't hack sendmail to handle it.

fax Experimental support for HylaFAX.

pop On Linux systems, POP support is provided by the popd, so the MAILER(pop) command is not used.

procmail Provides a procmail interface for the mailertable. Even though procmail is used as the Linux local mailer, the MAILER(procmail) command is not required.

mail11 Only used on DECNET mail networks that use the mail11 mailer.

phquery Provides CSO phone book (ph) directory service. User directory services are usually configured in the user mail agent, not in sendmail.

cyrus Provides a local mail delivery program that uses a mailbox architecture. cyrus and cyrusbb mailers are not widely used.

LOCAL_RULE

LOCAL_RULE_*n* heads a section of code to be added to ruleset *n*, where *n* is 0, 1, 2, or 3. The code that follows the LOCAL_RULE command is sendmail.cf rewrite rules. The one exception to this is the UUCPSMTP macro that maps UUCP host names to Internet host names. See the documentation that comes with the sendmail distribution if you have questions about UUCP configuration. The LOCAL_RULE command is rarely used.

LOCAL_CONFIG

LOCAL_CONFIG heads a section of code to be added to the sendmail.cf file after the local information section and before the rewrite rules. The section of code contains standard sendmail.cf configuration commands. This macro is rarely used.

HACKS

HACKS points to an m4 source file that contains site specific configuration information. HACKS are temporary fixes to temporary problems, yet they have an unfortunate way of becoming permanent. In general, the use of HACKS is discouraged.

Actually, I have never used the HACK macro and have never created a file in the HACK directory. I'm not sure when it would ever be needed considering the number of sendmail problems I have seen, none of which needed a HACK. My advice: "Don't use it."

SITECONFIG

This macro is only useful if you use UUCP for e-mail. SITECONFIG points to a source file that contains m4 SITE commands that define the UUCP sites connected to the local host. Such a file might look like the following:

```
SITE(byron)

SITE(keats)

SITE(shelley)
```

You create the m4 source file yourself and then invoke it with the SITECONFIG command. The SITECONFIG command to invoke the file shown above might be:

```
SITECONFIG(uucpsites, wren, U)
```

This command says that the local host wren reads the UUCP site names from the file uucpsites and stores them in class variable U.

I have not used UUCP for e-mail delivery for several years. Neither should you. UUCP has very little use in a world that is now fully networked with TCP/IP.

This concludes the discussion of m4 macros. The output of all of the files and commands that go into the m4 processor is a sendmail.cf file. The bulk of information about sendmail configuration is found in Chapter 7.

Appendices

PART 5

Index

Note to the reader: Throughout this index **boldfaced** page numbers indicate primary discussions of a topic. *Italicized* pages numbers indicate illustrations or tables.

Index

Sybex Books on the Web

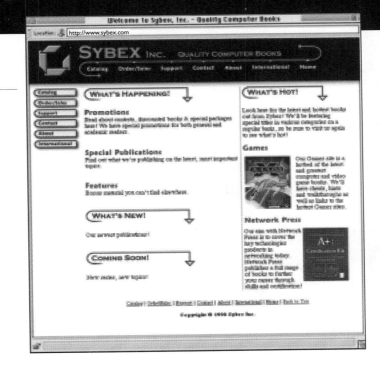

A t the dynamic and informative Sybex Web site, you can:

- view our complete online catalog
- preview a book you're interested in
- access special book content
- order books online at special discount prices
- learn about Sybex

www.sybex.com

SYBEX Inc. • 1151 Marina Village Parkway
Alameda, CA 94501 • 510-523-8233

TAKE YOUR CAREER TO THE NEXT LEVEL

with 24seven books from Network Press

- **This new series offers the advanced information you need to keep your systems and networks running 24 hours a day, seven days a week.**
- **On-the-job case studies provide solutions to real-world problems.**
- **Maximize your system's uptime—and go home at 5!**
- **$34.99; 7½" x 9"; 544–704 pages; softcover**

seven

TAKE YOUR CAREER TO THE NEXT LEVEL

with 24seven books from Network Press

- This new series offers the advanced information you need to keep your systems and networks running 24 hours a day, seven days a week.
- On-the-job case studies provide solutions to real-world problems.
- Maximize your system's uptime—and go home at 5!
- $34.99; 7½" x 9"; 544–704 pages; softcover

Paul Robichaux
0-7821-2531-X
Available 3rd Quarter 1999

Craig Hunt
0-7821-2506-9
Available 3rd Quarter 1999

Gary Govanus
0-7821-2509-3
Available 3rd Quarter 1999

Matthew Strebe
0-7821-2529-8
Available 3rd Quarter 1999

Craig Simmons, David Gardner
0-7821-2518-2
Available 3rd Quarter 1999

John Hales, Nestor Reyes
0-7821-2593-X
Available 4th Quarter 1999

THE ESSENTIAL RESOURCE FOR SYSTEMS ADMINISTRATORS

Visit the 24seven Web site at <u>www.24sevenbooks.com</u> for more information and sample chapters.

How to...